Red Hat® Linux®
Administra
A Beginner's G

Red Hat® Linux®
Administration
A Beginner's Guide

Michael Turner
Steve Shah

McGraw-Hill/Osborne

New York Chicago San Francisco
Lisbon London Madrid Mexico City
Milan New Delhi San Juan
Seoul Singapore Sydney Toronto

The **McGraw·Hill** Companies

McGraw-Hill/Osborne
2600 Tenth Street
Berkeley, California 94710
U.S.A.

To arrange bulk purchase discounts for sales promotions, premiums, or fund-raisers, please contact **McGraw-Hill**/Osborne at the above address. For information on translations or book distributors outside the U.S.A., please see the International Contact Information page immediately following the index of this book.

Red Hat® Linux® Administration: A Beginner's Guide

1234567890 CUS CUS 019876543
ISBN 0-07-222631-5

Publisher   Brandon A. Nordin
Vice President & Associate Publisher   Scott Rogers
Acquisitions Editor   Francis Kelly
Senior Project Editor   Betsy Manini
Acquisitions Coordinator   Martin Przybyla
Technical Editor   Josh Burke
Copy Editors   Robert Campbell, Emily Rader
Proofreaders   Stefany Otis, Marian Selig
Indexer   Valerie Haynes Perry
Computer Designers   George T. Charbak, Tabitha M. Cagan
Illustrator   Melinda Lytle, Michael Mueller, Lyssa Wald
Series Design   Jean Butterfield
Series Cover Design   Sarah F. Hinks

This book was composed with Corel VENTURA™ Publisher.

Dedicated to Amy, for her understanding,
and to Stephanie, who asked all the right questions.
I couldn't have done it without you.
—Michael Turner

About the Authors

Michael Turner is a systems administrator, software engineer, author, and all around geek with over twenty years experience behind a computer keyboard. He first started working with UNIX in 1988 and has been working with Linux professionally since 1995. He has managed computer networks with over 80,000 users and has written software that has flown on the Space Shuttle Discovery. Currently he is employed at Collabnet Inc. as an instantiation engineer working on the SourceCast collaborative development environment.

In his spare time he enjoys reading, watching independent films, listening to music, and playing with new technological gadgets. Free software advocacy and programming are also among his interests. He lives with his family in the Silicon Valley of California and shares his home with two cats, three snakes and one bearded dragon.

Steve Shah is the director of product management at Array Networks (www.arraynetworks.net) where he is responsible for the technical direction of traffic management and security products. His other author credits include contributions to *Unix Unleashed*, *Red Hat Linux Unleashed*, *Using Linux*, and *Content Delivery Networks*. Prior to Array Networks, Steve was a developer and systems administrator for several companies, including Alteon Web Systems and the Center for Environmental Research and Technology. Besides Linux, Steve has been responsible for a variety of operating systems including Solaris, Irix, FreeBSD, SunOS, HPUX, and the many flavors of Microsoft Window.

About the Technical Editor

Josh Burke, CISSP, is a network and security analyst with Boeing Employees Credit Union (BECU) near Seattle. He has held positions in networking, systems, and security over the past five years. A graduate of the business school at the University of Washington, Josh concentrates on balancing technical and business needs in the many areas of information security. His research interests include improving the security and resilience of the Domain Name System (DNS) and Internet routing protocol systems. Before joining BECU, Josh was a security and systems engineer at Internap Network Services.

Contents

PART II
Single-Host Administration

PART III
Internet Services

Acknowledgments

When I started this project, I seriously underestimated the amount of time and effort involved. Despite reading similar comments in the acknowledgment section of many other texts, it is still an exceedingly easy mistake to make. I work with this stuff every day, and I don't have a particularly hard time writing, so I thought, "how difficult can it really be?" Now I understand that when you read about an author thanking his friends and family for patience and understanding, it's not just because they're family and friends, but because it really does take more support and understanding from those folks than anyone really expects. Now I truly realize that without all these other people behind the scenes, it would not have been possible for this book to be in your hands.

First and foremost, I really appreciate everyone who helped, supported, or otherwise put up with me during this entire project. Someday I'll find a way to make it up to each of you. In addition, special thanks go out to Amy and Stephanie, both of whom went well above the call of duty in keeping me sane.

The people behind the scenes at McGraw-Hill/Osborne were also key to making this book happen. Betsy Manini and Franny Kelly were instrumental in making this work what it is. Josh Burke, Emily Rader, and Robert Campbell all earned many thanks for their work on this project. Michael Miller deserves special recognition for his contributions. My thanks to all of you.

I also would like to acknowledge all the companies who employed me working with Linux, without whom I wouldn't have gained the experience and knowledge that I hope to pass on to the readers of this volume. Special thanks to Collabnet for being such a cool place to work.

Introduction

Systems administrators are a unique bunch. As a group, we are probably the most significant consumers of reference and training books, and we probably demand the most from them (at least all of my peers do).

We're also a curious bunch. Most of my friends are gadget freaks (my wife included). We love to live on the edge of new technologies and find out what all the buzz is about before our users do. We like to do this for two very simple reasons: because it's fun and because we need to understand the technology before the CEO reads about it in *Business Week* and demands to know why we aren't running it.

The open source and free software movements seem to be a never-ending source of gadgets, and Linux is the overall platform of choice. In addition, Linux is becoming the buzz in the business world for several reasons. More and more we're seeing major corporations look into Linux in hopes of reducing costs and then sticking with it for more compelling reasons such as stability or flexibility.

Diehards will argue that Linux has been a buzz since the mid-1990s (it's been available since 1991). I personally started using Linux in 1995 when I was looking for a simple firewall solution for a company for which I was working; I wanted something that could be deployed with minimal cost. Over time, more and more project leaders at a variety of employers have found Linux to be the right tool for the job—not because of any coolness factor, but because the features and capabilities of Linux fit the needs at hand. It's somewhat validating to see some large corporations that only slowly move from their comfort zone starting to adopt Linux.

So, when IBM started porting DB2 to Linux, when Oracle ported its database platform to Linux, when SGI adopted Linux as its primary desktop operating system, and when even Dell made Red Hat Linux a preinstallation option on servers... well, that's what started the *real* buzz.

Who Should Read This Book

The title of this book says it's a "Beginner's Guide," and that's mostly true. What the title should really say is that it's a "Beginner's-to-Linux Guide," because the book does make a few assumptions about you, the reader.

First, it assumes you are already familiar with the Windows environment. At the very least, you should be a strong Windows user and know something about the networked Windows environment. Although you needn't be a Windows NT or 2000 expert, some exposure to NT/2000 will help your understanding of the hairier concepts. The book makes this assumption in order to avoid wasting time repeating what most folks from a Windows background already know, and instead focus on the new stuff that Linux brings to the table.

In addition to your Windows background, the book assumes that you're interested in having more information about the topics introduced here. After all, the book covers in 30 or 40 pages topics that have entire books devoted to them! So several chapters include references to other texts. Consider taking advantage of these references, no matter how advanced you think you're becoming, because there is always more to learn.

What's in This Book

Red Hat Linux Administration: A Beginner's Guide is organized into four parts. **Part I** is targeted at folks with no experience in Linux who want a hand installing it and getting rolling. You'll be introduced to some of the basic differences between Windows and Linux, and then walked through the basics of installation and software setup.

Part II is geared toward the administration of features common to all Linux systems, not just servers. Some of these chapters are really tutorials that help you use the system effectively, while others will delve into some of the more powerful concepts that set Linux (and UNIX in general) apart from other systems with which you may be familiar.

In **Part III**, you'll study all the services needed to run an Internet site. This includes the Domain Name System (DNS), the File Transfer Protocol (FTP), the Web, Simple Mail Transfer Protocol (SMTP) Mail, Post Office Protocol (POP) Mail, and Secure Shell (SSH).

Part IV goes in the opposite direction from Part III. Rather than studying services for everyone on the Internet, it examines services offered only to people on your internal network, such as the Network File System (NFS), the Network Information Service (NIS), and Samba.

Part I

Installing Linux as a Server

Module 1

Technical Summary of Linux Distributions and Windows

U nless you've been stranded on a deserted island somewhere or shunning the media and ignoring the trade press, you already have a pretty good idea of what Linux is and why you might be interested in it. To further your understanding of Linux, in this module you'll take a look at the technical differences between Linux and Windows 2000 (and its slightly enhanced successor, Windows .NET Server). This module also explains the GNU (GNU's Not UNIX) license, which may help you understand why much of Linux is the way it is.

CRITICAL SKILL
1.1 Describing Linux and Linux Distributions

Usually people understand Linux to be an entire package of developer tools, editors, GUIs, networking tools, and so forth. More formally, such packages are called *distributions*. You may have heard of the Linux distributions named Red Hat, SuSE, Mandrake, and Caldera, which have received a great deal of press and have been purchased for thousands of installations. Noncommercial distributions of Linux such as Debian are less well known outside certain technical circles, and while they have many happy users, they haven't reached the same scale of popularity as the commercial distributions.

What's interesting about all Linux distributions is that almost all of the tools with which they ship were not written by the companies themselves. Rather, other people have licensed their programs, allowing their redistribution with source code. By and large, these tools are also available on other variants of UNIX, and some of them are becoming available under Windows as well. The makers of the distribution simply bundle them up into one convenient package that's easy to install. (Some distribution makers also develop value-added tools that make their distribution easier to administer or compatible with more hardware, but the software that they ship is generally written by others.)

So if you consider a distribution to be everything you need for Linux, what then *is* Linux exactly? Linux itself is the core of the operating system: the *kernel*. The kernel is the program acting as Chief of Operations. It is responsible for such tasks as handling requests for memory, accessing disks, and managing network connections. The complete list of kernel activities could easily be a module in itself, and in fact, several books documenting the kernel's internal functions have been written.

The kernel is known as a nontrivial program. It is also what puts the Linux into all those Linux distributions. All distributions use the exact same kernel, and thus the fundamental behavior of all Linux distributions is the same.

What separates one distribution from the next is the value-added tools that come with each one. For example, Red Hat includes a very useful tool called *redhat-config-xfree86* that makes configuring the graphical interface a very straightforward task. Asking "Which distribution is better?" is much like asking "Which is better, Coke or Pepsi?" Almost all colas have the same basic ingredients—carbonated water, caffeine, and high-fructose corn syrup—thereby giving the similar effect of quenching thirst and bringing on a small caffeine-and-sugar buzz. In the end, it's a question of personal preference.

Project 1-1 Investigating Distributions

This book is an introduction to the use of one particular distribution of Linux: Red Hat Linux 8.0. It's a very good distribution, and it's especially popular in the United States. However, there are many other distributions, and most of them have something interesting to offer. In this project, you'll take a look at some of the other available distributions.

Step by Step

1. Using a Web browser, go to http://www.debian.org. Identify a primary distinguishing characteristic of the Debian distribution.

2. Now go to http://www.slackware.com to identify ZipSlack.

3. Identify the users primarily targeted by Turbolinux. (See http://www.turbolinux.com.)

4. In addition to Turbolinux, determine which companies are members of UnitedLinux (http://unitedlinux.com). Can you identify the primary objective of UnitedLinux?

5. Look at http://www.linux-mandrake.com and find the kernel version used in the latest Mandrake release.

6. Consider which hardware platforms are supported by Gentoo Linux (http://www.gentoo.org).

Project Summary

There is a world of information available on the distributions uncovered in this project, and on many more. If you want to find out more about them, a Google search (http://www.google.com) can uncover more nonmarketing information you might find useful. And of course, you shouldn't forget to see what Red Hat has to say about itself at http://www.redhat.com.

CRITICAL SKILL
1.2 Defining Free Software and the GNU License

In the early 1980s, Richard Stallman began a movement within the software industry. He preached (and still does) that software should be free. Note that by free, he doesn't mean in terms of price, but rather free in the same sense as freedom. This meant shipping not just a product, but the entire source code as well.

Stallman's policy was obviously a wild departure from the early eighties mentality of selling prepackaged software, but his concept of free software was in line with the initial distributions of UNIX from Bell Labs. Early UNIX systems did contain full source code. Yet by the late 1970s, source code was typically removed from UNIX distributions and could be acquired only by paying large sums of money to AT&T. The Berkeley Software Distribution (BSD) maintained a free version but had to deal with many lawsuits from AT&T until it could be proved that nothing in the BSD was from AT&T.

The idea of giving away source code is a simple one: A user of the software should never be forced to deal with a developer who might or might not support that user's intentions for the software. The user should never have to wait for bug fixes to be published. More important, code developed under the scrutiny of other programmers is typically of higher quality than code written behind locked doors. The greatest benefit of free software, however, comes from the users themselves: Should they need a new feature, they can add it to the program and then contribute it back to the source, so that everyone else can benefit from it.

From this line of thinking has sprung a desire to release a complete UNIX-like system to the public, free of license restrictions. Of course, before you can build any operating system, you need to build tools. And this is how the GNU project was born.

NOTE

GNU stands for GNU's Not UNIX—recursive acronyms are part of hacker humor. If you don't think it's funny, don't worry. You're still in the majority.

What Is the GNU Public License?

The most important thing to emerge from the GNU project has been the *GNU General Public License (GPL)*. This license explicitly states that the software being released is free, and that no one can ever take away these freedoms. It is acceptable to take the software and resell it, even for a profit; however, in this resale, the seller must release the full source code, including any changes. Because the resold package remains under the GPL, the package can be distributed free and resold yet again by anyone else for a profit. Of primary importance is the liability clause: The programmers are not liable for any damages caused by their software. More about GNU and the GPL can be found at http://www.gnu.org.

It should be noted that the GPL is not the only license used by free software developers (although it is arguably the most popular). Other licenses, such as BSD and Apache, have similar liability clauses but differ in terms of their redistribution. For instance, the BSD license allows people to make changes to the code and ship those changes without having to disclose the added code. (The GPL would require that the added code be shipped.) For more information about other open-source licenses, check out http://www.opensource.org.

The Advantages of Free Software

If the GPL seems a bad idea from the standpoint of commercialism, consider the recent surge of successful freeware packages—they are indicative of a system that does indeed work. This success has evolved for two reasons: First, as mentioned earlier, errors in the code itself are far more likely to be caught and quickly fixed under the watchful eyes of peers. Second, under the GPL system, programmers can release code without the fear of being sued. Without that protection, no one would ever release his or her code.

This concept of course begs the question of why anyone would release his or her work for free. The answer is simple: Most projects don't start out as full-featured, polished pieces of work. They may begin life as a quick hack to solve a specific problem bothering the programmer. As a quick-and-dirty hack, the code has no sales value. But when this code is shared with others who have similar problems and needs, it becomes a useful tool. Other program users begin to enhance it with features they need, and these additions travel back to the original program. The project thus evolves as the result of a group effort and eventually reaches full refinement. This polished program contains contributions from possibly hundreds if not thousands of programmers who have added little pieces here and there. In fact, the original author's code is likely to be little in evidence.

Here's another reason for the success of generally licensed software: Any project manager who has worked on commercial software knows that selling, marketing, supporting, documenting, packaging, and shipping can be more expensive than developing the software. A programmer carrying out a weekend lark to fix a problem with a tiny, kluged program lacks the interest, time, and backing money to turn that hack into a profitable product.

When Linus Torvalds released Linux in 1991, he released it under the GPL. As a result of its open charter, Linux has had a notable number of contributors and analyzers. This participation has made Linux very strong and rich in features. Torvalds himself estimates that since the v.2.2.0 kernel, his contributions represent only 5 percent of the total code base.

Since anyone can take the Linux kernel (and other supporting programs), repackage them, and resell them, some people have made money with Linux. As long as these individuals release the kernel's full source code along with their individual packages, and as long as the packages are protected under the GPL, everything is legal. Of course, this means that packages released under the GPL can be resold by other people under other names for a profit (and can in turn be resold again . . .).

In the end, what makes a package from one person more valuable than a package from another person consists of the value-added features, support channels, and documentation. Even IBM can agree to this; it's how they made the bulk of their money between the 1930s and 1970s: The money isn't in the product; it's in the services that go with it.

Ask the Expert

Q: Is it true that the operating system's correct name is GNU/Linux?

A: That depends upon whom you ask. Those with the GNU Project, having worked long and hard to create the tools that make an operating system useful (utilities, compilers, and applications), want their diligence recognized. Because nearly all "Linux" systems consist largely of GNU tools and the Linux kernel, this isn't unreasonable. On the other hand, many people feel that GNU/Linux is too awkward to use as the primary name for an operating system. In any event, the choice is up to you: Linux or GNU/Linux, it's all good.

Q: Linux is Red Hat, right?

A: Red Hat's Linux distribution is very popular, especially in the United States. However, many other excellent distributions exist, and none has the exclusive rights to Linux. I use Red Hat Linux, and presumably the reason you're reading this guide is so that you can use it, too. But once you become more comfortable with Linux, you can create your own distribution if you desire. The freedoms provided by the GPL allow you to customize and even sell Linux if you wish.

Q: Why do I have to pay for "free" software?

A: The short answer is you probably don't. Red Hat is one of many Linux distributions that allow free download, so if you have a high-bandwidth Internet connection, you can slurp down the files, burn some installation CDs, and install the software without paying one red cent. Many distributions are available on CDs from third parties who charge less than $5 each. Some people prefer to pay for support or to buy boxed versions of the software, either to support the company whose product they use, or to ensure that they get timely answers to their questions. Free Software does not mean you're entitled to have it without paying for it, but it does mean that if someone is entitled to have it, they can give it to you if they wish.

CRITICAL SKILL
1.3 Determining Technical Differences Between Windows and Linux

As you might imagine, the differences between Microsoft Windows 2000 or Windows .NET Server and the Linux operating systems cannot be completely discussed in the confines of this section. Throughout these modules, topic by topic, you'll examine the specific contrasts between the two systems. In some modules, you'll find that the text doesn't derive any comparisons, because a major difference doesn't really exist.

Before attacking the details, take a moment to discuss the primary architectural differences between the two operating systems. Historical differences between Linux and Windows are steadily disappearing, but some still persist.

Single Users vs. Multiusers vs. Network Users

Windows was designed according to the "one computer, one desk, one user" vision of Microsoft's cofounder Bill Gates. For the sake of discussion, I'll call this philosophy *single-user*. In this arrangement, two people cannot work in parallel running (for example) Microsoft Word on the same machine at the same time. Using Terminal Services in Windows 2000 or Windows XP allows remote use of one computer from another but is still bound by the single-user paradigm. The Windows .NET Server products, which are unfinished as of this writing, continue to add terminal features to enable more than one user to access the server simultaneously.

Linux borrows its philosophy from UNIX. When UNIX was originally developed at Bell Labs in the early 1970s, it ran on a PDP-7 computer that needed to be shared by an entire department. It required a design that allowed *multiple users* to log in to the central machine at the same time. Various people could edit documents, compile programs, and do other work at the exact same time. The operating system on the central machine took care of the "sharing" details, so that each user seemed to have an individual system. This multiuser tradition continues through today, on other UNIXs as well. And since Linux's birth in the early 1990s, it has supported the multiuser arrangement.

Today, the most common implementation of a multiuser setup is to support *servers*—systems dedicated to running large programs for use by many clients. Each member of a department can have a smaller workstation on the desktop, with enough power for day-to-day work. When they need to do something requiring significantly more CPU power or memory, they can run the operation on the server.

Linux, Windows 2000, and Windows .NET Server are all capable of providing services such as databases over the network. Users of this arrangement can be called *network users,* since they are never actually logged in to the server but rather send requests to the server. The server does the work and then sends the results back to the user via the network. The catch in this case is that an application must be specifically written to perform such server/client duties. Under Linux, a user can run any program allowed by the system administrator on the server without having to redesign that program. Most users find the ability to run arbitrary programs on other machines to be of significant benefit.

Separation of the GUI and the Kernel

Taking a cue from the Macintosh design concept, Windows developers integrated the graphical user interface (GUI) with the core operating system. One simply does not exist without the other. The benefit to this tight coupling of the operating system and the user interface is consistency in the appearance of the system. Although Microsoft does not impose rules as strict as Apple's with respect to the appearance of applications, most developers tend to stick with a basic look and feel among applications.

On the other hand, Linux (like UNIX in general) has kept the two elements—user interface and operating system—separate. The X Window System interface is run as a user-level application, which makes it more stable. If the GUI (which is very complex for both Windows and Linux) fails, Linux's core does not go down with it. The X Window System also differs from the 2000 GUI in that it isn't a complete user interface: It only defines how basic objects should be drawn and manipulated on the screen.

NOTE

Unfortunately, the lack of tight integration of The X Window System into Linux has a downside: While the operating system is very robust, X Windows is somewhat more prone to problems with certain hardware or graphics settings. The Linux version of the "three-finger salute" is CTRL-ALT-BACKSPACE, which kills X.

The most significant feature of the X Window System is its ability to transmit windows across a network and display them on another workstation's screen. This allows a user sitting on Host A to log in to Host B, run an application on Host B, and have all of the output routed back to Host A. It is possible for two people to be logged in to the same machine, running a

Linux equivalent of Microsoft Word (such as OpenOffice, WordPerfect, or StarOffice) at the same time. Even when using Terminal Services, Windows 2000 and Windows XP users are limited to a single user at a time running a given application and using the display.

In addition to the X Windows core, a window manager is needed to create a useful environment. Most Linux distributions (including Red Hat) come with several window managers and include support for GNOME and KDE, both of which are available on other variants of UNIX as well. When set as default, either GNOME or KDE offers an environment that is friendly even to the casual Windows user.

So which is better—Windows 2000 or Linux—and why? That depends on what you are trying to do. The integrated environment provided by Windows 2000 is convenient, and because it is more standardized, it is less complex than Linux, but it lacks the X Windows feature that allows applications to display their windows across the network on other workstations. Windows 2000's GUI is consistent but cannot be turned off, whereas X Windows doesn't have to be running (and consuming valuable memory) on a server.

The Network Neighborhood

The native mechanism for Windows folk to share disks on servers or with each other is through the Network Neighborhood. In a typical scenario, users *attach* to a share and have the system assign it a drive letter. As a result, the separation between client and server is clear. The only problem is that this method of sharing data is more people-oriented than technology-oriented: People have to know which servers contain which data.

Windows 2000 introduced a feature long available on UNIX systems: *mounting.* By mounting a share, Windows makes the share look as if it were just another directory located on the user's local disk. This gives the illusion that a single unified directory structure exists, completely local to the machine. Microsoft's Distributed File System (Dfs) allows a network-wide amalgamation of directories that can be configured and accessed as a directory tree. Windows .NET Server improves Dfs management features and allows a single server to host multiple Dfs trees.

Linux, using the Network File System (NFS), has supported the concept of mounting since its inception. This allows any directory to be "exported" for mounting on other systems. The mounted directory can be placed anywhere in the remote system's directory tree.

A common example of mounting partitions under Linux is with mounted home directories: The user's home directories reside on a server, and the client mounts the directories at boot time (automatically). So **/home** exists on the client, but the contents of **/home/username** exist on the server.

Under Linux NFS, users never have to know server names or directory paths, and their ignorance is your bliss! As with Dfs, there are no more questions about which server to connect to. Users need not know when the need arises to change the server configuration.

Under Linux, you can change the names of servers and adjust this information on client-side systems without making any announcements or having to reeducate users. Anyone who has ever had to reorient users to new server arrangements is aware of the repercussions that may occur. Module 8 discusses the Linux Automounter, which dynamically mounts and unmounts partitions on an as-needed basis.

Printing works in much the same way. Under Linux, printers receive names that are independent of the printer's actual host name. (This is especially important if the printer doesn't speak TCP/IP.) Clients point to a print server whose name cannot be changed without administrative authorization. Settings don't get changed without your knowing it. The print server can then redirect all print requests as needed. The Linux uniform interface will go a long way toward improving what may be a chaotic printer arrangement in your installation. It also means you don't have to install print drivers in several locations.

NOTE

If you intend to use Linux to serve Windows clients via the Samba package, you'll still have to deal with notifying users about server shares and printer assignments. You can read more about Samba in Module 18.

The Registry vs. Text Files

I think of the Windows Registry as the ultimate configuration database—thousands upon thousands of entries, very few of which are completely documented, some located on servers and some located on clients. While it is possible to edit Registry entries manually, the fact that one does so using a graphical tool doesn't make the process intuitive.

Consider this Windows .NET Server Registry setting: In HKEY_LOCAL_MACHINE\ SYSTEM\CurrentControlSet\Control\Session Manager\Memory Management\PrefetchParameters, set **EnablePrefetcher** to **0x00000003** to enable application and boot prefetching. Even assuming you know what prefetching is and want to enable it, that's a daunting configuration change, and not one that I remember offhand.

If you're not getting my message, I'm saying that the Windows Registry system is, at best, very difficult to manage. Although it's a good idea in theory, I've never emerged without injury from a battle with the Registry.

Linux does not have a registry. This is both a blessing and a curse. The blessing is that configuration files are most often kept as a series of text files (think of the Windows .INI files before the days of the Registry). This setup means you're able to edit configuration files using the text editor of your choice rather than tools like **regedit**. In many cases, it also means you can liberally comment those configuration files so that six months from now you won't forget why you set something up in a particular way. With most tools that come with Linux, configuration files exist in the **/etc** directory or one of its subdirectories.

The curse of a no-registry arrangement is that there is no standard way of writing configuration files. Each application or server can have its own format. Many applications are now coming bundled with GUI-based configuration tools, so you can do a basic setup easily and then manually edit the configuration file when you need to do more complex adjustments.

In reality, having text files to hold configuration information usually turns out to be an efficient method. Once set, they rarely need to be changed; even so, they are straight text files and thus easy to view when needed. Even more helpful is that it's easy to write scripts to read the same configuration files and modify their behavior accordingly. This is especially true when automating server maintenance operations, an ability that is crucial in a large site with many servers.

Because Linux configuration files are text files, configuring systems automatically can be done quickly and easily without special tools. Simple scripts can be written to set the configuration values, making deployment of a new operating system, software package, or utility very easy. Windows requires third-party software (often licensed on a per-machine basis, which can become very expensive for large projects) to perform similar feats.

Domains

For a group of Windows 2000 systems to work well together, they should exist in a domain. This requires a Windows 2000 Server system configured as a Domain Controller (DC). Domains are the basis of the Windows 2000 security model.

The basis of Linux's network security model is NIS, Network Information Service. NIS is a simple text file–based database that is shared with client workstations. Each primary NIS server establishes a domain. Any client workstation wanting to join this domain is allowed to do so, as long as it can set its domain name. To set the domain name, you must use the **root** user—Linux's equivalent to an Administrator user. Being part of the domain does not, however, immediately grant you rights that you would otherwise not have. The domain administrator must still add your login to the master NIS password list so that the rest of the systems in the network recognize your presence.

The key difference between NIS and Windows 2000 domains is that the NIS server by itself does not perform authentication the way a DC does. Instead, each host looks up the login and password information from the server and compares it to the user's entered information. It's up to the individual application to properly authenticate a user. Thankfully, the code necessary to authenticate a user is very trivial.

Another important difference is that NIS can be used as a general-purpose database and thus hold any kind of information that needs to be shared with the rest of the network. (This usually includes mount tables for NFS and e-mail aliases.) The only limitation is that each NIS map can have only one key, and the database mechanism doesn't scale well beyond about

20,000 entries. Of course, a site with 20,000 users shouldn't keep them all in a single NIS domain, anyway!

Neither Windows nor Linux requires use of domains for the base operating system to work. Nevertheless, they are key if you need to maintain a multiuser site with a reasonable level of security.

Active Directory

So how does NIS stack up to Active Directory? Good question. The answer is "it doesn't." Active Directory was designed to be much more than what NIS was designed for. This really places the two into different classes of applications.

Active Directory (AD) is designed to be a generic solution to the problem of large sites that need to have their different departments share administrative control—something that the older Windows NT Domain model did very poorly. (Setting up interdomain trusts under NT often required a great deal of patience and a willingness to fix "broken" trusts on a regular basis.) AD is also an opportunity for Microsoft to fix many of its broken naming schemes and move toward an Internet-centric scheme based on DNS. The result is quite beastly and requires a lot of time to master. Mark Minasi's book, *Mastering Windows 2000 Server, Second Edition* (Sybex, 2000), dedicates well over 100 pages to the subject. However, in a smaller network, most folks will find that it looks and feels mostly like the old-style NT domains with some new whiz-bang features thrown in for good measure.

Don't get me wrong, though—AD is a strong step in the right direction for Windows 2000 and presents solid competition for the Linux camp to think about how directory services can be better integrated into their designs. But despite what Microsoft tells you, AD will not solve all the world's problems, let alone all of yours, in one easy step.

So does Linux have anything that compares to AD? Yes, actually, it does. Several implementations of LDAP (Lightweight Directory Access Protocol) now exist for Linux, and work is actively being done to allow NIS to tie into LDAP servers. (The RADIUS authentication protocol is also becoming more common.) LDAP is also interesting because it uses the same underlying technology that Active Directory uses in Windows 2000 and Windows .NET Server. This means that, in theory, it is possible to share LDAP databases between both your UNIX and Windows systems and possibly unify authentication between them.

CRITICAL SKILL

1.4 Exploring Other Linux Resources

If you are interested in getting under the hood of the technology revolution (and it's always helpful to know how things work), I recommend the following texts:

- *Computer: A History of the Information Machine* by Martin Campbell-Kelly and William Aspray (Harper Collins, 1997)

- *A Quarter Century of Unix* by Peter Salus (Addison-Wesley, 1994)

Neither of these texts discusses Linux specifically. *A Quarter Century of Unix* does tell the Linux history up to the point where the system was just becoming a serious player. Peter Salus writes an interesting discussion of why Linus Torvalds saw a need to create Linux in the first place.

To get the scoop on Linux itself, start with the Linux home page at http://www.linux.org. For Linux-related news, http://linuxtoday.com is one of several good resources, and the "News for Nerds" at http://slashdot.org can be an entertaining—and often Linux-related—read.

Module Summary

In this module, you learned about three important topics: Linux distributions, the GNU license (GPL), and the major design differences between Windows 2000 or Windows .NET Server and Linux. Linux is a very powerful operating system, capable of many things. Perhaps its most important feature is being configurable—it's almost like Silly Putty! You can mold it into anything from basic to the most complex shapes. And part of the reward for working with Linux and other Free Software is that it is possible to solve all sorts of problems with many tools that others have made available. Be sure to keep this in mind as you read the remainder of this book and when you start working with Linux in any environment. Linux isn't just a productive, efficient operating system; it also gives you a chance to think creatively. As a Linux user, you won't have to rely on a commercial software vendor to provide you with the features you need; instead, you can learn to take a quick trip to the World Wide Web and find out if there isn't in fact a project already in existence that will solve your problem.

Module 1 Mastery Check

1. What part of the operating system is Linux?

2. What distinguishes one distribution from another?

3. What freedoms does the GPL confer?

   A. Freedom to access source code

   B. Freedom to redistribute the software

     C. Free technical support

     D. Free products

4. Describe the differences between single-user, multiuser, and network-user systems.

5. Which OS was developed as a single-user system?

6. Which OS was developed as a multiuser system?

7. Which OS is capable of supporting network users?

8. What are the performance implications of separating the GUI from the kernel?

9. Which of the following systems support mounting across networks:

     A. Attached File System (AFS)

     B. Linux File System (Lfs)

     C. Network File System (NFS)

     D. Distributed File System (Dfs)

10. In which directory do Linux configuration files usually reside?

11. What does NIS stand for?

12. What function does a DC perform that NIS does not?

13. What directory technology available on Linux is theoretically compatible with Microsoft's Active Directory?

14. Show a good place to start for more information about Linux.

Module 2

Installing Linux in a
Server Configuration

A key attribute in Linux's recent success is the remarkable improvement in installation tools. What once was a mildly frightening process many years back has now become almost trivial. Even better, there are many ways to install the software; CD-ROMs are no longer the only choice (although they are still the most common). Network installations are part of the default list of options as well, and they can be a wonderful help when installing a large number of hosts.

In most cases, designating a system as a server will enable more services than you want. A single Linux system is capable of providing all sorts of services: disk, printers, mail, news, web, chat, and more. Many of these services are turned on automatically. But the reality is that most servers are dedicated to performing one or two tasks, and any other installed services simply take up memory and drag on performance, as well as provide hackers another avenue of attack.

This module discusses the installation process as it pertains to servers. This requires you to do two things: differentiate between a server and a client workstation and streamline a server's operation in terms of its dedicated functions.

You will go through this process for Red Hat Linux, which you will find on the CD-ROM that came with this book.

CRITICAL SKILL
2.1 Performing Preinstallation Evaluation

Before getting into the actual installation phase, it is important that you take a moment and evaluate two things:

- The hardware the system is going to run on

- The server's ideal configuration to provide the services you need

Let's start by examining hardware issues.

Hardware

As with any operating system, before getting started with the installation process, you should determine what hardware configurations would work. Each commercial vendor publishes a hardware compatibility list (HCL) and makes it available on its web site. Red Hat's hardware support site is at http://hardware.redhat.com, where you can search a compatibility database for systems or components. In general, most popular Intel-based configurations work without difficulty.

A general suggestion that applies to all operating systems is to avoid cutting-edge hardware and software configurations. While they appear to be really impressive, they haven't had the maturing process some of the slightly older hardware has gone through. For servers, this usually isn't an issue, since there is no need for a server to have the latest and greatest toys, such as 3-D video cards. After all, your main goal is to provide a highly available server for your users, not to play Doom. (Although it should be noted that I, myself, during my less responsible days as a junior-level administrator, found that Linux is wonderfully stable even while running Doom and being a file server.)

Server Design

When a system becomes a server, its stability, availability, and performance become a significant issue. These three factors are usually improved through the purchase of more hardware, which is unfortunate. It's a shame to pay thousands of dollars extra to get a system capable of achieving in all three areas when you could have extracted the desired level of performance out of existing hardware with a little tuning. With Linux, this is not hard. Even better, the gains are outstanding!

The most significant design decision you must make when managing a server configuration is not technical but administrative. You must design a server to be *un*friendly to casual users. This means no cute multimedia tools, no sound card support, and no fancy web browsers (when at all possible). In fact, it should be a rule that casual use of a server is strictly prohibited— not only to site users but site administrators as well.

Another important aspect of designing a server is making sure that it has a good environment. As a system administrator, you must ensure the physical safety of your servers by keeping them in a separate room under lock and key (or the equivalent). The only access to the servers for nonadministrative personnel should be through the network. The server room itself should be well ventilated and kept cool. The wrong environment is an accident waiting to happen. Systems that overheat and nosy users who think they know how to fix problems can be as great a danger to server stability as bad software (arguably even more so).

Once the system is in a safe place, installing battery backup is also crucial. Backup power serves two key purposes: to keep the system running during a power failure so that it may gracefully shut down, thereby avoiding file damage or loss; and to ensure that voltage spikes, drops, and other noises don't interfere with the health of your system.

Here are some specific things you can do to improve your server situation:

- Take advantage of the fact that the graphical user interface is uncoupled from the core operating system, and avoid starting the X Window System (Linux's GUI) unless someone needs to sit at the console and run an application. After all, like any other application, X requires memory and CPU time to work, both of which are better off going to the server processes instead.

- Determine what functions the server is to perform, and disable all other functions. Not only are unused functions a waste of memory and CPU, they complicate the process of securing the server.

- Unlike some other operating systems, Linux allows you to pick and choose the features you want in the kernel. The default kernel will already be reasonably well tuned, so you won't have to worry about it; but if you do need to change a feature or upgrade the kernel, be picky about what you add and what you don't. Make sure you really need a feature before adding it.

NOTE

You may hear an old recommendation that you recompile your kernel to make the most effective use of your system resources. This is no longer true—the only reason to recompile your kernel is to upgrade or add support for a new device. Remember: Once a server is in use, don't change what's stable and performs reasonably well without a good reason.

Uptime

All of this chatter about taking care of servers and making sure silly things don't cause them to crash stems from a long-time UNIX philosophy: *Uptime is good. More uptime is better.*

The UNIX (Linux) **uptime** command tells the user how long the system has been running since its last boot, how many users are currently logged in, and how much load the system is experiencing. The last two are useful measures that are necessary for day-to-day system health and long-term planning. (For example, the server load has been staying high lately, so maybe it's time to buy a faster/bigger/better server.)

But the all-important number is how long the server has been running since its last reboot. Long uptimes are a sign of proper care, maintenance, and, from a practical standpoint, system stability. You'll often find UNIX administrators boasting about their server's uptimes the way you hear car buffs boast about horsepower. This is also why you'll hear UNIX administrators cursing at system changes (regardless of operating system) that require a reboot to take effect, even though applying the latest kernel security patch may justify that reboot. You may deny caring about it now, but in six months you'll probably scream at anyone who reboots the system unnecessarily. Don't bother trying to explain this phenomenon to a nonadmin, because they'll just look at you oddly. You'll just know in your heart that your uptime is better than theirs.

Dual-Booting Issues

If you are new to Linux, you may not be ready to commit to a complete system when you just want a test drive. All distributions of Linux can be installed on only certain partitions of your hard disk while leaving others alone. Typically, this means allowing Microsoft Windows to coexist with Linux.

Because you are focusing on server installations, the text will not cover the details of building a dual-booting system; however, anyone with a little experience in creating partitions on a disk should be able to figure this out. If you are having difficulty, you may want to refer to the installation guide that comes with your distribution or another one of the many available beginner's guides to Linux.

Some quick hints: If a Windows 95 or Windows 98 partition currently consumes an entire hard disk as drive C:, you can use the **fips** tool to repartition the disk. Simply defragment and then run **fips.exe**. If you are using Windows NT/2000 with NTFS and have already allocated all the disk with data on each partition, you may have to move data around a bit by hand to free up a partition. Don't bother trying to shrink an NTFS partition, though; because of its complexity, it doesn't like being resized, and doing so will lead to corruption.

NOTE

From the perspective of flexibility, NTFS doesn't sound like a good thing, but in reality it is. If you have to run a Windows server, use NTFS.

You may find using a commercial tool such as Partition Magic to be especially helpful, because it offers support for NTFS, FAT32, and regular FAT, as well as a large number of other file system types. Its user interface is also significantly nicer than **fips**.

If you're going to be installing a dual-boot system, install Linux last. If you install Windows last, it will clobber the boot information for your Linux system. If you install Linux last, it will recognize that you have Windows installed and let you choose which one you want to boot by default. Linux gets an "A" for citizenship.

Methods of Installation

With the improved connectivity and speed of both local area networks and Internet connections, it is becoming an increasingly popular option to perform installations over the network rather than using a local CD-ROM.

In general, you'll find that network installations become important once you've decided to deploy Linux over many machines and therefore require a fast installation procedure in which many systems can install at the same time.

Typically, server installations aren't well suited to automation, because each server usually has a unique task; thus, each server will have a slightly different configuration. For example, a server dedicated to handling logging information sent to it over the network is going to have especially large partitions set up for the appropriate logging directories, compared with a file server that performs no logging of its own. (The obvious exception is for server farms where you have large numbers of replicated servers. But even those installations have their nuances that require attention to detail specific to the installation.)

Because of this, you will focus exclusively on the technique for installing a system from a CD-ROM. Of course, once you have gone through the process from a CD-ROM, you will find performing the network-based installations to be very straightforward.

If It Just Won't Work Right . . .

You've gone through the installation procedure . . . twice. This book said it should work. The installation manual said it should work. The Linux guru you spoke with last week said it should work.

But it's just not working.

In the immortal words of Douglas Adams, *don't panic*. No operating system installs smoothly 100 percent of the time. (Yes, not even the Mac OS!) Hardware doesn't always work as advertised, combinations of hardware conflict with each other, that CD-ROM your friend burned for you has CRC errors on it (remember: it is legal for your buddy to burn you a copy of Linux!), or (hopefully not) the software has a bug.

With Linux, you have several paths you can follow for help. If you have purchased your copy from a commercial vendor such as SuSE or Red Hat, you can always call tech support and reach a knowledgeable person who is dedicated to working through the problem with you. If you didn't purchase a box set, you can purchase support from Red Hat and other distributors of Linux. Last, but certainly not least, is the option of going online for help. An incredible number of web sites are available to help you get started. They contain not only useful tips and tricks but also documentation and discussion forums where you can post your questions. Obviously, you'll want to start with the site dedicated to your distribution: www.redhat.com for Red Hat Linux. Other distributions have their own sites. Check your distribution for its appropriate web site information.

Here are some recommended sites for installation help:

- **comp.os.linux.admin** This is a newsgroup, not a web site. You can read it with a news client, or through the web at http://groups.google.com.

- **comp.os.linux.redhat** This is another newsgroup, but Red Hat Linux–specific.

- **linux.redhat** This is another Red Hat Linux newsgroup.

- **http://www.linuxdoc.org/** This site is a collection of wonderful information about all sorts of Linux-related topics, including installation guides. Just a warning, though: Not all documents are up to date. Be sure to check the date of any document's last update before following the directions. There is a mix of cookbook-style help guides as well as guides that give more complete explanations of what is going on.

- **http://linuxnewbie.org/** This site features "Newbie-ized Help Files" that help with a variety of hardware and software issues.

● **http://everythinglinux.org/**   Everything Linux, as you might expect, has a wide variety of resources for the Linux user, including how-to information and reviews.

Project 2-1 | Determining a Server's Functions

Before installing the Linux server, it's a useful exercise to determine exactly what purpose the server will serve. Even though you do not know all the functions available, you may have an idea of what is or isn't required of the server you plan to install. Knowing which specific functions are needed will ensure that the system has all the software it needs, and that it isn't bogged down or made exploitable by having unnecessary software installed.

Step by Step

1. Consider each of the following questions, making a list of services that are definitely needed or definitely not needed:

   ● Will this system's disk resources will be accessible for mounting by other systems using NFS? Will it provide print services?

   ● Which Internet-related services will this server provide? For example, will it be used as a web server? Will it provide mail, IRC, newsgroup, or other such services?

   ● Will the system be a database server?

   ● Will the system perform authentication tasks such as running as an LDAP or NIS server?

   ● Will the system perform any network functions by performing routing, firewalling, SNMP or traffic monitoring, or the like?

   ● Will program development take place on this system? Which languages will be used? What compilers, debuggers, libraries, and utilities are necessary?

   ● How will remote users access the system? Do they need FTP or telnet access? Will SSH or rlogin or rsh be used?

   ● Will the system be accessible from the console, and if so, is the X Window System necessary? How much work will be done in the GUI, and which windowing environments are required?

2. Looking at the list of requirements, make a note of any components that are implied by the must-have items. For example, a web and database server may require tools to interface from the web pages to the database, so Perl or PHP might be useful.

3. What documentation needs to be installed on this system? If it will be a developer or end-user resource, there may be more documentation requirements than if it will be just one of many systems in a large server farm.

(continued)

4. If this is a test server, what type of functions would you like to try? Make a note of each, and when it comes time to install the software, you may be able to find packages you didn't know existed.

Project Summary

You may feel that you don't yet know enough about Linux to determine what your server is going to do. But whether you go through this process before or after you first install Red Hat Linux, you'll find that it's a good way of focusing on real needs. Otherwise, looking at all the available packages can be a little like going grocery shopping on an empty stomach.

CRITICAL SKILL
2.2 # Installing Red Hat Linux

This section documents the steps necessary to install Red Hat Linux 8.0 on a stand-alone system. It will take a liberal approach to the process, installing all of the tools possibly relevant to server operations. Later modules explain each subsystem's purpose and help you determine which ones you really need to keep.

You have two ways to start the boot process: you can use a boot floppy or the CD-ROM. This installation guide assumes you will boot off the CD-ROM to start the Red Hat installation procedure. If you have an older machine not capable of booting off the CD-ROM, you will need to use a boot disk and start the procedure from there.

NOTE

Using the boot disk changes the order of some of the installation steps, such as which language to use and whether to use a hard disk or CD-ROM for installation. Once past the initial differences, you will find that the graphical steps are the same.

If your system supports bootable CD-ROMs, this is obviously the faster approach. If your distribution did not come with a boot disk and you cannot boot from the CD-ROM, you will need to create the boot disk. You will need a working installation of Windows to create the boot disk.

NOTE

Users who have a working UNIX operating system can use the **dd** command to create the boot image onto a floppy disk. Follow the instructions that came with your distribution for using the **dd** command with your floppy device.

Creating a Boot Disk

Once Windows has started and the CD-ROM is in the appropriate drive, open an MS-DOS Prompt window (Start | Program Menu | MS-DOS Prompt), which will give you a command shell prompt. Change over to the CD-ROM drive letter and go into the **dosutils** directory. There you will find the **rawrite.exe** program. Simply run the executable; you will be prompted for the source file and destination floppy. The source file will be on the same drive and is called **/images/boot.img**.

You can find more detail on this process at http://www.redhat.com/docs/manuals/linux/ RHL-8.0-Manual/install-guide/s1-steps-install-cdrom.html.

Starting the Installation

To begin the installation process, boot off the CD-ROM. This will present you with a splash screen introducing you to Red Hat 8.0. At the bottom of the screen will be a prompt that reads

```
boot:
```

If you do not press any key, the prompt will automatically time out and begin the graphical installation process. You can press ENTER to start the process immediately.

NOTE

If you have had some experience with Red Hat installations in the past and do not want the system to automatically probe your hardware, you can type in **expert** at the boot: prompt. For most installations, though, you will want to stick with the default.

If you don't have a mouse, or if the installer cannot find yours, you will be presented with a screen that asks whether you want to use the text mode installation or you want to help the installer figure out what kind of mouse you have. Use the TAB key to select which choice you want, and press ENTER to continue. If you proceed with the text mode, you will find that the basic steps to the installation are similar to those for the graphical interface, and you should be able to follow along with this installation guide. If you need additional help, you can visit Red Hat's help page for the text-mode installation at http://www.redhat.com/docs/manuals/linux/ RHL-8.0-Manual/install-guide/s1-guimode-textinterface.html.

Welcome to Red Hat Linux

The installer's first graphical screen welcomes you to Red Hat Linux (see Figure 2-1). The interface works much like any other GUI interface. Simply point to your selection and click.

Notice that context-sensitive help appears on the left side of the screen. If you don't want to see it, you can click the Hide Help button at the lower-left part of the screen. The Back button in the lower right of the screen is grayed out at this point, because there have been no prior options to select.

This screen isn't very challenging: there aren't any choices to be made. When you are ready to continue, click the Next button in the lower-right portion of the screen.

Choosing a Language

The first menu will ask which language you want to use to continue the installation process (see Figure 2-2). Once you have chosen the desired language, click Next to continue.

Figure 2-1 The first installer screen welcomes you to Red Hat Linux.

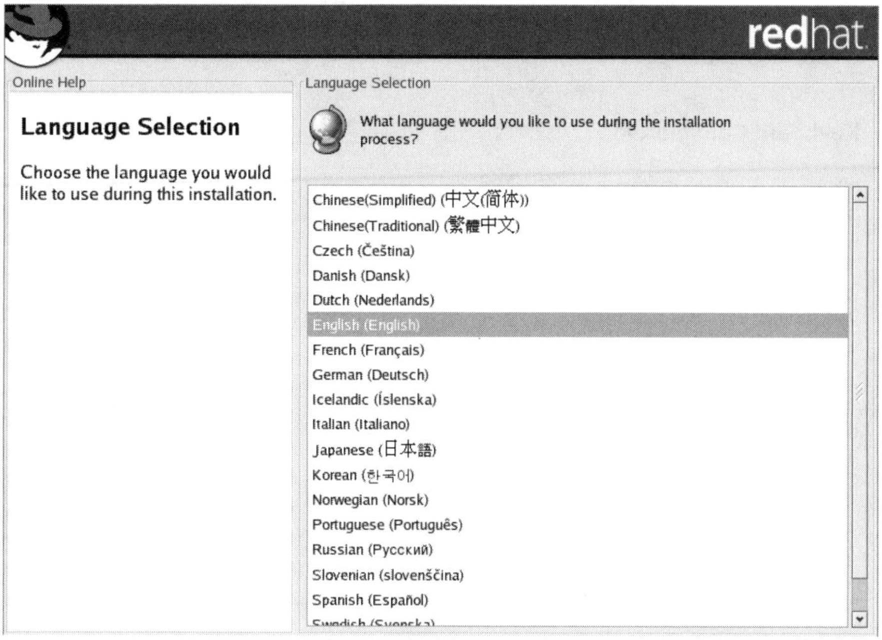

Figure 2-2 Select the language to be used during installation.

Selecting a Keyboard Type

This next menu enables you to select what kind of keyboard you have. For most people, the keyboard type will be selected according to language and geography (see Figure 2-3). A Dvorak keyboard layout may be selected here if you prefer it.

TIP

If you ever want to change your keyboard layout or type, you can run the program **/usr/bin/redhat-config-keyboard**.

When you are done, click Next to continue, or click Back to go back to the language selection menu.

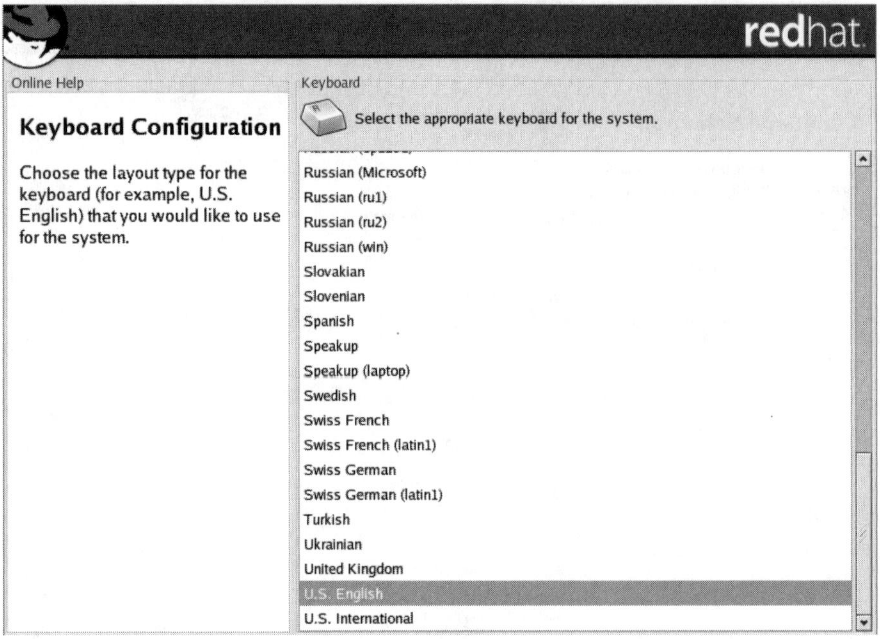

Figure 2-3 Select the preferred keyboard layout.

Selecting a Mouse

You now can select the type of mouse you want to use with the X Window environment. More than likely, the autoprobe will have been able to identify what kind of mouse you have.

If you need to help Linux, simply pick your mouse type from the top menu box (see Figure 2-4). The Generic settings work well in most cases, but you can scroll through the list of manufacturers and look for the maker of your particular mouse. Click on the triangle to the left of the vendor's name to open a new level of choices for that particular brand.

If you have a serial mouse, you will also need to select the serial port it is using, which you can do in the lower box of the screen.

If you have a two-button mouse, click Emulate 3 Buttons at the bottom of the screen, because some features of the X Window environment work with a three-button mouse only. The emulation allows you to click both buttons of a two-button mouse to simulate the third (middle) button.

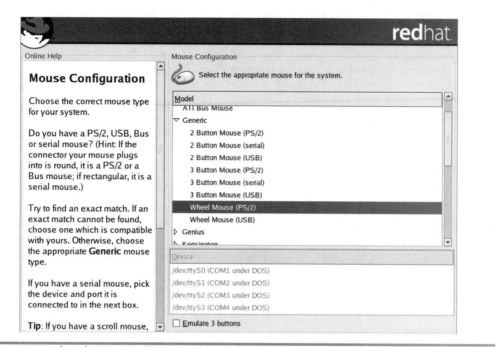

Figure 2-4 Select the mouse description that most closely matches your hardware.

TIP

If you change the type of mouse you have later, you can run
/usr/bin/redhat-config-mouse to reconfigure your mouse.

Installation Type

With the language and input devices selected, you are now ready to begin the actual installation phase of Red Hat Linux. You will see a screen that lets you pick how you want to install Red Hat Linux. If you are on an upgrade path, this selection is easy—simply click Upgrade and then click Next. You'll see some screens informing you of what is being currently upgraded.

This module assumes that you're doing a clean installation. This will wipe all the existing contents of the disk before freshly installing Red Hat 8.0.

CAUTION

I mean it. This process will lay waste to your hard disk and leave no data standing. So please perform this installation on a disk that doesn't hold the only copy of your late Great Aunt Sonia's world-champion pretzel recipe.

Note that under the Install button is an option to install Linux in a Server configuration (see Figure 2-5). This method has all of the packages selected for you, as well as a disk-partitioning scheme. While that can be a fine starting point for playing with Linux, for this module, you want to choose Custom so that you can fine-tune what you install and how you configure it.

Creating Partitions for Linux

Since you selected the custom installation, you will need to create partitions for Linux to install on. If you are used to the Windows installation process, you will find that this process is a little different from how you partition Windows into separate drives.

In short, each partition is *mounted* at boot time. The mount process makes the contents of that partition available as if it were just another directory on the system. For example, the root

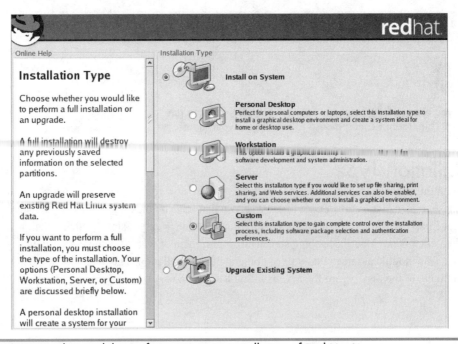

Figure 2-5 For this module, perform a Custom installation of Red Hat Linux.

directory (/) is the topmost directory in the structure. In a simple configuration (for example, the one performed when you choose the Automatically Partition option in a custom installation), the system's entire directory structure will be created on a single partition. More complicated configurations make more sense in most cases. For example, a standard Linux subdirectory called **/usr** will exist in the root directory, but it will have nothing in it. A separate partition can then be mounted such that going into the **/usr** directory will allow you to see the contents of the newly mounted partition (see Figure 2-6).

Since all of the partitions, when mounted, appear as a unified directory tree rather than as separate drives, the installation software does not differentiate one partition from another. All it cares about is into which directory each file goes. As a result, the installation process automatically distributes its files across all the mounted partitions, as long as the mounted partitions represent different parts of the directory tree where files are usually placed. Under Linux, the most significant grouping of files is in the **/usr** directory, where all of the actual programs reside. (In Windows terms, this is similar to **C:\Program Files**.)

Because you are configuring a server, you need to be aware of the additional large groupings of files that will exist over the life of the server. They are:

- **/usr**, where all of the program files will reside (similar to **C:\Program Files**).

- **/home**, where everyone's home directory will be (assuming this server will house them). This is useful for keeping users from consuming an entire disk and leaving other critical components without space (such as log files).

- **/var**, the final destination for log files. Because log files can be affected by outside users (for instance, individuals visiting a web site), it is important to partition them off so that no one can perform a Denial of Service (DoS) attack by generating so many log entries that the entire disk fills up.

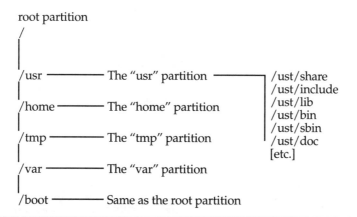

Figure 2-6 The contents of the **/usr** directory can be mounted on a separate partition from the root directory.

- **/tmp**, where temporary files are placed. Because this directory is designed so that it is writable by any user (similar to the **C:\Temp** directory under Windows), you need to make sure arbitrary users don't abuse it and fill up the entire disk; you ensure this by keeping it on a separate partition.

- **Swap**. This isn't a user-accessible file system, but it is where the virtual memory file is stored. Although Linux (and other UNIXs, as well) can use a normal disk file to hold virtual memory the way Windows does, you'll find that having it on its own partition improves performance.

Now you see why it is a good idea to create multiple partitions on a disk rather than a single large partition, which you may be used to doing under Microsoft Windows. As you become more familiar with the hows and whys of partitioning disks under Linux, you may choose to go back to a single large partition. At that point, of course, you will have enough knowledge of both systems to understand why one may work better for you than the other.

Now that you have some background on partitioning under Linux, let's go back to the installation process itself. The installation screen gives you three options (see Figure 2-7): automatically partition the disk, manually partition the disk with Disk Druid, or manually partition the disk with fdisk.

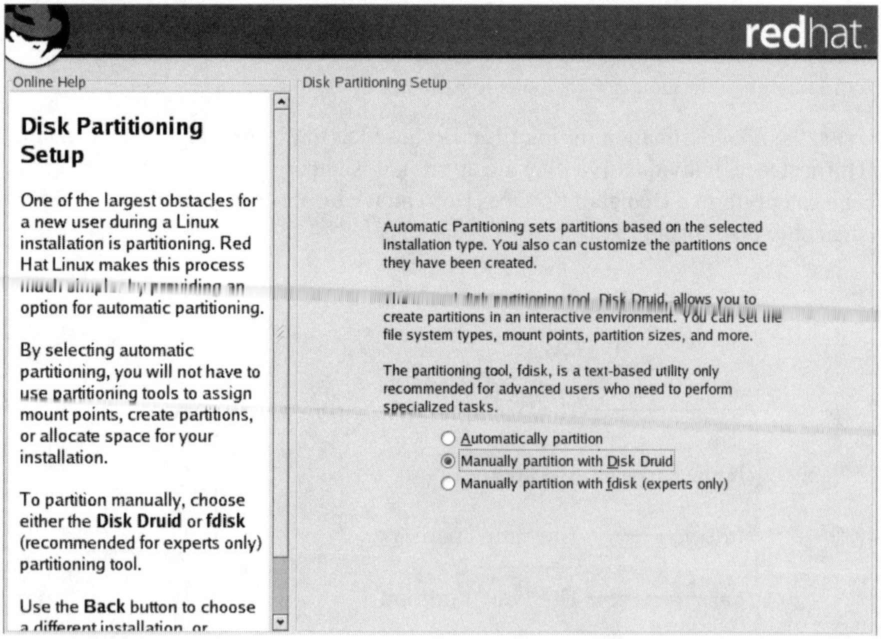

Figure 2-7 Hard disk partitions can be configured automatically, or manually using Disk Druid or fdisk.

You don't want to use the first option, because you want tight control over how the disk gets allocated in a server environment. And while using fdisk is extremely powerful, it can also be a bit daunting at first. (Don't worry: it is covered in Module 7.) So this leaves you with Disk Druid. Simply select Disk Druid and click Next. This will take you to Figure 2-8.

The Disk Druid partitioning tool was developed by Red Hat as an easy way to create partitions and associate them to the directories as which they will be mounted. When starting Disk Druid, you will see a graphical representation of the disk's partition layout, as well as detail on all of the existing partitions on your disk. Each partition entry will show the following information:

- **Device**   Linux associates each partition with a separate *device*. For the purpose of installation, you need to know only that under IDE disks, each device begins with **/dev/hd**X*Y*. Here, *X* is either:

  - **a** for IDE Master on the first chain
  - **b** for IDE Slave on the first chain
  - **c** for IDE Master on the second chain
  - **d** for IDE Slave on the second chain

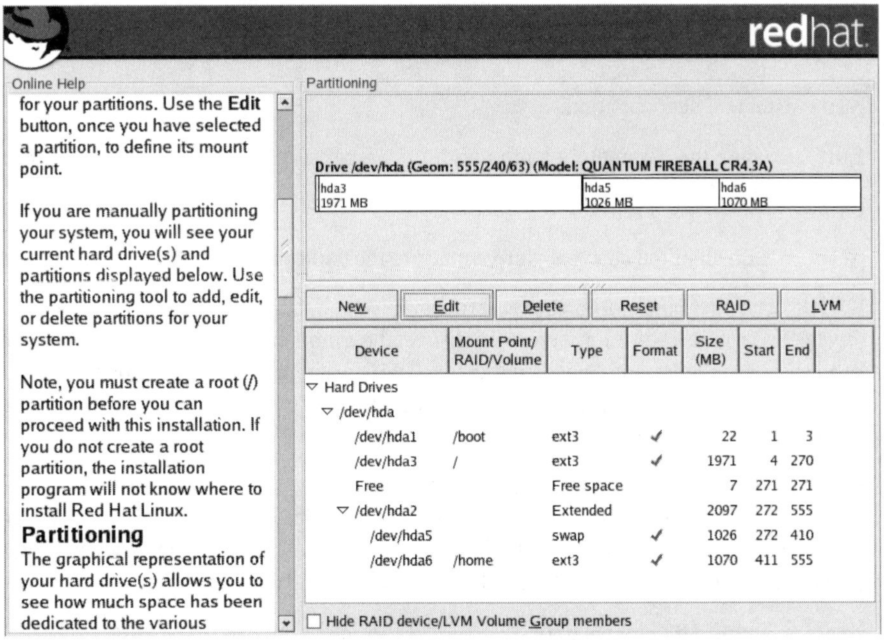

Figure 2-8 The Disk Druid starts by displaying the existing disk partitions.

Y is the partition number of the disk. For example, **/dev/hda1** is the first partition on the primary chain, primary disk. SCSI follows the same basic idea, except instead of starting with **/dev/hd**, each partition starts with **/dev/sd** and follows the format **/dev/sd***XY,* where *X* is a letter representing a unique physical drive (**a** is for SCSI id 1, **b** is for SCSI id 2, and so on). The *Y* represents the partition number. Thus **/dev/sdb4** is the fourth partition on the SCSI disk with id 2. The system is a little more complex than Windows, but each partition's location is explicit—no more guessing, "What physical device does E: correspond to?"

● **Mount point** The location where the partition is mounted. Initially, this should not contain any entries.

● **Type** The partition's type. Red Hat Linux's default type is ext3, but Disk Druid also understands many others, including FAT, FAT32, and NTFS.

● **Format** Indicates whether the partition will be formatted before Linux installation.

● **Size** Partition size in MB.

● **Start** Partition's initial cylinder number.

● **End** Partition's ending cylinder number.

In the middle of the screen are the buttons for controlling what you do with Disk Druid. These buttons are:

● **New** Create a new partition.

● **Edit** Change the parameters on the highlighted partition.

● **Delete** Delete the highlighted partition.

● **Reset** Undo all of the changes you've made to the partition table but have not committed to.

● **RAID** Use this button to create a partition in which data is distributed among multiple drives. This can be useful for increasing disk read performance or providing data redundancy. While this installation guide does not cover RAID installations, Red Hat provides extensive information on RAID concepts and configuration at http://www.redhat.com/docs/manuals/linux/RHL-8.0-Manual/custom-guide/ch-raid-intro.html.

● **LVM** The Logical Volume Manager (LVM) approach to disk space allocation is designed to make resizing the system's disk space easier on the fly. Configuring LVM is beyond the scope of this guide, but more information is available at http://www.redhat.com/docs/manuals/linux/RHL-8.0-Manual/custom-guide/ch-lvm.html.

● **Next** Commit all changes to disk.

● **Back** Abort all changes made using Disk Druid and exit the program.

NOTE

The changes made within Disk Druid are not committed to disk until you click Next.

Sizing Partitions   The exact amount of space you allocate to each partition depends on how much space you have and what you plan to do with it. All the same, there are some basic guidelines for sizing partitions in Red Hat Linux 8.0. If you install all the partitions suggested in this module, the basic sizing parameters look like this:

Partition	Minimum Size	Maximum Suggested Size
Swap	Same size as amount of installed RAM	Double the size of installed RAM
/	384MB	
/home	Depends on anticipated usage; 100MB	If you allocate it, they will fill it
/tmp	100MB	
/usr	Depends upon software and documentation to be installed; 2,000MB	
/var	256MB	

Adding a Partition   To create a new partition, click New. This will bring up a dialog box where each of the elements in the dialog box should resemble those in Figure 2-9:

- **Mount Point**   The directory where you want this partition to be automatically mounted at boot time.

- **File System Type**   The type of partition that will reside on that disk. By default, you will want to select ext3 except for the swap partition (which should be of type "swap").

- **Allowable Drives**   Specifies onto which drives the partition can be created.

- **Size (MB)**   The size of the partition in megabytes.

- **Additional Size Options**   If you know the exact size you wish to make the partition, select Fixed Size. The second option allows you to instead set a maximum size, while the last option allows Disk Druid to make the partition as large as possible.

- **Force to be a primary partition**   If this box is checked, the partition being added cannot be an "extended" partition. You are unlikely to have a reason to set this option; let Disk Druid configure the disk partition details.

- **Check for bad blocks**   If you have an old or questionable hard disk, it's worth setting this option, but it takes much longer to format the partition if you do. Once you are done entering all of the information, click OK to continue.

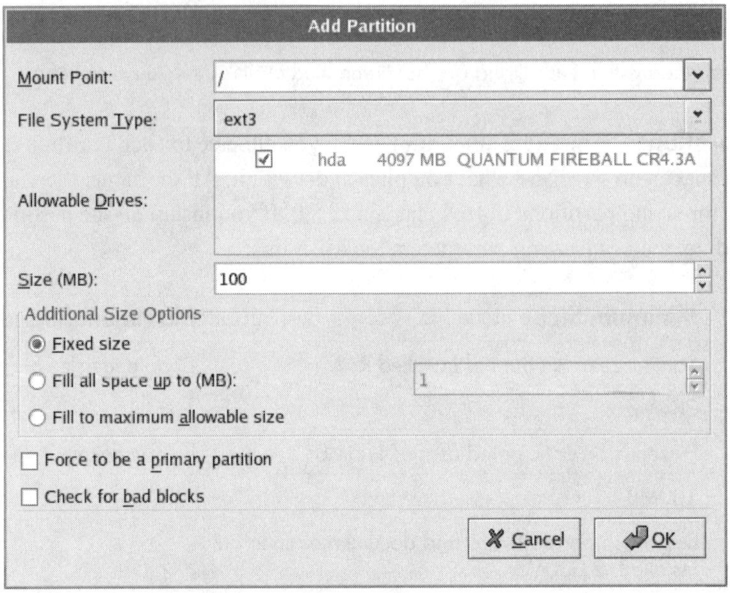

Add Partition		
Mount Point:	/	
File System Type:	ext3	
	☑ hda 4097 MB QUANTUM FIREBALL CR4.3A	
Allowable Drives:		
Size (MB):	100	

Additional Size Options
- ⦿ Fixed size
- ○ Fill all space up to (MB): [1]
- ○ Fill to maximum allowable size

- ☐ Force to be a primary partition
- ☐ Check for bad blocks

[✗ Cancel] [✓ OK]

Figure 2-9 Add a new partition using Disk Druid.

At a minimum, you need to have two partitions: one for holding all of the files and the other for swap space. Swap space is usually sized to be double the available RAM if there are fewer than 128MB of RAM, or the same size as the amount of RAM if there are more than 128MB.

Ideally, you will want to separate partitions for **/usr**, **/var**, **/home**, and **/tmp** in addition to a root partition. Obviously, you can adjust this equation according to the purpose of the server.

Other Partition Manipulation Tasks   Once you have gone through the steps of adding a partition, and you are comfortable with the variables involved (mount points, sizes, types, devices, and so on), the actual process of editing and deleting partitions is quite simple. Editing an entry means changing the exact same entries that you established when you added the partition, and deleting an entry requires only that you confirm that you really want to perform the deletion.

After you have configured the partitions and mount points as you want them, click Next to continue.

NOTE

One last detail that I have intentionally omitted is the process of adding network drive mounts (NFS). This requires a more complete explanation and is covered in Module 7.

Installing the Boot Loader

GRUB is the default *boot manager* for Red Hat Linux 8.0. If you aren't already familiar with what it does, a boot manager handles the process of actually starting the load process of an operating system. If you're familiar with Windows NT, you have already dealt with the NT Loader (NTLDR), which presents the menu at boot time, allowing you to select whether you want Windows NT or Windows NT (VGA only). You may also have run across NTLDR if you've set up a Windows machine in a dual boot configuration. GRUB performs the same function for Linux systems.

NOTE

Red Hat Linux also allows the use of the LILO boot loader, but GRUB is the default, and it works well, so it's used here.

The Red Hat tool's screen for setting up GRUB has three sections (see Figure 2-10). The top section includes a list of the bootable partitions and a button for changing the boot loader to LILO (or for not enabling a boot loader at all).

The middle block of this configuration screen allows you to select whether you want to enable password protection on the boot loader. You want to enable this to prevent

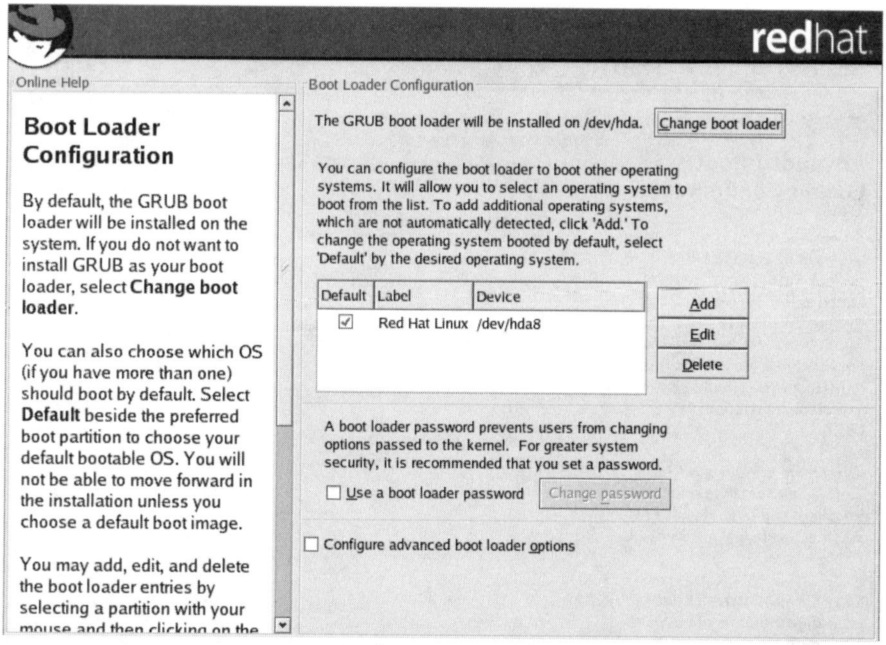

Figure 2-10 Configure the GRUB boot loader to boot Linux.

unauthorized access to the boot settings, so click the check box, which will bring up the password box as shown.

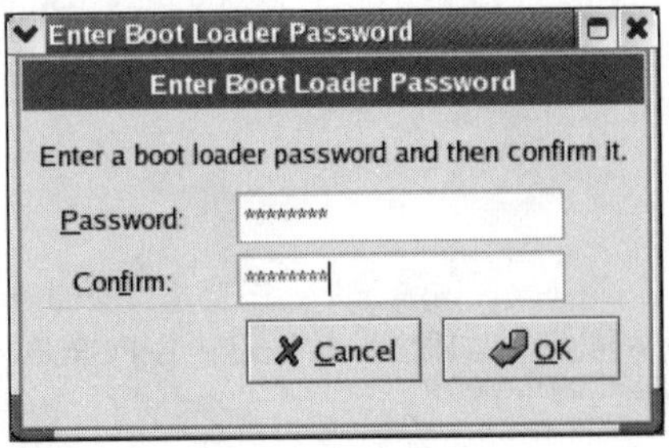

The check box in the last section of the boot loader configuration screen allows you to set somewhat more esoteric features of the boot loader. If you check the box and click Next, you will get an advanced configuration screen (see Figure 2-11).

GRUB sets up on the master boot record (MBR) or the first partition on which Linux resides. The MBR is the very first thing the system will read when booting a system. It is essentially the point where the built-in hardware tests finish and pass off control to the

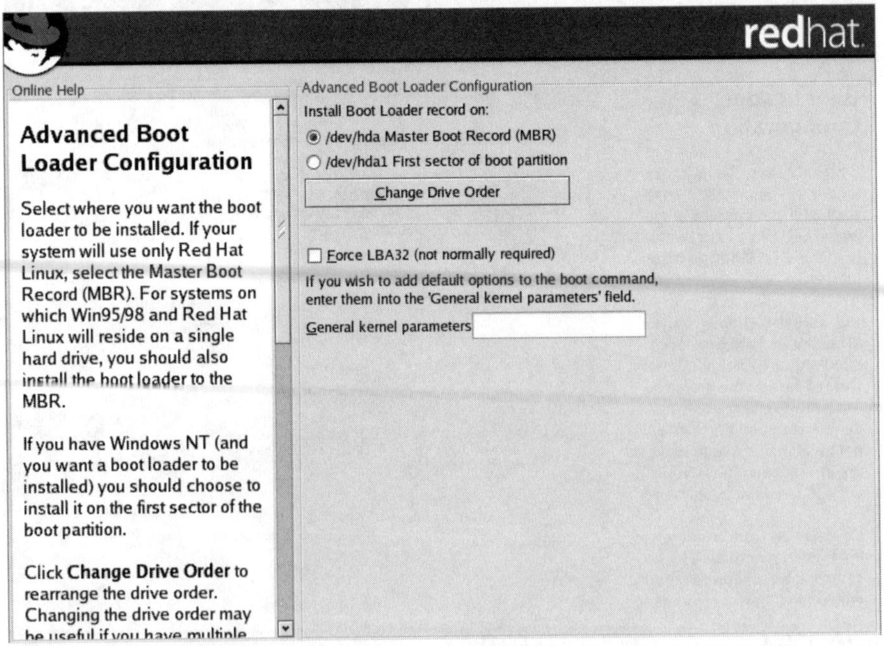

Figure 2-11 Set the boot loader's location and pass parameters to the kernel.

software. This is the default; if you allow GRUB to be installed here, its graphical boot menu will load when you power on or reboot your system, and it will allow you to select which operating system to load. In a server configuration, there may be choices of Linux kernels to load, but there should just be one operating system option!

NOTE

SMP-based systems will start with two boot image choices. The first choice, Red Hat Linux, is set up to support multiple processors. In the event that you encounter a problem with this configuration, Red Hat Linux-up will also be available; it will utilize only one processor, but at least it will get you up and going.

If you are already using another boot loader and prefer it, then you will want to place GRUB on the first sector of the root partition. This will allow your preferred boot loader to run first and then pass control off to GRUB, should you decide to start Linux. Figuring out how to notify your preferred boot loader that there's a new operating system available is up to you.

This screen also has an option to Force LBA32, which uses linear mode. This applies only to some SCSI drives or drives that are accessed in LBA mode, so unless you know that it applies to you, or are experimenting, leave the box unchecked.

The last option on this advanced configuration screen is a box that allows you to enter kernel parameters to be used at boot time. Most people can ignore this box. If the documentation for a particular feature or device requires you to pass a parameter here, add it; otherwise, leave it blank.

Setting Up Networking

Now Red Hat is ready to configure your network interface cards (see Figure 2-12).

Each interface card recognized by Linux will be listed in the table at the top of your screen. Ethernet devices are listed as eth0, eth1, eth2, and so on. You can select each interface and click Edit to configure it using DHCP or to set the IP address by hand, as shown.

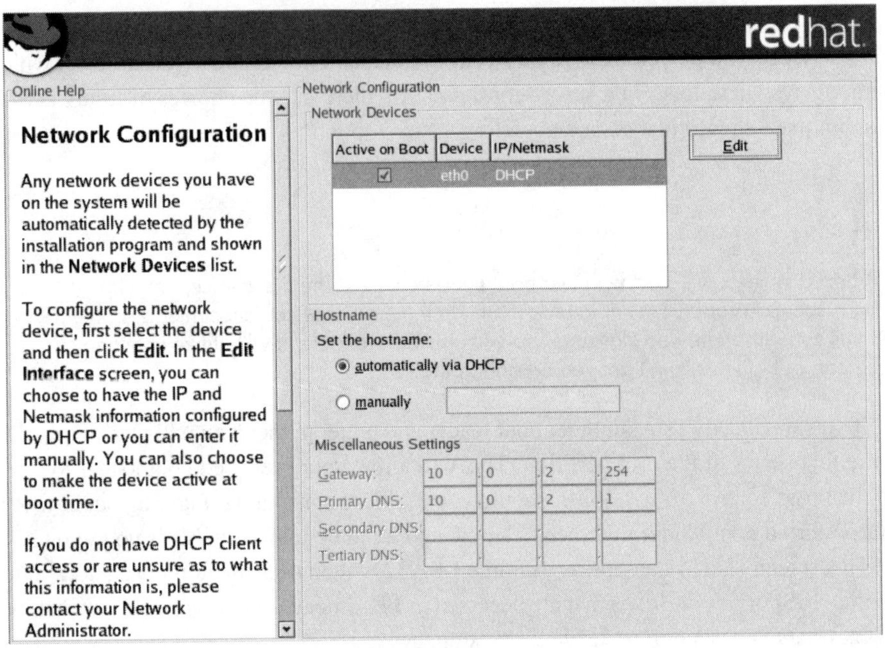

Figure 2-12 Configure network cards and IP settings.

If you choose to configure by hand, be sure to have the IP and netmask values handy.

Check the Activate On Boot button for a card if you want the interface to be enabled at boot time.

On the bottom half of the screen, you'll see the configuration choices for giving the machine a host name, a gateway, and related DNS information. If you have enabled DHCP on one of the network interfaces, you can opt to have the machine's name set from the DHCP server.

NOTE

Even if you are not part of a network, you can fill in the host name. If you don't fill in a host name, your computer will be known as localhost.

Once you have all of this filled in, simply click Next to continue.

Firewall Configuration

The next screen allows you to configure the firewall functionality of your Linux system (see Figure 2-13).

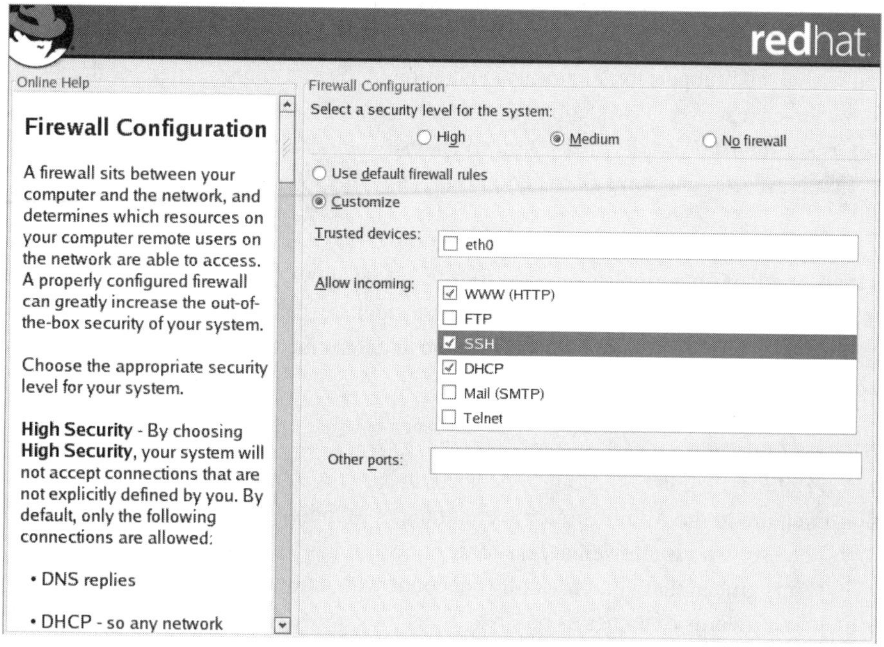

Figure 2-13 Configure the firewall properties on the Linux server.

How tightly or loosely you set access to the system will depend entirely on what type of function the server will perform. For example, if you want your system to serve as an NFS server so that other systems can mount its drives, you cannot set the high or medium security levels on this page. On the other hand, if you want this system to act as a web server without RealAudio content, the High security level may be the best choice.

If you don't plan to have access to the console of your Linux server, you should be sure to allow a method of managing the system remotely; enabling SSH can do this. You'll spend more time on configuring Red Hat Linux 8.0 to be secure in Module 9.

TIP

If it turns out you have over-constrained your server and are having problems accessing it or using it the way you intended, you can temporarily shut off the firewall using the command **/sbin/service iptables stop**, but be careful about doing so on a vulnerable network.

When you have configured the firewall properties to your satisfaction, click Next to continue installation.

Additional Language Support

If you wish to add support for languages in addition to the one you specified for the installation process, the next screen allows you to do so (see Figure 2-14). You can set up your Linux server as a virtual Tower of Babel if you so choose.

Click Next after choosing all the additional languages you need.

Time Zone Configuration

The time zone configuration screen (see Figure 2-15) allows you to select in which time zone the machine is located. If your system's hardware clock keeps time in UTC, be sure to click the System Clock Uses UTC button so that Linux can determine the difference between the two and display the correct local time.

Creating Accounts

The Red Hat Installation tool creates one account for you called **root**. This user account is similar in nature to the Administrator account under Windows 2000 and Windows .NET Server: The user who is allowed access to this account has full control of the system.

Thus, it is crucial that you protect this account with a good password. Be sure not to pick dictionary words or names as passwords, as they are easy to guess and crack.

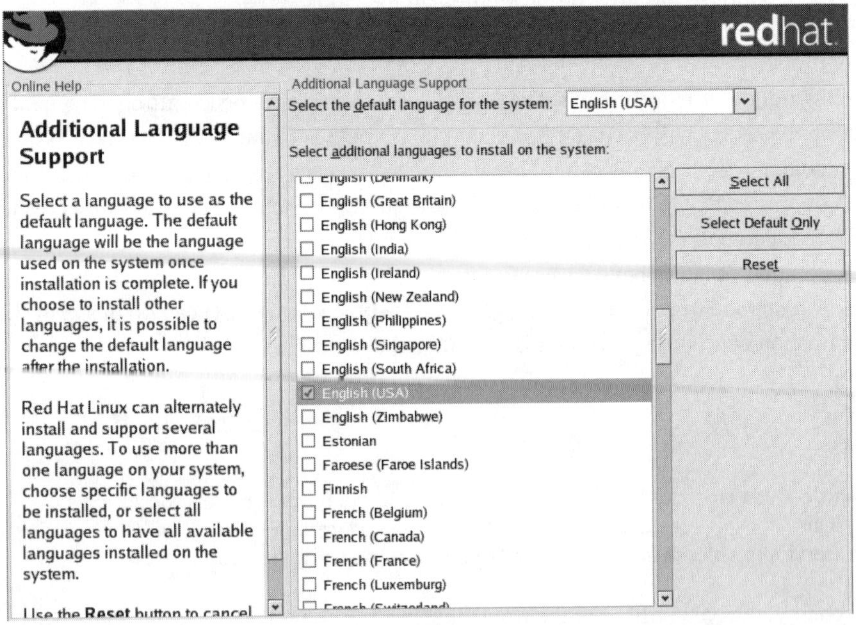

Figure 2-14 Add additional language support for multilingual environments.

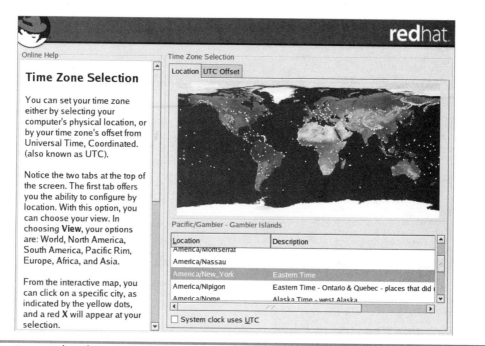

Figure 2-15 Select the correct time zone from the map or the text listing.

Part of protecting **root** means not allowing users to log in as the root user over the network. This keeps crackers from being able to guess your root password by using automated login scripts. In order to allow legitimate users to become the root user, you need to log in as yourself, and then use the **su** (switch user) command. Thus, setting the root password isn't enough if you intend to perform remote administration; you will need to set up a real user, as well.

In general, it is considered a good idea to set up a normal user to do day-to-day work anyway. This gives you the protection of not being able to accidentally break configuration files or other important components while you're just surfing the Net or performing nonadministrative tasks. The exception to this rule is, of course, certain server configurations where there should never be any users besides the root user (for example, firewalls).

In Figure 2-16, you see the screen that lets you set the root password as well as create new users.

Begin by picking a root password and entering it into the Root Password box at the top of the screen. Enter it again in the Confirm box right below; this protects you from locking yourself out of the system in case you make a typo. The text Root Password Accepted will appear below the password boxes once you have entered a password twice the same way.

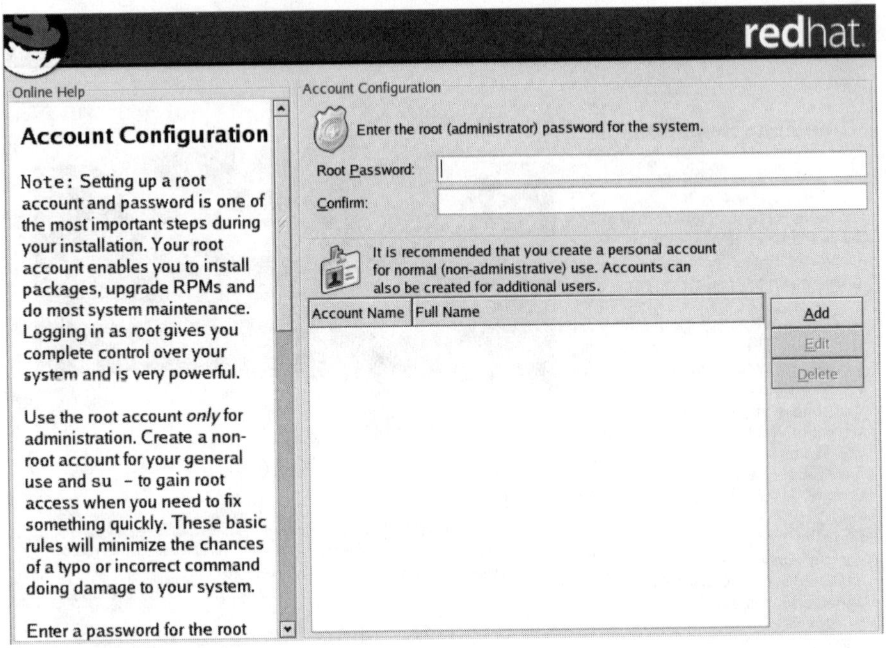

Figure 2-16 Set a strong password for the root user and add additional users.

NOTE

You do not need to add the root user.

The remainder of the screen is meant for creating new user accounts. To do so, simply click Add to bring up the Add A User Account window as shown.

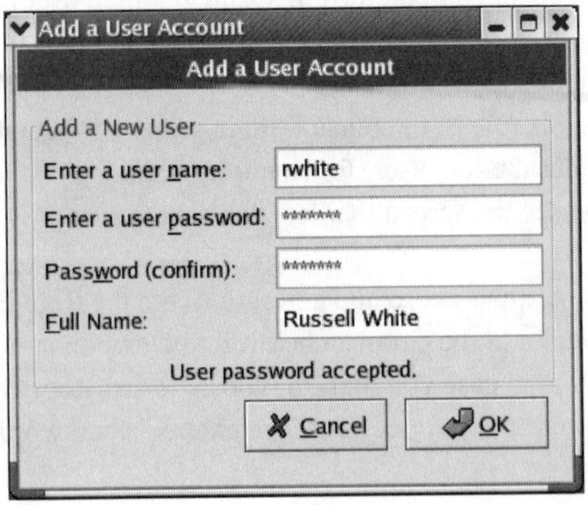

Enter the username in the Account Name box, the user's password in the Password and Password (confirm) boxes, and the user's real name in the Full Name box. Click OK to insert this new user into the list of user accounts. Repeat as desired and then click Next to continue.

NOTE

If you make any mistakes while adding new users, you can delete and edit them, as well.

Authentication Configuration

Linux keeps its list of users in the **/etc/passwd** file. Each system has its own copy of this file, and a user listed in one **/etc/passwd** file cannot log into another system unless that user has an entry in the other **/etc/passwd** file. To allow users to log in to any system in a network of computers, Linux can use the Network Information System (NIS) to handle remote password file issues.

In addition to listing users, the **/etc/passwd** file contains all of the passwords for each user in an encrypted format. For a very long time, this was acceptable because the process of attacking such files to crack passwords was so computationally expensive, it was almost futile to even try. Within the last few years, affordable PCs have gained the necessary computational power to present a threat to this type of security, and therefore a push to use *shadow passwords* has come. With shadow passwords, the actual encrypted password entry is not kept in the **/etc/passwd** file but rather in an **/etc/shadow** file. The **/etc/passwd** file remains readable by any user in the system, but **/etc/shadow** is readable by the root user only. Obviously, this is a good step up in security.

Another method to arise has been a technique utilizing the MD5 hashing function. (Don't worry about the details of MD5—all you need to concern yourself with is the fact that it is better than the stock method.) Unless you have a specific reason not to do this, be sure to check the Enable MD5 Passwords and Enable Shadow Passwords check boxes (see Figure 2-17).

If your site has an existing NIS infrastructure, enter the relevant NIS domain and server name in this window. If you don't know or if you want to deal with this later, you can safely ignore this step.

Another option is to use a Lightweight Directory Access Protocol (LDAP) server for storing passwords. This is ideal for an environment where you have many thousands of users accessing many servers and NIS doesn't cut it performance-wise. If you aren't sure about LDAP or whether you have an LDAP server, you can skip this step.

If you are in a Kerberos environment, you will need to enable the Kerberos authentication method. If you go this route, contact your Kerberos administrator for the appropriate realm names, KDC, and admin server. If you aren't sure about what Kerberos is, then you probably don't need it.

If you are in an established Windows environment and have an SMB server in use for authentication, the Linux system can also make use of this authentication method. If you're not sure about SMB authentication, skip it.

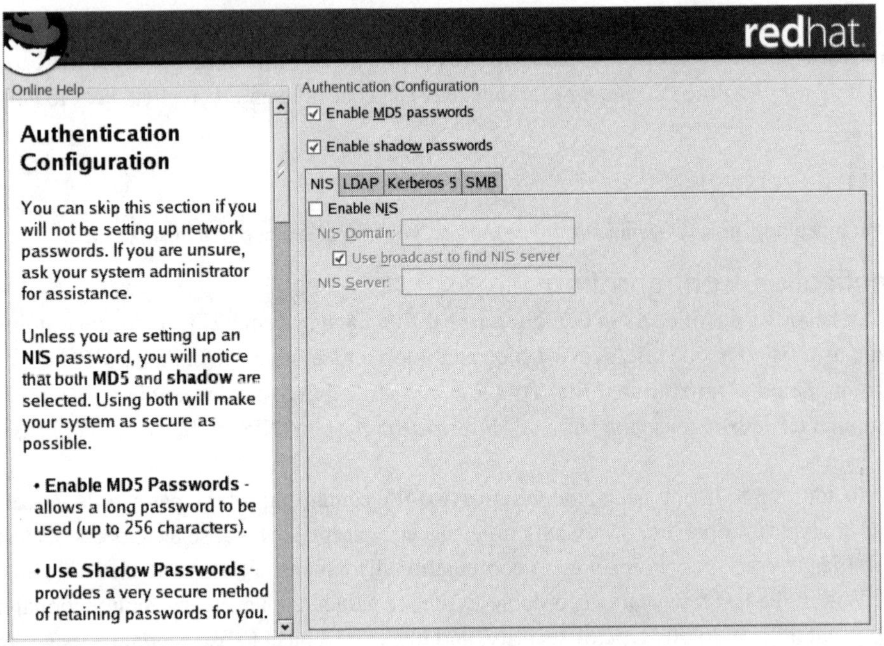

Figure 2-17 Configure authentication to use MD5 encrypted, shadow passwords, and to access any network authentication methods that apply.

Once you have selected all pertinent check boxes and filled out the relevant entries, click Next to continue to the next screen.

Selecting Package Groups

This is where you can select what packages get installed onto the system. Red Hat categorizes these packages into several high-level descriptions, enabling you to make a quick selection of what type of packages you want installed and to safely ignore the details. You can also choose to install all of the packages that come with Red Hat, but be warned: A full install is nearly 5GB of software!

NOTE

If you decide that you underestimated the amount of space you needed for software (which goes in **/usr**), you can click Back to repartition the system to make enough room for what you want.

Looking at the top-level group descriptions (Figure 2-18), you see the broadest set of options Red Hat gives you. You can simply pick the groups that interest you, or you can scroll

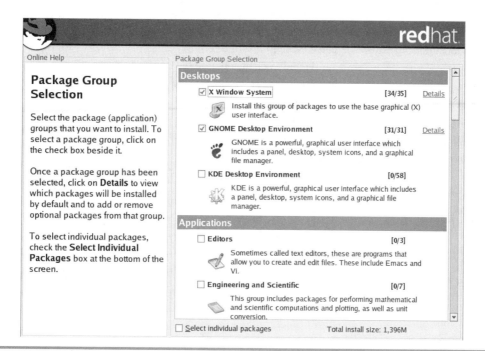

Figure 2-18 Select top-level groups of software to install prepared options.

to the bottom and pick Everything to have all of the packages installed; or you can click the Details link next to any selected group to select individual packages from that group.

If you choose to click a Details link, you'll see a screen like the one shown.

Each such screen lists the packages that are installed automatically, and then shows the optional packages that you can choose to install or omit.

If you check the Select Individual Packages button, you will see a screen like the one shown in Figure 2-19. The left side of the screen shows the functional groupings of packages, and the right side of the screen shows individual packages.

If you opt to select individual packages, Red Hat will go through and verify that all of the prerequisites necessary for these packages are met. If any are not met, you will be shown these packages in a screen that looks like Figure 2-20.

If there are any packages that need to be installed to allow all of your selected packages to work, simply make sure that the radio button labeled Install Packages To Satisfy Dependencies is selected.

Click Next when you're done picking packages.

About to Install

The installer now warns you (see Figure 2-21) that it's about to commence the drastic changes you've been selecting for your new server. If you're certain you've got things the way you want them, click Next.

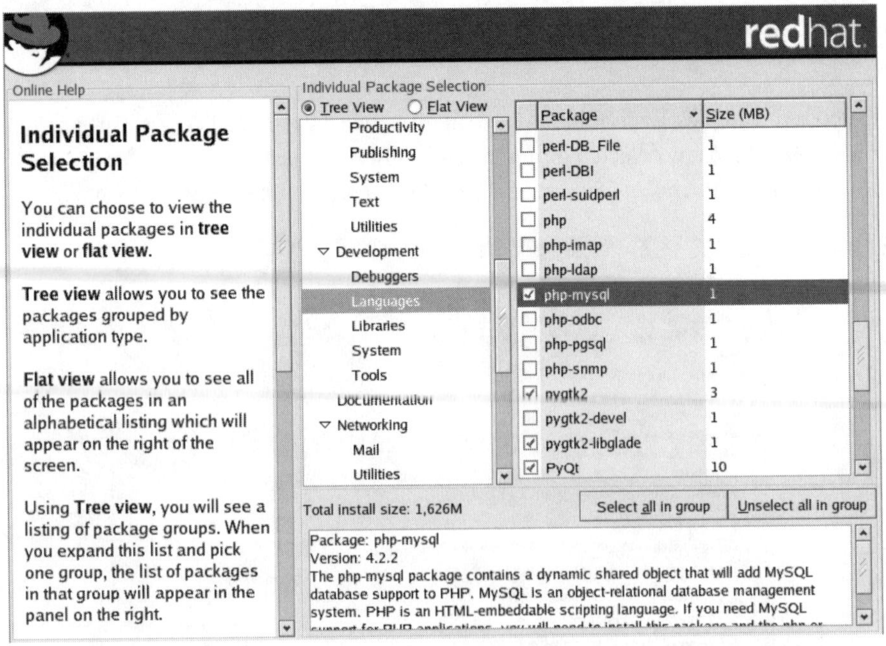

Figure 2-19 Select Individual Packages to precisely fine-tune your Linux installation.

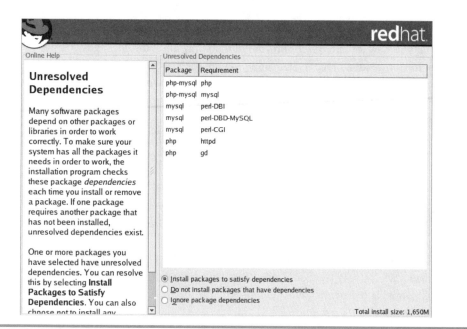

Figure 2-20 Red Hat Linux alerts you to unmet dependencies of packages you selected.

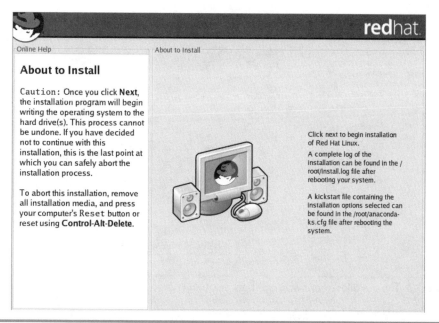

Figure 2-21 As Red Hat Linux is about to be installed, it checks to make sure you are ready.

Installation Begins

Red Hat will now go through the process of installing all of the packages you have selected as part of the installation process. Depending on the speed of your hard disk, CD-ROM, and machine, this could take from just a few minutes to more than 20 minutes. A status indicator (see Figure 2-22) will let you know how far the process has gotten and how much longer the system expects to take.

Once the installer has exhausted the files on the CD, it will eject the CD and prompt you for the next disc. Insert the next disc and click OK to continue.

Boot Disk Creation

Once the installation process is complete, Red Hat gives you the option of creating a boot disk. Unless you are familiar with recovering a Linux system already, it will make your life easier if you take a moment and create one.

Following the directions as shown in Figure 2-23, simply insert a blank disk into your drive and click Next. If you don't want to create a boot disk, click the button labeled Skip Boot Disk Creation, and then click Next.

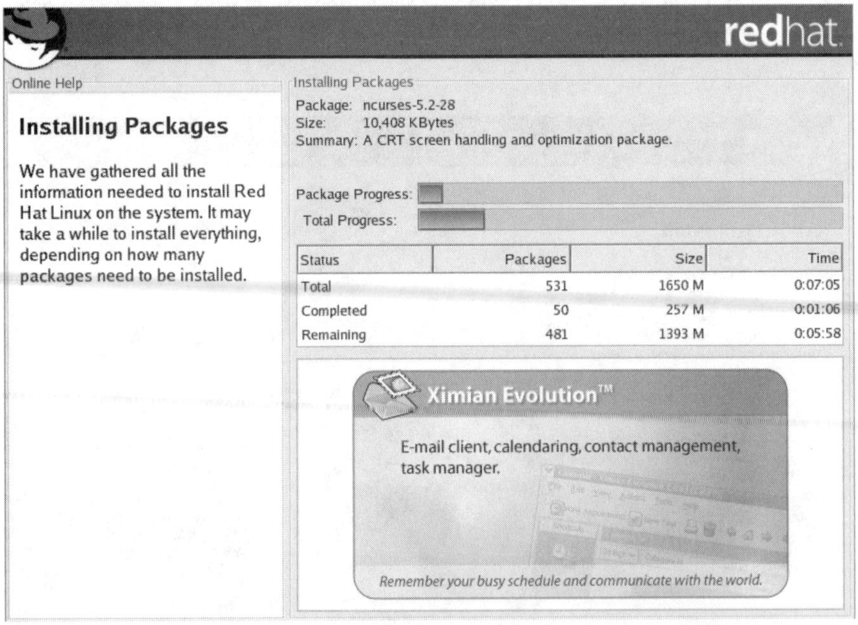

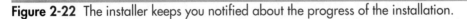

Figure 2-22 The installer keeps you notified about the progress of the installation.

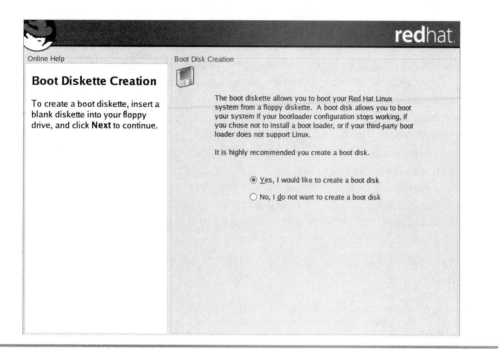

Figure 2-23 Create a boot disk to simplify system recovery.

WARNING

If you chose not to install a boot loader, you *must* create a boot diskette, or you won't be able to boot Linux.

Configuring the X Window System

The X Window System is the basis for the graphical user interface in Linux. It is what communicates with the actual video hardware. Programs such as KDE and GNOME (which you are more likely to have heard about; if not, read the next module) use the X Window System as a standard mechanism for communicating with the hardware.

What makes the X Window System interesting is that it is not coupled with the base operating system. In fact, the version of X that Linux uses, Xfree86, is also available for many other UNIX-based systems, such as those from Sun. This means it is possible to run a server without ever starting the graphical environment, and it is often a good idea to do so. By having the GUI turned off, you save memory and system resources that can instead be used for the actual server processes.

Of course, this doesn't change the fact that many nice administrative tools are available only under X, so getting it set up is still a good idea.

Red Hat will begin by trying to sense the type of graphics card you have (see Figure 2-24). If you have a nonbleeding-edge, brand-name card, you'll likely have the easiest time. If Linux cannot determine the type of video card and its memory, you can enter the necessary information directly.

Once the video card has been selected, click Next. The option to skip the X Window System is useful if you don't have a need for X, or if you want to configure it later. If that's the case, you can check the box to skip the X Window System and click Next.

The next screen displays a list of monitor manufacturers. Find your manufacturer and click the triangle to the left of its name to expand the list of monitor models (see Figure 2-25). Be sure to select the correct monitor make and model, or find a setting in the Generic list that is compatible with your monitor's video modes.

TIP

If you have an unusual monitor that isn't in Red Hat's database, have its frequency information available and enter it in the appropriate fields. Trying to send your monitor too high of a frequency can cause physical damage. This author managed to toast his first color monitor this way, back when monitors were far less robust and before the X Window System configuration tools existed.

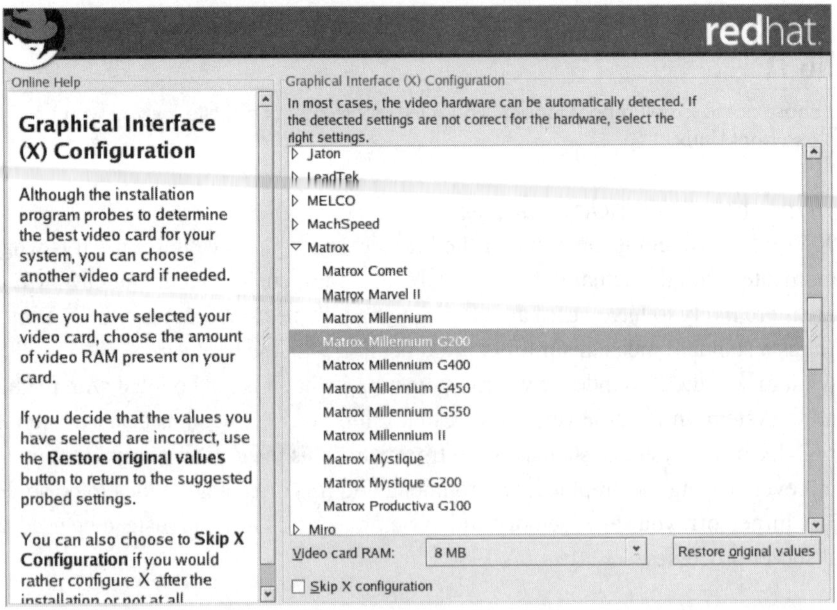

Figure 2-24 Red Hat Linux will attempt to automatically detect the graphics card.

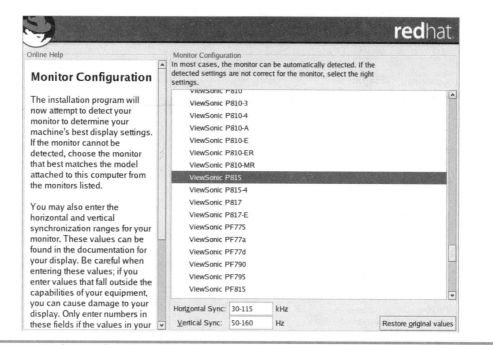

Figure 2-25 The installer allows you to select your monitor's manufacturer and model number or a generic equivalent.

Click Next to bring up a screen similar to Figure 2-26.

The drop-down lists show the color definitions and pixel resolutions supported by your display subsystem. Configure them to settings that you think will work, and then click the Test Setting button to see them in action. For some people, high-resolution settings are too high and make fonts hard to read. Displaying more colors generally makes the display look better, but may reduce performance.

The choice of using a graphical login is just that: You can have the X Window System automatically start up on boot so that the first login everyone sees is graphical instead of text based. This choice is often nice for the novice user who has a Linux system at his or her desk. However, it's not as sensible for use on a server, especially one you don't plan to use from the console much. When you're done selecting, click Next to continue.

Installation Completes

That's it! The installation process is over. You'll be prompted to click Next one more time to reboot the system. As the system reboots, be sure to remove any CD-ROMs or floppy disks you have in your system that are capable of booting before your hard disk does.

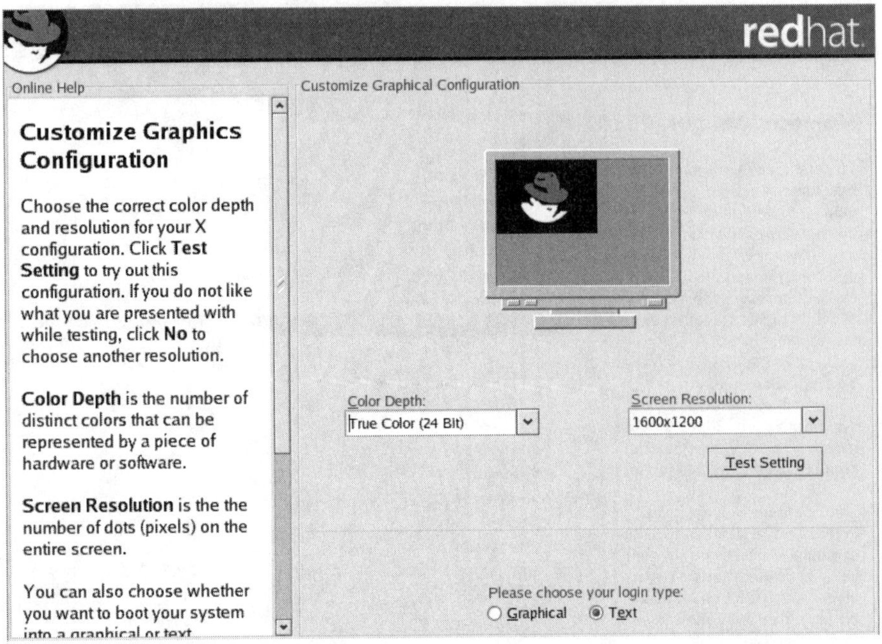

Figure 2-26 Configure and test the X Window System resolution settings.

Project 2-2 Installing a Server

While you've just covered the process of installing a server fairly exhaustively, you still have to put all the pieces together when you perform the real installation. Follow these steps to ensure good results!

Step by Step

1. Review your server hardware to make sure it meets the minimum system requirements and is on the Hardware Compatibility List.

2. Allocate an IP or DHCP address on your network for the server.

3. Check to see that you have adequate disk space to install and operate your software. You can check this precisely by starting the installation procedure and moving as quickly to the software installation step as possible. Without actually installing the software, select all the packages you wish to use. Make sure you check for dependencies if you select packages individually, as some dependencies can be very large.

4. Create a list of users for the system so that their accounts can be added during installation, if appropriate.

5. Determine the amount of space that users are likely to need in their home directories to make sure there will be enough room on that partition.

6. Perform the real installation, partitioning the disk as you've calculated, and installing the software you plan to use.

7. If you install and configure the X Window System, be sure to test it, especially if you use the default graphical login option.

8. Once the system restarts, see if it boots all the way up.

Project Summary

Experimenting with the Linux installation process isn't difficult, so it is possible to try several different options without expending too much energy. As will be described in Module 4, it's easy to add or remove software after the installation, so it's not necessary to have things perfect. But with a little investigation and some planning, the initial installation can be used right away.

Finding Additional Help

If you are still having problems with the installation, be sure to visit Red Hat's web site (http://www.redhat.com) and take a look at the manuals available for Red Hat 8.0 (http://www.redhat.com/docs/manuals/). There you will find the official installation guide for all possible variations in the installation process. You will also find the latest errata, security updates, and notes regarding the Red Hat 8.0 distribution.

Module Summary

This module described the process of building up a server, choosing the right hardware, establishing the right environment, and finally, installing Red Hat 8.0. All of the commentary before you got to the actual process of installing Red Hat Linux applies to any server you build, regardless of operating system.

The steps for installing Red Hat itself are also quite straightforward. Anyone who witnessed the procedure from prior versions should have noted how much easier the process has become and how many fewer configuration choices need to be made to get going. What makes Linux wonderful is that even though those options are no longer part of the installation process, you can still change them and tweak them to your heart's content once you've completed the install and have started the system for real.

Don't forget to search those places I mentioned earlier in the module if you need help, and once you become a Linux whiz, don't forget to help others.

2

Installing Linux in a Server Configuration

Project
2-2

Installing a Server

✓ Module 2 Mastery Check

1. What is the HCL, and why is it important?

2. List the three factors that are most important for a server.

3. Which of the following are effective means of configuring a Linux server?

    A. Recompiling the server's kernel

    B. Avoiding using the X Window System on the server

    C. Disabling unused functions

    D. Cooling the server with liquid nitrogen

    E. Loading as many modules in the kernel as possible

4. What command is used to determine how long a Linux system has been running?

5. What web site has guides and cookbook-style help for Linux?

6. What utility is used to create a Linux boot disk from a Windows system?

7. Name the utility used to configure each of these after Red Hat Linux 8.0 is installed on a system:

    A. X Window System

    B. Keyboard

    C. Mouse

8. In Linux terminology, how is the root directory identified?

9. What four subdirectories of the root directory are recommended for separate partitions?

10. How big should the swap file be?

    A. Double the size of the system RAM.

    B. If the system has less than 128MB of RAM, double the size of the system RAM. If the system has more than 128MB of RAM, then the same size as the system RAM.

    C. If the system has less than 128MB of RAM, then 128MB of swap. If the system has more than 128MB of RAM, then the same size as the system RAM.

    D. The same size as the system RAM.

11. How many boot options will a multiprocessing server system have after installation?

12. Describe the purpose of the Red Hat Linux-up boot option.

13. What command is used to become the root user?

14. What is a shadow password, and where is it stored?

15. Which of the following authentication methods are configurable during the Red Hat Linux installation procedure?

    A. Kerberos

    B. LDAP

    C. NIS

    D. RADIUS

    E. SMB

16. In rare instances, what could happen to a monitor set to run at frequencies it's not designed to handle?

Module 3

GNOME and KDE

GNOME and KDE have both received significant press because they offer a truly easy-to-use interface to UNIX-based operating systems, most notably Linux. In this module, you will go over various tips and tricks to make GNOME and KDE work better for you. Since most distributions come with one (or both) preinstalled, you won't have to deal with an installation or configuration process before you can jump in and start using them.

Before you get into the fun stuff, though, you need to step back and understand a little more about the X Window System and how it relates to GNOME and KDE. This will give you a better idea of the big picture of Linux and one of its fundamental architectural differences with Windows NT.

NOTE

It is unwise to run the X Window System as the root user, if for no other reason than that **root** should be used only when needed, and giving the root user its own desktop configuration invites overuse. If you did not create an additional non-root user during Red Hat installation, you can skip to Module 5 to see how to do so before continuing this module. All of the changes you read about here can apply to any user, including **root**.

CRITICAL SKILL
3.1 Understanding the X Window System's Origins

The designers of UNIX-based operating systems, like Linux, take a very different view of the world when it comes to user environments than do those behind Microsoft Windows or even Macintosh OS. UNIX folk believe the interface they present the user should be 100 percent independent of the core operating system. As a result, Linux's kernel is completely decoupled from its user interface. This allows you to select the interface that works best for you, rather than be stuck with the dictated vision of someone else or potentially random "market research."

More important, however, is the stability that comes from having such a large program independent of the core operating system. If the GUI crashes under Windows or Mac OS, you have to reboot. Under Linux, you can kill the GUI and restart it without affecting any other services being offered by the system (such as network file services).

In the mid-1980s, an OS-independent foundation for graphical user environments was created and called the X Window System. "X" (as it is commonly abbreviated) simply defines the method by which applications can communicate with the graphical hardware. Also established was a well-defined set of functions programmers could call on to perform basic window manipulation.

NOTE

The implementation of the X Window System used by Linux is XFree86. Information about the XFree86 project and its configuration can be found at http://www.xfree86.org.

The simple definition of how windows are drawn and mouse clicks are handled did not include any model of how the windows should look. (In fact, the X Window System in its natural state has no real appearance. It doesn't even draw lines around windows!) Control of appearance was passed off to an external program called a *window manager.* The window manager took care of drawing borders, using color, and making the environment pleasant to the eye; the window manager was required only to use standard calls to the X subsystem to draw on the screen. The window manager *did not* dictate how the application itself utilized the windows. This meant application programmers had the flexibility to develop a user interface most intuitive for the application.

Because the window manager was external to the X subsystem, and the X application programmers interface (API) was open, any programmer who wanted to develop a new window manager could, and many did. In the context of today, we might associate this form of openness with MP3 players, like Winamp, that allow developers to build "skins" for the base player.

The icing on the cake was the relationship between applications and X. Typical applications were written to communicate directly with X, thereby working with any window manager the user opted to use. Figure 3-1 shows this relationship.

The Downside

As technically interesting and versatile as the X Window System is, it is a pain in the backside to program for. A Windows programmer might equate programming for X to programming for the original MS Windows prior to the visual tools and MFC libraries. For example, a simple program to bring up a window, display the text "Hello World," and then offer a button to allow the user to quit could easily be several hundred lines long under both X and MS Windows!

And here the UNIX folks took a lesson from the Macintosh OS and MS Windows families (who, it should be noted, borrowed their ideas from Xerox's work back in the late 1970s): Failure to offer a reasonably consistent user interface for both the user and the programmer that is easy to use and easy to develop for means a loss of user base.

Commercial UNIX vendors tried to fix this problem with the Common Desktop Environment so that their users would get a consistent look and feel, and an improved library for X called Motif was developed, as well. For Linux, both of these developments presented a problem, because they went against the ideal of being open source. To make matters even more unpleasant, they weren't much better than what was available before.

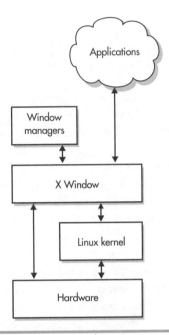

Figure 3-1 The relationship between the X Window System, window managers, applications, and the core operating system

Enter KDE and GNOME

With unfriendly programming environments and unfriendly user interfaces, X had the potential to one day turn into a legacy interface. This would be extremely unfortunate, because it offers a design that was (and still is) leaps and bounds better than other commercial offerings. The protocol is open, which means anyone who wants to write an X client or X server is welcome to. And, of course, one of the best features of X is that it allows applications to be run on one host but be displayed on another host.

NOTE

Despite what you might hear in newsgroups and on web sites, the two groups are not "at war" with each other. Rather, they welcome the open competition. Each group can feed off of each other's ideas, and in turn, both groups can offer two excellent choices for us, the users.

In the latter 1990s, two groups came out of the woodwork with solutions to the problems with the X Window System: GNOME and KDE. *KDE* offers a new window manager and necessary libraries to make writing applications for it much easier. *GNOME* offers a general framework for other window managers and applications to work with it. Each has its own ideas for how things should work, but because they both work on top of the X Window System, they are not entirely incompatible

What This Means for You

The key words in the preceding paragraph were "not entirely incompatible." In order for KDE and GNOME to offer features such as drag and drop, they must offer a uniform way for applications to communicate with each other and a set of developer libraries to do so. The good news is that the two methods are being reconciled so as to offer ever-increasing interoperation. In fact, Red Hat Linux 8.0 is designed to hide their differences more than ever before. The bad news is that this burgeoning compatibility is still a work in progress, and thus the Linux desktop is not as integrated as Apple's OS X or Microsoft's Windows XP.

What this means for applications can be a little confusing. Depending on the functionality the application calls on from its libraries, it may still work in the other environment as long as the libraries exist. One example is the **ksysv** program, used by the root user for controlling the services that run on a system. It was written with KDE in mind, but because the functionality it relies on is 100 percent available in the library, a system that is running GNOME but has KDE libraries available (such as Red Hat) will allow the application to run without a problem. On the other hand, if an application relies on the KDE window manager itself, the application will not work under GNOME.

This means that picking one environment over the other has the possibility of locking you out of getting to use certain applications. If you aren't sure about what you like better, try both. At one time, people may have perceived the objective as deciding which of the two environments was the best match, but it is becoming more clear that there are significant advantages to making both available and using the best tools and methods from each. You will still have to see which you like better for running as your primary environment, but that's a personal choice. What I use is irrelevant. What you like is what matters. And that's what having two competing systems is all about.

CRITICAL SKILL
3.2 Using and Customizing GNOME

GNOME (GNU Network Object Model Environment) offers a complete desktop environment and application framework to make development as well as use easier. What makes GNOME different from KDE is how it achieves these goals. Unlike KDE, GNOME does not provide a window manager. GNOME provides development libraries and session management—foundation features that we as users don't see. On top of this foundation is a window manager that takes care of the general appearance of the desktop. The default window manager is Metacity, but there are several choices available.

NOTE

According to the official web site, the correct pronunciation of GNOME is guh-NOME. This is because the G in GNOME stands for GNU, and the correct pronunciation of GNU is "guh-new." In the same paragraph, the GNOME team states that no one will be offended if you pronounce it "NOME."

From a developer's point of view, GNOME is very interesting. It defines its interfaces with the rest of the world through the CORBA technology. Thus, any development system that can communicate using CORBA can be used to develop GNOME-compliant applications. (For more information, see their developer's web pages at http://www.gnome.org.)

For users, this holds the potential for many applications to be developed to take advantage of the features in GNOME. Of course, like KDE, GNOME also works with existing X applications quite nicely.

NOTE

You're starting with GNOME because it is selected by default during the Red Hat installation process. If you haven't already installed GNOME, you can consult Module 4 for more information on installing software.

Starting the X Window System and GNOME

If you are using Red Hat Linux and have opted for its defaults, you already have GNOME installed as your default GUI. Depending on how X is configured, you may already have a graphical login prompt. In that case, logging in will automatically place you in the X Window System environment. If you have a text-based login, simply run **startx** in order to bring X up, like so:

```
[rwhite@tedford ~]$ startx
```

This should bring up a screen that looks something like Figure 3-2.

How do you know that GNOME has started? In past versions of Red Hat Linux, the GNOME and KDE desktops looked rather different, but Red Hat has used the same icon set and similar desktop configuration options to make the differences less marked. However, if you start X for the first time on a Red Hat Linux 8.0 system and move the cursor over the

Figure 3-2 Red Hat Linux 8.0 runs GNOME with the Bluecurve theme by default.

Red Hat icon in the lower left-hand corner, you'll see pop-up text that says "GNOME Menu" if the GNOME desktop is loaded.

If the default GUI that starts is not GNOME, you can change your personal settings to use GNOME by editing the **.xinitrc** file in your home directory. Begin by trying to exit out of the window manager. If you are in KDE, click the red hat in the lower left-hand corner to bring up a menu. In that menu should be an option to log out. If you're really stuck, you can also press CTRL-ALT-BACKSPACE to kill the underlying X system. This will bring you back into text mode. Edit the .xinitrc file using your favorite editor. If you don't have a favorite, try **pico**, like so:

```
[rwhite@tedford ~]$ pico .xinitrc
```

NOTE

If you aren't familiar with **pico**, don't worry. All of the available commands are always shown at the bottom of the screen. Any command that starts with the caret symbol (^) means you use the CTRL key along with other keys specified. For example, ^X means CTRL-X.

Most likely, the file will be empty. If that is the case, simply add the following content:

```
#!/bin/sh
gnome-session
```

If the file is not empty, go to the very last line. It will probably begin with the string **exec**, which tells the system to execute a program. Change that line so that it reads **gnome-session** instead.

GNOME Basics

If you are familiar with GUI interfaces such as Microsoft Windows, the GNOME desktop should make you feel right at home. There are two significant differences: the first is that there is no My Computer icon on the desktop. This is because Linux does not have the concept of separate drive letters for each partition. Rather, all of the partitions are made available in a single directory tree, thereby eliminating the need to select a drive.

The second big difference is the panel at the bottom of the screen. This panel is similar to the Windows XP taskbar; it shows what applications are currently running, as well as the date and time, and the red hat button at the left side of the panel is similar to the Start button. The big difference is that this panel is completely configurable: You can move things around in it, dock dynamic applications, set up shortcuts to other applications, and move around your virtual desktops. As in Windows, you can set it to automatically hide itself when it's not in use. And if you don't want it in the way for a particular task, you can click arrow buttons at each end of the panel and it will slide out of the way until you click the arrow button again.

By default, the buttons available on the panel are, from left to right, the Start Menu, web browser (Mozilla), e-mail manager (Evolution), word processor (OpenOffice.org Writer), presentation tool (OpenOffice.org Impress), spreadsheet (OpenOffice.org Calc), and a workspace switcher for moving between virtual desktops. On the left-hand side of the panel are Red Hat's "critical updates notifier" and a clock.

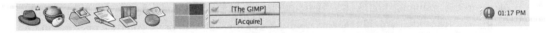

If you want to change the panel's appearance, right-click on any blank portion of the panel. This will bring up a menu as shown; its submenus allow you to configure various aspects of the panel, including being able to dock running programs into it (applets) and set up new shortcuts (launchers).

⊕ <u>A</u>dd to Panel   ▸
⊖ <u>D</u>elete This Panel...
🗒 <u>P</u>roperties
▢ <u>N</u>ew Panel   ▸
◎ <u>H</u>elp
☆ <u>A</u>bout Panels
☆ About <u>G</u>NOME

The blank space on the desktop is not wasted space; you can right-click anywhere on the empty desktop in GNOME to bring up this menu. Select one of the options to open a window to browse the contents of your system, or add a folder or application launcher icon to your desktop, or open a terminal window.

New <u>W</u>indow
<u>N</u>ew Folder
New <u>L</u>auncher
New T<u>e</u>rminal
<u>S</u>cripts   ▸

Clean <u>U</u>p by Name

✂ Cu<u>t</u> Files
🗐 <u>C</u>opy Files
📋 <u>P</u>aste Files

Dis<u>k</u>s   ▸

Use <u>D</u>efault Background
Change Desktop <u>B</u>ackground

The GNOME Start Here Icon

On the GNOME desktop are a Trash icon, a Home icon (a link to the current user's home directory), and the Start Here icon. Options available in the Preferences setting under the Start Here icon enable you to control the appearance and behavior of GNOME, similar to the way that the Windows Control Panel works.

TIP

If you aren't sure what a particular button does, simply leave the mouse pointer on the button for a few seconds. A small description will pop up right next to the pointer. The description will automatically disappear once you move the mouse off the button.

If you don't see the Start Here icon on your desktop, you can try clicking the Red Hat icon on the bottom-left corner of your screen. This will bring up a menu containing the Preferences option. Selecting Preferences will bring up a submenu with various configuration options (shown in Figure 3-3).

In this section, you will step through several common tasks. They should give you an idea of what can be done and the typical method for figuring out how to do it. As was mentioned earlier, the interface is very Windows-like, so learning to get around in it should be relatively easy.

Changing the Background

To change your background settings, click the Background option. This will bring up a panel that looks like Figure 3-4.

Figure 3-3 The Preferences options allow you to configure various desktop features.

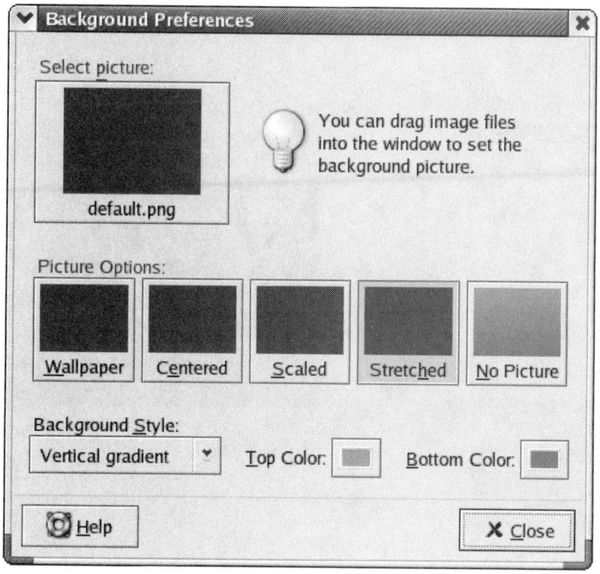

Figure 3-4 Set the background in Red Hat Linux's GNOME desktop.

The Background window enables you to control the background color and wallpaper. The Select picture option enables you to choose from a list of images to use for the background, or you can drag an image file into the Background window to use it instead. The image can be handled in several different ways; the Picture Options show what the desktop will look like if each option is selected.

If you like, you can set the background to use no picture, and instead select a single color, or select two colors and do a horizontal or vertical gradient between them. To select the colors, click one of the color boxes; this will bring up a color wheel from which you can choose any color you like.

Setting the Screen Saver

To set the screen saver under GNOME, click the Desktop menu and then the Screensaver menu. This will bring up a panel that looks like Figure 3-5.

Once there, choosing a screen saver is very easy. Simply select the mode you want to use—no screen saver, screen-blanking only, one screen saver, or a random screen saver from a list of possibilities. A sample of what a screen saver will look like will appear in the Description

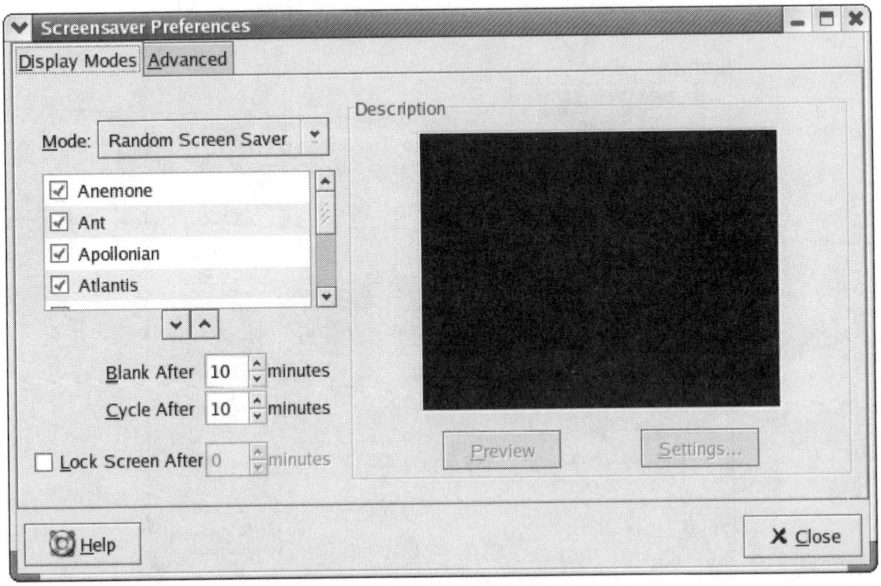

Figure 3-5 Set the screen saver in Red Hat Linux's GNOME desktop.

area, located in the same window. If the screen saver has customizable settings, they can be set by clicking the Settings button. The global screen saver settings allow you to select how long the system should wait before starting the screen saver and how long it should wait before it moves to another screen saver (if you have enabled multiple screen savers). You can also set the system to "lock" the screen after some time elapses; when the lock turns on, the current user's password must be entered to unlock the screen.

Under the Advanced tab, you'll find power management features to try to save power when the system is not in use, diagnostics settings, and other configuration options.

Themes

Themes are the way GNOME allows you to configure the appearance of your window manager. These changes go beyond simply changing colors; they can change the appearance of the desktop, windows, borders, and fonts for all applications. (Users of Mac OS 8 or Winamp should be at home with this technology.) If you aren't sure how significant a change you can make, visit http://art.gnome.org, http://themes.freshmeat.net, or http://www.themedepot.org.

To get to the Themes menu in GNOME, simply go to the Preferences menu and then click the Themes icon. This will bring up a panel that looks like Figure 3-6.

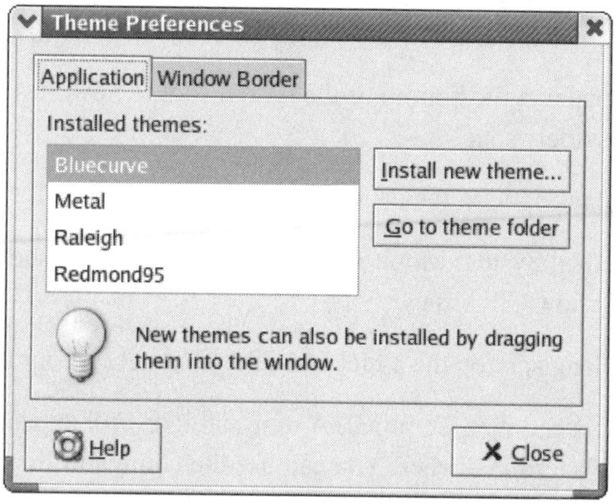

Figure 3-6 Select a theme in Red Hat Linux's GNOME desktop.

By default, Red Hat Linux 8.0 starts with the Bluecurve theme. Several additional themes are available with the Red Hat installation. If you are interested in adding a nonstandard theme, you can download new ones. You can drag and drop new themes into the Theme Preferences window's Application tab, and you can customize window borders under the . . . surprise! . . . Window Border tab.

Project 3-1 Customizing a GNOME Desktop

Desktop configuration is a very personal issue, as each user seems to have a particular favored way of doing things. Without trying some changes, however, it's hard to know how one *can* do things. You now know enough to tweak a GNOME desktop a bit; in this project, you'll change some commonly altered configuration settings.

Step by Step

1. From the default GNOME desktop, right-click on a blank space on the panel.

2. Click the Properties menu item.

3. You can use this page to reposition the panel to any of the four edges of the desktop, but leave the location alone for now. In the Size drop-down menu, select Small (36 pixels).

4. Check the Show/Hide Buttons box.

(continued)

5. Check the Arrows on the Hide Buttons box.

6. Click Close. The panel at the bottom of the screen should now be shorter, and its icons smaller and more widely spaced.

7. Right-click on a blank spot on the panel and select Add To Panel.

8. Select Utility and then System Monitor. A system monitor area should appear on the panel; it will graphically show CPU usage.

9. Right-click on a blank spot on the panel and select Launcher from the menu.

10. Select System Tools and then Terminal. A terminal icon will appear on the panel; clicking this icon will open a terminal where you can use the command-line interface.

11. Right-click on a blank spot on the panel and select Launcher from the menu again.

12. Select the Office menu and then Project Management. A Mr. Project icon should appear on the panel; this tool is still under development, but it is similar in concept to Microsoft Project.

13. Right-click on a blank spot on the panel and select New Panel.

14. Select the Menu Panel option, and a menu bar should appear at the top of the desktop. Applications and actions can be invoked from this menu bar, and it can also hold additional launchers, applets, and utilities.

15. Right-click on the new menu panel at the top of the screen.

16. Select Add To Panel, and then the Accessories menu, and the Stock Ticker option. A stock ticker area should appear on the menu panel.

17. Right-click on the stock ticker area on the panel and select Preferences. A configuration page should appear.

18. Type **RHAT** in the New Symbol field.

19. Click the Add button, and then click Close. In five minutes, the Red Hat stock price should begin scrolling in the stock ticker area, along with the default index information.

20. Move the icons on the panels by left-clicking them and then dragging them to the desired locations.

(continued)

Project Summary

This project illustrates one way to customize a desktop. While a system monitor utility might be quite useful if you're going to be logged in to a server much of the time, the stock ticker feature is not likely to be there for solid business reasons. The reality is that the options you select will have relatively little to do with how your Linux server runs, but they can have a large impact on how efficiently and comfortably you can use its GUI. Experimentation in this regard won't hurt anything, so take a little time to explore further.

CRITICAL SKILL
3.3 Using and Customizing KDE

KDE, like GNOME, is a desktop environment (the K Desktop Environment). It is slightly different from typical window managers: Instead of just describing how the interface should look, KDE also provides a set of libraries that, if used, allow an application to take advantage of some of the special features the window manager has to offer. These include drag-and-drop support, standardized printing support, and so on.

The flip side to this technique of window management is that once an application is designed to run with KDE, it requires KDE in order to work. This is a big change from earlier window managers where applications are independent of the window manager.

From a programmer's point of view, KDE offers a library that is much easier to work with and more powerful than using the vanilla X interface. KDE also offers a standardized object-oriented framework that allows one set of tools to build on another, something that was not available with X alone. Of course, in order for a user to employ applications that use this great library functionality, the KDE libraries must be installed on the user's system, so in absolute terms, the expanded functionality offered by the libraries comes with a cost of portability. Because KDE is very widely included as the default windowing environment in commercial Linux distributions, that cost may not be too great.

For this section, I will assume that KDE has already been installed on your system. See Module 4 for information on how to install additional software if you did not opt to install KDE initially.

NOTE

For more details and information on KDE, visit their web site at http://www.kde.org.

Starting the X Window System and KDE

When setting up the X Window System, you may have had a choice of starting up the system straight into X. If so, all you need to do is log in and you're there—you're using KDE and X. If that option was not selected, you will have a text-based login prompt. To get into the X environment, simply log in and run **startx**, like so:

```
[rwhite@tedford ~]$ startx
```

In a few moments, you will be in KDE. Your screen will probably look something like Figure 3-7.

Notice that things look extremely similar to the default GNOME desktop. The icons are the same (but there may be a few extras, depending on the floppy and CD drives you have on your system). So how do you tell if KDE has started? One way to tell using the default Red Hat Linux 8.0 configuration is to move the cursor over the Red Hat icon in the lower left-hand corner. If the pop-up text that appears after a few moments says "Start Applications," you are in KDE.

Figure 3-7 Red Hat has a highly customized KDE desktop.

If the pop-up text on your screen doesn't look like that but says "GNOME Menu" instead, then you need to edit the file that decides which window manager you start. To do this, exit out of GNOME by clicking the red hat in the lower-left corner of the screen and selecting Log Out. This will bring you back into text mode. Edit the **.xinitrc** file using your favorite editor. If you don't have a favorite, try **pico**, like so:

```
[rwhite@tedford ~]$ pico .xinitrc
```

NOTE

If you aren't familiar with **pico**, don't worry. All of the available commands are always shown at the bottom of the screen. Any command that starts with the caret symbol (^) means you use the CTRL key along with other keys specified. For example, ^X means CTRL-X.

Most likely, unless you created the contents of the file when looking at the GNOME desktop, the file will be empty. If that is the case, simply add the following content:

```
#!/bin/sh
startkde
```

If the file is not empty, go to the very last line. It will probably begin with the string **exec**, which tells the system to execute a program. Change that line so that it reads **startkde** instead.

Changing the Desktop Environment for All Users

While creating or changing the **.xinitrc** file for each user is one option, you can set the default desktop environment for all users by editing one file. Using your favorite editor or pico, you can create or edit the **/etc/sysconfig/desktop** file so that it specifies the correct desktop. You'll need to be the root user to do this, since it's a system configuration file. If you want KDE to be the default desktop environment, edit **/etc/sysconfig/desktop** so that it contains:

```
DESKTOP="KDE"
```

If, on the other hand, you want to use GNOME by default, you can either empty the contents of the **/etc/sysconfig/desktop** file, delete the file completely, or set its contents to be:

```
DESKTOP="GNOME"
```

KDE Basics

KDE shares many qualities with other graphical desktops, such as Windows or Mac OS. It has a desktop on which files and folders can exist. One key point to note is that because Linux places all of the hard disks on the system into a unified directory tree, you won't find a special icon allowing you to browse a particular disk as you can under My Computer.

At the bottom of the screen, you will find the *kpanel*. In non–Red Hat versions of the KDE software, the Red Hat icon is replaced by the KDE "K" logo. Regardless of the icon on it, this button is similar to the Windows Start button. By clicking it, you will be presented with a menu showing you a number of applications that can be started by simply clicking the appropriate menu entry.

The kpanel is similar to the Windows XP menu in that it is also a shortcut bar to commonly used applications. You can configure the bar to have any shortcuts you like by clicking the Red Hat panel button, selecting the Preferences option, then the Look and Feel menu, and selecting Panel. Under this menu, you will find a number of configuration options.

If you want to hide the panel altogether, you can do so by enabling and clicking the arrow at the far right or left side of the panel. This will make the panel hide in that direction. Click the arrow again to bring the panel back. Red Hat Linux does not enable these arrows by default, so you must select the Hiding tab in the Panel menu, and check the appropriate Hide Buttons boxes.

The KDE Control Center

The KDE Control Center is a lot like the Control Panel for Windows (see Figure 3-8).

The Control Center offers an impressive array of tools for configuring KDE to your heart's delight. This includes support for a variety of themes, colors, backgrounds, screen savers, certain applications, and certain types of hardware. The best way to see all it has to offer is to go through it and play—this is one of the rare opportunities you have as a system administrator to play with the interface without breaking your system.

In this section, you will step through several common tasks, giving you an idea of what can be done and the typical method for figuring out how to do it. As mentioned earlier, the interface is very Windows-like, so getting around in it should be relatively easy.

NOTE

KDE's background and themes can be changed in much the same way GNOME's background and themes are (from the Preferences menu, select Look and Feel, and then Desktop or Theme Manager). For KDE-based themes beyond the set included with Red Hat Linux 8.0, check out www.kde-look.org, http://themes.freshmeat.net, or http://www.themedepot.org.

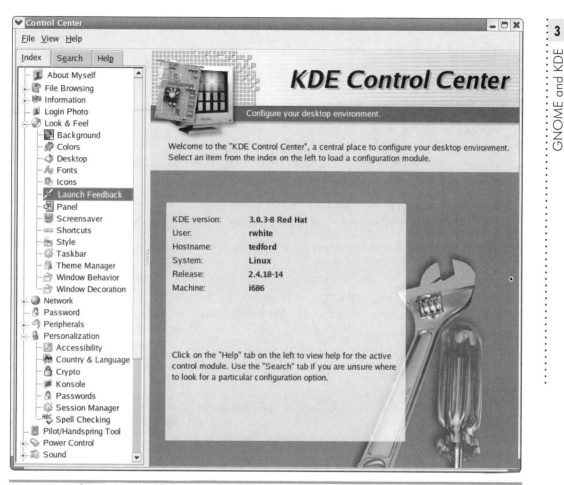

Figure 3-8 The KDE Control Center is a single place from which to manage a variety of system and desktop features.

Using Multiple Desktops

One of the most powerful tools you have at your disposal is the virtual desktop. The only dangerous thing about it is your aggravation when you work on systems that don't have this feature.

The essence of virtual desktops is that they allow you to effectively have multiple screens at the same time. All you need to do is select which screen you want to use by clicking the virtual desktop selector at the bottom of the screen.

Red Hat Linux 8.0's KDE installations default to four virtual screens. If you want to adjust that, do the following:

1. Open the Control Center.

2. Select Look and Feel.

3. Select Panel.

4. Select Number of Desktops from the tab-style window on the right side of the Control Center.

5. Move the Visible slider to the right to increase the number of desktops. (Of course, you can also move it left to reduce the number of desktops.)

6. Click the Apply button at the bottom of the window to make the changes take effect.

If each desktop has a specific purpose, you can also change the label of the desktop by highlighting it and changing the desktop name field on the same panel. In Figure 3-9, you can see that Desktop 1 has been renamed Administration and Desktop 2 has been renamed OpenOffice, while the other desktops have remained untouched.

TIP

If you prefer keyboard shortcuts, you can set up a shortcut that allows you to move from one desktop to another in the Control Center under the Look and Feel | Shortcuts menu. Simply click the action you want (switch desktop) and then select the key combination you want to use to move around. Like a lot of folks who used the fvwm window manager for a long time, I personally prefer using the CTRL-arrow key to jump from one desktop to another.

Starting Other Applications

Many applications are available from the panel menu; simply clicking the Red Hat icon and browsing through what's available is probably the best way of familiarizing yourself with what is available by default. But although a wide array of software is available there, you may find that a tool you're looking for can't be found in the generic menus.

There are multiple ways to start a new application. As a system administrator, you are likely to have a command window up (better known as an "Xterm"), so you may find it convenient to simply run the application from there. In fact, most of this book assumes you are running applications from that prompt. Simply open a terminal window box by clicking the Red Hat logo menu, selecting System Tools, and then clicking Terminal. This starts up konsole, which

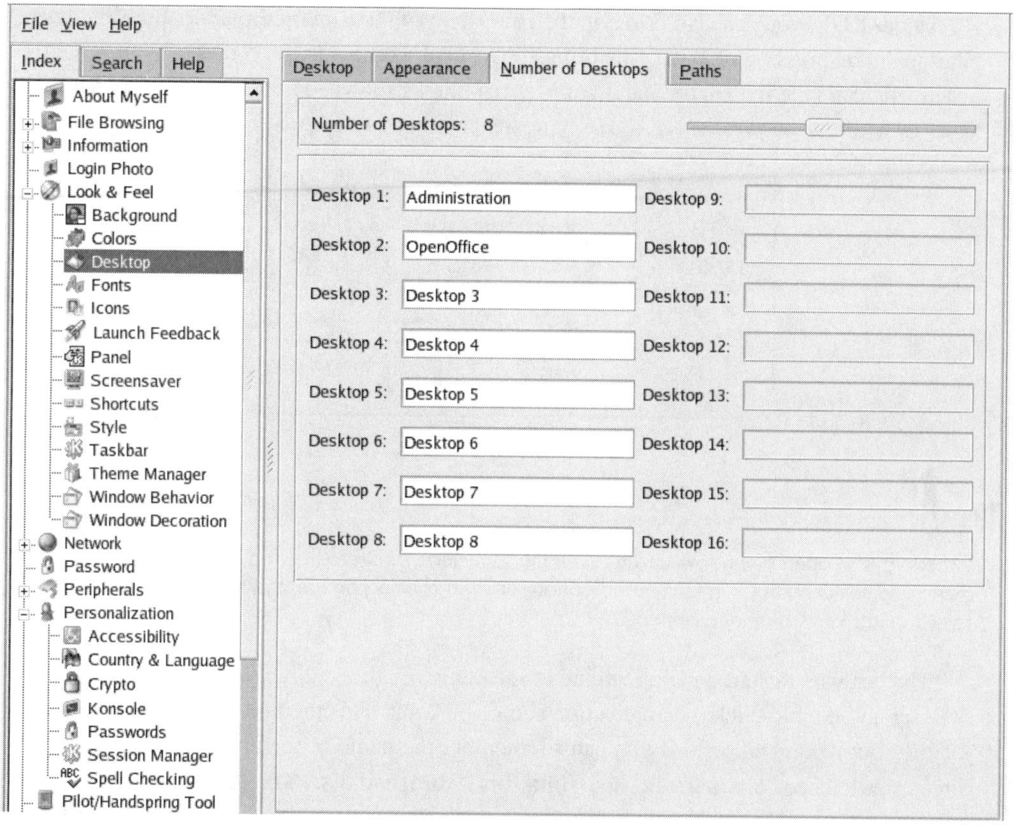

Figure 3-9 Select the number of virtual desktops available within KDE.

is functionally equivalent to an Xterm. Once konsole is open, you can type the name of the command you wish to run there and press ENTER.

NOTE

Many commands discussed in this book must be run from a terminal window.

Under KDE, you can also bring up the equivalent of the Run option under the Windows Start menu by pressing ALT-F2. This brings up a small window in the center of your screen where you can type in the command you want to run, as shown. The window automatically goes away once you press ENTER to execute the command or ESC to abort.

TIP

Other ways to open a window to run a command include going to the Red Hat logo menu and selecting the Run Command option, or right-clicking on the desktop and selecting the Run Command option.

The last way to start an application is to search through the directory listing using the file browser and double-click the application name you want. This method is, of course, the most tedious, but it can be useful if you can't remember the name of the application. Common directories to check are **/usr/bin**, **/usr/sbin**, **/bin**, **/sbin**, and **/usr/X11R6/bin**.

Changing the Color Scheme

If you're fussy about your desktop environment, you'll probably want to change the appearance of your desktop color scheme. You can use the Red Hat logo menu and select the Preferences option, and then Desktop. You can also use KDE's Control Center. Begin by bringing the Control Center up, going to the Look and Feel menu, and then clicking the Colors option in the left window. This will bring up a window that looks like Figure 3-10.

Simply click the color combination you like best. I like the default Bluecurve look, but if you prefer one of the other settings, you can select it instead. If you want to create a new combination, click the Add button underneath the list and give your new settings a name. Highlight this setting and then select the color you want to give each widget in the right side of the panel. For example, to change the color of normal text, open the Widget Color drop-down box. Select Normal Text. The bar underneath the drop-down box will show the current color. Click the bar to bring up a color wheel so that you can select the new color you like best.

As always, click Apply once you are done.

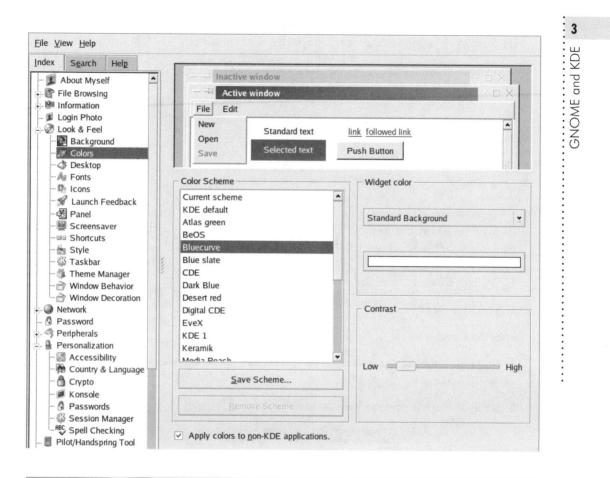

Figure 3-10 Change the color scheme for the KDE desktop.

Setting Up More Fonts

New to Red Hat Linux 8.0 is a partially automated way to add fonts to either the GNOME or KDE desktop. Both environments can use antialiased fonts, and although some people like the default fonts, others have complained loudly about them. If you're accustomed to using certain fonts in Windows, you'll be happy to know that some of them can be used in GNOME or KDE without too much trouble. You can get some of the standard Windows fonts from http://corefonts.sourceforge.net.

To make the fonts available within the X Window System, copy the font files to the **.fonts** subdirectory in your home directory, and run the **fc-cache** script:

```
[rwhite@tedford ~]$ cp *.TTF ~/.fonts
[rwhite@tedford ~]$ fc-cache ~/.fonts
```

If you want to make the fonts available for all users on a system, you can (as **root**) put the files in the **/usr/share/fonts** directory instead:

```
[root@tedford /root]# cp *.TTF /usr/share/fonts
[root@tedford /root]# fc-cache /usr/share/fonts
```

If you do this in an Xterm or on a command line within X, you'll have to log out of the desktop environment and start X again for the fonts to be available. So if you install the Verdana font family on your Linux system, you can make it the default font by following these steps:

1. Open the Control Center.

2. Select Look and Feel.

3. Select Fonts.

4. Select the Choose button to the left of the General font listing from the tab-style window on the right side of the Control Center.

5. Scroll down and select the Verdana entry.

6. Click OK to return to the fonts list.

7. Click the Apply button at the bottom of the window to make the changes take effect.

Using Added Fonts in OpenOffice

This process will make the fonts available to most KDE- and GNOME-based programs, but they will not be available to all X programs, including OpenOffice. While you probably won't be using OpenOffice on your Red Hat Linux Server very much, I'll tell you how to load the fonts for use there anyway.

1. Use the Run Command option to open a command window, and enter **oopadmin**. Don't be surprised if it takes a few moments for the OpenOffice printer administration tool to load.

2. When it does, click the Fonts button to list the installed fonts.

3. Click the Add button to add the new font directory.

4. Click the . . . button to open the graphical representation of the system's directory structure.

5. Find the correct parent directory and type **.fonts** after it (files and directories that start with a period are "hidden," so you won't be able to select the **.fonts** directory from the list).

6. Click Select All to select all the fonts in the directory.

```
Add Fonts                                              [x]
 ┌─────────────────────────────────┐   ┌──────────┐
 │ Verdana, Bold, Italic (Verdanaz.TTF)│   │    OK    │
 │ Verdana, Bold (Verdanab.TTF)    │   └──────────┘
 │ Verdana, Italic (Verdanai.TTF)  │   ┌──────────┐
 │ Verdana, Regular (Verdana.TTF)  │   │  Cancel  │
 │                                 │   └──────────┘
 │                                 │   ┌──────────┐
 │                                 │   │ Select All│
 │                                 │   └──────────┘
 └─────────────────────────────────┘
 Source directory
 ┌─────────────────────────────────┐  ┌──┐
 │ /home/rwhite/.fonts/            │  │..│
 └─────────────────────────────────┘  └──┘
 ☐ Create soft links only

 Please select the folder from which you want to import fonts. Add the selected fonts
 by clicking the OK button.
```

7. Click OK to add all the selected fonts.

8. A message will pop up telling you how many fonts were added. Click OK to continue.

9. Click Close to close the Fonts window.

10. Click Close to close the OpenOffice printer administration tool.

The fonts you added will now be available for use within the OpenOffice programs. This is very different from the situation in most Windows applications, where making the fonts available within the operating system will automatically allow the applications to use them.

Project 3-2 Customizing a KDE Desktop

In Project 3-1, you customized a GNOME desktop by following detailed instructions. Now that you have more background on desktop configuration, and more experience altering it, let's try some more unusual effects. Use a system set up to use the KDE desktop environment for this project.

Step by Step

1. From the KDE desktop, enable the Desktop menu. Start by right-clicking on the desktop, and find the appropriate menu item.

2. Enable file previews for HTML and text files. Use the KDE Control Center or right-click on the desktop to configure the desktop settings.

3. Change the focus policy. From the Control Center's Window Behavior entry, change KDE from its default of having "focus" (the active window or area) being wherever you clicked last, as in Windows systems. Instead, have focus follow the mouse cursor, whether it has clicked somewhere or not, as on UNIX systems.

4. Also in the Window Behavior configuration area, set the desktop's treatment of double-clicking the title bar. By default, double-clicking a window's title bar will *shade* the window, that is, roll the window up so that only the title bar is showing. You can set KDE to make a double-click maximize the window instead. Do so.

5. From the Launch Feedback section of the Control Center, enable the busy cursor behavior so that KDE behaves more like Windows XP. When an application is loading, the cursor shows that application's icon, so you know it's working on something.

(continued)

6. Change the icon set from the default Red Hat Bluecurve set to the Conectiva Crystal Icon theme. You should be able to find the configuration tool to do this in the Control Center.

Project Summary

Again, these customizations may not be to your liking. In particular, if you are used to Microsoft Windows' focus policy, having focus follow the mouse can be disorienting. However, it can be very useful to have focus follow the mouse, as it allows you to actively use two overlapping windows when clicking on the windows to change focus might obscure information you need.

Module Summary

In this module, you learned about the X Window System environment, specifically KDE and GNOME. These are some key points:

- The X Window System environment is *not* part of the core operating system.

- Window managers run on top of X, and you can pick whatever window manager works best for you.

- The KDE environment is a combination of both a window manager and an application framework for developing GUI applications.

- KDE's control panel, called the Control Center, can be found by clicking the K icon in the lower-left corner of the window.

- KDE's web site is http://www.kde.org.

- GNOME defines an application framework for other window managers and libraries. Therefore, you can use multiple window managers, such as Enlightenment and Window Maker.

- GNOME's web site is http://www.gnome.org.

GNOME and KDE represent significant advancements in the quality of graphical user interfaces for Linux and UNIX as a whole. Hopefully, the comfort of working in these two environments is enough to convince even more folks to turn their dual-boot configurations into single-boot Linux configurations.

3

GNOME and KDE

Project
3-2

Customizing a KDE Desktop

Module 3 Mastery Check

1. What percentage of Linux's GUI is built into the kernel?

2. What is a window manager?

3. Can you run KDE applications within GNOME?

4. What command is used to start the X Window System?

5. What files can be edited to change the GUI that runs when you start X?

6. Which of the following are not standard icons on the Red Hat Linux 8.0 panel:

   A. Start Menu

   B. Spreadsheet

   C. Presentation Tool

   D. System Monitor

   E. Email Program

   F. Web Browser

   G. Terminal Emulator

   H. Word Processor

7. How do you add a program to the panel in GNOME?

8. What is GNOME's web site?

9. Name one place to get different themes for GNOME.

10. What is KDE's web site?

11. Name one place to get different themes for KDE.

12. How do you add a program to the panel in KDE?

13. What is the name of the default set of look and feel elements in Red Hat Linux 8.0?

14. Into what directories can new fonts be added to the system?

15. What is the name of the script to run to add new fonts to the system?

Module 4

Installing Software

87

Given that a great deal of systems administration centers on installing the software necessary to provide a service, it is important that you consider the mechanisms for installing new packages as well as compiling those packages that ship as source code.

In general, most applications have very similar installation patterns. Keeping an eye out for the typical sources of information, as well as maintaining a healthy dose of common sense, will make most installation processes go smoothly. Thus, the intent of this module is not only to show cookbook formulas for installing certain types of packages, but also to include troubleshooting strategies.

In this module, you will learn the two most common methods of installation: using the Red Hat Package Manager (RPM) and compiling the source code yourself. All of the commands entered in this module are entered as the root user. The easiest way to do this is to log in as **root**. (Module 6 will show you how to change your user ID to someone else's ID using the **su** command.) In general, if you have logged in as someone other than **root**, go to the command line or open a terminal window. At the prompt, type **su - root** there.

CRITICAL SKILL
4.1 Using the Red Hat Package Manager

The Red Hat Package Manager's primary function is to allow the installation and removal of files (typically precompiled software). It is easy to use, and several graphical interfaces have been built around it to make it even easier. Red Hat, Mandrake, and other distributions use this tool to distribute their software. In fact, almost all of the software mentioned in this book is available in RPM form. The reason for going through the process of compiling software yourself in other modules is that you can use compile-time options that are not available in an RPM.

Basically, an RPM file is a collection of all the files necessary for a particular program to run. It also includes descriptions of the program, version information, and the necessary scripts to perform the installation itself.

NOTE

In this context, I am assuming that the RPM files contain precompiled binaries. Several groups, such as Red Hat, also make source code available as an RPM, but it is uncommon to download and compile source code in this fashion.

The RPM tool performs general management of all of the RPM packages that are installed on a given host. This includes tracking which packages are installed, their version numbers, and their file locations. All of this information is kept in a simple database file on the host.

In general, software that comes in the form of an RPM is less work to install and maintain than software that needs to be compiled. The trade-off is that by using an RPM, you accept the default parameters supplied in the RPM. In most cases, these defaults are acceptable. However, if you need to be more intimately aware of what is going on with a service, you may find that compiling the source yourself will prove more educational about what package components exist and how they work together.

But assuming that all you want to do is install a simple package, RPM is perfect. There are several great resources for RPM packages, including the following:

- http://www.rpmfind.net

- http://www.freshrpms.net

- http://www.linuxapps.com

- ftp://ftp.redhat.com/pub/contrib

Of course, if you are interested in more details about RPM itself, you can visit the RPM web site at http://www.rpm.org. RPM comes with Red Hat Linux (and derivatives) as well as Caldera Linux. If you aren't sure if RPM comes with a particular distribution, check with your vendor.

NOTE

Although the name of the package manager says "Red Hat," the software can be used with other distributions as well. In fact, RPM has even been ported to other operating systems, such as Solaris and IRIX! The source code to RPM is open-source software, so anyone can take the initiative to make the system work for them.

Installing a New Package

The easiest way to install a new package is to use the **–i** option with **rpm**. For example, if you downloaded a package called **bc-1.06-10.i386.rpm** and wanted to install it, you would type

```
[root@tedford /root]# rpm -i bc-1.06-10.i386.rpm
```

If the installation went fine, you would not see any errors or messages. This is the most common method of installing RPMs. On the other hand, if the package already existed, you would see this message:

```
error: package bc-1.06-10 is already installed
```

Some packages rely on other packages. A KDE applet, for example, may depend on KDE libraries having already been installed. In those instances, you will get a message indicating which packages need to be installed first. Simply install those packages and then come back to the original package.

If you need to upgrade a package that already exists, use the –**U** option, like so:

```
[root@tedford /root]# rpm -U bc-1.06-10.i386.rpm
```

Some additional command-line options to **rpm** are listed in Table 4-1.

For example, to force the installation of a package regardless of dependencies or other errors, you would type:

```
[root@tedford /root]# rpm -ivh --force --nodeps packagename.rpm
```

where *packagename.rpm* is the name of the package being installed. Because of the –**h** and –**v** options, the command will also keep you apprised of its progress as the installation progresses.

Command-Line Option	Description
--force	This is the sledgehammer of installation. Typically, you use it when you're knowingly installing an odd or unusual configuration, and RPM's safeguards are trying to keep you from doing so. The **--force** option tells rpm to forgo any sanity checks and just do it, even if it thinks you're trying to fit a square peg into a round hole. Be careful with this option.
–h	Prints hash marks to indicate progress during an installation. Use with the –**v** option for a pretty display.
--percent	Prints the percentage completed to indicate progress. It is handy if you're running rpm from another program, such as a Perl script, and you want to know the status of the install.
--nodeps	If rpm is complaining about missing dependency files, but you want the installation to happen anyway, passing this option at the command line will cause rpm to not perform any dependency checks.
--test	This option does not perform a real installation; it just checks to see whether an installation would succeed. If it anticipates problems, it displays what they'll be.
–v	Tells rpm to be verbose about its actions.

Table 4-1 Common RPM Command-Line Options

Querying a Package

Sometimes it is handy to know which packages are currently installed and what they do. You can do that with the RPM query options.

To list all installed packages, simply type

```
[root@tedford /root]# rpm -qa
```

Be ready for a long list of packages! If you are looking for a particular package name, you can use the **grep** command to specify the name (or part of the name) of the package, like so:

```
[root@tedford /root]# rpm -qa | grep -i 'bc'
```

NOTE

The **–i** parameter in **grep** tells it to make its search case-insensitive.

If you just want to view all of the packages one screen at a time, you can use the **more** command, like so:

```
[root@tedford /root]# rpm -qa | more
```

To find out which package a particular file belongs to, type

```
[root@tedford /root]# rpm -qf /usr/bin/bc
```

where you substitute the name of the file that you want to check on for **/usr/bin/bc**.

To find out the purpose of a package that is already installed, you must first know the name of the package (taken from the listing in **rpm –qa**) and then specify it, like so:

```
[root@tedford /root]# rpm -qi bc
```

where you can substitute any *packagename* in place of **bc**.

To find out what files are contained in a package, type

```
[root@tedford /root]# rpm -ql bc
```

where you can replace **bc** with any *packagename* you want information about.

You can also identify information about and a list of files included in an uninstalled package by including the **–p** option to look at an RPM package file:

```
[root@tedford /root]# rpm -qilp bc-1.06-10.i386.rpm | more
```

Notice that this command combines the **–i** and **–l** options; the resulting output is likely to be long, so the **more** command was added to display one screen of information at a time. Press the ENTER key to display the next screen of data.

Uninstalling a Package

Uninstalling packages with RPM is just as easy as installing them. In most cases, all you will need to type is

```
[root@tedford /root]# rpm -e packagename
```

where *packagename* is the name of the package as listed in **rpm -qa**.

Progress Check

1. What command-line option is used with the **rpm** command to install an RPM package?

2. What command-line option is used to upgrade an RPM package?

3. What command-line options, used in combination, show the installation progress?

4. How can you list all installed packages on a system, displaying them one screen at a time?

---

1. Use the **rpm –i** option to install a package.
2. Use the **rpm –U** option to upgrade a package.
3. Use the **–v** and **–h** options with either **–i** or **–U** to show installation progress. These options can be combined: **rpm –Uvh** *packagename*.
4. The command: **rpm –qa | more** will list the names of all packages installed on a system, one screen at a time.

Project 4-1 Installing Webmin

One popular system management tool available under Linux and several flavors of UNIX is called Webmin. Webmin provides a variety of functionality for administrators, especially those who want to manage multiple servers. Installing Webmin can be useful not only for practicing RPM installation skills, but also for practicing system management skills you'll learn about in later modules.

Step by Step

1. Go to the Webmin site at http://webadmin.sourceforge.net.

2. Find the download area and download the latest Webmin RPM package. If you download from a system with RealPlayer installed, you may have to shift-click or right-click the download package to download it, because RealPlayer may want to "play" the RPM package.

3. Install the Webmin RPM package using **rpm –ivh**. (You'll have to specify the name of the RPM package file.) You should see the preparation process start and move to 100 percent. The Webmin package will note the operating system version being run, and then install its contents. When installation is finished, you should be told what address to put into a web browser to log in to Webmin as **root**.

4. Point your browser to **http://*yourservername*:10000** and log in using the **root** account and its password. Set *yourservername* to be the name of the server as described by the Webmin installation message.

5. Have a look around Webmin and see what options are available!

Project Summary

Installing software via RPM is very easy! Now that you have an operational Webmin package, you can experiment with it. If you don't want to use it, you can uninstall it using **rpm –e webmin**. To find more potentially interesting RPM packages, you can check out some of the sites mentioned earlier in this module.

redhat-config-packages

If you like a good GUI tool to help simplify your life, look to **redhat-config-packages**. It performs all of the functions of the command-line RPM tool, without forcing you to remember command-line parameters. Of course, this comes at the price of not being scriptable, but that's why we have the command-line version, too. To run the graphical package management tool, go to the Red Hat menu, and from System Settings, select Packages. You can also go to a command line and run:

```
[rwhite@tedford ~]$ redhat-config-packages
```

Either way you start the package manager, it will check to see if you are the root user. If you are not, it will open a window like the one shown, in which you can enter the root password to run the utility with **root**'s permissions.

```
┌──────────────────────────────────────────────────┐
│ ✔ Query                                        ✖ │
├──────────────────────────────────────────────────┤
│   ⚷    You are attempting to run "redhat-config-packages" │
│        which requires administrative privileges, but more │
│        information is needed in order to do so.  │
│                                                  │
│   Password for root    [ ******** ]              │
│                                                  │
│                    [ ✖ Cancel ]   [ ⤶ OK ]       │
└──────────────────────────────────────────────────┘
```

Once you have successfully entered the root password, the package manager will check to see what packages are already installed on the system. You will be able to select packages for installation or removal in exactly the same way you did during the Red Hat Linux 8.0 installation. This is a welcome update to the look and feel of the package manager. As during installation, whole groups of packages can be selected (see Figure 4-1), or specific packages can be manipulated.

Project 4-2 Getting Apt

The Debian distribution and a few others use a non-RPM package manager that adherents much prefer to RPM. The Debian package manager, *apt,* does a better job of handling dependencies automatically than RPM does. Some people like to use apt on their RPM-based systems, too, and so the folks at the Conectiva distribution made a version available that handles RPM installations. Now the same thing is available for Red Hat users. To install and use apt, you'll have to build upon your RPM installation skills.

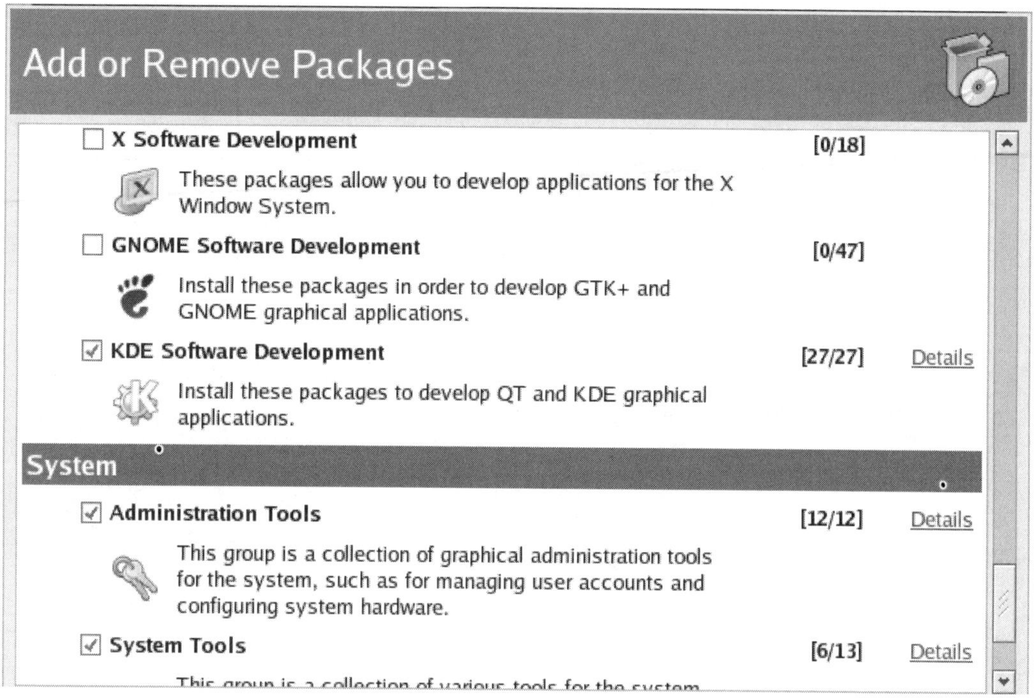

Add or Remove Packages

☐ **X Software Development**   [0/18]

These packages allow you to develop applications for the X Window System.

☐ **GNOME Software Development**   [0/47]

Install these packages in order to develop GTK+ and GNOME graphical applications.

☑ **KDE Software Development**   [27/27]   Details

Install these packages to develop QT and KDE graphical applications.

System

☑ **Administration Tools**   [12/12]   Details

This group is a collection of graphical administration tools for the system, such as for managing user accounts and configuring system hardware.

☑ **System Tools**   [6/13]   Details

This group is a collection of various tools for the system

Figure 4-1 The **redhat-config-packages** tool uses the same interface as the package selector used during Red Hat Linux 8.0 installation.

Step by Step

1. Go to http://psyche.freshrpms.net and find the apt package.

2. Download the apt package and install it (as **root**) using **rpm –ivh**.

3. Run **apt-get update** to download package information from the freshrpms.net site.

4. Run **apt-get –f install** to verify apt's installation integrity.

5. Download an apt GUI manager by running **apt-get install synaptic**.

6. Test the synaptic installation by running **synaptic**.

(continued)

Project Summary

Many other packages can be installed from the command line using **apt-get install** and specifying the package name, or by using the synaptic GUI shown.

For some purposes, such as loading the many desktop-enhancing files available from freshrpms.net, these tools are even easier than RPM. Many server installations might not be good guinea pigs for using apt, however. Consider whether you want to be using non–Red Hat packages on a server you want to run mission-critical services. In the end, installing apt is not only a way of practicing use of RPMs, it's also a way of starting to think about security policies, which I'll address in more detail in Module 9.

CRITICAL SKILL
4.2 Compiling Software Yourself

One of the key benefits of open-source software is that you have the source code in your hands. If the developer chooses to stop working on it, you can continue. If you find a problem, you can fix it. In other words, you are in control of the situation and not at the mercy of a commercial developer you can't control. But having the source code means you need to be able to compile it, too. Otherwise all you have is a bunch of text files that can't do much.

Although almost every piece of software in this book is available as an RPM, you should step through the process of compiling it yourself so that you can pick and choose compile-time options, which is something that you can't do with RPMs. Thus, it's a good idea to become comfortable with compiling packages yourself.

In this section, you will step through the process of compiling the KDirStat package, a graphical tool for viewing directory sizes. You can download KDirStat from http://kdirstat.sourceforge.net. KDirStat is a typical package; you'll find that most other packages that you need to compile follow the same general pattern.

NOTE

KDirStat is not an essential package for managing your Red Hat Linux system; its functionality is similar to that of the **du** utility, which provides disk usage information for the directories you specify.

Getting and Unpacking the Package

Software that comes in source form is often made available as a *tarball*—that is, it is archived into a single large file and then compressed. The tools used to do this are **tar** and **gzip** or **bzip2**; **tar** handles the process of combining many files into a single large file, and **gzip** or **bzip2** is responsible for the compression.

NOTE

Do not confuse **gzip** and **bzip2** with WinZip. They are different programs that use different methods of compression. It should be noted, though, that WinZip does know how to handle tarballs.

Typically, a single directory is selected in which to build and store tarballs. This allows the system administrator to keep the tarball of each package in a safe place in the event he or she needs to pull something out of it later. It also lets all the administrators know which packages are installed on the system in addition to the base system. A good directory for this is **/usr/local/src**, since software local to a site is generally installed in **/usr/local**. The downside of using the **/usr/local/src** directory to store source code is that the root user must be used to build the software there, not just install it. In most cases, software installed from tarballs *can* be built by a normal user and then installed by the root user, but because of the default directory permissions in **/usr/local/src**, normal users cannot build the software there.

When unpacked, most tarballs create a new directory for all of its files. The KDirStat tarball (**kdirstat-2.2.0.tgz**), for example, creates the subdirectory **kdirstat-2.2.0**. Most packages follow this standard. If you find a package that does not follow it, it is a good idea to create a subdirectory with a reasonable name and place all the unpacked source files there. This allows multiple builds to occur at the same time without the risk of the two builds conflicting.

TIP

While tarballs often end in **.tar.gz** or **.tar.bz2**, you may also see files ending in **.tgz**. These are also tarballs; their file extension is a sort of contraction of **.tar** and **.gz**.

Begin by downloading the KDirStat source tarball. You can fetch it from its web site at http://kdirstat.sourceforge.net/.

To unpack the KDirStat tarball, first become **root**, and then move the file into the **/usr/local/src** directory, like so:

```
[rwhite@tedford ~]$ su -
[root@tedford /root]# mv ~rwhite/kdirstat-2.2.0.tgz /usr/local/src
```

Once there, use the **cd** command to change directories to **/usr/local/src**, like so:

```
[root@tedford /root]# cd /usr/local/src
```

Then unpack the tarball with the following command:

```
[root@tedford src]# tar -xvzf kdirstat-2.2.0.tgz
```

The **z** parameter in the **tar** command invokes **gzip** to decompress the file before the untar process occurs. The **v** parameter tells **tar** to show the name of the file it is untarring as it goes through the process. This way, you'll know the name of the directory where all the sources are being unpacked. You should now have a directory called **/usr/local/src/kdirstat-2.2.0**. You can test this by using the **cd** command to move into it:

```
[root@tedford src]# cd /usr/local/src/kdirstat-2.2.0
```

Looking for Documentation

Once you are inside the directory with all of the source code, begin looking for documentation. *Always read the documentation that comes with the source code!* If there are any special compile directions, notes, or warnings, they will most likely be mentioned here. You will save yourself a great deal of agony by reading the relevant files first.

So then, what are the relevant files? Typically there are two files in a distribution: README and INSTALL, both of which are located in the root of the source code directory. The README file generally includes a description of the package, references to additional documentation (including the installation documentation), and references to the author of the package. The INSTALL file typically has directions for compiling and installing the package.

These are not, of course, absolutes. Every package has its quirks. The best way to find out is to simply list the directory contents and look for obvious signs of additional documentation. In the case of KDirStat, there is a file named README, and another named INSTALL. Some packages use different capitalization: readme, README, ReadMe, and so on; some introduce variations on a theme: README.1ST or README.NOW, and so on.

Another common place for additional information is a subdirectory that is appropriately called "doc" or "documentation." In the case of KDirStat, the doc directory contains source files for building the documentation.

To view a text file, use the **more** command:

```
[root@tedford kdirstat-2.2.0]# more README
```

To view the text file in an editor, use the **pico** command:

```
[root@tedford kdirstat-2.2.0]# pico README
```

TIP

To get a quick list of all the directories in a source tree, enter the command:
```
[root@tedford kdirstat-2.2.0]# ls -l | grep drwx
```

Configuring the Package

Most packages ship with an autoconfiguration script; it is safe to assume they include one unless their documentation says otherwise. These scripts are typically named "configure," and they take parameters. There are a handful of stock parameters that are available across all configure scripts, but the interesting stuff occurs on a program-by-program basis. Each package will have a handful of features that can be enabled or disabled or that have special values set at compile time, and they must be set up via **configure**.

To see what configure options come with a package, simply run

```
[root@tedford kdirstat-2.2.0]# ./configure --help
```

Yes, those are two dashes (--) before the word "help." The configure command will usually return a list (sometimes a very long list) of options that can be set when running the configuration script.

One commonly available option is **--prefix**. This option allows you to set the base directory where the package gets installed. By default, most packages use **/usr/local**. Each component in the package will install into the appropriate directory in **/usr/local**. For example, the KDirStat executable is called kdirstat, which by default gets installed into **/usr/local/kde/bin**.

With all of the options you want set up, a final run of **configure** will create a special type of file called a *makefile*. Makefiles are the foundation of the compilation phase.

Compiling Your Package

Compiling your package is the easy part. All you need to do is run **make**, like so:

```
[root@tedford kdirstat-2.2.0]# make
```

The **make** tool reads all of the makefiles that were created by the configure script. These files tell **make** which files to compile and the order in which to compile them—which is crucial, since there could be hundreds of source files.

Depending on the speed of your system, the available memory, and how busy it is doing other things, the compilation process could take a while to complete, so don't be surprised.

As **make** is working, it will display each command it is running and all of the parameters associated with it. This output is usually the invocation of the compiler and all of the parameters passed to the compiler—it's pretty tedious stuff that even the programmers were inclined to automate!

If the compile goes through smoothly, you won't see any error messages. Most compiler error messages are very clear and distinct, so don't worry about possibly missing an error.

If you do see an error, don't panic. Most error messages don't reflect a problem with the program itself, but usually with the system in some way or another. Typically, these messages are the result of inappropriate file permissions (see the **chmod** command in Module 6), or files that cannot be found. In the latter case, make sure your path has at the very least the **/bin**, **/sbin**, **/usr/bin**, **/usr/sbin**, **/usr/local/bin**, **/usr/local/sbin**, and **/usr/X11R6/bin** directories in it. You can see your path by issuing the following command:

```
[root@tedford kdirstat-2.2.0]# echo $PATH
```

See Module 6 for information on environment variables so that you can set your path correctly.

Another potential pitfall is the set of packages you installed on your system. If you aren't a programmer, you might have foregone installing the development tools for KDE and the X Window System. If you do that, programs such as KDirStat, which rely on functionality contained in the library packages installed with those tools, may not be able to build and run. If you think this might be a possibility, you can use **redhat-config-packages** to install the development software.

In general, slow down and read the error message. Even if the format is a little odd, it may explain what is wrong in plain English, thereby allowing you to quickly fix it. If the error is still confusing, look at the documentation that came with the package to see if there is a mailing list or e-mail address you can contact for help. Most developers are more than happy to provide help, but you need to remember to be nice and to the point. (In other words, don't start an e-mail with a one paragraph rant about why their software is terrible!) You can also sometimes find hints simply by doing a web search on the most concise and relevant-looking error message you see.

Installing the Package

Similar to the compile stage, the installation stage typically goes smoothly. In most cases, once the compile is done, all you need to run is

```
[root@tedford kdirstat-2.2.0]# make install
```

This will start the installation script (which is usually embedded in the makefile). Because **make** displays each command as it is executing it, you will see a lot of text fly by. Don't worry about it—it's perfectly normal. Unless you see an error message, the package is installed.

If you do see an error message, it is most likely because of permissions problems. Look at the last file it was trying to install before failure, and then go check on all the permissions required to place a file there. You may need to use the **chmod**, **chown**, and **chgrp** commands for this step; see Module 6 for additional details.

Running the Package

Depending on the options you fed into the autoconfiguration process, and the defaults, the installed software can be several places. While the most common place for software to install itself is the **/usr/local/bin** directory, many packages have their own ideas about where is most appropriate. For example, the KDirStat executable is installed by default in **/usr/local/kde/bin**. This is a perfectly acceptable location, but it's not in the default Red Hat Linux path, so you won't be able to execute it without doing some more work.

There are three common ways of running software that isn't installed in the path. You can invoke the executable with path information specified, which is the simplest one-time solution. You can add the executable directory to the path, which is the easiest long-term solution. You can add a link to the executable from a directory already in the path, which can be tidy. Use any of these three options to run the **kdirstat** command and bring up the tool (see Figure 4-2).

Running with Path Information

The quick and dirty way of seeing whether the software runs (to test it or evaluate it to see if you like it and want to make more permanent arrangements) is to specify the path information when you run it. While trying to run **kdirstat** without the path specified wouldn't do anything but generate an error message, running the following command will start the utility:

```
[rwhite@tedford ~]$ /usr/local/kde/bin/kdirstat
```

Name	Subtree Percentage	Percentage	Subtree Total	Own Size	Items	Files	Subdirs	Last Change
/usr			2.19 GB	4.0 kB	136454	125834	7925	2002-10-17 11:06:09
lib		39.7%	891.0 MB	48.0 kB	24103	21590	1479	2002-10-17 10:52:50
share		23.1%	1.1 GB	4.0 kB	77998	72081	4762	2002-10-17 10:52:50
local		11.1%	249.5 MB	4.0 kB	12895	11960	915	2002-10-17 11:06:09
bin		7.7%	172.3 MB	44.0 kB	2223	1933	0	2002-10-17 10:52:49
src		5.2%	117.8 MB	4.0 kB	8025	7667	356	2002-10-03 15:43:35
X11R6		4.3%	96.4 MB	4.0 kB	6092	5840	165	2002-10-17 10:52:52
include		1.2%	26.9 MB	8.0 kB	4621	4380	215	2002-10-17 10:52:50
sbin		0.8%	10.2 MB	8.0 kB	303	250	0	2002-10-11 16:09:25
libexec		0.4%	9.1 MB	4.0 kB	84	76	7	2002-10-03 07:23:30
kerberos		0.1%	3.3 MB	4.0 kB	95	56	13	2002-10-03 06:57:41
games		0.0%	21.4 kB	4.0 kB	1	1	0	2002-10-03 07:00:45
dict		0.0%	4.0 kB	4.0 kB	0	0	0	1996-02-06 13:04:01
etc		0.0%	4.0 kB	4.0 kB	0	0	0	1996-02-06 13:04:01
<Files>		0.0%	10 Bytes		1	0		2002-10-03 06:47:01

Figure 4-2 Start **kdirstat** to show the relative usage of directories on the Linux system.

The downside of this solution is that it's irritating and inefficient to have to type all that path information every time you want to run the tool. Fortunately, there are other options.

TIP

If you set up a desktop icon or a panel or menu entry for a program, you can enter its full path information and not have to worry about retyping it. For a program like KDirStat, which is useful only within X, that's probably the best option.

Adding the Executable Directory to the Path

As in Windows, the Linux *path* is a list of directories in which the system looks for executable files. The programs you have already learned of, such as **tar** and **gzip**, exist in directories that are already in the system's path, so you don't have to know their precise location to run them. (In Module 6, you'll look at some commands that can help you find precisely where a program is in your path.)

If you have a directory that you want to add to the path, you can either add it on the fly or add it in a configuration file to make the change permanent. If you wanted to add the **/usr/local/kde/bin** directory to the path using the Bash shell, you could use this command:

```
[rwhite@tedford ~]$ export PATH = $PATH:/usr/local/kde/bin
```

This command tells Bash to make the PATH environment variable available everywhere, and redefines its contents to be the original contents plus the **/usr/local/kde/bin** directory at the end. This will work fine if you just want to use KDirStat during the current login session, but as soon as you log out, this modification will be lost.

To make the path change persist, you can edit a user's ~/.**bash_profile** file. Use pico or another text editor to add the new directory to the list. To make the path alteration system-wide, you can become **root** and add the new pathname to the **/etc/profile** file.

Linking to the Executable

You can also run the program by linking to it from a directory that's already in the path. You can see which directories are in your path using the following command:

```
[rwhite@tedford ~]$ echo $PATH
```

One of the directories that should be in your path is **/usr/local/bin**. Module 6 has more information on paths, so if this brief overview feels inadequate, you can get more information there. To create a link from **/usr/local/bin** to the KDirStat executable in **/usr/local/kde/bin**, use the following command (as **root**):

```
[root@tedford /root]# ln -s /usr/local/kde/bin/kdirstat /usr/local/bin
```

This creates a symbolic link named "kdirstat" in **/usr/local/bin**, so when you try to run the program, the system will find the link in the path and execute the file from its original, linked location.

Cleaning Up

Once the package is installed, you can do some cleanup to get rid of all the temporary files created during the installation. Some makefiles include rules for deleting all the files that are created during a build, and you can use that option (usually **make clean**) to return the source directory to its original state.

```
[root@tedford kdirstat-2.2.0]# make clean
```

If you have retained the original source code tarball, it is okay to simply get rid of the entire directory from which you compiled the source code. In the case of KDirStat, you would get rid of **/usr/local/src/kdirstat-2.2.0**. Begin by going one directory level above the directory you want to remove. In this case, that would be **/usr/local/src**.

```
[root@tedford kdirstat-2.2.0]# cd /usr/local/src
```

Now use the **rm** command to remove the actual directory, like so:

```
[root@tedford src]# rm -rf kdirstat-2.2.0
```

CAUTION

The **rm** command, especially with the **–rf** parameter, is very dangerous. It recursively removes an entire directory without stopping to verify any of the files. Run as the root user, this has the potential to really cause problems on your system. Be very careful and make sure you are erasing what you mean to erase. There is no "undelete" command.

Progress Check

1. List the standard sequence of commands for building and installing software from a tarball.

2. Name two common names of text files containing information about a tarball.

---

1. The standard sequence of commands is **./configure**, **make**, **make install**. Bonus point and a gold star if you remembered to **make clean** or **rm –rf** the build directory afterward.
2. README and INSTALL are two of your best bets for useful information inside a tarball.

Project 4-3   Building and Installing Kgraphspace

You have already built one directory information tool, but there are plenty more utilities available for your benefit and enjoyment. In this project, you'll build another KDE- and disk space–related program called Kgraphspace. It displays a pie chart showing the space usage of each mounted partition, plus a directory tree showing the size of the contents of each branch of the tree.

Step by Step

1. Go to the http://kgraphspace.sourceforge.net site and find the version for KDE 3. (At the time this is being written, that version is 0.3.0-pre1.)

2. Download the Kgraphspace tarball. For the purposes of this project, don't use an RPM, even if one is available.

3. Become the root user using the **su -** command.

4. Change directories to the source repository: **cd /usr/local/src**.

5. Unpackage the tarball into **/usr/local/src**. Since the tarball is packaged using **bzip2** compression, use **tar xvjf** with the tarball name. The **–j** option tells tar to use **bunzip2** to uncompress the file.

6. Change directories into the directory created by unpackaging the tarball.

7. Read the contents of the README and INSTALL files. Use **more README** and **more INSTALL**.

8. Run the configuration script: **./configure**.

9. Build the software: **make**.

10. Install the software: **make install**.

11. Clean up after yourself: **make clean**.

12. Look for the executable in **/usr/local/kde/bin**, and use one of the techniques described in this module to run the file in your GUI desktop environment.

Project Summary

As long as you have the development tools and the X and KDE libraries required to build this package, it should be very easy to do so. If you encounter problems, the first place to go is into the **redhat-config-packages** tool to ensure that you have all the necessary tools and libraries installed. Unless you're cramped for disk space, installing each full group will be easiest. Now you're ready to find some software you really want to download, build, install, and use!

Module Summary

In this module, you learned how to install software under Linux using the RPM method and by compiling software yourself. Hopefully, this information should alleviate any fears you have of dealing with an open-source system!

These are the key points to remember:

● The typical install command with RPM is **rpm –i** *packagename.rpm*.

● The typical upgrade command with RPM is **rpm –U** *packagename.rpm*.

● The typical package remove command with RPM is **rpm –e** *packagename*.

● Most source code is shipped as *tarballs,* which can be unpacked with the **tar** command.

● Once the package is untarred, reading the documentation that comes with it is very important.

● Configure the package with the **./configure** command.

● Compile the software by running the **make** command.

● Install compiled software by running the **make install** command.

Module 4 Mastery Check

1. List the **rpm** command's arguments used to install, upgrade, and delete packages.

2. What command could you use to find out which package the **/bin/gzip** file belongs to?

3. Once you knew what package the **/bin/gzip** file belonged to, how could you uninstall it?

4. What **rpm** option can be used to install a package, even if the system thinks it should not be installed?

5. What **rpm** options can be used to perform a "dry run" of a package installation without actually installing the software?

6. Which of the following commands will list the files contained in an installed RPM package?

    A. rpm -qlp bc

    B. rpm -ql bc-1.06-10.i386.rpm

    C. rpm -ql mysql

    D. rpm -qa | grep "mysql"

7. Which graphical tool allows you to manage packages within KDE or GNOME?

8. In what Start Menu button would you find the tool in question 7?

9. Name at least two web sites from which you can get software to add to your Red Hat Linux system.

10. Describe a tarball.

11. How might you tell from a filename that it is a tarball?

12. What command would you run to see options available from a standard configure script?

13. Name one downside to using **/usr/local/src** as the repository for tarballs and their contents.

14. Which is the correct order for a standard software build?

    A. config, make, make clean, make install

    B. make clean, ./configure, make, make install

    C. make clean, make, make install, ./configure

    D. ./configure, make, make install, make clean

15. How can you find out what directories are in the current path?

16. If you have decided you don't need a directory created by unpacking a tarball, how can you remove the directory and its contents?

Part II

Single-Host Administration

Module 5

Managing Users

U nder Linux, every file and program must be owned by a *user.* Each user has a unique identifier called a *user ID (UID).* Each user must also belong to at least one *group,* a collection of users established by the system administrator. Users may belong to multiple groups. Like users, groups have unique identifiers called *group IDs (GIDs).*

The accessibility of a file or program is based on its UIDs and GIDs. A running program inherits the rights and permissions of the user who invokes it. (SetUID and SetGID, discussed in "SetUID and SetGID Programs" later in this module, create an exception to this rule.) Each user's rights can be defined in one of two ways: a *normal user* or the *root user.* Normal users can access only what they own or have been given permission to run; permission is granted either because the user belongs to the file's group or because the file is accessible to all users. The root user is allowed to access all files and programs in the system, whether or not **root** owns them. The root user is often called a *superuser.*

If you are accustomed to Windows, you can draw parallels between that system's user management and Linux's user management. Linux UIDs are comparable to Windows SIDs (system IDs), for example. You may find that, in contrast to Windows, the Linux security model is maddeningly simplistic: Either you're **root** or you're not. Normal users cannot have root privileges in the same way normal users can be granted Administrator access under NT. You'll also notice the distinct absence of Access Control Lists (ACLs) in Linux. Which system is better? Depends on what you want and whom you ask.

In this module, you will examine the technique of managing users for a single host. Managing users over a network will be discussed in Module 17. You'll begin by exploring the actual database files that contain information about users. From there you'll examine the system tools available to manage the files automatically.

CRITICAL SKILL
5.1 # Understanding Linux Users

In Linux, everything has an owner attached to it. Given this, it is impossible for a Linux system to exist without users! At the very least, it needs one root user; however, most Linux distributions ship with several special users set up. These users work well as self-documentation tools, since each user owns all of the files related to his or her username—for example, the user **www** is set up to own all files related to World Wide Web service. These users are configured in a way that grants access only to a select few, so you do not have to worry about their abuse.

TIP

When possible, run applications without root privileges. (The Apache server, for example, knows how to give up root privileges before it starts accepting connections.) The benefit of doing this is that if an application is found to have a security problem, it cannot be exploited to gain system privileges.

A few things need to be set up for a user's account to work correctly. In this section, you'll learn about those items and why they need to be there. The actual process of setting up accounts is discussed in "Employ User Management Tools," later in the module.

Home Directories

Every user who actually logs in to the system needs a place for configuration files that are unique to the user. This place, called a *home directory,* allows each user to work in a customized environment without having to change the environment customized by another user—even if both users are logged in to the system at the same time. In this directory, users are allowed to keep not only their configuration files but their regular work files as well.

For the sake of consistency, most sites place home directories at **/home** and name each user's directory by his or her login name. Thus, if your login name were **rwhite**, your home directory would be **/home/rwhite**. The exception to this is for system accounts, such as a root user's account. Here, home directories are usually set to be either / or something specific to the need for that account (e.g., the **www** account may want its home directory set to **/usr/local/apache** if the Apache web server is installed). The home directory for **root** is traditionally / with most variants of UNIX. Many Linux installations use **/root**.

The decision to place home directories under **/home** is strictly arbitrary—but it does make organizational sense. The system really doesn't care where you place home directories so long as the location for each user is specified in the password file (discussed in "The /etc/passwd File," later in this module). You may see some sites use **/users** or break up the **/home** directory by department, thereby creating **/home/engineering, /home/accounting, /home/admin**, etc., and then have users located under each department. (For example, Dr. Lee from engineering would be **/home/engineering/blee**.)

Passwords

Every account should either have a password or be tagged as impossible to log in to. This is crucial to your system's security—weak passwords are often the cause of compromised system security.

The original philosophy behind passwords is actually quite interesting, especially since we still rely on a significant part of it today. The idea is simple: Instead of relying on protected files to keep passwords a secret, the system would encrypt the password using an AT&T-developed (and National Security Agency–approved) algorithm called Data Encryption Standard (DES) and leave the encrypted value publicly viewable. What originally made this secure was that the encryption algorithm was computationally difficult to break. The best most folks could do was a brute-force dictionary attack where automated systems would iterate through a large dictionary and rely on the tendency of users to pick English words for their passwords. Many people tried to break DES itself, but since it was an open algorithm that anyone could study, it was made very bulletproof before it was actually deployed.

When users entered their passwords at a login prompt, the password they entered would be encrypted. The encrypted value would then be compared against the user's password entry. If the two encrypted values matched, the user was allowed to enter the system. The actual algorithm for performing the encryption was computationally cheap enough that a single encryption wouldn't take too long. However, the tens of thousands of encryptions that would be needed for a dictionary attack would take prohibitively long. Along with the encrypted passwords, the password file could then also keep information about the user's home directory, UID, shell, real name, and so on without anyone's having to worry about system security being compromised if any application run by any user would be allowed to read it.

But then a problem occurred: Moore's Law on processor speed doubling every 18 months held true, and home computers were becoming fast enough that programs were able to perform a brute-force dictionary attack within days rather than weeks or months. Dictionaries got bigger and the software got smarter. The nature of passwords needed to be reevaluated.

Shadow passwords were one solution. In the shadow password scheme, the encrypted password entries were removed from the password file and placed in a separate file called **shadow**. The regular password file would continue to be readable by all users on the system, and the actual encrypted password entries would be readable only by the root user. (The login prompt is run with root permissions.) Why not just make the regular password file readable by **root** only? Well, it isn't that simple. By having the password file open for so many years, the rest of the system software that grew up around it relied on the fact that the password file was always readable by all users. Changing this would simply cause software to fail.

Another solution has been to improve the algorithm used to perform the encryption of passwords. Some distributions of Linux, including Red Hat Linux 8.0, have followed the path of the FreeBSD operating system and used the MD5 scheme. This has increased the complexity of being able to crack passwords, which, when used in conjunction with shadow passwords, works quite well. (Of course, this is assuming you make your users choose good passwords!)

TIP

Choosing good passwords is always a chore. Your users will inevitably ask, "What then, O, Almighty System Administrator, makes a good password?" Here's your answer: a nonlanguage word (not English, not Spanish, not German, not human-language word), preferably with mixed case, numbers, and punctuation. Unfortunately, if a password is too hard to remember, most people will quickly defeat its purpose by writing it down and keeping it in an easily viewed place. So better make it memorable! I prefer the technique of choosing a phrase and then picking the first letter of every word in the phrase. Thus, the phrase "my hero Glenn Seaborg talked to me" becomes mhGSt2m. The phrase is memorable (for fans of radioisotopes, anyway), even if the resulting password isn't.

Shells

When users log in to the system, they expect an environment that can help them be productive. This first program that users encounter is called a *shell.* If you're used to the Microsoft side of the world, you might equate this to command.com, Program Manager, or Explorer (not to be confused with Internet Explorer, which is a web browser).

Under UNIX, most shells are text based. The shell discussed in further detail in Module 6 is the default shell for the root user, the Bourne Again Shell, or BASH for short. Linux comes with several shells from which to choose—you can see most of them listed in the **/etc/shells** file. Deciding which shell is right for you is kind of like choosing a favorite beer—what's right for you isn't right for everyone, but still, everyone tends to get defensive about his or her choice!

What makes UNIX so interesting is that you do not have to stick with the list of shells provided in **/etc/shells**. In the strictest of definitions, the password entry for each user doesn't list what shell to run so much as it lists what program to run first for the user. Of course, most users prefer that the first program run be a shell, such as BASH.

Startup Scripts

Under DOS, you may have grown used to having the **autoexec.bat** and **config.sys** files run automatically when you started up the system. Since DOS was a single-user system, the two programs not only performed system functions such as loading device drivers, but they also set up your working environment.

UNIX, on the other hand, is a multiuser environment. Each user is allowed to have his or her own configuration files; thus the system appears to be customized for each particular user, even if other people are logged in at the same time. The configuration file comes in the form of a *shell script*—a series of commands executed by the shell that starts when a user logs in. In the case of BASH, it's the file **.bashrc**. (Yes, there is a period in front of the filename— filenames preceded by periods, also called *dot files,* are hidden from normal directory listings unless the user uses a special option to list them.) You can think of shell scripts in the same light as batch files, except shell scripts can be much more capable. The **.bashrc** script in particular is similar in nature to **autoexec.bat**.

When you create a user's account, you should provide a default set of dot files to get the user started. If you use the tools that come with Linux, you don't need to worry about creating these files—the tools automatically do this for you. However, there is nothing stopping you from customizing these files to make them site specific. For example, if you have a special application that requires an environment variable to be set, you can add that to the dot files that are copied to new user's home directories.

Mail

Creating a new user means not only creating the user's home directory and setting up the environment. It also means making it possible for the user to send and receive e-mail. Setting up a mailbox under Linux is quite easy, and if you use the tools that come with Linux to create the account, you don't even have to do this yourself!

Mailboxes are kept in the **/var/spool/mail** directory. Each user has a mailbox that is based on his or her login name. Thus, if a user's login is **bwoodall**, his mailbox will be **/var/spool/ mail/bwoodall**. All mailboxes should be owned by their respective owners with the permissions set such that others cannot read its contents. (See the **chown**, **chmod**, and **chgrp** commands in Module 6 for details on how to do this.)

An empty mailbox is a zero-length file. To create a zero-length file anywhere in the system, you simply use the **touch** command like so:

```
[root@tedford /root]# touch myfile
```

This will create a new file called **myfile** in the current directory.

Progress Check

1. What is the usual location for user home directories?

2. What was the original encryption scheme used for passwords?

3. Name a BASH shell configuration filename.

4. Where would you expect to find user **mpawlawski**'s mailbox?

Managing User Databases

If you're already used to Windows 2000 or .NET Server user management, you're familiar with the Active Directory tool that takes care of the nitty-gritty details of the user database. This tool is convenient, but it makes developing your own administrative tools trickier, since the only other way to read or manipulate user information is through a series of LDAP calls.

---

1. The usual location for user home directories is **/home**.

2. The Data Encryption Standard (DES) was originally used for encrypting passwords.

3. The **.bashrc** file is a BASH configuration file (as is **/etc/profile**, although the latter isn't covered here).

4. You would find **mpawlawski**'s mailbox at **/var/spool/mail/mpawlawski**.

In contrast, Linux takes the path of traditional UNIX and keeps all user information in straight text files. This is beneficial for the simple reason that it allows you to make changes to user information without the need of any other tool than a text editor such as **pico**. In many instances, larger sites take advantage of these text files by developing their own user administration tools so that they can not only create new accounts but also automatically make additions to the corporate phone book, web pages, and so on.

However, users and groups working with UNIX style for the first time may prefer to stick with the basic user management tools that come with the Linux distribution. You'll learn about those tools in "Employ User Management Tools" later in this module. For now, you'll examine how Linux's text files are structured.

The /etc/passwd File

The **/etc/passwd** file stores the following information for each defined user:

- Login name
- Encrypted password entry
- UID
- Default GID
- Name (sometimes called GECOS)
- Home directory
- Login shell

The file contains one user per line, and each entry for the user is delimited by a colon. For example:

```
rwhite:boQavhhaCKaXg:100:102:Russell White:/home/rwhite:/bin/tcsh
```

Earlier in this module, you learned about the details of the password entry. In the preceding code listing, you can actually see what a DES-encrypted password looks like (the information following the first column). Many sites disable accounts by altering the encrypted password entry so that when the disabled account's user enters her password, it won't match the value in the password file. The guaranteed method of altering passwords for this reason is to insert an asterisk (*) into the entry. The preceding entry, for example, could be altered to **boQavhhaCKaXg***.

TIP

When disabling accounts in this manner, you may find it helpful not only to add an asterisk character, but also to add a string to indicate why the account was disabled in the first place. For example, if you catch a user downloading proprietary software, you could disable his account by changing the encrypted entry to **boQavhhaCKaXg*caught violating rules**.

The UID must be unique for every user, with the exception of the UID zero. Any user who has a UID of zero has root (Administrative) access and thus has full run of the system. Usually, the only user who has this specific UID has the login **root**. It is considered bad practice to allow any other users or usernames to have a UID of zero. This is notably different from the Windows NT 2000, and .NET Server models, in which any number of users can have Administrative privileges.

NOTE

Some distributions of Linux reserve the UID −1 (also written as 65535) or the UID −2 (65534) for the user nobody. Red Hat uses the latter.

The user's name can be any free-form text entry. Although it is possible for nonprintable characters to exist in this string, it is considered bad practice to use them. Also, the user's name may not span multiple lines.

NOTE

Although the entire line for a user's password entry may not span multiple lines, it may be longer than 80 characters.

The user's home directory appears as discussed earlier in this module. Ditto for the last entry, the user's shell. A complete password file for a system, then, might look like this:

```
root:AgQ/IJgASeW1M:0:0:root:/root:/bin/bash
bin:*:1:1:bin:/bin:
daemon:*:2:2:daemon:/sbin:
adm:*:3:4:adm:/var/adm:
lp:*:4:7:lp:/var/spool/lpd:
sync:*:5:0:sync:/sbin:/bin/sync
shutdown:*:6:0:shutdown:/sbin:/sbin/shutdown
halt:*:7:0:halt:/sbin:/sbin/halt
mail:*:8:12:mail:/var/spool/mail:
```

```
news:*:9:13:news:/var/spool/news:
uucp:*:10:14:uucp:/var/spool/uucp:
operator:*:11:0:operator:/root:
games:*:12:100:games:/usr/games:
gopher:*:13:30:gopher:/usr/lib/gopher-data:
ftp:*:14:50:FTP User:/home/ftp:
pop:*:15:15:APOP Admin:/tmp:/bin/tcsh
nobody:*:99:99:Nobody:/:
rwhite:Kss9Ere9b1Ejs:500:500:Russell White:/home/rwhite:/bin/tcsh
mpawlawski:bfCAblvZBIbFM:501:501:Mike Pawlawski:/home/mpawlawski:/bin/bash
bwoodall:*:502:502:Brent Woodall:/home/bwoodall:/bin/bash
michael:sMs7sG0rhWdoU8VabYG7M2:503:503:Michael Turner:/home/michael:/bin/zsh
```

The /etc/shadow File

The speed of home computers began making dictionary attacks against password lists easier for hackers to accomplish. This led to the separation of the encrypted passwords from the **/etc/passwd** file. The **/etc/passwd** file would remain readable by all users, but the passwords kept in the **/etc/shadow** file would be readable only by those programs with root privileges, such as the login program. An *x* is typically placed in the password field of **/etc/passwd** to indicate that the encrypted password actually exists in the shadow file.

In addition to the encrypted password field, the **/etc/shadow** file contains information about password expiration and whether the account is disabled. The format of each line in the **/etc/shadow** file contains the following:

- Login name

- Encrypted password

- Days since Jan. 1, 1970, that the password has been changed

- Days before the password may be changed

- Days after which the password must be changed

- Days before the password is about to expire that the user is warned

- Days after the password is expired that the account is disabled

- Days since Jan. 1, 1970, that the account has been disabled

- Reserved field

Each user has a one-line entry with a colon delimiter. Here's an example:

```
rwhite:boQavhhaCKaXg:10750:0:99999:7:-1:-1:134529868
```

Entries with a **–1** imply infinity. In the case where a **–1** appears in the field indicating the number of days before a password expires, you are effectively tagging a user as never having to change his or her password.

The /etc/group File

As you know, each user belongs to at least one group, that being the user's default group. Users may then be assigned to additional groups if needed. The **/etc/passwd** file contains each user's default GID. This GID is mapped to the group's name and other members of the group in the **/etc/group** file. The format of each line in the **/etc/group** file is

- Group name
- Encrypted password for the group
- GID number
- Comma-separated list of member users

Again, each field is separated from the preceding one by a colon. An entry looks similar to this:

```
project:baHrE1KPNjrPE:102:rwhite,hdc
```

Also like the **/etc/passwd** file, the group file must be world-readable so that applications can look for associations between users and groups. Group names should not exceed eight characters, and the GID should be unique for each group. Finally, the comma-separated list of users is used only for users for whom particular groups are not their default group.

If you want to include a group that does not have a password, you can set the entry like this:

```
project:baHrE1KPNjrPE:102:rwhite,hdc
```

If you want a group to exist, but you don't want to allow anyone to change his working group to this group (good for applications that need their own group but no valid reason exists for a user to be working inside that group), use an asterisk in the password field. For example:

```
project:*:102:
```

Progress Check

1. Name the fields stored in the **/etc/passwd** file.

2. Name the fields stored in the **/etc/shadow** file.

3. Name the fields stored in the **/etc/group** file.

CRITICAL SKILL
5.3 Employing User Management Tools

The wonderful part about having password database files that have a well-defined format in straight text is that it is easy for anyone to be able to write his or her own management tools. Indeed, many site administrators have already done this in order to integrate their tools along with the rest of their organization's infrastructure. They can start a new user from the same form that lets them update the corporate phone and e-mail directory, LDAP servers, web pages, and so on. Of course, not everyone wants to roll their own tools, which is why Linux comes with several prewritten tools that do the job for you.

In this section, you'll learn about user management tools that work from both the command-line interface and the graphical user interface (GUI). Of course, learning how to use both is the preferred route, for you never know under what circumstances you may one day find yourself adding users.

Command-Line User Management

You can choose from among six command-line tools to perform the same actions performed by the GUI tool: **useradd**, **userdel**, **usermod**, **groupadd**, **groupdel**, and **groupmod**. The obvious advantage to using the GUI tool is ease of use. However, the disadvantage is that actions that can be performed with it cannot be automated. This is where the command-line tools become very handy.

---

1. The **/etc/passwd** file contains the following colon-delimited fields: login name; encrypted password; UID; default GID; full user name; home directory; and login shell.

2. The **/etc/shadow** file contains the following colon-delimited fields: login name; encrypted password; days since Jan. 1, 1970, that the password was changed; days before the password may be changed; days after which the password must be changed; days before the password is about to expire that the user is warned; days after the password is expired that the account is disabled; days since Jan. 1, 1970, that the account has been disabled; and a reserved field.

3. The **/etc/group** file contains the following colon-delimited fields: group name; encrypted password for the group; GID number; and a comma-separated list of member users.

NOTE

Linux distributions other than Red Hat may have slightly different parameters than the tools used here. To see how your particular installation is different, read the man page for the particular program in question.

useradd

As the name implies, **useradd** allows you to add a single user to the system. Unlike the GUI tool, it offers no interactive prompts. Instead, all parameters must be specified on the command line. Here's how you use this tool:

```
useradd [-c comment] [-d homedir] [-e expire date] [-f inactive time]
[-g initial group] [-G group[,...]] [-m [-k skeleton dir]] [-M]
[-s shell] [-u uid [-o]] [-n] [-r] login
```

Don't be intimidated by this long list of options! You'll examine them one at a time and discuss their relevance.

Before you dive into these options, take note that anything in the square brackets is optional. Thus, to add a new user with the login **rwhite**, you could issue a command as simple as this:

```
[root@tedford /root]# useradd rwhite
```

Default values are used for any unspecified values. (To see the default values, simply run **useradd -D**; the module will describe how to change the defaults shortly.) Table 5-1 shows the command options and their descriptions.

Option	Description
−c comment	Allows you to set the user's name in the GECOS field. As with any command-line parameter, if the value includes a space, you will need to put quotes around the text. For example, to set the user's name to Russell White, you would have to specify **−c "Russell White"**.
−d homedir	By default, the user's home directory is **/home/login** (for example, if the login is rwhite, the home directory would be **/home/rwhite**). When creating a new user, the user's home directory gets created along with the user account. So if you want to change the default to another place, you can specify the new location with this parameter—for example, **−d /home/sysadmin/rwhite**.
−e expire-date	It is possible for an account to expire after a certain date. By default, accounts never expire. To specify a date, be sure to place it in *MM/DD/YY* format (specify 00 for the year 2000 for this system)—for example, use **−e 04/01/03** for the account to expire on April 1, 2003.

Table 5-1 Options for the useradd Command

Option	Description
–f inactive-time	This option specifies the number of days after a password expires that the account is still usable. A value of 0 (zero) indicates that the account is disabled immediately. A value of –1 will never allow the account to be disabled, even if the password has expired (for example, **–f 3** will allow an account to exist for three days after a password has expired). The default value is –1.
–g initial-group	Using this option, you can specify the default group the user has in the password file. You can use a number or name of the group; however, if you use a name of a group, the group must exist in the **/etc/group file**—for example, **–g project**.
–G group[,...]	This option allows you to specify additional groups to which the new user will belong. If you use the **–G** option, you must specify at least one additional group. You can, however, specify additional groups by separating them with commas. For example, to add a user to the project and admin groups, you should specify **–G project,admin**.
–m [–k skel-dir]	By default, the system automatically creates the user's home directory. This option is the explicit command to create the user's home directory. Part of creating the directory is copying default configuration files into it. These files come from the **/etc/skel** directory by default. You can change this by using the secondary option **–k skel dir**. (You must specify **–m** in order to use **–k**.) For example, to specify the **/etc/adminskel** directory, you would use **–m –k /etc/adminskel**.
–M	If you used the –m option, you cannot use **–M**, and vice versa. This option tells the command *not* to create the user's home directory.
–n	Red Hat Linux creates a new group with the same name as the new user's login as part of the process of adding a user. You can disable this behavior by using this option.
–s shell	A user's login shell is the first program that runs when a user logs in to a system. This is usually a command-line environment, unless you are logging in from the X login screen. By default, this is the Bourne Shell (**/bin/bash**), though some folks like other shells such as the Turbo C Shell (**/bin/tcsh**). This option lets you choose whichever shell you would like to run for the new user upon login. (A list of shells is available in **/etc/shells**.)
–u uid	By default, the program will automatically find the next available UID and use it. If for some reason you need to force a new user's UID to be a particular value, you can use this option. Remember that UIDs must be unique for all users.
Login	Finally, the only parameter that *isn't* optional! You must specify the new user's login name.

Table 5-1 Options for the useradd Command (continued)

For example, to create a new user whose name is Mike Pawlawski, who is a member of the admin and support groups (default group admin), and who prefers using the Turbo C Shell and wants the login name **mpawlawski**, you would use this line:

```
[root@tedford /root]# useradd -c "Mike Pawlawski" -g admin -G support \
> -s /bin/tcsh mpawlawski
```

userdel

The **userdel** command does the exact opposite of **useradd**—it removes existing users. This straightforward command has only one optional parameter and one required parameter:

```
userdel [-r] username
```

By running the command with only the user's login specified on the command line, for example, **userdel rwhite**, all of the entries in the **/etc/passwd** and **/etc/shadow** files, and references in the **/etc/group** file, are automatically removed. By using the optional parameter (for example, **userdel -r rwhite**) all of the files owned by the user in his home directory are removed as well.

usermod

The **usermod** command allows you to modify an existing user in the system. It works in much the same way as **useradd**. The exact command-line usage is as follows:

```
usermod [-c comment] [-d homedir] [-m] [-e expire date]
[-f inactive time] [-g initial group]
[-G group[,...]] [-l login] [-s shell]
[-u uid] login
```

Every option you specify when using this command results in that particular parameter being changed about the user. All but one of the parameters listed here are identical to the parameters documented for the **useradd** program. That one option is –l.

The –l option allows you to change the user's login name. This and the –u option are the only options that require special care. Before changing the user's login or UID, you must make sure the user is not logged in to the system or running any processes. Changing this information if the user is logged in or running processes will cause unpredictable results.

Here's an example of using **usermod** to change user **mpawlawski** such that his comment field reads Number Nine instead of Mike Pawlawski.

```
[root@tedford /root]# usermod -c "Number Nine" mpawlawski
```

groupadd

The group commands are similar to the user commands; however, instead of working on individual users, they work on groups listed in the **/etc/group** file. Note that changing group information does not cause user information to be automatically changed. For example, if you remove a group whose GID is 100 and a user's default group is specified as 100, the user's default group would not be updated to reflect the fact that the group no longer exists.

The **groupadd** command adds groups to the **/etc/group** file. The command-line options for this program are as follows:

```
groupadd [-g gid] [-r] [-f] group
```

Table 5-2 shows command options and their descriptions.

Option	Description
–g *gid*	Specifies the GID for the new group as *gid*. By default, this value is automatically chosen by finding the first available value.
–r	By default, Red Hat searches for the first GID that is higher than 499. The **–r** options tell **groupadd** that the group being added is a system group and should have the first available GID under 499.
–f	When adding a new group, Red Hat Linux will exit without an error if the specified group to add already exists. By using this option, the program will not change the group setting before exiting. This is useful in scripting cases where you want the script to continue if the group already exists.
group	This option is required. It specifies the name of the group you want to add to be *group*.

Table 5-2 Options for the groupadd Command

Suppose, for example, that you want to add a new group called research with the GID 800. To do so, you would type the following command:

```
[root@tedford /root]# groupadd -g 800 research
```

groupdel

Even more straightforward than **userdel**, the **groupdel** command removes existing groups specified in the **/etc/group** file. The only usage information needed for this command is

```
groupdel group
```

where **group** is the name of the group to remove. For example, if you wanted to remove the research group, you would issue this command:

```
[root@tedford /root]# groupdel research
```

groupmod

The **groupmod** command allows you to modify the parameters of an existing group. The options for this command are

```
groupmod -g gid -n group-name group
```

where the **–g** option allows you to change the GID of the group, and the **–n** option allows you to specify a new name of a group. Additionally, of course, you need to specify the name of the existing group as the last parameter.

For example, if the superman research group wanted to change its name to batman, you would issue the command:

```
[root@tedford /root]# groupmod -n batman superman
```

Project 5-1 Creating a User Directory

Seeing the user management tools in the abstract is all well and good, but when the rubber hits the road, you'll have users and groups to organize and implement in your own environment. In this project, you'll be working with a list of employees from a small company to configure the user directory properly.

Step by Step

1. Begin by getting a handle on the employees and their groupings. In this company, there are two primary organizations: the research and development group, and the customer support group. Each group will need to share files and resources internally. The research group consists of three users: **blee**; **dalbers**; and **pdedood**. The support group consists of five users: **dgranda**; **jwang**; **pvenet**; **dnenni**; and **mmiller**.

2. There are some secondary organizational groupings that will require configuration. Three of the users serve in executive officer roles and will need to share private information not accessible by the other users. These executives are: **dalbers**; **dnenni**; and **pdedood**.

3. Another secondary grouping is among the application engineers. Users **dgranda**, **jwang**, and **mmiller** will need to run the bug tracking and documentation databases.

4. One final grouping is among administrative users. Users **blee**, **dalbers**, and **mmiller** have account information, support contract information, router passwords, and other data that will need to be kept confidential.

5. Arrange the users by primary and secondary groups.

6. Now use the **groupadd** command to add each of the groups described in steps 1–4.

7. Use the **useradd** command to add each of the user accounts and make them members of their primary group and any additional groups of which they should be members.

Project Summary

Half the battle in this project is simply organizing the group information so that all users are mapped to the correct groups. The mechanics of adding groups and users are straightforward. Note that you don't have the users' full names, so you can omit the **-c** option when using the **useradd** command.

Using redhat-config-users to Manipulate Users and Groups

The **redhat-config-users** utility can be used to create, delete, and modify users and groups on a Red Hat Linux 8.0 system.

To start **redhat-config-users**, be sure you have started the X environment. You can start the utility by going to the Red Hat icon on the panel and selecting System Settings, and then Users and Groups. If you prefer, you can start the program by entering the command **redhat-config-users** from a terminal window.

If you are not logged on as the root user (and you shouldn't be, remember), you will be prompted for the root password. Once **redhat-config-users** has started, you will see the contents of the current user database, which may look like Figure 5-1.

From this window, you can perform the three basic functions: add, modify, and delete users and groups.

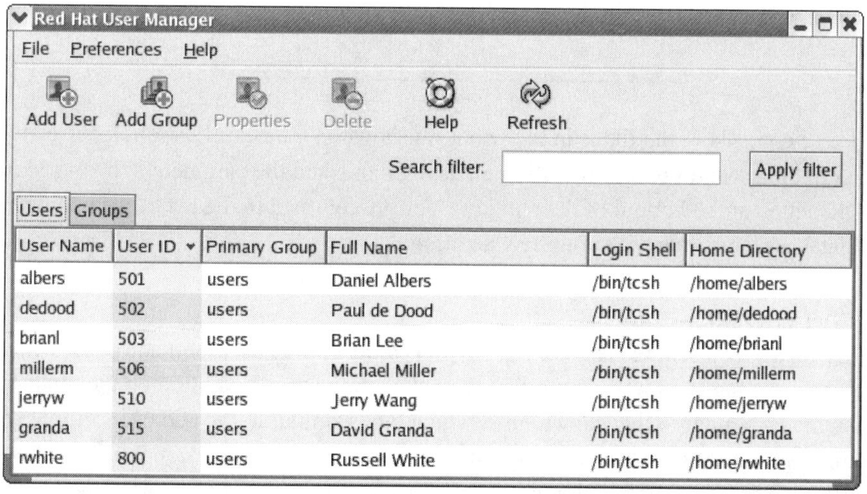

Figure 5-1 The redhat-config-users tool lists the contents of the current user database.

Adding a User

To add a user, begin by clicking the Add User button on the **redhat-config-users** toolbar. This will change the window, as shown here.

These contents of the fields in the windows shown in the next illustration correlate to the entries in the **useradd** program. After you have established the parameters to your liking, click the OK button at the bottom of the window. You are returned to the list of the contents of the user database, complete with your new addition.

Modifying a User

Modifying a user's settings is quite simple. In **redhat-config-users**'s main window, select the user whose settings you wish to modify, then click the Properties button on the toolbar. You'll see a window similar to that shown next, which looks similar to the add user settings, except that there are some additional tabs for further configuring the user account. Under the Account Info tab, you can set an expiration date for the account or lock the account immediately. The Password Info tab allows you to enable password expiration and set the related fields in the **/etc/passwd** file. Finally, the Groups tab lists all available groups and allows you to check or uncheck boxes to configure the user's group membership.

All the fields in the window are modifiable. After all of the modifications are made, click OK. You'll be returned once more to the main window and the list of users.

NOTE

Before you change a user's login or UID, make sure the user is not logged in or running any processes.

Deleting a User

To delete a user, click the username from the user list and click the Delete button on the **redhat-config-users** toolbar. This will immediately delete the user account without any further warnings or messages.

Adding a Group

To add a new group, click the Groups tab in the main window. This will reveal the list of current groups.

If you click Add, you'll see a window like the one shown, in which you can fill in the name of a new group to be created.

You can also specify the GID if you wish, although the system can automatically provide a GID. After you're finished, click OK, and you will be brought back to the list of groups, which should include the new group you added.

Modifying a Group

Similar to modifying a user, to modify a group you simply select the name of the group you wish to edit from the group list and click Properties to open a window similar to the add group window. This time, the fields will be filled out with the group's existing values. Simply change the fields you want and click OK for the changes to take effect.

Deleting a Group

To delete a group, select the group from the list of groups in the main **redhat-config-users** window. Click Delete Group to remove the group from the database.

Project 5-2 Handling Reorganization

It seems that reorganization is a standard business practice even during good times, so juggling users and groups is a skill you'll be wise to practice. In this project, you'll take the company described previously through a reorganization, adding, modifying, and removing users and groups as necessary using the **redhat-config-users** tool.

Step by Step

1. Open the user and group database developed in Project 5-1 using the **redhat-config-users** utility.

2. The company is now organized into four primary groups: executives; research; applications; and sales.

3. The executives are **pdedood**, **rolson**, and **cbenefield**.

4. The researchers are **blee**, **bjohnson**, and **tbantac**.

5. The applications staff members are **jwang**, **dgranda**, and **iwiinikka**.

6. The sales staff consists of **dnenni**, **pvenet**, and **kmadsen**.

7. Each executive is also a member of one of the other groups. The research group is headed by **pdedood**. The applications group is headed by **rolson**. The sales group is headed by **cbenefield**.

8. Determine the groups that no longer exist, and delete them.

9. Determine the users who no longer exist, and delete them.

10. Add new groups and users.

11. Ensure that each user is a member of the correct primary and secondary groups.

Project Summary

There's not much different about the process of organizing users and groups once you know where they belong. In a real reorganization, unfortunately, there tend to be misunderstandings, unspoken assumptions, and other communications and planning problems that muddy the process somewhat. On the technical side, you should also be aware of the ramifications of deleting users and groups who owned files on the system. Learn more about that in the section called "Handle Orphaned Files."

CRITICAL SKILL
5.4 Running Programs as Other Users

Normally, when a program is run by a user, it inherits all of the rights (or lack thereof) that the user has. If the user can't read the **/var/log/messages** file, neither can the program. Note that this permission can be different than the permissions of the user who owns the program file (usually called *the binary*). For example, the **ls** program (which is used to generate directory listings) is owned by the root user. Its permissions are set such that all users of the system can run the program. Thus, if the user **rwhite** runs **ls**, that instance of **ls** is bound by the permissions granted to the user **rwhite**, not **root**.

SetUID and SetGID Programs

However, there is an exception. Programs can be tagged with what's called a *SetUID bit,* which allows a program to be run with permissions from the program's owner, not the user who is running it. Using **ls** as an example again, setting the SetUID bit on it and having the file owned by **root** means that if the user **rwhite** runs **ls**, that instance of **ls** will run with root permissions, not with **rwhite**'s permissions. The *SetGID bit* works the same way, except instead of applying to the file's owner, it is applied to the file's group setting.

To enable the SetUID bit or the SetGID bit, you need to use the **chmod** command, which is covered in detail in Module 6. To make a program SetUID, prefix whatever permission value you are about to assign it with a 4. To make a program SetGID, prefix whatever permission you are about to assign it with a 2. For example, to make the **/bin/ls** a SetUID program (which is a bad idea, by the way), you would use this command:

```
[root@tedford /root]# chmod 4755 /bin/ls
```

NOTE

Avoid running programs SetUID root if at all possible. This is one common way in which systems can be compromised, because too much trust is conferred upon a mere mortal user.

Using sudo

Running programs SetUID root is a dangerous business that can make a system more prone to being exploited. A bug in a program being run SetUID root can allow an unscrupulous user or an attacker to gain full root access, which is a Very Bad Thing (VBT). A better option for running programs as someone else is to use the **sudo** command.

The **sudo** ("superuser do") command allows you to configure extremely limited parameters for running certain programs as **root**. To configure a command for use by **sudo**, use the **visudo** command, which is an editor that checks the syntax of your configuration and prevents another user from clobbering the file while you're editing it.

```
[root@tedford /root]# visudo
```

Running **visudo** allows you to edit the **/etc/sudoers** file (don't edit it directly; always use **visudo** to change this file). The contents of the **/etc/sudoers** file look a bit like this:

```
# sudoers file.
# This file MUST be edited with the 'visudo' command as root.
# See the sudoers man page for the details on how to write a sudoers file.
# Host alias specification
# User alias specification
# Cmnd alias specification
# Defaults specification
# User privilege specification
root       ALL=(ALL) ALL
# Uncomment to allow people in group wheel to run all commands
# %wheel    ALL=(ALL)      ALL
# Same thing without a password
```

```
# %wheel   ALL=(ALL)       NOPASSWD: ALL

rwhite  localhost=/sbin/shutdown -h now
```

The last line of the file allows user **rwhite**, on the local system only, to run the **shutdown** command to halt the computer immediately. Notice that the command is described complete with specific options; this is the only version of this command that **rwhite** can run. When users attempt to use **sudo**, the activity is logged in the **syslog** file, about which more is said in Module 8.

CRITICAL SKILL
5.5 # Handling Orphaned Files

A file is always owned, no matter what. But what happens when a file's owner's UID doesn't map to an entry in the **/etc/passwd** file? This can happen, for example, when you remove users as you did in Project 5-2.

When a user is created, it gets a new and unique UID. Any files created by that user are owned by that user. To keep things easy, Linux doesn't use the user's name, but the UID, to set file ownership. The system then uses the **/etc/passwd** file to perform a mapping between the user's UID and login so that it can make directory listings more human readable.

So what happens when a user is removed from the **/etc/passwd** file but files still exist that were owned by him? Nothing special, really. The most visible effect will be when you perform a directory listing on the file in question. Instead of showing you the owner of the file, it'll show a number. This number represents the UID that owns this file. If a new user is created with the same UID as the old user, the same UID will show up as the owner, making it appear as if the new user owns the file. Because of this behavior, it is important that you make sure you delete all of the files owned by a user when removing that user's account.

CRITICAL SKILL
5.6 # Using Pluggable Authentication Modules (PAM)

One of the problems with the UNIX method of authentication is that it is always the same thing no matter what—passwords. While this worked great for a very long time, people have needed to become more sophisticated for a variety of reasons. This led to a number of very ugly hacks to abstract the authentication mechanism. Taking a cue from Solaris, Linux folks created their own implementation of *Pluggable Authentication Modules (PAM)*.

The idea behind PAM is that instead of applications reading the password file, they would simply ask PAM to perform the authentication. PAM could then use whatever authentication mechanism the system administrator wanted. For many sites, the mechanism of choice is still a simple password file. And why not? It does what we want. Most users understand the need for it, and it's a well-tested method to get the job done. However, some sites have needed to expand on this.

A popular example of exceptions to the rule is still password-based, but instead of using standard UNIX passwords, another method of storing passwords was needed. For some sites, this is based on a database, thereby allowing for a larger number of users. For others, it is adapting to an existing system (like an NT server acting as a PDC).

This section describes how PAM is set up under Red Hat Linux. The placement of files may not be exactly the same in every other distribution, but the underlying configuration files and concepts still apply.

How PAM Works

PAM is to other programs as a DLL is to a Windows application—it is just a library. When programs need to perform authentication on someone, they call a function that exists in the PAM library.

When invoked, PAM checks the configuration file for that application. If there isn't a configuration file, it uses a default configuration file. This configuration file tells the library what types of checks need to be done in order to authenticate the user. Based on this, the appropriate module is called on. (Red Hat folks can see these modules in the **/lib/security** directory.)

This module can check any number of things. It can simply check the **/etc/passwd** file or the **/etc/shadow** file, or it can perform a more complex check like calling on a LDAP server.

NOTE

The PAM web site (http://www.kernel.org/pub/linux/libs/pam/) offers a complete list of available modules.

Once the module has made the determination, an "authenticated/not authenticated" message is passed back to the calling application.

If this feels like a lot of steps for what should be a simple check, you're almost correct. While it feels like a lot of steps, each module here is very small and does its work very quickly. From a user's point of view, there should be no noticeable performance difference between an application that uses PAM and one that does not. From a system administrator's and developer's point of view, the flexibility this scheme offers is incredible and a very welcome addition.

PAM's Files and Their Locations

On a Red Hat–style installation, PAM puts her configuration files in certain places. These file locations and their definitions are listed in Table 5-3.

Looking at the list of file locations in Table 5-3, one has to ask why PAM needs so many different configuration files. "One configuration file per application? That seems crazy!"

File Location	Definition
/sbin/pam_filter	Filters that have the opportunity to examine all of the input and output from a user and a running application. This is a very discrete way of setting up logs and traps, but it is rarely used.
/sbin	Supplementary tools that may be called on from library functions.
/lib	The actual PAM library that manages the authentication process. Depending on the application's configuration, it calls on the appropriate module in the **/lib/security** directory.
/lib/security	Dynamically loaded authentication modules called by the actual PAM library.
/usr/include/security	Special header files for developers.
/etc/security	Configuration files for the modules located in **/lib/security**.
/etc/pam.d	Configuration files for each application that uses PAM. If an application that uses PAM does not have a specific configuration file, the default is automatically used.

Table 5-3 PAM Configuration File Locations

Well, maybe not. The reason PAM allows this is that not all applications are created equal. For instance, a POP mail server that uses the Qpopper mail server may want to allow all of a site's users to fetch mail, but the login program may only want to allow certain users to be able to log in to the console. To accommodate for this, PAM needs a configuration file for POP mail that is different from the configuration for the login program.

Configuring PAM

The configuration files described here are the ones located in the **/etc/pam.d** directory. If you want to change the configuration files that apply to specific modules in the **/etc/security** directory, you should consult the documentation that came with the module. (Remember, PAM is just a framework. Specific modules can be written by anyone.)

The nature of a PAM configuration file is very interesting because of its "stackable" nature. That is, every line of a configuration file is evaluated during the authentication process (with the exceptions shown next). Each line specifies a module that performs some authentication task and returns either a success or failure flag. A summary of the results is returned to the application program calling PAM.

NOTE

By "failure," I do not mean the program did not work. Rather, I mean that when some process was done to verify whether a user could do something, the return value was "NO." PAM uses the terms "success" and "failure" to represent this information that is passed back to the calling application.

Each file consists of lines in the following format:

```
module_type    control_flag    module_path    arguments
```

where *module_type* represents one of four types of modules: **auth**, **account**, **session**, or **password**. Comments must begin with the hash (#) character. Table 5-4 lists these module types and their functions.

The *control_flag* allows you to specify how you want to deal with the success or failure of a particular authentication module. The control flags are described in Table 5-5.

The *module_path* specifies the actual directory path of the module that performs the authentication task. For a full list of modules, visit PAM's web site (http:// www.kernel.org/ pub/linux/libs/pam).

The final entry in a PAM configuration line is *arguments*. These are the parameters passed to the authentication module. Although the parameters are specific to each module, there are some generic options that can be applied to all modules. These arguments are described in Table 5-6.

An Example PAM Configuration File

Let's examine a sample PAM configuration file, **/etc/pam.d/login**:

```
#%PAM-1.0
auth       required    /lib/security/pam_securetty.so
auth       required    /lib/security/pam_pwdb.so shadow nullok
auth       required    /lib/security/pam_nologin.so
account    required    /lib/security/pam_pwdb.so
password   required    /lib/security/pam_cracklib.so
password   required    /lib/security/pam_pwdb.so shadow nullok use_authtok
session    required    /lib/security/pam_pwdb.so
```

You can see that the first line begins with a hash symbol and is therefore a comment. Thus you can ignore it. Let's go on to line 2.

```
auth       required    /lib/security/pam_securetty.so
```

Module Type	Function
auth	Instructs the application program to prompt the user for a password and then grants both user and group privileges.
account	Performs no authentication but determines access based on other factors such as time of day or location of the user. For example, the **root** login can be given only console access this way.
session	Specifies what, if any, actions need to be performed before or after a user is logged in (for example, logging the connection).
password	Specifies the module that allows users to change their passwords (if appropriate).

Table 5-4 PAM Module Type Descriptions

Control Flag	Description
required	If this flag is specified, the module *must* succeed in authenticating the individual. If it fails, the returned summary value must be failure.
requisite	This flag is similar to **required**; however, if **requisite** fails authentication, modules listed after it in the configuration file are not called, and a failure is immediately returned to the application. This allows you to require certain conditions to hold true before even accepting a login attempt (for example, the user is on the local area network and cannot come from over the Internet).
sufficient	If a **sufficient** module returns a success and there are no more **required** or **sufficient** control flags in the configuration file, PAM returns a success to the calling application.
optional	This flag allows PAM to continue checking other modules even if this one has failed. You will want to use this when the user is allowed to log in even if a particular module has failed.

Table 5-5 PAM Authentication Module Control Flags

Since the **module_type** is **auth**, PAM will want a password. The **control_flag** is set to **required**, so this module must return a success, or the login will fail. The module itself, **pam_securetty.so**, verifies that logins on the **root** account can only happen on the terminals mentioned in the **/etc/securetty** file. There are no arguments on this line.

```
auth        required     /lib/security/pam_pwdb.so shadow nullok
```

Similar to the first **auth** line, line 3 wants a password for authentication, and if the password fails, the authentication process will return a failure flag to the calling application.

Argument	Description
debug	Sends debugging information to the system logs.
no_warn	Does not give warning messages to the calling application.
use_first_ pass	Does not prompt the user for a password a second time. Instead, the password they entered the first time determine their eligibility to enter the system. (This is for configurations where two different modules require a password to continue.)
try_first_ pass	This option is similar to **use_first_ pass**, where the user is not prompted for a password the second time. However, if the existing password causes the module to return a failure, the user is then asked to enter a second password, and the module is tried again.
use_mapped_ pass	Passes the password from a previous module into the current one, much like **use_first_ pass**. However, the password is then used to generate an encryption or decryption key.

Table 5-6 PAM Authentication Module Parameters

The **pam_pwdb.so** module checks the **/etc/passwd** file and with the **shadow** parameter, it checks the **/etc/shadow** file as well. The **nullok** parameter tells it that having no password is okay. (Normally empty passwords mean that the account is locked.)

```
auth        required     /lib/security/pam_nologin.so
```

In line 4, the **pam_nologin.so** module checks for the **/etc/nologin** file. If it is present, only **root** is allowed to log in; others are turned away with an error message. If the file does not exist, it always returns a success.

```
account     required     /lib/security/pam_pwdb.so
```

In line 5, since the **module_type** is **account**, the **pam_pwdb.so** module acts differently. It silently checks that the user is even allowed to log in (e.g., "has their password expired?"). If all the parameters check out okay, it will return a success.

```
password    required     /lib/security/pam_cracklib.so
```

The **module_type** of **password** in line 6 means that this module will only be applied during password changes. The **pam_cracklib.so** module performs a variety of checks to see whether a password is "too easy" to crack by potential intruders.

```
password    required     /lib/security/pam_pwdb.so shadow nullok
use_authtok
```

Line 7 offers another example of the versatility of the **pam_pwdb.so** module. With the **module_type** set to **password**, it will perform the actual updating of the **/etc/passwd** file. The **shadow** parameters tell it to check for the existence of the **/etc/shadow** file and update that file if it does exist. The **nullok** parameter allows users to change their passwords from empty entries to real passwords. The last option, **use_authtok**, forces **pam_pwdb.so** to use the password retrieved from a previous **module_type** entry of **password**.

```
session     required     /lib/security/pam_pwdb.so
```

The final usage of the **pam_pwdb.so** module is for **module_type session**. This time, it sends login successes and failures to the system logs.

The "Other" File

As mentioned earlier, if PAM cannot find a configuration file that is specific to an application, it will use a generic configuration file instead. This generic configuration file is called **/etc/pam.d/ other**. By default, the "other" configuration file is set to a paranoid setting so that all authentication attempts are logged and then promptly denied. It is recommended you keep it that way.

"Doh! I Can't Log In!"

Don't worry—screwing up a setting in a PAM configuration file happens to everyone. Consider it part of learning the ropes. First thing to do: Don't panic. As when dealing with most configuration errors under Linux, you can fix things by booting into single-user mode (see Module 8) and fixing the errant file.

If you've screwed up your login configuration file and need to bring it back to a sane state, here is a safe setting you can put in:

```
auth        required     /lib/security/pam_unix_auth.so
account     required     /lib/security/pam_unix_acct.so
password    required     /lib/security/pam_unix_passwd.so
session     required     /lib/security/pam_unix_session.so
```

This setting will give Linux the default behavior of simply looking into the **/etc/passwd** file for a password. This should be good enough to get you back in, where you can make the changes you meant to make!

Debugging PAM

Like many other Linux services, PAM makes excellent use of the system log files. (You can read more about them in Module 8.) If things are not working the way you want them to work, begin by looking at the end of the log files and see if PAM is spelling out what happened. More than likely, it is. You should then be able to use this information to change your settings and fix your problem.

TIP

If you are running in X, you can monitor the log file in real time by using the **tail** command in a window like so:

```
[root@tedford /root]# tail -f /var/log/messages
```

where **/var/log/messages** is the name of the log file that you want to monitor. If you aren't sure which file to check, start with **/var/log/messages**. Then check the **/var/log** directory and see what other files are there. You can use the **tail** command with any of them. In another window, try doing what you are testing out. If PAM generates any messages, you will see them in your **tail** window immediately.

Module Summary

This module documents the nature of users under Linux. Much of what you read here also applies to other variants of UNIX, which makes administering users in heterogeneous environments much easier with different UNIXs than NT/UNIX.

Following are the most significant issues covered in this module:

- Each user gets a unique UID.

- Each group gets a unique GID.

- The **/etc/passwd** file maps UIDs to usernames.

- Linux handles encrypted passwords in multiple ways.

- Linux includes tools that help you administer users.

- Should you decide to write your own tools to manage the user databases, you'll now understand the format for doing so.

- PAM, the Pluggable Authentication Modules, is Linux's generic way of handling multiple authentication mechanisms.

These changes are pretty significant for an administrator coming from the Windows environment and can be a little tricky at first. Not to worry, though—the UNIX security model is quite straightforward, so you should quickly get comfortable with how it all works.

If the idea of getting to build your own tools to administer users appeals to you, definitely look into books on the Perl scripting language. It is remarkably well suited for manipulating tabular data (such as the **/etc/passwd** file). With Perl's networking facilities and NT/2000 support, Linux even lets you build a cross-platform **adduser** tool that can create and set up both UNIX and NT accounts. With so many books on Perl out there, each with a slightly different angle and assuming a slightly different level of programming background, it's tough to make a single book recommendation. Take some time and page through a few books at your local bookstore.

Module 5 Mastery Check

1. To what does GID refer?

2. To what does UID refer?

3. What improved encryption scheme can be used to encrypt passwords in Red Hat Linux 8.0?

4. In which file would you find the encrypted passwords that use the scheme alluded to in Question 1?

5. Which users can view the contents of the file referenced in Question 3?

6. What character can be added to a password field to disable the password so that a user cannot log into the system?

7. By default, in which directory are the configuration files stored for use when a user is added to the system?

8. When adding a system group, how can you tell the system to use the first available GID lower than 499?

9. How could you remove all a user's files when removing the user's account?

10. Which of the following can be used to graphically manage users and groups in Red Hat Linux 8.0?

   A. redhat-config-group

   B. redhat-config-users

   C. Xusers

   D. KuserGroupManager

11. What does it mean to run a program SetUID root?

12. What command provides somewhat more security than using SetUID root?

13. What command is used to configure a system to use the command referred to in Question 12?

14. What does it mean if a directory listing shows files that are owned by a number instead of a name?

15. Where would you find configuration files for programs that use PAM?

16. What are the four types of PAM modules?

17. Describe the four PAM control flags.

Module 6

The Command Line

Over time, it's been UNIX's command-line options that have given the system its power and flexibility. Casual observers of UNIX gurus are often astounded at the results of a few carefully entered commands. Unfortunately, this power makes UNIX less intuitive to the average user. For this reason, graphical user interfaces (GUIs) have become the de facto standard for many UNIX tools.

More experienced users, however, find that it is difficult for a GUI to present all of the available options. Typically, doing so would make the interface just as complicated as the command-line equivalent. The GUI design is often oversimplified, and experienced users ultimately return to the comprehensive capabilities of the command line.

TIP

Debating the merits of the interfaces is pointless. Each has its weaknesses and benefits. In the end, the person who chooses to master both methods will come out ahead.

Before you begin your study of the command-line interface under Linux, understand that this module is far from an exhaustive resource. Rather than trying to cover all the tools without any depth, this Module describes thoroughly a handful of tools believed to be most critical for day-to-day work.

NOTE

For this module, assume that you are logged in, can become the root user, and have started the X Window System environment. (Most of these commands, however, will work without X running, if you log in to the console instead.) You can open a terminal window by going to the Red Hat menu and then selecting System Tools and then Terminal. All of the commands you enter in this module should be typed into the window that appears after the Terminal icon is selected.

CRITICAL SKILL
6.1 Switching Users: su

Once you have logged in to the system as one user, you need not log out and back in again in order to assume another identity (the root user, for instance). Instead, use the **su** command to switch. This command has only two command-line parameters, both of which are optional.

Running **su** without any parameters will automatically try to make you the root user. You'll be prompted for the root password and, if you enter it correctly, will drop down to a root shell. If you are already the root user and want to switch to another ID, you don't need to enter the new password when you use this command.

For example, if you're logged in as yourself and want to switch to the root user, type this command:

```
[michael@workbox michael]$ su
```

If you're logged in as **root** and want to switch to, say, user **rwhite**, enter this command:

```
[root@workbox michael]# su rwhite
```

The optional hyphen (-) parameter tells **su** to switch identities and run the login scripts for that user. For example, if you're logged in as **root** and want to switch over to user **rwhite** with all of his login and shell configurations, type this command:

```
[root@workbox michael]$ su - rwhite
```

Some of the commands covered in this module can be used only as **root**. It's a bad practice to do all of your work logged in as **root**, however. You should assume **root** only when you need to. Commands like **su** make it easier to become **root** to do the things you need and leave it behind when you're finished.

CRITICAL SKILL
6.2 Using the BASH Shell

In Module 5, you learned that one of the parameters for a user's password entry is that user's *login shell,* which is the first program that runs when a user logs in to a workstation. The shell is comparable to the Windows Program Manager, except that the shell program used, of course, is arbitrary.

A *shell* is simply a program that provides an interface to the system. The original shell common among UNIX systems was the Bourne shell, commonly referred to as *sh.* The Bourne Again Shell (BASH) is a free software shell based on the original Bourne shell, but with a few enhancements. It is a command-line-only interface containing a handful of built-in commands, the ability to launch other programs, and the ability to control programs that have been launched from it (job control). Think of it as a command.com or a cmd on steroids.

A variety of shells exist, most with similar features but different means of implementing them. Again for the purpose of comparison, you can think of the various shells as web browsers; among several different browsers, the basic functionality is the same—displaying content from the Web. In any situation like this, everyone proclaims that their shell is better than the others, but it all really comes down to personal preference.

In this section, you'll examine some of BASH's built-in commands. A complete reference on BASH could easily be a book in itself, so in this module, you'll stick with the commands that most affect the daily operations of a systems administrator. However, I do recommend that you eventually study BASH's operations. There's no shortage of excellent books on the topic.

Job Control

When working in the BASH environment, you can start multiple programs from the same prompt. Each program is a *job*. Whenever a job is started, it takes over the *terminal*. (This is a throwback to the days when actual dumb terminals such as VT-100s and Wyse-50s were used to interface with the machine.) On today's machines, the terminal is either the straight-text interface you see when you boot the machine or the window created by the X Window System on which BASH runs. (A terminal interface in X is called a pseudo tty, or pty for short.) If a job has control of the terminal, it can issue control codes so that text-only interfaces (the pine mail reader, for instance) can be made more attractive. Once the program is done, it gives full control back to BASH, and a prompt is redisplayed for the user.

Not all programs require this kind of terminal control, however. Some, including programs that interface with the user through the X Window System, can be instructed to give up terminal control and allow BASH to present a user prompt, even though the invoked program is still running. In the following example, Mozilla receives such an instruction, represented by the ampersand suffix:

```
[michael@workbox michael]$ mozilla &
```

Immediately after you press ENTER, BASH will present a prompt. This is called *backgrounding* the task. Folks who remember Windows NT prior to version 4 will remember having to do something similar with the Start command.

If a program is already running and has control of the terminal, you can make the program give up control by pressing CTRL-Z in the terminal window. This will stop the running job altogether and return control to BASH so that you can enter new commands.

At any given time, you can find out how many jobs BASH is tracking by typing this command:

```
[michael@workbox michael]$ jobs
```

The running programs that are listed will be in one of two states: running or stopped. If a job is stopped, you can start it running in the background, thereby allowing you to keep control of the terminal. Or a stopped job can run in the foreground, which gives control of the terminal back to that program.

To run a job in the background, type

```
[michael@workbox michael]$ bg number
```

where **number** is the job number you want to background. If you omit the number, the most recent job is assumed. To run a job in the foreground, type

```
[michael@workbox michael]$ fg number
```

where **number** is the job number you want in the foreground. Again, omitting the number will refer to the most recently stopped job.

NOTE

You cannot (usefully) background a task that requires interaction through the terminal window.

Environment Variables

Every instance of a shell that is running has its own "environment"—settings that give it a particular look, feel, and, in some cases, behavior. These settings are typically controlled by *environment variables*. Some environment variables have special meanings to the shell, but there is nothing stopping you from defining your own and using them for your own needs. It is with the use of environment variables that most shell scripts are able to do interesting things and remember results from user inputs as well as program's outputs. If you are already familiar with the concept of environment variables in Windows NT/2000/.NET Server, you'll find that many of the things that you know about them will apply to Linux as well; the only difference is how they are set, viewed, and removed.

Display Environment Variables

To list all of your environment variables, use the **printenv** command. For example:

```
[michael@workbox michael]$ printenv
```

To show a specific environment variable, specify the variable as a parameter to **printenv**. For example, here is the command to see the environment variable OSTYPE:

```
[michael@workbox michael]$ printenv OSTYPE
```

Setting Environment Variables

To set an environment variable, use the following format:

```
[michael@workbox michael]$ variable=value
```

where **variable** is the variable name, and **value** is the value you want to assign the variable. For example, here is the command to set the environment variable FOO with the value BAR:

```
[michael@workbox michael]$ FOO=BAR
```

Once the value is set, use the **export** command to finalize it. The format of the **export** command is as follows:

```
[michael@workbox michael]$ export variable
```

where *variable* is the name of the variable. In the example of setting FOO, you would enter this command:

```
[michael@workbox michael]$ export FOO
```

TIP

With BASH you can combine the steps for setting an environment variable with the export command, like so:
```
[michael@workbox michael]$ export FOO=BAR
```

If the value of the environment variable you want to set has spaces in it, surround the variable with quotation marks. Using the preceding example, to set FOO to "Welcome to the BAR of FOO.", you would enter

```
[michael@workbox michael]$ export FOO="Welcome to the BAR of FOO."
```

Unsetting Environment Variables

To remove an environment variable, use the **unset** command:

```
[michael@workbox michael]$ unset variable
```

where *variable* is the name of the variable you want to remove. For example, here is the command to remove the environment variable FOO:

```
[root@tedford]# unset FOO
```

NOTE

This section assumed that you are using BASH. There are many other shells to choose from; the most popular alternatives are C-Shell (csh) and its brother Turbo C-Shell (tcsh), which use different mechanisms for getting and setting environment variables. For more information, read the manual page (see "The man Command" section later in this module) for the shell you prefer. I document BASH here because it is the default shell of all new Linux accounts.

Pipes

Pipes are a mechanism by which the output of one program can be sent as the input to another program. Individual programs can be chained together to become extremely powerful tools.

Let's use the **grep** program to provide a simple example of pipes usage. The **grep** utility, given a stream of input, will try to match the line with the parameter supplied to it and display only matching lines. For example, if you were looking for all environment variables containing the string "OSTYPE", you could enter this command:

```
[michael@workbox michael]$ printenv | grep "OSTYPE"
```

The vertical bar (|) character represents the pipe between **printenv** and **grep**.

The command shell under Windows also utilizes the pipe function. The primary difference is that all commands in a Linux pipe are executed concurrently, whereas Windows runs each program in order, using temporary files to hold intermediate results.

Redirection

Through *redirection,* you can take the output of a program and have it automatically sent to a file. The shell rather than the program itself handles this process, thereby providing a standard mechanism for performing the task. (Using redirection is much easier than having to remember how to do this for every single program!)

Redirection comes in three classes: output to a file, append to a file, and send a file as input.

To collect the output of a program into a file, end the command line with the greater than symbol (>) and the name of the file to which you want the output redirected. If you are redirecting to an existing file and you want to append additional data to it, use two > symbols back-to-back (>>) followed by the filename. For example, here is the command to collect the output of a directory listing into a file called **/tmp/directory_listing**:

```
[michael@workbox michael]$ ls > /tmp/directory_listing
```

Continuing this example with the directory listing, you could append the string "Directory Listing" to the end of the **/tmp/directory_listing** file by typing this command:

```
[michael@workbox michael]$ echo "Directory Listing" >> /tmp/directory_listing
```

The third class of redirection, using a file as input, is done by using the less than sign (<) followed by the name of the file. For example, here is the command to feed the **/etc/passwd** file into the **grep** program:

```
[michael@workbox michael]$ grep 'root' < /etc/passwd
```

Command-Line Shortcuts

One of the difficulties in moving to a command-line interface, especially from command-line tools such as command.com, is working with a shell that has a good number of shortcuts. These refinements may surprise you if you're not careful. This section explains the most common of the BASH shortcuts and their behaviors.

Filename Expansion

Under UNIX-based shells such as BASH, wildcards on the command line are expanded *before* being passed as a parameter to the application. This is in sharp contrast to the default mode of operation for DOS-based tools, which often have to perform their own wildcard expansion. The UNIX method also means that you must be careful where you use the wildcard characters.

The wildcard characters themselves in BASH are identical to those in command.com: the asterisk (*) matches against all filenames, and the question mark (?) matches against single characters. If you need to use these characters as part of another parameter for whatever reason, you can *escape* them by preceding them with a backslash (\ ) character. This causes the shell to interpret the asterisk and question mark as regular characters instead of wildcards.

NOTE

Most UNIX documentation refers to wildcards as regular expressions. The distinction is important since regular expressions are substantially more powerful than just wildcards alone. All of the shells that come with Linux support regular expressions. You can read more about them either in the shell's manual page or in the book *Mastering Regular Expressions* by Jeffrey E. F. Friedl (O'Reilly & Associates, 1997).

Environment Variables as Parameters

Under BASH, you can use environment variables as parameters on the command line. (Although command.com does this as well, it's not a common practice and thus is an often forgotten convention.) For example, issuing the parameter **$ FOO** will cause the value of the FOO environment variable to be passed rather than the string "$ FOO".

Multiple Commands

Under BASH, multiple commands can be executed on the same line by separating the commands with semicolons (;). For example, to execute this sequence of commands on a single line

```
[michael@workbox michael]$ ls -l
[michael@workbox michael]$ cat /etc/passwd
```

you could instead type this:

```
[michael@workbox michael]$ ls -l ;cat /etc/passwd
```

Backticks

How's this for wild: You can take the output of one program and make it the parameter of another program. Sound bizarre? Well, time to get used to it—this is one of the most useful and innovative features available in all UNIX shells.

Backticks (`) allow you to embed commands as parameters to other commands. As an example, this can be used to take a number sitting in a file and pass that number as a parameter to the **kill** command. A typical instance of this occurs when the DNS server, **named**, needs to be killed. When **named** starts, it writes its process identification number into the file **/var/run/named.pid**. Thus, the generic way of killing the **named** process is to look at the number in **/var/run/named.pid** using the **cat** command, and then issue the **kill** command with that value. For example:

```
[root@workbox /root]# cat /var/run/named.pid
253
[root@workbox /root]# kill 253
```

One problem with killing the **named** process in this way is that it cannot be automated—we are counting on the fact that a human will read the value in **/var/run/named.pid** in order to **kill** the number. Another issue isn't so much a problem as it is a nuisance: It takes two steps to stop the DNS server.

Using backticks, however, you can combine the steps into one *and* do it in a way that can be automated. The backticks version would look like this:

```
[root@workbox /root]# kill `cat /var/run/named.pid`
```

When BASH sees this command, it will first run **cat /var/run/named.pid** and store the result. It will then run **kill** and pass the stored result to it. From your point of view, this happens in one graceful step.

NOTE

So far in this module, you have looked at features that are internal to BASH. The remainder of the module explores several common commands accessible outside of BASH.

Reviewing Command-Line Documentation

Linux comes with two superbly useful tools for making documentation accessible: **man** and **info**. Currently, a great deal of overlap exists between these two documentation systems because many applications are moving their documentation to the **info** format. This format is considered superior to **man** because it allows the documentation to be hyperlinked together in a web-like way, but without actually having to be written in HTML format.

The **man** format, on the other hand, has been around for decades. For thousands of utilities, their man (short for *manual*) pages are their only documentation. Furthermore, many applications continue to utilize **man** format because many other UNIX-like operating systems (such as Sun Solaris) use **man** format.

Both the **man** and **info** documentation systems will be around for a long while to come. I highly recommend getting comfortable with them both.

TIP

Red Hat, like many other distributions, also includes a great deal of documentation in the **/usr/share/doc** directory.

The man Command

You read quite early in this book that man pages are documents found online that cover the use of tools and their corresponding configuration files. The format of the **man** command is as follows:

```
[michael@workbox michael]$ man program_name
```

where ***program_name*** identifies the program you're interested in. For example:

```
[michael@workbox michael]$ man ls
```

While reading about UNIX and UNIX-related information sources (newsgroups and so forth), you may encounter references to commands followed by numbers in parentheses— for example, **ls(1)**. The number represents the *section* of the manual pages (see Table 6-1). Each section covers various subject areas, to accommodate the fact that some tools (such as **printf)** are commands in the C programming language as well as command-line commands.

To refer to a specific **man** section, simply specify the section number as the first parameter and then the command as the second parameter. For example, to get the C programmers' information on **printf**, you'd enter this:

```
[michael@workbox michael]$ man 3 printf
```

To get the command-line information, you'd enter this:

```
[michael@workbox michael]$ man 1 printf
```

By default, the lowest section number gets displayed first.

Unfortunately, this organization is sometimes difficult to use. You may find it helpful to use the graphical interface for this library of documentation, developed as part of the GNOME project; it's called **gnome-help**. If you have installed GNOME on a system, you can always start it from a terminal window yourself with this command:

```
[michael@workbox michael]$ gnome-help
```

Manual Section	Subject
1	User tools
2	System calls
3	C library calls
4	Device driver information
5	Configuration files
6	Games
7	Packages
8	System tools

Table 6-1 Man Page Section Descriptions

TIP

A handy option to the **man** command is **-k** preceding the command parameter. With this option, **man** will search the summary information of all the man pages and list pages matching your specified command, along with their section number. For example:

```
[michael@workbox michael]$ man -k printf
```

The texinfo System

Another common form of documentation is *texinfo*. Established as the GNU standard, texinfo is a documentation system similar to the hyperlinked World Wide Web format. Because documents can be hyperlinked together, texinfo is often easier to read, use, and search.

To read the texinfo documents on a specific tool or application, invoke **info** with the parameter specifying the tool's name. For example, to read about **emacs**, type:

```
[michael@workbox michael]$ info emacs
```

In general, you will want to verify that a man page exists before using **info** (there is still a great deal more information available in **man** format than in texinfo). If you run **info** on a command that isn't described in texinfo but does have a man page, the information from **man** is often displayed. On the other hand, some man pages will explicitly state that the texinfo pages are more authoritative and should be read instead.

While **info** is a much more powerful system, it's also more complex as a result. A good starting place may be:

```
[michael@workbox michael]$ info info
```

Alternatively you may want to start **info**, and press CTRL-H to bring up the help menu, and then press H to start the built-in tutorial.

CRITICAL SKILL
6.4 # Understanding File Listings, Ownerships, and Permissions

Managing files under Linux is different than managing files under Windows 2000/.NET, and radically different from managing files under Windows 95/98. This section discusses basic file management tools for Linux. We'll start with specifics on some useful general-purpose commands and then step back and look at some background information.

Listing Files: ls

The **ls** command is used to list all the files in a directory. Of more than 26 available options, the ones listed here are the most commonly used. The options can be used in any combination. See the texinfo page for a complete list.

Option for ls	Description
–l	Long listing. In addition to the filename, shows the file size, date/time, permissions, ownership, and group information.
–a	All files. Shows all files in the directory, including hidden files. Names of hidden files begin with a period.
–1	Single column listing.
–R	Recursively lists all files and subdirectories.

To list all files in a directory with a long listing, type this command:

```
[michael@workbox michael]$ ls -la
```

To list a directory's nonhidden files that start with *A,* type this:

```
[michael@workbox michael]$ ls A*
```

File and Directory Types

Under Linux (and UNIX in general), almost everything is abstracted to a file. Originally this was done to simplify the programmer's job. Instead of having to communicate directly with device drivers, special files (which look like ordinary files to the application) are used as a bridge. Several types of files accommodate all these file uses.

Normal Files

Normal files are just that—normal. They contain data or executables, and the operating system makes no assumptions about their contents.

Directories

Directory files are a special instance of normal files. Directory files list the location of other files, some of which may be other directories. (This is similar to folders in Windows.) In general, the contents of directory files won't be of importance to your daily operations, unless you need to open and read the file yourself rather than using existing applications to navigate directories. (This would be similar to trying to read the DOS File Allocation Table directly rather than using command.com to navigate directories, or using the findfirst/findnext system calls.)

Hard Links

Each file in the Linux file system gets its own *i-node*. An i-node keeps track of a file's attributes and its location on the disk. If you need to be able to refer to a single file using two separate filenames, you can create a *hard link*. The hard link will have the same i-node as the original file and will therefore look and behave just like the original. With every hard link that is created, a *reference count* is incremented. When a hard link is removed, the reference count is decremented. Until the reference count reaches zero, the file will remain on disk.

NOTE

A hard link cannot exist between two files on separate partitions. This is because the hard link refers to the original file by i-node, and a file's i-node may differ among file systems.

Symbolic Links

Unlike a hard link, which points to a file by its i-node, a *symbolic link* points to another file by its name. This allows symbolic links (often abbreviated *symlinks*) to point to files located on other partitions, even other network drives.

Block Devices

Since all device drivers are accessed through the file system, files of type *block device* are used to interface with devices such as disks. A block device file has three identifying traits:

- It has a major number.

- It has a minor number.

- When viewed using the ls -l command, it shows **b** as the first character of the permissions.

For example:

```
[michael@workbox michael]$ ls -l /dev/hda
brw-rw----   1 root     disk        3,   0 May  5  1998 /dev/hda
```

Note the **b** at the beginning of the file's permissions; the **3** is the major number, and the **0** is the minor number.

A block device file's major number identifies the represented device driver. When this file is accessed, the minor number is passed to the device driver as a parameter telling it which device it is accessing. For example, if there are two serial ports, they will share the same device driver and thus the same major number, but each serial port will have a unique minor number.

Character Devices

Similar to block devices, *character devices* are special files that allow you to access devices through the file system. The obvious difference between block and character devices is that block devices communicate with the actual devices in large blocks, whereas character devices work one character at a time. (A hard disk is a block device; a modem is a character device.) Character device permissions start with a **c**, and the file has a major and a minor number. For example:

```
[michael@workbox michael]$ ls -l /dev/ttyS0
crw-------   1 root      tty        4,  64 May  5  1998 /dev/ttyS0
```

Named Pipes

Named pipes are a special type of file that allows for interprocess communication. Using the **mknod** command (discussed later in this module), you can create a named pipe file that one process can open for reading and another process can open for writing, thus allowing the two to communicate with one another. This works especially well when a program refuses to take input from a command-line pipe, but another program needs to feed the other one data and you don't have the disk space for a temporary file.

For a named pipe file, the first character of its file permissions is a **p**. For example:

```
[michael@workbox michael]$ ls -l mypipe
prw-r--r--   1 root      root           0 Jun 16 10:47 mypipe
```

Changing Ownership: chown

The **chown** command allows you to change the ownership of a file to someone else. Only the root user can do this. (Normal users may not give away file ownership or steal ownership from another user.) The format of the command is as follows:

```
[root@workbox /root]$ chown [-R] username filename
```

where ***username*** is the login of the user to whom you want to assign ownership, and ***filename*** is the name of the file in question. The ***filename*** may be a directory as well.

The **–R** option applies when the specified ***filename*** is a directory name. This option tells the command to recursively descend through the directory tree and apply the new ownership not only to the directory itself, but to all of the files and directories within it.

Changing Groups: chgrp

The **chgrp** command-line utility lets you change the group settings of a file. It works much like **chown**. Here is the format:

```
[root@workbox /root]# chgrp [-R] groupname filename
```

where *groupname* is the name of the group to which you want to assign *filename* ownership. The *filename* may be a directory as well.

The **–R** option applies when the specified *filename* is a directory name. As with **chown**, the **–R** option tells the command to recursively descend through the directory tree and apply the new ownership not only to the directory itself, but also to all of the files and directories within it.

Changing Mode: chmod

Permissions are divided into four parts. The first part is represented by the first character of the permission. Normal files have no special value and are represented with a hyphen (-) character. If the file has a special attribute, it is represented by a letter. The two special attributes you are most interested in here are directories (**d**) and symbolic links (**l**).

The second, third, and fourth parts of a permission are represented in three-character chunks. The first part indicates the file owner's permission. The second part indicates the group permission. The last part indicates the world permission. In the context of UNIX, "world" means all users in the system, regardless of their group settings.

What follows are the letters used to represent permissions and their corresponding values. When you combine attributes, you add their values. The **chmod** command is used to set permission values.

Letter	Permission	Value
R	Read	4
W	Write	2
X	Execute	1

Although **chmod** does have more readable formats for permissions, it's important that you understand the numbering scheme because it is used in programming. In addition, not everyone uses the letter-naming scheme. It is often assumed that if you understand file permissions, you understand the numeric meanings as well.

What follows are the most common combinations of the three permissions. Other combinations, such as –**wx**, do exist, but they are rarely used.

Letter	Permission	Value
---	No permissions	0
r--	Read only	4
rw-	Read and write	6
rwx	Read, write, and execute	7
r-x	Read and execute	5
--x	Execute only	1

For each file, three of these three-letter chunks are grouped together. The first chunk represents the permissions for the owner of the file, the second chunk represents the permissions for file's group, and the last chunk represents the permissions for all users on the system. Table 6-2 describes some common file permission setups.

Permission	Numeric Equivalent	Description
-rw-------	600	Owner has read and write permissions. Set for most files.
-rw-r--r--	644	Owner has read and write permissions; group and world have read-only permission. Be sure you want to let other people read this file.
-rw-rw-rw-	666	Everyone has read and write permissions. Not recommended; this combination allows the file to be accessed and changed by anyone, anywhere on the system.
-rwx------	700	Owner has read, write, and execute permissions. Best combination for programs the owner wishes to run (files that result from compiling a C or C++ program).
-rwxr-xr-x	755	Owner has read, write, and execute permissions. Everyone else has read and execute permissions.
-rwxrwxrwx	777	Everyone has read, write, and execute privileges. Like the 666 setting, this combination should be avoided.
-rwx--x--x	711	Owner has read, write, and execute permissions; everyone else has execute-only permissions. Useful for programs that you want to let others run but not copy.
drwx------	700	This is a directory created with the **mkdir** command. Only the owner can read and write into this directory. Note that all directories must have the executable bit set.

Table 6-2 Common File Permission Descriptions

Permission	Numeric Equivalent	Description
drwxr-xr-x	755	This directory can be changed only by the owner, but everyone else can view its contents.
drwx--x--x	711	A combination for keeping a directory world-readable but restricted from access by the **ls** command. File can be read only by someone who knows the filename.

Table 6-2 Common File Permission Descriptions *(continued)*

CRITICAL SKILL
6.5 Managing and Manipulating Files

This section covers the basic command-line tools for managing files and directories. Most of this will be familiar to anyone who has used a command-line interface. These are the same old functions, but with different command names.

Copying Files: cp

The **cp** command is used to copy files and has a substantial number of options. See its man page for additional details. By default, this command works silently, displaying status information only if an error condition occurs. Here are the most common options for **cp**:

Option for cp	Description
–f	Force copy; do not ask for verification.
–I	Interactive copy; before each file is copied, verify with user.

To copy **index.html** to **index-orig.html**, use the following command:

```
[michael@workbox michael]$ cp index.html index-orig.html
```

To interactively copy all files ending in **.html** to the **/tmp** directory, type this command:

```
[michael@workbox michael]$ cp -i *.html /tmp
```

Moving Files: mv

The **mv** command is used to move files from one location to another. Files can be moved across partitions as well. That requires a copy operation to occur, so such a move may take longer. These are the most common options for **mv**:

Option for mv	Description
–f	Force move
–l	Interactive move

To move all files from **/usr/src/myprog/bin/*** to **/usr/bin**, use this command:

```
[root@workbox /root]# mv /usr/src/myprog/bin/* /usr/bin
```

There is no explicit rename tool, so you can use **mv**. To rename **/tmp/blah** to **/tmp/bleck**, type this command:

```
[michael@workbox michael]$ mv /tmp/bleck /tmp/blah
```

Linking Files: ln

The **ln** command lets you establish hard links and soft links. (See "File and Directory Types" earlier in this module.) The general format of **ln** is as follows:

```
[michael@workbox michael]$ ln original_file new_file
```

Although **ln** has many options, you'll never need to use most of them. The most common option, **–s**, creates a symbolic link instead of a hard link.

To create a symbolic link so that **/usr/bin/myadduser** points to **/usr/local/bin/myadduser**, issue this command:

```
[root@workbox /root]# ln -s /usr/local/bin/myadduser /usr/bin/myadduser
```

Project 6-1   Creating an Export Area

Part of using a Linux system as a file server is preparing its directory structure to share files. Unless your plan is to allow everybody to access everything, you'll have to set up the structure to limit access to ensure security and make the system easier to navigate for users. In this project, you will add an export area with subdirectories configured with permissions for access by different departments.

Step by Step

1. As the root user, use the **mkdir** command to create a subdirectory of / for the files to be exported to other systems. Use the directory name **/export**.

(continued)

2. Configure the directory to be visible to everyone but editable only by the administrator. Using the **chmod** command, set permissions on the **/export** directory to allow read permissions for everyone, but restricting write permissions to the directory owner alone.

3. Within the export directory, create directories for the executives, researchers, applications staff, and sales staff to share their files internally.

4. Set group ownership on each directory to the corresponding user group (see the groups defined in Project 5-2). Use the **chgrp** command.

5. Set the permissions on the directories so that the executives alone can read and write in their shared directory, and so that members of all four groups can read the contents of the other directories, but only each group's members can write to each group's directory.

6. Test access by using the **su -** command to log in as another user temporarily. See if you can create files in directories in which the user has write permission. Make sure you can't create files in directories in which the user lacks write permission.

Project Summary

Real-world file access rules can be much more complicated than this, but changing group ownership and membership and changing directory permissions is key to managing data directories. Be sure that you create your export area on a disk partition that has ample space for the files you expect to be sharing with others. Once the area is set up the way you want it, with only a little more work (described in later modules), you'll be able to have local users, NFS access, FTP access, or HTTP access provided as needed.

Finding a File: find

The **find** command lets you search for files according to various criteria. Like the tools you have already considered, **find** has a large number of options that you can read about on its man page. Here is the general format of **find**:

```
[michael@workbox michael]$ find start_dir [options]
```

where *start_dir* is the directory from which the search should start. Table 6-3 shows the most common options used with **find**.

To find all files in **/tmp** that have not been accessed in at least seven days, use the following command:

```
[root@workbox /tmp]# find /tmp -atime 7 -print
```

Option for find	Description
-mount	Do not search file systems other than the one from which search starts.
-atime *n*	File was accessed at least *n**24 hours ago.
-ctime *n*	File was changed at least *n**24 hours ago.
-inum *n*	File has i-node *n*.
-amin *n*	File was accessed *n* minutes ago.
-cmin *n*	File was changed *n* minutes ago.
-empty	File is empty.
-mmin *n*	File was modified *n* minutes ago.
-mtime *n*	File was modified *n**24 hours ago.
-nouser	File's UID does not correspond to a real user in **/etc/passwd**.
-nogroup	File's GID does not correspond to a real group in **/etc/group**.
-perm *mode*	File's permissions are exactly set to **mode**.
-size *n[bck]*	File is at least *n* blocks/characters/kilobytes. One block equals 512 bytes.
-print	Print the filenames found.
-exec *cmd*	On every file found, execute **cmd**. Important: Be sure to always follow every **cmd** with the \; characters, or BASH will become confused.
-name *name*	File's name should be **name**. You can use regular expressions here.

Table 6-3 Common Options for the **find** Command

Type this command to find all files in **/usr/src** whose names are **core** and to remove them:

```
[root@workbox src]# find /usr/src -name core -exec rm
```

To find all files in **/home** which end in **.jpg** and are over 100K in size, issue this command:

```
[root@workbox /root]# find /home -name "*.jpg" -size 100k
```

The -exec Parameter

One of the most useful parameters to **find** is **-exec**. It allows **find** to execute a command on any file it finds. The name of the file is passed to the command using the string "{}", and the end of the command is entered as \;. For example, to look for the string 'tcp' in all of the header files in **/usr/include/netinet** using **grep**, use this command:

```
[root@workbox /root]# find /usr/include/netinet -name "*.h" -exec grep
    'tcp' {} \; -print
```

Converting and Copying a File: dd

The **dd** command reads the contents of a file and sends it to another file. What makes it different from **cp** is that **dd** can perform on-the-fly conversions on the file and accept data from a tape or floppy drive or other device. When **dd** accesses a device, it does not assume anything about the file system but instead pulls the data in a raw format. Thus, **dd** can be used to generate images of disks even if the disk is of foreign format.

Table 6-4 shows the most common parameters for **dd**.

To generate an image of a floppy disk (especially useful for foreign file formats), use the following command:

```
[michael@workbox michael]$ dd if=/dev/fd0 of=/tmp/floppy_image
```

File Compression: gzip

NOTE
The **gzip** command does not share file formats with either PKZip or WinZip; however, WinZip can decompress **gzip** files.

Option for dd	Description
If=*infile*	Specifies the input file as *infile*.
Of=*outfile*	Specifies the output file as *outfile*
count=*blocks*	Specifies *blocks* as the number of blocks on which **dd** should operate before quitting.
ibs=*size*	Sets the block size of the input device to be *size*.
obs=*size*	Sets the block size of the output device to be *size*.
Seek=*blocks*	Skips *blocks* number of blocks on the output.
Skip=*blocks*	Skips *blocks* number of blocks on the input.
Swab	Converts big-endian input to little endian or vice versa.

Table 6-4 Common Options for the **dd** Command

In the original distributions of UNIX, the tool to compress files was appropriately called **compress**. Unfortunately, the algorithm was patented by someone hoping to make a great deal of money. Instead of paying out, most sites sought and found another compression tool with a patent-free algorithm: **gzip**. Even better, **gzip** consistently achieves better compression ratios than **compress** does. Another bonus: Recent changes have allowed **gzip** to uncompress files that were compressed using the **compress** command.

TIP

The filename extension usually identifies a file compressed with **gzip**. These files typically end in .gz (files compressed with **compress** end in .Z).

Optional parameters used most often with **gzip** are as follows; see the man page for a complete list:

Option for gzip	Description
–c	Write compressed file to the **stdout** (thereby allowing the output to be piped to another program)
–d	Decompress
–r	Recursively find all files that should be compressed
–9	Best compression
–1	Fastest compression

Note that **gzip** compresses the file in place, meaning that after the compression process, the original file is removed, and the only thing left is the compressed file.

NOTE

While the **bzip2** command produces better compression than **gzip**, it is still used less often, not only because people are more familiar with **gzip**, but also because its compression algorithm is more complex and thus slower for compressing and uncompressing files.

To compress a file and then decompress it, use this command:

```
[michael@workbox michael]$ gzip myfile
[michael@workbox michael]$ gzip -d myfile.gz
```

Issue this command to compress all files ending in **.html** using the best compression possible:

```
[michael@workbox www]$ gzip -9 *.html
```

Making Special Files: mknod

As discussed earlier, Linux accesses all of its devices through files. A file that the system understands as an interface to a device must be of type block or character and have major and minor numbers. To create this kind of file with the necessary values, you use the **mknod** command. The **mknod** command can also be used to create named pipes.

Here's the command format:

```
[root@workbox /root]# mknod name type [major] [minor]
```

where *name* is the name of the file; *type* is either **b** for block device, **c** for character device, or **p** for named pipe. If you choose to create a block or character device (when installing a device driver that requires it), you need to specify the *major* and *minor* numbers. The documentation accompanying that driver should tell you what values to use for the major and minor numbers.

To create a named pipe called **/tmp/mypipe**, use this command:

```
[root@workbox /root]# mknod /tmp/mypipe p
```

Creating a Directory: mkdir

The **mkdir** command in Linux is identical to the same command in other UNIXs, as well as in MS-DOS. The only option available is **–p**, which will create parent directories if none exist. For example, if you need to create **/tmp/bigdir/subdir/mydir** and the only directory that exists is **/tmp**, using **–p** will cause **bigdir** and **subdir** to be automatically created along with **mydir**.

To create a directory called **mydir**, use this command:

```
[michael@workbox michael]$ mkdir mydir
```

NOTE

The **mkdir** command cannot be abbreviated to **md** as it can be under DOS.

Removing Directory: rmdir

The **rmdir** command offers no surprises for those familiar with the DOS version of the command; it simply removes an existing directory. The directory must be empty before you can remove it. The only command-line parameter available for this is **–p**, which removes parent directories as well. For example, in a directory named **/tmp/bigdir/subdit/mydir**, if you want to get rid of all the directories from **bigdir** to **mydir**, you'd issue this command alone:

```
[root@tedford /tmp]# rmdir -p bigdir/subdir/mydir
```

To remove a directory called **mydir**, you'd type this:

```
[michael@workbox michael]$ rmdir mydir
```

NOTE

The **rmdir** command cannot be abbreviated to **rd** as it can under DOS.

Showing Present Working Directory: pwd

It is inevitable that you will sit down in front of an already logged-in workstation and not know where you are in the directory tree. To get this information, you need the **pwd** command. It has no parameters, and its only task is to print the current working directory. The DOS equivalent is typing **cd** alone on the command line; however, the BASH **cd** command takes you back to your home directory.

To get the current working directory, use this command:

```
[michael@workbox src]# pwd /usr/local/src
```

Tape Archive: tar

If you are familiar with the WinZip program, you are accustomed to the fact that the compression tool reduces file size but also consolidates files into compressed archives. Under Linux, this process is separated into two tools: **gzip** and **tar**.

The **tar** program combines multiple files into a single large file. It is separate from the compression tool, so it allows you to select which compression tool to use or whether you even want compression. Additionally, **tar** is able to read and write to devices in much the same way **dd** can, thus making **tar** a good tool for backing up to tape devices.

NOTE

Although the name of the **tar** program includes the word "tape," it isn't necessary to read or write to a tape drive when creating archives. In fact, you'll rarely use **tar** with a tape drive in day-to-day situations (backups aside). The reason it was named **tar** in the first place was that when it was originally created, limited disk space meant that tape was the most logical place to put archives. Typically, the **–f** option in **tar** would be used to specify the tape device file, rather than a traditional UNIX file. You should be aware, however, that you can still **tar** straight to a device.

Here's the structure of the **tar** command, its most common options, and several examples of its use:

```
[michael@workbox michael]$ tar [commands and options] filename
```

Option for tar	Description
–c	Create a new archive.
–t	View the contents of an archive.
–x	Extract the contents of an archive.
–f	Specify the name of the file (or device) in which the archive is located.
–v	Be verbose during operations.
–z	Use **gzip** to compress or decompress the file.
–i	Use **bzip2** to compress or decompress the file.

To create an archive called **apache.tar** containing all the files from **/usr/src/apache**, use this command:

```
[root@workbox src]# tar -cf apache.tar /usr/src/apache
```

To create an archive called **apache.tar** containing all the files from **/usr/src/apache**, and to show what is happening as it happens, enter the following:

```
[root@workbox src]# tar -cvf apache.tar /usr/src/apache
```

To create a **gzip**ped compressed archive called **apache.tar.gz** containing all of the files from **/usr/src/apache**, and to show what is happening as it happens, issue this command:

```
[root@workbox src]# tar -cvzf apache.tar.gz /usr/src/apache
```

To extract the contents of a **gzip**ped **tar** archive called **apache.tar.gz**, and to show what is happening as it happens, use this command:

```
[michael@workbox michael]$ tar -xvzf apache.tar.gz
```

If you like, you can also specify a physical device to **tar** to and from. This is handy when you need to transfer a set of files from one system to another and for some reason you cannot create a file system on the device. (Or sometimes it's just more entertaining to do it this way.) To create an archive on the first floppy device, you would enter this:

```
[root@workbox src]$ tar -cvzf /dev/fd0 /usr/src/apache
```

To pull that archive off of a disk, you would type

```
[root@workbox src]# tar -xvzf /dev/fd0
```

Concatenating Files: cat

The **cat** program fills an extremely simple role: to display files. More creative things can be done with it, but nearly all of its usage will be in the form of simply displaying the contents of text files—much like the **type** command under DOS. Because multiple filenames can be specified on the command line, it's possible to concatenate files into a single, large continuous file. This is different from **tar** in that the resulting file has no control information to show the boundaries of different files.

To display the **/etc/passwd** file, use this command:

```
[michael@workbox michael]$ cat /etc/passwd
```

To display the **/etc/passwd** file and the **/etc/group** file, issue this command:

```
[michael@workbox michael]$ cat /etc/passwd /etc/group
```

Type this command to concatenate **/etc/passwd** with **/etc/group** into the file **/tmp/complete**:

```
[michael@workbox michael]$ cat /etc/passwd /etc/group > /tmp/complete
```

To concatenate the **/etc/passwd** file to an existing file called **/tmp/orb**, use this:

```
[michael@workbox michael]$ cat /etc/passwd >> /tmp/orb
```

Displaying a File One Screen at a Time: more or less

The **more** command works in much the same way the DOS version of the program does. It takes an input file and displays it one screen at a time. The input file can come either from its **stdin** or from a command-line parameter.

Additional command-line parameters, though rarely used, can be found in the man page. To view the **/etc/passwd** file one screen at a time, use this command:

```
[michael@workbox michael]$ more /etc/passwd
```

To view the directory listing generated by the **ls** command one screen at a time, enter this:

```
[michael@workbox michael]$ ls | more
```

An enhanced version of the **more** command was created, and named **less**. In addition to displaying one screen at a time, **less** will allow you to move backward through a file as well as forward. When you get to the end of the file, **less** doesn't automatically exit the way **more** does (after all, you may still want to scroll back). To exit out of **less**, press **q**. Once again, see the man page if you want to know all the available options.

```
[michael@workbox michael]$ less /etc/passwd
[michael@workbox michael]$ ls | less
```

Disk Utilization: du

You will often need to determine where and by whom disk space is being consumed, especially when you're running low on it! The **du** command allows you to determine the disk utilization on a directory-by-directory basis. Here are some of the options available:

Option for du	Description
−c	Produce a grand total at the end of the run.
−h	Print sizes in human readable format.
−k	Print sizes in kilobytes rather than block sizes. (Note: Under Linux, one block is equal to 1K, but this is not true for all UNIXs.)
−s	Summarize. Print only one output for each argument.
−x	Skip directories that are on other file systems.

To display the amount of space each directory in **/home** is taking up in human readable format, use this command:

```
[root@tedford /root]# du -sh /home/*
```

Showing the Directory Location of a File: which

The **which** command searches your entire path to find the name of the file specified on the command line. If the file is found, the command output includes the actual path of the file. This command is used to locate fully qualified paths.

Use the following command to find out which directory the **ls** command is in:

```
[michael@workbox michael]$ which ls
```

You may find this similar to the **find** command. The difference here is that since **which** searches only the path, it is much faster. Of course, it is also much more limiting than **find**, but if all you're looking for is a program, you'll find it to be a better choice of commands.

Locating a Command: whereis

The **whereis** tool searches your path and displays the name of the program and its absolute directory, the source file (if available), and the man page for the command (again, if available).

To find the location of the program, source, and manual page for the command **grep**, use this:

```
[michael@workbox michael]$ whereis grep
```

Disk Free: df

The **df** program displays the amount of free space, partition by partition. The drives/partitions must be mounted in order to get this information. NFS information can be gathered this way, as well. Some parameters for **df** are listed here; additional (rarely used) options are listed in the **df** manual page.

Option for df	Description
–h	Generate free space amount in human readable numbers rather than free blocks.
–l	List only the locally mounted file systems. Do not display any information about network-mounted file systems.

To show the free space for all locally mounted drivers, use this command:

```
[michael@workbox michael]$ df -l
```

To show the free space in a human-readable format for the file system in which your current working directory is located, enter

```
[michael@workbox michael]$ df -h .
```

To show the free space in a human-readable format for the file system on which **/tmp** is located, type this command:

```
[michael@workbox michael]$ df -h /tmp
```

Synchronizing Disks: sync

Like most other modern operating systems, Linux maintains a disk cache to improve efficiency. The drawback, of course, is that not everything you want written to disk will have been written to disk at any given moment.

To schedule the disk cache to be written out to disk, you use the **sync** command. If **sync** detects that writing the cache out to disk has already been scheduled, the kernel is instructed to immediately flush the cache. This command takes no command-line parameters.

Type this command to ensure the disk cache has been flushed:

```
[root@workbox /root]# sync ;   sync
```

CRITICAL SKILL
6.6 # Tracking and Terminating Processes

Under Linux (and UNIX in general), each running program comprises at least one process. From the operating system's standpoint, each process is independent of the others. Unless it specifically asks to share resources with other processes, a process is confined to the memory and CPU allocation assigned to it. Processes that overstep their memory allocation (which could potentially corrupt another running program and make the system unstable) are immediately killed. This method of handling processes has been a major contributor to the stability of UNIX systems: User applications cannot corrupt other user programs or the operating system.

This section describes the tools used to list and manipulate processes. They are very important elements of a system administrator's daily work.

Listing Processes: ps

The **ps** command lists all the processes in a system, their state, size, name, owner, CPU time, wall clock time, and much more. There are many command-line parameters available; the ones most often used are described in Table 6-5.

Option for ps	Description
–a	Show all processes with a controlling terminal, not just the current user's processes.
–r	Show only running processes (see the description of process states later in this section).
–x	Show processes that do not have a controlling terminal.
–u	Show the process owners.
–f	Display parent/child relationships among processes.
–l	Produce a list in long format.
–w	Show a process's command-line parameters (up to half a line).
–ww	Show all of a process's command-line parameters, despite length.

Table 6-5 Common **ps** Command Options

The most common set of parameters used with the **ps** command is **–auxww**. These parameters show all the processes (regardless of whether they have a controlling terminal), each process's owners, and all the processes' command-line parameters. Let's examine the output of an invocation of **ps –auxww**.

```
USER      PID  %CPU %MEM   VSZ   RSS TTY      STAT START    TIME COMMAND
root        1   0.0  0.3  1096   476 ?        S    Jun10    0:04 init
root        2   0.0  0.0     0     0 ?        SW   Jun10    0:00 [kflushd]
root        3   0.0  0.0     0     0 ?        SW   Jun10    0:00 [kpiod]
root        4   0.0  0.0     0     0 ?        SW   Jun10    0:00 [kswapd]
root        5   0.0  0.0     0     0 ?        SW<  Jun10    0:00 [mdrecoveryd]
root      102   0.0  0.2  1068   380 ?        S    Jun10    0:00 /usr/sbin/
                                                                apmd -p 10 -w 5
bin       253   0.0  0.2  1088   288 ?        S    Jun10    0:00 portmap
root      300   0.0  0.4  1272   548 ?        S    Jun10    0:00 syslogd -m 0
root      311   0.0  0.5  1376   668 ?        S    Jun10    0:00 klogd
daemon    325   0.0  0.2  1112   284 ?        S    Jun10    0:00 /usr/sbin/atd
root      339   0.0  0.4  1284   532 ?        S    Jun10    0:00 crond
root      357   0.0  0.3  1232   508 ?        S    Jun10    0:00 inetd
root      371   0.0  1.1  2528  1424 ?        S    Jun10    0:00 named
root      385   0.0  0.4  1284   516 ?        S    Jun10    0:00 lpd
root      399   0.0  0.8  2384  1116 ?        S    Jun10    0:00 httpd
xfs       429   0.0  0.7  1988   908 ?        S    Jun10    0:00 xfs
root      467   0.0  0.2  1060   384 tty2     S    Jun10    0:00 /sbin/
                                                                mingetty tty2
```

```
root        468   0.0   0.2   1060    384  tty3      S    Jun10    0:00 /sbin/
                                                                        mingetty tty3
root        469   0.0   0.2   1060    384  tty4      S    Jun10    0:00 /sbin/
                                                                        mingetty tty4
root        470   0.0   0.2   1060    384  tty5      S    Jun10    0:00 /sbin/
                                                                        mingetty tty5
root        471   0.0   0.2   1060    384  tty6      S    Jun10    0:00 /sbin/
                                                                        mingetty tty6
root        473   0.0   0.0   1052    116  ?         S    Jun10    0:01 update
                                                                        (bdflush)
root        853   0.0   0.7   1708    940  pts/1     S    Jun10    0:00 BASH
root       1199   0.0   0.7   1940   1012  pts/2     S    Jun10    0:00 su
root       1203   0.0   0.7   1700    920  pts/2     S    Jun10    0:00 BASH
root       1726   0.0   1.3   2824   1760  ?         S    Jun10    0:00 xterm
root       1728   0.0   0.7   1716    940  pts/8     S    Jun10    0:00 BASH
root       1953   0.0   1.3   2832   1780  ?         S    Jun11    0:05 xterm
root       1955   0.0   0.7   1724    972  pts/10    S    Jun11    0:00 BASH
nobody     6436   0.0   0.7   2572    988  ?         S    Jun13    0:00 httpd
nobody     6437   0.0   0.7   2560    972  ?         S    Jun13    0:00 httpd
nobody     6438   0.0   0.7   2560    976  ?         S    Jun13    0:00 httpd
nobody     6439   0.0   0.7   2560    976  ?         S    Jun13    0:00 httpd
nobody     6440   0.0   0.7   2560    976  ?         S    Jun13    0:00 httpd
nobody     6441   0.0   0.7   2560    976  ?         S    Jun13    0:00 httpd
root      16673   0.0   0.6   1936    840  pts/10    S    Jun14    0:00 su -michael
michael   16675   0.0   0.8   1960   1112  pts/10    S    Jun14    0:00 -zsh
root      18243   0.0   0.9   2144   1216  tty1      S    Jun14    0:00 login --
                                                                        rwhite
rwhite    18244   0.0   0.8   1940   1080  tty1      S    Jun14    0:00 -tcsh
```

The very first line of the output provides column headers for the listing, as follows:

- **Column 1: USER**   Who owns what process.

- **Column 2: PID**   Process identification number.

- **Column 3: %CPU**   Percentage of the CPU taken up by a process. Note: For a system with multiple processors, this column will add up to more than 100 percent.

- **Column 4. %MEM**   Percentage of memory taken up by a process.

- **Column 5: VSZ**   The amount of virtual memory a process is taking.

- **Column 6: RSS**   The amount of actual (resident) memory a process is taking.

- **Column 7: TTY**   The controlling terminal for a process. A question mark in this column means the process is no longer connected to a controlling terminal.

- **Column 8: STAT**   The state of the process:

- **S**   Process is sleeping. All processes that are ready to run (that is, being multitasked, and the CPU is currently focused elsewhere) will be asleep.

- **R**   Process is actually on the CPU.

- **D**   Uninterruptible sleep (usually I/O related).

- **T**   Process is being traced by a debugger or has been stopped.

- **Z**   Process has gone zombie. This means either (1) the parent process has not acknowledged the death of its child using the **wait** system call; or (2) the parent was improperly **kill**ed, and until the parent is completely **kill**ed, the **init** process (see Module 8) cannot reap the child itself. A zombied process usually indicates poorly written software.

In addition, the STAT entry for each process can take one of the following modifiers: W = No resident pages in memory (it has been completely swapped out); < = High-priority process; N = Low-priority task; L = Pages in memory are locked there (usually signifying the need for real-time functionality).

- **Column 9: START**   Date the process was started.

- **Column 10: TIME**   Amount of time the process has spent on the CPU.

- **Column 11: COMMAND**   Name of the process and its command-line parameters.

Showing an Interactive List of Processes: top

The **top** command is an interactive version of **ps**. Instead of giving a static view of what is going on, **top** refreshes the screen with a list of processes every two to three seconds (user adjustable). From this list, you can reprioritize processes or **kill** them. Figure 6-1 shows a **top** screen.

The **top** program's main disadvantage is that it's a CPU hog. On a congested system, this program tends to complicate system management issues. Users start running **top** to see what's going on, only to find several other people running the program as well, slowing down the system even more.

By default, **top** is shipped so that everyone can use it. You may find it prudent, depending on your environment, to restrict **top** to **root** only. To do this, change the program's permissions with the following command:

```
[root@workbox /root]# chmod 0700 /usr/bin/top
```

```
 Shell - Konsole <5>                                                  _ □ ✕

 Session  Edit  View  Settings  Help

 [icons]

  9:38pm  up 12:17, 10 users,  load average: 0.12, 0.05, 0.01
 102 processes: 101 sleeping, 1 running, 0 zombie, 0 stopped
 CPU0 states:  3.2% user,  3.3% system,  0.0% nice, 92.3% idle
 CPU1 states:  2.1% user,  2.2% system,  0.0% nice, 95.0% idle
 Mem:   513468K av,  465184K used,   48284K free,    OK shrd,  56164K buff
 Swap: 1044216K av,      OK used, 1044216K free               275136K cached

  PID USER     PRI  NI  SIZE  RSS SHARE STAT %CPU %MEM   TIME COMMAND
 7193 root      5 -10 61284  17M  3308 S <   2.9  3.4  0:43 X
 7769 millerm  15   0  2868 2868  2380 S     1.7  0.5  0:00 screenshot
 7768 rwhite   16   0  1064 1064   840 R     1.3  0.2  0:00 top
 7267 millerm  15   0 54052  13M 11096 S     0.9  2.6  0:06 kdeinit
 7720 millerm  15   0 54408  13M 11596 S     0.7  2.7  0:01 kdeinit
 7294 millerm  15   0 56344  15M 12788 S     0.5  3.1  0:12 kdeinit
 1113 xfs      16   0  3520 3520   920 S     0.3  0.6  0:14 xfs
 7248 millerm  15   0 51852  11M  9692 S     0.3  2.2  0:04 kdeinit
 7504 millerm  15   0 17292  16M  4204 S     0.3  3.3  0:03 gimp
 7263 millerm  15   0 53888  13M 11184 S     0.1  2.6  0:00 kdeinit
 7291 millerm  15   0 54496  13M 11768 S     0.1  2.7  0:04 kdeinit
 7304 millerm  15   0  4292 4292  3688 S     0.1  0.8  0:00 pam-panel-icon
 7308 millerm  16   0 54508  13M 11576 S     0.1  2.7  0:01 kdeinit
    1 root     15   0   480  480   428 S     0.0  0.0  0:04 init
    2 root     OK   0     0    0     0 SW    0.0  0.0  0:00 migration_CPU0
    3 root     OK   0     0    0     0 SW    0.0  0.0  0:00 migration_CPU1
    4 root     15   0     0    0     0 SW    0.0  0.0  0:00 keventd
    5 root     34  19     0    0     0 SWN   0.0  0.0  0:00 ksoftirqd_CPU0
    6 root     34  19     0    0     0 SWN   0.0  0.0  0:00 ksoftirqd_CPU1
    7 root     15   0     0    0     0 SW    0.0  0.0  0:02 kswapd
    8 root     25   0     0    0     0 SW    0.0  0.0  0:00 bdflush
    9 root     15   0     0    0     0 SW    0.0  0.0  0:00 kupdated
   10 root     25   0     0    0     0 SW    0.0  0.0  0:00 mdrecoveryd
   16 root     25   0     0    0     0 SW    0.0  0.0  0:00 scsi_eh_0
   19 root     15   0     0    0     0 SW    0.0  0.0  0:03 kjournald
   75 root     16   0     0    0     0 SW    0.0  0.0  0:00 khubd
  167 root     15   0     0    0     0 SW    0.0  0.0  0:00 kjournald
  455 root     15   0  1024 1024   711 S    0.0  0.1  0:00 dhclient
  494 root     15   0   536  536   456 S    0.0  0.1  0:00 syslogd
```

Figure 6-1 The top command gives an updated view of running processes.

Sending a Signal to a Process: kill

This program's name is misleading: it doesn't really kill processes. What it *does* do is send *signals* to running processes. The operating system, by default, supplies each process a standard set of *signal handlers* to deal with incoming signals. From a system administrator's standpoint, the most important handlers are for signals number 9 and 15, kill process and terminate process, respectively. When **kill** is invoked, it requires at least one parameter: the process identification number (PID) as derived from the **ps** command. When passed only the PID, **kill** sends signal 15. Some programs intercept this signal and perform a number of actions so that they can shut down cleanly. Others just stop running in their tracks. Either way, **kill** isn't a guaranteed method for making a process stop.

Signals

The optional parameter available for **kill** is *–n,* where the *n* represents a signal number. As system administrators, we are most interested in the signals 9 (kill) and 1 (hang up).

The kill signal, 9, is the impolite way of stopping a process. Rather than asking a process to stop, the operating system simply kills the process. The only time this will fail is when the process is in the middle of a system call (such as a request to open a file), in which case the process will die once it returns from the system call.

The hang up signal, 1, is a bit of a throwback to the VT100 terminal days of UNIX. When a user's terminal connection dropped in the middle of a session, all of that terminal's running processes would receive a hang up signal (often called a SIGHUP or HUP). This gave the processes an opportunity to perform a clean shutdown or, in the case of background processes, to ignore the signal. These days, a HUP is used to tell certain server applications to go and reread their configuration files (you'll see this in action in several of the later modules). Most applications simply ignore the signal.

Security Issues

The power to terminate a process is obviously a very powerful one, making security precautions important. Users may kill only processes they have permission to kill. If non-root users attempt to send signals to processes other than their own, error messages are returned. The root user is the exception to this limitation; **root** may send signals to all processes in the system. Of course, this means **root** needs to exercise great care when using the **kill** command.

Examples of kill

Use this command to terminate process number 2059:

```
[root@workbox /root]# kill 2059
```

For an almost guaranteed kill of process number 593, issue this command:

```
[root@workbox /root]# kill -9 593
```

Type this to send the HUP signal to the **init** program (which is always PID 1):

```
[root@workbox /root]# kill -1 1
```

| Project 6-2 | Checking Your Processes |

Let's take a break from the theory of process management to see what processes are running on your Linux system. In this project, you'll try to discover documentation and configuration information about active processes by using some of the commands described in this module.

Step by Step

1. From within X, check the most active processes on your Linux system. Use the **top** command from a terminal window to see what's taking up the most CPU activity.

2. Note the most active process names and open another terminal window to see what information you can gather about those top processes. Use the **which** command to see where the executables are located. Use the **man** and **info** commands to determine whether there are command-line documents available for each of the most active processes.

3. Try to determine whether these programs have related files. Sometimes this information can be found in the SEE ALSO section of the **man** page for the program. Look especially for man section 5 references.

4. Try using the **find** command with the **-name** option and a regular expression to see if there are related configuration files in the /**etc** directory, spool or log files in the /**var** directory, or program files in the /**usr**, /**sbin**, or /**bin** directories.

5. Try to find configuration files that aren't named like the program itself by performing a **grep** for the program's name through the contents of the /**etc** directory.

6. Use the **more** command to view any configuration files brought to light by your efforts in steps 4 and 5.

7. Continue your investigation to the less-active programs by running the **ps** command and repeating steps 2–6.

Project Summary

Some of the programs that come with Red Hat Linux 8.0 have useful documentation in the /**usr/share/doc** directory, so that may be a good place to look for information about the programs that run on your system. However, even though README files and even web searches can often turn up exactly the information you need, being able to do a little sleuthing on your own can be invaluable in certain circumstances!

CRITICAL SKILL
6.7 Using Miscellaneous Command-Line Tools

The following tools don't fall into any specific category covered in this module. They all make important contributions to daily system administration chores.

Showing the System Name: uname

The **uname** program produces some system details that may be helpful in several situations. Maybe you've managed to remotely log in to a dozen different computers and have lost track of where you are! This tool is also helpful for script writers, because it allows them to change the path of a script according to the system information.

Here are the command-line parameters for **uname**:

Option for uname	Description
−m	Print the machine hardware type (such as i686 for Pentium Pro and better architectures).
−n	Print the machine's host name.
−r	Print the operating system's release name.
−s	Print the operating system's name.
−v	Print the operating system's version.
−a	Print all of the above.

To get the operating system's name and release, enter the following command:

```
[michael@workbox michael]$ uname -s -r
```

NOTE

The **−s** option may seem wasted (after all, we know this is Linux), but this parameter proves quite useful on almost all UNIX-like operating systems, as well. At an SGI workstation, **uname −s** will return IRIX, or SunOS at a Sun workstation. Folks who work in heterogeneous environments often write scripts that will behave differently according to the OS, and **uname** with **−s** is a consistent way to determine that information.

Learning Who Is Logged In: who

On systems that allow users to log in to other users' machines or special servers, you will want to know who is logged in. You can generate such a report by using the **who** command:

```
[michael@workbox michael]$ who
```

The **who** report looks like this:

```
michael    tty1       Jun 14 18:22
rwhite     pts/9      Jun 14 18:29 (:0)
root       pts/11     Jun 14 21:12 (:0)
root       pts/12     Jun 14 23:38 (:0)
```

A Variation on who: w

The **w** command displays the same information that **who** does and a whole lot more. The details of the report include who is logged in, what their terminal is, where they are logged in from, how long they've been logged in, how long they've been idle, and their CPU utilization. The top of the report also gives you the same output as the **uptime** command.

Networking Tools

If you are starting your experience with Linux in an already networked environment, you may find some of these tools handy for getting around.

CAUTION

These networking tools are useful, but allowing **telnet, rsh**, remote X, and **ftp** connections to a server can be risky from a security standpoint. See Module 9 for more information on securing a Linux server.

telnet

As was mentioned in earlier modules, Linux understands the concept of multiple users logged in to the same workstation at the same time. So in order to allow for someone to log in to another host from remote, the **telnet** command was created.

The format of the command is as follows:

```
[rwhite@workbox rwhite]$ telnet gregory
```

where **gregory** is the name of another computer running either Linux or a variant of UNIX. Once you run the command, you will get a login prompt from that machine. Logging in to that machine enables you to run programs on the other host just as if you were running them on your own. If you aren't sure where you are logged in, use the **uname** command (discussed earlier) to find out where you are.

Due to security concerns, **telnet** has fallen out of favor as a method for logging in to remote machines (see Module 15 for a better alternative). However, because of its ability to send and receive ASCII text over a network port, **telnet** is still very useful as a diagnostic tool. You'll see some examples of this in later modules.

Remote Shell: rsh

As you've seen with **telnet**, you must enter a username and password in order to log in to another host. For many people who found the need to log in to other hosts often, this became a nuisance. They wanted the other host to automatically trust them so that when issued a remote login request, the system would allow them access without asking for a login and password. The double-win with a feature like that is the ability to automate tasks that require one host to invoke a program on another host.

To accommodate this, the **rsh** command was created. In its simplest form, specify the name of the host you wish to log in to the way you would for **telnet**. For example:

```
[rwhite@workbox rwhite]$ rsh gregory
```

If you set up your configuration files so that **gregory** knows to trust you, the system will automatically give you a shell prompt. If the configuration file does not automatically trust you, you will need to enter your password again.

To set up the configuration file, edit the **.rhosts** file (yes, there is a period in front of the filename) in your home directory. When there, create a line that looks like this:

```
host_to_trust    your_username
```

If you want to be able to **rsh** from **workbox** to **gregory** without being prompted for a password, you would create the following file in an **.rhosts** file in your home directory on **gregory**:

```
workbox rwhite
```

And you'd be ready to go!

Once again, **rsh** is covered here for completeness, but before you decide to use it for anything serious, I recommend that you explore **ssh** in Module 15.

Remote X Displays

In Module 1, I said that X offers the ability to display content on other hosts' screens. This makes it possible to log in to a server that has a special program on it and have the display redirected to the screen in front of you.

Allowing this to happen is a two-step process. The first step is telling your machine that it should allow connections from another host for X displays. This is done with the **xhost** command:

```
[michael@workbox michael]$ xhost +ungerer
```

where **ungerer** is the name of the host you want to allow X displays to come from in addition to your own host.

Now that you have allowed **ungerer** to display to your host, log in to **ungerer**, and set your DISPLAY environment variable like so:

```
[michael@ungerer michael]$ DISPLAY="workbox:0"; export DISPLAY
```

This will redirect all X displays to the host workbox. If you have two hosts to try this with, an easy test to see if it worked is to start a web browser on the remote host and watch it display its content on your host. Neat trick, isn't it?

Once you are done with whatever work is required to allow other hosts to display to your screen, you need to explicitly disallow future connections like so:

```
[michael@workbox michael]$ xhost -ungerer
```

If you want to disallow everyone, you can use the following shortcut:

```
[michael@workbox michael]$ xhost -
```

CAUTION

Issuing the command **xhost +** is dangerous because it allows anyone to connect to your machine and display things on it. While this most often leads only to practical jokes, the potential for something more serious to happen is there. Be sure to specify from which hosts you allow X connections, and remember to undo it when you are done.

Mail Preferences: mail, pine, and mutt

Like everyone else, Linux folk need to read their e-mail. And as you can imagine, you have plenty of choices as to how. Although there are many GUI-based POP mail readers, this module covers command-line tools.

The one tool that you will always be able to find is called—you guessed it—**mail**. Simply run **mail** from the command line like so:

```
[michael@workbox michael]$ mail
```

and you'll see what mail you have available to read. Because this tool does not require any screen formatting, it is well suited for those instances where you are troubleshooting a host so broken it has no terminal control.

To exit the **mail** program, type **q** and press ENTER. If you want more information about **mail**, check out its man page. As you'll see, for a tool that looks very simple, it actually offers quite a bit of capability.

Another popular tool is **pine**, which actually takes control of your terminal window and makes the display look much nicer. Being a fully menu-driven program where all of your options are always listed on a menu in front of you, **pine** tends to be a very popular choice for people new to UNIX.

From a practical point of view, **pine** is ideal for communicating with people who use all sorts of other mail tools, since it understands all of the popular standards in use today (such as MIME attachments). The **pine** program also offers a very powerful filing system with which you can archive your mail easily and find it again at a later date.

My personal favorite mail tool is **mutt**. To quote **mutt**'s author, "All mail clients suck. This one just sucks less." **mutt** is another tool that looks simple on the outside but offers a wealth of capability. Unlike **pine**, **mutt** is much less menu-oriented. For folks who are used to the UNIX environment, this is a very welcome feature because it allows for very efficient use. Doubly useful is that **mutt** offers excellent memory management and can therefore handle extremely large mailboxes. More than once, I've used **mutt** to clean up someone's mailbox that Outlook choked on.

ftp

Linux offers a very handy command-line version of the FTP client. Anyone used to the Windows version of the FTP client that runs under command.com will feel right at home with this, since the Windows version adopted the standard commands in use by the UNIX community since the late 70s.

To start the FTP client, simply run **ftp** at the command line like so:

```
[michael@workbox michael]$ ftp remotehostname
```

where ***remotehostname*** is the name of the host that you would like to FTP to/from.

6.8 Editing Text Files

Editors are by the far the bulkiest of common tools, but they are also the most useful. Without them, making any kind of change to a text file would be a tremendous undertaking. Regardless of your Linux distribution, you will have gotten a few editors. You should take a few moments to get comfortable with them before you're busy fighting another problem.

NOTE

Although all of the editors listed here come with Red Hat 8, not all of them are installed by default. You may have to specifically install one that you find you like and isn't one of the defaults.

vi

The **vi** editor has been part of UNIX-based systems since the 1970s, and its interface shows it. It is arguably one of the last editors to actually use a separate command mode and data entry mode; as a result, most newcomers find it unpleasant to use. But before you give **vi** the cold shoulder, take a moment to get comfortable with it. In difficult situations, you may not have a pretty graphical editor at your disposal, and **vi** is ubiquitous across all UNIX systems.

The version of **vi** that ships with Linux distributions is VIM (VI iMproved). It has a lot of what made **vi** popular in the first place and many features that make it useful in today's typical environments (including a graphical interface if X is running).

To start **vi**, simply type

```
[michael@workbox michael]$ vi
```

The easiest way to learn more about **vi** is to start it and enter **:help**. If you ever find yourself stuck in **vi**, press the ESC key several times and then type **:qu!** to force an exit without saving. If you want to save the file, type **:wq**.

emacs

It has been argued that **emacs** is an operating system all by itself. It's big, feature-rich, expandable, programmable, and all-around amazing. If you're coming from a GUI background, you'll probably find **emacs** a pleasant environment to work with at first. On its cover, it works like Notepad in terms of its interface. Yet underneath is a complete interface to the GNU development environment, a mail reader, a news reader, a web browser, and even a psychiatrist (well, not exactly).

To start **emacs**, simply type

```
[michael@workbox michael]$ emacs
```

Once **emacs** has started, you can visit the psychiatrist by pressing ALT-X and then typing **doctor**. To get help using **emacs**, press CTRL-H. If you want to save a file press CTRL-X and then CTRL-S. To exit **emacs**, use CTRL-X followed by CTRL-C.

joe

Of the editors listed here, **joe** most closely resembles a simple text editor. It works much like Notepad and offers on-screen help. Anyone who remembers the original WordStar command set will be pleasantly surprised to see that all those brain cells hanging on to CTRL-K commands can be put back to use with **joe**.

To start **joe**, simply type

```
[michael@workbox michael]$ joe
```

pico

The **pico** program is another editor inspired by simplicity. Typically used in conjunction with the **pine** mail reading system, **pico** can also be used as a stand-alone editor. Like **joe**, it can work in a manner similar to Notepad, but **pico** uses its own set of key combinations. Thankfully, all available key combinations are always shown at the bottom of the screen.

To start **pico**, simply type

```
[michael@workbox michael]$ pico
```

CRITICAL SKILL
6.9 Reviewing Linux File System Standards

One argument you hear regularly against Linux is that there are too many different distributions, and that multiple distributions lead to fragmentation. This fragmentation will eventuate in different, incompatible Linux versions.

This is, without a doubt, complete nonsense that plays on "FUD" (Fear, Uncertainty, and Doubt). These types of arguments usually stem from a misunderstanding of the kernel and distributions. However, the Linux community has realized that it has grown past the stage of informal understandings about how things *should* be done. As a result, two types of standards are actively being worked on.

The first standard is the File Hierarchy Standard (FHS). This is an attempt by many of the Linux distributions to standardize on a directory layout so that developers have an easy time making sure their applications work across multiple distributions without difficulty. As of this writing, Red Hat is almost completely compliant, and it is likely that most other distributions are as well.

The other standard is the Linux Standard Base Specification (LSB). Like the FHS, the LSB is a standards group that specifies what a Linux distribution should have in terms of libraries and tools.

A developer who only assumes that a Linux machine complies with the LSB and FHS is guaranteed to have an application that will work with all Linux installations. All of the major distributors have joined these standards groups, including organizations like Red Hat, Caldera, SuSE, Debian, Mandrake, and Turbo Linux. This should ensure that all desktop distributions will have a certain amount of common ground that a developer can rely on.

From a system administrator's point of view, these standards are interesting but not crucial to administering a Linux network. However, it never hurts to learn more about both. For more information on the FHS, go to their web site at http://www.pathname.com/fhs. To find out more about the LSB, check out http://www.linuxbase.org.

Module Summary

In this module, you learned about Linux's command-line interface through BASH, many command-line tools, and a few editors. As you continue through this book, you'll find many references to the information in this module, so be sure that you get comfortable with working at the command line. You may find it a bit annoying at first, especially if you are used to a GUI for performing many of the basic tasks mentioned here—but stick with it. You may even find yourself eventually working faster at the command line than with the GUI!

Obviously, this module can't cover all the command-line tools available to you as part of your default Linux installation. I highly recommend taking some time to look into some of the reference books available, which give complete documentation on this subject. *Linux: The Complete Reference,* Fourth Edition, by Richard Peterson (McGraw-Hill/Osborne, 2001) is an excellent choice for a solid, thorough guide that covers everything available on your Linux system. For a helpful but less comprehensive approach to the considerable detail of Linux systems, try *Linux in a Nutshell,* Third Edition, edited by Ellen Siever (O'Reilly & Associates, 2000). In addition, there are a wealth of texts on shell programming at various levels and from various points of view. Get whatever suits you; shell programming is a skill well worth learning even if you don't do system administration.

Module 6 Mastery Check

1. How would you find out which jobs you are running in a BASH session?

2. How would you move one of the jobs identified in question 1 to the foreground of the session?

3. Match the following functions with these symbols: **&**, |, >, >>, <, ;, `` ` ``

   A. Use a file as input

   B. Use the output of a command as a parameter to another command

   C. Output data from a program to a file

   D. Provide the output of one program as input to another program

   E. Execute two programs consecutively from the same command line

   F. Execute a command without giving it control of the terminal

   G. Append program data to a file

4. What command would you use to view the manual page on the **passwd** program?

5. What command would you use to view the manual page for the **/etc/passwd** file?

6. Identify the contents of the following directory listing:

   ```
   crw-rw----   1 millerm users 27,  18 Dec 17 16:10 zqft2
   -r--------   1 root    rwhite 19005 Dec 18 20:55 usage.out
   drw-rw---- 30 rwhite   admin   4096 Dec 18 21:37 routerconfig/
   lrwxrwxrwx   1 root    root      27 Dec  9 09:59 a.txt -> /tmp/a.txt
   prw-r--r--   1 tbantac tbantac    0 Dec  4 11:41 flicker
   brw-rw----   1 root    disk   13, 73 Dec 17 16:10 xdb9
   ```

   A. What is the name of the normal file?

   B. What is the name of the directory?

   C. What is the name of the symbolic link?

   D. What is the name of the block device?

   E. What is the name of the character device?

F. What is the name of the named pipe?

G. Which is owned by user **rwhite**?

H. Which is owned by group **rwhite**?

I. Which is readable only by user **root**?

J. Which can be read or written by the group "admin"?

7. What commands and options would you use to change the file README to be owned by user **rwhite** and group **rwhite**?

8. What command and options would you use to set that same README file to allow read/write access by its owning user and group, and readable by the rest of the world?

9. What command-line instruction would you use to locate all files named README in the **/usr** directory and its subdirectories?

10. How would you create a compressed archive file named **etc.tar.gz** in **/root** that preserves the contents of the **/etc** directory?

11. What command would you use to identify the program that runs when you type "top?"

12. How would you identify the disk usage on a system's local disks only?

13. What signal number is used to kill processes with extreme prejudice?

14. How would you find out what users are currently logged in to the system?

15. What key combination starts help in the **emacs** editor?

16. What command string starts help in the **vi** editor?

Module 7

File Systems

inux is built upon the foundation of *file systems*. They are the mechanisms by which the disk gets organized, providing all of the abstraction layers above sectors and cylinders. In this module, you'll learn about the composition and management of these abstraction layers supported by the default Linux file system, ext2, and its more robust counterpart, ext3.

This module covers the many aspects of managing disks. This includes creating partitions, establishing file systems, automating the process by which they are mounted at boot time, and dealing with them after a system crash. In addition to the basics, you'll grow acquainted with some of the more complex features of Linux, such as mounting network file systems, managing quotas, and the Autofs service.

NOTE

Before beginning your study of this module, you should already be familiar with files, directories, permissions, and owners in the Linux environment. If you haven't yet read Module 6, it's best to read that module before continuing.

CRITICAL SKILL
7.1 Understanding File Systems

Let's begin by going over the structure of file systems under Linux. It will help to clarify your understanding of the concept and let you see more easily how to take advantage of the architecture.

i-Nodes

The most fundamental building block of many UNIX file systems (including Linux's ext2/ext3) is the *i-node*. An i-node is a control structure that points either to other i-nodes or to data blocks.

The control information in the i-node includes the file's owner, permissions, size, time of last access, creation time, group ID, etc. (For the truly curious, the entire kernel data structure is available in **/usr/src/linux/include/linux/ext3_fs.h**—assuming, of course, that you have the source tree installed in the **/usr/src** directory.) The one thing an i-node *does not* keep is the file's name.

As mentioned in Module 6, directories themselves are special instances of files. This means each directory gets an i-node, and the i-node points to data blocks containing information (filenames and i-nodes) about the files in the directory. The i-nodes are used to provide *indirection* so that more data blocks can be pointed to—which is why each i-node does not contain the filename. (Only one i-node works as a representative for the entire file; thus it would be a waste of space if every i-node contained filename information.) Each indirect block can point in turn to other indirect blocks if necessary.

Superblocks

The very first piece of information read from a disk is its *superblock*. This small data structure reveals several key pieces of information, including the disk's geometry, the amount of available space, and, most important, the location of the first i-node. Without a superblock, a file system is useless.

Something as important as the superblock is not left to chance. Multiple copies of this data structure are scattered all over the disk to provide backup in case the first one is damaged. Under Linux's ext2 file system, a superblock is placed after every *group* of blocks, which contains i-nodes and data. One group consists of 8,192 blocks; thus the first redundant superblock is at 8193, the second at 16385, and so on.

ext3

The ext2 file system is a well-tested subsystem of Linux and has had the time to be very well optimized. However, other file systems that were considered experimental when ext2 was created have matured and become available to Linux.

There are four file systems one might consider to replace the aging ext2: ext3, ReiserFS, XFS, and JFS. All four of these file systems offer features that might be tempting in various circumstances, but the most important enhancement offered by all four is called *journaling*. Traditional file systems (such as ext2) must search through the directory structure, find the right place on disk to lay out the data, and then lay out the data. (Linux can also cache the whole process, including the directory updates, thereby making the process appear faster to the user.)

The problem with this method of doing things is that in the event of an unexpected crash, the **fsck** program has to go in and follow up on all of the files that are on the disk in order to make sure that they don't contain any dangling references (for example, i-nodes that point to other, invalid i-nodes or data blocks). As disks expand in size and shrink in price, the availability of these large capacity disks means more of us will have to deal with the aftermath of having to **fsck** a large disk. And as anyone who has had to do that before can tell you, it isn't fun. The process can take a long time to complete, and that means downtime for your users.

With journaling file systems, the new way of getting data out to disk, instead of finding the right place, the file system simply writes the data out in any order it can, as fast as it can. Each time, it logs the location of these data blocks. You can think of it as being like using the same spiral notebook for multiple classes without prepartitioning the notebook. It would be wiser to simply take notes for each class in chronological order instead of grouping all of one class together. A journaled file system is like such a notebook, with the beginning of the notebook containing an index telling you which pages contain all the notes for a single class. Once the data is written, the file system can go move things around to make them optimal for reading without risking the integrity of the file.

What this means to you as a system administrator is that the amount of time it takes for the disk to write out data is much less, while at the same time the safety of getting the data written out to disk quickly means that in the event of a system crash, you won't need to run **fsck** exhaustively. Even when you do run **fsck**, it only has to check recently modified data, so instead of interminable times, you'll find that the checks go very quickly.

So which of the four journaling systems should you choose? That call is entirely up to you. But the only one I'll talk about here is ext3, which is the default file system in Red Hat Linux 8.0.

Ask the Expert

Q: Is the ext3 file system the best option for my system?

A: I don't know.

Q: Thanks so much. Okay, how does ext3 compare to the other three journaling file systems you mentioned?

A: That's an easier question to answer. Because of its close compatibility with ext2, the ext3 file system lacks some of the features the other journaling file systems implemented because they didn't have to worry about backward compatibility.

For example, the largest file you can create in an ext3 file system is 2,048GB. That's mighty large, but if you expect to need something larger, you may want to consider any of the other three, which can handle files that are orders of magnitude larger. That is, they could do so if the Linux kernel supported file systems larger than 2,048GB, which is not the case with the kernel distributed with Red Hat Linux 8.0.

Q: Okay, that's more helpful. What are the relative strengths of the file systems?

A: Obviously, ext3 is great from the basis of compatibility. If you already have a Linux partition, you can add journaling functionality to it without pain. If you have a system that uses many small files, ReiserFS (see http://www.namesys.com/) may be just the ticket; it can fit more data onto a partition and handle it much faster than ext2/ext3. If you're looking for a super-high-capacity file system with very good performance, the XFS file system is your choice. Unfortunately, as I mentioned before, Linux won't immediately let you take advantage of the storage scale made possible by XFS (see http://oss.sgi.com/projects/xfs/). Your other option, JFS (see http://www-124.ibm.com/jfs/), is less quick with small files than ReiserFS and not as fast with large files as XFS, but it offers good all-around performance. Check out the resources I've mentioned here and see what sounds good to you.

Yes, I claimed earlier that ext2 was the default Linux file system, but when you install Red Hat you'll find that the partitions default to ext3 unless you set them to something different. And that's a good thing, for the reasons I just explained. Installing journaling file systems by default was one way Red Hat attempted to answer some of Linux's critics, who noted that other operating systems already had that capability.

CRITICAL SKILL
7.2 Managing File Systems

The process of managing file systems is trivial—that is, the management becomes trivial *after* you have memorized all aspects of your networked servers, disks, backups, and size requirements with the condition that they will never again have to change. In other words, managing file systems isn't trivial at all.

There aren't many technical issues involved in file systems. Once the systems have been created, deployed, and added to the backup cycle, they do tend to take care of themselves for the most part. What makes them tricky to manage are the administrative issues—such as users who refuse to do housekeeping on their disks, and cumbersome management policies dictating who can share what disk and under what condition, depending of course on the account under which the disk was purchased, and . . . (It sounds frighteningly like a *Dilbert* cartoon strip, but there is a good deal of truth behind that statement.)

Unfortunately, there's no cookbook solution available for dealing with office politics, so this section will stick to the technical issues involved in managing file systems—that is, the process of mounting and unmounting partitions, dealing with the **/etc/fstab** file, and performing file-system recovery with the **fsck** tool.

Mounting and Unmounting Local Disks

Linux's strong points include its flexibility and the way it lends itself to seamless management of file locations. Partitions are mounted so that they appear as just another subdirectory. Even a substantial number of file systems look, to the user, like one large directory tree. This characteristic is especially helpful to the administrator, who can relocate partitions to various servers but can have the partitions still mounted to the same location in the directory tree; users of the file system need not know about the move at all.

The file-system management process begins with the root directory (see Figure 7-1). The partition containing the kernel and core directory structure is mounted at boot time. This single partition needs to have all the required utilities and configuration files to bring the system up to single-user mode. Many of the directories on this partition are empty.

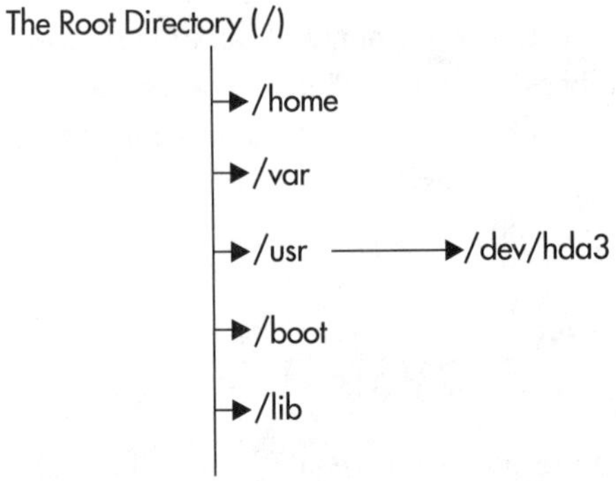

The Root Directory (/)

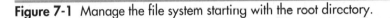

    ▶ /home

    ▶ /var

    ▶ /usr ⟶ ▶ /dev/hda3

    ▶ /boot

    ▶ /lib

Figure 7-1 Manage the file system starting with the root directory.

As the boot scripts run, additional partitions are mounted, adding to the structure of the file system. The mount process overlays a single subdirectory with the directory tree of the partition it is trying to mount. For example, let's say that **/dev/hda1** is the root partition. It has the directory **/usr,** which contains no files. The partition **/dev/hda3** contains all the files that you want in **/usr,** so you mount **/dev/hda3** to the directory **/usr**. Users can now simply change directories to **/usr** to see all the files from that partition. The user doesn't need to know that **/usr** is actually a separate partition.

Keep in mind that when a new directory is mounted, the **mount** process hides all the contents of the previously mounted directory. So in the **/usr** example, if the root partition did have files in /usr before mounting **/dev/hda3,** those **/usr** files would no longer be visible. (They're not erased, of course—once **/dev/hda3** is unmounted, the **/usr** files would become visible once again.)

Using the mount Command

Like many command-line tools, the **mount** command has myriad options, most of which you won't be using in daily work. You can get full details on these options from the **mount** man page. In this section, you'll explore the most common uses of the command.

The structure of the **mount** command is as follows:

```
mount [options] device directory
```

where **[options]** may be any of those shown in Table 7-1.

The **options** available for use with the **mount –o** parameter are shown in Table 7-2.

The following **mount** command mounts the **/dev/hda3** partition to the **/usr** directory with read-only privileges:

```
[root@tedford /root]# mount -o ro /dev/hda3 /usr
```

Unmounting File Systems

To unmount a file system, use the **umount** command. Here's the command format:

```
umount [-f] directory
```

where **directory** is the directory to be unmounted. For example:

```
[root@tedford /root]# umount /usr
```

unmounts the partition mounted on the **/usr** directory.

Option for mount	Description
–a	Mounts all the file systems listed in **/etc/fstab** (this file is examined later in this section).
–t *fstype*	Specifies the type of file system being mounted. Linux can mount file systems other than the ext2/ext3 standard, most notably FAT, VFAT, and FAT32. The **mount** command can usually sense this information on its own.
–o *options*	Specifies **options** applying to this **mount** process. These are usually options specific to the file system type (options for mounting network file systems may not apply to mounting local file systems).

Table 7-1 Common Options for the **mount** Command

Option for the mount –o Parameter (for Local Partitions)	Description
Ro	Mounts the partition as read-only.
Rw	Mounts the partition as read/write (default).
Exec	Permits the execution of binaries (default).
Noatime	Disables update of the access time on i-nodes. For partitions where the access time doesn't matter (such as news spools), this improves performance.
Noauto	Disables automatic mount of this partition when the –a option is specified (applies only to the /etc/fstab file).
Nosuid	Disallows application of **setuid** program bits to the mounted partition.
Remount	Remounts an already-mounted file system with the now-current settings. This is an alternative to unmounting and remounting a partition to update its settings (for example, changing the partition from read-only to read/write).
loop	The loopback option allows you to mount a file as if it was a device. For example, you could mount an ISO of a CD image without having to burn it to a CD-ROM.
sb=n	Tells **mount** to use block **n** as the superblock on an ext2/ext3 file system.

Table 7-2 Options for the **mount –o** Command

TIP

The command name is **umount**, with no "n." What it does is "unmount," but that's not its name.

When the File System Is in Use   There's a catch to **umount**: If the file system is in use (that is, when someone has a file open on that partition), you won't be able to unmount that file system. To get around this, you have three choices:

- You can use **lsof** or **fuser** to determine which processes are keeping the files open, and then kill them off or ask the process owners to stop what they're doing. (Read about the **kill** parameter in **fuser** on the **fuser** man page.) If you choose to kill the processes, be sure you understand the repercussions of doing so (read: don't get fired for doing this).

GUI Mounting

Users can make use of the Disk Management tool from one of the Red Hat desktop environments to mount and unmount certain devices. If you're working with CD-ROM or floppy drives within the GUI, you can select the System Tools option from the Red Hat menu and start Disk Management. As you can see from the illustration, its very simple interface won't allow you to mount or unmount the system partitions you're dealing with in this module, but it's a straightforward way to (for example) swap CDs. Just click the mount button to mount a disc, and click the unmount button to unmount it.

- You can use the –f option with **umount** to force the unmount process. Any processes with open files on the partition will be left hanging, and data may be lost.

- The safest and most proper alternative is to bring the system down to single-user mode and then unmount the file system. In reality, of course, you don't always get this luxury.

The /etc/fstab File

As mentioned earlier, **/etc/fstab** is a configuration file that **mount** can use. This file contains a list of all partitions known to the system. During the boot process, this list is read and the items in it are automatically mounted.

Here's the format of entries in the **/etc/fstab** file:

```
/dev/device /dir/to/mount      fstype    parameters    fs_freq
fs_passno
```

Table 7-3 defines each element in an **/etc/fstab** entry.

Here is a sample **/etc/fstab** file:

```
/dev/hda2           /              ext3    defaults      1 1
/dev/hda8           /home          ext3    defaults      1 2
/dev/hda7           /tmp           ext3    defaults      1 2
/dev/hda5           /usr           ext3    defaults      1 2
/dev/hda6           /var           ext3    defaults      1 2
/dev/hda1           /usr/local     ext3    defaults      1 2
/dev/hda3           swap           swap    defaults      0 0
```

```
/dev/fd0          /mnt/floppy       ext3      noauto          0 0
/dev/cdrom        /mnt/cdrom        iso9660   noauto,ro       0 0
/dev/hdc          /mnt/cdrom2       iso9660   noauto,ro       0 0
none              /proc             proc      defaults        0 0
none              /dev/pts          devpts    mode=0622       0 0
```

Let's take a look at a few details of **/etc/fstab** that haven't been mentioned yet, most notably the entry of **swap** for **/dev/hda3**, and the **none** for **/proc** and **/dev/pts**. In general, you'll never have to touch these file systems once the system is installed, so don't worry about them.

- The **/dev/hda3** partition is where virtual memory resides. Unlike in Microsoft Windows and similar systems, in Linux the virtual memory can be kept on a separate partition from the root partition. This is done to improve performance, since the swap partition can obey rules different than a normal file system. Since the partition doesn't need to be backed up or checked with **fsck** at boot time, the last two parameters on it are zeroed out. (Note that a swap partition can be kept in a normal disk file, as well. See the man page on **mkswap** for additional information.)

- The **none** entry in conjunction with **/proc** is for the **/proc** file system. This is a special file system that provides an interface to kernel parameters through what looks like any other file system. Although it appears to exist on disk, it really doesn't—all the files represent something that is in the kernel. Most notable is **/dev/kcore**, which is the system memory abstracted as a file. People new to the **/proc** file system often mistake this for a large unnecessary file and accidentally remove it, which will cause the system to malfunction in many glorious ways. Unless you are sure you know what you are doing, it's a safe bet to leave all the files in **/proc** alone.

- The last entry in a **/etc/fstab** file, **/dev/pts**, is for a new mechanism to improve implementation for network terminal support (**ptys**). This entry is necessary if you intend to allow remote login to your host via **rsh, telnet, rlogin,** or **ssh.**

/etc/fstab File Entry	Definition
/dev/device	Indicates the partition to be mounted (e.g., **/dev/hda3**).
/dir/to/mount	Designates the directory on which to mount the partition (e.g., **/usr**).
Fstype	Specifies the type of file system (e.g., ext3).
parameters	Indicates the parameters to be supplied in the **-o** option of the **mount** command.
Fs_freq	Tells the **dump** command how often the file system needs to be backed up.
Fs_passno	Tells the **fsck** program at boot time to determine the order in which the file systems should be checked. (Note that all file systems are checked before they are mounted.)

Table 7-3 Contents of an **/etc/fstab** Entry

TIP

When mounting partitions with the **/etc/fstab** configured, you can run the **mount** command with only one parameter: the directory you wish to mount to. The **mount** command checks **/etc/fstab** for that directory; if found, **mount** will use all parameters that have already been established there. For example, here's the command to mount a CD-ROM given the **/etc/fstab** shown earlier:

```
[root@tedford /root]# mount /mnt/cdrom
```

Using fsck

The **fsck** tool, short for **F**ile **S**ystem **C**hec**K**, is used to diagnose and repair file systems that may have become damaged in the course of daily operations. Such repairs are usually necessary after a system crash in which the system did not get a chance to fully flush all of its internal buffers to disk. (Although this tool's name bears a striking resemblance to one of the expressions often uttered after a system crash, that this tool is part of the recovery process is *strictly* coincidence.)

Usually, the system runs the **fsck** tool automatically during the boot process (much in the same way Windows runs Scandisk) if it detects a partition that was not cleanly unmounted. Linux makes an impressive effort to automatically repair any problems it runs across and in most instances does take care of itself. The robust nature of the ext3 file system helps in such situations. Nevertheless, it may happen that you get this message:

```
Your system appears to have shut down uncleanly
Press Y within 5 seconds to force file system integrity check
```

If you press Y, you'll see messages appear on the screen telling you how the check is proceeding. The system will tell you what file system is being checked and how far the check has progressed. You may see messages such as these:

```
recovering journal
clearing orphaned inode
```

These messages are normal; **fsck** is just doing its thing.

If you find that a file system is not behaving as it should (log messages are excellent hints to this situation), you may want to run **fsck** yourself on a running system. The only downside is that the file system in question must be unmounted in order for this to work. If you choose to take this path, be sure to remount the file system when you are done.

NOTE

The name **fsck** isn't the proper title for the ext2/ext3 repair tool; it's actually just a wrapper. The **fsck** wrapper tries to determine what kind of file system needs to be repaired and then runs the appropriate repair tool, passing any parameters that were passed to **fsck**. In ext2 and ext3, the real tool is called **e2fsck**. When a system crash occurs, you may need to call **e2fsck** directly rather than relying on other applications to call it for you automatically.

Parameters Available for e2fsck

The parameters available for **e2fsck** are shown in Table 7-4.

For example, to run **e2fsck** on the /dev/hda3 file system, you would run:

```
[root@tedford /root]# e2fsck /dev/hda3
```

To force a check and automatically answer Yes to any prompts that come up, you would enter this command:

```
[root@tedford]# e2fsck -f -y /dev/hda3
```

TIP

You won't find an "e3fsck" command. The ext2 and ext3 file systems are so similar that the **e2fsck** command works on both of them.

Parameter for e2fsck	Description
-b *superblock*	Specifies the superblock number from which **e2fsck** should read partition information. In most instances, **e2fsck** is able to find it at block 1, but if that block becomes corrupted, you'll need to specify an alternative number. Superblocks occur at every 8,192 blocks, so the next superblock is at 8,193, then 16,385, and so on.
-c	Runs the **badblocks** program on the disk before running **e2fsck**. This searches the entire disk block-by-block and verifies the block's integrity. This is a very thorough way of checking a disk, but it is *extremely* time consuming.
-j *journal*	Sets the location of the external journal file, which is ordinarily hidden to avoid deletion and backup, which don't make sense for its contents.
-f	Forces a check to run even if it thinks the file system is already clean.
-y	Tells **e2fsck** to automatically assume that all prompts from **e2fsck** are to be answered Yes.

Table 7-4 Options for the **e2fsck** Command

What If I Get Errors?

First, relax. The **fsck** check rarely finds problems that it cannot correct by itself. When it does ask for human intervention, telling **fsck** to execute its default suggestion is often enough. Very rarely does a single pass of **e2fsck** not clear up all problems.

On the rare occasions when a second run is needed, it *should not* turn up any more errors. If it does, you are most likely facing a hardware failure. Remember to start with the obvious: Check for reliable power and well-connected cables. Anyone running SCSI systems should verify that they're using the correct type of terminator, that cables aren't too long, that SCSI IDs aren't conflicting, and that cable quality is adequate. (SCSI is especially fussy about the quality of the cables.)

The lost+found Directory

Another rare situation is when **e2fsck** finds segments of files that it cannot rejoin with the original file. In those cases, it will place the fragment in the partition's **lost+found** directory. This directory is located where the partition is mounted, so if **/dev/hda3** is mounted on **/usr,** then **/usr/lost+found** correlates to **/dev/hda3.**

Anything can go into a **lost+found** directory—file fragments, directories, and even special files. When normal files wind up there, a file owner should be attached, and you can contact the owner and see if they need the data (typically, they won't). If you encounter a directory in **lost+found**, you'll most likely want to try to restore it from the most recent backups rather than trying to reconstruct it from **lost+found**.

At the very least, **lost+found** tells you if anything became dislocated. Again, such errors are extraordinarily rare.

CRITICAL SKILL

7.3 Adding and Partitioning a Disk

The process of adding a disk under Linux on the Intel (x86) platform is relatively easy. Assuming you are adding a disk that is of similar type to your existing disks (e.g., adding an IDE disk to a system that already has IDE drives or adding a SCSI disk to a system that already has SCSI drives), the system should automatically detect the new disk at boot time, and all that is left is partitioning it and creating a file system on it.

If you are adding a new type of disk (like a SCSI disk on a system that has only IDE drives), you may need to compile in support for your SCSI card to the kernel. (Note that most Linux distributions come with support for many popular SCSI cards as part of the standard installation. If you didn't recompile the kernel from the original installation, it is unlikely that you will need to recompile the kernel to add support.) To compile in support for a new type of disk, see Module 9. Be sure to step through all of the relevant menus and mark the appropriate driver to be compiled either into the base kernel or as a module (assuming it can be compiled as a module).

Once the disk is in place, simply boot the system and you're ready to go. If you aren't sure about whether the system can see the new disk, run the **dmesg** command and see whether the driver loaded and was able to find your disk. For example:

```
[root@tedford /root]# dmesg | more
```

Overview of Partitions

For the sake of clarity, and in case you need to know what a partition is and how it works, let's do a brief review of this subject. Every disk must be *partitioned. Partitions* divide up the disk, and each segment acts as a complete disk by itself. Once a partition is filled, it cannot (without special software) automatically overflow onto another partition. Usually, the process of partitioning a disk accomplishes one of two goals: Either the user needs two different operating systems installed and each operating system requires its own partition, or it may be prudent that the usage of space on one partition not interfere with space dedicated to other tasks on other partitions.

An example of the latter occurs in user home directories. When users of the system are not the administrators of the system, the administrator must ensure that users don't consume the entire disk for their personal files. This takes up room needed for logging purposes and temporary files, causing the system to misbehave. To prevent this, a special partition is created for user files so that they don't overflow into protected system space.

NOTE

It is acceptable to partition a disk so that only one large partition is taking up the entire disk. But beware: If this is the boot partition, the entire partition must fit within the 1024 cylinder boundary, or you may not be able to boot. See Module 8 for more information.

Where Disks Exist

Under Linux, each disk is given its own device name. IDE disks start with the name **/dev/hd***X*, where *X* can range from *a* through *z*, with each letter representing a physical device. For example, in an IDE-only system with one hard disk and one CD-ROM, both on the same IDE chain, the hard disk would be **/dev/hda**, and the CD-ROM would be **/dev/hdb**. Disk devices are automatically created during system installation.

When partitions are created, new devices are used. They take the form of **/dev/hd***XY*, where *X* is the device letter (as just described), and *Y* is the partition number. Thus, the first partition on the **/dev/hda** disk is **/dev/hda1**, the second partition would be **/dev/hda2**, and so on.

SCSI disks follow the same basic scheme as IDE, except instead of starting with **/dev/hd**, they start with **/dev/sd**. Therefore, the first partition on the first SCSI disk would be **/dev/sda1**, the second partition on the third SCSI disk would be **/dev/sdc2**, and so on.

Creating Partitions

CAUTION

The process of creating partitions is irrevocably destructive to the data already on the disk. Before creating, changing, or removing partitions on any disk, you must be very sure of what's on the disk being modified, and you need to have a backup if that data is still needed.

During the installation process, you probably used a "pretty" tool to create partitions. Unfortunately, Linux platforms don't ship with a standard utility for creating and managing partitions. A basic mechanism that does exist on all Linux distributions is **fdisk**. Though it's small and somewhat awkward, it's a reliable partitioning tool. Furthermore, in the event you need to troubleshoot a system that has gone really wrong, you should be familiar with basics such as **fdisk**. The only real downside to **fdisk** is its lack of a user interface.

For this sample run, assume that you want to partition the **/dev/hdb** device, a 340MB IDE hard disk. (Yes, they do still exist.) You begin by running **fdisk** with the **/dev/hdb** parameter:

```
[root@tedford /root]# fdisk /dev/hdb
```

which outputs a simple prompt:

```
Command (m for help):
```

Let's use **m** to see what your options are. This menu is reasonably self-explanatory:

```
Command (m for help): m
Command action
   a   toggle a bootable flag
   b   edit bsd disklabel
   c   toggle the dos compatibility flag
   d   delete a partition
   l   list known partition types
   m   print this menu
   n   add a new partition
   o   create a new empty DOS partition table
   p   print the partition table
   q   quit without saving changes
   s   create a new empty Sun disklabel
   t   change a partition's system id
   u   change display/entry units
   v   verify the partition table
   w   write table to disk and exit
   x   extra functionality (experts only)
Command (m for help):
```

You begin by looking at the existing partition, using the **p** command (print the partition table):

```
Command (m for help): p
Disk /dev/hdb: 16 heads, 63 sectors, 665 cylinders
Units = cylinders of 1008 * 512 bytes
   Device Boot    Start      End    Blocks   Id  System
/dev/hdb1    *        1      664   334624+    6  FAT16
Command (m for help):
```

You have a little legacy system here, don't you think? Time to upgrade this disk—start by removing the existing partition using the **d** command (delete a partition):

```
Command (m for help): d
Partition number (1-4): 1
Command (m for help):
```

And use the **p** (print the partition table) command to verify the results:

```
Command (m for help): p
Disk /dev/hdb: 16 heads, 63 sectors, 665 cylinders
Units = cylinders of 1008 * 512 bytes
   Device Boot    Start      End    Blocks   Id  System
Command (m for help):
```

No partition there. Time to start creating partitions. For the sake of discussion, pretend this disk is large enough to accommodate a full workstation configuration. To set this up, you need to create the partitions shown in Table 7-5.

So now that you know which partitions to create, let's do it! Start with the root partition. Given that you have only 340MB to work with, keep root small—only 35MB.

```
Command (m for help): n
Command action
   e   extended
   p   primary partition (1-4)
p
Partition number (1-4): 1
First cylinder (1-665, default 1): 1
Last cylinder or +size or +sizeM or +sizeK (1-665, default 665): +35M
Command (m for help):
```

Notice the first prompt is for whether you want a primary or extended partition. This is because of a goofy mess created long ago (pre-Linux) when hard disks were so small that no one thought more than four partitions would ever be needed. When disks got bigger and backward-compatibility was an issue, we needed a trick to accommodate more partitions.

Partition	Description
/	The root partition is for those core system files necessary to bring a system to single-user mode. Once established, the partition's contents shouldn't vary at all and definitely shouldn't need to grow. The intent is to isolate this file system from other file systems, to prevent interference with core operations.
/usr	This partition is used for system software such as user tools, compilers, X, and so forth. Because you may one day need to find a bigger home for your system software, you put this in a separate partition.
/var	The /var partition is used to hold files that change a lot—this usually includes spool directories (mail, print, etc.) and log files. What makes this partition worrisome is that external events can make its contents grow beyond allocated space. Log files from a web server, for instance, can grow quickly and beyond your control. To keep these files from spilling over into the rest of your system, it's wise to keep this partition separate. (A type of attack via the network can be mounted by artificially generating so much activity on your server that the disk fills up with system logs and the system behaves unreliably.)
/tmp	Similar to /var, files in /tmp can unexpectedly consume substantial space. This can occur when users leave files unattended or application programs create large temporary files. Either way, maintaining this partition is a good safety mechanism.
/home	If you need to store home directories on your disk, especially for users whose disk consumption needs to be restricted, you'll definitely want to have this separate partition.
swap	The swap partition is necessary to hold virtual memory. Although it isn't required, swap is often a good idea in case you do exhaust all your physical RAM. In general, you'll want this partition to be the same size as your RAM.

Table 7-5 Partition Descriptions and Configuration

The last partition would be an "extended" partition, unseen by the user but able to contain additional partitions.

The next question: Which partition number? (You can see the limit of four primary partitions as part of the question.) You start with one, picking the default starting cylinder, and then specify that you want 25MB allocated to it.

To create the second partition for swap, type the following:

```
Command (m for help): n
Command action
   e   extended
   p   primary partition (1-4)
p
Partition number (1-4): 2
First cylinder (68-665, default 68): 68
Last cylinder or +size or +sizeM or +sizeK (52-665, default 665): +16M
Command (m for help):
```

This time, the prompts are identical to those used for the previous partition, with slightly different numbers. However, by default, **fdisk** is creating ext2 partitions. You need this partition to be of type **swap**. To do this, use the **t** (change partition type) command:

```
Command (m for help): t
Partition number (1-4): 2
Hex code (type L to list codes): L
 0   Empty              16  Hidden FAT16      61  SpeedStor        a6  OpenBSD
 1   FAT12              17  Hidden HPFS/NTF   63  GNU HURD or Sys  a7  NeXTSTEP
 2   XENIX root         18  AST Windows swa   64  Novell Netware   b7  BSDI fs
 3   XENIX usr          24  NEC DOS           65  Novell Netware   b8  BSDI swap
 4   FAT16 <32 <N       3c  PartitionMagic    70  DiskSecure Mult  c1  DRDOS/secFAT-
 5   Extended           40  Venix 80286       75  PC/IX            c4  DRDOS/secFAT-
 6   FAT16              41  PPC PReP Boot      80  Old Minix        c6  DRDOS/secFAT-
 7   HPFS/NTFS          42  SFS                81  Minix / old Lin  c7  Syrinx
 8   AIX                4d  QNX4.x             82  Linux swap       db  CP/M / CTOS .
 9   AIX bootable       4e  QNX4.x 2nd part    83  Linux            e1  DOS access
 a   OS/2 Boot Manag    4f  QNX4.x 3rd part    84  OS/2 hidden C:   e3  DOS R/O
 b   Win95 FAT32        50  OnTrack DM         85  Linux extended   e4  SpeedStor
 c   Win95 FAT32 (LB    51  OnTrack DM6 Aux    86  NTFS volume set  eb  BeOS fs
 e   Win95 FAT16 (LB    52  CP/M               87  NTFS volume set  f1  SpeedStor
 f   Win95 Ext'd (LB    53  OnTrack DM6 Aux    93  Amoeba           f4  SpeedStor
10   OPUS               54  OnTrackDM6         94  Amoeba BBT       f2  DOS secondary
11   Hidden FAT12       55  EZ-Drive          a0  IBM Thinkpad hi  fe  LANstep
12   Compaq diagnost    56  Golden Bow        a5  BSD/386          ff  BBT
14   Hidden FAT16       5c  Priam Edisk
Hex code (type L to list codes): 82
Changed system type of partition 2 to 82 (Linux swap)
Command (m for help):
```

The first question is, of course, what partition number do you want to change to? Since you want the second partition to be the swap, you entered **2**. The next prompt is a bit more cryptic: the hexadecimal code for the correct partition. Since people don't remember hex codes very well, the **L** command lists all available partition types. You spot 82 for Linux Swap, so enter that, and you're done.

NOTE

It used to be that Linux's swap partition was limited to 128M. This is no longer the case. You can create a single swap partition as large as 2GB. You can create multiple swap partitions if you like.

Now to create **/usr**. Make it 100MB in size:

```
Command (m for help): n
Command action
   e    extended
   p    primary partition (1-4)
p
Partition number (1-4): 3
First cylinder (85-665, default 85): 85
Last cylinder or +size or +sizeM or +sizeK (85-665, default 665): +100M
Command (m for help):
```

So at this point, you have three partitions: **root**, **swap**, and **/usr**. You can see them by entering the **p** command:

```
Command (m for help): p
Disk /dev/hdb: 16 heads, 63 sectors, 665 cylinders
Units = cylinders of 1008 * 512 bytes
   Device Boot    Start        End      Blocks   Id  System
/dev/hdb1              1         51       25672+  83  Linux
/dev/hdb2             52         84       16632   82  Linux swap
/dev/hdb3             85        288      102816   83  Linux
Command (m for help):
```

Now you need to create the extended partition to accommodate **/tmp**, **/var**, and **/home**. Do so using the **n** command, just as for any other new partition:

```
Command (m for help): n
Command action
   e    extended
   p    primary partition (1-4)
e
Partition number (1-4): 4
First cylinder (289-665, default 289): 289
Last cylinder or +size or +sizeM or +sizeK (289-665, default 665): 665
Command (m for help):
```

Instead of designating a megabyte value for the size of this partition, you enter the last cylinder number, thus taking up the remainder of the disk. Let's see what this looks like:

```
Command (m for help): p
Disk /dev/hdb: 16 heads, 63 sectors, 665 cylinders
Units = cylinders of 1008 * 512 bytes
   Device Boot    Start        End      Blocks   Id  System
/dev/hdb1              1         51       25672+  83  Linux
/dev/hdb2             52         84       16632   82  Linux swap
/dev/hdb3             85        288      102816   83  Linux
/dev/hdb4            289        665      190008    5  Extended
Command (m for help):
```

Now you're ready to create the last three partitions:

```
Command (m for help): n
First cylinder (289-665, default 289): 289
Last cylinder or +size or +sizeM or +sizeK (289-665, default 665): +100M
Command (m for help): n
First cylinder (493-665, default 493): 493
Last cylinder or +size or +sizeM or +sizeK (493-665, default 665): +45M
Command (m for help): n
First cylinder (585-665, default 585): 585
Last cylinder or +size or +sizeM or +sizeK (585-665, default 665): 665
Command (m for help):
```

Note that for the very last partition, you again specified the last cylinder instead of a megabyte value, so that you are sure that you have allocated the entire disk. One last **p** command shows you what your partitions now look like:

```
Command (m for help): p
Disk /dev/hdb: 16 heads, 63 sectors, 665 cylinders
Units = cylinders of 1008 * 512 bytes
   Device Boot    Start       End    Blocks   Id  System
/dev/hdb1             1        51     25672+  83  Linux
/dev/hdb2            52        84     16632   82  Linux swap
/dev/hdb3            85       288    102816   83  Linux
/dev/hdb4           289       665    190008    5  Extended
/dev/hdb5           289       492    102784+  83  Linux
/dev/hdb6           493       584     46336+  83  Linux
/dev/hdb7           585       665     40792+  83  Linux
Command (m for help):
```

Perfect. Commit the changes to disk and quit the **fdisk** utility by using the **w** (write table to disk and exit) command:

```
Command (m for help): w
The partition table has been altered!
Calling ioctl() to re-read partition table.
Syncing disks.
WARNING: If you have created or modified any DOS 6.x
partitions, please see the fdisk manual page for additional
information.
[root@tedford /root]#
```

If you needed to write an **/etc/fstab** file yourself for this configuration, it would look something like this:

```
/dev/hdb1          /           ext3      defaults   1 1
/dev/hdb2          swap        swap      defaults   0 0
/dev/hdb3          /usr        ext3      defaults   1 2
/dev/hdb5          /home       ext3      defaults   1 2
/dev/hdb6          /var        ext3      defaults   1 2
/dev/hdb7          /tmp        ext3      defaults   1 2
none               /proc       proc      defaults   0 0
none               /dev/pts    devpts    mode=0622  0 0
```

Making File Systems

With the partitions created, you need to put file systems on them. (If you're accustomed to Microsoft Windows, this is akin to formatting the disk once you've partitioned it.)

Under Linux, you use two tools for this process: **mke2fs** to create ext3 file systems, and **mkswap** to create swap file systems. There are many command-line parameters available for the **mke2fs** tool, many of which are needed only if you have an unusual situation. And if you have such an unusual need, I'm confident you don't need this text for guidance on creating file systems!

The only command-line parameter you'll usually have to set is the partition onto which the file system should go. To create a file system on the **/dev/hdb3** partition, you would issue the command

```
[root@tedford /root]# mke2fs -j /dev/hdb3
```

The **-j** parameter tells **mke2fs** that you want to set the file system up with a journal file; in other words, that this is an ext3 partition rather than an ext2 partition. Omit the **-j**, and you'll create an ext2 partition instead.

NOTE

To convert the ext2 file system to an ext3 file system, run the command **tune2fs -j /dev/hdb3** (of course, substituting your partition name for **/dev/hdb3**). To convert an ext3 file system to ext2, edit the **/etc/fstab** file so that the partition is listed as ext2, then unmount the partition and mount it again.

Setting up swap space with the **mkswap** command is equally straightforward. The only parameter needed is the partition onto which the swap space will be created. To create swap space on **/dev/hdb2**, you would use

```
[root@tedford /root]# mkswap /dev/hdb2
```

Project 7-1 To Journal, or Not to Journal?

In this project, you'll be taking your very fine, very stable Linux system, and monkeying shamelessly with it. You'll convert a partition from the default ext3 file system to the nonjournaling ext2 file system, and then convert it back. Do this on a test server that nobody else is using. You shouldn't lose any data, but there's no sense in taking any risks.

Step by Step

Exit the GUI on your Red Hat Linux 8.0 system and become the root user at a console prompt.

1. Look at the contents of your **/etc/fstab** file, and on a piece of paper, note the name of the partition on which **/home** is mounted. If you make a mistake in the text editor, you can restore the setting from your note.

2. Make sure nobody else is using the partition you plan to modify by running the **fuser -v /home/*** command.

3. Edit the **/etc/fstab** file and convert the file system type entry on the /home configuration line from **ext3** to **ext2**. Save the file. It wouldn't hurt to check again to see whether any users have snuck back on the system.

4. Unmount the file system on **/home** using the **umount** command.

5. Mount the file system on **/home** using the **mount** command.

6. You now have an ext2 file system instead of an ext3 file system. Try remounting the **/home** file system read-only and forcing an **fsck** to see how long the process takes.

7. Edit the **/etc/fstab** file again to set **ext2** back to **ext3**.

8. Just telling the system that **/home** should have an ext3 file system isn't enough; you must create a journal file for the file system. Use the **tune2fs -j** *home_part* command, where *home_part* is the device name of the partition you wrote down in step 2.

9. Check again for interloping users, and then remount the **/home** file system. You now have an ext3 file system again. Amuse yourself further, if you wish, by remounting the file system read-only and seeing what happens if you force an **fsck** on it.

Project Summary

The answer to the question is an unequivocal "journal." Your life will be much better, the sky will be much brighter, and your systems will run much better if you use ext3 than if you use ext2. However, the process of migrating between the two file systems isn't difficult, and it should give you an idea of what's involved in working with file systems in general.

CRITICAL SKILL

7.4 Using Network File Systems

Network file systems make it possible for you to dedicate systems to serving disks while letting clients handle the compute-intensive tasks of users. Centralized disks mean easier backup solutions and ready physical security. Under Linux (and UNIX as a whole), disk centralization is accomplished through the Network File System (NFS). In this section, you'll learn about client-side issues of NFS, leaving the server-side issues until later in this book (Module 16).

Mounting NFS Partitions

Mounting NFS partitions works much the same way as mounting local partitions. The only difference is in how the partition is addressed. On local disks, partitions are addressed by their device name, such as **/dev/hda1**. In NFS mounts, partitions are referenced by their hostnames and export directories. Thus, if the server named ungerer is allowing your host to mount the directory **/export/SL1200/MK2** and you want to mount this to **/projects/topsecret1**, you would use this command:

```
[root@tedford /root]# mount ungerer:/export/SL1200/MK2
/projects/topsecret1
```

As you can see, it's not necessary for your local directory to have the same name as the server's directory.

With NFS come some additional options you can use in conjunction with the **mount** command's **-o** option, as shown in Table 7-6.

Here's an example of an NFS mount in the **/etc/fstab** file:

```
denon:/export/DN2000F  /proj/DN2k nfs bg,intr,hard,wsize=8192,rsize=8192 0 0
```

Option for the mount –o Parameter (for NFS Partitions)	Description
soft	"Soft mounts" the partition. If the server fails, the client will time out after a designated interval and cause the requested operation to fail.
hard	"Hard mounts" the partition. The client will wait as long as it takes for the server to come back after a failure. If the server comes up, no data will be lost.
timeo=n	Sets the time-out value to be **n** seconds.

Table 7-6 Options for the **mount –o** Parameter for NFS Partitions

Option for the mount –o Parameter (for NFS Partitions)	Description
wsize=*n*	Sets the write buffer size to **n** bytes. Default is 1024; recommended value is 8192.
rsize=*n*	Sets the read buffer size to **n** bytes. Default is 1024; recommended value is 8192.
bg	Backgrounds the mount. If the mount does not initially work, lets the mount process go into the background and keep trying. If you are placing any NFS mount points in an **/etc/fstab** file, you should definitely include this option.

Table 7-6 Options for the **mount –o** Parameter for NFS Partitions *(continued)*

Using the autofs Service

As your site grows, you'll find that maintaining mount tables becomes increasingly complicated. You may find it appropriate to standardize on a particular set of NFS mounts for all systems to save yourself some work, but this has the side effect of wasting system resources for both the client and server.

To combat this problem, you can use the *autofs service,* also known as the *automounter.* As its name implies, it automatically mounts file systems as they are needed. When it is used in conjunction with NIS (see Module 17), you can produce a centralized set of maps that apply to your entire site, deploying the autofs service to mount only those partitions needed by users at the time they are needed.

A good example of this is home directories. Say that for a variety of technical reasons, my company currently needs to allow everyone in engineering to put their home directories on their local systems rather than having them all reside on a central server. However, we want to allow anyone to be able to log in to anyone else's system and have their home directory available to them. If we were to use **/etc/fstab** for this, every new person in engineering would require a lot of people to get their /etc/fstabs updated, which is bound to be an error-prone task. Even worse, having to mount several dozen home directories every time would be a waste of resources, especially if other engineers are not logging in to other people's machines all the time.

By using the autofs service in conjunction with NIS, I can maintain a very simple **/etc/fstab** on each host and run the autofs daemon. When someone logs in to the system, the login program will try to access her home directory. The autofs service will intercept this request, go look up where that user's home directory is located, mount it, and then let the login process continue. The process happens so quickly the user doesn't realize that her home directory was just dynamically mounted for her. Once the user logs off, autofs will notice that there hasn't been any activity on that partition for a while and automatically unmount it. Neat, huh?

And of course, conveniently, all popular distributions of Linux are currently shipping with the autofs subsystem already set up, ready to accept your configuration files.

The Slightly Bigger Picture

Let's begin by taking a closer look at the steps taken by the autofs service so that you better understand how it works.

When autofs starts, it looks for a file called **/etc/auto.master**. This file tells it what *maps* it will need to read for what directory. For example, the **auto.master** file might contain an entry that looks like this:

```
/home            auto.home
```

This tells autofs that for any directory accessed in the **/home** directory, it should consult the **/etc/auto.home** file to find out what partition it should mount.

The **auto.home** file is called a *mapfile*. Mapfiles in this context are simply text files that map user's names to the location of their home directories. The first column of the file contains the *key,* which is simply the user's login. This value is what is used to search the mapfile.

```
rwhite           orb:/export/home/rwhite
```

In this example, rwhite is the key.

Combining the two files together (**auto.master** and **auto.home**), the autofs service will do the following when someone tries to access the directory **/home/rwhite**:

1. Check if **/home/rwhite** is already mounted.

2. If not, create the directory **/home/rwhite**.

3. Mount **orb:/export/home/rwhite** to **/home/rwhite**.

Don't worry if it takes you a few minutes to wrap your head around this concept—it isn't terribly intuitive. But once you get it and see why this feature is useful, you'll wonder how you ever managed a network without it.

Starting the autofs Service

Because the way you're using autofs to mount partitions across the network relies on NFS, before using it you'll need to be sure you can do normal NFS mounts. Once you have this working, just make a simple change to your startup scripts to deploy the autofs service. The easiest way to do this is to run the **redhat-config-services** utility to enable the daemon. Simply start the configuration tool and mark the **autofs** check box as shown.

If you need to start autofs by hand, run this command:

```
[root@tedford /root]# service autofs start
```

Use this same command to stop the autofs daemon, by changing the **start** option to **stop**. You can also update the configuration files and have the daemon reread them by replacing the **start** option to **reread**.

Configuring /etc/auto.master

The autofs service's primary configuration file is **/etc/auto.master**. The format of this file is as follows:

```
#
# Sample /etc/auto.master file
# (lines which begin with a '#' are comments)
#
/mount/point        map-file        global options
/home               auto.home
/usr/local          auto.local
/misc               auto.misc
```

The first column tells you the mount point; the second column lists the files containing details about the mapping for that mount point; and the last column contains any NFS options you want to apply to all mounts.

The map files look a little different from the **auto.master** file. For example, here's the **auto.misc** file:

```
#
# auto.misc
#
# This is an automounter map and it has the following format
```

```
# key [ -mount-options-separated-by-comma ] location
# Details may be found in the autofs(5) manpage
kernel          -ro,soft,intr            ftp.kernel.org:/pub/linux
cd              -fstype=iso9660,ro        :/dev/cdrom
# the following entries are samples to pique your imagination
#floppy         -fstype=auto              :/dev/fd0
#floppy         -fstype=ext2              :/dev/fd0
#e2floppy       -fstype=ext2              :/dev/fd0
#jaz            -fstype=ext2              :/dev/sdc1
```

Here, the first column is the key, the second column holds the **mount** options, and the last column is the location from which to mount. If the location entry begins with a colon, it's a signal to the system that the mount is local. Thus, **/misc/cd** would mount **/dev/cdrom** with the following **mount** options:

```
-fstype=iso9660,ro
```

NOTE

Unlike NFS, which requires that the directory already exist in order for you to mount it, the autofs service does not. In the case of the **/misc** mount point, all that needs to exist is the **/misc** directory. All subdirectories would be created by the autofs daemon as needed.

If you change any of the map files while autofs is running, you'll need to restart the autofs service so that it can reread the configuration files. This is done by using autofs as follows:

```
[root@tedford /root]# /etc/init.d/autofs reload
```

CRITICAL SKILL

7.5 Managing Quotas

In any multiuser environment, you're bound to run across users who—either refusing to play fair or because they're oblivious to common courtesy—practice the fine art of disk hogging, taking up more than a reasonable amount of disk space.

This problem can be managed in several ways. The first and most obvious solution is to beg and plead. This rarely works. The second approach is peer pressure: You regularly and publicly post the amounts of disk space being hogged by these users. If people are at all sensitive to what others think of them, this may work. The final and most successful technique is to institute *disk quotas,* allowing each user to consume a certain amount of disk space and no more. Enforcement is done by the operating system.

Disk quotas are usually the best option for system administrators, because the quotas are automated and don't require that you confront the offending users. However, technical and/or political barriers may be standing in the way of using them. (For instance, the CEO may not like being told she can use only 5MB of the server disk space.) Quotas are, of course, optional—your system will be quite happy to hum along without them. Whether they will work in your environment is up to you and your management.

Preparing a Disk for Quotas

Preparing to use disk quotas works in two steps. Step 1 is to make the necessary settings in the **/etc/fstab** file and add the necessary files in each partition for which you want quota control. Step 1 must be repeated for every partition you want under quota control. Step 2 is to run the **quotacheck** command to set up the quotas on each of the partitions you've configured.

Configuring Individual Partitions

Disk quotas work on either a per-user or per-group basis, with each partition allowing for their own quotas. For example, it's possible for all users to have a quota associated with their home directories on one partition and another quota on another partition for a group project they're part of.

For each partition on which you want a quota, you'll need to set up the **usrquota** option and the **grpquota** option, and then remount the partition.

The usrquota Option   Edit the **/etc/fstab** file so that, for each partition needing quotas, the **mount** options contain the **usrquota** option. For example, if **/dev/hda5** is mounted to the **/home** directory and you want that directory to have user quotas, the **/etc/fstab** entry would be something like this:

```
/dev/hda5     /home     ext3     defaults,usrquota  1    1
```

The grpquota Option   Partitions needing group quota support should have the **grpquota** option in the **/etc/fstab** file, just like the **usrquota** option as just described. (Note that it's acceptable to have both options enabled.) For example, if **/dev/hda5** is mounted to the **/home** directory and you want that directory to have group quotas, the **/etc/fstab** entry would be similar to this:

```
/dev/hda5     /home     ext3     defaults,grpquota  1    1
```

Remount the partition   Now you simply need to remount the partition using **umount** and **mount**. While this act alone won't make your quota system ready to use, you can't skip this step! To continue this example, remounting **/home** on the **/dev/hda5** partition would look like this:

```
[root@tedford /root]# umount /home
[root@tedford /home]# mount /home
```

Running quotacheck to Enable Quotas

After you have reconfigured and remounted the partitions, you have to tell Red Hat Linux to initialize the database files, examine the file system for usage, and turn on quotas. Use the **quotacheck** command to perform all these actions:

```
[root@tedford /root]# quotacheck -avug
```

The **-avug** options tell **quotacheck** to run on **a**ll file systems with quotas enabled, with **v**erbose output so you know what it's doing, and for both **u**ser- and **g**roup-based quotas.

TIP

Red Hat recommends rerunning the **quotacheck** command periodically. You can do this by running a "cron" job on a weekly basis (see Module 8 for more about cron jobs).

Configuring Quota Settings

Creating, modifying, and removing quotas on either a per-user or per-group basis is done via the **edquota** command. In this section, you'll look at the usage of this command and run through some examples as well. First, some terminology:

- **Soft Limit**   This requested limit is placed on a user or group. If the user's account exceeds the soft limit, a grace period can be imposed as to how long the account can exist over the soft limit. During this time phase, users can be warned that their accounts are over the limit.

- **Hard Limit**   This limit is imposed by the operating system and cannot be overrun. Any attempts to write data beyond the hard limit are denied.

- **Grace Period (Time Limit)**   When a user's account exceeds the soft limit, a clock starts tracking. After the grace period expires, the user cannot access the account. The length of this grace period should depend on the environment. A common value is one week. To keep the account from being disabled, the user needs to remove or compress files until his or her disk consumption falls below the soft limit.

Command-Line Options of edquota

The **edquota** command has only three options when used to manage per-user quotas:

–u *login*	Sets the quota information for the named user.
–t	Sets the grace period of a partition. Use it in conjunction with **–u** or **–g** to set all the grace periods for users or groups, respectively. Note: If users/groups exist on the same partition, they cannot have different grace periods.

−g group	Sets the quota information for the named group.
−p login	Allows you to clone one user's (user *login*) information to another user. Must be set in conjunction with the **−u** option.

When you invoke the **edquota** command, it brings up the configuration information for the particular user, group, or grace period you want to add or edit. By default, the **vi** editor is used to display human-readable information. If you prefer another editor, such as **emacs** or **pico**, you can simply change the EDITOR environment variable before running **edquota**. For example, if you're using BASH (the root user's default shell), you would enter this command:

```
[root@tedford]# export EDITOR=pico
```

Once the **edquota** information is on screen, you can edit it, save the document, and quit. The **edquota** process takes that information and places it into the database. Note that **edquota** uses the **/etc/passwd** file to determine the location of a user's home directory.

Examples of edquota

To place a quota on user **blee**, I would use the following command:

```
[root@tedford]# edquota -u blee
```

This will bring up the editor with a file that looks like the following:

```
Quotas for user blee:
   /dev/hda2: blocks in use: 0, limits (soft = 0, hard = 0)
              inodes in use: 0, limits (soft = 0, hard = 0)
```

Zeros in all the limits means there is no quota on **blee**'s account at the moment. Notice that there is a limit value for i-nodes as well as blocks. Remember that one block is equal to 1K under Linux, and i-nodes are the control information needed to store files. You will usually need only a few i-nodes per file, and more as the file grows larger.

So to set **blee**'s soft block limit to 5000, the hard block limit to 6000, the soft i-node limit to 2500, and the hard i-node limit to 3000, I would edit the file to look like this:

```
Quotas for user blee:
   /dev/hda2: blocks in use: 0, limits (soft = 5000, hard = 6000)
              inodes in use: 0, limits (soft = 2500, hard = 3000)
```

CAUTION

The **edquota** command generates a unique name for the temporary file used to edit this information. Keep this file—do not write over the **quota.user** or **quota.group** file with this information! The **edquota** utility will take care of integrating quota information into those two files for you.

To change the quota for **blee**, rerun **edquota -u blee** and change the limits.

Another example of using **edquota** is to clone one user's settings to apply to another user. For example, if you want to clone the user **dalbers** so that user **dedood** gets the same quota values, you would enter this command:

```
[root@tedford]# edquota -p dalbers dedood
```

Here's one more example: To apply quota settings to a large number of users at once, you can use a little one-line script to do it. Let's assume that all of the affected users have their UIDs at greater than (or equal to) 500, and that at least one user has had his or her quota set up manually. For our example, we'll call this user **artc**. The magic line is

```
[root@tedford]# edquota -p artc `awk -F: '$3 >> 499 print $1' /etc/passwd`
```

Managing Quotas

Once you have your quotas enabled and working, there are three tools available to help you manage things: **quotacheck**, **repquota**, and **quota**.

The quotacheck Command

The **quotacheck** command verifies the integrity of the quota database. In the script presented earlier for turning on the quota subsystem, you started by running this script with the **-avug** option set.

The options you can pass to **quotacheck** are as follows:

–v	Turns on verbose mode. This presents useful and interesting information as the quota databases are checked.
–u *uid*	Checks the allocation of the user whose UID is *uid*.
–g *gid*	Checks the allocation of all users whose GID is *gid*.
–a	Checks all file systems that have quotas (as determined by the **/etc/fstab** file).
–r	Used in conjunction with **–a.** Checks all partitions with quotas, except the root partition.

The repquota Command

The **repquota** command generates a summary report of quota usage on the system. This command takes the following options:

–a	Reports on all file systems.
–v	Reports on all quotas, even if there is no usage.
–g	Reports on quotas for groups only.
–u	Reports on quotas for users only.

The quota Command

Finally, the **quota** command is for users. It allows them to view the quota limitations placed on them. It takes the following options:

-g	Prints quotas on groups of which the user is a member.
-u	Prints quota information about the specific user (default).
-v	Prints quota information as it pertains to the user for all file systems that support quotas.
-q	Prints a message to the user if he is over quota.

For example, if user **rwhite** were to run **quota –v**, he would see this:

```
[rwhite@tedford ~]% quota -v
Disk quotas for user rwhite (uid 500):
     File system  blocks   quota   limit   grace   files   quota  limit  grace
      /dev/hda8        0       0       0                0       0      0
      /dev/hdb1        0    5000    5100                0    1000   1100
```

Project 7-2   Setting Up autofs

In this project, you'll set up the autofs daemon and set quotas for a group of users. If you can configure your Red Hat Linux test system to be similar to the situation described, that will help, but if not, bend the details to fit your situation.

Consider the following situation: User **pdedood** purchased the Linux system you're managing (named tedford), and has several projects running on it. He also wants users **jwang**, **dalbers**, and **blee** to be able to use space on the system, but he doesn't want them filling up his disk. The server, tedford, has a **/home** partition with 8GB of space. The other users already have accounts on tedford, and their Linux workstations can already mount **/home** via NFS, but the users complain that mounting tedford manually is difficult. Make everybody happy.

Step by Step

1. The first step is to configure the disk quotas on tedford. There's no sense in allowing the users easy access until the necessary restrictions are in place. Enable group-based disk quotas on the server by editing the **/etc/fstab** file as described in this module.

2. Remount the partition and enable quotas on the system by running the **quotacheck** command with the appropriate options.

3. Configure the group quota using a suitable **edquota** command.

4. On each remote system, create an **/etc/auto.home** file to automount tedford's **/home** partition in the remote system's **/home** directory.

5. On each remote system, create an entry in **/etc/auto.master** to consult **/etc/auto.home** if it does not already exist.

6. Update the autofs daemon on each workstation with the new configuration information.

7. Test each workstation by attempting to access tedford's home directory where the automounter put it in the local **/home** directory.

Project Summary

This type of project is the meat and potatoes of Linux system administration. Managing partitions and disk space are two of the common (if somewhat mundane) aspects of system administration. This is where monitoring disk usage, including free space, is vital. If you notice that users are filling up the system's disk space (and they will), you can plan your next steps: expand storage capacity, add or tighten disk quotas, or start randomly deleting user files. Use the skills you've developed in this module to avoid that last option.

Module Summary

In this module, you covered the process of administering your file systems, from creating them to applying quotas to them. With this information, you're armed with what you need in order to manage a commercial-level Linux server in a variety of environments.

Like any operating system, Linux undergoes changes from time to time. Although the designers and maintainers of the file systems go to great lengths to keep the interface the same, you'll find some alterations cropping up from time to time. Sometimes they'll be interface simplifications. Others will be dramatic improvements in the file system itself. Keep your eyes open for these changes. Linux provides a superb file system that is robust, responsive, and in general a pleasure to use. Take the tools described in this module and find out for yourself.

Project
7-2

Setting Up autofs

✓ *Module 7 Mastery Check*

1. What is the point of having i-nodes?

2. What is a superblock?

3. What feature distinguishes the ext2 and ext3 file systems?

4. What file contains information on how to mount the partitions on a system?

5. What are the six entries on each line of the file referred to in Question 4?

6. What commands are used to mount and unmount partitions?

7. How could you remount the **/dev/hda5** partition, which is currently mounted read/write, as read-only?

8. What command could be used to run a check on a file system that appears to be clean?

9. What happens to file segments that cannot be reunited during a file system check?

10. What would the device name of the fifth SCSI disk on a system? What would be the name of its first partition?

11. What command can be used to delete or create partitions?

12. What is the system type number for a partition of the type "Linux swap?"

13. What command would be used to create the file system on a partition of the type described in Question 12?

14. Describe the command used to create an ext3 file system on **/dev/hda1**.

15. Show the **mount** command used to mount server gregory's **/export/foo** directory on the local server's **/mnt/foo** directory using NFS?

16. What is the automounter's primary configuration file? What does it contain?

17. Which is the correct procedure for setting up quotas?

   A. Edit /etc/edquota, run **quotacheck**, and then edit /etc/fstab.

   B. Edit /etc/fstab, run **edquota**, and then run **quotacheck**.

   C. Run **quotacheck**, edit /etc/fstab, and then run **edquota**.

   D. Edit /etc/fstab, run **quotacheck**, and then run **edquota**.

18. Name the command used to summarize quota usage on a file system.

Module 8

Core System Services

As operating systems have become more complex, the process of starting up and shutting down has become more comprehensive. Anyone who has undergone the transition from a straight DOS-based system to a Windows 2000 or XP system has experienced this transition firsthand: Not only is the core operating system brought up and shut down, but also an impressive list of services must be started and stopped. Like Windows, Linux comprises an impressive list of services that are turned on as part of the boot procedure.

In this module, you step through the processes of starting up and shutting down the Linux environment and its basic services. Regardless of distribution, network configuration, and overall system design, every Linux system has four core services: **init**, **inetd** or **xinetd**, **syslog**, and **cron**. The functions performed by these services may be simple, but they are also fundamental.

In this module, you'll learn about each one of the core services and its corresponding configuration file. You'll also grow acquainted with the scripts that automate the starting and stopping of services during the boot and shutdown processes. I'll show you how to specify which services get started at boot time, and I'll introduce the process of writing your own scripts to control services.

CRITICAL SKILL

8.1 Configuring the Boot Manager

GRUB, the GRand Unified Boot loader, is a boot manager. It allows you to boot multiple operating systems. In addition to booting multiple operating systems, with GRUB (or LILO, the LInux LOader, the other boot manager supported out-of-the-box by Red Hat Linux 8.0), you can choose various kernel configurations or versions to boot. This is especially handy when you're trying kernel upgrades before adopting them. What's the difference between LILO and GRUB?

LILO reads a configuration file (**/etc/lilo.conf**) that specifies which partitions are bootable and, if a partition is Linux, which kernel to load. When the **/sbin/lilo** program runs, it takes this partition information and rewrites the boot sector with the necessary code to present the options as specified in the configuration file. At boot time, a prompt (usually **lilo:**) is displayed, and you have the option of specifying the operating system. (Usually, a default can be selected after a time-out period.) LILO loads the necessary code from the selected partition and passes full control over to it.

While GRUB performs the same tasks, it offers greater functionality than LILO. For example, there are more commands available at the **grub>** prompt. You don't really want to use either boot loader's prompt if you can avoid it (if, like the rest of us, you want your systems to install and run effortlessly), but because GRUB can read ext2 and ext3 partition data, it is possible to access disk data without even booting into the operating system. A further consequence of being able to read ext2 file system data is that GRUB can automatically find any updates to its configuration. LILO, on the other hand, must be run every time you change something, or it won't update its configuration information.

NOTE

If you have a reason to use LILO, that's okay, but because GRUB is more feature-laden, nicer-looking, and the Red Hat Linux default, I'm going to assume you want to use it, and that you've already installed it. In future versions of Red Hat, it may be the only option. If you haven't already installed it, do so (see Module 4 for more information on installing software). When you do, it will automatically become your boot manager. It's pushy, but good.

Configuring GRUB

The GRUB configuration file in Red Hat Linux 8.0 is **/boot/grub/grub.conf**, and it is automatically populated during the installation process. This sample file tells you a few things:

```
# grub.conf generated by anaconda
#
# Note that you do not have to rerun grub after making changes to this file
# NOTICE:  You have a /boot partition.  This means that
#          all kernel and initrd paths are relative to /boot/, eg.
#          root (hd0,0)
#          kernel /vmlinuz-version ro root=/dev/hda2
#          initrd /initrd-version.img
#boot=/dev/had
default=0
timeout=10
splashimage=(hd0,0)/grub/splash.xpm.gz
password --md5 $1$MXñpqCÿÅ$tmRR3o30M46mNXLbM5rci0
title Red Hat Linux (2.4.18-14smp)
  root (hd0,0)
  kernel /vmlinuz-2.4.18-14smp ro root=LABEL=/ hdd=ide-scsi
  initrd /initrd-2.4.18-14smp.img
title Red Hat Linux-up (2.4.18-14)
  root (hd0,0)
  kernel /vmlinuz-2.4.18-14 ro root=LABEL=/ hdd=ide-scsi
  initrd /initrd-2.4.18-14.img
```

First, the comment line at the beginning of the file notes that it was generated by anaconda (the Red Hat installer). It also mentions that GRUB does not need to be rerun to update changes to its configuration file (this message is included because LILO *does* require rerunning after every configuration change). It also notes that **/boot** is on its own partition and points out that the boot-related files will be found on that partition.

GRUB Device Names

If you've just gotten used to the device names described in Module 7, there's more bad news. While Linux calls the first IDE hard disk **hda** and the second SCSI hard disk **sdb**, GRUB uses its own identification system. The first hard disk is **hd0**, whether it's IDE, SCSI, or Zoroastrian. The second hard disk is **hd1**, and so on. If you specify the device name in this way, GRUB understands you to be referring to the entire drive. More specifically, you are referring to the *Master Boot Record (MBR)* on that drive. This sector describes what to load first in order to start the operating system. Once loaded, the program stored in the MBR is expected to take over the boot process. To specify a partition, you add a comma and a partition number, starting from 0. In other words, the third partition on the fourth hard disk would be known as **hd3,2**.

GRUB Configuration Commands

In the **/boot/grub/grub.conf** file you started reviewing, the first few lines after the comments gave some cryptic but important instructions. They told GRUB to use the first boot entry as the default, and to start from that entry if no other input was received within ten seconds. They also specified a splash screen graphic and gave an MD5-encrypted password required to alter the boot loader configuration. After that come two boot entries, each of which has a title that appears as an option when GRUB starts up, a "root" partition for GRUB to load to read files, a kernel file to load, and a RAM disk. These commands can be found in Table 8-1.

In Project 8-1, you'll have the opportunity to change a few of the configuration settings on the boot loader to see what impact they have.

GRUB Command	Description
kernel	Points to the kernel file used to boot the system and any options to pass to the loaded kernel.
root	Mounts the specified device and partition as GRUB's root partition.
default	Sets the default boot entry, which is used if the time-out time is reached. The number refers to a title command, with 0 pointing to the first title in the configuration file, 1 pointing to the second title command, and so on.
fallback	Defines the title entry to use if the initial boot attempt fails.
hiddenmenu	Hides the GRUB menu. If the user does not unhide the menu by pressing the ESC key at startup, the time-out time will elapse and the default entry will be loaded.
password	Requires that the user know the password (which is MD5-encrypted in this file) to edit the boot loader configuration.
timeout	Sets the time limit after which GRUB will automatically load the default entry.
splashimage	Points to the image presented when GRUB starts.
title	Provides a name for a group of configuration commands. This name is displayed on GRUB's boot menu.
initrd	Points to the initial RAM disk used during booting.

Table 8-1 GRUB Configuration Commands

CAUTION

Apply a liberal dose of common sense in following this module with a real system. As you experiment with modifying startup and shutdown scripts, bear in mind that it is possible to bring your system to a nonfunctional state that cannot be recovered by rebooting. Don't try new processes on production systems; make backups of all the files you wish to change; and most important, have a boot disk ready in case you make an irreversible change.

Running LILO

The LILO configuration file is **/etc/lilo.conf**. In most cases, you won't need to modify the file in any significant way. When you do need to change this file, the options are quite plain and simple to follow. Let's begin by reviewing a simple configuration. The file shown here is probably quite similar to what is already in your default **lilo.conf** file:

```
boot=/dev/hda
prompt
timeout=50
image=/boot/vmlinuz-2.4.18-14
        label=linux
        root=/dev/hda2
        read-only
other = /dev/hda1
        label = dos
        table = /dev/hda
```

The first line, **boot=/dev/hda**, tells LILO where to write the boot sector. Usually, this is the first sector of the boot drive: **/dev/hda** for IDE-based disks, and **/dev/sda** for SCSI-based disks. The next command is **prompt**. This instruction tells LILO to give the **lilo:** prompt at boot time. At this prompt, the user can either type in the name of the boot image that is to start, or press TAB to list the available options. By default, LILO will wait indefinitely for user input unless a time-out command is specified.

The **timeout=50** command tells LILO to wait for 50 deciseconds (5 seconds) before selecting the default boot image and starting the boot process.

The next line begins a small block. The line

```
image=/boot/vmlinuz-2.4.18-14
```

indicates a specific boot image. This being the first block, it will be the default boot image. The image to boot is the file **/boot/vmlinuz-2.4.18-14**, which is a Linux kernel. Inside the block is the line **label=linux**, which is the name that is displayed if the user asks for a list of available boot options at the **lilo:** prompt.

Also inside the block is the line

```
root=/dev/hda2
```

which tells LILO the partition on which the **/boot/vmlinuz-2.4.18-14** file is located.

Adding a New Kernel to Boot

Part of the process of compiling new kernels to boot requires adding an entry into the **/boot/grub/grub.conf** or **/etc/lilo.conf** file so that the boot loader knows about the new kernel. More important, this entry allows you to keep the existing, working configuration in case the new kernel doesn't work as you'd like it to. You can always reboot and select an older kernel that does work.

For the sake of discussion, I'll assume you've compiled the 2.5.44 kernel because you want to try the new Plug and Play patches. You have compiled the new kernel, **vmlinuz-2.5.44**, and it is placed in the **/boot** directory. Your first step is to append the relevant information to the **/boot/grub/grub.conf** or **/etc/lilo.conf** file.

Adding a New Kernel For GRUB

The new section would look something like this in **/boot/grub/grub.conf**:

```
title Scary New Kernel (2.5.44)
root (hd0,0)
    kernel /vmlinuz-2.5.44 ro root=LABEL=/ hdd=ide-scsi
    initrd /initrd-2.5.44.img
```

When you reboot, the Scary New Kernel option will be available (but not the default).

NOTE

You need the **initrd** line only to load a SCSI driver or to support the ext3 module, but if you need it, use the **mkinitrd** command to create the file.

Adding a New Kernel for LILO

For LILO-based systems, the configuration file could be updated with the following block:

```
image=/boot/vmlinuz-2.5.44
    label=linux-2.5.44
    root=/dev/hda1
    read-only
```

Once the **/etc/lilo.conf** file is edited and saved, you need to run **/sbin/lilo** to update the boot loader. The result will look something like this:

```
[root@tedford /boot]# lilo
Added linux *
Added linux-2.5.44
```

LILO has taken the information from **/etc/lilo.conf** and written it into the appropriate boot sector.

Project 8-1 Modifying Your GRUB Configuration

This is a good time for you to do a little test tweaking of your GRUB configuration. In this project, you'll change some of the optional settings in the **/boot/grub/grub.conf** file. You'll need GRUB loaded on a system you can reboot a few times, so make sure you don't have any active users whose work will get trashed.

Step by Step

1. As the root user, using your favorite text editor, open your **/boot/grub/grub.conf** file. Unless you have an SMP system or a multi-OS configuration, you'll have only one GRUB **title** entry. Look at the configuration entries for that entry (or your default Linux entry, if you've got multiple titles). From the **boot** entry listed, determine which hard disk and partition hold your **/boot** partition.

2. If you change where the **kernel** and **initrd** parameters point, this boot entry won't work any more, so leave them alone. However, you can alter the **title** entry if you wish. Customize it with your name or a pithy saying.

3. Without making any other changes, see what you've wrought. Restart your Linux system and see how the GRUB menu looks.

4. Once you've started the system again, log back in as root and edit the configuration file again. Start by making sure the **title** entry you changed is something respectable enough that your mother wouldn't be offended. Not that I don't trust you.

5. Now turn your attention to the global options (the ones that don't appear in a **title** entry). Double the **timeout** setting. Add a line with the **hiddenmenu** option all by itself.

6. Restart the system again and see what the boot loader looks like in stealth mode. See if you can open the menu by pressing the ESC key.

(continued)

7. Re-edit the configuration file to undo any undesired changes. You won't have to reboot the system or run any utilities to have the updates take effect the next time the system is restarted.

Project Summary

This project will be even more interesting once you can add your own custom-compiled kernels to the system. Until you learn about that, it's important that you be comfortable with using the GRUB menu, and that you know about the contents of the **/boot/grub/grub.conf** file. While you shouldn't have to touch either one in a production environment (especially if you update the kernel only with Red Hat's packages), you never know when knowledge of the boot loader will come in handy.

CRITICAL SKILL
8.2 # Knowing the Boot Process

Once the boot manager has started and you have selected a Linux kernel to boot, that kernel is loaded. Keep in mind that no operating system exists in memory at this point, and PCs (by their unfortunate design) have no easy way to access all of their memory. Thus, the kernel must load completely into the first megabyte of available RAM. In order to accomplish this, the kernel is compressed. The head of the file contains the code necessary to bring the CPU into protected mode (thereby removing the memory restriction) and decompress the remainder of the kernel.

Kernel Execution

With the kernel in memory, it can begin executing. It knows only whatever functionality is built into it, which means any parts of the kernel compiled as modules are useless at this point. At the very minimum, the kernel must have enough code to set up its virtual memory subsystem and root file system (usually, the ext2 or ext3 file system). Once the kernel has started, a hardware probe determines what device drivers should be initialized. From here, the kernel can *mount* the root file system. (You could draw a parallel of this process to that of Windows' being able to recognize and access its C: drive.) The kernel mounts the root file system and starts a program called **init**.

The init Process

The **init** process is the first nonkernel process that is started, and therefore it always gets the process ID number of 1. **init** reads its configuration file, **/etc/inittab**, and determines the *runlevel* where it should start. Essentially, a runlevel dictates the system's behavior. Each level (designated by an integer between 0 and 6) serves a specific purpose. A runlevel of **initdefault** is selected if it exists; otherwise, you are prompted to supply a runlevel value.

Runlevel	Description
0	Halt the system
1	Enter single-user mode (no networking is enabled)
2	Multiuser mode, but without NFS
3	Full multiuser mode (normal operation)
4	Unused
5	Same as runlevel 3, except using an X login rather than a text-based login
6	Reboot the system

Table 8-2 Runlevels as Found in **/etc/inittab**

The runlevel values as used by Red Hat are shown in Table 8-2.

When it is told to enter a runlevel, **init** executes a script as dictated by the **/etc/inittab** file. The default runlevel depends on whether you indicated the system should start with a text-based or X login during the installation phase.

NOTE

Don't start a server in runlevel 5. It's not morally wrong, but it's silly to have any GUI processes running on a system that isn't supposed to be running its GUI on a regular basis.

Progress Check

1. What is the default boot loader in Red Hat Linux 8.0, and what is its primary configuration file?

2. What is the standard runlevel for a server?

1. The **GRUB** boot loader is used by default in Red Hat Linux 8.0, and its configuration file is found at **/boot/grub/grub.conf**.

2. Runlevel 3 is the standard runlevel used for servers.

Learning about the init Service

The **init** process is the patron of all processes. It is *always* the first process that gets started, and its process ID is always 1. Should **init** ever fail, the rest of the system will most definitely follow suit.

The **init** process serves two roles: The first is being the ultimate parent process. Because **init** never dies, the system can always be sure of its presence and, if necessary, make reference to it. The need to refer to **init** usually happens when a process dies before all of its spawned children processes have completed. This causes the children to inherit **init** as their parent process. A quick execution of the **ps –af** command will show a number of processes that will have a parent process ID (PPID) of 1.

The second job for **init** is to handle the various runlevels by executing the appropriate programs when a particular runlevel is reached. This behavior is defined by the **/etc/inittab** file.

The /etc/inittab File

The **/etc/inittab** file contains all the information **init** needs for starting runlevels. The format of each line in this file is as follows:

```
id:runlevels:action:process
```

NOTE

Lines beginning with the number symbol (#) are comments. Take a peek at your own **/etc/inittab**, and you'll find that it's already liberally commented. If you ever do need to make a change to **/etc/inittab** (and it's unlikely that you'll ever need to), you'll do yourself a favor by including liberal comments to explain what you've done.

Table 8-3 explains the significance of each of the four items in the **/etc/inittab** file's line format.

/etc/inittab Entry	Description
id	A unique sequence of 1–4 characters that identifies this entry in the **/etc/inittab** file.
runlevels	The runlevels at which the process should be invoked. Some events are special enough that they can be trapped at all runlevels (for instance the CTRL-ALT-DEL key combination to reboot). To indicate that an event is applicable to all runlevels, leave *runlevels* blank. If you want something to occur at multiple runlevels, simply list all of them in this field. For example, the *runlevels* entry **123** specifies something that runs at runlevels 1, 2, and 3.

Table 8-3 Entries in the **/etc/inittab** File

/etc/inittab Entry	Description
action	Describes what action should be taken. Options for this field are explained in Table 8-4.
process	Names the process (program) to execute when the runlevel is entered.

Table 8-3 Entries in the **/etc/inittab** File *(continued)*

Table 8-4 defines the options available for the ***action*** field in the **/etc/inittab** file.

Values for *action* Field in /etc/inittab File	Description
respawn	The process will be restarted whenever it terminates.
wait	The process will be started once when the runlevel is entered, and **init** will wait for its completion.
once	The process will be started once when the runlevel is entered; however, **init** won't wait for termination of the process before possibly executing additional programs to be run at that particular runlevel.
boot	The process will be executed at system boot. The ***runlevels*** field is ignored in this case.
bootwait	The process will be executed at system boot, and **init** will wait for completion of the boot before advancing to the next process to be run.
ondemand	The process will be executed when a specific runlevel request occurs. (These runlevels are **a**, **b**, and **c**.) No change in runlevel occurs.
initdefault	Specifies the default runlevel for **init** on startup. If no default is specified, the user is prompted for a runlevel on console.
sysinit	The process will be executed during system boot, before any of the **boot** or **bootwait** entries.
powerwait	If **init** receives a signal from another process that there are problems with the power, this process will be run. Before continuing, **init** will wait for this process to finish.
powerfail	Same as **powerwait**, except that **init** will not wait for the process to finish.

Table 8-4 Action Options for **/etc/inittab**

Values for *action* Field in /etc/inittab File	Description
powerokwait	If **init** receives the same type of signal as **powerwait**, when a file called /etc/powerstatus exists with the string "OK" in it, this process will be executed, and **init** will wait for its completion.
ctrlaltdel	The process is executed when **init** receives a signal indicating that the user has pressed CTRL-ALT-DEL. Keep in mind that most X servers capture this key combination, and thus **init** will not receive this signal if X is active.

Table 8-4 Action Options for **/etc/inittab** (continued)

Now take a look at a sample line from an **/etc/inittab** file:

```
# If power was restored before the shutdown kicked in, cancel it.pr:
12345:powerokwait:/sbin/shutdown -c "Power Restored; Shutdown Cancelled"
```

In this case:

- **pr** is the unique identifier.

- **1, 2, 3, 4**, and **5** are the runlevels from which this process can be activated.

- **powerokwait** is the condition under which the process is run.

- The **/sbin/shutdown . . .** command is the process.

The telinit Command

The mysterious force that tells **init** when to change runlevels is the **telinit** command. This command takes two command-line parameters: One is the desired runlevel that **init** needs to know about, and the other is **-t** *sec*, where *sec* is the number of seconds to wait before telling **init**.

CRITICAL SKILL
8.4 Configuring and Using the xinetd Process

The **inetd** and **xinetd** programs are daemon processes. You probably know that daemons are special programs that, after starting, voluntarily release control of the terminal from which they started. The only mechanism by which daemons can interface with the rest of the system is through interprocess communication (IPC) channels, by sending entries to the system-wide log file, or by appending to a disk file.

Starting with version 7.0, the Red Hat distribution has been using a newer version of **inetd** called **xinetd**. The **xinetd** program accomplishes the same task as the older **inetd** program, but it includes a new configuration file format and some additional features.

The role of **xinetd** is as a "superserver" for other network server-related processes, such as **telnet** and **ftp**. It's a simple philosophy: Not all server processes (including those that accept new **telnet** and **ftp** connections) are called upon so often that they require a program to be running in memory all the time. So instead of constantly maintaining potentially dozens of services loaded in memory waiting to be used, they are all listed in **xinetd**'s configuration file, **/etc/xinetd.conf**. On their behalf, **xinetd** listens for incoming connections. Thus only a single process needs to be in memory.

A secondary benefit of **xinetd** falls to those processes needing network connectivity but whose programmers do not want to have to write it into the system. The **xinetd** program will handle the network code and pass incoming network streams into the process as its standard input (**stdin**). Any of the process's output (**stdout**) is sent back to the host that has connected to the process. This is primarily useful for programmers or those who want to make a script available on the network.

As a general rule of thumb, low-volume services (such as Telnet) are usually best run through **xinetd**, whereas higher-volume services (such as Web servers) are better run as a stand-alone process that is always in memory ready to handle requests.

The /etc/xinetd.conf File

The **/etc/xinetd.conf** file consists of a series of blocks that take the following format:

```
blockname
{
    variable = value
}
```

where **blockname** is the name of the block that is being defined, **variable** is the name of a variable being defined within the context of the block, and **value** is the value assigned to the **variable**. Every block can have multiple variables defined within.

One special block exists which is called "default." Whatever variables are defined within this block are applied to all other blocks that are defined in the file.

An exception to the block format is the **includedir** directive, which tells **xinetd** to go read all the files in a directory and consider them to be part of the **/etc/xinetd.conf** file.

Any line that begins with a number sign (#) is the start of a comment. The stock **/etc/xinetd.conf** file that ships with Red Hat 8.0 looks like this:

```
#
# Simple configuration file for xinetd
#
# Some defaults, and include /etc/xinetd.d/

defaults
{
        instances               = 60
        log_type                = SYSLOG authpriv
        log_on_success          = HOST PID
        log_on_failure          = HOST
        cps                     = 25 30

}

includedir /etc/xinetd.d
```

Don't worry if all of the variables and values aren't familiar to you yet; you will go over those in a moment. First make sure you understand the format of the file.

In this example, the first four lines of the file are comments explaining what the file is and what it does. After the comments, you see the first block: **defaults**. The first variable that is defined in this block is **instances**, which is set to the value of 60. Five variables in total are defined in this block, the last one being **log_on_failure**. Since this block is titled **defaults**, the variables that are set within it will apply to all future blocks that are defined. Finally, the last line of the file specifies that the **/etc/xinetd.d** directory must be examined for other files that contain more configuration information. This will cause **xinetd** to read all of the files in that directory and parse them as if they were part of the **/etc/xinetd.conf** file.

Variables and Their Meanings

The variable names that are supported by **xinetd** are shown in Table 8-5.

Variable	Description
ID	This attribute is used to uniquely identify a service. This is useful because services exist that can use different protocols and need to be described with different entries in the configuration file. By default, the service ID is the same as the service name.

Table 8-5 The Variable Names Supported by **xinetd**

Variable	Description
Type	Any combination of the following values may be used: **RPC** if this is an RPC service, **INTERNAL** if this service is provided by **xinetd**, or **UNLISTED** if this is a service not listed in the **/etc/services** file.
Disable	This is either the value **yes** or **no**. A **yes** value means that although the service is defined, it is not available for use.
socket_type	Valid values for this variable are **stream** to indicate that this service is a stream-based service, **dgram** to indicate that this service is a datagram, or **raw** to indicate that this service uses raw IP datagrams. The **stream** value refers to connection-oriented (TCP) data streams (for example, **telnet** and **ftp**). The **dgram** value refers to datagram (UDP) streams (for example, the **tftp** service is a datagram-based protocol). Other protocols outside the scope of TCP/IP do exist; however, you'll rarely encounter them.
Protocol	Determines the type of protocol (either **tcp** or **udp**) for the connection type.
Wait	If this is set to **yes**, only one connection will be processed at a time. If this is set to **no**, multiple connections will be allowed by running the appropriate service daemon multiple times.
User	Specifies the username under which this service will run. The username must exist in the **/etc/passwd** file.
Group	Specifies the group name under which this service will run. The group must exist in the **/etc/group** file.
Instances	Specifies the maximum number of concurrent connections this service is allowed to handle. The default is no limit if the **wait** variable is set to **nowait**.
Server	The name of the program to run when this service is connected.
server_args	The arguments passed to the server. In contrast to **inetd**, the name of the server should not be included in **server_args**.
only_from	Specifies the networks from which a valid connection may arrive. (This is the built-in TCP Wrappers functionality.) You can specify this in one of three ways: a numeric address, a host name, or a network address with netmask. The numeric address can take the form of a complete IP address to indicate a specific host (such as 192.168.1.1). However, if any of the ending octets are zeros, the address will be treated like a network where all of the octets that are zero are wildcards (for instance, 192.168.1.0 means any host that starts with the numbers 192.168.1). Alternatively, you can specify the number of bits in the netmask after a slash (for instance, 192.168.1.0/24 means a network address of 192.168.1.0 with a netmask of 255.255.255.0).
no_access	The opposite of **only_from** in that instead of specifying the addresses from which a connection is valid, this variable specifies the addresses from which a connection is invalid. It can take the same type of parameters as **only_from**.

Table 8-5 The Variable Names Supported by **xinetd** (continued)

Variable	Description

log_type	Determines where logging information for that service will go. There are two valid values: **SYSLOG** and **FILE**. If **SYSLOG** is specified, you must also specify to which syslog facility to log, as well (see "Managing the syslogd Daemon," later in this module, for more information on facilities). For example, you can specify:
	`log_type = SYSLOG local0`
	Optionally, you can include the log level, as well. For example:
	`log_type = SYSLOG local0 info`
	If **FILE** is specified, you must specify to which filename to log. Optionally, you can also specify the soft limit on the file size. The soft limit on a file size is where an extra log message indicating that the file has gotten too large will be generated. If the soft limit is specified, a hard limit can also be specified. At the hard limit, no additional logging will be done. If the hard limit is not explicitly defined, it is set to be 1% higher than the soft limit. An example of the **FILE** option is as follows:
	`log_type = FILE /var/log/mylog`

log_on_success	Specifies which information is logged on a connection success. The options include **PID** to log the process ID of the service that processed the request, **HOST** to specify the remote host connecting to the service, **USERID** to log the remote username (if available), **EXIT** to log the exit status or termination signal of the process, or **DURATION** to log the length of the connection.
Port	Specifies the network port under which the service will run. If the service is listed in **/etc/services**, this port number must equal the value specified there.
Interface	Allows a service to bind to a specific interface and be available only there. The value is the IP address of the interface that you wish this service to be bound to. An example of this is binding less secure services (such as Telnet) to an internal and physically secure interface on a firewall and not allowing it the external, more vulnerable interface outside the firewall.
Cps	The first argument specifies the maximum number of connections per second this service is allowed to handle. If the rate exceeds this value, the service is temporarily disabled for the second argument number of seconds. For example: `cps = 10 30` This will disable a service for 30 seconds if the connection rate ever exceeds 10 connections per second.

Table 8-5 The Variable Names Supported by **xinetd** *(continued)*

You do not need to specify all of the variables in defining a service. The only required ones are:

- **socket_type**
- **user**
- **server**
- **wait**

An Example of a Service Entry

You can see several of the variables in this standard **xinetd** entry:

```
# default: off
# description: An echo server. This is the tcp \
# version.
service echo
{
  disable = yes
  type        INTERNAL
  id          echo-stream
  socket_type   = stream
  protocol    = tcp
  user    = root
  wait    = no
}
```

In Red Hat Linux 8.0, you can find this entry in **/etc/xinetd.d/echo**.

Progress Check

1. To which directory does the **/etc/xinetd.conf** file point?

2. Why might there be few entries in that directory?

---

1. The default **/etc/xinetd.conf** file has an **includedir** statement that includes the contents of the **/etc/xinetd.d** directory, so individual configuration files are stored there.

2. There would be few entries in that directory if the system supports few of the server processes that **xinetd** manages. For example, if you don't have **ftp**, **finger**, and **telnet** on your system as a security measure, their configuration files aren't installed, either.

Managing the syslogd Daemon

With so much going on at any one time, especially with services that are disconnected from a terminal window, it's necessary to provide a standard mechanism by which special events and messages can be logged. Linux uses the **syslogd** daemon to provide this service.

The **syslogd** daemon provides a standardized means of performing logging. Many other UNIXs employ a compatible daemon, thus providing a means for cross-platform logging over the network. This is especially valuable in a large heterogeneous environment where it's necessary to centralize the collection of log entries to gain an accurate picture of what's going on. You could equate this system of logging facilities to the Windows System Logger.

The log files that **syslogd** stores to are straight text files, usually stored in the **/var/log** directory. Each log entry consists of a single line containing the date, time, host name, process name, process PID, and the message from that process. A system-wide function in the standard C library provides an easy mechanism for generating log messages. If you don't feel like writing code but want to generate entries in the logs, you have the option of using the **logger** command.

As you can imagine, a tool with **syslogd**'s importance is something that gets started as part of the boot scripts. Every Linux distribution you would use in a server environment will already do this for you.

Invoking syslogd

If you do find a need to either start **syslogd** manually or modify the script that starts it up at boot, you'll need to be aware of **syslogd**'s command-line parameters, shown in Table 8-6.

Parameter	Description
–d	Debug mode. Normally, at startup, **syslogd** detaches itself from the current terminal and starts running in the back ground. With the **–d** option, **syslogd** retains control of the terminal and prints debugging information as messages are logged. It's extremely unlikely that you'll need this option.
–f config	Specifies a configuration file as an alternative to the default **/etc/ syslog .conf**.
–h	By default, **syslogd** does not forward messages sent to it that were really destined for another host. *Caution:* If you use this parameter, you run the risk of being used as part of a denial of service attack.
–l hostlist	This option lets you list the hosts for which you are willing to perform logging. Each host name should be its simple name, not its fully qualified domain name (FQDN). You can list multiple hosts, as long as they are separated by a colon; for example, `-l gregory:tedford:ungerer`.

Table 8-6 Command-Line Parameters for **syslogd**

Parameter	Description
–m interval	By default, **syslogd** generates a log entry every 20 minutes as a "just so you know, I'm running" message. This is for systems that may not be busy. (If you're watching the system log and don't see a single message in over 20 minutes, you'll know for a fact that something has gone wrong.) By specifying a numeric value for interval, you can indicate the number of minutes **syslogd** should wait before generating another message.
–r	By default, as a security precaution, the **syslogd** daemon refuses messages sent to it from the network. This command-line parameter enables this feature.
–s domainlist	If you are receiving **syslogd** entries that show the entire FQDN, you can have **syslogd** strip off the domain name and leave just the host name. Simply list the domain names to remove in a colon-separated list as the parameter to the **–s** option. For example, `-s x-files.com:conspiracy.com:wealthy.com`

Table 8-6 Command-Line Parameters for **syslogd** (continued)

The /etc/syslog.conf File

The **/etc/syslog.conf** file contains the configuration information that **syslogd** needs to run. This file's format is a little unusual, but the default configuration file you have will probably suffice unless you begin needing to seek out specific information in specific files or sent to remote logging machines.

Log Message Classifications

Before you can understand the **/etc/syslog.conf** file format itself, you have to understand how log messages get classified. Each message has a *facility* and a *priority*. The facility tells you from which subsystem the message originated, and the priority tells you how important the message is. These two values are separated by a period.

Both values have string equivalents, making them easier to remember. The string equivalents for facility and priority are listed in Tables 8-7 and 8-8, respectively.

Facility String Equivalent	Description
auth	Authentication messages.
authpriv	Essentially the same as **auth**.
cron	Messages generated by the **cron** subsystem (see "Using the cron Program," later in this module).
daemon	Generic classification for service daemons.
kern	Kernel messages.
lpr	Printer subsystem messages.
mail	Mail subsystem messages (including per mail logs).

Table 8-7 Log Message Facility Descriptions

Facility String Equivalent	Description
mark	Obsolete, but you may find some books that discuss it; **syslogd** simply ignores it.
news	Messages through the NNTP subsystem.
security	Same thing as **auth**; should not be used.
syslog	Internal messages from **syslog** itself.
user	Generic messages from user programs.
uucp	Messages from the UUCP (UNIX to UNIX CoPy) subsystem.
local0–local9	Generic facility levels whose importance can be decided according to your needs.

Table 8-7 Log Message Facility Descriptions *(continued)*

NOTE

The priority levels are in the order of severity according to **syslogd**. Thus **debug** is not considered severe at all, and **emerg** is the most crucial. For example, the combination facility-and-priority string **mail.crit** indicates there is a critical error in the mail subsystem (for example, it has run out of disk space). **syslogd** considers this message more important than **mail.info**, which may simply note the arrival of another message.

Priority String Equivalent	Description
debug	Debugging statements.
info	Miscellaneous information.
notice	Important statements, but not necessarily bad news.
warning	Potentially dangerous situation.
warn	Same as **warning**; should not be used.
Err	An error condition.
Error	Same as **err**; should not be used.
Crit	Critical situation.
Alert	A message indicating an important occurrence.
Emerg	An emergency situation.

Table 8-8 Log Message Priority Descriptions

The **syslogd** process also understands wildcards. Thus, you can define a whole class of messages; for instance, **mail.*** refers to all messages related to the mail subsystem.

Format of /etc/syslog.conf

Here is the format of each line in the configuration file:

```
facility/priority combinations separated by commas
file/process/host to log to
```

For example:

```
kern.info, kern.emerg /ver/log/kerned
```

The location to which **syslogd** can send log messages is also quite flexible. It can save messages to files and send messages to FIFOs, to a list of users, or (in the case of centralized logging for a large site) to a master log host. To differentiate these location elements, the following rules are applied to the location entry:

- If the location begins with a slash (/), the message is going to a file.

- If the location begins with a pipe (|), the message is going to a FIFO.

- If the location begins with an @, the message is going to a host.

Table 8-9 shows examples of location entries according to these rules.

Location Style	Description
/var/log/logfile	A file. Note: If you prefix the filename with a dash, **syslogd** will not synchronize the file system after the write. This means you run the risk of losing some data if there is a crash before the system gets a chance to flush its buffers. On the other hand, if an application is being overly verbose about its logging, you'll gain performance using this option. Remember: If you want messages sent to the console, you need to specify **/dev/console**.
|/tmp/mypipe	A pipe. This type of file is created with the **mknod** command (see Module 7). With **syslogd** feeding one side of the pipe, you can have another program running that reads the other side of the pipe. This is an effective way to have programs parsing log output, looking for critical situations, so that you can be paged if necessary.
@@loghost	A host name. This example will send the message to **loghost**. The **syslogd** daemon on **loghost** will then record the message.

Table 8-9 Log Message Destination Descriptions

If you enter no special character before the location entry, **syslogd** assumes that the location is a comma-separated list of users who will have the message written to their screen.

If you use an asterisk (*), **syslogd** will send the message to all of the users who are logged in. As usual, any line that begins with a number symbol (#) is a comment.

Now take a look at some examples of configuration file entries:

```
# Log all the mail messages in one place.
mail.* /var/log/maillog
```

This example shows that all priorities in the mail facility should have their messages placed in the **/var/log/maillog** file.

Consider the next example:

```
# Everybody gets emergency messages, plus log them on another
# machine.
*.emerg                                    @loghost,rwhite,bwoodall,root
```

In this example, you see that any facility with a log level of **emerg** is sent to another system running **syslogd** called **loghost**. Also, if the user **bwoodall**, **rwhite**, or **root** is logged in, the message being logged is written to the user's console.

You can also specify multiple selectors on a single line for a single event. For example:

```
*.info;mail.none;authpriv.none
/var/log/messages
```

Using redhat-logviewer

There's nothing wrong with reading a few text files in the **/var/log** directory, if that's where you have your log messages going. However, you can also use the **redhat-logviewer** utility within a GUI to bring up the pretty interface shown in Figure 8-1.

You can start the utility by typing its name in a terminal window, or by going to the System Tools menu and selecting System Logs. Either way, you'll bring up a window like the one in Figure 8-1. If you customize your log file locations, you can still use the graphical log viewer; just go to the viewer's Edit menu and select Preferences. From there, you can set alert levels and log file paths.

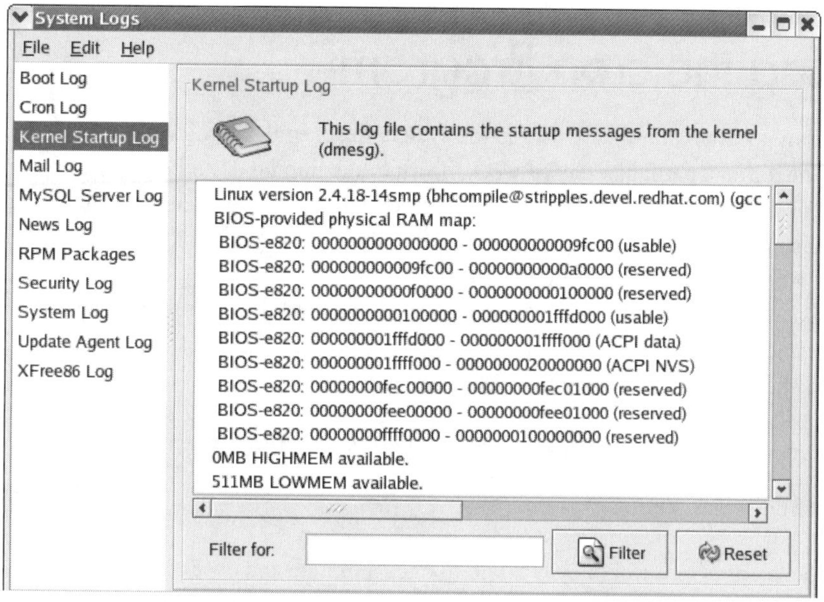

Figure 8-1 Use the **redhat-logviewer** to browse and search log files.

Progress Check

1. How could you start **syslogd** and tell it to accept log messages for the hosts "peanut" and "chocolate"?

2. Which priority string is considered the most urgent?

---

1. Running from the command line, or editing the startup file, use **syslogd –l peanut:chocolate**.
2. The **emerg** priority level is the most urgent.

CRITICAL SKILL
8.6 # Using the cron Program

The **cron** program allows any user in the system to schedule a program to run on any date, at any time, or on a particular day of week, down to the minute. Using **cron** is an extremely efficient way to automate your system, generate reports on a regular basis, and perform other periodic chores. (Not-so-honest uses of **cron** include having it invoke a system to have you paged when you want to get out of a meeting!)

Like the other services you've considered in this module, **cron** is started by the boot scripts and is most likely already configured for you. A quick check of the process listing should show it quietly running in the background:

```
[root@tedford /root]# ps auxw | grep cron | grep -v grep
root        341  0.0  0.0  1284   112 ?        S    Jun21   0:00 crond
[root@tedford /root]#
```

The **cron** service works by waking up once a minute and checking each user's **crontab** file. This file contains the user's list of events that they want executed at a particular date and time. Any events that match the current date and time are executed.

The **crond** command itself requires no command-line parameters or special signals to indicate a change in status.

The crontab File

The tool that allows you to edit entries to be executed by **crond** is **crontab**. Essentially, all it does is verify your permission to modify your **cron** settings and then invoke a text editor so that you can make your changes. Once you're done, **crontab** places the file in the right location and brings you back to a prompt.

Whether or not you have appropriate permission is determined by **crontab** by checking the **/etc/cron.allow** and **/etc/cron.deny** files. Neither of these files exists by default in Red Hat Linux 8.0, and therefore they are not consulted. However, if either of these files exists, a user must be explicitly listed there for their actions to be effected. For example, if the **/etc/cron.allow** file exists, your username must be listed in that file in order for you to be able to edit your **cron** entries. On the other hand, if the only file that exists is **/etc/cron.deny**, unless your username is listed there, you are implicitly allowed to edit your **cron** settings.

The file listing your **cronjobs** (often referred to as the **crontab** file) is formatted as follows. All values must be listed as integers.

Minute Hour Day Month DayOfWeek Command

If you want to have multiple entries for a particular column (for instance, you want a program to run at 4:00 A.M., 12:00 P.M., and 5:00 P.M.), then you need to have each of these time values in a comma-separated list. Be sure not to type any spaces in the list. For the program running at 4:00 A.M., 12:00 P.M., and 5:00 P.M., the *Hour* values list would read **4,12,17**. Notice that **cron** uses military time format.

For the *DayOfWeek* entry, 0 represents Sunday, 1 represents Monday, and so on, all the way to 6 representing Saturday.

Any entry that has a single asterisk (*) wildcard will match any minute, hour, day, month, or day of week when used in the corresponding column.

When the dates and times in the file match the current date and time, the command is run as the user who set the **crontab**. Any output generated is e-mailed back to the user. Obviously, this can result in a mailbox full of messages, so it is important to be thrifty with your reporting. A good way to keep a handle on volume is to output only error conditions and have any unavoidable output sent to **/dev/null**.

Next look at some examples. The following entry runs the program **/usr/bin/ping –c 5 zaphod** every four hours:

```
0 0,4,8,12,16,20 * * * /usr/bin/ping -c 5 zaphod
```

Here is an entry that runs the program **/usr/local/scripts/backup_level_0** at 10:00 P.M. on every Friday night:

```
0 22 * * 5 /usr/local/scripts/backup_level_0
```

And finally, here's a script to send out an e-mail at 4:01 A.M. on April 1 (whatever day that may be):

```
1 4 1 4 * /bin/mail mpawlawski@cyberbears.org < /home/rwhite/joke
```

NOTE

When **crond** executes commands, it does so with the **sh** shell. Thus, any environment variables that you might be used to may not work within **cron**.

Using the kron GUI

While you should be able to decipher and create your own **crontab** entries, there is a nice tool for making the job easier that's included with Red Hat Linux 8.0. The **kron** program (see Figure 8-2) can be run by entering its name from a terminal window or by selecting Task

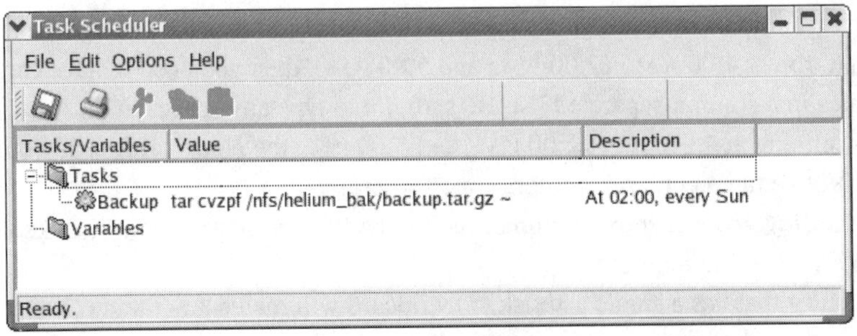

Figure 8-2 Use the **kron** tool to manage scheduled jobs.

Scheduler from the System Tools menu. It puts a pretty face on some of the harder-to-remember aspects of cron jobs, especially their periodicity. If you're comfortable with using **crontab**, you'll find **kron** a little clumsy, but if you're just getting comfortable with scheduled jobs in Linux, it can be very helpful.

To create a new scheduled task, go to the Edit menu and select New. This will bring up a configuration window as shown in Figure 8-3, in which you can enter the command, its schedule, and a descriptive comment.

The /etc/cron.* Directories

Another facility for making **crontab** more approachable is Red Hat's use of the **/etc/cron.***
directories. There are four of these directories:

- /etc/cron.hourly
- /etc/cron.daily
- /etc/cron.weekly
- /etc/cron.monthly

The executable contents of each of these directories are run each hour, day, week, or month; you don't have to specify when the jobs run. This is perfect for those cases when you don't care exactly when the jobs run, only how frequently they run.

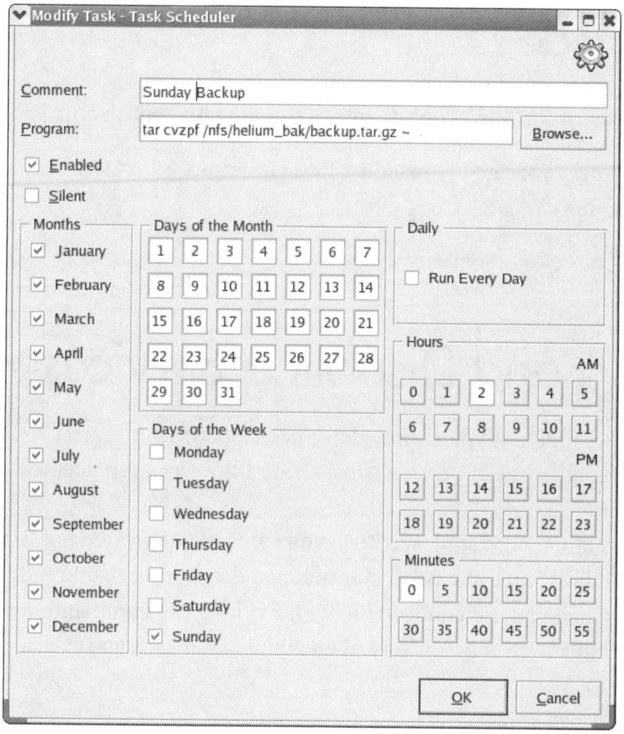

Figure 8-3 Add a scheduled job using **kron**.

There's nothing magical about any of these directories; they are merely holding areas, and the **/etc/crontab** file makes them work the way they do. Inside that file are the following lines:

```
01 * * * * root run-parts /etc/cron.hourly
02 4 * * * root run-parts /etc/cron.daily
22 4 * * 0 root run-parts /etc/cron.weekly
42 4 1 * * root run-parts /etc/cron.monthly
```

These instructions run the **run-parts** script periodically with the name of one of the periodic directories, and **run-parts** in turn runs all the programs in the directory.

Progress Check

1. When will each of the **/etc/crontab** entries run the **run-parts** script?

2. Would you expect your newly installed Red Hat Linux 8.0 system to have **/etc/cron.allow** and **/etc/cron.deny** files?

Enabling and Disabling Services

At times, you may find that you simply don't need a particular service to be started at boot time. This is especially true if you are considering Linux as a replacement for a Windows File and Print server.

As described in the preceding sections, you can cause a service not to be started by simply renaming the symbolic link in a particular runlevel directory; rename it to start with a **K** instead of an **S**. Once you are comfortable with working the command line and the symbolic links, you'll find this to be a quick way of enabling and disabling services.

Graphical Service Managers

While getting your feet wet in this process, however, you may find the graphical interface introduced in Module 7 easier to deal with. To start it, simply open a terminal window and type in the **redhat-config-services** command, or from System Settings menu, select Services. A window will pop up displaying all of your options, including a help section if you need it (see Figure 8-4).

Although the GUI tool is a nice way to do this task, you may find yourself in a situation where there is no graphical interface (for instance, you have logged in to a colocated server and cannot redirect X through the firewall). There is an interactive console-based tool available, called **ntsysv**, for turning the service defaults on or off. You run **ntsysv** as the root user, and it provides a simple interface (see Figure 8-5) in which an asterisk means the service will start when the system boots, and no asterisk means the service does not automatically start when the system boots.

---

1. The first line runs every hour, at one minute past the hour. The second line runs every day at 4:02 A.M. The third line runs every Sunday at 4:22 A.M. The fourth line runs on the first day of each month at 4:42 A.M.

2. No, the **/etc/cron.allow** and **/etc/cron.deny** files are not created during the Red Hat Linux 8.0 installation.

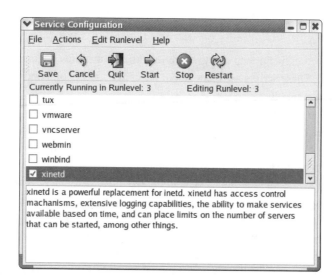

Figure 8-4 Use the **redhat-config-services** tools to enable and disable services.

If you want to do more than turn a service switch on and off, or if you don't have access to the "ncurses" text-GUI library required to run **ntsysv**, you'll need to get under the hood a little further. In that case, you will need to know about the **/etc/rc.d** directory.

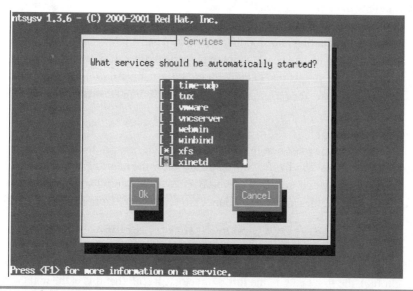

Figure 8-5 Use the **ntsysv** command to determine which services start when the system boots.

rc Scripts

The preceding section mentioned that the **/etc/inittab** file specifies which scripts to run when runlevels change. These scripts are responsible for either starting or stopping the services that are particular to the runlevel.

Because of the number of services that need to be managed, **rc** scripts are used. The main one, **/etc/rc**, is responsible for calling the appropriate scripts in the correct order for each runlevel. As you can imagine, such a script could easily become extremely uncontrollable! To keep this from happening, a slightly more elaborate system is used.

For each runlevel, a subdirectory exists in the **/etc** directory. These runlevel subdirectories follow the naming scheme of **rcX.d**, where *X* is the runlevel. For example, all the scripts for runlevel 3 are in **/etc/rc3.d**.

In the runlevel directories, symbolic links are made to scripts in the **/etc/init.d** directory. Instead of using the name of the script as it exists in the **/etc/init.d** directory, however, the symbolic links are prefixed with an **S** if the script is to start a service, or with a **K** if the script is to stop (or kill) a service. (See Module 6 for information on symbolic links.) Note that these two letters are case sensitive. You must use capitals or the startup scripts will not recognize them.

In many cases, the order in which these scripts are run makes a difference. (You can't use DNS to resolve host names if you haven't yet configured a network interface!) To enforce order, a two-digit number is suffixed to the **S** or **K**. Lower numbers execute before higher numbers; for example, **/etc/S50inet** runs before **/etc/S55named** (**S50inet** configures the network settings, and **S55named** starts the DNS server).

The scripts pointed to in the **/etc/init.d** directory are the workhorses; they perform the actual process of starting and stopping services. When **/etc/rc** runs through a specific runlevel's directory, it invokes each script in numerical order. It first runs the scripts that begin with a **K**, and then the scripts that begin with an **S**. For scripts starting with **K**, a parameter of **stop** is passed. Likewise, for scripts starting with **S**, the parameter **start** is passed.

Disabling a Service

To disable a service, you must first find out two things: the name of the service and the runlevel at which it starts. More than likely, you'll already know the name of it, and also more than likely, the service is started in both runlevels 3 and 5. If you aren't sure about the runlevel, use the **find** command (described in Module 6) to find it. For example,

```
[root@tedford rc.d]# find . -name "*nfs*" -print
```

will find all files containing the string "nfs". You'll likely get three hits (locations containing the sought file), the first being in the **init.d** directory. Recall that this is the main script that does the work, though it is not directly called. You do not want to remove this script, in the event that you want to enable it again in the future. Going back to the results of the **find** command, you'll see that you got two hits in the **rc3.d** and **rc5.d** directories.

To remove the service, simply **cd** into each of those directories and rename the symlink so that instead of starting with an **S**, it starts with a **K**. By renaming the symlink, you'll be able to come back later and easily enable it without having to try and figure out the correct order that entry should be in (for instance, should it be **S35nfs** or **S45nfs**?).

Enabling a Service

Enabling a service works just like disabling a service. You find the scripts that actually run at the appropriate runlevels, except instead of changing them from an **S** to a **K**, you'll change them *to* an **S** from a **K**.

If the symlink you are looking for does not exist but the appropriate script in the **init.d** directory does exist, you can simply add a new symlink in the **rc3.d** and **rc5.d** directories. Be sure to use the correct format for the filename (see previous sections for details).

Starting and Stopping Services

To start or stop a service from the command line, the quick and dirty way to do things is to use the **service** command. Become the root user and run:

```
[root@tedford /root]# service --status-all
```

This command shows the currently stopped and running services (complete with process ID numbers for running services). To start a service that isn't running, simply tell that service to start:

```
[root@tedford /root]# service nfs start
```

Telling a service to stop works predictably:

```
[root@tedford /root]# service nfs stop
```

You can also check the status of a single service (the full list can be overwhelming):

```
[root@tedford /root]# service nfs status
```

Other commands supported by the specific service can be used as well, including **restart** to stop and start the service, or **reload** to reread the configuration file (although sometimes these two commands are synonymous, as in the script you'll look at in the next section).

Writing Your Own rc Script

In the course of keeping a Linux system running, you will, at some point, need to modify the startup or shutdown scripts. There are two roads you can take to doing this:

● If your change is to be effected at boot time only, and the change is small, you may want to simply edit the **/etc/rc.local** script. This script gets run at the very end of the boot process.

● On the other hand, if your addition is more elaborate and/or requires that the shutdown process explicitly stop, you should add a script to the **/etc/init.d** directory. This script should take the parameters **start** and **stop** and act accordingly.

Of course, the first option, editing the **/etc/rc.local** script, is the easier of the two. To make additions to this script, simply open it in your editor of choice and append the commands you want run at the end. This is good for simple one- or two-line changes.

If you do need a separate script, however, you will need to take the second option. The process of writing an **rc** script is not as difficult as it may seem. Let's step through it using an example, to see how it works. (You can use this example as a skeleton script, by the way, changing it to add anything you need.)

Assume you want to start a special program that pops up a message every 60 minutes and reminds you that you need to take a break from the keyboard (a good idea if you don't want to get carpal tunnel syndrome!). The script to start this program will include the following:

● A description of the script's purpose (so you don't forget it a year later!)

● Verification that the program really exists before trying to start it

● Acceptance of the **start** and **stop** parameters and performance of the required actions

Given these parameters, here's the script you will write. (Notice that lines starting with a number sign (#) are only comments and not part of the script's actions, except for the first line.)

```
#!/bin/sh
#
# Carpal          Start/Stop the Carpal Notice Daemon
#
# description: Carpald is a program which wakes up every 60 minutes and
#              tells us that we need to take a break from the keyboard
#              or we'll lose all functionality of our wrists and never
#              be able to type again as long as we live.
# processname: carpald

# Source function library.
. /etc/rc.d/init.d/functions
```

```
[ -f /usr/local/sbin/carpald ] || exit 0

# See how we were called.
case "$1" in
  start)
        echo -n "Starting carpald: "
        daemon carpald

        echo
        touch /var/lock/subsys/carpald
        ;;
  stop)
        echo -n "Stopping carpald services: "
        killproc carpald

        echo
        rm -f /var/lock/subsys/carpald
        ;;
  status)
        status carpald
        ;;
  restart|reload)
        $0 stop
        $0 start
        ;;
  *)
        echo "Usage: carpald start|stop|status|restart|reload"
        exit 1
esac

exit 0
```

Once you have a new script written, simply add the necessary symbolic links (symlinks, as described in Module 6) from the appropriate runlevel directory to have the script either start or stop. In the sample script, you want it to start only in either runlevel 3 or runlevel 5. This is because it assumes these are the only two runlevels during which you will do normal day-to-day work. Lastly, you want the daemon to be shut down when you go to runlevel 6 (reboot). Here are the commands you enter to create the required symlinks:

```
[root@tedford /root]# cd /etc/rc3.d
[root@tedford rc3.d]# ln -s ../init.d/carpal S99carpal
[root@tedford rc3.d]# cd ../rc5.d
[root@tedford rc5.d]# ln -s ../init.d/carpal S99carpal
[root@tedford rc5.d]# cd ../rc6.d
[root@tedford rc6.d]# ln -s ../init.d/carpal K00carpal
```

Notice that for runlevels 3 and 5, you used the number 99 after the **S** prefix; this ensures that the script will be one of the last things to get started as part of the boot process. For runlevel 6, you wanted the opposite—**carpald** should shut down before the rest of the components. (The sequence for starting components generally goes from most critical to least critical, whereas shutting components down goes from least critical to most critical.)

Seems rather elaborate, doesn't it? Well, the good news is that because you've set up this **rc** script, you won't ever need to do it again. More important, the script will automatically run during startup and shutdown and be able to manage itself. The long-term benefits are well worth the overhead up front.

Project 8-2 Creating an rc Script

This module presents an example of an **rc** script created for a repetitive stress warning message. In this project, you'll write an **rc** script for a daemon that monitors a directory and maintains an archive of its contents. For this project, assume that there exists a program, **/usr/local/sbin/arch_data**, that detects changes in a specified directory and creates an archive of that directory's contents. The program is called this way: **/usr/local/sbin/arch_data** *monitored-directory archive-directory*.

Step by Step

1. Become **root** to edit the file **/etc/init.d/arch_data** in your preferred text editor.

2. This will be a shell script, so you need to tell the system that's the case by starting the file with the string **#!/bin/sh**.

3. Add a comment explaining the purpose of this script and the program it points to. You might want to add additional helpful information, such as what arguments are passed to the program, the date you're writing it, and your name.

4. Tell the script to make use of the functions Red Hat has already provided in the **/etc/init.d/functions** file by adding the string **. /etc/init.d/functions**.

5. Make sure the **arch_data** program exists; if it doesn't, exit.

6. Set the variable MON_DIR to the name of the directory to be monitored: **MON_DIR="/export/research/current"**.

7. Set the variable SAVE_DIR to the name of the directory to hold the changes: **SAVE_DIR="/export/research/archive"**.

8. Set up the **case** statement to read the **rc** instruction, which will be in the **$1** variable.

(continued)

9. If the instruction is **start**, then **echo** a message indicating that the service is starting, and run the **daemon** command on **arch_data**, passing $MON_DIR and $SAVE_DIR so the archive program knows what to do. Use the **touch** command to create the **/var/lock/subsys /arch_data** lock file.

10. If the instruction is **stop**, then print a message indicating that the service is stopping, and run the **killproc** command on **arch_data** program to stop it. Delete the lock file you created.

11. If the instruction is **status**, then run the **status** command on **arch_data**.

12. If the instruction is **restart** or **reload**, then stop, then start **arch_data**.

13. If the instruction is anything else, print a message listing the valid instructions and exit with an error.

14. Don't forget to close the case statement and exit without an error.

15. Add links to the new script so that it starts and shuts down properly in runlevels 2, 3, and 5.

Project Summary

If you've never done any script programming, this may not be the world's easiest project. That's okay, but be sure to look at the example in this module to help clarify things. You can also look at the contents of the **/etc/init.d** directory for some more advanced examples. Each of those scripts makes use of functions defined in the **/etc/init.d/functions** file (including **killproc**, **status**, and **daemon**), and you can polish your script by following some of the examples you see there.

By storing the program's input arguments, *monitored-directory* and *archive-directory*, in variables at the beginning of the script, you make configuration changes easier. But it would be even better to create a configuration file to hold those values (for instance, **/etc/arch_data.conf**) so that changing the daemon's configuration wouldn't require editing the startup script.

Instead of using a background process as you did in this project, you might tackle the same problem by using a **cron** job to periodically check the contents of the directory and update the archive if there are changes. The difference would be in functionality: our mythical backup process is activated by changes in the directory, while the **cron** job would be activated at a set time. But that's food for thought: one of the beautiful aspects of Linux is the opportunity to use different tools to solve the same problem.

Module Summary

This module discussed the five core services that come with every Linux system. These services do not require network support and can vary from host to host, making them very useful, since they can work regardless of whether or not the system is in multiuser mode.

A quick recap of the module:

- GRUB is Red Hat Linux's default boot loader; it is responsible for starting the operating system and uses the **/boot/grub/grub.conf** configuration file. Red Hat also supports the LILO boot loader, which uses the **/etc/lilo.conf** configuration file but, unlike GRUB, needs to be told each time that configuration file is changed.

- The boot process is responsible for getting the operating system running in one of the defined runlevels.

- The **init** process is the father of all processes in the system with a PID of 1. It also controls runlevels and can be configured through the **/etc/inittab** file.

- The **xinetd** process is the "new" version of the classic **inetd** superserver. It listens to server requests on behalf of a large number of smaller, less frequently used services. When it accepts a request for one of those services, **xinetd** starts the actual service and quietly forwards data between the network and actual service. Its configuration file is **/etc/xinetd.conf**.

- The **syslog** process is the system-wide logging daemon. Along with log entries generated by the system, **syslog** can accept log messages over the network (so long as you enable that feature). Its configuration file is **/etc/syslog.conf**.

- The **cron** service allows you to schedule events to take place at certain dates and times, which is great for periodic events such as backups and e-mail reminders. All the configuration files on which it relies are handled via the **crontab** program.

- System services are controlled by **rc** scripts, which can be created, modified, or controlled via GUI or the command line.

✓
Module 8 Mastery Check

1. Name the four core services that run on a Linux system.

2. If you look at a GRUB configuration file, how can you tell how many boot options will be displayed on the boot loader menu?

3. What would GRUB call the fourth partition on the first hard disk?

4. How can you bring up the GRUB boot menu if it is hidden?

5. What command is used to notify GRUB of changes to its configuration?

6. Give the number of the runlevel that starts with a graphical login screen.

7. What value could be given to **telinit** to send the system to single-user mode?

8. List the four fields on a line in the **/etc/inittab** file.

9. What action defined in the **/etc/inittab** file sets the system's default runlevel?

10. What action defined in the **/etc/inittab** file determines how the system responds to the CTRL-ALT-DEL keystroke combination?

11. What file would you edit and what change would you make to limit minor service concurrent connections to a default of 20?

12. How could you edit that same file to limit the services to five connections per second, and set a service lockout period of one minute when that limit is exceeded?

13. What change would you make to reduce the frequency of default **syslogd** log entries to one hour?

14. Which logging priority would you expect to generate the most messages?

15. Name two ways to run the program **foo** once per week.

16. In which order will these commands be run when the system starts up?

    A. S30foo

    B. K30bar

    C. S01biz

    D. K99bat

Module 9

Securing an
Individual Server

You don't have to look hard to find that someone has discovered yet another new and exciting way to break into your systems. Sites such as http://www.securityfocus.com and mailing lists such as BugTraq regularly announce such new exploits. And making the situation even more troublesome for system administrators is the proliferation of "script kiddies." These individuals do not themselves possess the technical knowledge to break into other sites; they use prebuilt scripts instead, motivated by the adolescent thrill of impressing friends and being a nuisance. The positive result of this behavior is that the Linux community has become very responsive to security issues that come up. In several cases, security patches have been made available within 24 hours of the announcement of a vulnerability.

In this module, you'll learn about basic techniques for securing your server. If you follow these tips, you'll be more likely to keep out the script kiddies. But be advised: No system is perfect. New holes are discovered daily, and new tools to launch attacks come out more often than we'd like to imagine. Securing your systems is much like fighting off disease—as long as you maintain basic hygiene, you're likely to be okay, but you'll never be invulnerable.

Nearly all system administration texts today have to cover these topics, explaining which of the neat, network-friendly features you have to turn off so that crackers can't abuse them. No matter what operating system you manage, if you have users, you may encounter misuse. In this module, I'll help you make it more difficult for the abusers to make headway on your systems.

CRITICAL SKILL
9.1 # Keeping Your System up2date

It's swell that programmers are slaving away like busy worker bees to close security holes as they surface. That's also useless to you if you never update your system to reflect the changes they're making. Red Hat is kind enough to package up security fixes for the software it distributes, and it makes those packages available to you in a couple of ways.

Making use of these updates is an excellent way of ensuring that known exploits for the software you need to use can't be made into open doors for those who attack your systems. Whether you pay for support via the Red Hat Network and configure your systems to install the security fixes automatically, or you simply download security updates as they become available, installing these upgrades is mandatory for ensuring that your systems are as secure as they can be.

Using the Red Hat Network

The easiest way to manage Red Hat package updates, for security fixes or anything else, is to use the Red Hat Network (RHN). You can sign up for this service at http://rhn.redhat.com; there is an annual fee required to entitle more than one system to updates (boxed software releases come with varying periods of additional free RHN access). When you installed Red

Hat Linux 8.0, it automatically installed the Red Hat Network Registration Client, which you can start by going to the panel's main menu button and running the following command from a terminal window:

```
[rwhite@tedford ~]$ up2date
```

TIP

Even if you're not interested in joining Red Hat Network yet, you can try it out. You can receive a free demonstration entitlement by creating an account and registering a system.

Upgrading Using up2date

The first time you execute the **up2date** command, you'll see a configuration screen to enable you to begin the process of registering your server with the Red Hat Network, as shown in the following illustration. If you run the command as a non-root user, you'll first have to enter the root password.

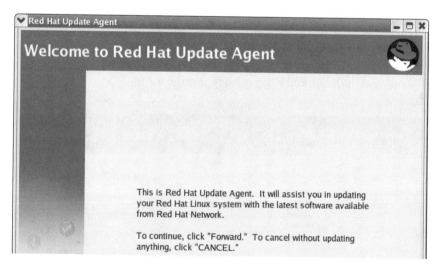

Click the Forward button to continue with the configuration process. You'll get another graphical screen (see Figure 9-1) with some lengthy text describing Red Hat's privacy statement. Read it yourself, typos and all, but the bottom line is that you have some control over the information that Red Hat collects, but they'll collect your hardware and package inventory and your IP address.

If you click the Forward button again, you'll finally arrive at the registration screen (shown in Figure 9-2), at which you can enter existing Red Hat Network user or organization account information, or create a user account. You may have to try multiple usernames if your choices turn out to be popular. Click Forward to continue.

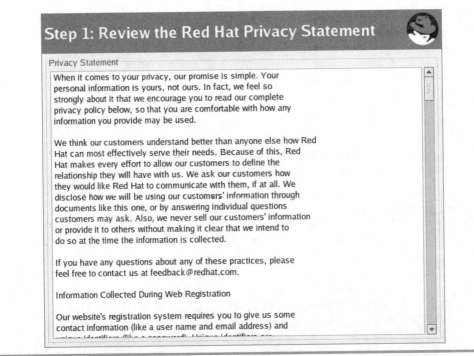

Figure 9-1 Read and decipher Red Hat's privacy statement.

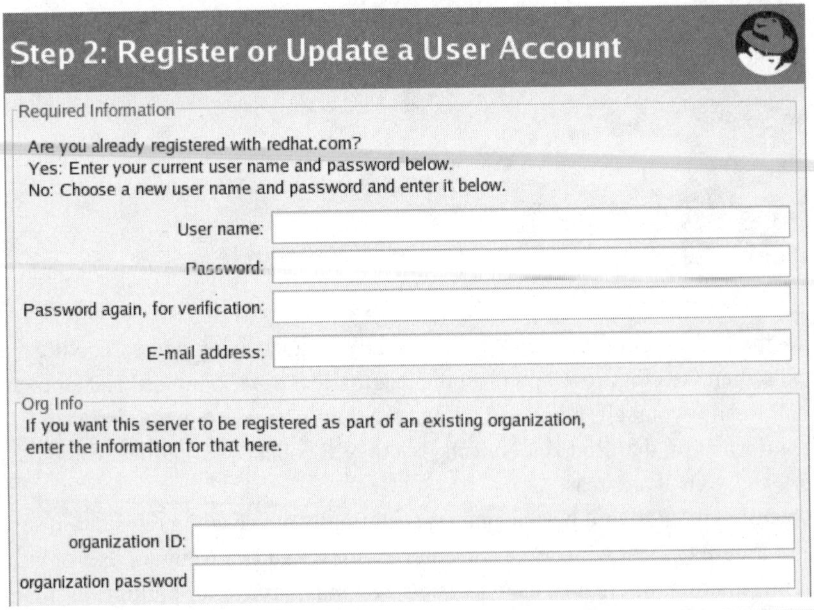

Figure 9-2 Register a user name and password with the Red Hat Network.

On the next screen, you'll find a list of the hardware on your system, plus an editable field in which you can enter the name of the system, or give it an identification number, or both. You can uncheck the box to avoid sending your hardware configuration information to Red Hat if you so choose. Click Forward to move on.

Step 3: Register a System Profile - Hardware

A Profile Name is a descriptive name that you choose to identify this System Profile on Red Hat Network web pages. Optionally, include a computer serial or identification number.

Profile name: tedford

Hardware information is important to determine what updated software and drivers are relevant to this system. The minimum set of information you can include will contain your system's architecture and Red Hat Linux version.

☑ Include information about hardware and network

Included information

Red Hat Linux version: 8.0	CPU model: Pentium III (Katmai)
Hostname: tedford	CPU speed: 500 MHz
IP address: 10.0.2.52	Memory: 512 megabytes

Additional hardware information including PCI devices, disk sizes and mount points will be included in the profile.

The following screen, shows a list of the packages found on the system. If you want this information sent to Red Hat, leave the boxes checked. You can unselect individual packages or the whole lot of them as you see fit. Click Forward when you're ready.

Step 3: Register a System Profile - Packages

RPM information is important to determine what updated software packages are relevant to this system.

☑ Include RPM packages installed on this system in my System Profile

Below is a list of packages present on your system that RPM knows about:

Package Name	Version	Release
☑ 4Suite	0.11.1	10
☑ GConf	1.0.9	6
☑ GConf2	1.2.1	3
☑ Glide3	2001052	19
☑ LPRng	3.8.9	6
☑ MAKEDEV	3.3.1	2
☑ ORBit	0.5.13	5
☑ ORBit2	2.4.1	1
☑ Omni	0.7.0	6
☑ Omni-foomatic	0.7.0	6
☑ PyXML	0.7.1	6

When the next screen comes up (shown in the following illustration), you'll get one last chance to avoid sending the collected data to Red Hat. If you've changed your mind, click the Back button to change things or the Cancel button to exit **up2date**. Otherwise, click Forward.

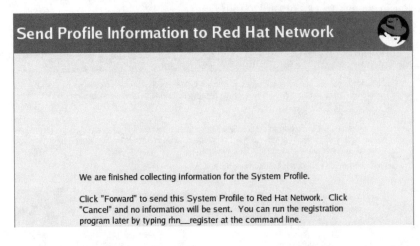

If you continued, and I hope you did, you will get a list of Red Hat update channels that apply to your system, shown next. The **up2date** command shows the list of update channels to which the system is subscribed. The Red Hat Linux 8.0 channel suited to your system will be listed and enabled. Click Forward to continue.

The next screen (in Figure 9-3) gives you a list of available update packages that have been flagged to be skipped. By default, this includes all kernel packages. If you want to install some or all of the packages listed here, click the appropriate boxes for the packages you want. Click Forward when you're ready.

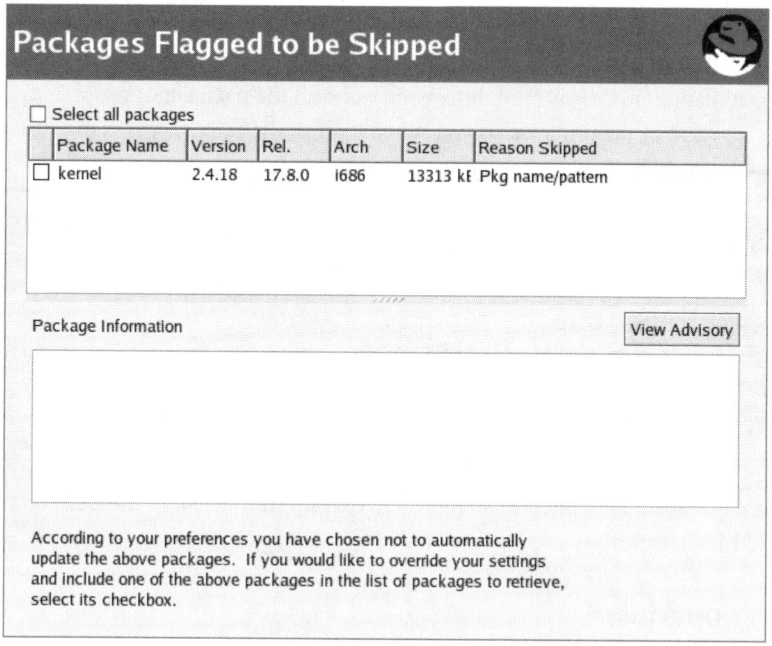

Packages Flagged to be Skipped

☐ Select all packages

Package Name	Version	Rel.	Arch	Size	Reason Skipped
☐ kernel	2.4.18	17.8.0	i686	13313 kE	Pkg name/pattern

Package Information   [View Advisory]

According to your preferences you have chosen not to automatically
update the above packages. If you would like to override your settings
and include one of the above packages in the list of packages to retrieve,
select its checkbox.

Figure 9-3 The up2date command lists update packages scheduled to be skipped.

The following screen shows the available package updates that apply to your system.
As with previous screens, you can opt to include all the packages or select them one by one.
After selecting the packages you want, click Forward.

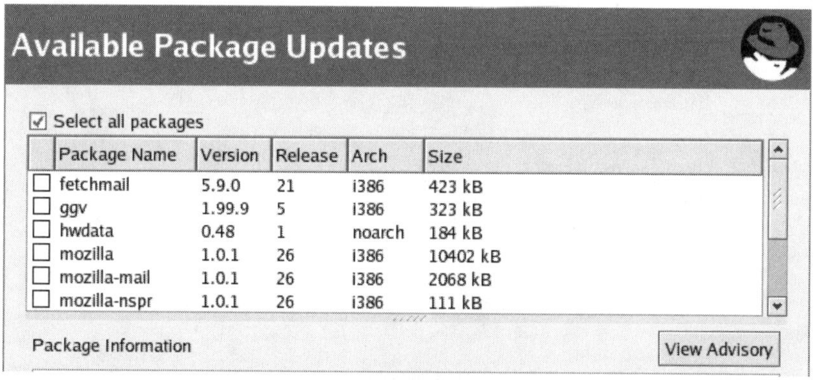

Available Package Updates

☑ Select all packages

Package Name	Version	Release	Arch	Size
☐ fetchmail	5.9.0	21	i386	423 kB
☐ ggv	1.99.9	5	i386	323 kB
☐ hwdata	0.48	1	noarch	184 kB
☐ mozilla	1.0.1	26	i386	10402 kB
☐ mozilla-mail	1.0.1	26	i386	2068 kB
☐ mozilla-nspr	1.0.1	26	i386	111 kB

Package Information   [View Advisory]

The **up2date** program will now retrieve the packages you selected. This may take a while
if there are lots of updates or if you have limited bandwidth. Grab a Mountain Dew, trim your

fingernails, or go over a few mastery checks while you're waiting. When the packages have downloaded, the Forward button will be enabled. Click it to continue on to install the packages.

The installation process is straightforward; as with the package download, **up2date** will keep you apprised of the progress so far. When the installation process is done, you'll be able to click the Forward button again to bring up a screen listing the updates that have been installed.

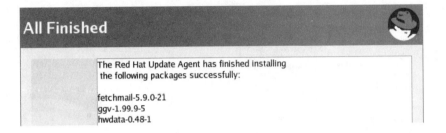

From this screen, click the Finish button to exit **up2date** back to the desktop of your up-to-date Linux server!

Configuring up2date

If your network uses an HTTP proxy system, or if you want to make other changes to the **up2date** utility's default configuration, you can use the **up2date-config** program to set up things the way you want them. Invoke the program using the following command:

```
[root@tedford ~]$ up2date-config
```

This command brings up the configuration screen shown in the following illustration. The contents of the General tab allow you to point to a proxy server and enter your authentication information.

You can also set the package retrieval options from the Retrieval/Installation tab (shown in Figure 9-4). If you want to check the authenticity of the upgrade packages, prevent installation

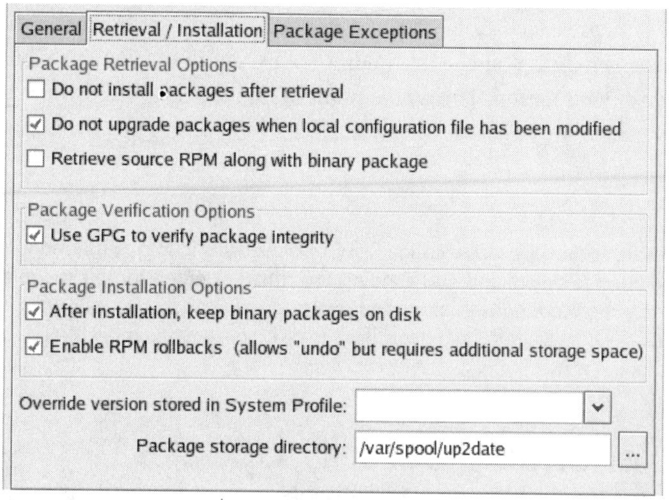

Figure 9-4 Configure package retrieval and installation options in up2date-config.

of the packages (just download them), or enable "undo" operations for upgrades about which you have second thoughts, you can do those things here.

If you want the **up2date** program to download kernel upgrade packages by default, you can make that configuration change from the Package Exceptions tab, shown in Figure 9-5.

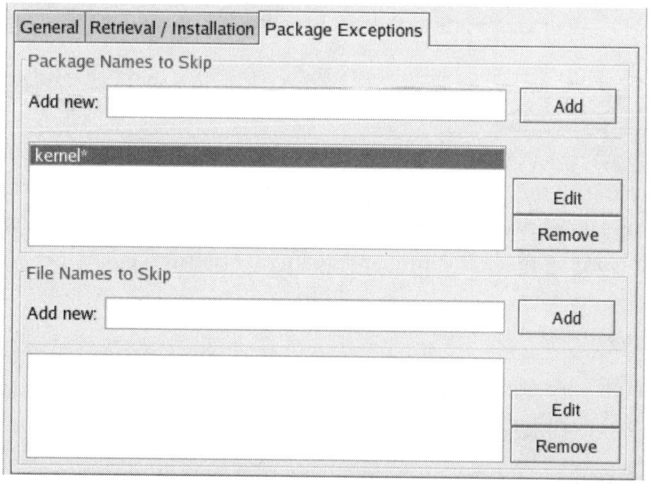

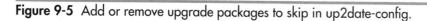

Figure 9-5 Add or remove upgrade packages to skip in up2date-config.

By default, the kernel-related packages are not automatically downloaded, so there should already be an entry in the skip list. You can add additional exceptions if you wish, but don't do this unless you have a good reason. The whole point of this tool is to keep your system up to date.

NOTE

You can also initiate system upgrades via the RHN web interface at http://rhn.redhat.com. The systems will need to be entitled and running the **rhnsd** daemon for this to work properly, but it can be more convenient than having to touch each of many systems to perform updates. Of course, running **rhnsd** itself may have security implications, but if you've got to choose, **rhnsd** is the lesser of two evils.

Manually Performing Security Updates

You don't have to be a Red Hat Network subscriber or use the **up2date** command to keep your system up to date. Instead, you can track Red Hat Linux 8.0 security updates from Red Hat's web site at https://rhn.redhat.com/errata/rh8-errata.html. Follow these steps to update your system the manual way:

1. Find the packages you need on the web site.

2. Download them from the web site to your system.

3. Verify their authenticity by checking their GNU Privacy Guard keys using the **rpm –K *.rpm** command in the download directory.

4. Run the package upgrades as described in Module 4.

Project 9-1 Getting Your System up2date

You've seen the screens in this module; now see them on your very own Linux server's screen. In the course of this project, you will create a Red Hat Network account, register your computer, and update its packages. Even if you have already burned your one demonstration run of **up2date**, you can make this project a reality by registering another account name.

Step by Step

1. Run the **up2date** program to set up your account and register your Red Hat Linux 8.0 system (if you haven't already).

2. Select at least one, but not all, of the available packages for download.

3. Once the packages have been downloaded, install them.

4. Now that you've used the "manual" version of the **up2date** process, check to see if the RHN daemon process is activated. If it isn't, start it up.

5. Log onto your account at http://rhn.redhat.com and find your registered system. Set it up to perform the remainder of the upgrade installations.

6. The RHN daemon process checks for updates every two hours by default. Track the progress of the update you scheduled using the Red Hat Network web site.

7. Once the packages are listed as having been updated, check a list of the locally installed packages and look for the updated versions.

8. If the kernel has been upgraded during this process, reboot and ensure that the system still comes up properly.

Project Summary

Now that was an easy project. Maintaining packages on a Red Hat Linux server is not difficult, because of the automation that the Red Hat Network provides. If you do lots of customization of startup scripts or make other significant changes, you may run into problems because certain packages won't be upgraded (otherwise they would clobber your changes). This can cascade into a larger problem if the nonupgrading packages are required for other upgrades to be installed. Fortunately, this problem can be avoided by using tools to change the startup scripts, rather than moving them around willy-nilly.

CRITICAL SKILL
9.2 Understanding TCP/IP
and Network Security

This module assumes you have experience configuring a system for use on a TCP/IP network. Because the focus here is on network security and not an introduction to networking, this section discusses only those parts of TCP/IP affecting your system's security.

The Importance of Port Numbers

Every host on an IP-based network has at least one IP address. In addition, every Linux-based host has many individual processes running. Each process has the potential to be a network client, a network server, or both. Obviously, if a packet's destination were identified with the IP address alone, the operating system would have no way of knowing to which process the packet's contents should be delivered.

To solve this problem, TCP/IP adds a component identifying a TCP (or UDP) *port*. Every connection from one host to another has a *source port* and a *destination port*. Each port is labeled with an integer between 0 and 65535.

In order to identify every unique connection possible between two hosts, the operating system keeps track of four pieces of information: the source IP address, the destination IP address, the source port number, and the destination port number. The combination of these four values is guaranteed to be unique for all host-to-host connections. (Actually, the operating system tracks a myriad pieces of connection information, but only these four elements are needed to uniquely identify a connection.)

The host initiating a connection specifies the destination IP address and port number. Obviously, the source IP address is already known. But the source port number, the value that will make the connection unique, is assigned by the source operating system. It searches through its list of already open connections and assigns the next available port number. By convention, this number is always greater than 1024 (port numbers from 0 to 1023 are reserved for system uses). Technically, the source host can also select its source port number. In order to do this, however, another process cannot have already taken that port. Generally, most applications let the operating system pick the source port number for them.

Knowing this arrangement, you can see how source Host A can open multiple connections to a single service on destination Host B. Host B's IP address and port number will always be constant, but Host A's port number will be different for every connection. The combination of source and destination IPs and port numbers (a 4-tuple) is therefore unique, and both systems can have multiple independent data streams (connections) between each other.

Port Dangers

For a server to offer services, it must run programs that listen to specific port numbers. Many of these port numbers are called *well-known services* because the port number associated with a service is an approved standard. For example, port 80 is the well-known service port for the HTTP protocol.

All these ports allowing incoming connects are not just an opportunity for productive, predictable use of your system, they're also an opportunity for the unscrupulous or clueless to gain unintended access on your system. Legitimate users' systems know the default port numbers for the services you'll offer, but so will crackers' tools. So by default, you'll want to restrict access as much as possible, allowing only your real users to access your system.

In "Using the netstat Command," later in this module, you'll look at the **netstat** command as an important tool for network security. When you have a firm understanding of what port numbers represent, you'll be able to easily identify and interpret the network security statistics provided by the **netstat** command.

For More Information on TCP/IP

There are many great books that discuss TCP/IP in greater detail. The *Network Administrator's Reference* by Tere' Parnell and Christopher Null (/McGraw-Hill/Osborne, 1999) is a good place to start. This book discusses network administration from a high-level point of view and is a solid text all by itself (despite being very Windows NT–centric). It discusses TCP/IP but doesn't get too far into the nuts and bolts.

The ultimate TCP/IP "bible" (referenced by network developers and administrators around the world) is W. Richard Stevens' *TCP/IP Illustrated* series (Addison-Wesley, 1994–96). These books step you through TCP/IP and related services in painstaking detail. As a systems administrator, you'll be interested mostly in *Volume 1: The Protocols,* which addresses the suite of protocols and gives a strong explanation of IP stacks. If there's a kernel-hacker inside of you who's curious about TCP/IP implementation, check out Stevens' line-by-line analysis of the BSD network code in *Volume 2: The Implementation.* (Although there's little resemblance between Linux's networking code and the code documented in *Volume 2,* the general guidance and philosophy offered are still invaluable.)

Another excellent book, *TCP/IP Network Administration* by Craig Hunt (O'Reilly & Associates, 2002), is a solid network administration reference. It has a much greater breadth of topics (but less technical depth) than Stevens' *Volume 1.*

Finally, if you're responsible for implementing a firewall (and I recommend you do implement one), the O'Reilly & Associates text on firewall design, *Building Internet Firewalls* (O'Reilly & Associates, 2000), edited by D. Brent Chapman, et al., is a good one.

CRITICAL SKILL
9.3 Using Tracking Services

The services provided by a server are what make it a server. These services are provided by processes that bind to network ports and listen to incoming requests. For example, a web server might start a process that binds to port 80 and listens for requests to download the pages of a site. Unless a process exists to listen to a specific port, Linux will simply ignore packets sent to that port.

NOTE

Remember that when a process makes a request to another server, it opens a connection on a port, as well. The process is, in effect, listening to data coming in from that port. However, on the client the process knows to whom it's talking because it initiated the request. The client process will automatically ignore any packets sent to it that do not originate from the server to which it's connected.

This section discusses the usage of the **netstat** command, a tool for tracking network connections (among other things) in your system. It is, without a doubt, one of the most useful debugging tools in your arsenal for troubleshooting security and day-to-day network problems.

Using the netstat Command

To track what ports are open and what ports have processes listening to them, you use the **netstat** command. For example:

```
[root@tedford /root]# netstat -natu
Active Internet connections (servers and established)
Proto Recv-Q Send-Q Local Address        Foreign Address       State
tcp       1      0 209.179.251.53:1297   199.184.252.5:80   CLOSE_WAIT
tcp       1      0 209.179.251.53:1296   199.184.252.5:80   CLOSE_WAIT
tcp      57      0 209.179.158.93:1167   199.97.226.1:21    CLOSE_WAIT
tcp       0      0 192.168.1.1:6000      192.168.1.1:1052   ESTABLISHED
tcp       0      0 192.168.1.1:1052      192.168.1.1:6000   ESTABLISHED
tcp       0      0 0.0.0.0:4242          0.0.0.0:*             LISTEN
tcp       0      0 0.0.0.0:1036          0.0.0.0:*             LISTEN
tcp       0      0 0.0.0.0:1035          0.0.0.0:*             LISTEN
tcp       0      0 0.0.0.0:1034          0.0.0.0:*             LISTEN
tcp       0      0 0.0.0.0:1033          0.0.0.0:*             LISTEN
tcp       0      0 0.0.0.0:1032          0.0.0.0:*             LISTEN
tcp       0      0 0.0.0.0:1031          0.0.0.0:*             LISTEN
tcp       0      0 0.0.0.0:1024          0.0.0.0:*             LISTEN
tcp       0      0 0.0.0.0:6000          0.0.0.0:*             LISTEN
tcp       0      0 0.0.0.0:80            0.0.0.0:*             LISTEN
tcp       0      0 0.0.0.0:515           0.0.0.0:*             LISTEN
tcp       0      0 192.168.1.1:53        0.0.0.0:*             LISTEN
tcp       0      0 127.0.0.1:53          0.0.0.0:*             LISTEN
tcp       0      0 0.0.0.0:98            0.0.0.0:*             LISTEN
tcp       0      0 0.0.0.0:113           0.0.0.0:*             LISTEN
tcp       0      0 0.0.0.0:23            0.0.0.0:*             LISTEN
tcp       0      0 0.0.0.0:21            0.0.0.0:*             LISTEN
tcp       0      0 0.0.0.0:111           0.0.0.0:*             LISTEN
udp       0      0 0.0.0.0:1024          0.0.0.0:*
```

```
udp        0        0 192.168.1.1:53          0.0.0.0:*
udp        0        0 127.0.0.1:53            0.0.0.0:*
udp        0        0 0.0.0.0:111             0.0.0.0:*

[root@tedford /root]#
```

By default (with no parameters), **netstat** will provide all established connections for both network and domain sockets. That means you'll see not only the connections that are actually working over the network, but also the interprocess communications (which, from a security monitoring standpoint, are not useful). So in the command illustrated, you have asked **netstat** to show you all ports (**–a**), whether they are listening or actually connected, for TCP (**–t**) and UDP (**–u**). You have told **netstat** not to spend any time resolving hostnames from IP addresses (**–n**).

In the **netstat** output, each line represents either a TCP or UDP network port, as indicated by the first column of the output. The Recv-Q (receive queue) column lists the number of bytes received by the kernel but not read by the process. Next, the Send-Q column tells you the number of bytes sent to the other side of the connection but not acknowledged.

The fourth, fifth, and sixth columns are the most interesting in terms of system security. The Local Address column tells you your own server's IP address and port number. Remember that your server recognizes itself as 127.0.0.1 and 0.0.0.0 as well as its normal IP address. In the case of multiple interfaces, each port being listened to will show up on both interfaces and thus as two separate IP addresses. The port number is separated from the IP address by a colon. In the output from the preceding **netstat** example, one Ethernet device has the IP address 192.168.1.1, and the PPP connection has the address 209.179.251.53. (Your IP addresses will vary depending on your setup.)

The fifth column, Foreign Address, identifies the other side of the connection. In the case of a port that is being listened to for new connections, the default value will be 0.0.0.0:*. This IP address means nothing, since you're still waiting for a remote host to connect to you!

The sixth column tells you the State of the connection. The man page for **netstat** lists all of the states, but the two you'll see most often are LISTEN and ESTABLISHED. The LISTEN state means there is a process on your server listening to the port and ready to accept new connections. The ESTABLISHED state means just that—a connection is established between a client and server.

Security Implications of netstat's Output

By listing all of the available connections, you can get a snapshot of what the system is doing. You should be able to explain and justify *all* ports listed. If your system is listening to a port that you cannot explain, this should raise suspicions.

If you've been using your memory cells for other purposes and haven't memorized the services and their associated port numbers, you can look up the matching info you need in the

/etc/services file. However, some services (most notably those that use the portmapper) don't have set port numbers but are valid services. To see which process is associated with a port, use the **–p** option with **netstat**. Be on the lookout for odd or unusual processes using the network. For example, if the BASH shell is listening to a network port, you can be fairly certain that something odd is going on.

Finally, remember that you are interested only in the destination port of a connection; this tells you which service is being connected to and whether it is legitimate. Unfortunately, **netstat** doesn't explicitly tell you who originated a connection, but you can usually figure it out if you give it a little thought. Of course, becoming familiar with the applications that you do run and their use of network ports is the best way to determine who originated a connection to where. In general, you'll find that the rule of thumb is that the side whose port number is greater than 1024 is the side that originated the connection. Obviously, this general rule doesn't apply to services typically running on ports higher than 1024, such as X (port 6000).

Shutting Down Services

One purpose for the **netstat** command is to determine what services are enabled on your servers. Making Linux easier to install and manage right out of the box has led to more and more default settings that are unsafe, so keeping track of services is especially important.

When you're evaluating which services should stay and which should go, answer the following questions:

1. *Do I need the service?* The answer to this question is very important. In most situations, you should be able to disable a great number of services that start up by default. A stand-alone Web server, for example, should not need to run NFS.

2. *If I do need the service, is the default setting secure?* This question can also help you eliminate some services—if they aren't secure and they can't be made secure, then chances are they should be removed. The Telnet service, for instance, is often a candidate for early removal because it requires that passwords be sent over the network without encryption.

3. *Does the service software need updates?* All software needs updates from time to time, such as that on web and FTP servers. This is because as features get added, new security problems creep in. So be sure to remember to track the server software's development and get upgrades installed as soon as security bulletins are posted.

Shutting Down an xinetd Service

To shut down a service that is started via the **xinetd** program, simply edit the service's configuration file in **/etc/xinetd** and set disable equal to Yes. See Module 8 for more information on **xinetd**. Send a SIGUSR2 signal to reload **xinetd**. Red Hat Linux makes this simple using the following command:

```
[root@tedford /root]# service xinetd reload
```

NOTE

If you have a system using the older **inetd**, edit the **/etc/inetd.conf** file and comment out the service you no longer want. To designate the service as a comment, start the line with a number sign (#). Remember to send the HUP signal to **inetd** once you've made any changes to the **/etc/inetd.conf** file.

Shutting Down Non-xinetd Services

If a service is not run by **xinetd**, then a process that is probably started at boot time is running it. The easiest way to stop that from happening is to edit the startup service list using the **redhat-config-services** GUI tool or the **ntsysv** command from the command line as described in Module 8. You can also manually change the symlink. Go to the **/etc/rc.d/** directory and in one of the **rc*.d** directories, find the symlinks that point to the startup script. (See Module 8 for information on startup scripts.) Rename the symlink to start with an X instead of S. Should you decide to restart a service, it's easy to rename it again starting with an S. If you have renamed the startup script but want to stop the currently running process, use the **service** command to tell the process to **stop**. For example, here is the command to kill a **portmap** process:

```
[root@tedford /root]# service portmap stop
```

NOTE

As always, be sure of what you're killing before you kill it, especially on a production server.

A Note about the syslogd Service

One non-**inetd** service that will pop up on **netstat** output but can be safely ignored is **syslogd**. This service has historically defaulted to binding to a network port and listening for network messages to log. Because of the danger of logging arbitrary messages from a network, Linux developers have added a mechanism whereby **syslogd** logs requests sent from other hosts only if it has been started with the –**r** option. By default, **syslogd** does not start with –**r**, so you can safely let it remain on your system.

Monitoring Your System

The process of tying down your server's security isn't just for the sake of securing your server; it gives you the opportunity to see clearly what normal server behavior should look like. After all, once you know what normal behavior is, unusual behavior will stick out like a sore thumb. (For example, if you turned off your Telnet service when setting up the server, seeing a log entry for Telnet means something is very wrong!)

Commercial packages that perform monitoring do exist and may be worth checking out for your site as a whole, but I'll leave the discussions of their capabilities to *Network World* or *InfoWorld*. Here, you'll take a look at a variety of other excellent tools that help you accomplish the monitoring of your system. Some of these tools come with all Linux distributions; some don't. All are free and easily acquired.

Making the Best Use of syslog

In Module 8, you explored syslog, the system logger that saves messages from various programs into a set of text files for record-keeping purposes. By now, you've probably seen the type of log messages you get with syslog. These include security-related messages such as who has logged in to the system, when they logged in, and so forth.

As you can imagine, it's possible to analyze these logs to build a time-lapse image of the utilization of your system services. This data can also point out questionable activity. For example, why was the host crackerboy.nothing-better-to-do.net sending so many web requests in such a short period of time? What was he looking for? Has he found a hole in the system?

Log Parsing

Doing periodic checks on the system's log files is an important part of maintaining security. Unfortunately, scrolling through an entire day's worth of logs is a time-consuming and unerringly boring task that reveals few meaningful events. To ease the drudgery, pick up a text on a scripting language (such as Perl) and write small scripts to parse out the logs. A well-designed script works by throwing away what it recognizes as normal behavior and showing everything else. This can reduce thousands of log entries for a day's worth of activities down to a manageable few dozen. This is an effective way to detect attempted break-ins and possible security gaps. Hopefully, it'll become entertaining to watch the script kiddies trying and failing to break down your walls.

You may also want to look into the logwatch program that comes with Red Hat 8. This simple program can be configured to create reports based on your log activity and mail them to the administrator. It's certainly not the perfect solution, but it may be a good starting point. Read the man page for more details.

Storing Log Entries

Unfortunately, log parsing may not be enough. If someone breaks into your system, it's likely that your log files will be promptly erased—which means all those wonderful scripts won't be able to tell you a thing. To get around this, consider dedicating a single host on your network to storing log entries. Configure your **/etc/syslog.conf** file to send all of its messages to this single host, and configure the host so that it's listening only to the syslog port (514). In most instances, this should be enough to gather, in a centralized place, the evidence of any bad things happening.

If you're *really* feeling paranoid, consider attaching a DOS-based PC to the serial port of the loghost and, using a terminal emulation package such as Telix, recording all of the messages sent to the loghost. (You can also use another Linux box running **minicom** in log mode—just be sure *not* to network this second Linux box!) Have **/etc/syslog.conf** configured to send all messages to a **/dev/ttyS0** if you're using COM1 or **/dev/ttyS1** if you're using COM2. And, of course, do *not* connect the DOS system to the network. This way, in the event the loghost also gets attacked, the log files won't be destroyed. The log files will be safe residing on the DOS system, which is impossible to log in to without physical access.

For the highest degree of monitoring capability, connect a parallel-port printer to the DOS system and have the terminal emulation package echo everything it receives on the serial port to the printer. Thus, if the DOS system fails or is damaged in some way by an attack, you'll have a hard copy of the logs. (Note that a serious drawback to using the printer for logging is that you cannot easily search through the logs. If you choose to set up this arrangement, consider also keeping an electronic copy for easier searching.)

TIP

Consider using a package like **swatch** to page you when it sees a log entry that indicates trouble. You can find out more about it at http://www.oit.ucsb.edu/~eta/swatch/.

Monitoring Bandwidth with MRTG

Monitoring the amount of bandwidth being used on your servers produces some very useful information. The most practical use for it is justifying the need for upgrades. By showing system utilization levels to your managers, you'll be providing hard numbers to back up your claims. Your data can be easily turned into a graph, too—and managers like graphs! Another useful aspect of monitoring bandwidth is to identify bottlenecks in the system, thus helping you to better balance the system load. But the most useful aspect of graphing your bandwidth is to identify when things go wrong.

Once you've installed a package such as MRTG (Multi-Router Traffic Grapher, available in Red Hat Linux 8.0) to monitor bandwidth, you will quickly get a criterion for what "normal" looks like on your site. A substantial drop or increase in utilization is something to investigate. Check your logs, and look for configuration files with odd or unusual entries.

COPS

The COPS tool (Computer Oracle and Password System) provides a simple and automated way of checking for unusual settings in the system. Such checks include looking for SetUID programs in home directories, unusual permission settings on home directories, configuration files that expose your system to outside access without authorization, and so on.

One of the most significant features of COPS is that it is designed to be automatically run from a **cron** entry (see Module 8 for more about **cron**) every night. The report, if there is anything to report, is e-mailed to you.

You can research and download the latest and greatest version of COPS at ftp://ftp.cert.org/pub/tools.

Tripwire

Tripwire, distributed as a standard Red Hat Linux 8.0 package, takes a very paranoid approach to security: If something changes, Tripwire tells you. This comprehensive protection removes the opportunity for someone to place a "backdoor" or "time bomb" in your system.

Tripwire generates MD5 checksums of every file on your system and saves them in an encrypted format. When you want to check on differences, you can recall the saved checksums and compare all of the files on the system to their known good MD5 checksum. Differences are reported.

The idea here is for you to perform an install and then ready a system for network deployment. But before actually putting the system onto the network, you run the Tripwire tool to generate and store all of the checksums. You can be confident that your list of MD5 checksums is safe in its encrypted domicile.

The process of setting up a Tripwire arrangement is time consuming. And if you use it on a system you're fiddling with, you'll get lots and lots of change notifications. However, short of cutting off network connectivity, it's hard to tighten up a system any more than this.

Nessus

Nessus is a very flexible security scanner with a modular architecture that helps it keep up with the latest threatening developments. While it's not the final word in threat assessment (there isn't one), it's very capable and full-featured, with a variety of scanning and reporting options. See http://www.nessus.org for more information. You can also install Nessus via a package from http://freshrpms.net, but be mindful that third-party packages could introduce vulnerabilities of their own. Sort of makes you want to disconnect your computers from the rest of the world, if you focus too much on this security stuff, doesn't it?

Nessus is a client/server tool for which you'll have to set up a server process, add users who are allowed to run scans, and then launch a GUI to configure an "attack" to identify vulnerabilities. By default, Nessus doesn't try to crash the host you're testing, but you might want to be careful about which potential vulnerabilities you test. Running a denial of service attack as a test of a production server during business hours might be a career-limiting move.

SATAN

SATAN, the System Administrator Tool for Analyzing Networks, was released in the mid-1990s to a flurry of press suggestions that it was a hacker's toolkit. And SATAN's author, Dan Farmer, more or less declared that it *was* a hacker's toolkit—but for system administrators rather than evildoers.

SATAN works by probing your network for potential security holes. This program is especially interesting because it can be run from both inside (for you) and outside of your network (against you). It's an effective way of exposing firewall gaps when you run it from the outside, and an excellent investigation of internal weaknesses when run from an inside host.

Although SATAN is a bit older and doesn't identify many of the newer attacks that are employed today, it does do many of the "twist the door handle and see if it's open" checks that are no less important. You should assume that others will run SATAN against you, so be sure you know where your own weaknesses are and get them fixed as quickly as possible.

Like COPS, SATAN is available from ftp://ftp.cert.org/pub/tools.

Ask the Expert

Q: **I'm interested in learning more about system security in general. What can I read on the subject?**

A: There's tons of information available, so the biggest problem is sorting out what you really want to find out about. Red Hat has a Security Guide document that discusses a variety of security issues. Look at the HTML version at https://www.redhat.com/docs/manuals/linux/RHL-8.0-Manual/security-guide/. I'm fond of the policy documents available at http://www.sans.org/newlook/resources/policies/policies.htm, from the SysAdmin, Audit, Network, Security (SANS) Institute, and the Auditing Linux document at http://www.sans.org/SCORE/checklists/AuditingLinux.doc.

(continued)

Q: You mention several security-related tools; are there more I should know about?

A: The Linux Intrusion Detection System, which is software for bolstering the security of a Linux system's operation, is worth looking into at http://www.lids.org. There are also "hardened" Linux distributions, including Bastille Linux (http://www.bastille-linux.org), which is an add-on for other distributions (including Red Hat Linux 8.0) designed to tighten security for you. Furthermore, if you follow the link sections of the web sites listed in "Find Helpful Resources Online," later in this module, you'll find a wide range of additional materials to peruse.

Q: I've heard that Linux is much more secure than Windows. Is it that secure?

A: There have been lots of arguments on this subject, with people going so far as to count the number of vulnerability reports on each operating system. Unfortunately, this is rarely an apples-to-apples comparison, and debating the issue won't make your servers, whether from Microsoft, Red Hat, or somebody else, any more secure. Instead, spend your efforts on becoming knowledgeable about what the real risks are. Spend some time browsing the sites mentioned in this module; they'll give you some solid information on what to do with the systems you have.

Q: But I need to know which operating system is most secure so that I can use it and not have to worry.

A: But unfortunately, you'll always have to worry. The only way to secure a computer system is to turn it off and lock it up. Even then, it could be compromised by someone with a lock pick set and a UPS. So unless you plan to dump your computers in a smelting furnace (alongside any rogue T-1000 terminators you run across), you're going to need to exert some effort keeping on top of their security.

Project 9-2 Running a Nessus Scan

There are lots of interesting tools available for scanning systems for vulnerabilities. It's quite instructive to see the output from such a tool, to see what somebody else might find out about your system.

While there may be other pressing issues to consider first (I'll explain a few of them in "Be Aware of Security Miscellany" later in this module), scanning a system doesn't take long, and just reading the explanation of the results can be an excellent learning experience.

Step by Step

1. Obtain and install Nessus. Using the http://freshrpms.net site's prebuilt packages is the easiest way, but you can practice your software building and installation skills (from Module 4) by downloading the source code from http://www.nessus.org. Install all the packages or build both server and client software.

2. Once Nessus is installed, create a certification for the server using the **/sbin/nessus-mkcert** command.

3. Add a Nessus user with the **nessus-adduser** command.

4. Start the **nessusd** service.

5. Start the client program, **nessus**, and point it to the host system running **nessusd**.

6. Log in as the Nessus user you added.

7. Configure the scan to use whichever plug-ins sound interesting. The default settings work pretty well, but remember not to bombard an important server.

8. Select a target system and scan away.

9. Look at the resulting report, double-clicking on the network and host information that appears to get to the target system's results.

10. Decide whether you'll need to disable any services, apply any updates, or perform other security-related housecleaning based on your results.

Project Summary

Running Nessus is not at all hard, so installing and configuring it may be the most difficult part. By now you should be an old pro at setting up software on your Linux system! Avail yourself of help online if you get stuck, and refer to the man pages, or even type **nessus** at a prompt and press TAB to see which auto-completion options are available. Also, remember that you're performing a vulnerability scan in this project. That may not be allowed by your Internet service provider or hosting site, so be careful, Linux administrator, whose drapes you're peeking through. Even owners of other servers on an internal network can become fairly agitated and unruly if they catch you scanning their systems. As well they might!

9

Securing an Individual Server

Project
9-2

Running a Nessus Scan

Employing a Checklist

If you don't keep track of the systems you administer, you never know what's going on with them. Using a simple checklist can help keep you aware of security issues that need to be bolted down on every system, not just the one you practiced on while reading this module! Table 9-1 shows a sample checklist that you can modify to meet your own needs.

Rule	Security Measure
1.	Use software to enhance safety
1.1	Set password protection on your boot loader
1.2	When installing, keep the Red Hat default of using shadow passwords with MD5 encryption
1.3	Enable PAM
1.4	Use OpenSSH rather than **rlogin** and **rsh** (see Module 15 for more on OpenSSH)
1.5	Install and configure Tripwire, and monitor its output
1.6	Use **up2date** or a manual process to ensure that update packages are installed from a secure site
1.7	Periodically use a vulnerability scanner to keep yourself and your systems honest
2.	Configure the system to enhance safety
2.1	Do not open file and directory permissions any wider than necessary, especially executable and configuration files
2.2	Do not use SetUID root permissions
2.3	Disable reboots using the CTRL-ALT-DEL key combination (in the **/etc/inittab** file)
2.4	Use restrictive settings on Apache, DNS, FTP, SMTP, POP/IMAP, printing, and NFS configurations (and only enable these servers as needed)
2.5	Configure iptables firewalling as appropriate
3.	Restrict or eliminate vulnerable software
3.1	Do not use **xinetd** services unless necessary
3.2	Disable the **rlogin** and **rsh** commands; use OpenSSH instead
3.3	Disable unnecessary processes listening on ports
4.	Use your brain
4.1	Limit access to the physical server

Table 9-1 Sample Security Consciousness Checklist

Rule	Security Measure
4.2	Maintain backups, emergency boot disks, and configuration information
4.3	Avoid having too many people know root passwords
4.4	Use secure passwords for all your accounts

Table 9-1 Sample Security Consciousness Checklist *(continued)*

CRITICAL SKILL
9.6 Finding Helpful Resources Online

As with TCP/IP, substantially more security information is available than I can cover in this module. The best way to go about keeping yourself and your system up to snuff is to regularly visit web sites that discuss such matters and join mailing lists that make regular announcements of developments in this area.

CERT

The first and foremost site for reliable and timely information on system security is the Computer Emergency Response Team (CERT). The CERT Web site, http://www.cert.org, maintains frequent announcements and a plethora of tools for protecting your site. Even more impressive is CERT's phone response team, which will help you deal with attacks against your site if you aren't sure about what to do. The CERT Web page tells you how to contact them.

At the very least, you'll want to join the CERT mailing list or subscribe to the comp.security .announce newsgroup; that's where moderated announcements from CERT are sent. You'll rarely ever see more than one or two announcements a month, so don't worry about getting your already full mailbox crammed with even more stuff!

BugTraq

Another good source of general system information is the BugTraq mailing list. This list gets regular traffic, but because it is moderated, you don't have to worry about useless flame wars consuming your mailbox. The discussions aren't specifically about security, but rather about serious bugs that affect all types of systems. As a systems administrator, you'll find many other useful tidbits here as well. For information on subscribing to the BugTraq list, go to http://www.securityfocus.com/forums/bugtraq/faq.html. At this site, you'll also find archives of past discussions.

Linux Security

As its name implies, this site, found at http://www.linuxsecurity.com, is focused on Linux- and Open Source–software security. It links to articles illustrating all manner of security-related topics, and it has extensive links to tools, how-to documentation, and other useful fodder for the Linux administrator with a security jones. While the bulk of the site features links to other useful resources, including discussion forums, there is also original material available here.

Security Focus

The Security Focus Web site (http://www.securityfocus.com) is a full-disclosure site on security issues pertinent to all operating systems. The site is actively maintained; additions to its list of security issues occur almost daily. It also has links to security-related stories around the Internet and some interesting and entertaining articles.

CRITICAL SKILL
9.7 # Being Aware of Security Miscellany

Before we jump into the next module, I want to bring up three security issues that have nothing to do with Linux but are and forever will be problematic.

The first is *security through obscurity*. This phrase describes the behavior of people who foolishly believe that by not telling anyone about what's there or how something is done, they are keeping their system secure. This is simply not true. Programs can be reverse-engineered, and probes can tell more about the insides of a system or network than we'd ever want revealed. A classic example of why security through obscurity doesn't work is PGP (Pretty Good Privacy, http://www.pgp.com). Because of its source code, and because underlying algorithms have been revealed to the world and thereby examined by countless cryptography experts, PGP is considered the most secure means of storing information. No proprietary cryptography system has ever reached this level of trust before.

The second issue is *social engineering,* the process by which a would-be intruder starts with a telephone before taking to the keyboard. It's remarkable what one can learn by making a few phone calls, showing the slightest bit of authority, and asking unsuspecting people for information. Reporters often use this technique for getting the inside scoop on news stories, because they know the average insider is far less likely to be ready to handle probing questions than is a public relations representative. Social engineering also works for questions about passwords, network infrastructure, operating systems, and so on.

The only way to help keep social engineering from getting through your site's security is by keeping your system's users educated and aware. They should be warned against revealing critical information to anyone who calls up asking for it. Policies need not be complicated to be effective—for example, "The MIS department will never ask for your password. If anyone does ask for your password, report it immediately."

Finally, there is the issue of *physical security.* That is, making sure that only trustworthy individuals have physical access to the machine. The reason this is critical is that once a person has physical access, it is possible for them to do anything with it—from the simple action of turning off a critical server (a potentially lethal move in the .com world) to the more insidious act of putting a tap onto your network connection so that all of its traffic can be monitored, passwords stolen, and so on. Of course, these two are extremes. A realistic "attack" in this situation can be as simple as the attacker booting your system with a boot disk, mounting your root file system, and adding an account for herself so that she can remotely access your system with ease at a later date. And of course, there is simple theft: you could find that your system suddenly doesn't have RAM anymore or you're missing those new (and expensive) CPUs.

My point: You can have all the best electronic security systems you want, but the wrong person with physical access to a machine can cut through all of them with ease. Keep your machines protected.

Module Summary

Security is one of those topics about which you can never say enough. In the course of writing this module, I considered touching on many topics that were clearly beyond the scope of the book. Exploring most of these subjects would require adding many more modules.

Don't fail to take an assertive role in exploring the issues of your system's security. It is an annoyingly time-consuming task, but it is one that cannot be ignored in this era of complex networks and operating systems. If your environment is like most today, you're probably running several different operating systems and need to contend with security for all of them.

✓ Module 9 Mastery Check

1. What command connects a Red Hat Linux 8.0 system with updates at the Red Hat Network?

2. What process can be run to collect update requests from the Red Hat Network web site?

3. What is the address of the Red Hat Network web site?

4. What command allows you to configure proxy settings and other preferences for the Red Hat update process?

5. Give the expression used to verify the GPG key on the file **foobar-server.2.3-4.rpm**.

6. What range of IP ports is reserved for system use?

7. What options for the **netstat** command will list all listening or connected ports for TCP, plus their associated processes?

8. What three questions should you ask yourself when evaluating which services to enable on a server?

9. How can you shut down the **xinetd** program if it's unneeded?

10. What port number is the syslog port, and what is it used for?

11. Name the utility that notifies you of any changes to files on your system.

12. What is the name of the Nessus server process?

13. Explain the concept of security through obscurity. How well does it work?

14. What is social engineering, and how does it pertain to security?

15. What measures can you think of to improve a server's physical security?

Part III

Internet Services

Module 10

The Domain
Name Service (DNS)

Would the World Wide Web have become such a smashing success if you had to read "http://204.71.200.68" on the side of a bus rather than "http://www.yahoo.com"? Probably not. The need to map those long numerical IP addresses into people-friendly format has been an issue with TCP/IP since its creation in the 1970s. Although this translation isn't mandatory, it does make the network much more useful and easy to work with for most of us.

Initially, IP address-to-name mapping was done through the maintenance of a **hosts.txt** file that was distributed via the File Transfer Protocol (FTP) to all the machines on the Internet. As the number of hosts grew (starting back in the early 1980s), it was soon clear that a single person maintaining a single file of all of those hosts was not a realistic way to manage the association of IP addresses to host names. To solve this problem, a distributed system was devised in which each site maintained information about its own hosts. One host at each site would be considered "authoritative," and that single host address would be kept in a master table that could be queried by all other sites. This is the essence of the Domain Name System (DNS).

A hierarchical format is used so that, at each level, responsibility can be directed to a server responsible for that portion of the Domain Name System. For example, if your computer wanted to contact the machine known as **www.domain.com**, the following queries would occur:

1. Your computer would start with the "top-level domain," consult the server answering for all of .com, and ask who was authoritative for all of the host names at domain.com.

2. Your computer would receive an answer such as "dns1.domain.com 209.92.33.130". Your computer would then ask **dns1.domain.com**, "What is the IP address for **www.domain.com**?"

3. That server would answer with the IP address of the requested machine.

4. With the IP address in hand, your computer could begin direct communication with **www.domain.com**.

If this seems like a lot of extra work to get something as simple as another host's IP address, realize that the only other choice would be to have a central site maintaining a master list of all hosts (numbering in the tens of millions) and having to update those host names tens of thousands of times a day—simply impossible! Even more important to consider are the needs of each site. One site may need to maintain a private DNS server because its firewall requires that IP addresses not be visible to outside networks, while the inside network must be able to find hosts on the Internet. If you're stunned by the prospect of having to manage this for every host on the Internet, then you're getting the picture.

In this module, we will discuss DNS in depth, so you'll have what you need to configure and deploy your own DNS servers for whatever your needs may be.

NOTE

In this module, you will see the terms "DNS server" and "name server" used interchangeably. Technically, "name server" is a little ambiguous because it can apply to any number of naming schemes that resolve a name to a number and vice versa. In the context of this module, "name server" will always mean a DNS server unless otherwise stated.

CAUTION

This module uses as examples many host names, domain names, and IP addresses that really do exist. Please be kind and do NOT configure your DNS server with their settings!

CRITICAL SKILL
10.1 Understanding the History Behind DNS: The /etc/hosts File

Not all sites run DNS servers. Not all systems need DNS servers. In sufficiently small sites with no Internet connectivity, it's reasonable for each host to keep its own copy of a table matching all of the host names in the local network with their corresponding IP addresses. This table is stored in the **/etc/hosts** file.

TIP

Even in hosts that have access to a DNS server, you may want to keep a hosts file locally, where a particular host can look up an IP address before going out to the DNS server. Typically, this is done so that the system can keep track of hosts it needs for booting so that even if the DNS server may become unavailable, the system can still boot. A less-obvious reason might be that you want to give a host a name but you don't want to (or can't) add an entry to your DNS server. At the very least you should have the **localhost** entry, the machine's own identity, and any Dynamic Host Configuration Protocol (DHCP) servers you may need. The IP address to find the DNS server(s) is taken care of elsewhere, as we shall see shortly.

The **/etc/hosts** file keeps its information in a simple tabular format. The IP address is in the first column, and all the related host names are in the second column. Only white space separates the entries. Pound symbols (#) at the beginning of a line represent comments. Here's an example:

```
#
# Host table for my internal network
#
```

```
127.0.0.1 localhost localhost.localdomain
192.168.1.1 mybox # the real ip for this box
192.168.1.3 toybox # Heidi's Mac (MacOS X)
192.168.1.6 workhorse # local DHCP and NFS (Linux)
192.168.1.7 assimilator # Win2k
192.168.1.8 gatekeeper # Firewall/Router (Linux)
192.168.1.9 challange # OpenBSD toy
192.168.1.20 scribe # Printer
```

You can also modify this file through Red Hat's **neat** GUI Network Configuration tool. You can find this by selecting Network under the Server Settings submenu, or by typing **neat** at the command line. Yes, the actual command name for the tool is **neat**, in case you just thought I was just commenting on its usefulness. You'll find that the tab labeled Hosts provides a view of the **/etc/hosts** file. The buttons on the right will allow you to perform most of your desired modifications to the entries in the table, but unfortunately this tool has no provision for maintaining comments and has a tendency to munge the comments you entered with your text editor.

In general, your **/etc/hosts** file should contain at the very least the necessary host-to-IP mappings to allow your system to boot up if the DNS server is not responding.

CRITICAL SKILL
10.2 Exploring the Guts of DNS

In this section, we'll explore some background material necessary to your understanding of the installation and configuration of a DNS server and client.

Domains and Hosts

Up until now, you've most likely referenced sites by their fully qualified domain name (FQDN), like this one: www.hyperreal.org. Each string between the periods in this FQDN is significant. Starting from the right end and moving to the left, you have first the top-level domains (.org, .com, .net, .mil, .gov, .edu, .int) and the two-letter country codes such as .us for the United States.

Ask the Expert

Q: Should we be expecting new top-level domains in the future?

A: Getting a new top-level domain approved is a difficult process. As of this writing, several new top-level domains have been given a go (.biz and .info, for example), but they are not in wide use as yet.

Q: Who approves top-level domains?

A: The Internet Corporation for Assigned Names and Numbers (ICANN) is a nonprofit corporation that has taken over management of the Domain Name System and root servers.

Q: Since I can put any information in my DNS server, what will prevent me from creating my own top-level domain?

A: A number of groups actually try to create or manage their own top-level domains such as OpenNIC (http://www.opennic.unrated.net) or AlterNIC (http://www.alternic.org). The problem with this approach is that unless you point your DNS server at that organization's root servers, you won't see the names they claim to manage. As long as ICANN's root servers are the only ones listed in the default BIND (Berkeley Internet Name Domain) configuration, the usefulness of these extra top-level domains is limited at best.

From these top-level domains come actual organizational boundaries. Companies, Internet service providers (ISPs), educational communities, and nonprofit groups typically acquire unique names under one or more of the domains. Here are a few examples: redhat.com, mit.edu, planetoid.org, hyperreal.org, theorb.com, collab.net, and linux.org. Assignment of these names is done by companies like register.com and networksolutions.com under the authority of the Internet Assigned Naming Authority (IANA).

Visually, you can imagine the DNS format as an upside-down tree, as shown in Figure 10-1. The root of the tree is a simple period; this is the period that's supposed to occur after every FQDN. Thus the proper FQDN for www.linux.org is really www.linux.org. (with the root period at the end). Most applications have come to assume that the user will not place the suffixing period.

All domains are placed in *root servers,* DNS servers scattered around the entire world. Each server contains the entire mapping of domain names up to two layers deep (linux.org, redhat.com, and so on) to their *primary name servers.* A primary name server for a domain is simply a DNS server that knows about all hosts and subdomains existing under its domain. For example, the root servers know that the primary name server for redhat.com is 66.187.233.210. That's all the root server knows about redhat.com. (Well, that's not technically true.) It also knows a couple of backup, or *secondary,* name servers to try if the first one is down. But the point is, that it has no idea what IP address belongs to www.redhat.com or ftp.redhat.com. To find out about the hosts existing inside of redhat.com, you have to ask the DNS server at 66.187.233.210. When asked about redhat.com, the DNS server at 66.187.233.210 knows only about the hosts inside redhat.com and nothing else. If you ask it about **whitehouse.gov**, it will turn around and ask the primary name server for **whitehouse.gov**. (See the information about caching name servers in "Configuring Servers" later in this module.)

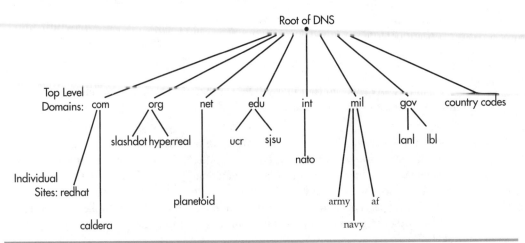

Figure 10-1 A visual representation of the DNS hierarchy, two layers deep

By keeping DNS distributed in this manner, the task of keeping track of all the hosts connected to the Internet is delegated to each site taking care of its own information. The central repository listing of all the primary name servers, called the *root server,* is the only list of existing domains. Obviously, a list of such critical nature is itself mirrored across multiple servers and multiple geographic regions. For example, an earthquake in Japan may destroy the root server for Asia, but all the other root servers around the world can take up the slack until it comes back online. The only difference noticeable to users is likely to be a slightly higher latency in resolving domain names. Pretty amazing, isn't it?

So now that you know how domains get resolved, you can begin to see the separation of hosts and domains. The host name is the very first word before the first period in an FQDN. This is usually the name of the actual machine you're asking about. For example, in the FQDN taz.hyperreal.org, the host name is taz, and the domain name is hyperreal.org. When a user sitting somewhere far away (in Internet terms) asks, "What's the IP address of **taz.hyperreal .org**?" the root servers will tell the user to ask **ns.hyperreal.org**. When **ns.hyperreal.org** is asked the same question, it can authoritatively answer "209.133.83.22".

Subdomains

Just when you get comfortable with that notion, you'll run across a site like **www.cs.ucr.edu**. And then you may ask yourself, "What's the host name component, and what's the domain name component?"

Welcome to the wild and mysterious world of subdomains. Hopefully you remember what was mentioned earlier about domain names being hierarchical. With a little digging, you'll find that www (everything before the first dot) is still the name of the host. And you'll find that, as expected, the root name servers only know which server to ask for ucr.edu. The folks at **ucr**, however, have so many computers, that it makes sense that they would further subdivide their domain into smaller sections. So when asked, the name server for **ucr** will point you to the name server for any of these subsections, including the one named **cs**. The name server for the **cs** department can then be queried to find the IP address for the host **www**. In this example, **cs** is considered a *subdomain* of the **ucr** domain. Figure 10-2 shows how this fits into the DNS tree. A subdomain exhibits all the properties of a domain, except that it has delegated a subsection of the domain instead of all the hosts at a site.

To make this clearer, let's follow the path of a DNS request. A query starts with the top-level domain **edu**. Within **edu** is **ucr.edu**, and three authoritative DNS servers for **ucr.edu** are found. Let's pick (at random) the **ns2.ucr.edu** server to be contacted and ask about **www.cs.ucr.edu**. **ns2.ucr.edu**'s DNS configuration is such that for anything ending with a **cs.ucr.edu**, the server must contact **momo.cs.ucr.edu** to get an authoritative answer. The request for **www.cs.ucr.edu** is then passed on to **momo.cs.ucr.edu**, which returns 138.23.169.15.

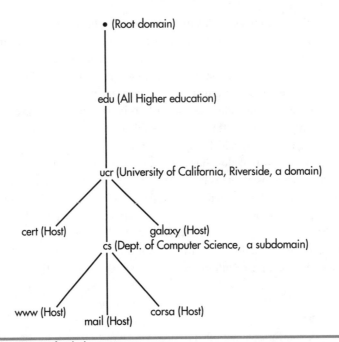

Figure 10-2 Delegation of subdomains

Note that when a site name appears to reflect the presence of subdomains, it does not mean that subdomains in fact exist. Although the host name specification rules do not allow periods, the BIND name server has always allowed them. (BIND is described in the upcoming section "Installing a DNS Server.") Thus, in effect, it creates something that looks like a subdomain but doesn't actually use a separate DNS server. Whether or not a subdomain exists is handled by the configuration of the DNS server for the site.

in-addr.arpa Domain

DNS allows resolution to work in both directions. *Forward resolution* converts names into IP addresses, and *reverse resolution* converts IP addresses back into host names. The process of reverse resolution relies on the **in-addr.arpa** domain.

As explained in the preceding section, domain names are resolved by looking at each component from right to left, with the suffixing period indicating the root of the DNS tree. Very few top-level domains exist, but each level going down the tree fans out. Following this logic, IP addresses must have a top-level domain as well. This domain is called the **in-addr.arpa**.

IP addresses are also hierarchical. Each number between the dots, sometimes referred to as an "octet," further subdivides the address space and can be assigned to a subgroup to manage. Unlike FQDNs however, IP addresses are resolved from left to right. This results in some slightly strange syntax when mapped into the domain space, as the IP address has to be reversed to be found under the **in-addr.arpa** domain. For example, the IP address 138.23.169.15 would become 15.169.23.138.in-addr.arpa when you want to look up its host name. Figure 10-3 gives you a visual example of reverse resolution of an IP address.

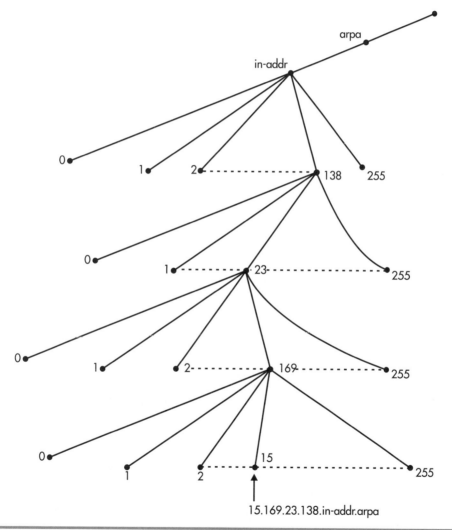

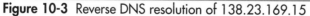

Figure 10-3 Reverse DNS resolution of 138.23.169.15

NOTE

If the **in-addr.arpa** domain sounds a bit strange, you might be interested to know that it's a carryover from the Internet's early days as a research project for the United States Department of Defense. ARPA stands for Advanced Research Projects Agency. The **in-addr** part will make a bit more sense when you see the syntax for how IP addresses are assigned in BIND.

Types of Servers

DNS servers come in three flavors: primary, secondary, and caching. *Primary servers* are the ones considered authoritative for a particular domain. An *authoritative server* is the one on which the domain's configuration files reside. When updates to the domain's DNS tables occur, they are done on this server.

Secondary servers work as backups and as load distributors for the primary name servers. Primary servers know of the existence of secondary servers and send them periodic updates to the tables. When a site queries a secondary name server, the secondary responds with authority. However, because it's possible for a secondary to be queried before its primary can alert it to the latest changes, some people refer to secondary servers as "not quite authoritative." Realistically speaking, you can generally trust secondary servers to have correct information. (Besides, unless you know which is which, you cannot tell the difference between a query response received from a primary and one received from a secondary.)

Caching servers contain no configuration files for any particular domain. Rather, the first time a client host requests a caching server to resolve a name, that server will go and query an authoritative server for the domain, but it will remember (by keeping a local copy of) the result. The next time a request is made for that same info, it will notice that it already has the answer, and if the data is fairly recent there is no need to wait for an authoritative server to respond. The locally cached answer can be used. Practically speaking, caching servers work quite well because of the temporal nature of DNS requests. That is, if you've asked for the IP address to hyperreal.org, you are likely to do so again in the near future. (The Web has made this even more likely.) Clients can tell the difference between a caching server and a primary or secondary server, because when a caching server answers a request, it answers it "nonauthoritatively." In the real world, a DNS server can be configured to act with a specific level of authority for a particular domain, and differently for another. For example, a server can be primary for domain.com but be secondary for example.net. Commonly, DNS servers will act as caching servers, even if they are also primary or secondary for any other domains.

Progress Check

1. _____ domains signify organizational boundaries.

2. Name each level of host or domain of the following address: **www.worldscollide.org**.

3. Domain names are

   A. Formatted

   B. In a time line

   C. Hierarchical

   D. All of the above

CRITICAL SKILL

10.3 Installing a DNS Server

Red Hat comes with the option to install a DNS server when the system is installed for the first time, though you can also install the RPMS at a later time. The DNS server of choice for Linux and for almost all UNIX servers is BIND, the Berkeley Internet Name Domain server. (At one point, a rumor floated around the Internet that Windows NT's name server bore striking similarity to BIND. This rumor was never confirmed or denied.) As of this writing, the latest BIND version is 9.2, which conveniently is also what Red Hat 8 currently uses.

NOTE

Because of the critical nature of the BIND software, it was taken over by the Internet Software Consortium (ISC) to ensure its continued development. You can find out more about the ISC at http://www.isc.org. The ISC is also in charge of development of a DHCP server as well as the INN news server.

---

1. Top-level domains signify organizational boundaries.

2. In order, **www** is the host, **worldscollide** is the domain name, and **org** is the top-level domain.

3. **C.** Domain names are hierarchical.

BIND 9 was a major rewrite that introduced some significant changes over BIND 8, and some administrators have been slow to make the conversion. If your organization has a reason to remain with an older version of BIND, you will either have to find an RPM of the appropriate version or be willing to compile it yourself. If you're installing BIND for the first time, there is no reason not to start with BIND 9. Regardless of which branch you're tracking, keep an eye out for new releases. New bugs and security issues are discovered from time to time and should be corrected. Of course, new features are released, as well, but unless you have a need for them, those releases are less critical. All new BIND releases are available at http://www .isc.org, or you can get an updated RPM from Red Hat.

NOTE

Although freely available with full source code to anyone who wishes to download it, BIND has the benefit of the ISC's commercial-quality management and support. Of course you'll have to pay for the commercial-level support, but the software supported by their commercial-level contracts is the same software you can download free.

Along with the BIND server itself, you'll find a few tools that you'll use for setting up and testing your name server. These tools are actually part of a separate RPM called bind-utils, in case you want to install them on a machine that doesn't need to run its own DNS server.

Starting DNS at Boot Time

Since the default installation of BIND on Red Hat is pretty minimal, it's not terribly useful out of the box. As a result, it's not started by default when you boot your machine. We're going to configure it in the next few pages, but before we do so, let's make sure that it starts automatically when the server does. There are two easy ways to do this. The first is through the simple GUI interface for services. Hopefully you'll remember the Service Configuration tool from Module 4. While BIND is a complete package including both the name server, a name resolver, and various tools, the name server is the piece we're looking to start at boot time. This server is called *named* (pronounced "name-dee"), which is short for "name daemon." When you bring up the Service Configuration tool, if you have BIND properly installed, you can enable named by clicking the appropriate check box for each runlevel you are interested in, as shown in the following illustration. I'd suggest that unless you have other specific requirements, you now enable it for runlevels three through five.

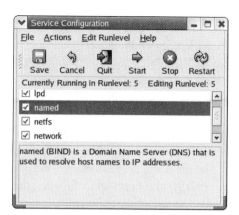

Now suppose that you have your DNS server locked away in a server room somewhere and you don't have immediately available all the comforts of a modern GUI desktop. Perhaps you're even accessing the box through some form of remote console utility. Fortunately, you recall what you learned earlier in this book about init scripts and using symlinks to start and stop services at a particular runlevel. So to enable named in runlevel 5, for example, you simply navigate to **/etc/rc5.d** and replace the K45named symlink with an S55named symlink.

NOTE

If you're wondering where I pulled the symlink numbers from in this example, I did steal them from what Red Hat's Service Configuration tool would have used, but any valid values would have worked. However, don't overlook interactions between services if you find the need to choose your own values.

Hurry Up Already! And What Are We Skipping in the Process?

If all you're looking for is a simple configuration for a simple situation, take a look at the cookbook solutions in "Putting It All Together" at the end of the module. One of them may be exactly what you are looking for. Of course, I still recommend reading through the module to understand how BIND interprets the configuration files so that you can more easily troubleshoot problems in the future.

If you do take the time to read the documentation that comes with BIND, you may wonder why I don't cover several of the features that are new to BIND, such as Secure DNS (DNSSEC) and IPv6 (Internet Protocol, version 6) support. The reason is simple: those are very heavy topics that require a significant background to understand. Both of their discussions more or less merit a book of their own. It's unfortunate that DNS has become this complex, but the Internet isn't the friendly place it used to be, either.

BIND Documentation

BIND comes with a lot of great documentation, and I highly recommend taking the time to go through it. It's hardly light reading, but it will make you a better systems administrator and a better DNS administrator. And the world needs as many good sysadmins as it can get!

In addition to what can be found in the man and info pages, there is a wealth of information installed under /**usr/share/doc/bind-9.2.1** (adjusting the version number as necessary to match the RPM you've installed). The best way to read through the multiple HTML page files is to point your web browser to them, read them and click a link to bring up another, and so on. This is because several of the files are written in HTML (Hypertext Markup Language) and are much easier to read than their text counterparts. (By easier to read, I mean easier on the eye. The content is identical.)

Of the directories in the **doc** directory, the most important documentation is the **arm** subdirectory. In there you will find the BIND Administrators Reference Manual. As the title suggests, ARM is a reference manual and not a tutorial, but as you need more complex configurations out of your DNS server, you will find it a very valuable resource.

CRITICAL SKILL
10.4 Configuring Clients

In this section and the next, we'll delve into the wild and exciting process of configuring DNS clients and servers! Okay, maybe they're not that exciting but there's no denying their significance to the infrastructure of any networked site, so it's best if you can get a few warm and fuzzy feelings about DNS configurations.

Client-Side DNS (a.k.a. the Resolver)

So far, we've been studying servers and the DNS tree as a whole. The other part of this equation is, of course, the client—the host that is contacting the DNS server to resolve a host name into an IP address.

Under Linux, the client side of DNS is handled by the *resolver*. This is actually part of a library of C programming functions that gets linked to a program when the program is started.

Because all of this happens automatically and transparently, the user doesn't have to know anything about it. It's simply a little bit of magic that let's the user start browsing the Internet.

From the system administrator's perspective, configuring the DNS client isn't magic, but it's very straightforward. There are only two files involved: **/etc/resolv.conf** and **/etc/ nsswitch.conf**.

The /etc/resolv.conf File

The **/etc/resolv.conf** file contains the information necessary for the client to know what its local DNS server is. (Every site should have, at the very least, its own caching DNS server.) This file has two lines: The first line indicates the default search domain, and the second indicates the IP address of the host's name server.

The *default search domain* applies mostly to sites that have their own local servers. When the default search domain is specified, the client side will automatically append this domain name to lookups in case it is a bare host name or a local subdomain. For example, if we specify our default domain to be yahoo.com and then try to connect to the host name *my,* the client software will automatically try contacting my.yahoo.com. Using the same default, if we try to contact the host **www.stat.net**, the software will try **www.stat.net.yahoo.com** (a perfectly legal host name), find that it doesn't exist, and then try **www.stat.net** alone (which does exist).

Of course, you may supply multiple default domains. However, doing so will slow the query process a bit, because each domain will need to be checked. For instance, if both **yahoo.com** and **stanford.edu** are specified, and we perform a query on **www.stat.net**, we'll get three queries: **www.stat.net.yahoo.com**, **www.stat.net.stanford.edu**, and **www.stat.net**.

The format of the **/etc/resolv.conf** file is as follows:

```
search domainname
nameserver IP-address
```

where *domainname* is the default domain name to search, and *IP-address* is the IP address of your DNS server. For example, here's my **/etc/resolv.conf** file:

```
search collab.net
nameserver 127.0.0.1
```

Thus when I contact zaphod.collab.net, I only need to specify **zaphod** as the host name. Since I run a name server on my own machine, I specify the local host address.

If you're using the **neat** tool, the entries in the DNS tab correspond to the information in **/etc/resolv.conf**.

TIP

If you use DHCP to get your IP address, be sure you understand the effect that it will have on files like **/etc/resolv.conf** before you spend a lot of time customizing those files. Otherwise, you may find that all your hard work has disappeared the next time you boot. For more information, see Module 20.

The /etc/nsswitch.conf File

The **/etc/nsswitch.conf** file tells the system where it should look up certain kinds of configuration information (services). When multiple locations are identified, the **/etc/nsswitch.conf** file also specifies the order in which the information can best be found. Typical configuration files that are set up to use **/etc/nsswitch.conf** include the password file, group file, and hosts file.

The format of the **/etc/nsswitch.conf** file is simple: The service name comes first on a line (note that **/etc/nsswitch.conf** applies to more than just host name lookups), followed by a colon. Then come the locations that contain the information. If multiple locations are identified, the entries are listed in the order in which the system should perform the search. Valid entries for locations are files: **nis, dns, [NOTFOUND]**, and **nisplus**. Comments begin with a pound symbol (#).

NOTE

Patches can be found to make other schemes, such as the Lightweight Directory Access Protocol (LDAP), into valid entries in **nsswitch.conf**. Unfortunately, the details of such extensions are beyond the scope of this book.

For example, if you open the file with your favorite editor, you'll see a line similar to this:

```
hosts: files nisplus nis dns
```

This line tells the system that all host name lookups should first start with the **/etc/hosts file**. If the entry cannot be found there, **NISPLUS** is checked. If the host cannot be found via **NISPLUS**, regular **NIS** is checked, and so on. It's possible that **NISPLUS** isn't running at your site and you want the system to check **DNS** records before it checks **NIS** records. In this case, you'd change the line to

```
hosts:     files dns nis
```

And that's it. Save your file, and the system automatically detects the change.

The only recommendation for this line is that the hosts file (**files**) should always come first in the lookup order.

What's the preferred order for NIS and DNS? This is very much dependent on the site. Whether you want to resolve host names with DNS before trying NIS will depend on whether the DNS server is closer than the NIS server in terms of network connectivity, if one server is faster than another, firewall issues, site policy issues, and other such factors.

Using [NOTFOUND]

In the **/etc/nsswitch.conf** file, you'll see entries that end in **[NOTFOUND]**. This is a special directive that allows you to stop the process of searching for information after the system has failed all prior entries. For example, if your file contains the line

```
hosts: files nis [NOTFOUND] dns
```

the system will try to look up host information in the **/etc/hosts** file, and then in NIS. If, after searching files, a search of NIS returned an answer of "not found", then no further searching is performed. If, however, NIS was not able to be searched (perhaps the NIS server was down, for example), then searching will continue to the DNS server. This allows you to distinguish between an authoritative "no" and a failed search attempt. For more advanced configuration options, consult the man page for **nsswitch.conf**. NIS is covered in more detail in Module 17.

Progress Check

1. What type of program handles the client side of DNS?

2. What are some examples of valid directives in **nsswitch.conf**?

CRITICAL SKILL

10.5 Getting Ready for DNS Servers: The named.conf File

The **named.conf** file is the main configuration file for BIND, and it is located by default in the **/etc** directory. Based on this file's specifications, BIND determines how it should behave and what additional configuration files, if any, must be read.

This section of the module covers what you need to know to set up a general-purpose DNS server. You'll find a complete guide to the configuration file format in BIND's documentation.

The general format of the **named.conf** file is as follows:

```
statement {
     options;      // comments
};
```

The *statement* tells BIND we're about to describe a particular facet of its operation, and *options* are the specific commands applying to that statement. The curly braces are required so that BIND knows which options are related to which statements; there's a semicolon after every option and after the closing curly brace. An example of this is as follows:

```
options {
    directory "/var/named";    // put config files in /var/named
};
```

---

1. A resolver handles the client side of DNS.
2. **nis**, **dns**, **[NOTFOUND]**, and **nisplus** are some examples of valid directives in **nsswitch.conf**.

The Specifics

This section documents the most common statements you will see in a **named.conf** file. The best way to tackle this is to give it a skim but then treat it as a reference guide for later sections. If some of the directives seem bizarre or don't quite make sense to you during the first pass, don't worry. Once you see them in use in later sections, the hows and whys will quickly fall into place.

I can almost hear you saying it: "Why is this stuff so ugly to configure? Don't they have a GUI for this? Can't this be simplified?" Well, yes and no. There is a GUI tool included with Red Hat, and we'll cover its use a bit later in the module. However, the hard part here is not the configuration file, but the concepts; and no GUI can simplify that for you. But once you understand the concepts, the configuration file will feel much more sane, and so will the options in the GUI. If, while you're glancing through this section, you feel very lost, you may just want to skip to the next section and see these files in action. Then come back and actually see what the files are doing in better detail.

Comments

Comments may be in one of the following formats:

Format	Indicates
//	C++-style comments
/*...*/	C-style comments
#	Perl and UNIX shell script-style comments

In the case of the first and last styles (C++ and Perl/UNIX shell), once a comment begins, it continues until the end of the line. In regular C-style comments, the closing */ is required to indicate the end of a comment. This makes C-style comments easier for multiline comments. In general, however, you can pick the comment format that you like best. No one style is better than another.

TIP

Even though there are multiple comment styles that will work, if you mix and match too much you're more likely to confuse both yourself and other admins that have to read your files later. It is recommended that you pick a style that works well for you and stick with it.

statement Keywords

Some of the most common **statement** keywords are:

Keyword	Description
acl	Access Control List—determines what kind of access others have to your DNS server.
include	Allows you to include another file and have that file treated like part of the normal **named.conf** file.
logging	Specifies what information gets logged and what gets ignored. For logged information, you can also specify where the information is logged.
options	Addresses global server configuration issues.
controls	Allows you to declare control channels for use by the **rndc** utility.
server	Sets server-specific configuration options.
zone	Defines a DNS zone (discussed in further detail in "Zones," later in the module).

ACLs

Access Control Lists (ACLs) allow you to specify a group of addresses as having access or no access to your DNS server. Each group gets a name, and you can use this name in other configuration options. The entries in an **acl** statement do not themselves change the behavior of BIND.

There are four default ACLs: **any** specifies all hosts; **none** denies all hosts; **localhost** allows the IP address of all interfaces on this BIND system; and **localnet** allows any host on a network for which this system has an interface.

To specify your own ACL, use this format:

```
acl name_of_your_acl {
       address-list
};
```

where *name_of_your_acl* is the name of the ACL you wish to define and *address-list* is the list of addresses defined by ACL. By default, everything is denied (for this ACL only), so you just add a list of the addresses having access. This address list contains individual addresses separated by semicolons. An individual address can be formatted in one of three ways:

● Dotted decimal notation (192.168.1.2).

● IP prefix notation (192.168.2/24), where the /24 represents the number of "on" bits in the netmask. For example, /24 represents the netmask 255.255.255.0. Most network gear allows this type of address specification. See Part V of this book for further discussion of netmasks and IP notations.

- The name of an existing ACL. References to ACLs that are defined later in the file (*forward references*) are not allowed.

To negate an address, place an exclamation mark (!) in front of it. Address lists are evaluated from left to right, and the first matching expression wins. So if you specify an address as being accessible before you specify the negation, that address will be allowed access. For example, let's say you want to allow access to everyone on the 192.168.1 network access except 192.168.1.2.

```
192.168.1/24; !192.168.1.2;
```

will still give access to 192.168.1.2, because it's allowed through by the first expression of 192.168.1/24. To deny 192.168.1.2 but allow the rest of 192.168.1/24, you need to specify the address list as follows:

```
!192.168.1.2; 192.168.1/24
```

Here is a sample ACL statement:

```
acl punks {
# These people thought it was funny to replace salt for the sugar
# next to the coffee machine. Little do they know to NEVER make the
# sysadmin unhappy... Mu-ha-ha-ha!
        !192.168.1.45; !192.168.1.74;
};
acl our_network {
        punks; 192.168.1/24; 192.168.2/24; // everybody but punks
};
```

Note that defining an ACL does not automatically put it to use. It simply allows you to refer to the addresses as a group instead of repeating a list of addresses over and over again.

The include Statement

If you find that your configuration file is starting to grow unwieldy, you may want to consider breaking up the file into smaller components. Each file can then be included into the main **named.conf** file. Note that you cannot use the **include** statement inside another statement.

Here's an example of an **include** statement:

```
include "/var/named/acl.conf";
```

CAUTION

To all you C and C++ programmers out there: Be sure not to begin **include** lines with the pound symbol (#), despite what your instincts tell you! That symbol is used to start comments in the **named.conf** file. (Believe me when I say this error is a very frustrating bug to track down!)

The logging Statement

The **logging** statement is used to specify what information you want logged, and where. When this statement is used in conjunction with the **syslog** facility, you get an extremely powerful and configurable logging system. The items logged are a number of statistics about the status of **namcd**. By default, they are logged to the **/var/log/messages** file.

Unfortunately, the configurability of this logging statement comes at the price of some additional complexity, but the default logging set up by **named** is good enough for most uses. If you want to reconfigure the logging process, read the BIND Administrators Reference Manual.

Configuration Options

Many options are available for your BIND configuration; these are listed in Table 10-1. Obviously, you don't need to specify all of these options in order to make your system work, but it's good to know what the choices are if you need to do some additional configuration. In general, don't change the defaults for these options unless you have an explicit reason to do so.

Option	Description
`directory path-name;`	Location of the rest of the **named** configuration files.
`named-xfer path-name;`	Path name to the **named-xfer** program. By default, this is **/usr/sbin/named-xfer**.
`dump-file path-name;`	Path name of the file to which the **named** server should dump database information when the server receives a signal from the **ndc** program (**ndc dumpdb**).
`memstatistics-file path-name;`	Path name of the file to which memory usage statistics are written to on exit, if the **deallocate-on-exit** option (defined in this table) is set to Yes. By default, the filename is **named.memstats**.

Table 10-1 BIND Configuration Options

Option	Description
pid-file *path-name*;	Path name of the file to which the **named** server writes its process ID immediately after startup. Default is **/var/run/named.pid**. This file is used by the **ndc** program.
statistics-file *path-name*;	Path name of the file into which the server appends statistics information when the **ndc stats** command is run.
auth-nxdomain *yes/no*;	If you specify Yes (the default), the server will always answer authoritatively on domain queries for which it is authoritative. Caution: Do not specify No unless you really know what you're doing.
deallocate-on-exit *yes/no*;	When set to Yes, the server will write out a complete report of memory allocation. Results in a longer shutdown time but is useful for analysis of memory usage. Default is No.
fake-iquery *yes/no*;	Default is No. If Yes, the server will simulate the obsolete IQUERY query type. Like the **auth-nxdomain** option, don't turn this on unless you know what you're doing.
fetch-glue *yes/no*;	Yes (the default) tells the server to fetch (and cache) the necessary records to answer queries about domains on which it is not authoritative. Setting this to No, along with the **recursion** option, prevents your cache from growing and becoming corrupted by malicious attacks. However, clients have to do more work for each query.
host-statistics *yes/no*;	Tells BIND whether to keep track of statistics for each host that queries it. Although the information is useful, the tracking consumes substantial memory; thus the default is No.
multiple-cnames *yes/no*;	The specification for DNS tables does not allow for CNAME records to point to other CNAME records, so the default for this option is No. Since older versions of BIND did allow this, you can enable this backward compatibility by choosing Yes for this option. (CNAME records are host aliases, discussed in "DNS Records Types" later in the module.)
notify *yes/no*;	Default is Yes. Causes a primary DNS server to send a NOTIFY message informing all the primary server's secondaries that its tables have been updated. The NOTIFY message causes the secondaries to perform zone transfers (to get the latest information from the primary) almost immediately.

Table 10-1   BIND Configuration Options *(continued)*

Option	Description
recursion *yes/no;*	If Yes (the default), the server will attempt to traverse the DNS tree to get information about a requested IP address. This takes the load off the client to perform the same task. (See the **fetch-glue** option for reasons to turn recursion off.)

forwarders { *ip-list;* }	Specifies a list of IP addresses to be queried if the current server does not have the answer to a request. Forwarders are optional; the addresses generally come from an upstream provider. Example *ip-list* (with fictitious addresses):
	forwarders {
	        192.168.8.24;
	        192.168.3.12;
	};

forward *first/only;*	Only applicable if you have set up **forwarders** (see previous listing). The default setting, First, causes the server to query forwarders for unknown information before going out on its own to resolve a request. By changing this option to Only, the server will look to forwarders only and not attempt to resolve any addresses by itself.
check-names *type* **action;**	Verifies the integrity of domain names based on their client contexts. Values for *type*: **master** = primary name servers; **slave** = secondary name servers; **response** = caching servers and clients. Values for *action*: **ignore** = no checking; **warn** = respond by generating a log entry; **fail** = generate a log entry and refuse to respond to the query. Defaults: **Check-names** *master* **fail;** **Check-names** *slave* **warn;** **Check-names** *response* **ignore;** The **check-names** option can be specified in the **zone** statement, in which case it overrides the configuration setup in the **options** statement for that particular zone. When used in the **zone** statement, do not specify *type*, because it can be derived from the **zone** information.
allow-query { *address-list;* };	Specifies which IP addresses are allowed to generate queries to the server. By default, all hosts are allowed. Separate addresses in *address-list* with semicolons (same format as for **acl**, discussed earlier in this section). You can refer to **acls** by name in this *address-list*, as well.

Table 10-1 BIND Configuration Options *(continued)*

Option	Description
`allow-transfer { address-list; }`	Specifies which hosts can perform a zone transfer with your DNS server. In general, this list will include only hosts that are secondaries for your primaries. By default, anyone can perform a zone transfer, but I recommend you restrict this to only those with a legitimate reason to do so.
`listen-on { address-list; }`	By default, the **named** server will listen to port 53 for DNS queries on all interfaces, but you can change this by specifying other addresses in **address-list**. Format is the same as for **acl** address list explained earlier. To select which port **named** will listen to, add **port portnum** right after the **listen-on** statement but before the first curly brace. Value for **portnum** is the port number you want named to listen to. For example: **Listen-on port 1031 {192.168.1.1;};** tells BIND to listen to port 1031 for DNS queries, on the interface configured to be 192.168.1.1. And **listen-on { 192 .168.1.1; };** tells BIND to listen to its default port 53 for DNS queries, on the interface configured to be 192.168.1.1.
`query-source address address\ port port;`	When a server needs to contact another DNS server, it goes by default to any of the IP addresses on the system, and the source port is a random high port (port numbers 1024 to 65535). If you need a particular configuration to allow your DNS server through a firewall, you can specify a specific source **address** and **port** of origin for the message. If you need to specify one but not the other, you can use the wildcard (*) character. For example, the statement **query-source address * port 53**; says to send the query from whatever IP address **named** wants to use but from port 53 explicitly.
`max-transfer-time-in number;`	Specifies the number of minutes a zone transfer can run before it is terminated. Default is 120 minutes.
`transfer-format\ one-answer/many-answers;`	When the **named** process answers a request, it sends back only one answer at a time (the default), even though there may be space to pack multiple answers into one transfer. This is because old versions of BIND and other DNS servers still in use do not support multiple responses. If you know your DNS server will be working only with other BIND 8.x servers, you can change this option to **many-answers** for improved performance.

Table 10-1 BIND Configuration Options *(continued)*

Option	Description
`transfers-in number;`	Maximum number of inbound zone transfers that can be running concurrently. Default is 10. Increasing this value may speed up the process of updates at the expense of increasing system load.
`transfers-out number`	Maximum number of outbound zone transfers that can be running concurrently. Default is 10. As of this writing, this option is parsed by BIND but is not yet in use.
`transfers-per-ns number;`	Maximum number of inbound zone transfers that can be running concurrently from a single remote name server. Default is 2. Can be increased at the expense of more load on the remote name server.
`coresize size;`	If **named** crashes, Linux will generate a **coredump**, an image of the memory used by the program at the instant it crashed. Data can be used for "post mortem" analysis by programmers. Be aware: This image may be quite large; if you're short on disk space for the DNS system, consider limiting the core file size. Default under Linux is unlimited. The *size* parameter can be specified in bytes (no suffix), K, MB, or GB. For example, all of the following are the same value, 1 gigabyte: **coresize 1073741824**; **coresize 1048576K**; **coresize 1024M**; and **coresize 1G**; .
`datasize datasize;`	Specifies memory allocated for **named**. Default under Linux = as much memory as you have. The *datasize* value follows the same conventions as the *size* value for **coresize**. Thus **1073741824** is the same as **1048576K** is the same as **1024M** is the same as **1G**.
`files number;`	Maximum number of files **named** can open at once. Be aware: The more files BIND has open at once, the more its performance is affected by having to deal with all those file handles. (C programmers are familiar with this issue because of the **select** system call.)
`stacksize number;`	Maximum amount of memory **named** can take off the system stack (used to track temporary variables in a program). Default under Linux is no limit. For *number*, follow the same conventions as for **coresize** and **datasize**.
`cleaning-interval number;`	Specifies interval between server's removals of expired records from the cache. Default is every 60 minutes. If set to 0, no periodic cleaning will occur.

Table 10-1 BIND Configuration Options *(continued)*

Option	Description
`interface-interval number;`	By default, the server scans the list of interfaces on the system every 60 minutes. If `listen-on` is enabled (defined earlier in this table), `named` begins listening for DNS requests on any new interfaces it finds. If an interface has disappeared, `named` will stop listening to requests on that interface. If this option is set to 0, the server will check for available interfaces only when `named` is started up.
`statistics-interval number;`	Specifies how often the `named` server generates server statistics and deposits them to the log file. Default is every 60 minutes. If set to 0, no statistics are generated.

`topology { address-list; };`	When multiple forwarders exist, `named` shows preference to servers assumed to be closer than others. By default, the `named` server shows preference to itself and then to servers on the same subnet. You can specify another order of preference (the order of the `address-list`). You can also embed sublists representing a group of addresses. For example, in this configuration,
	`topology {`
	    `192.168.3.12;`
	        `{ 192.168.11.25; 192.168.42/24; }`
	        `192.168.8.24;`
	`};`
	first choice is given to 192.168.3.12, equal preference is shown to 192.168.11.25 and all hosts on the 192.168.42.0 network, and last preference is given to 192.168.8.24.

Table 10-1   BIND Configuration Options *(continued)*

The server Statement

The **server** statement tells BIND specific information about other name servers it might be dealing with. The format of the **server** statement is as follows:

```
server ip-address {
     bogus yes/no;
     transfer-format one-answer/many-answers;
};
```

where *ip-address* is the IP address of the server in question.

The first item in the statement, **bogus**, tells the server whether or not the other server is sending bad information. This is useful in the event you are dealing with another site that may be sending you bad information due to a misconfiguration. The default is "no". The second item, **transfer-format**, tells BIND whether this server can accept multiple answers in a single query response, or whether each answer should be sent separately. The many-answers option is much more efficient, but typically only servers running BIND version 8.*x* or later can handle this mode.

A sample **server** entry might look like this:

```
server 192.168.3.12 {
     bogus no;
     transfer-format many-answers;
};
```

Zones

The **zone** statement allows you to define a DNS zone the definition of which is often confused. Here is the fine print: *A DNS zone is not the same thing as a DNS domain*. The difference is subtle, but important.

Let's review: Domains are designated along organizational boundaries. A single organization can be separated into smaller administrative subdomains. Each subdomain gets its own zone. All of the zones collectively form the entire domain.

For example, the .bigcompany.com is a domain. Within it are the subdomains .engr .bigcompany.com, .marketing.bigcompany.com, .sales.bigcompany.com, and .admin.bigcompany .com. Each of the four subdomains has its own zone. And .bigcompany.com has some hosts within it that do not fall under any of the subdomains; thus it has a zone of its own. As a result, .bigcompany.com is actually composed of five zones in total.

In the simplest model, where a single domain has no subdomains, the definition of zone and domain are the same in terms of information regarding hosts, configurations, and so on.

The process of setting up zones in the **named.conf** file is discussed in the following section.

CRITICAL SKILL
10.6 Configuring Servers

Time for *big fun*: configuring a name server! Oh, you don't think it's fun? Well, wait until you find out how much people get paid for knowing this stuff.

Earlier, you learned about the differences between primary, secondary, and caching name servers. Briefly, primary name servers contain the databases with the latest DNS information for a zone. When a zone administrator wants to update these databases, the primary name server gets the update first, and the rest of the world asks it for updates. Secondary servers explicitly keep track of primaries, and primary servers notify the secondaries when changes occur. Primaries and secondaries are considered equally authoritative in their answers. Caching name servers have no authoritative records—only cached entries.

Updating the named.conf File for a Primary Zone

The most basic syntax for a zone entry is as follows:

```
zone domain-name {
      type master;
      file path-name;
};
```

The *path-name* refers to the file containing the database information for the zone in question. For example, to create a zone for the domain **example.org**, where the database file is located in **/var/named/example.org.db**, we would use the following:

```
zone "example.org" {
      type master;
      file "example.org.db";
};
```

Note that the value of the **directory** option in the **named.conf** file will automatically prefix the **example.org.db** filename. So if we designated **directory** as **/var/named**, the server software will automatically look for **example.org**'s information in **/var/named/example.org.db**.

Now that's just the *forward reference,* the mechanism by which others can look up a name and get the IP address. It is proper Net behavior to also supply a reverse for IP-to-host name mapping (also necessary if you want to send e-mail to some sites!). To do this, you provide an entry in the **in-addr.arpa** domain.

As we mentioned in our earlier discussion, the format of an **in-addr.arpa** entry is the first three octets of your IP address, reversed, followed by **in-addr.arpa**. Assuming that the network address for example.org is **192.168.1**, the **in-addr.arpa** domain would be **1.168.192.in-addr.arpa**. Thus the **zone** statement in the **named.conf** file would be as follows:

```
zone "1.168.192.in-addr.arpa" {
      type master;
      file "example.org.rev";
};
```

NOTE

This example assumes that you're doing the reverse for an entire Class C block of 255 IP addresses. Doing reverse mapping for a different size netblock is possible, but more complicated than what we'll cover here. The BIND documentation and a thorough understanding of netmasks should provide what you need if you find yourself in such a situation.

Now that you have your **named.conf** entries ready, it's time to actually write the **example.org.db** and **example.org.rev** files.

Additional Options

Primary domains may also use some of the configuration choices from the **options** statement. These options are

- check-names
- allow-update
- allow-query
- allow-transfer
- notify
- also-notify

Using any of these options in a zone configuration will affect only that zone. See the "Configuration Options" subsection in the discussion of **named.conf**, earlier in this module, for more information on how these options work.

Updating the named.conf for a Secondary Zone

The zone entry format for secondary servers is very similar to that of master servers. For forward resolution, here is the format:

```
zone domain-name {
    type slave;
    masters  IP-address-list; ;
};
```

where the *domain-name* is the exact same name as the primary name server, and the *IP-address-list* is the list of IP addresses where the primary name server for that zone exists.

A recommended additional option you can list in a secondary zone configuration is

```
file path-name;
```

where *path-name* is the full path location of where the server will keep copies of the primary's zone files. By keeping a local copy, you can reduce bandwidth needs for updates and improve performance.

Additional Options

A secondary zone configuration may also use some of the configuration choices from the **options** statement. These options are

- check-names
- allow-update
- allow-query
- allow-transfer
- max-transfer-time-in
- notify
- also-notify

See the "Configuration Options" subsection in the discussion of **named.conf**, earlier in this module, for more information on how these options work.

Updating the named.conf File for a Caching Zone

A caching configuration is the easiest of all configurations. It's also required for every DNS server configuration, even if you are running a primary or secondary server. This is necessary in order for the server to recursively search the DNS tree to find other hosts on the Internet.

The two zone entries you need are for the cache and for making the local-host entry primary for itself. Here's the first entry:

```
zone "." {
     type hint;
     file "named.ca";
};
```

The line **type hint;** specifies that this is a caching zone entry, and the line **file "named.ca";** specifies the file that will prime the cache with entries pointing to the root servers. (This **named.ca** file comes with the BIND package. You can also find the latest file at ftp://rs.internic.net.)

The second zone entry is as follows:

```
zone "0.0.127.in-addr.arpa"  {
     type master;
```

```
            file "named.local";
};
```

This is the reverse entry for resolving the local host address back to the local host name. The **named.local** file contains the following:

```
$TTL 86400
@        IN      SOA     localhost. root.localhost. (
                                2002103100  ; Serial
                                28800       ; Refresh
                                14400       ; Retry
                                3600000     ; Expire
                                86400  )    ; Minimum
         IN      NS      localhost.

1        IN      PTR     localhost.
```

If this doesn't make sense to you yet, don't worry. Just know that this is enough for a caching server. The following sections will help you make sense of this file.

DNS Records Types

Okay, I kind of lied. You aren't ready to create the **example.org.db** and **example.org.rev** files—not quite yet. First you need to understand all the record types for DNS: SOA, NS, A, PTR, CNAME, MX, TXT, and RP.

SOA: Start of Authority

The SOA record starts the description of a site's DNS entries. The format of this entry is as follows:

```
domain.com. IN SOA ns.domain.com. hostmaster.domain.com. (
    2002112400          ; serial number
    10800               ; refresh rate in seconds (3 hours)
    1800                ; retry in seconds (30 minutes)
    1209600             ; expire in seconds (2 weeks)
    604800      )       ; minimum in seconds (1 week)
```

The first line contains some details we need to pay attention to:

- **domain.com.** is of course to be replaced with your domain name. Notice that last period at the end of domain.com.? It's supposed to be there—indeed, the DNS configuration files are extremely picky about it. The ending period is necessary for the server to differentiate relative host names from fully qualified domain names (FQDNs); for example, to differentiate between **box** and **box.example.org**. If you forget that trailing period, you may find your server thinking it's answering for *domain*.com.*domain*.com. While that would be a valid subdomain, it's probably not what you intended. If you've been peeking ahead at the example files, you may have noticed that this first occurrence of the domain name is often replaced by a single @ sign. This is a very common shorthand found in zone files when the domain exactly matches the origin specified in the zone statement in your **named.conf** file.

- **IN** tells the name server that this is an Internet record. There are other types of records, but it's been years since anyone has had a need for them. We can safely ignore them.

- **SOA** tells the name server that this is the Start of Authority record.

- **ns.domain.com.** is the FQDN for the name server for this domain (the server where this file will finally reside). Again, watch out and don't miss that trailing period.

- **hostmaster.domain.com.** is the e-mail address for the domain administrator. Notice the lack of an @ in this address. The @ symbol is replaced with a period. Thus, the e-mail address referred to in this example is **hostmaster@domain.com**. The trailing period is used here, too.

The remainder of the record starts after the opening parenthesis on the first line. The first line is the serial number. It is used to tell the name server when the file has been updated. Watch out—forgetting to increment this number when you make a change is a mistake frequently made in the process of managing DNS records. (Forgetting to put a period in the right place is another common error.)

TIP

Although you can use nearly any number in the serial number field, choosing a meaningful value makes it easier to maintain and spot mistakes. One very popular method is to use the current date formatted in the following order: YYYYMMDD*xx*. The tail-end *xx* is an additional two-digit number starting with 00, so if you make multiple updates in a day, you can still provide a constantly increasing number.

The second line in the list of values is the refresh rate in seconds. This value tells the secondary DNS servers how often they should query the primary server to see if the records have been updated. If you know you will be making changes in the near future, changing this to a smaller value will help keep all the name servers in sync. For daily usage where you don't expect many changes, a higher value will help keep network traffic manageable.

The third value is the retry rate in seconds. If the secondary server tries but cannot contact the primary DNS server to check for updates, the secondary server tries again after the specified number of seconds.

The fourth value is intended for secondary servers that have cached the zone data. It tells these servers that if they cannot contact the primary server for an update, they should discard the value after the specified number of seconds. One to two weeks is a good value for this interval.

The final value, **minimum**, tells caching servers how long they should wait before expiring an entry if they cannot contact the primary DNS server. Five to seven days is a good guideline for this entry.

NOTE
Don't forget to place the closing parenthesis after the final value.

NS: Name Server

The NS record is used for specifying which name servers maintain records for this zone. The format of this record is as follows:

```
IN NS           ns1.domain.com.
IN NS           ns2.domain.com.
```

You can have as many backup name servers as you'd like for a domain—at least two is a good idea. Most ISPs are willing to act as secondary DNS servers if they provide connectivity for you.

A: Address Record

The A record is used for providing a mapping from host name to IP address. The format of an A address is simple:

```
host name           IN A            IP-Address
```

For example, an A record for the host box.example.org, whose IP address is 192.168.1.2, would look like this:

```
box                 IN A            192.168.1.2
```

Note that any host name is automatically suffixed with the domain name listed in the SOA record, unless this host name ends with a period. In the foregoing example for **box**, if the SOA record above it is for example.org, then box is understood to be **box.example.org**. If we were to change this to box.example.org (without a trailing period), the name server would understand it to be box.example.org.example.org. So if you want to use the FQDN, be sure to suffix it with a period.

PTR: Pointer Record

The PTR record is for performing reverse name resolution, thereby allowing someone to specify an IP address and determine the corresponding host name. The format for this record is very similar to the A record, except with the values reversed:

```
IP-Address      IN PTR      host name
```

The *IP-Address* can take one of two forms: just the last octet of the IP address (leaving the name server to automatically suffix it with the information it has from the **in-addr.arpa** domain name) or the full IP address, which is suffixed with a period. The *host name* must have the complete FQDN. For example, the PTR record for the host **box** would be as follows:

```
192.168.1.2.     IN PTR      box.example.org.
```

MX: Mail Exchanger

The MX record is in charge of telling other sites about your zone's mail server. If a host on your network generated an outgoing mail with its host name on it, someone returning a message would not send it back directly to that host. Instead, the replying mail server would look up the MX record for that site and send the message there instead.

When Internet sites were primarily composed of UNIX-based systems, with Sendmail configured as a NULL host forwarding to a mail hub, lack of an MX record was okay. But as more non-UNIX systems joined the Net, MX records became crucial. If **pc.domain.com** sends a message using its PC-based mail reader (which cannot accept SMTP mail), it's important that the replying party have a reliable way of knowing the identity of **pc.domain.com**'s mail server.

The format of the MX record is as follows:

```
domainname.  IN MX weight host name
```

where *domainname.* is the domain name of the site (with a period at the end, of course); the *weight* is the importance of the mail server (if multiple mail servers exist, the one with the smallest number has precedence over those with larger numbers); and the *host name* is, of course, the name of the mail server. It is important that the host name have an A record, as well. Here's an example entry:

```
domain.com.     IN MX 10 mailserver1
                IN MX 20 mailserverbackup
```

Typically, MX records occur at the top of DNS configuration files. If a domain name is not specified, the default name is pulled from the SOA record.

CNAME: Canonical Name

CNAME records allow you to create aliases for host names. This is useful when you want to provide a highly available service with an easy-to-remember name and still give the host a real name.

Another popular use for CNAMEs is to "create" a new server with an easy-to-remember name without having to invest in a new server at all. An example: A site has a mail server named mailhost in a UNIX-like tradition. As non-UNIX people come into the Internet picture, they assume the mail server will be called mail; to accommodate this assumption, a CNAME is created rather than renaming the server, so that all requests to the host named mail will transparently resolve to mailhost.

Here's the format for the CNAME record:

```
new host name   IN CNAME   old host name
```

For example, for the mail-to-mailhost mapping just mentioned, our entries might look like this:

```
mailhost     IN A       192.168.1.10
mail         IN CNAME   mailhost
```

CAUTION

It is a very bad practice to point an MX record to a CNAME record. The official DNS specification document explicitly prohibits this. BIND may allow it, but only to keep backward compatibility with a broken feature from the past.

RP and TXT: The Documentation Entries

Sometimes it's useful to provide contact information as part of your database—not just as comments, but as actual records that others can query. This can be accomplished using the RP and TXT records.

A TXT record is a free-form text entry into which you can place whatever information you deem fit. Most often, you'll only want to put contact information in these records. Each TXT record must be tied to a particular host name. For example:

```
hhgttg.planetoid.org.  IN TXT "Contact: Marvin"
                       IN TXT "SysAdmin/Android"
                       IN TXT "Voice: 800-555-1212"
```

The RP record was created as an explicit container for a host's contact information. This record states who is the responsible person for the specific host; here's an example:

```
hhgttg.planetoid.org.   IN RP marvin.domain.com. planetoid.org.
```

As useful as these records may be, they are a rarity these days, because it is perceived that they give away too much information about the site that could lead to social engineering–based attacks. You may find such records helpful in your internal DNS servers, but you should probably leave them out of anything that one could query from the Internet.

CRITICAL SKILL
10.7 Putting It All Together

So now we have the entries we need in the **named.conf** file, and we know about all the DNS record types. It's time to create the actual database that will feed the server.

The database file format is not too strict, but some conventions have jelled over time. Sticking to these conventions will make your life easier and will smooth the way for the administrator who takes over your creation.

TIP

Comment liberally. In this file, comment lines begin with a semicolon. Although there isn't a lot of mystery about what's going on in a DNS database file, a history of the changes is a useful reference about what was being accomplished and why.

Every database file must start with a $TTL entry. This entry tells BIND what the time-to-live (TTL) value is for each individual record. (The TTL in the SOA record is for the SOA record only.) After the $TTL entry is the SOA record and at least one NS record, everything else is optional. (Of course, "everything else" is what makes the file useful!) You may find the following general format helpful to follow:

```
$TTL
SOA record
NS records
MX records
A and CNAME records
```

For example, here is a complete zone configuration file for a single domain with four hosts and a time-to-live setting of 604,800 seconds (1 week):

```
$TTL 604800
@        IN        SOA       domain.com.   hostmaster.domain.com. (
                             2002112400   ; serial number
                             10800        ;Refresh every 3 hours
                             1800         ;Retry every 30 minutes
                             1209600      ;Expire in 2 weeks
                             604800 )     ;Minimum 1 week
```

```
                  IN      NS       ns.domain.com.
                  IN      MX 10    mail.domain.com.
imp               IN      A        192.168.1.1    ; Internet gateway
mail              IN      A        192.168.1.2    ; mail server
technics          IN      A        192.168.1.3    ; web server
www               IN      CNAME    technics
ns                IN      A        192.168.1.4    ; name server
peanutbutter      IN      A        192.168.1.5    ; firewall
```

And here is the corresponding reverse file:

```
$TTL 604800
@   IN   SOA 1.168.192.in-addr.arpa. hostmaster.domain.com. (
                      2002112400        ; Serial
                      10800             ; Refresh rate (3 hours)
                      1800              ; Retry (30 minutes)
                      1209600           ; Expire (2 weeks)
                      604800 )          ; Minimum (1 week)
                  IN      NS       ns.domain.com.
1                 IN      PTR      imp.domain.com.
2                 IN      PTR      mail.domain.com
3                 IN      PTR      technics.domain.com
4                 IN      PTR      ns.domain.com
5                 IN      PTR      peanutbutter.domain.com.
```

A Complete Configuration

So far, we've given you snippets of configuration files. Hopefully that has been enough to give you the big DNS picture and provide plenty of guidance for coming up with your own configuration file. Then again, a nice example never hurts.

Following is a complete configuration for a primary domain (**domain.com**) that also acts as a secondary to a friend, **example.com**. In exchange, the **example.com** domain acts as our secondary. We allow zone transfers to occur between our two sites, but not with any other sites. The **domain.com** site's ISP provides DNS service as well, to which we forward requests when we cannot resolve information ourselves. We haven't reproduced the **named.ca** file here, as you really don't want to change the one that was supplied to you.

Here is the **named.conf** file:

```
options {
  directory "/var/named";
  forwarders {
            192.168.2.1;
            192.168.2.2;
  };
  allow-transfer  {
```

```
                    10.0.0.1;    // ns1.example.com
                    10.0.0.2;    // ns2.example.com
    };
};

//
// a caching only name server config
//
zone "." {
        type hint;
        file "named.ca";
};

zone "0.0.127.in-addr.arpa" {
        type master;
        file "named.local";
};

//
// our primary information
//
zone "domain.com"  {
        type master;
        file "named.domain.com.";
};
zone "1.168.192.in-addr.arpa" {
        type master;
        file "named.rev";
};

//
// our secondary information for example.com
//
zone "example.com" {
        type slave;
        file "example.com.cache";
        masters  { 10.0.0.1; 10.0.0.2; };
};
```

Here is the **/var/named/named.local** file:

```
$TTL 86400
@       IN      SOA     localhost. root.localhost.  (
                                2002112400 ; Serial
                                28800      ; Refresh every 8 hours
```

```
                                  14400        ; Retry every 4 hours
                                  3600000      ; Expire in ~6 weeks
                                  86400 )      ; Minimum 1 day
            IN      NS      localhost.

1           IN      PTR     localhost.
```

Here is the **/var/named/named.domain.com** file:

```
$TTL 86400
@        IN      SOA     domain.com.  hostmaster.domain.com. (
                         2002112400 ; serial number
                         10800    ;Refresh every 3 hours
                         1800     ;Retry every 30 minutes
                         1209600 ;Expire in 2 weeks
                         604800 ) ;Minimum 1 week
                 IN      NS      ns.domain.com.
                 IN      MX 10   mail.domain.com.
imp              IN      A       192.168.1.1    ; Internet gateway
mail             IN      A       192.168.1.2    ; mail server
technics         IN      A       192.168.1.3    ; web server
www              IN      CNAME   technics
ns               IN      A       192.168.1.4    ; name server
peanutbutter     IN      A       192.168.1.5    ; firewall
```

Here is the **/var/named/named.rev** file:

```
$TTL 604800
@   IN   SOA 1.168.192.in-addr.arpa. hostmaster.domain.com. (
                         2002112400       ; Serial
                         10800            ; Refresh rate (3 hours)
                         1800             ; Retry (30 minutes)
                         1209600          ; Expire (2 weeks)
                         604800 )         ; Minimum (1 week)
                 IN      NS      ns.domain.com.
1                IN      PTR     imp.domain.com.
2                IN      PTR     mail.domain.com
3                IN      PTR     technics.domain.com
4                IN      PTR     ns.domain.com
5                IN      PTR     peanutbutter.domain.com.
```

We don't have to create any files to be secondary for **example.com**. We only need to add the entries we already have in the **named.conf** file.

And that's it: a complete configuration for a primary domain.

Now just as a bonus for those who have all the nice GUI stuff set up on their DNS server, we'll cover how to create that same domain by using Red Hat's GUI tool.

Project 10-1   Configuring a Domain Using the GUI Tool

In this project we will create the same domain as explained in the last section. However, we will be using Red Hat 8's GUI tool to do the configuration. You will need to have the X Window System on your DNS server in order to perform the configuration in this way.

Step by Step

1. Launch the tool by either selecting Domain Name Service from the Server Settings submenu, or launch it from the command line as **redhat-config-bind**. You'll notice that the **localhost** and caching part is already filled in and set up for you. Unfortunately that's all that can be set up automatically without your attention.

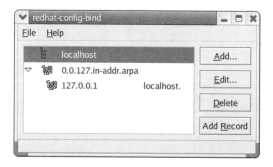

2. Click the Add button on the right, and select Forward Master Zone from the dialog box to start configuring our primary zone.

3. Enter **domain.com** into the text widget (or substitute your own domain name) and click OK.

4. You'll move on to a dialog box called Name to IP Translations. You'll probably recognize the entries on this dialog box as corresponding to the SOA section at the top of your zone file. You will probably want to update the Contact address at the very least.

5. If you're looking to modify the time values related to your zone, look for the Time Settings button near the middle of the dialog box. The defaults are usually an adequate starting point, however.

6. The bottom half of the dialog box shows records you have defined for the zone. The default for a new zone will be just the domain name—**domain.com**, in our example. Click the Edit button while that entry is highlighted, and you'll have the opportunity to add name servers and mail exchangers for the zone.

Project
10-1

(continued)

7. You may notice the opportunity at the bottom to enter an IP address for **domain.com**. Yes, that can be a valid host name with its own IP address, even if you have other hosts under it. Click OK when you've finished with any entries on that dialog box.

8. Once you've finished with the domain-wide entries, you can click Add from the Name to IP Translations dialog box and enter our other entries for the zone from the preceding steps. Be sure to set the Record Resource correctly for each entry.

9. Once you have all the hosts entered for **domain.com**, you can click Add again for the reverse zone.

10. Finally you can enter the details of a *slave zone* (another term for a secondary zone) set up for our friends at example.com. Click Add as before but select Slave Zone this time. Enter **example.com** in the text widget and click OK.

11. Fill in the master server we're pulling from, and then click OK.

Project Summary

That's all there is to setting up a secondary.

From the tree widgets on the main GUI window, you can directly edit not only each zone setup, but also directly edit individual entries within the zone. Be sure you understand the difference between the Add button and the Add Record button in this window. Use the Add button for creating a new zone, and Add Record for entries within the highlighted zone.

(continued)

Once again, you'll notice that the GUI tool is sadly lacking when it comes to letting you comment your files.

Progress Check

1. What must all zone file entries start with?

2. According to the author, which configuration is the easiest?

CRITICAL SKILL
10.8 Using the DNS Toolbox

This section describes a few tools that you'll want to get acquainted with as you work with DNS. They'll help you to troubleshoot problems more quickly.

rndc

In BIND 9, the older Name Daemon Controller program **ndc** has been replaced by **rndc**, the Remote Name Daemon Controller. Using this tool for reloading **named** after a configuration change or other administrative tasks is considered preferable to issuing a kill -HUP. It also provides the ability to remotely manage servers securely. A simple use would be

```
[root@tux /etc]# rndc reload zone
```

The BIND documentation has more information on changing the default configuration of this tool for more advanced tasks. This tool takes a bit more work to set up than its predecessor, but if you're working with BIND on a regular basis, it will be worth your time. If you infrequently touch your name server, you may be able to get by with just restarting BIND from its init script in **/etc/init.d/** when you make a configuration change.

host

The **host** tool is really the master of all DNS tools. By learning all of the features **host** has to offer, you can eliminate the need to learn several of the smaller tools that come with BIND.

1. $TTL.
2. A caching configuration is the easiest.

Long-time users of **nslookup** may be surprised to see their old friend being put away. Well, the news isn't as bad as you think—the BIND team is simply trying to leave less overlap between its tools.

In its simplest use, **host** allows you to resolve host names into IP addresses from the command line. For example:

```
[root@tux root]# host theorb.com
theorb.com has address 209.133.83.16
```

We can also use **host** to perform reverse lookups. For example:

```
[root@tux root]# host 209.133.83.16
16.83.133.209.IN-ADDR.ARPA domain name pointer taz.hyperreal.org
```

This can lead to all kinds of interesting discoveries. In this case, we see that **theorb.com** is the same as **taz.hyperreal.org**. It is likely that **taz.hyperreal.org** is also "virtually hosting" other domains, as well.

TIP

If you are familiar with **nslookup**, don't worry, it's still there. However, since the BIND group is trying to move people away from it, consider using the **dig** tool (discussed next) instead when you need to find out about records other than A and PTR, or when you need to query servers other than your own.

dig

The domain information gopher, **dig**, is a great tool for gathering information about DNS servers. The typical format of the **dig** command is

```
[root@tux /root]# dig @server domain query-type
```

where **@server** is the name of the DNS server you want to query, **domain** is the domain name you are interested in querying, and **query-type** is the name of the record you are trying to get (A, MX, NS, SOA, HINFO, TXT, or ANY).

For example, to get the **mx** record for the domain **whitehouse.gov** from the DNS server **ns1.ucsd.edu**, you would run:

```
[root@ford /root]# dig @ns1.ucsd.edu whitehouse.gov mx
```

The program **dig** is incredibly powerful. You should read the man page that was installed with **dig** to learn how to use some of its more advanced features.

whois

The **whois** command is used for determining ownership of a domain. Information about a domain's owner isn't a mandatory part of its records, nor is it customarily placed in the TXT or RP records. So you'll need to gather this information using the **whois** technique, which reports the actual owner of the domain, as well as the owner's snail-mail address, e-mail address, and technical contact phone numbers.

```
[root@ford root]#  whois collab.net

Whois Server Version 1.3

Domain names in the .com, .net, and .org domains can now be registered
with many different competing registrars. Go to http://www.internic.net
for detailed information.
    Domain Name: COLLAB.NET
    Registrar: NETWORK SOLUTIONS, INC.
    Whois Server: whois.networksolutions.com
    Referral URL: http://www.networksolutions.com
    Name Server: NS.HYPERREAL.ORG
    Name Server: NS1.COLLAB.NET
    Name Server: NS2.COLLAB.NET
    Name Server: NS3.COLLAB.NET
    Updated Date: 05-nov-2001
>>> Last update of whois database: Thu, 26 Oct 2000 06:47:54 EDT <<<
The Registry database contains ONLY .COM, .NET, .ORG, .EDU domains and
Registrars.

Found crsnic referral to whois.networksolutions.com.

The Data in the VeriSign Registrar WHOIS database is provided by VeriSign for
information purposes only, and to assist persons in obtaining information about
or related to a domain name registration record.  VeriSign does not guarantee
its accuracy.  Additionally, the data may not reflect updates to billing contact
information.  By submitting a WHOIS query, you agree to use this Data only
for lawful purposes and that under no circumstances will you use this Data to:
(1) allow, enable, or otherwise support the transmission of mass unsolicited,
commercial advertising or solicitations via e-mail, telephone, or facsimile; or
(2) enable high volume, automated, electronic processes that apply to VeriSign
(or its computer systems).  The compilation, repackaging, dissemination or
other use of this Data is expressly prohibited without the prior written
consent of VeriSign.  VeriSign reserves the right to terminate your access to
the VeriSign Registrar WHOIS database in its sole discretion, including
without limitation, for excessive querying of the WHOIS database or for failure
to otherwise abide by this policy.  VeriSign reserves the right to modify these
terms at any time.  By submitting this query, you agree to abide by this policy.
Registrant:
Collaboration Networks Inc. (COLLAB6-DOM)
    8000 Marina Blvd, Suite 600
    Brisbane, CA 94005
    US
```

```
Domain Name: COLLAB.NET

Administrative Contact, Technical Contact:
    Hostmaster General  (JB1348-ORG)          hostmaster@COLLAB.NET
    Collabnet
    8000 Marina Blvd, Suite 600
    Brisbane, CA 94005
    US
    650-228-2500
    Fax: 650-228-2501

Record expires on 13-May-2003.
Record created on 13-May-1999.
Database last updated on 17-Aug-2002 03:38:04 EDT.

Domain servers in listed order:

NS1.COLLAB.NET              64.125.134.21
NS2.COLLAB.NET              64.125.178.141
NS3.COLLAB.NET              63.211.145.15
NS.HYPERREAL.ORG           209.133.83.22
```

Keeping the **whois** information up-to-date for your own domain is very important. Should an extraordinary event occur, such as your site being attacked or turned into a spam relay, you'll most likely be contacted via telephone before via e-mail. In such situations, not having current, relevant information can cause you a great deal of harm.

Other References

Obviously, any protocol that's been around as long as DNS can't be summarized in a few short pages. If you need to explore DNS beyond what has been discussed in this module, I highly recommend the following texts:

- *DNS and BIND,* Fourth Edition, by Paul Albitz and Cricket Liu (O'Reilly & Associates, 2001) does a superb job of getting into the truly hairy details of DNS. If you're looking to subdomain, do DNS load balancing, or basically do anything out of the ordinary, pick up this book. Modules like the one you're reading are a great way to get up and running with a reasonably solid understanding, but it is books like *DNS and BIND* that make you fly.

- For more low-level details about how it all works under the covers, see *TCP/IP Illustrated, Volume 1: The Protocols,* by Richard Stevens (Addison-Wesley, 1994–1996). It contains a chapter dedicated to DNS, with a packet-by-packet analysis and fundamental explanations of how it all works.

There are several RFCs related to DNS, most notably 1034 and 1035. Several are included with the BIND documentation and can be found in the **/usr/share/doc/bind-9.2.1/rfc/** directory on Red Hat. You can also get them online from http://www.rfc-editor.org. If you're curious about the bleeding edge, visit the Internet Engineering Task Force (IETF) at http://www.ietf .org to see what they are up to.

Module Summary

In this module, we covered all of the information you'll need to get various types of DNS servers up and running. We discussed

- Name resolution over the Internet

- The **/etc/hosts** file

- The process of configuring a Linux client to use DNS

- Configuring DNS servers to act as primary, secondary, and caching servers

- The record types needed to establish a site

- Most of the configuration options in the **named.conf** file

- Tools for use in conjunction with the DNS server to do troubleshooting

- Additional sources of information

With the information available in the BIND documentation on how the server should be configured, along with the actual configuration files for a complete server presented in this module, you should be able to go out and perform a complete installation from start to finish.

Like any software, nothing is perfect, and problems can occur with BIND and the related files and programs discussed here. Don't forget to check out web sites as well as the various newsgroups dedicated to DNS and BIND for additional information.

You will find plenty of people who can help you work through your problems. Remember to help someone else after you've learned it yourself!

Module 10 Mastery Check

1. What is a primary name server?

2. What is the central repository listing of all primary servers called?

3. How are subdomains used?

4. How many types of name servers are there? List each and explain what they do.

5. What does the server statement tell BIND?

6. Name five record types for DNS. What does each do and what do the symbols stand for?

7. What is CNAME used for?

8. What is BIND?

9. True or False? Domains are designated along organizational boundaries.

10. How do you negate an address in a DNS configuration file?

Module 11

Transferring Files with FTP

The File Transfer Protocol (FTP) has existed for the Internet since around 1971. Remarkably, the protocol has undergone very little change since then. Clients and servers, on the other hand, have been almost constantly improved and refined. There are a number of good FTP clients installed with your Red Hat system, ranging from the original **ftp**, to the more advanced command-line client **lftp**, to the graphical clients like **gftp**. If you've worked with FTP servers on UNIX before, you might be a bit surprised to find that your Red Hat installation doesn't use the Washington University FTP daemon (**wu-ftpd**) by default, but instead includes the Very Secure FTP daemon (**vsftpd**).

Red Hat uses the **vsftpd** server on its own machines, and that's also what the company now includes as the default FTP server for Red Hat 8. The "vs" stands for "very secure," but as the authors of the program point out, that is a design goal and not a guarantee. In part because of its lightweight design, **vsftpd** has also proven itself to be stable and scalable under heavy usage. The servers behind ftp.redhat.com have withstood 15,000 concurrent connections across their server pool using **vsftpd**, with individual servers handling more than 2,500 concurrent downloads. Security-conscious organizations, such as the SANS (SysAdmin, Audit, Network, Security) Institute and IBM, are also recommending **vsftpd**. In addition, there is at least anecdotal evidence that it is noticeably faster than **wu-ftpd**.

CAUTION

Like most other services, **vsftpd** is only as secure as you make it. The authors of the program have provided all of the necessary tools to make your site secure, but a bad configuration can cause your site to become open. Remember to double-check your configuration and test it out before going live. FTP servers are a popular target for attackers, so keeping up on the latest bug fixes and patches for public servers is critical.

In this module, I will discuss how to configure **vsftpd** for private access as well as anonymous access, and will show how to use it to set up virtual domains.

CRITICAL SKILL
11.1 Defining the Mechanics of FTP

The act of transferring a file from one computer to another may seem trivial, but in reality it is not—at least, not if you're doing it right. In this section, you walk through the details of the FTP client/server interaction. While this information isn't crucial to being able to get an FTP server up and running, it is important when you need to consider security issues and troubleshooting issues—especially troubleshooting issues that don't clearly manifest themselves as FTP related. ("Is it the network, or is it FTP?")

Client/Server Interactions

When an FTP client wants to connect to an FTP server, it takes two random high ports (a port number greater than 1024)—one for a "control" connection and one for a "data" connection. It then initiates a connection from the port it chose as "control" to port number 21 on the server. (Port 21 is the ubiquitous FTP server port defined in the FTP standard, so that's where the server daemon will listen for new connections.) As part of the initial negotiation, the client also tells the server which other high port the client has selected. Once the connection is established, the client can log in and issue commands to go through the FTP server's directories.

When the client makes a request to transfer a file, the server initiates a connection from its own port number 20 to the port on the client that was specified earlier. The original connection is left open so that the client and server can send additional "out of band" messages to each other (to abort the transfer, for example). Figure 11-1 illustrates this two-channel communication.

This design, conceived in the early 1970s, assumed something that was reasonable to assume for a long period of time on the Internet: Internet users are a friendly bunch. This was indirectly protected by the fact that the National Science Foundation (NSF) funded the Internet backbone, and therefore no commercial organizations were allowed on to it unless they were working in conjunction with a research institute. Academic- and government-funded research labs made up most of the users.

Around 1990–1991, the NSF stopped footing the bill for the Internet backbone, and the Internet went commercial. At first, it wasn't a big deal. Then the World Wide Web came along and the Net's population exploded—along with its security problems.

Many sites have now taken to using firewalls to protect their internal networks from the Big Bad Internet. Firewalls, however, consider arbitrary connections from high ports on the Internet to high ports on the internal network to be a very bad thing (and rightfully so). As a result, many firewalls implement application-level proxies for FTP that keep track of FTP requests and open up those high ports when needed to receive data from a rcmote site.

Of course, not all firewalls are that smart. Many sites rely on packet-filtering firewalls, which don't really understand the data going through them but know that data being sent to

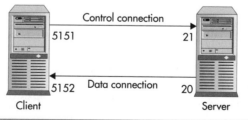

Figure 11-1 Port connections for FTP running in "normal mode"

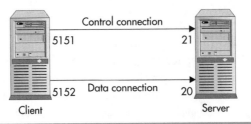

Figure 11-2 Port connections for FTP running in "passive mode"

arbitrary high ports is bad and thus bounces them out. This type of firewall promptly breaks FTP, because FTP relies on being able to open a connection back with the client on a high port. A typical symptom of this behavior occurring is that when a client appears to be able to connect to the server without a problem, the connection seems to hang whenever an attempt to transfer data occurs.

Now think back to when FTP was originally created and bandwidth was at a premium. When someone wanted to get a file transferred from host A to host B while sitting at host C, the process of transferring the file from host A to C and then from C to B would waste an incredible amount of bandwidth. So the designers of the FTP protocol came up with a solution: make it possible for someone sitting on host C to transfer a file from host A to host B directly. This was done via a *passive transfer*.

Passive transfers are accomplished by having the client side, rather than the server side, initiate the connection for data transfer, as shown in Figure 11-2. In the three-machine scenario, one of the servers is put into passive mode, and the other is left in normal mode. The normal-mode machine can then initiate a data connection to the passive-mode machine, as shown in Figure 11-3. This sort of thing doesn't happen too often in the real world anymore, but passive mode still exists, and we can use it for other purposes. For example, passive mode can also be used between just two machines. From the standpoint of firewalls, this allows the client to remain securely behind a firewall without the need for complex rules for allowing connections back in.

Progress Check

1. What are two types of FTP clients that come with Red Hat 8?

2. _____ originally funded the Internet backbone.

---

1. Two types of FTP clients that come with Red Hat 8 are a command line such as **lftp** and a graphical client such as **gftp**.
2. The National Science Foundation (NSF) funded the Internet backbone.

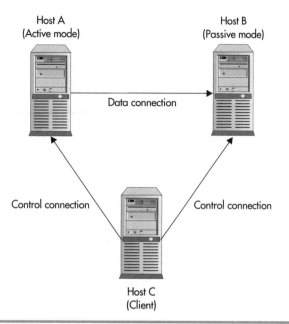

Host A
(Active mode)

Host B
(Passive mode)

Data connection

Control connection

Control connection

Host C
(Client)

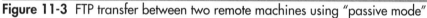

Figure 11-3 FTP transfer between two remote machines using "passive mode"

CRITICAL SKILL
11.2 Setting Up vsftp

The **vsftp** server doesn't have quite as many configuration options as some of its competitors, focusing instead on doing the basics well. It should be sufficient for most FTP needs, and much of what's missing can be considered "frills" or can be accomplished in other ways. I'm going to cover how to set up a working server for both user and anonymous access throughout the rest of this module. In addition to the **vsftp rpm**, you'll probably want to check that you also have installed an FTP client and the **anonftp** package.

```
[root@tux /root]# rpm -qa | grep ftp
lftp-2.5.2-4
anonftp-4.0-12
ftp-0.17-15
vsftpd-1.0.1-7
gftp-2.0.13-4
```

The **anonftp** package isn't really an FTP server in itself, but it provides a framework for setting up an anonymous FTP server with **vsftpd** or another FTP daemon.

CAUTION

As I've mentioned, FTP was designed in the early days of the Internet and doesn't have many of the security features we've come to expect from modern Internet usage. When we talk about the security of servers like **vsftpd**, we're talking mostly about its resilience against directed attacks. All of the data transferred over an FTP session, including passwords, is still sent unencrypted. As a result, FTP is not recommended for use in insecure environments, or for sensitive data. You should probably look into more secure protocols, such as Secure Shell (SSH)/Secure Copy (SCP), if you have to transfer files with better protection. Only anonymous-style FTP servers should be exposed to the Internet.

Read the READMEs

You'll find that **vsftp** comes with several documentation files in straight text format located under **/usr/share/doc/vsftpd-1.0.1/**. These give a good overview of the security and design considerations in **vsftpd**. I highly recommend taking a few minutes to read through this documentation. The configuration options will make much more sense if you understand how they fit into the whole package. It also is helpful to have read the documentation that comes with the package *before* heading off to any discussion forums with questions.

Fixing Your xinetd.conf File

As you might recall from Module 8, the **/etc/inetd.conf** file is managed by the **xinetd** program, which acts as a kind of "superserver," listening for network requests on behalf of many server applications and starting a server application once it detects a connection request for it. If its configuration file **/etc/xinetd.conf** gets changed, you need to send the **xinetd** process a signal to tell it to reload its configuration file.

Red Hat comes with a configuration file for **vsftpd** in the **/etc/xinetd.d/** directory, but is disabled by default. If you enable **vsftpd** in the Service Configuration tool, shown in the following illustration, the disable directive line in the **xinetd.d** file for **vsftpd** changes from "disable = yes" to "disable = no."

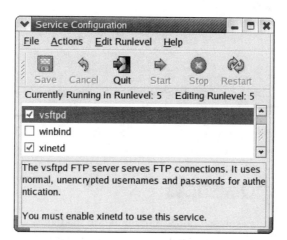

If you're not using the Service Configuration tool, you can make the same change with your favorite text editor. The resulting file should look similar to the following:

```
# default: off
# description: The vsftpd FTP server serves FTP connections. It uses \
#        normal, unencrypted usernames and passwords for authentication.
service ftp
{
        disable = no
        socket_type             = stream
        wait                    = no
        user                    = root
        server                  = /usr/sbin/vsftpd
        nice                    = 10
}
```

Now we need to tell **xinetd** to reread all of its configuration files. The easiest way to do this is to run

```
[root@tux /root]#  /etc/init.d/xinetd reload
```

You can also force it to reread its configuration by sending it a **SIGUSR1**, as follows.

```
[root@tux /root]# kill -SIGUSR1 `cat /var/run/xinetd.pid`
```

You should now be able to **ftp** to your own system. Don't worry if you can't log in yet—you'll get to those details in the next section—but at the very least you should be able to get an FTP login prompt.

```
[michael@tux michael]$ ftp localhost
Connected to localhost (127.0.0.1).
220 ready, dude (vsFTPd 1.0.1: beat me, break me)
Name (localhost:michael):
```

CRITICAL SKILL
11.3 Configuring vsftpd

The **vsftpd** package comes with a sample configuration file that is very easy to modify for your needs. Your default **conf** file should look something similar to the following.

```
# Example config file /etc/vsftpd.conf
#
# The default compiled in settings are very paranoid. This sample file
# loosens things up a bit, to make the ftp daemon more usable.
#
# Allow anonymous FTP?
anonymous_enable=YES
#
# Uncomment this to allow local users to log in.
local_enable=YES
#
# Uncomment this to enable any form of FTP write command.
write_enable=YES
#
# Default umask for local users is 077. You may wish to change this to 022,
# if your users expect that (022 is used by most other ftpd's)
local_umask=022
#
# Uncomment this to allow the anonymous FTP user to upload files. This only
# has an effect if the above global write enable is activated. Also, you will
# obviously need to create a directory writable by the FTP user.
#anon_upload_enable=YES
#
# Uncomment this if you want the anonymous FTP user to be able to create
# new directories.
#anon_mkdir_write_enable=YES
#
# Activate directory messages - messages given to remote users when they
# go into a certain directory.
dirmessage_enable=YES
#
# Activate logging of uploads/downloads.
xferlog_enable=YES
#
```

```
# Make sure PORT transfer connections originate from port 20 (ftp-data).
connect_from_port_20=YES
#
# If you want, you can arrange for uploaded anonymous files to be owned by
# a different user. Note! Using "root" for uploaded files is not
# recommended!
#chown_uploads=YES
#chown_username=whoever
#
# You may override where the log file goes if you like. The default is shown
# below.
#xferlog_file=/var/log/vsftpd.log
#
# If you want, you can have your log file in standard ftpd xferlog format
xferlog_std_format=YES
#
# You may change the default value for timing out an idle session.
#idle_session_timeout=600
#
# You may change the default value for timing out a data connection.
#data_connection_timeout=120
#
# It is recommended that you define on your system a unique user which the
# ftp server can use as a totally isolated and unprivileged user.
#nopriv_user=ftpsecure
#
# Enable this and the server will recognize asynchronous ABOR requests. Not
# recommended for security (the code is non-trivial). Not enabling it,
# however, may confuse older FTP clients.
#async_abor_enable=YES
#
# By default the server will pretend to allow ASCII mode but in fact ignore
# the request. Turn on the below options to have the server actually do ASCII
# mangling on files when in ASCII mode.
# Beware that turning on ascii_download_enable enables malicious remote parties
# to consume your I/O resources, by issuing the command "SIZE /big/file" in
# ASCII mode.
# These ASCII options are split into upload and download because you may wish
# to enable ASCII uploads (to prevent uploaded scripts etc. from breaking),
# without the DoS risk of SIZE and ASCII downloads. ASCII mangling should be
# on the client anyway..
#ascii_upload_enable=YES
#ascii_download_enable=YES
#
# You may fully customise the login banner string:
#ftpd_banner=Welcome to blah FTP service.
#
# You may specify a file of disallowed anonymous e-mail addresses. Apparently
# useful for combatting certain DoS attacks.
#deny_email_enable=YES
# (default follows)
```

```
#banned_email_file=/etc/vsftpd.banned_emails
#
# You may specify an explicit list of local users to chroot() to their home
# directory. If chroot_local_user is YES, then this list becomes a list of
# users to NOT chroot().
#chroot_list_enable=YES
# (default follows)
#chroot_list_file=/etc/vsftpd.chroot_list
#
# You may activate the "-R" option to the builtin ls. This is disabled by
# default to avoid remote users being able to cause excessive I/O on large
# sites. However, some broken FTP clients such as "ncftp" and "mirror" assume
# the presence of the "-R" option, so there is a strong case for enabling it.
#ls_recurse_enable=YES
pam_service_name=vsftpd
```

The example file is fairly well commented, so you can probably figure out how to get the basics working just by reading through it. You will cover some of the most important features in the next few sections, including some not mentioned in the default **config** file. You may want to refer back to this file as you read through the descriptions of the following options.

General Configuration Options

Before you cover the different access options available, you should familiarize yourself with some of the basic configuration choices. This section provides only a brief reference, but you can further explore topics that are relevant to your setup.

connect_from_port_20   This option determines whether the data connection uses port 20 (when operating in normal mode). It may come as some surprise that the default is "no." The reason for this is part of **vsftpd**'s security model. By not requiring a low-number port, parts of the daemon can run in a less privileged mode. The tradeoff is that some clients have a security model that insists the connection come from port 20, so in our example file this option has been set to "yes."

pasv_enable   This option enables the use of passive mode and defaults to "yes." Disable it if, for some reason, you want to prevent passive mode from being used.

pasv_promiscuous   One of **vsftpd**'s security precautions involves making sure that in passive mode the data connection is coming from the same IP address as the control connection. Enabling this option would bypass that precaution. There may be a reason to do so if you're planning on performing one of those three-way FTP sessions mentioned at the beginning of this module, or if you're using some form of secure tunneling scheme that it interferes with. Otherwise you should probably leave it disabled.

port_enable   This enables normal (nonpassive) mode connections. In this case *port* refers to the practice of the client passing along the port number it has chosen for the data connection. Turn this off if you want to allow only passive mode connections. The default is "yes."

ftpd_banner   This gives you the option to change the message that's displayed when you first connect to the server. Unlike some other **ftpd** servers, **vsftpd** has you add your new message right here in the **config** file. Including your software's name and version number here is considered by some to be a security risk and is not advised. There is currently a one-line limit on the banner message.

dirmessage_enable   Enabling this means that when users change into a new directory, they'll be shown the contents of a text file (**.message** by default) if it exists. This is useful for providing per-directory information to users. This has been enabled in the example file. If you want to display a different file than .message, look at the **message_file** option.

write_enable   Just as you might expect, this enables writing operations in the **ftp** directories. This is necessary if you're going to allow uploads of any kind. There are, of course, security implications of doing this, and it's suggested that you leave this turned off unless you really need it.

xferlog_enable   Logging is your best asset as an administrator. This option will record all transfers to the log file. Note that **vsftpd** doesn't use **syslog**. This is enabled in the example configuration.

xferlog_std_format   This will toggle between a "standard" format used by some other FTP servers, notably **wu-ftp**, and **vsftpd**'s own format. The default is "no," but the example configuration changes this to "yes" to take advantage of existing log parsers that may be aware of the standard format.

xferlog_file   If you need to change where the log file is written, this is the option you're looking for. The default is **/var/log/vsftpd.log**.

pam_service_name   This is the string that **pam** will use as the service name when authenticating. The default is **ftp**, but this has been changed to **vsftp** in the example file to be less ambiguous. For more information on **pam**, see Module 9.

Controlling Access to FTP

Being able to control who may and who may not enter your FTP server is a crucial aspect of server management. You may want to allow users with an account on the box to log in as themselves. You may want to allow only anonymous, password-less logins. Perhaps you want both. There are options to control whether new files can be uploaded or only downloads can be performed. You can even limit actions based on certain lists of users.

Anonymous Access

Under the UNIX model, every process must have an owner. In the case of an anonymous FTP user, this owner should have minimal file access rights and only be able to see the files in the designated public FTP area. Even though this setup is taken care of by the **anonftp** package under Red Hat, it's still something to keep in mind when deciding which options and permissions to set. Also keep in mind that so-called anonymous access still requests a username and password, but the server recognizes the username of **anonymous** or **ftp** as being special and will accept any password for them. Customarily, the users e-mail address is requested as the password on anonymous access, but no real validation is performed.

anonymous_enable   This is obviously the most important of the options related to an anonymous setup. The default for this option is "yes," so you really only have to worry about it if you want to disable anonymous access.

anon_world_readable_only   This option defaults to "yes" under the assumption that from time to time the anonymous FTP user may own files that you don't want the world to have access to. When enabled, anonymous users will only be allowed to download files that are world readable. Change the value to "no" if you want to allow downloading of all files readable by the FTP user.

Ask the Expert

Q: How can we ensure that anonymous users enter their real e-mail addresses?

A: You cannot ensure that anonymous users enter their real e-mail addresses because FTP only provides authentication for users with accounts. Anonymous users can be truly anonymous. If you need gated access for users who do not have real accounts, you will probably need to use something fancier than FTP.

anon_upload_enable   This is set to "no" by default. If you change this to "yes" and also have the **write_enable** option set, anonymous users will be able to upload files. The anonymous FTP user must still have write permissions in the desired location.

anon_mkdir_write_enable   This will allow anonymous users to create new directories if the **write_enable** option is also on. The anonymous FTP user must have write permissions in the parent directory. The default is "no."

anon_other_write_enable   This controls deleting and renaming of files by anonymous users. You probably don't want to change this from its default value of "no."

chown_uploads   This option will allow you to have all anonymous uploads automatically changed to be owned by a certain user. This can be useful for security.

chown_username   This is the user to whom files are **chown**ed to if you enabled the previous option. The default is **root**, so you may want to change that to a dedicated user.

Authenticated User Access

Here's where we get into the issue of allowing users with accounts on the server to log in as themselves. The lack of general security in the FTP protocol means that the server usually tries to compensate with features like user ID remapping and **chroot**ed jails. This makes configurations potentially trickier than you might expect.

local_enable   This is the primary option to allow logins from people with local accounts. You have to change this to "yes" to make most of the following options relevant.

guest_enable   This will remap all nonanonymous logins to a specified "guest" user account. This can be a useful security option for some configurations.

guest_username   This is the username to map as **guest** if you enable the previous option. The default is **ftp**.

userlist_enable   Turn this option to "yes" if you want to limit who can log in based on a list in a file. You can either allow only those names listed, or you can deny those listed, depending on the following option.

userlist_deny   This option is only consulted if the previous option is enabled. It defaults to "yes," which will deny user accounts that are listed in the file. Changing this option to "no" reverses the meaning of the list so that only those listed can log in.

userlist_file   And this option specifies the file referred to by the preceding two options. The default is **/etc/vsftpd.user_list**. It is instructive to at least examine the accounts that Red Hat has listed here by default.

Configuring Host Access

While some FTP daemons will provide direct support for blocking certain hosts, the proper place for that kind of activity is in the access control files **hosts.allow** and **hosts.deny**. Place an entry in either or both of these files to adjust the access according to your needs. An example configuration might be

```
/etc/hosts.allow
vsftpd: LOCAL 10.1.42.0/24 *.my.domain.com
```

```
/etc/hosts.deny
vsftpd: ALL
```

The access control files are very flexible, but if they don't quite meet your needs for some reason, you can also adjust the settings in **xinetd.conf**. For more information on the **hosts.allow** and **hosts.deny** files, see Module 8.

CRITICAL SKILL
11.4 Configuring a Virtual FTP Server

Even though the FTP protocol doesn't support name-based virtual servers the way the Hypertext Transfer Protocol (HTTP) does, you can still set up multiple FTP servers on the same host so long as each server has its own IP address. To distinguish between the different "servers," we'll be taking advantage of **xinetd** once again. This section assumes that you have already configured an IP alias and fudged the Address Resolution Protocol (ARP) table correctly. (This is discussed later in this book in Part V, "Advanced Linux Networking.") This quick jumpstart on the process assumes you have one Ethernet card and want to add a single virtual IP address:

1. Make sure your new IP address exists in both the local host table (**/etc/hosts**) and your DNS table. (In this example, we'll call the host "earth.")

2. Run the **ifconfig** command to configure the eth0:0 device with the appropriate address, **netmask**, and **broadcast**. For example, to configure the 192.168.1.42 device on eth0:0, you would use the following command:

```
ifconfig eth0:0 192.168.1.42 netmask 255.255.255.0 broadcast 192.168.1.255
```

3. Fudge the ARP table. You will need your Ethernet card's hardware address for this. Run the **ifconfig –a** command to get this information. Assuming your Ethernet card's hardware address is 00:10:4B:CB:15:9F, type the following command:

```
arp -s earth 00:10:4B:CB:15:9F pub
```

With your virtual IP address established, you now need to create a configuration similar to that of your main site. In this example, I'll assume that you've put your new configuration file at **/etc/vsftpd.earth.conf**. You may decide to create a new directory structure for this or overlap with the existing configuration. We're going to take advantage of two features to make this all work together. The first is the ability to pass **vsftpd** the name of the **config** file you want it to use on the command line. The second is the use of the **bind** directive in **xinetd.conf** to limit an instance to a specific IP address.

```
service ftp
{
        disable = no
        socket_type        = stream
        wait               = no
        user               = root
        server             = /usr/sbin/vsftpd
        nice               = 10
        bind               = 192.168.1.41
        server_args     = /etc/vsftpd.main.conf
}

service ftp
{
        disable = no
        socket_type        = stream
        wait               = no
        user               = root
        server             = /usr/sbin/vsftpd
        nice               = 10
        bind               = 192.168.1.42
        server_args     = /etc/vsftpd.earth.conf
}
```

Ask the Expert

Q: Why do you need a separate IP address for each virtual server in FTP when you do not with some other protocols such as HTTP?

A: HTTP actually passes the uniform resource locator (URL) as part of your request. Domain names can be extracted from the URL, and the server can act on that information accordingly. The design of the FTP protocol does not support passing a URL to the server; thus the only method the server can use to determine where the original request was directed is based on the IP address the request arrives on.

With a configuration similar to this, **xinetd** will start **vsftpd** with a different configuration file depending on which interface the connection comes in on. Don't forget to restart **xinetd** after you make changes to its configuration.

Progress Check

1. Why is the default "no" when connecting from port 20?

2. How do you change the option where the log file is written?

Project 11-1   Setting Up Your FTP Server

Now that you've covered the basics, you should have no problem getting your FTP server up and running. This project will walk you through this process, but it should all seem like a simple review after working through the previous sections.

(continued)

---

1. **vsftp** has the default "no" as part of its security; by not requiring the low number port, parts of the daemon can run in a less-privileged mode.

2. You change the option where the log file is written using the **xferlog_file** option.

Step by Step

1. Set up **xinetd** as described earlier. The easiest way to do this is just to edit the file **/etc/xinetd.d/vsftpd** with your favorite text editor and set the disable directive to "no."

2. Now point your editor at the **config** file **/etc/vsftpd.conf**. Examine the default configuration settings and see if they apply to your situation. Pay special attention to **anonymous_enable** and **local_enable**. Review the previous sections or the man page if you're unsure about a particular option.

3. Examine the settings in **/etc/hosts.allow** and **/etc/hosts.deny** to make sure that they are appropriate for your setup.

4. Restart **xinetd** by typing **/etc/init.d/xinetd restart**.

5. Test your server by trying to log in. The simplest way is to just type **ftp localhost** on the command line and supply an appropriate username and password when prompted.

Project Summary

The **vsftp** server is very simple to set up and run. Most of the configuration values have reasonable defaults. Be sure to test your server, and if something doesn't work as expected, review your configuration carefully.

Module Summary

The Very Secure FTP daemon (**vsftpd**) is a powerful FTP server offering all of the basic features one would need for running a commercial FTP server in a secure manner. This module, discussed the process of configuring the **wu-ftpd** server. Specifically, it covered these topics:

- The most important configuration options for **vsftpd**

- Details about the FTP protocol and its effects on firewalls

- Establishing virtual FTP servers

- Setting up anonymous FTP servers

- Setting up a normal-users-only FTP server

This information is enough to keep your FTP server humming for quite a while. Of course, like any printed media about software, this text will age, and the information will slowly but surely become obsolete. Please be sure to visit the **vsftpd** web site (http://vsftp.beasts.org) from time to time to learn about not only the latest developments but also the latest documentation.

✓

Module 11 Mastery Check

1. How does a passive transfer differ from an active transfer?

2. How should you check to see if your FTP server is secure, and why is this important?

3. What are two different ways in which you can control who can access your server?

4. What is requested as a password for an anonymous login?

5. True or False? When a client makes a request to transfer a file and the data connection is initiated, the control connection closes immediately.

6. True or False? The **pasv_enable** option enables the use of passive mode, and it defaults to "yes."

7. What is FTP?

8. Why does Red Hat choose to use **vsftpd**?

9. Where are the documentation files for **vsftp**?

10. What is the **ftpd_banner** option for configuring the FTP server?

11. Why is the **anon_world_readable_only** default set to "yes"?

12. What does setting the configuration option **userlist_enable** allow the server to do?

13. Where would you place the name of a host that you wanted to explicitly allow or deny access to?

14. Why is passive mode important?

15. Does **vsftpd** support virtual FTP servers?

16. Can **vsftpd** be run as a standalone daemon?

Module 12

Setting Up Your Web Server Using Apache

In this module, I discuss the process of installing and configuring the Apache HTTP Server (http://httpd.apache.org) on your Linux server. Apache is free software released under its own Berkeley Software Distribution (BSD)-style license. According to one of the most respected statistics on the Net (published by Netcraft Ltd., http://www.netcraft.com/survey), Apache has a market share of more than 60 percent. This level of respect from the Internet community comes from the following benefits and advantages provided by the Apache server software:

- It is stable.

- Several major web sites, including www.amazon.com and www.generalelectric.com, are using it.

- The entire program and related components are open source.

- It works on a large number of platforms (all popular variants of UNIX, some of the not-so-popular variants of UNIX, and even Windows).

- It is extremely flexible.

- It has shown itself to be more secure than most of the alternatives.

Before I get into the steps necessary to configure Apache, I will review some of the fundamentals of the Hypertext Transfer Protocol (HTTP) as well as some of the internal workings of Apache, such as its process ownership model. This information will help us understand why Apache is set up to work the way it does.

NOTE

Although the term "Apache" has long been used rather loosely to refer to the Apache Foundation's **httpd** server, the Apache Foundation has started branching out into a number of other programming endeavors. Its other programs are typically referred to by their full names, such as "Apache FOP" or "Apache Jakarta." The other projects of the Apache Foundation are beyond the scope of this book, so whenever I refer to a program as "Apache," you can be sure I am talking about the **httpd** server. For more information on the Apache Foundation, see http://www.apache.org.

CRITICAL SKILL
12.1 Explaining the Mechanics of HTTP

The Hypertext Transfer Protocol (HTTP) is, of course, a significant portion of the foundation for the World Wide Web, and Apache is the server implementation of the HTTP protocol. Browsers such as Netscape Navigator, Mozilla, Opera, and Microsoft Internet Explorer are client implementations of HTTP.

As of this writing, the HTTP protocol is at version 1.1 and is documented in RFC 2616 (for details, go to http://www.ietf.org/rfc/rfc2616.txt).

NOTE

Some people tend to confuse HTTP and HTML. Keep in mind that the Hypertext Markup Language (HTML) is the format that web pages are written in, while HTTP is the transfer protocol for moving those pages (among other things) from the server to your browser.

Headers

When a web client connects to a web server, the client's default method of making this connection is to contact the server's TCP port 80. Once connected, the web server says nothing; it's up to the client to issue HTTP-compliant commands for its requests to the server. Along with each command comes a *request header,* which includes information about the client. For example, when using Mozilla under Linux as a client, a web server will receive the following information from a client:

```
GET / HTTP/1.1
Host: localhost:80
User-Agent: Mozilla/5.0 (X11; U; Linux i686; en-US; rv:1.0.0) Gecko/20020809
Accept:
text/xml,application/xml,application/xhtml+xml,text/html;q=0.9,text/plain;q=0.8,video/
x-mng,image/png,image/jpeg,image/gif;q=0.2,text/css,*/*;q=0.1
Accept-Encoding: gzip, deflate, compress;q=0.9
Accept-Charset: ISO-8859-1, utf-8;q=0.66, *;q=0.66
Keep-Alive: 300
Connection: keep-alive
```

The first line contains the HTTP **GET** command, which asks the server to fetch a file. The remainder of the information is a collection of *key: value* pairs that make up the header. This tells the server about the client, the kind of file formats the client will accept, and so forth. Many servers use this information for logging purposes, as well as to determine what can and cannot be sent to the client.

Along with the request header, additional headers may be sent. For example, when a client uses a hyperlink to get to the server site, a header entry showing the client's originating site will also appear in the header.

When it receives a blank line, the server knows a request header is complete. Once the request header is received, it responds with the actual requested content, prefixed by a server header. The server header tells the client information about the server, the amount of data the client is about to receive, and the type of data coming in. For example, when sent to a default installation of the Apache HTTP server under Red Hat 8, the request header shown in the preceding code listing results in the following server response header.

```
HTTP/1.1 200 OK
Date: Mon, 28 Oct 2002 12:59:42 GMT
Server: Apache/2.0.40 (Red Hat Linux)
Last-Modified: Sat, 07 Sep 2002 12:17:54 GMT
ETag: "16411d-20-c571d380"
Accept-Ranges: bytes
Content-Length: 33
Keep-Alive: timeout=15, max=100
Connection: Keep-Alive
Content-Type: text/html; charset=ISO-8859-1
```

The response header is followed by a blank line and then the actual content of the transmission.

Nonstandard Ports

The default port for HTTP requests is port 80, but you can also configure a web server to use a different (arbitrarily chosen) port that is not in use by another service. This allows sites to run multiple web servers on the same host, each server on a different port. Some sites use this arrangement for multiple configurations of their web servers, to support various types of client requests.

When a site runs a web server on a nonstandard port, you can see that port number in the site's uniform resource locator (URL). For example, this address,

http://www.redhat.com/

with an added port number, would read

http://www.redhat.com:80/

CAUTION

Don't make the mistake of going for "security through obscurity." If your server's on a nonstandard port, that doesn't guarantee that Internet troublemakers won't find your site. Because of the automated nature of tools used to attack a site, it takes fewer than 100 lines of C code to scan a server and find which ports are running web servers. Using a nonstandard port does not keep your site "secure."

Process Ownership and Security

As discussed in other modules, running a web server under UNIX means that you get to deal with the Linux (and UNIX in general) model. In terms of permissions, that means each process has an owner, and that owner has limited rights on the system.

Whenever a program (process) is started, it inherits the permissions of its parent process. For example, if you're logged in as root, the shell in which you're doing all your work has all the same rights as the root user. In addition, any process you start from this shell will inherit all the permissions of that root. Processes may give up rights, but they cannot gain rights.

NOTE

There is an exception to the Linux inheritance principle: Programs configured with the SetUID bit (see the **chmod** command in Module 6) do not inherit rights from their parent process, rather, they start with the rights specified by the owner of the file itself. For example, the file containing the program **su** (**/bin/su**) is owned by root and has the SetUID bit set. If the user michael runs the program **su**, that program doesn't inherit the rights of michael but instead will start with the rights of root.

How Apache Processes Ownership

To perform network setups, the Apache HTTP server must start with root permissions. Specifically, it needs to bind itself to port 80 so that it can listen for requests and accept connections, and only root can take control of low numbered ports. Once it does this, Apache can give up its rights and run as a nonroot user, as specified in its configuration files. Although, many implementations select the user "nobody" for this purpose, Red Hat has created a special user and group, both named "apache," just for this role.

Running as user apache, the Apache **httpd** server can read only the files that user apache has permission to read. Thus, if a file's permissions are set so that they are readable only by the file's owner, the owner must be apache. For any file that you want available to user apache but don't want to change its ownership, set that file's permission to world readable:

```
chmod a+r filename
```

where *filename* is the name of the file.

Security is especially important for sites that use CGI scripts. By limiting the permissions of the web server, you decrease the likelihood that someone can send a malicious request to the server. And the server processes and corresponding CGI scripts can break only what they can access. As user apache, the scripts and processes don't have access to the same key files that root can access. (Remember that root can access everything, no matter what the permissions.)

CAUTION

In dealing with CGI scripts, most successful attacks on sites are typically possible because of improperly configured web servers or poorly written CGI scripts.

Ask the Expert

Q: If I do have CGI scripts on my server, what precautions should I take to make them more secure?

A: In the event that you decide to allow CGI scripts on your server, pay strict attention to how they are written. Be sure it isn't possible for input coming in over the network to make the CGI script do something it shouldn't.

Progress Check

1. What special user and group name does Red Hat use for running apache?

2. Why is security for root important?

CRITICAL SKILL
12.2 Setting Up the Apache HTTP Server

Installing Apache HTTP Server can be as simple as selecting the Web Server option when installing your system. If you're adding Apache by hand, the packages you're most interested in are **httpd**, and optionally **httpd-manual** and **redhat-config-httpd**. Merely installing the base packages will give you basic web-serving capabilities, but you've barely scratched the surface of Apache's capabilities.

Changes in Apache 2

Red Hat 8 includes Apache version 2 which introduces many changes from the long standing 1.3 series. If you're familiar with past versions of Apache, you should at least browse through the differences in the newer version. Some of the highlights of Apache 2 include:

POSIX threading	A hybrid setup that uses multiple threads as well as multiple processes to improve scalability for some configurations.
Multi-Processing Module	A new mechanism for taking advantage of the native capabilities of whichever platform the server is running on.

---

1. To run apache, Red Hat uses the user and group name "apache."

2. The security for root is important because root can access any and all files no matter what permissions are set on those files.

New module API	Significant changes and improvements over the 1.3 API for writing Apache extensions. Expected to alleviate some of the module ordering problems sometimes encountered with the old system and provide other new capabilities.
IPv6	IPv6 sockets and address strings are now supported.
Filtering	Modules can now be written to act upon data as it's being passed to or from the server. External programs can be hooked in as well.
Multilanguage error responses	Error messages sent back to the browser can be customized for multiple languages (using the "server-side includes" feature).
More powerful regular expressions	Perl 5–style regular expressions are now supported throughout.

Apache Modules

Part of what makes Apache so powerful and flexible is that its design allows extensions through modules. Apache comes with many modules by default and automatically includes them in the default installation.

If you are interested in extending Apache's capability, visit http://httpd.apache.org/docs-2.0/mod/ to see what other modules are available for inclusion as well as directions on adding them to your installation. To give you some idea of what kinds of things third parties are doing with modules, visit http://modules.apache.org. Be careful, however. Due to the significant changes in the module API for Apache 2, modules written for 1.3 won't work directly with the newer Apache. There are many interesting modules floating around that have not yet been updated for Apache 2.

Starting Up and Shutting Down Apache

One of the nicest features of Linux is its ability to start up and shut down system services without needing to reboot. This is easy to do in the Apache server.

The **apachectl** utility can be used to start, stop, and restart your daemon, as well as check your config files for syntactical errors, reload configuration changes, or report server status. If you're going to be spending any serious time with Apache, you should really become familiar with this tool.

To start Apache manually, use this command:

```
[root@www root]# /usr/sbin/apachectl start
```

To shut down Apache, enter this command:

```
[root@www root]# /usr/sbin/apachectl stop
```

Starting Apache at Boot Time

If you're changing the start or stop runlevels for Apache from the GUI **redhat-config-services** tool, the entry you want to look for is **httpd**. If on the other hand, you're looking to manipulate the symlinks by hand, you might consider using **S85httpd** and **K15httpd**, just to keep in sync with the GUI tool.

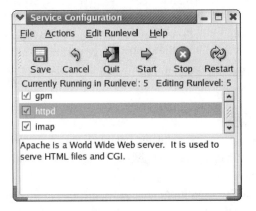

```
[root@www rc3.d]# rm K15httpd
[root@www rc3.d]# ln -s ../init.d/httpd S85httpd
```

For details on startup and shutdown scripts, see Module 8.

Testing Your Installation

You can perform a quick test on your Apache installation using a default home page. To do this, start up the server (if necessary) using the following command:

```
[root@www /root]# /usr/sbin/apachectl start
```

Apache comes with a default home page for testing purposes. To find out if your Apache installation went smoothly, start a web browser and tell it to visit your machine. For example, for a machine with the host name tesla.some-domain.com, you would visit http://tesla.some-domain.com. There you should see a simple web page whose title is "Test Page." If you don't, check your Apache installation and startup to make sure you didn't encounter any errors in the process.

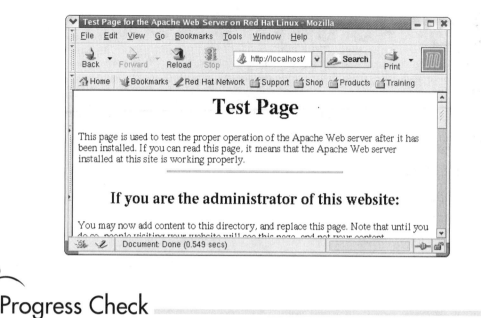

Progress Check

1. What utility is used to start and stop Apache?

2. How can you test your Apache installation?

CRITICAL SKILL

12.3 Configuring Apache

Apache supports a rich set of configuration options that, unlike Sendmail, are sensible and easy to follow. This makes it a simple task to set up the web server in various configurations.

This section walks through a basic configuration. The default configuration is actually quite good and (believe it or not) works right out of the box, so if the default is acceptable to you, simply start creating your HTML documents! Apache allows several common customizations. After we step through the creation of a simple web page, you'll see how you can make those common customizations in the Apache configuration files.

---

1. The **apachectl** utility is used to start and stop Apache.
2. You can test your Apache installation by starting a web browser and pointing it at your machine.

Project 12-1 Creating a Simple Root-Level Page

If you like, you can start adding files to Apache right away in the **/var/www/html** directory for top-level pages. Any files placed in that directory should be world readable.

When no page is explicitly requested, Apache's default web page is **index.html**. Let's take a closer look at changing the default home page so that it reads "Welcome to my Red Hat web server."

Step by Step

1. In your favorite text editor, create or open a file named **index.html** under the directory **/var/www/html/**.

2. Enter the following text:

```
<html>
      <head>
            <title>Welcome to my web server</title>
      </head>
      <body>
            <h1>Welcome to my Red Hat web server.</h1>
      <body>
</html>
```

3. Save the file and exit your favorite text editor.

4. As **root**, at a command line type **chmod 644 /var/www/html/index.html**.

5. Point your web browser at your site again, or refresh the page if you are already at the location. You should see your new page in your browser.

Project Summary

You have just created a simple web page with HTML that you can later modify using the above steps to suit your needs. Index.html was chosen in the above example because it will be the default page loaded when no specific page is specified in the URL.

Apache Configuration Files

The configuration files for Apache are located in the **/etc/httpd/conf** directory. There you may see a number of files, but the only one you're concerned with right now is **httpd.conf**. The best way to learn more about the configuration is to read the **httpd.conf** file. The default installation file is heavily commented, explaining each entry, its role, and the parameters you can set.

NOTE

You may have noticed when you created the **index.html** file earlier, that there was no **index.html** page previously in that directory. You may be wondering where the "Test Page" you saw earlier came from? A close examination of **httpd.conf** will reveal the trick. When you request the root directory from the server, and if there is no **index.html** page in that directory, the server is configured to return a different file instead of just presenting you with an error. That file lives at **/var/www/error/noindex.html**. Even if you don't yet understand all the directives used in **httpd.conf**, this should at least hint at the sort of flexibility you can look forward to.

Common Configuration Changes

The default configuration settings work just fine right out of the box and need no modification. Nevertheless, most site administrators will want to at least be familiar with the alterations described in this section.

Changing Host Names

At many sites, servers fulfill multiple purposes. An intranet web server that isn't getting heavy usage, for example, should probably share its usage allowance with another service. In such a situation, the computer name www implied above wouldn't be a good choice, because it suggests that the machine has only one purpose.

It's better to give a server a neutral name and then establish DNS CNAME entries or multiple host name entries in the **/etc/hosts** file. In other words, you can give the system several names for accessing the server, but it needs to know only about its real name. Consider a server whose host name is dioxin.eng.domain.org that is to be a web server, as well. You might be thinking of giving it the host name alias www.eng.domain.org. However, since dioxin will know itself only as dioxin, users who visit www.eng.domain.org will be confused by seeing in their browsers that the server's real name is dioxin.

Ask the Expert

Q: What happened to **access.conf** and **srm.conf**?

A: Earlier versions of Apache used these two files in addition to **http.conf** for configuration. It sometimes became confusing to know which directives belonged to which files. These files were actually a holdover from the old National Center for Supercomputing Applications (NCSA) web server. The features of these files have now been merged into **httpd.conf** to simplify administration.

Apache provides a way to get around this using the ServerName directive. By specifying what you want Apache to return as the host name of the web server, a system with a name like dioxin can have an alias of www, invisible to users of the site. Here is an example of the ServerName directive:

```
ServerName www.eng.domain.org
```

Server Administrator

It's often a good idea, for a couple of reasons, to use an e-mail alias for a web site's administrator. First, there may be more than one administrator. By using an alias, it's possible for the alias to expand out to a list of e-mail addresses. Second, if the current administrator leaves, you don't want to have to make the rounds of all those web pages and change the name of the site administrator.

Assuming you have set up the e-mail alias so that www@*domain*.com represents your web administrator(s) (see Module 13 for doing this in Linux), you need to edit the ServerAdmin line in the **httpd.conf** file so that it reads as follows:

```
ServerAdmin www@domain.com
```

Prefork MPM

As I mentioned earlier, the Multi-Processing Module (MPM) is a new feature in Apache that allows closer integration with the native networking features of each operating system. The trick is that, unlike regular Apache modules, you can only select one MPM, and you have to do so when Apache is compiled. While some of the available MPMs are just not relevant to us on Linux (**mpm_winnt**, for example) there are still a few different features implemented at the MPM level. The hybrid process/threading model I mentioned earlier is one example. For compatibility reasons, the Apache package included with Red Hat has been compiled with the prefork MPM, as it follows the same process model that was used in the Apache 1.3 series. Unfortunately, if you want to use a different MPM, you'll have to recompile Apache. Even sticking with the prefork MPM, there are a number of settings that you can adjust for performance.

Using the prefork model, Apache will start a number of processes and have them wait around for incoming connections. Each process can handle a number of requests from the same client. When the load grows, more processes are forked to handle the additional connections. When the load dies down, extraneous idle processes are killed off. With this in mind, the following options should start to make more sense.

This is the number of processes that Apache will fork as a starting point when it first starts up:

```
StartServers        8
```

Apache will always keep at least this many processes around:

```
MinSpareServers     5
```

This is the upper limit for idle processes:

```
MaxSpareServers    20
```

If there are more than these, Apache starts killing off some of them.

Apache will not start more processes than this maximum, even if the site is extremely busy:

```
MaxClients         150
```

This limits the number of client requests that a single process will handle:

```
MaxRequestsPerChild  1000
```

IP Address and Port Selection

By default, Apache is set up to wait for connections to port 80 on any IP address assigned to the machine. If you want to change that behavior, you'll be interested in the Listen directive. With this you can change what port is listened to or limit which IP addresses (assuming you have more than one) attention is paid to, as shown in the following examples:

```
Listen 8080
```

```
Listen 192.168.0.42:80
```

Modules

As I mentioned earlier, loading modules to add additional functionality is where Apache's real power shines through. This is accomplished with the LoadModule directive, specifying the module name (as indicated in its documentation) and the location of the library file. There are a good number of modules enabled in the default configuration, and it may be worth commenting out some of the ones you're not really using. (In case it's not already obvious, **httpd.conf** uses # as its comment character.)

```
LoadModule cgi_module modules/mod_cgi.so
#LoadModule speling_module modules/mod_speling.so
```

Directory and Alias

You may have noticed by now that there are a number of HTML-like bracketed directives in **httpd.conf**, especially when there is a need to specify suboptions. The most prominent of these is the **<directory>...</directory>** block, which allows you to specify a different set of options for a particular directory than for the rest of your site. This is most helpful for grouping a set of files with special needs together, such as Common Gateway Interface (CGI) programs. You will also find this often used in conjunction with the Alias directive, which allows you to map a portion of your web space to a particular physical directory (separate from your document root).

```
Alias /icons/ "/var/www/icons/"
```

```
<Directory "/var/www/icons">
```

```
        Options Indexes MultiViews
        AllowOverride None
        Order allow,deny
        Allow from all
</Directory>
```

Executable Scripts

The ScriptAlias directive works much like Alias, with the notable exception that accessing any file in the ScriptAlias directory will cause it to be executed rather than blindly returned to the client.

```
ScriptAlias /cgi-bin/ "/var/www/cgi-bin/"
```

NOTE

Obviously, it's impossible to cover everything about the Apache HTTP server in a few short pages. The software's online manual comes with the distribution and will give you the information you need. It's written in HTML, so you can access it in a browser. Simply point to **http://localhost/manual/** or check out **http://httpd.apache.org/docs-2.0/**.

Configuring Virtual Domains

One of the most used features of Apache is its ability to support virtual domains—that is, to allow multiple domains to be hosted from the same IP address. This is accomplished thanks to the HTTP 1.1 protocol, which specifies the desired site in the HTTP header rather than relying on the server to know what site to fetch based on its IP address.

NOTE

Don't forget that it is not merely enough to configure a virtual domain using Apache. You must also get the domain itself from a company that sells domain names like Register.com. Once you have the domain name, you can either use your registrar's DNS server or you can set up your own DNS server. Either way, you will need to establish the necessary entries so that www.*yourdomain*.com points to your web server. Of course, if you are just playing around and don't want to set up a site for real, you can simply set up a local DNS server and create fictitious domains and IP addresses, or even just add the necessary entries to the **/etc/hosts** file.

To set up a new virtual domain, open the **httpd.conf** file in your favorite text editor and scroll toward the end of the file. The **NameVirtualHost** directive needs to be uncommented to allow Apache to differentiate client requests by the supplied domain name.

```
NameVirtualHost *
```

The * means that this will apply to all IP addresses Apache is listening to. Just below that you will find an example of a virtual host entry that has been commented out and looks something like this:

```
# VirtualHost example:
# Almost any Apache directive may go into a VirtualHost container.
# The first VirtualHost section is used for requests without a known
# server name.
#
#<VirtualHost *>
#     ServerAdmin webmaster@dummy-host.example.com
#     DocumentRoot /www/docs/dummy-host.example.com
#     ServerName dummy-host.example.com
#     ErrorLog logs/dummy-host.example.com-error_log
#     CustomLog logs/dummy-host.example.com-access_log common
#</VirtualHost>
```

Simply clone this entry and substitute in your own information. Many of the settings available for the basic server can have different values specified for each virtual host or can inherit the values used by the main server configuration. For example, a virtual host entry could look like this:

```
#
# Virtual Host Settings for company1.com and sideproject.org
#
<VirtualHost *>
  ServerName company1.com
  ServerAdmin webmaster@company1.com
  DocumentRoot /var/www/company1/html
  ErrorLog /var/log/httpd/company1/error_log
  CustomLog /var/log/httpd/access_log common
</VirtualHost>

<VirtualHost *>
  ServerName sideproject.org
  ServerAdmin webmaster@sideproject.org
  DocumentRoot /var/www/sideproject/html
  ErrorLog /var/log/httpd/sideproject/error_log
  CustomLog /var/log/httpd/access_log common
</VirtualHost>
```

Note that you have to do this for each host you want visible. So if you want to have both example.com and www.example.com resolve to the same web page, you need to set up a second virtual host setting for www.example.com, as well. (Both **www.example.com** and **example.com** can have the same configuration information, but they must remain separate virtual host entries.)

Once you have the information in there, simply restart Apache using the **/usr/sbin/apachectl** restart command, and you're off!

GUI Configuration

Now that you have a basic grasp of Apache configuration, let's take a quick peek at Red Hat's GUI tool option. You can find it on the menu as HTTP Server under the Server Settings submenu, or you can launch it from the command line as **redhat-config-httpd**.

On the Main tab, you will find some of the basic settings discussed earlier, including setting the server name, the server admin, and what IP addresses and ports to listen to. The Performance Tuning tab will give you some access to connection parameters, but as you may notice, it's not as fine-grained as what you've seen in the **httpd.conf** file.

The Virtual Hosts tab is where things really get interesting. Even if you're not planning to host multiple sites off of the same machine, you'll find that "Default Virtual Host" is where you'll set a number of options that may have seemed missing from the "Main" configuration at first glance. Editing one of the virtual hosts (default or otherwise) will give you access to options concerning document Root Directory location, logging, and per-directory options, among others.

The GUI tool, of course, doesn't express the depth of configuration that Apache is capable of. If you want to enable (or disable) additional modules, for example, you still have to edit **httpd.conf** by hand. And as usual, the Red Hat GUI tool doesn't play nice with hand editing, pushing you toward choosing one method or the other. If you need to make only the most basic changes to the default setup however, then the GUI tool may be just what you want.

CRITICAL SKILL
12.4 Performing Basic Troubleshooting with Apache

The process of changing configurations (or even the initial installation) can sometimes not work as smoothly as we'd like. Thankfully, Apache does an excellent job at reporting why it failed in its error log file.

The error log file is located in your log's directory. If you are running a stock Red Hat installation, this is in the **/var/log/httpd** directory. In this directory, you will find a number of files, the most notable of which are **access_log** and **error_log**.

The **access_log** file is simply that—a log of which files have been accessed by people visiting your web site. It contains information about whether the transfer completed successfully, where the request originated (IP address), how much data was transferred, and what time the transfer occurred. This is a very powerful way of determining the usage of your site.

The **error_log** file contains all of the errors that occur in Apache. Note that not all errors that occur are fatal—some are simply problems with a client connection from which Apache can automatically recover and continue operation. However, if you started Apache but still cannot visit the web site, then take a look at this log file to see why Apache may not be responding. The easiest way to see the last 10 error messages is to use the **tail** command, like so:

```
[root@www httpd]# tail -10 error_log
```

If you need to see more log information than that, simply change the number 10 to the number of lines that you do need to see. If that number of lines exceeds the length of your screen, you can pipe the output through less so that you can see one screen at a time, like so:

```
[root@www httpd]# tail -100 error_log | less
```

This will display the last 100 lines of the error log, one screen at a time.

Module Summary

This module covered the process of arranging your own web server using Apache from the ground up. This module by itself is enough to get you going with a top-level page and a basic configuration.

I highly recommend taking some time to page through the Apache manual. It is well written, concise, and flexible enough so that you can set up just about any configuration imaginable.

In addition to the manual documentation, several good books about Apache have been written. *Apache: The Definitive Guide*, Second Edition, by Ben Laurie, et al. (O'Reilly & Associates, 1999), covers the details of Apache very well. Even though this book has not yet been updated for the new features in Apache 2, the majority of the information is still very relevant. The text focuses on Apache only, so you don't have to wade through hundreds of pages to find what you need.

✔

Module 12 Mastery Check

1. How does the server name directive help reduce user confusion?

2. How does the prefork model work?

3. How many MPM modules can you include on a server?

4. What mechanism does Apache provide for adding features to the server?

5. Which of the following features are new to Apache 2?

   A. POSIX threading

   B. Multi-Processing Module

   C. Support for IPv6

   D. Filtering modules

   E. All of the above

6. What is the definition of HTTP?

7. Name some of the following benefits and advantages provided by Apache.

8. True or False? Each virtual host in Apache requires its own IP address.

9. True or False? The **error_log** file contains all of the errors that occur in Apache.

10. True or false? In dealing with multiple domain names, every domain name you would like visible on the Apache sever requires a virtual host stanza in the configuration file.

Module 13

Sending Mail
with SMTP

377

The Simple Mail Transfer Protocol (SMTP) is the accepted standard for mail transport across the Internet. Anyone who wants to have a mail server capable of sending and receiving mail across the Internet must be able to support it. Many internal networks have also taken to using SMTP for their private mail services because of its platform independence and availability across all popular operating systems.

In this module, we'll first discuss the mechanics of SMTP as a protocol and its relationship to other mail-related protocols, such as the Post Office Protocol (POP) and the Internet Message Access Protocol (IMAP). Then we'll discuss the Internet's most popular mail server, Sendmail, as well as one of the more popular alternatives, Postfix. As part of our discussion, we'll go over several popular configurations and conclude with some references to where you can get more information.

CRITICAL SKILL
13.1 # Discovering the Mechanics of SMTP

The SMTP protocol defines the method by which mail is sent from one host to another. That's it. It does not define how the mail should be stored. It does not define how the mail should be picked up or displayed by the recipient. Nothing.

SMTP's strength is its simplicity, and that is due to the dynamic nature of networks during the early 1980s. (The SMTP protocol was originally defined in 1982.) People were linking networks together with everything short of bubble gum and glue. SMTP was the first mail standard that was independent of the transport mechanism. This meant that people using TCP/IP networks could use the same format to send a message as someone using some other networking protocol.

SMTP is also independent of operating systems, which means each system can use its own style of storing mail without worrying about how senders of messages store their mail. You can draw parallels to how the phone system works: each phone service provider has its own independent accounting system; however, they all have agreed on a standard way to link their networks together so that calls can go from one network to another transparently.

Rudimentary SMTP Details

Ever had a "friend" who sent you an e-mail on behalf of some government agency informing you that you owe taxes from the previous year, plus additional penalties? Somehow a message like this ends up in a lot of people's mailboxes around April 1, better known as April Fool's Day. Well, guess what? I'm going to show you how they did it. Even more fun, how you can do it yourself. (Not that I would advocate such behavior, of course.)

The purpose of this example is to show how the SMTP protocol sends a message from one host to another. After all, more important than learning how to forge an e-mail is learning how to troubleshoot mail-related problems. So in this example, you are acting as the sending host, and whichever machine you connect to is the receiving host.

The SMTP protocol requires only that a host be able to send straight ASCII text to another host. Typically, this is done by contacting the SMTP port (port 25) on a mail server. You can do this using the Telnet program. For example:

```
[michael@cubicle /]# telnet mailserver 25
```

where the host *mailserver* is the recipient's mail server. As you may be aware, the Telnet program's main purpose is to log in remotely to other machines. There are a number of reasons that it's no longer a good choice for doing that, some of which are covered in Module 14, but the biggest one is also what makes Telnet a good debugging tool for other protocols. That is, Telnet sends plain ASCII text to a network port. The "25" that follows *mailserver* in the preceding example tells Telnet that you want to communicate with the server's port 25 rather than the normal port 23. (Port 23 is used for remote logins, and port 25 is for the SMTP server.)

The mail server will respond with a greeting message such as this:

```
220 mail.example.com ESMTP Postfix
```

You are now communicating directly with the SMTP server.

Although there are many SMTP commands, the four worth noting are

- **helo**

- **mail from:**

- **rcpt to:**

- **data**

The **helo** command is used when a client introduces itself to the server. The parameter to **helo** is the host name that is originating the connection. Of course, most mail servers take this information with a grain of salt and double-check it themselves. For example:

```
helo super-duper-strong-coffee.com
```

If you aren't coming from the **super-duper-strong-coffee.com** domain, many mail servers will respond by telling you that they know your real IP address, but they will not stop the connection from continuing. (Some mail servers include a comment about why you didn't use a truthful **helo** statement.)

The **mail from:** command requires the parameter of the sender's e-mail address. This tells the mail server the e-mail's origin. For example,

```
mail from: dilbert@example.com
```

means the message is from **dilbert@example.com**.

The **rcpt to:** command also requires the parameter of an e-mail address. This e-mail address is of the recipient of the e-mail. For example,

```
rcpt to: pointy-hair-boss@example.com
```

means the message is destined to **pointy-hair-boss@example.com**.

Now that the server knows who the sender and recipient are, it needs to know what message to send—that is done by using the **data** command. Once issued, the server will expect the entire message with relevant header information, followed by a period on a line by itself (technically, a **<CR><LF>.<CR><LF>** sequence, for those that are curious about such details). Continuing the example, **dilbert@domain.com** might want to send the following message to **pointy-hair-boss@example.com**:

```
data
354 End data with <CR><LF>.<CR><LF>
From: Dilbert <dilbert@domain.com>
To: Pointy Hair Manager <pointy-hair-boss@domain.com>
Subject: On time and within budget.
Date: Sat, 1 Apr 2003 04:01:00 -0700 (PDT)

Just an fyi, boss. The project is not only on time, but it is within
budget too!

.
250 queued as 26F7B1D01A2
```

And that's all there is to it. To close the connection, enter the **quit** command.

This is the basic technique used by applications that send mail—except, of course, they usually use C code rather than Telnet, but the actual content sent between the client and server remains the same.

Project 13-1 Using telnet to Examine SMTP

Now that we've shown you how SMTP works, we're going to walk through a first-hand example. This project assumes that you have a working mail server (not necessarily on your own machine) that you can reach. You'll need to fill in your own correct information in the places indicated.

Step by Step

1. First, **telnet** to port 25 on the mail server where you normally receive mail. Replace your own server name in the following example.

```
telnet mailserver.my-domain-name.com 25
```

2. Next, type **helo** followed by the name of the server you're pretending to be. Using the host name of the machine you're working on is probably not a bad idea. Whether any checking is done on this value will depend entirely on the paranoia of the server you're connecting to. If you use the name of the machine you're connecting from, you shouldn't have any problems.

```
helo my-hostname.my-domain-name.com
```

3. Enter the **mail from:** now. Remember from the previous section that this identifies the sender of the message. If you're dealing with a properly paranoid mail server, this value should at least be a valid e-mail address. You can use your own e-mail address here.

```
mail from: myself@my-domain-name.com
```

4. Now enter the e-mail address of the recipient, after the **rcpt to:** command. This will again be your own e-mail address for this test.

```
rcpt to: myself@my-domain-name.com
```

5. Next comes the **data** command:

```
data
```

6. Finally we get to the meat of the e-mail. If you want this message to actually be readable with standard mail software, you'll need to have proper headers. Start with entering the simple headers shown here:

```
From: myself@my-domain-name.com
To: myself@my-domain-name.com
Subject: Project 13-1
```

7. Enter a blank line to separate the headers from the body of the message.

8. Type any message body that you like; then enter a period on a line by itself to end the message.

```
This is really cool. I can test my mail servers just like this.
.
```

8. Type **quit** to close the connection.

9. Fire up your favorite mail reader and see if your message arrived.

Project Summary

This project not only gave you a real-world example of an SMTP session, but illustrates a simple method for testing your mail servers if you're experiencing problems. Hopefully you'll have the restraint necessary not to misuse this ability next April first.

SMTP vs. POP and IMAP

SMTP is often confused with POP and/or IMAP, so we'll try to clarify what it all means:

- SMTP is a transport protocol for sending messages *only*. A user cannot connect to an SMTP server to read his or her mail.

- POP and IMAP are just the opposite. A client *can* use POP or IMAP to read mail off a server, but the client host *cannot* send e-mail with POP or IMAP. For more information on POP and IMAP, see Module 14.

What often confuses some people is the fact that the actual machine running the SMTP server software can be the same machine running the POP or IMAP server software. This is because SMTP uses a different port to send mail than POP or IMAP use to retrieve mail. (It's often convenient to consolidate your mail functions onto a single server like this.)

Progress Check

1. Which of the following are SMTP commands:

   A. helo

   B. mail from:

   C. rcpt to:

   D. data

   E. All of the above

2. What is used to indicate the end of a data command?

Exploring Sendmail

Sendmail is the original cross-network electronic mail transfer program. When competing network architectures gave way to the TCP/IP-based Internet, Sendmail's immense configurability kept its foothold as the default server for e-mail. Many years later, Sendmail is still the de facto standard for Internet mail, and is used by many large sites such as Yahoo!,

---

1. E. helo, mail from:, rcpt to:, and data are all SMTP commands.
2. The end of a data command is marked with a period on a line by itself (**<CR><LF>.<CR><LF>**).

Earthlink, and AOL. It has been estimated that if you send an e-mail message across the Internet, you have a 75-80 percent chance that it will touch Sendmail at some point on its journey. Sendmail is also the default e-mail server on Red Hat 8.

In all likelihood, Sendmail will be the single most difficult program you will have to configure as a UNIX administrator. The main configuration file is so cryptic that it's considered bad form to try to edit it directly.

In the next couple of sections, we're going to try to distill down enough of this important program to allow you to set up a basic configuration for your own use.

Security Implications

Like any other large server software, Sendmail's internal structure and design are complex and require a considerable amount of care during development. It is not surprising, then, that over its long history, it has had a somewhat spotty security record. In recent years, however, the developers of Sendmail have taken a very paranoid approach to their design to help alleviate these issues. Basically, they ship the package in a very tight security mode and leave it to you to loosen it up as much as you need to loosen it up for your site. This means the responsibility falls to you of making sure you keep the software properly configured (and thus not vulnerable to attacks).

Some issues to keep in mind when deploying any mail server are

- When an e-mail is sent to the server, what programs will it trigger?

- Are those programs securely designed?

- If they cannot be made secure, how can you limit their damage?

- Under what permissions do those programs run?

In Sendmail's case, we need to back up and examine its architecture. Mail service has three distinct components. The *mail transfer agent (MTA)* handles the process of getting the mail from one site to another; Sendmail is an MTA. The *mail delivery agent (MDA)* is what takes the message, once received at a site, and gets it to the appropriate user mailbox. Finally, the *mail user agent (MUA)* is what the user sees, such as the Evolution, Outlook, and Pine programs. An MUA is responsible only for reading mail and allowing users to compose mail.

Sendmail works as an MTA only, passing the task of performing local mail delivery to another external program. This allows each operating system or site configuration to use its own custom tool if necessary (that is, to be able to use a special mailbox storage mechanism).

In many configurations, sites prefer using the Procmail program to perform the actual mail delivery (MDA) because of its advanced filtering mechanism. Many older configurations have stayed with their default **/usr/bin/mail** program to perform mail delivery. The security issues in using that particular program vary from operating system to operating system, due to interactions with other parts of the system.

Ask the Expert

Q: How does a system like Microsoft Exchange Server or Lotus Domino fit into this scheme?

A: Systems like these not only accept mail, but handle delivery as well. They've essentially integrated MTA and MDA functionality into one system. If you consider Exchange Server's web interface, it is an MUA as well.

Because Sendmail must run as the **root** user in order to bind to port 25 and accept mail there, its child processes by default run with the same level of permissions. This means the MDA must be of a secure design—and ditto for any other program that can get spawned from Sendmail through the use of mail aliases and forwarding files. (We will discuss this in "The aliases File," later in this module.)

Recently, Sendmail has started shipping with a tool called **smrsh** (SendMail Restricted Shell). This special shell restricts what the child process can do and thus can help keep any programs spawned by Sendmail from doing bad things as the **root** user. If you ever find yourself needing to process mail using an external program, you should consider using **smrsh** as a wrapper to prohibit bugs in your program from being exploited to do potentially dangerous things.

Sendmail itself is an open-source package, giving it the benefit of public scrutiny for bugs, security flaws, and other such design issues. It has been this way from the day it was released in the early 1980s. The base version of Sendmail is free and can be used both commercially and noncommercially. Many large sites, such as Yahoo!, use Sendmail and believe in its design methodology.

In the late 1990s, Eric Allman, the creator of Sendmail, started a company called Sendmail Inc., which sells a commercial version of the package. The commercial version of the package is different from the free version only in terms of configuration tools, installation tools, support, and documentation. The actual mail server software is the same.

Recommended Texts

One of Sendmail's biggest features is also one of its biggest problems: configurability. (One might even argue the same for UNIX-based operating systems as a whole.) Obviously, we can't cover everything about Sendmail in this module; instead, we give you the information necessary to set up the most common configurations and hopefully supply enough base knowledge for you to be able to pursue more complex designs with confidence.

If you decide to take on the challenge of understanding more about Sendmail, check out the one truly authoritative book on the beast: *Sendmail*, Third Edition, by Bryan Costales and Eric Allman (O'Reilly & Associates, 1997). The book's coauthor, Eric Allman, was the main developer of Sendmail. The downside to this text is that it's *huge*—more than 1,100 pages. This is *not* an introductory text! However, if you ever find yourself posting a question about Sendmail on an Internet discussion forum, be ready to hear at least one person telling you to get this book. (The book is also affectionately called "The Bat Book" because of the bat pictured on its cover.)

You've probably got another two or three books on system administration sitting on your bookshelf that cover Sendmail, as well—it would be naive of me to think otherwise. One difference you may find between what I cover and what they cover is that I won't be getting into the details of all the commands in the **sendmail.cf** configuration file. This is because most configuration options should be doable through the use of the configuration macros that come with Sendmail. In fact, if you open **sendmail.cf** with your favorite text editor, you'll find a big warning about not editing the **.cf** file directly. Not only are the macros easier for you, they also make it easier for your successors to know what you've done with the system, rather than having to worry that they are going to break some minor (undocumented) tweak you did by upgrading. If you do decide to read up more on the format of the **sendmail.cf** file, be sure to understand that a handful of pages is not going to be complete enough for you to be able to seriously play with the rule sets defined in the configuration file. As always, use good sysadmin common sense and back up any files before making changes.

The Sendmail web site is actually quite an impressive collection of useful information regarding Sendmail. You will find the Sendmail FAQ, pointers to useful electronic documentation, and, of course, links to the commercial version of the software, at http://www.sendmail.com. I highly recommend you read through the FAQ even if you don't understand all of it or don't even have a question that needs to be answered yet. That way, when you do run across a problem, you will have a better idea of what help you can find at the web site.

Installing Sendmail

As you may have guessed, there is a mail server option in the package management GUI tool. If you didn't select it during the initial install, you can launch the GUI tool as Packages under the System Settings menu, or from the command line as **redhat-config-packages**. Checking the Mail Server option will include Sendmail, but since we want to change Sendmail's configuration, there's an additional package that we'll need to add. If you pull up the **details** link, you'll see an option called **sendmail-cf**. This contains many of the components we'll need for the next section when we configure Sendmail using its **M4** macros. These packages also contain a number of auxiliary tools, outlined in Table 13-1, which you may find useful with Sendmail. If you're installing by hand, you'll want to make sure that you have the **sendmail** and the **sendmail-cf rpms**. It also probably won't hurt to install the **sendmail-doc** package while you're at it.

Tool	Description
mailstats	This program presents the statistics that Sendmail tracks on its performance and throughput in a human readable form.
mail.local	This is a simple mail delivery agent. (Instead, consider using Procmail, which is discussed later in "The Sendmail Macros.")
makemap	To increase performance, Sendmail keeps many of its tables in database format. This, of course, requires that there be a tool to convert the tables (as we create them using a text editor) into the database format. **makemap** is that tool.
praliases	The Sendmail aliases file allows you to create alternative e-mail addresses for your users, among many other things. (See "The aliases File" on **/etc/aliases** later in this module.) Although I can't figure out any really good use for this tool, especially since the aliases file is kept in a human-readable format, it is possible to use it to dump the aliases file by using **praliases**.
smrsh	The **smrsh** tool (and corresponding feature in Sendmail) is a great way to help secure Sendmail. It essentially restricts Sendmail so that it can run only those programs placed in a special directory. If a program isn't there, it can't be run. This keeps outsiders from trying to send Sendmail bogus information in hopes of executing a malicious operation. It is highly recommended you use this feature in Sendmail. (How to use this feature is discussed in "smrsh," later.)

Table 13-1 Sendmail Peripheral Programs

Configuring Sendmail with .mc Files

Sendmail configuration files are notoriously complex, which has a lot to do with Sendmail's history as the ultimate glue between disparate mail systems during the 1980s. The *rule sets* that define Sendmail's behavior allow for headers to be rewritten and even special action to be taken on particular header entries. This level of configurability, along with the fact that it was free and distributed with source code, made Sendmail the standard mail server for hosts on the Internet.

You might expect that as the need for connecting disparate mail systems came to a close, the configuration file would be simplified—but it wasn't. This was because of the number of people who used the flexibility of Sendmail to create powerful messaging solutions that would not be possible with any other mail server. And so we still use the basic structure of the Sendmail configuration file, almost 20 years after it was originally designed.

NOTE

This is not to say that the actual format of the configuration file has remained identical. It hasn't. Several changes have been made as far as new parameters to certain commands, and so on.

What made Sendmail's configuration semi-tolerable is the set of macros that were developed to make the process of generating configuration files much easier. Sendmail allows you to use the M4 macro language, which was originally developed in the 1970s and thus is available across all variants of UNIX (including Linux) to convert a relatively short and simple configuration file, which is much easier to understand by humans, into a formal configuration file.

In this section, we will go through the process of developing the correct macro file for your site's needs.

TIP

The ultimate authority on writing **.mc** files comes from the developers of Sendmail. If you have the **sendmail-doc rpm** installed, you'll find a file called **/usr/share/doc/ sendmail/README.cf**, which documents all the macros that come with Sendmail. While you may find this document overwhelming at first, it covers everything necessary to configure Sendmail via the M4 macros.

Enough M4 for Sendmail

The M4 language is actually a complete macro language (read the information page on M4 using the **info** command, for the complete documentation); however, the Sendmail configuration file needs only a small subset of commands in order to build a complete configuration file. This section documents what those commands are and how to use them.

Any commands you use in this section should be placed in a straight text file ending with a **.mc** extension, such as **myconfig.mc**. The next section discusses how to convert the **.mc** file into a configuration file that Sendmail understands, called **sendmail.cf**.

CAUTION

M4 is a stream-based language, which means it doesn't have the concept of lines. As a result, any time it sees a command it recognizes, it will expand it, regardless of context. This means that any references to commands in comments must be quoted.

include

The **include** directive allows you to add the contents of other files to your own. We're going to use this feature to suck in the Sendmail macros that we'll need later in the file.

```
Include(`/usr/share/sendmail-cf/m4/cf.m4')
```

divert

The **divert** command tells M4 to ignore a specified section of input. This allows you to place free-form comments in your macro file, which is a great way to document your work: You can explain *why* you are setting the parameters you are setting, so those future administrators who need to deal with your work will understand the reasoning behind the setup.

To mark the beginning of a comment block, use

```
divert(-1)
```

To mark the end of a comment block, use

```
divert(0)
```

For example:

```
divert(-1)
#
# mysite.mc - Sendmail configuration file
# Here's where we make all the changes that we want to end up
# in sendmail.cf
#  Last updated by wally on 2002/10/01
#
divert(0)
```

dnl

This instruction is as close as M4 gets to understanding anything about lines. The **dnl** instruction stands for *d*elete through *n*ew *l*ine, and its purpose is to eliminate unnecessary white space between macro expansions. Sometimes **dnl** also gets used as an improvised method for in-line comments. You'll see it used liberally in the .mc files that come with Sendmail. Note that using **dnl** is not required.

define

The **define** command is a basic building block that allows you to give values to a variable. The format of the command is

```
define (`variable', `value')
```

For example, to set ALIAS_FILE to **/etc/aliases**, you would use

```
define (`ALIAS_FILE', `/etc/aliases')
```

undefine

This command is the opposite of the **define** command—it takes a variable that has already been defined and undoes the setting. It is useful in situations where a predefined macro that comes with Sendmail has all the settings you want except for one or two that you don't. In these cases, you can undefine the settings you don't want rather than define a new macro by hand.

For example, if you don't expect to ever relay mail over the UNIX to UNIX copy protocol (UUCP), you might want to undefine the variables associated with UUCP transfers.

```
undefine (`UUCP_RELAY')
```

Using Quotes

As you may have noticed by now, string definition must be in single quotes. These quotes are important to M4 in order to process strings correctly. The beginning quote mark should be the back-tick character (`). This is often found on the same key as the tilde character (~). The end of the quote should be a single quote (') that is often shared with the double quote character ("). For example:

```
OSTYPE(`linux')
```

The Sendmail Macros

M4 by itself doesn't make configuring Sendmail any easier—it's the macros that ship with the Sendmail package that you can use from within an M4 script that make it easier. In this section, we discuss those macros.

Before reading this section, take a moment to look at the **.mc** files that come with Sendmail so that you know what's there. Don't worry if it doesn't make sense yet—seeing what's there and then reading this section will make things work a little more smoothly than the other way around. The main file we'll be concerned with here is **/etc/mail/sendmail.mc**, but it may also be interesting to browse through all of the **.mc** files in the **/usr/share/sendmail-cf/cf/** directory.

OSTYPE

The OSTYPE macro must be used before any of the other macros discussed in this section. It sets up the minimum number of definitions necessary for the particular operating system specified. In our case, we simply need to supply the string **linux** as its parameter, like so:

```
OSTYPE(`linux')
```

By using this macro, we spare ourselves from having to configure a number of default settings by hand. You can view the specific features in the **/usr/share/sendmail-cf/ostype/linux.m4** file that comes with Sendmail.

DOMAIN

If you are configuring a large number of mail servers for a single site, you may want to look into setting up a domain macro for your site. (See the **/usr/share/sendmail-cf/domains/** directory for examples.) These macros are essentially site-specific entries that you can set up and share across your network so that other administrators do not have to repeat certain configuration options.

For example, if you wanted to set up a domain configuration for your site and call it **mysite.m4**, you would use the DOMAIN macro as follows:

```
DOMAIN(`mysite')
```

For most sites, this is unnecessary and not worth the extra work of setting up a new domain entry in the **domains** directory.

MAILER

In the first section, we discussed the differences between mail transfer agents (MTAs) and mail delivery agents (MDAs). Sendmail is an MTA only, and thus it requires another program to perform the actual mail delivery. The MAILER macro allows you to specify the program that will perform the delivery of messages.

There are three mailers we are interested in: **local**, **smtp**, and Procmail. The **local** mailer is meant for messages that need to be delivered to local mailboxes. The **smtp** mailer is for messages that need to be relayed to other sites instead of delivered locally. For example, if you have a single mail server and many clients in your network, you may want to configure your firewall so that the only host that is allowed to communicate through the firewall on the SMTP port (25) is your mail server. This means all of the clients on your network need to relay through your mail server, thus the need for an SMTP mailer.

The last mailer is the most interesting. Procmail is an extremely flexible general-purpose mail-filtering tool. Best of all, it is written with security issues in mind, which makes Procmail an excellent replacement for the default local mailer that comes with Linux.

NOTE

Sendmail supports more mailers than I have presented here; however, their usage is more likely to be the exception rather than the rule. If you are running into exceptions, it is better that you read through the **README.cf** file yourself rather than depend on my interpretation (and simplification) of it.

For example, to use the **smtp** mailer for relays and Procmail for local delivery, you need the following lines in your **.mc** file:

```
MAILER(`procmail')
MAILER(`smtp')
```

NOTE

You must have a mailer macro in your **.mc** file.

MASQUERADE_AS

It is often necessary to give the illusion that all e-mail originates from the same location when it really may not (for example, UNIX hosts doing their own e-mail service but relaying through your server to be sent to the Internet). This is most often used to strip host names from the beginning of a fully qualified domain name, such as converting **mail.example.net** into **example.net**. In such cases, you should use the MASQUERADE_AS macro to set up host name masquerading. The format of this command is as follows:

```
MASQUERADE_AS(domainname)
```

where *domainname* is the name of the domain you want the messages to masquerade as.

EXPOSED_USER   The EXPOSED_USER macro works in conjunction with the MASQUERADE_AS macro to set up exceptions to the masquerading for specific users. For example, you'd probably want to know the real host name if the message originated from the **root** user. The usage of EXPOSED_USER is

```
EXPOSED_USER(usernames)
```

where *usernames* is a comma-separated list of users who should not be masqueraded.

For example, to make all of your mail appear as if it is coming from **example.net** except for mail coming from the **root** user, you need the following lines in your **.mc** file:

```
MASQUERADE_AS(`example.net')
EXPOSED_USER(`root')
```

FEATURE

Sendmail comes with a number of features that need to be explicitly enabled. Each feature that you want enabled should be enabled through the FEATURE macro, like so:

```
FEATURE(`feature_name')
```

where *feature_name* is the name of the feature that you wish to enable. In this section, we will go through a list of many of the features that Sendmail supports.

use_cw_file   If your mail server is known by multiple names, you need to let Sendmail know. This was originally communicated in a special macro placed inside the final configuration file, but that practice made it much more difficult to make changes. This feature tells Sendmail to look for the list of mail server names in the **/etc/mail/local-host-names** file. The format of the file is simply a list of host names, one host name per line.

This feature differs from masquerading because **use_cw_file** tells Sendmail for which host names to accept mail, whereas masquerading tells Sendmail which host names it can send mail to.

use_ct_file   Sendmail has a command-line option that allows you to change an outgoing message's sender name to something other than your own. By default, Sendmail allows only the **root** user to do this without generating a warning in the mail header. Using this feature, you can add more people to the list of trusted users by adding them to the **/etc/mail/trusted-users** file. The format of the file is one user per line.

redirect   When users leave the system, it is often necessary to provide forwarding information for them. This is done using the redirect feature in Sendmail. Messages sent to *address*.REDIRECT@*mailserver* have an SMTP code sent back to the mail sender telling them to forward e-mail to *address*. This is done using the **/etc/mail/aliases** file (discussed in "The aliases File" later in the module) to set up an alias for the user who has departed. For example, if the user **asok** has left, and his new e-mail address is **asok@example.net**, you can set up an entry in the **/etc/mail/aliases** file that looks like this:

```
asok:     asok@example.net.REDIRECT
```

Now, when mail is received for the user **asok**, the sender automatically gets a message sent back to him indicating that the user's new e-mail address is **asok@example.net**.

mailertable   If you are performing virtual hosting, you may want to route your e-mail in a different way, depending on the domain to which it is being sent. The **mailertable** feature allows you to do this in the **/etc/mail/mailertable** file, where each line is in the format

```
receiverhost                mailer:hostname
```

where *receiverhost* is the host for which you are receiving mail, *mailer* is the mailer (as defined with the MAILER macro), and *hostname* is the machine onto which you want to pass the message. The *receiverhost* has some additional flexibility—namely, it can have wildcard host names. This is done by prefixing the *receiverhost* string with a period, which tells Sendmail to allow an arbitrary host name to be in front of the *receiverhost* string. For example, if we specified *receiverhost* to be **.domain.com**, it would accept messages destined to **anything.domain.com**. If *receiverhost* is not prefixed with a period, then the complete host name must match.

For example, to relay all messages sent to any host in the **.example.com** domain to the host **mail.outsourced-mail-server.com**, you would create an entry that looks like this:

```
.example.com                    smtp:mail.outsourced-mail-server.com
```

TIP

Although it is probably just coincidence, Sendmail was created a mere 20 miles north of the base of Silicon Valley, a mystical land where mergers and acquisitions happen daily. And as luck may have it, Sendmail's **mailertable** feature is very well suited to instances where a merger or acquisition has created an immediate need for a single mail server to accept mail for more than one domain name. Another popular use for this feature is for the purpose of relaying mail through a DMZ. Thus the firewall can be configured to pass mail through only if the originating IP address is the relay host.

The **mailertable** file must be turned into Sendmail's database format before it can be used. This is done via the **makemap** program that gets compiled along with Sendmail. To use it with the **mailertable** file, we would say

```
[root@mail /etc]# makemap hash /etc/mail/mailertable
```

domaintable   The **domaintable** feature allows you to tell Sendmail to map one domain name to another domain name transparently. This is useful when your site changes its domain name. Once you enable it with the **FEATURE** command, you will need to set up the database containing the name information mapping. The database is typically **/etc/mail/domaintable**. The format of this file is

```
old-name.com       some-new-name.com
```

Like the **mailertable**, Sendmail requires this table to be converted into a database format using the **makemap** command, like so:

```
[root@mail /etc]# makemap hash /etc/mail/domaintable
```

always_add_domain   This feature tells Sendmail to always add your domain name to all delivered mail, even if it is being delivered locally. This is a good way to ensure a uniform appearance of e-mail addresses to all people, regardless of whether they are inside or outside of your domain.

virtusertable   If you are hosting virtual domains, you will quickly find yourself facing name space collisions among e-mail addresses. The **virtusertable** feature allows you to get around this by setting up a special mapping of e-mail addresses to real usernames. Thus, it becomes possible for there to be multiple **info** e-mail addresses (**such as info@domain.com, info@example.net**, and so on) hosted on the same system.

The format of the **virtusertable** is as follows:

```
fake-address           real-address
```

where *fake-address* is the address that you need to host, and *real-address* is where the e-mail is actually sent. So if you are hosting **domain.com** and **example.net**, you might do something like

```
info@domain.com domain-info@real-domain.com
info@example.net example-info@real-domain.com
```

so that any messages sent to **info@domain.com** get sent to **domain-info@real-domain.com** instead, and **info@example.net** gets sent to **example-info@real-domain.com**.

You can set up the additional flexibility of having the right column entry not have a username but have the **@domain.com** portion. This results in any messages sent to any username to **@domain.com** being forwarded to a single address. For example

```
@@example.net        alice@alices-real-domain.com
```

will cause any messages sent to any user **@example.net** to have her messages forwarded to **alice@alices-real-domain.com**.

This table is like the other tables we've discussed, in that it needs to be converted into the database format using the **makemap** command, like so:

```
[root@mail /etc]# makemap hash /etc/virtusertable
```

nullclient   If you have UNIX machines in your network and want them all to relay their e-mail through a central server, you will need to configure them so that they are *null clients*. Telling Sendmail that it is a null client is essentially asking it to remove its intelligence and pass the buck over to a central server. While this may appear bizarre, it's actually a good idea, because it allows you to centralize mail service. Null clients relay all of their messages to the mail hub (sometimes referred to as a "*smart host*"), which takes care of proper delivery, even if the delivery stays local to your network. This feature also enables you to perform centralized logging of mail activity.

To specify a mail hub, use the following **define** statement in conjunction with the FEATURE macro:

```
define(`MAIL_HUB', `mailhubhost')
```

where *mailhubhost* is the name of the host acting as the mail hub. For example:

```
FEATURE(`nullclient')
define(`MAIL_HUB', `mail.example.com')
```

where **mail.example.com** is the mail hub.

local_procmail

local_procmail   This feature tells Sendmail to use Procmail as the local mailer. It can take up to three arguments: the path to Procmail (defaults to **/usr/local/bin/procmail**), parameters to Procmail (defaults to **-Y -a** *hostname* -d *username*), and flags for the mailer. Realistically speaking, all you need to do is specify the location of Procmail. Don't worry about the parameters to Procmail unless you have a special need and have read the corresponding Procmail parameters. For example:

```
FEATURE(`local_procmail', `/usr/bin/procmail')
```

smrsh   One of Sendmail's security problems is that we, the people who configure it, make mistakes. One of the most common mistakes is setting up programs that can be run through an alias expansion in an insecure manner that can be exploited by remote users. We are effectively hitting ourselves in the foot with a hammer.

Sendmail tries to take away the hammer with the SendMail Restricted Shell (**smrsh**). It is a very simplified shell that has limited functionality, and therefore fewer things can be exploited because of a misconfiguration.

This feature accepts a parameter specifying where **smrsh** is located. If **smrsh** is in the **/usr/sbin** directory, we would specify

```
FEATURE(`smrsh', `/usr/sbin/smrsh')
```

promiscuous_relay   By default, Sendmail does not allow any site to relay mail through your site. This is done to protect you from spammers using your systems as a hopping point. If, for some really strange reason, you have to allow random people to relay through your mail server, you can use this feature.

CAUTION

Allowing random people to relay through your server is a very bad idea. It opens up your site to denial of service (DoS) attacks, theft of bandwidth, and the nightmare of getting floods of e-mail coming from angry recipients of unsolicited e-mail. Before opening up your system like this, understand the implications!

relay_entire_domain   Sendmail's default behavior is to relay mail only from hosts listed in the **access** database (discussed in "Spam Control: The access Database," later in this module). By using this feature, you allow any host from within your domain to relay through you.

relay_based_on_MX   This feature tells Sendmail to look up the DNS MX record of a host that is asking to relay through you. If Sendmail finds that the host's MX record is the same host that Sendmail is running on, the message will be accepted for relaying.

accept_unqualified_senders   Normally, Sendmail refuses mail from e-mail addresses that are unqualified. For example, mail from **alice@example.com** is acceptable, but mail from **alice** alone is not. Using this feature tells Sendmail *not* to require that sender e-mail addresses be qualified.

accept_unresolvable_domains   Sendmail defaults to verifying that the sender's domain name is resolvable via DNS. This keeps people from forging e-mail from noncxisting domains. If your site has a limited view of the Internet DNS namespace for some reason (such as if you're behind a firewall), you will want to use this feature to tell Sendmail to accept messages from unresolvable domains.

access_db   This feature enables the **access** database, which allows you to specify whether you want to accept, reject, drop, or reject with a special code all of your incoming e-mail, based on source domain or e-mail address. We explore the configuration file for this feature in greater detail in "Spam Control: The access Database" later in this module, when we discuss spam control.

blacklist_recipients   There are some users who should never receive e-mail, such as **nobody**, **bin**, or **lp**. You can blacklist these users so that they cannot receive e-mail by using this feature in combination with the **access_db** feature.

   The way blacklist configuration works with the **access_db** is discussed later in "Spam Control: The access Database."

Configurable Parameters

Sendmail offers a number of configurable parameters for its features. In this section, we review these parameters and explain what they are used for and their default values. You'll find that, for the most part, the defaults are perfectly good, and you won't need to change anything.

   You can see the very long list of configurable options in the **README.cf** file. However, many of those options are so incredibly rarely used that you'll probably even forget they are there when you're done with this module. Because of that, Table 13-2 sticks to the most common options.

Option Name	Description	Default
confMAILER_ NAME	The name used for internally-generated mail (typically for error messages for returned mail).	MAILER-DAEMON
confDOMAIN_ NAME	Your domain name. You should set this option only if Sendmail cannot determine your domain name by itself.	No default
confCW_FILE	The full path to the file containing host names that the server may be known as (see the use_cw_file feature).	**/etc/sendmail.cw**
confCT_FILE	The full path to the file containing trusted users (see the use_ct_file feature).	**/etc/sendmail.ct**
confCR_FILE	The full path to the relay-domains file. This is the list of domains for which Sendmail will relay. (You should use the access_db feature instead.)	**/etc/mail/relay-domains**
confALIAS_ WAIT	When the mail **aliases** file is updated, it must be converted to the internal database format with the **newaliases** command. This parameter tells Sendmail how long to wait for **newaliases** to run before rebuilding the database itself.	10 minutes (10m)
confMIN_ FREE_BLOCKS	The number of free blocks the mail storage partition must have for Sendmail to accept new messages. This option allows Sendmail to protect the system from sudden bursts of e-mail.	100 blocks, where 1 block (under Linux) is equal to 1K
confMAX_ MESSAGE_SIZE	The maximum message size (in bytes) that Sendmail will accept.	Infinite
confAUTO_ REBUILD	Specifies if Sendmail should automatically rebuild the aliases database if needed.	False
confLOG_ LEVEL	Specifies Sendmail's level of logging. The higher the level number, the more logging performed. The level codes are as follows: 0 Minimal logging 1 Serious system failures and potential security problems 2 Lost communication (network problems) 3 Transient errors, malformed addresses, forward/include errors 4 Minor failures, out-of-date alias databases, connection rejections via check_rule sets 5 Message collection statistics 6 Creation of error messages, **VRFY** and **EXPN** commands 7 Delivery failures (host or user unknown, and so on) 8 Successful deliveries and alias database rebuilds 9 Messages being deferred 10 Database expansion (alias, forward, and user database lookups) 11 NIS errors and end-of-job processing 12 All SMTP connections 13 Bad user shells and files with improper permissions	Log level 9

Table 13-2 Sendmail's Most Common Configurable Parameters

13

Sending Mail with SMTP

Option Name	Description	Default
confME_TOO	When a message is sent to an alias that has the sender as a member of the list (such as the user hdc sends a message to management, which expands to the users hdc, julia, and ceo), this option determines whether the message should be sent to the sender, too.	False (does not send message back to sender)
confTO_INITIAL	Timeout period Sendmail should wait when connecting to remote sites to send mail.	5 minutes (5m)
confTO_IDENT	Timeout period Sendmail should wait when trying to identify the username of someone trying to send mail to it via the IDENT protocol.	30 seconds (30s)
confTO_QUEUEWARN	Timeout period before a user is told that her message being relayed through Sendmail is being deferred because the remote site cannot be contacted.	4 hours (4h)
confSMTP_LOGIN_MSG	The greeting message sent to someone trying to connect to Sendmail. Some sites have taken to customizing this string so that remote sites don't know what kind of mail server is really being run. In essence, this is security through obscurity, where the underlying philosophy is, "Why tell them what you don't have to?" Just understand that obscuring the type of mail server does not mean a cracker will not get through if they are determined enough.	Host name of the server, the version of Sendmail, and the version of the Sendmail configuration file
confDOUBLE_BOUNCE_ADDRESS	If an error occurs, Sendmail delivers an e-mail notice to the site administrator. The site administrator is defined by this option. Most sites leave the default alone and use an alias to route messages to the system administrator.	Postmaster

Table 13-2 Sendmail's Most Common Configurable Parameters *(continued)*

NOTE

Some of the parameters in the configuration file represent time values. The format of these values is a number followed by a letter, where the letter is either *s* for seconds, *m* for minutes, *h* for hours, or *d* for days. For example, **10m** is 10 minutes, **3d** is 3 days, and so on.

For example, to set the path for the Procmail program to **/usr/bin/procmail**, we would use

```
define(`PROCMAIL_MAILER_PATH', `/usr/bin/procmail')
```

A Complete Sample Configuration

Here is the complete **.mc** file used to build the Red Hat 8 configuration:

```
VERSIONID('linux setup for Red Hat Linux')dnl
OSTYPE('linux')
define('confDEF_USER_ID', ''8:12'')dnl
undefine('UUCP_RELAY')dnl
undefine('BITNET_RELAY')dnl
define('confAUTO_REBUILD')dnl
define('confTO_CONNECT', '1m')dnl
define('confTRY_NULL_MX_LIST',true)dnl
```

```
define('confDONT_PROBE_INTERFACES',true)dnl
define('PROCMAIL_MAILER_PATH', '/usr/bin/procmail')dnl
define('STATUS_FILE', '/var/log/sendmail.st')dnl
define('UUCP_MAILER_MAX', '2000000')dnl
define('confUSERDB_SPEC', '/etc/mail/userdb.db')dnl
dnl define('confPRIVACY_FLAGS', 'authwarnings,novrfy,noexpn')dnl
dnl define('confTO_QUEUEWARN', '4h')dnl
dnl define('confTO_QUEUERETURN', '5d')dnl
dnl define('confQUEUE_LA', '12')dnl
dnl define('confREFUSE_LA', '18')dnl
FEATURE('smrsh', '/usr/sbin/smrsh')dnl
FEATURE('mailertable', 'hash -o /etc/mail/mailertable')dnl
FEATURE('virtusertable', 'hash -o /etc/mail/virtusertable')dnl
FEATURE(redirect)dnl|
FEATURE(always_add_domain)dnl
FEATURE(use_cw_file)dnl
FEATURE(local_procmail)dnl
FEATURE('access_db')dnl
FEATURE('blacklist_recipients')dnl
dnl We strongly recommend to comment this one out if you want to
dnl protect yourself from spam. However, the laptops and users on
dnl computers that do not have 24x7 DNS do need this.
FEATURE('accept_unresolvable_domains')dnl
dnl FEATURE('relay_based_on_MX')dnl
MAILER(smtp)dnl
MAILER(procmail)dnl
```

Compiling Macros into a Configuration File

Once you have all of your macros put into a **.mc** file, you are ready to convert it into a complete configuration file that Sendmail can understand. The process is wonderfully straightforward. Invoke the **m4** processor, passing it the name of your macro file, and redirect the output to the name of the resulting file that you want to use.

```
[root@mail mail]# m4 myconfig.mc > sendmail.cf
```

And that's it. The file **sendmail.cf** has been created and is ready to use. If you're really curious, you might peek at the resulting **sendmail.cf** and see how it compares with the macro file you started with.

Beyond the Primary Configuration File

Reading through the features that Sendmail offers us, we saw that there are many features that enable and disable the usage of additional configuration files. Some of these files are very straightforward and are explained in a sentence or two in the previous section. But there are two files in particular that are nontrivial: the **aliases** file and the **access** database file. In this section, we examine their formats and learn how to write our own.

The aliases File

Sendmail's mail **aliases** file is one of Sendmail's most powerful features. It allows you to create mailing lists, give users alternative e-mail aliases, and even pipe e-mail directly to external applications. Though some newer systems prefer to move the **aliases** file to **/etc/mail/aliases**, Red Hat has chosen to leave it in its traditional location at **/etc/aliases**.

The format of the **aliases** file is reasonably straightforward. All comment lines begin with a pound symbol (#), and the remainder of the line is free-form. Lines may also be blank to help define logical blocks.

Each alias must begin with the alias's name, followed immediately by a colon. The remainder of the line is what Sendmail will expand that address to be. The content of the line can be one of six things: another alias, a list of aliases, another user, a list of users, a file, or an external application. Aliases and usernames can be intermixed. Any aliases referenced on the right side of the colon must have been previously defined.

Assume the **domain example.com** has the users **boss**, **alice**, **asok**, **wally**, **bob**, **mordac**, and **dilbert**. Let's look at a few examples and see what some of these aliases can be set up to do.

● We want a simple alias for **boss**. Since she is the CEO, we will set up an alias as follows:

```
ceo: boss
```

Now any mail sent to **ceo@example.com** will transparently be sent to **boss**.

● We want to create an alias for three of our departments: **engineering**, **mis**, and **management**. We can create the aliases as follows:

```
engineering: dilbert, wally
mis: mordac, bob
management: bob, alice, ceo
```

Any mail sent to **management@example.com** will automatically be forwarded to the users **alice**, **bob**, and **ceo**. The **ceo** address will get expanded to **boss**.

● We want to create the alias **everybody** so that any mail sent to it will automatically be forwarded to all of the departments. We can do that with the following alias:

```
everybody: engineering, mis, management
```

E-mail sent to **everybody@domain.com** will be expanded to **engineering**, **mis**, and **management**. Each of these aliases will expand to their respective users, with the management alias having one more expansion to convert **ceo** to **boss**.

Are you following the trend here?

- If we want all of the mail sent to a particular address to be copied to a file, we simply begin the right side of an alias with a forward slash character (/), indicating that the rest of the line is a filename. So if we want messages sent to **log@example.com** to be placed into a file called **/tmp/log**, we would set an alias, like so:

```
log: /tmp/log
```

- If we want to pipe all of the e-mail sent to a particular alias to an external program, we can do so through this file. Assume that the external program is **/etc/smrsh /external_program**.

```
abuse: "|/etc/smrsh/external_program"
```

NOTE

You will need to be sure to place your binaries in the correct directory so that **smrsh** knows they are there. Under a standard Red Hat installation, this would be the directory **/etc/smrsh**.

Once you have finished creating the **aliases** file, you will need to use the **newaliases** command to convert the file into a database format that Sendmail can quickly read. To do so, simply type

```
[root@mail /etc]# newaliases
```

Spam Control: The access Database

Sendmail allows you to use the **/etc/mail/access** file to list special actions for particular domain names, host names, IP addresses, and users. This feature is especially interesting because it unifies all of Sendmail's spam-control mechanisms into a single configuration file.

The format of the file is simple: lines that begin with a pound symbol (#) are comments, blank lines are allowed, and the rest of the lines contain the actual configuration information.

The default features of using the **access_db** allow you to list either the host name, domain name, IP address, or e-mail address, and specify whether you want a specific action on e-mail originating from there. The actions are listed in Table 13-3.

Let's look at a few examples that illustrate the features listed in Table 13-3:

- To reject all messages from **annoying-web-site.com**, your entry would be

```
annoying-web-site.com                    REJECT
```

- To discard all messages from **badperson@badpeople.com**, you would use

```
badperson@badpeople.com                  DISCARD
```

- To relay all messages from the 138.23.0.0 network, you would use

  ```
  138.23                                    RELAY
  ```

- To reject all messages from **spamathon.com** with the SMTP message "550 No Spam Here.", you would use

  ```
  spamathon.com                             550 No Spam Here.
  ```

- You can also blacklist an individual address:

  ```
  spamsender@badpeople.com                       550 Been blacklisted.
  ```

We can put all of these examples together into a single file:

```
#
# /etc/mail/access
# Rules for accepting/denying mail from various sites.
#
annoying-web-site.com                REJECT
badperson@badpeople.com              DISCARD
138.23                               RELAY
spamathon.com                        550 No Spam Here.
spamsender@badpeople.com                  550 Been blacklisted...
```

Action	Description
OK	Accepts the message even if there are other rules that would otherwise reject it. For example, if you enable the feature to deny messages from domain names that cannot be resolved to an IP address, you can specify a specific exception domain using the **OK** action.
RELAY	Unless explicitly turned on, the default Sendmail configuration does not relay messages for other domains. This action overrides that rule for a specific domain.
REJECT	Refuses all messages from this site/person. This will cause a brief message to be sent back to the sender informing him or her that the message was rejected.
DISCARD	Discards the message entirely. No message is sent back to the sender. For all he/she knows, the message was accepted.
SMTP-code message	SMTP-code must be a valid SMTP code as specified in RFC 821. **message** can be any text you want returned along with **SMTP-code**.

Table 13-3 access_db Features

Progress Check

1. Name two mail delivery agents (MDAs) that can be used with Sendmail.

2. Why is allowing any site to relay e-mail through your server a bad idea?

CRITICAL SKILL
13.3 Choosing Postfix

Among the many criticisms commonly leveled against Sendmail, the biggest ones are its security, complexity, and performance. A number of programs have sprung up to try to address these (among other) criticisms, in hopes of doing a better job than Sendmail. Among the competitive replacements, one of the most popular (and the only one we'll cover here) is Postfix.

Postfix was created at IBM's T. J. Watson Research Center by Wietse Venema with the intention of being fast, easy to configure, and secure. Originally known as VMailer, and then as IBM Secure Mailer, the program finally settled on the name Postfix in 1998. While Postfix is most known for its security approach, it also claims to be three times faster than its closest competitor.

Postfix is often compared with **qmail**, another MTA replacement with a strong security focus. But while Postfix borrows a number of architecture ideas from **qmail**, they differ in at least one important way. Postfix strives to be a drop-in replacement for Sendmail, to make migrating as painless as possible. As a result, Postfix directly supports a number of Sendmail files, such as **/etc/aliases**, **/var/spool/mail**, and ~/.forward. Since Postfix tries to be simple to configure, however, it does not try to support **sendmail.cf**.

Unlike Sendmail's monolithic architecture, Postfix is made up of a dozen or so small programs that each perform a single, specific task. In addition to the security advantage of making it easier to find unwanted side effects in a small, simple program, this also provides a great deal of flexibility. Machines that don't need a specific function (such as local delivery, for example) can easily omit that daemon from their install. The majority of the component pieces are run without any special privileges, so even if an attacker does manage to break them, the potential damage is minimized. Also because of security concerns, the individual Postfix programs don't really trust data passed to them, even if it's from another part of Postfix, but instead validate for themselves (where applicable) any data passed to them.

---

1. The local **mail** program and Procmail are two that are mentioned.

2. Allowing anyone to relay e-mail through your server opens your server up to being used for spam by unscrupulous people.

Installing Postfix

Although Postfix is included with Red Hat 8, it's included as an alternative to the well-entrenched Sendmail program, and unlike Sendmail, you have to specifically select to install Postfix. This can be done either during the initial install or through the **redhat-config-packages** GUI tool, which can be selected from the desktop menu by choosing System Settings from the main menu, and then selecting Packages. If you prefer the command line, you can just type **redhat-config-packages**. Now find the Mail Server group and open the Details dialog box. Here, among the extra packages, you can select postfix. If you're installing RPMS by hand, the package you're interested in is also just called postfix. No additional packages should be necessary, but there is at least one or two more that you may find useful. In **redhat-config-packages**, under the Server Configuration Tools group, you'll find two utilities near the bottom of the list: **redhat-switchmail** and **redhat-switchmail-gnome**. These correspond to the RPMS of the same name and are discussed in the next section.

Switching MTAs

Since Postfix was designed to be a drop-in replacement for Sendmail, it mimics not only Sendmail's purpose but much of Sendmail's visible form as well. Because of Sendmail's long heritage as the standard UNIX mail program, it's not uncommon to have other programs that take advantage of Sendmail's presence to handle mail-related functions rather than try to implement it internally. This means that for command-line interfaces, like **newaliases** or sendmail, Postfix must provide similar working equivalents. Normally, it's expected that if you install something like Postfix, you won't have Sendmail installed at the same time, so there isn't much worry about name collisions. Notice however that we didn't remove the Sendmail package when we installed Postfix in the previous section. That's because Red Hat has moved the real programs to places that won't collide when both packages are installed and then uses symlinks to connect the name you're expecting, such as "**sendmail**," to the correct real program.

NOTE

It may seem confusing at first to realize that Postfix includes a program named "**sendmail**." As long as you realize that this is just a compatibility interface, it shouldn't trouble you for too long. A number of the other programs in Postfix are also named the same as their Sendmail counterparts; the others just don't seem quite as strange when you first transition.

This is where those extra packages mentioned in the last section come in. Installing Postfix doesn't automatically change the symlinks, since it's possible that you have Sendmail already working; and you probably have to do some configuration before Postfix is ready to take over. Red Hat supplies two programs that will manage switching between Sendmail and Postfix (or back again) when you're ready to make that transition. Both programs perform exactly the same function, except that one of them takes advantage of GNOME to bring up a GUI dialog box, and the other is purely text based. Launching either of these will allow you to choose which MTA you would like to have active on your system, Sendmail or Postfix. You can bring this tool up from the main menu by selecting System Settings followed by Mail Transport Agent Switcher. From the command line you can launch either **redhat-switchmail** or **redhat-switchmail-nox**. The **redhat-switchmail** program will bring up the GNOME-based dialog box shown in the following illustration, if it's installed, or the text variant otherwise, while **redhat-switchmail-nox** will always bring up the non-GUI "no X" version. This utility will take care of any symlinks that need to be moved, including making sure that the correct startup script is used.

You will now want to bring up the Service Configuration tool (or examine the symlinks yourself). Even though the **switchmail** programs will make sure the correct option appears in the Service Configuration tool, it doesn't synchronize the startup runlevels with what you had set for the previous MTA, so you will want to make sure that your new selection starts and stops where you expect it to.

The Structure of Postfix

We touched briefly on the fact that Postfix is comprised of a multitude of small, specific-purpose programs. Postfix also uses multiple queues to store messages that are in various stages of being processed. This may look complex at first glance, but the steps are roughly the same as what Sendmail performs internally, except that in Postfix the process has been separated into its component pieces. In this section we'll discuss the overall structure of Postfix, as well as its components and queues, in a little more detail.

The program called **master** is the main Postfix overseer. This daemon will remain resident, and its whole purpose is to launch other pieces of Postfix as they're needed. Most of the other programs mentioned are launched when needed, and they close when they're finished with their tasks and not expecting to be needed again soon.

An e-mail message arriving across the network is received by the program called **smtpd** and is then passed on to a daemon named **cleanup**. It is the **cleanup** program's responsibility to sanity-check the format and addresses in the message to make sure they all are in a form that the other Postfix components will understand. If some very basic transformations need to be performed, such as expanding a bare host name into a fully qualified domain name, the message is passed to the **trivial-rewrite** daemon, which then passes it back to **cleanup** with the addresses properly expanded. Once all the addresses have been checked, **cleanup** will drop the message into a queue called **incoming**, and notify the queue manager of the waiting message.

A message generated locally with the **sendmail** program will be passed along to the **postdrop** daemon. (Remember, we're talking about **sendmail**, the compatibility interface, here—not the Sendmail MTA.) The purpose of the **postdrop** daemon is to deliver messages into the **maildrop** queue. This task has been separated out into its own program to better protect the **maildrop** queue. The **postdrop** program has write access to the **maildrop** queue through the use of the **set-group** ID bit, which is considered risky to give to **sendmail** directly. For added security, **postdrop** has its own group ID rather than sharing one with the other Postfix components. A daemon named **pickup** will then be responsible for collecting messages from the **maildrop** queue, performing some basic formatting sanity checks, and passing them along to **cleanup**. The messages will then make their way toward the **incoming** queue just like messages that arrived over **smtp**.

E-mails are retrieved from the **incoming** queue for routing by the queue manager. This was traditionally performed by a program called **qmgr**, and much of Postfix's documentation will reference **qmgr**, but a new version called **nqmgr** promises better scheduling, particularly in the presence of large mailing lists. Red Hat uses the newer **nqmgr** by default, and for our purposes here, we'll consider them to be interchangeable.

Messages being processed by either variant of **qmgr** are moved into the **active** queue. The **active** queue is intentionally limited in size, to prevent excessive load on the mail server, even under heavy mail conditions. Messages leave the **active** queue to be delivered, or if they can't be delivered they are deferred. E-mail that can't be delivered immediately for one reason or another, is deferred for a later delivery, going into a separate queue named (you guessed it) **deferred**. When there is space in the **active** queue, a new message from each of the **incoming** and **deferred** queues is pulled into the **active** queue by **qmgr**.

If an e-mail is destined for local delivery, **qmgr** passes it to the **local** daemon, which will drop it into the user's mailbox or pass it along to an external delivery program such as Procmail. Messages bound for other servers are passed instead to the **smtp** program, which is responsible for transferring the e-mail to the next server. A third delivery option exists just in case neither of the preceding options fit your needs. The Postfix **pipe** command can pass your message along to an external program for special processing (see Figure 13-1).

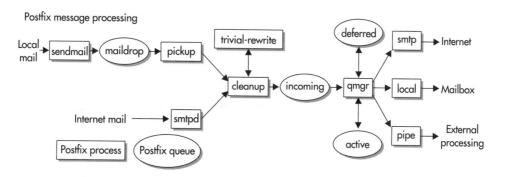

Figure 13-1 Simplified diagram of Postfix mail delivery process

There are other programs and queues used by Postfix, such as a daemon for sending bounce notifications, but these are the basic parts used in normal mail delivery. It's not critical that you know all the details of this system, but understanding the basic process will help with configuration, and any troubleshooting that you may have to do.

Configuration

Fortunately, the default configuration supplied with Red Hat is pretty usable. Of course, no one configuration is right for everyone, so it's also fortunate that the Postfix config files are relatively easy to read. Most of the files you will need are located in the **/etc/postfix** directory, and most of the files in that directory are lookup tables for various features. The two actual configuration files are **master.cf** and **main.cf**. These are both regular text files, and lines beginning with a pound symbol (#) are treated as comments.

The master.cf File

As you may have guessed already, the **master.cf** file correlates to the Postfix **master** daemon that we covered in the previous section. You will probably rarely need to modify this file, but understanding it may help you see how all the pieces tie together. Remember that it's the **master** daemon's job to start the various pieces of Postfix when they're required. The **master.cf** file is where you specify what programs get started and specify some parameters about each. Each line in the file represents a particular function that Postfix has to perform, most of which you will recognize from our discussion on the structure of Postfix.

Each line is made up of eight fields that describe the process that **master** should run for a particular function. The first field is the name of the service and must match one of the built-in values that Postfix will understand. The last field is the command to run for that service. The command specified must be a program written specifically to work with the Postfix system, which at the moment means they most likely will be one of the daemons that came with the

Postfix package (and it explains why most of the commands exactly match the service name). If you recall our earlier discussion about **nqmgr** as a replacement for the original **qmgr**, you may be interested to notice the entry for the **qmgr** service. You'll see a line commented out that would run the old **qmgr** (still included with the Postfix distribution), followed immediately by an entry for the newer **nqmgr**. If, for example, you had a previous Postfix installation that used the old **qmgr**, and you weren't ready to deploy the **nqmgr** yet for some reason, you could just change the comment on those two lines and maintain the previous behavior.

The second field specifies how the service receives its data. The **unix** designation refers to using UNIX sockets to communicate between processes. Processes that use a named pipe will specify **fifo** here, and processes that actually listen to Internet ports will specify **inet**. You may notice that this field is what differentiates the incoming **smtp** service (which uses the **smtpd** program to listen on an Internet port) and the outgoing **smtp** service (which uses the **smtp** program to take data in from a **unix** socket and send it out over the Internet to the next server).

The remaining fields have the option of using just a hyphen (–) to specify that you want the default value. For example, the third field is labeled "private" and refers to the program's ability to communicate with programs or services outside of Postfix. The default is not to share data outside of Postfix, and most of the entries have just a – in that field. It doesn't make any sense, however, to place this restriction on a process that is supposed to be listening to an Internet port, for example, so an **n** is placed in this field.

The **unprivileged** field defaults to running processes as the **postfix** user, unless an **n** here is used to indicate services that need special privileges (i.e., **root**). The **chroot** field specifies whether to run the process in a **chroot**ed jail based in your Postfix queue directory (**/var/spool/postfix** by default).

The **wakeup** field is used by processes that need to occasionally check one of the queues to see if there is work for it to do. For example, the value of 60 for the **pickup** service means that once a minute the **pickup** program is started to check for messages in the **maildrop** queue.

As an aid in keeping system resources under control, the **maxprocess** field defaults to 50. This means that no more than 50 instances of a given service will be running at the same time. There are a few services that have special needs in this area, however. It's important that the **bounce, cleanup**, and **defer** services have a value of 0 to indicate no limit, or it's possible for Postfix to become stuck under a heavy load. If **qmgr** and **pickup** are not kept at 1 you will begin to see duplicate messages being delivered.

```
# ============================================================================
# service type  private unpriv  chroot  wakeup  maxproc command + args
#               (yes)   (yes)   (yes)   (never) (50)
# ============================================================================
smtp    inet    n       -       y       -       -       smtpd
#smtps  inet    n       -       n       -       -       smtpd
#  -o smtpd_tls_wrappermode=yes -o smtpd_sasl_auth_enable=yes
#submission     inet    n       -       n       -       -       smtpd
#  -o smtpd_enforce_tls=yes -o smtpd_sasl_auth_enable=yes
```

```
#628     inet   n   -   n   -       -   qmqpd
pickup   fifo   n   -   y   60      1   pickup
cleanup  unix   n   -   y   -       0   cleanup
#qmgr    fifo   n   -   n   300     1   qmgr
qmgr     fifo   n   -   y   300     1   nqmgr
#tlsmgr  fifo   -   -   n   300     1   tlsmgr
rewrite  unix   -   -   y   -       -   trivial-rewrite
bounce   unix   -   -   y   -       0   bounce
defer    unix   -   -   y   -       0   bounce
flush    unix   n   -   y   1000?   0   flush
smtp     unix   -   -   y   -       -   smtp
showq    unix   n   -   y   -       -   showq
error    unix   -   -   y   -       -   error
local    unix   -   n   n   -       -   local
virtual  unix   -   n   y   -       -   virtual
lmtp     unix   -   -   y   -       -   lmtp
```

The main.cf File

This file is where you specify nearly all of your configuration settings for Postfix. The default **main.cf** that accompanies Red Hat 8 is very well commented, and you should be able to get a good understanding just from reading through the file. Entries in the **main.cf** file are simple *key = value* pairs, and most of them are intuitively named. The one extra trick available here is that for a value parameter you can refer to a previously set value by prefixing its key with a dollar sign ($). For example:

```
myorigin = $mydomain
```

The **myorigin** variable specifies what gets appended to unqualified usernames. In this example, the value of **myorigin** is set to the same value that the **mydomain** variable is set to. This has the advantage that if your domain name changes, you don't have to change multiple values in different places in the config file. In addition, a number of the variables have intelligent defaults. If **$mydomain** wasn't previously set in the preceding example, the default value is the domain name of the server it's running on. Most of the important options are listed next.

mail_006Fwner   This specifies what username will be the designated owner of Postfix queue directories. The default is the user named **postfix**.

default_p0072ivs   The user listed here is assumed by Postfix when writing to files or external programs. It is probably best to leave this at the default user **nobody**.

setgid_group   This specifies the directory group ID of the **maildrop** queue, and the group ID used by the **postdrop** program to write to that queue. Under Red Hat the default is the group **postdrop**.

myhostname Here is the fully qualified domain name of your server. By default this will be the value set as the host name of your server, so you may not have to set this value explicitly.

mydomain Much like the previous setting, this will default to the domain portion of your fully qualified domain name. You may need to set this specifically with some subdomain configurations.

myorigin E-mail with unqualified usernames will have this value appended to the address. By default this will assume the same value as **mydomain**.

masquerade_domains Here is your option for stripping the extraneous host name from your users' mail before it goes out into the wild Internet. See the discussion of masquerading, earlier in this module.

```
masquerade_domains = example.com
```

masquerade_exceptions Anyone that you don't want to have masqueraded by the previous option should be listed here. At the very least, you probably won't want to masquerade **root**.

```
masquerade_exceptions = root
```

inet_interfaces Here you can limit what network interfaces Postfix will pay attention to. The default is to listen to all interfaces on the machine. For a machine on which you don't expect to receive mail from external sources, you may want to change this to **localhost** or **127.0.0.1**.

```
inet_interfaces = all
```

mydestination For the purposes of accepting mail to be delivered locally, Postfix needs to know all the names that refer to the server. Do not list virtual domains here without reading the next section about how virtual domains are handled in Postfix. You will want to list all aliases for the current machine. If this is the mail server for the whole domain, you'll want to list that here as well. Multiple aliases can be separated by commas, as in

```
mydestination = $myhostname, localhost.$mydomain, $mydomain
```

relay_domains This lists all domains that your server will accept mail for. This differs from **mydestination** in that **mydestination** only lists domains accepted for local delivery, whereas **relay_domains** will also list domains you act as secondary for.

```
relay_domains = $mydestination, secondary.example.org
```

mynetworks   If you want to relay outbound mail from your local network, you must list that network in this parameter. Set this value carefully to avoid becoming a spam relay. Multiple networks can be separated by commas.

```
mynetworks = 10.1.2.0/24, 127.0.0.0/8
```

alias_maps   Postfix supports the same aliases table that Sendmail uses. Red Hat points this to **/etc/postfix/aliases** to avoid stomping on your Sendmail configuration. If you want to use your existing **aliases** file, you'll want to specify it here. The format of this variable takes one additional value, however. Unlike Sendmail, Postfix supports more than one method of indexing the contents of your **aliases** file, and so you have to specify which database format you want to use. You can also specify more than one source, and they will be consulted in the order listed.

```
alias_maps = hash:/etc/aliases, nis:mail.aliases
```

alias_database   This designates alias maps that Postfix has control over. This is different from the preceding setting in that **alias_maps** lists all the sources that Postfix should consult when resolving aliases, while **alias_database** lists all the sources that should be rebuilt when you run the **newaliases** command.

```
alias_database = hash:/etc/aliases
```

virtual_maps   Postfix supports a virtual table that works much like an enhanced aliases table. See the upcoming section "Aliases, Virtual Domains, and Fancy Addresses" for more details.

```
virtual_map = hash:/etc/postfix/aliases
```

canonical_maps   Canonical maps can be used to map fancy e-mail addresses to real users. See the upcoming section "Aliases, Virtual Domains, and Fancy Addresses" for more details.

```
canonical_maps = hash:/etc/postfix/canonical
```

mail_spool_directory   If you're planning to use traditional user mailboxes in **/var/spool/mail**, you probably don't have to touch this variable at all. If you want to move that spool directory to another location, you can specify it here:

```
mail_spool_directory = /var/mail
```

home_mailbox   If you want to avoid having a communal mail spool directory for all users, another option is to drop mail into each user's home directory. This variable specifies the name of the mailbox within each user's home directory.

```
home_mailbox = Mailbox
```

mailbox_command   Yet another option is to pass locally delivered mail to an external service. The Procmail program is a popular choice.

```
mailbox_command = /usr/bin/procmail
```

header_checks   This is a spam-control option that lets you blacklist known spammers. The value will be the name of a regular expression lookup table that can be matched against the headers of incoming e-mail. We aren't going to delve into the world of regular expressions here; but if you think you could use this feature, it'll be worth your time to read through the documentation.

```
header_checks = regexp:/etc/postfix/my-blacklist-file
```

Applying Your Changes

Unlike Sendmail, you won't need to stop and restart your Postfix server when you make changes to the configuration. You will want to let the server know that a change has been made. You can accomplish this with the same script you use to start or stop Postfix by hand, except that you specify the **reload** option.

```
[root@mail postfix]# /etc/init.d/postfix reload
```

Aliases, Virtual Domains, and Fancy Addresses

As part of Postfix's goal of being a drop-in replacement for Sendmail, it fully supports a Sendmail-style **aliases** file. Changes to the **aliases** file can be compiled into a format that Postfix understands using the **newaliases** command, just as you would under Sendmail. (You can also use the native **postalias** command for the same purpose if you prefer.) In addition, Postfix supports a few other lookup tables that seem similar at first glance.

The virtual table is used to map users in virtual domains to local usernames. There are two main modes for supporting virtual domains in Postfix. The first is Sendmail-style virtual domains. In this mode, virtual domains are listed in the **mydestination** variable and are treated the same as local domains. Specifically all users' aliases and mailing lists will exist in all domains. For example, if you had an entry in **main.cf** like this

```
mydestination = $mydomain, example.com, example.net
```

then the local user **bob** would receive e-mail sent to **bob@example.com** and **bob@example.net**. If these were supposed to go to different users, then you could set up the **virtual** table to deliver the right mail to the right user. The **virtual** table will handle entries of the form *alias username* in much the same way that the **aliases** table does, and you may wish to place some of those entries here if they're related to other virtual domain information contained in the **virtual** table. (There's a definite advantage to reducing the number of files you have to read to find related entries.) The real advantage of the **virtual** table, however, is when you want to map *alias@virtual.domain.com* to a local user.

```
#  map bob's alias here just to keep all of bob's entries in one place
dinosaur bob
#  let's separate each of bob's mail to the correct recipient
bob@example.com bob1
bob@example.net robert
```

The second form of virtual domain handling is known as Postfix-style virtual domains. With this style, the virtual domains each have their own nonoverlapping namespace. Local users, aliases, and mailing lists don't automatically exist in the virtual domains. The only addresses that exist in the virtual domain will be those explicitly listed in the **virtual** table. For this style you don't list the domain in **main.cf**, but instead you have a rather unusual entry in the **virtual** table. Remember that the **virtual** table (like most of the map tables in Postfix) consists of *key = value* pairs separated by white space. A key in the form of *virtual.domain.com* will indicate that Postfix should deliver to usernames indicated for that domain even though it's absent from the **mydestinations** variable. The value specified with that key in the **virtual** table entry is irrelevant for anything other than making the line a valid entry, which leaves you with a rather strange-looking entry of the form *virtual.domain.com anything*. (This is a limitation of the hashing that gets performed on these tables rather than a direct limitation of Postfix.)

```
# we only want one address to be valid in this domain
example.org foobar
info@example.org marketing@example.com
```

TIP

It's tempting to want to indent sections like the one in the last example. Attempting to do so will break your virtual aliasing, however. Postfix treats any line that begins with white space as a continuation of the previous line. This does come in handy, however, when you have some really long entries to break up.

The other lookup map that seems suspiciously like **aliases** is the **canonical** table. The **canonical** table is used for mapping a user to a fancier e-mail address.

```
boss@example.com pointy.haired.boss@example.com
```

This looks a lot like the **aliases** file at first glance, but the **aliases** entries only guide a message to the correct recipient. Entries in the **canonical** table will be used to rewrite all the headers in an e-mail, including outgoing e-mails. In the preceding example, if boss sends an e-mail out, all references to her real username including From: headers and the envelope sender address are rewritten to appear as if they came from **pointy.haired.boss@example.com**. A popular use is to map *username* to *Firstname.Lastname@example.com*.

Updating Map Tables

Just as changes to the **aliases** files need to be compiled into a format the MTA can understand, so do the other lookup tables. You'll notice that most of the lookup tables in **/etc/postfix** have a corresponding **.db** file. (Other formats are possible, but we won't cover that here. Read the Postfix documentation if you want more details about using a different data format.) The command for compiling a table after you've changed one of the files is **postmap**, and you'll need to tell it which file you've just changed. For example:

```
[root@mail postfix]# postmap /etc/postfix/virtual
```

Typically, Postfix will start using the new values in a few minutes without any further assistance. If you want to tell Postfix to look for the change right away, however, send it the **reload** command.

```
[root@mail postfix]# /etc/init.d/postfix reload
```

Remember always to use the **postmap** command after any changes you make to the lookup tables, just as you would use **newaliases** (or **postalias**) after changing the **aliases** table.

Additional Reading

Even though Postfix is not nearly as complicated or as configurable as Sendmail can be, there is still a lot more to it than we can cover in this brief module. The included documentation is pretty good at getting you through most configurations; but if you're considering particularly complex or advanced configurations, you may consider looking at one of the books available. Richard Blum's book *Postfix* (Sam's Publishing, 1999) is a thorough examination of implementing Postfix on a Linux server. Other, more generic, administration texts may have a chapter or two on Postfix but won't have the depth that a dedicated book will provide.

Progress Check

1. When Sendmail or Postfix accepts a message, it immediately places it:

   A. In a storage file

   B. In a mailbox

   C. In a queue

   D. All of the above

CRITICAL SKILL
13.4 Solving Real-Life MTA Issues

E-mail is usually the most often used service at any site. Given the frequency of its usage, you are bound to run across situations where you need to get some more information about the mail system. Although many of these situations aren't MTA-specific problems (disk and network problems are more often the culprit), knowing about some of the peripheral tools that come with Sendmail and Postfix can be helpful in debugging the problem.

In this section, we go over some of these tools and instances where you might use them.

mailq

When Sendmail or Postfix accepts a message, it immediately places it in a queue. This allows these programs to accept mail faster than it can be processed—a feature crucial in high-volume environments.

Because a message gets queued for later processing, users can experience delays between sending a message and having it arrive at the destination. After all, there may be several queues between the sender and receiver, each with its own queue length, processing time, and bandwidth limitations—not to mention an inability to connect to the next server in the chain.

In any case, it is important to find out how long the queue is for your server. This can be done using the **mailq** command, like so:

```
[root@mail /root]# mailq
```

This will list all of the messages in the queue, their message identifiers, whom the messages are from, and where they are going.

---

1. **C.** Messages are immediately placed in a queue.

Is the MTA Running?

When mail seems especially slow, you may begin to question whether the mail server is even running! The quick way to check this from any host on your network is to try to **telnet** to your mail server's port 25, as we did in the first section of this module. You should see a response from the server in a timely manner. If the response is slow, it may be due to a few possibilities:

● *The mail server is very busy.* This can be checked by logging into the server and running the **uptime** command. This command will report three values representing the current load average, the load average from 5 minutes ago, and the load average from 15 minutes ago. These load averages represent the average number of processes that are waiting for CPU time. A value higher than 1.0 for each processor means that the system has more things to do than it has time to do, and that means a process has to wait longer before the CPU can get to it. Periodic bursts are normal, but a sustained load significantly greater than the number of processors means you need to look into a bigger, faster mail server solution.

● *The mail server is so busy that the MTA has stopped processing messages.* This is a way of keeping the server from spiraling out of control. Instead of increasing the load by processing messages, it simply queues them for future processing. This can make mail delivery times substantially greater.

● *DNS is broken.* A typical sign of a broken DNS is *extremely* sluggish performance even though the load average is near zero. Delays of minutes before server response are caused by the server making a DNS request and then having to wait until the timeout before giving up on resolving a host name or an IP address and continuing on the best it can. In the case of message delivery, this means leaving the messages in the queue until DNS is repaired.

● *Out of spool space.* An MTA can be quickly stumped when it runs out of disk space. A quick check of disk space allocation with the **df** command can reveal if this is a problem. (See Module 6 for more information on **df**.)

If the MTA is not responding at all, you may need to restart it. To do so, try using the startup script. For Sendmail:

```
[root@mail /root]# /etc/init.d/sendmail restart
```

For Postfix:

```
[root@mail /root]# /etc/init.d/postfix restart
```

Where Are Queues and Spools Kept?

Sendmail maintains only one queue, and that queue is stored in **/var/spool/mqueue** under Linux. The mail spools themselves are stored in **/var/spool/mail**, where each user's mail spool is stored in a file with his login name. Postfix also delivers to **/var/spool/mail** by default, but it uses subdirectories under **/var/spool/postfix** for each of its queues. (You shouldn't have any trouble matching subdirectories to their respective queue by name.)

Because the mail spool and mail queue can grow due to inputs from users and people outside of your network, it is possible that file space can get used up unexpectedly, causing the MTA to get grumpy about not having enough working space. For this reason, it is a good idea to keep these spools on their own partitions or otherwise carefully adjust their quotas (especially **/var/spool/mail**). By doing so, users outside your network cannot bring the entire system down if they send messages that are too large; they can only affect the MTA's behavior.

Of course, it doesn't matter how or why the disk space is no longer available: If it isn't there, programs will not behave. So be sure to check for this problem when you notice abnormal behavior.

How to Remove Entries from the Queue

In your life as a system administrator, you are bound to run across a user who insists on doing something incredibly crazy—like mailing a 100MB movie file halfway around the world to his buddy who has a very slow connection.

In those cases, you may need to purge an entry in the queue by hand. To do this, you need to first find out which message is the troublemaker. Sometimes it is obvious, as in the case of a large message in a queue directory or **mailq**—the file size will stick out like a sore thumb. Other times, it takes a bit of intuition when looking at the mail queue with the **mailq** command. A message that has been sitting in the queue for days is unlikely to be delivered successfully and may need to be purged because it is causing the MTA to spend time needlessly trying to send it. In either case, you should see the message ID number. (This is the mixture of letters and numbers you see in the **mailq** output.)

With Sendmail you will just remove the offending message directly from the queue. You should be able to identify the message in the mail queue by looking for the filenames that contain the message ID. A quick way to do that is

```
[root@mail /root]# ls -l /var/spool/mqueue | grep messageID
```

where *messageID* is the ID number of the troublemaker.

With this information, you are ready to remove the file from the queue. Simply use the **rm** command to remove the queue file. For example, if you found that message ID RAA735 was causing problems, you could remove that message like so:

```
[root@mail /root]# rm -i /var/spool/mqueue/*RAA735
```

Don't forget to check to see if Sendmail is still working correctly after you do this. If Sendmail happened to be working on that particular piece of mail when you removed it, Sendmail may need to be restarted.

Postfix provides a slightly smoother alternative with its **postsuper** tool, and you don't even need to restart the server. The **postsuper** utility provides a number of options for queue management beyond just deleting messages, and you're encouraged to read its documentation. For our purposes here, we're just going to use the **–d** option to remove the offending message.

```
[root@mail /root]# postsuper -d F1B441D01A8
```

Flushing the Queue

If your site loses connectivity with the rest of the world (for instance, if your Internet connection is down), your MTA will quietly accept messages from your users for future delivery. When Sendmail or Postfix finds that it can once again contact other servers, it will quietly start processing the queue itself.

In most instances, you can leave the server alone and let it work through its queue. Sendmail and Postfix both do a great job of regulating themselves and making sure they process their queue without overwhelming the system or your network connection.

However, there are instances when you need the MTA to hurry up and get through its queue faster. One instance might be if the outage was long enough that it would take your MTA unreasonably long to process the queue at its normal rate, especially given the flood of new e-mails coming into the system. (After all, other sites trying to contact your mail server patiently queued their messages until they could connect. Now they're all delivering!)

In these instances, you need the MTA to churn through its queue much more quickly. To force Sendmail or Postfix to process its queue immediately, use the **sendmail –q** option. For example, to ask Sendmail to process its queue, you would enter

```
[root@mail /root]# sendmail -q
```

With Postfix you can either enter that exact same command, or use the native **postqueue** method. (Either command runs the exact same program.)

```
[root@mail /root]# postqueue -f
```

Mail Logging

Keeping track of how much mail goes through your system is useful for two reasons: It provides a history of activity on the server, which is good when trying to track down bad behavior on the system (or bad behavior of the users on the system!); and it provides a quantifiable metric for the demands placed on the server. The latter is especially handy when trying to convince those with the spending power that a server needs to be upgraded!

Both Sendmail and Postfix use the **syslog** mechanism for logging its activity. Red Hat comes preconfigured so that any messages sent to **syslog** that are from the mailer are placed into a separate log file called **/var/log/maillog**. (You may want to check your **/etc/syslog.conf** file if you wish to make changes to that setup.) On a system that passes hundreds to thousands of messages a day, these logs will grow very quickly. Be sure you have a method of rotating your logs. (Red Hat Linux comes preconfigured to do this.) If you are doing this by hand, simply rename the current log file to something new (for example, **maillog** to **maillog.old**), and then create an empty new file called **maillog**. Once the files are set up, restart the **syslog** daemon so that it knows what to do with the new files.

Module Summary

In this module, you learned how to configure the Sendmail mail server, as well as the alternative Postfix mail server. Although it can appear intimidating at first, it doesn't take long to gain an understanding of how an MTA works.

The most important things you should carry with you from this module are

- Sendmail is configured using a series of macros written in the M4 macro language. Most of these macros come predefined with the Sendmail source code.

- All of the features you need are specified, using these macros, into a file that ends with a **.mc** extension. Once this macro file is created, you "compile" it into the final configuration file, **/etc/mail/sendmail.cf**.

- A configuration file outside of **/etc/mail/sendmail.cf** is usually stored as a straight text file and then converted into a database format so that Sendmail can refer to it quickly.

- There are very few binaries related to Sendmail. The server application itself is a single file called **sendmail**, located at **/usr/sbin/sendmail**.

- Postfix attempts to provide a secure, fast replacement for Sendmail that is easy to configure. Postfix attempts to be compatible with Sendmail where it makes the most sense.

- Postfix is made up of a number of small, single-purpose programs that all work together to send mail. Postfix tries to limit the privileges given to most of those processes.

- The **/etc/postfix/main.cf** file is where the majority of configuration is performed, but you may occasionally have a reason to make adjustments in **/etc/postfix/master.cf** as well.

As we've seen, Sendmail is one very powerful program that can handle some remarkable configurations. If your configuration needs are not quite as extreme, Postfix provides an alternative option with a focus on security.

✓ Module 13 Mastery Check

1. What does the SMTP protocol do?

2. Which of the following possible SMTP commands requires the parameter of the e-mail address of the sender of the e-mail:

   A. helo

   B. mail from:

   C. rcpt to:

   D. data

   E. All of the above

3. Explain the difference between SMTP and IMAP?

4. Why is Sendmail more secure now than in previous versions?

5. What is the most common mail delivery agent?

6. What are the three basic components of mail service?

7. What character signifies the start of a string definition?

   A. A single quote (')

   B. A double quote (")

   C. A backtick (`)

   D. All of the above

8. The _____ variable in Postfix specifies what gets appended to unqualified usernames.

9. Where are the queues and spools kept?

10. True or False? Both Sendmail and Postfix use the **syslog** mechanism for logging their activity.

11. True or False? Sendmail and Postfix use the M4 language to configure themselves.

Module 14

Using POP and IMAP for E-Mail Retrieval

n the old days of the Internet, there were a few large UNIX (or other multiuser time sharing) machines that were always connected. Your e-mail got delivered to a mailbox on whichever machine it was that you typically used, and when you logged in you could run e-mail client software directly on the local mailbox. Then gradually, the old methods gave way to the new upstarts. Many PCs and Macs, for example, were not even running UNIX, which represented remote users that were only infrequently connected. This required some rethinking of how e-mail retrieval worked; and new protocols were created, including the Post Office Protocol (POP) and the Internet Message Access Protocol (IMAP).

NOTE

POP and IMAP are protocols for receiving mail from a server for reading. Sending outgoing mail still requires your e-mail client to use SMTP to talk to other mail servers. For more information on SMTP, refer to Module 13.

CRITICAL SKILL
14.1 Comparing the POP and IMAP Protocols

The Post Office Protocol, or POP for short, was the first widespread attempt to solve remote e-mail access, and is still in common use today. For users on machines that either aren't capable of running a full Simple Mail Transfer Protocol (SMTP) server, or are not permanently connected, a "Post Office" machine is used. The Post Office machine is connected to the Internet full time and receives e-mail on behalf of its users via SMTP. E-mail is delivered to a local mailbox on the Post Office machine just as if it was the user's login machine under the old model. Sometime later the user connects from her workstation and the user's e-mail client will contact the POP server on the Post Office machine and transfer any waiting messages to the user's workstation. The user can then read or otherwise process e-mail on her local workstation. This very simple system has served e-mail users well for many years.

The Internet Message Access Protocol, or IMAP for short, was designed to overcome some of the limitations of POP. Instead of transferring all e-mail to the client's workstation, IMAP retains the users e-mail on the server. The method used by POP is sometimes referred to as "offline" because once you've transferred your waiting messages, you could theoretically be disconnected while you read through your e-mail. The method primarily used with IMAP is considered "online" because it expects that you're connected the whole time that you're reading your e-mail. (This should not be confused with the sort of permanent connection expected from the old style SMTP-only model. IMAP is still a "connect when you want to read mail" type of protocol.) When you connect to an IMAP server, the headers of your new e-mail are downloaded to your e-mail client. As you browse through your new mail and select a message to read, the body of that message is transferred to your workstation. Deletion, read/unread status, and other status flags are synced back to the server. If this all seems like a more complicated protocol, it is. But only the server and client programs need to worry about that, and it results in some definite advantages over using POP.

Advantages of IMAP over POP

IMAP is a superset of POP, and it can do everything that POP can (though it doesn't always do it in quite the same way). In addition, IMAP introduces a number of new features.

It's becoming increasingly more common for people to use more than one computer. One at work, another at home, and perhaps a laptop when traveling. POP doesn't lend itself well to checking mail on multiple machines, and your e-mail ends up spread out across all the different clients machines. Some POP clients try to partially account for this by having a "leave mail on server" option; but POP's inability to indicate read messages means downloading the same message multiple times, which is an inelegant solution at best. IMAP was designed with multiple clients in mind. Since the status of which e-mails have been read and which haven't (among other things) is stored on the server, you don't have to wade through seen messages even if you're connecting from a client machine you've never used before.

Conservation of bandwidth may not seem like a huge deal in this day of ubiquitous high-speed connections, until you're traveling and have your laptop on a slow dial-up connection and that 10MB attachment isn't nearly as critical as the information in the messages immediately after it. Because IMAP only transfers the actual messages you request, you don't have to wait for (or pay for) downloading spam, large attachments, or other e-mails you're not immediately interested in. You can even download some MIME parts of a message and not others.

Multiple mail folders allow for better organization of your saved mail. While POP accounts for only a single INBOX, IMAP allows for multiple mailbox folders to be manipulated directly from your mail client. You can create, delete, rename and transfer or copy messages between different mailbox folders. Depending on you server setup, you may even be able to have hierarchical mailbox folders that contain both messages and other mailbox subfolders within them.

IMAP supports shared folders. Not only can more than one person access the shared folders, but IMAP will manage concurrent access. This is particularly useful for role-based accounts, such as a **webmaster@*example*.com** or a help desk support mailbox, which may be accessed by multiple administrators.

Searching is built in to the protocol. Searches are performed on the server side to again reduce the amount of data that needs to be transferred. Matching result sets are then returned to the client for selection. This can be a huge win for large archival mailboxes, and shouldn't be underestimated.

While a POP client that is kept online for long periods of time can be configured to poll the server occasionally for new mail, IMAP avoids this problem altogether. A client connected to an IMAP server can be notified directly of any new mail that arrives.

Just in case the basic status indicators of read/unread, answered, important, and so on, aren't sufficient for your needs, IMAP allows user-defined Status flags. This means you can mark messages in ways that are uniquely meaningful to you and your needs.

IMAP can even support non–e-mail applications. For example, you may set up a documentation repository as an anonymous read-only IMAP folder. This could then be available to your entire company and accessed with any IMAP client.

When the client performs its initial handshake with the server, it negotiates which capabilities are supported by both machines, and which are not. This structure makes it easy to add optional features to IMAP gradually, without a major upheaval to the protocol. For example, during the initial handshake, clients and servers can negotiate support for start-TLS–style encrypted connections, something that was not in the original IMAP specification.

For those with pay-by-the-minute Internet connections, or other specialized circumstances that make POP's "offline" mode seem attractive, IMAP offers a "disconnected" mode. In this mode, all new mail is copied down to the client for local processing. Deletions and status changes are kept recorded by the client, and synced back to the server next time you connect. While this trades off connection time for bandwidth usage, it will still maintain many of the other advantages of using IMAP, such as a centralized mail store accessible by multiple clients, or custom status flags.

Ask the Expert

Q: Wow! IMAP sounds so cool. Are there any issues to consider when installing all these features?

A: Even though the IMAP specification supports a large set of features, you're still dependant on these features being implemented in your server and client software. Not all client software supports all of the more esoteric or recently proposed features of the protocol. Some server or mailbox configurations can also limit the features available for use.

TIP

Even though IMAP often involves less bandwidth than blindly downloading everything, its download-as-you-go approach can make it seem more sluggish to former POP users that are used to a "hit the Get Mail button, go for coffee, then come back and read mail" approach. These users may be good candidates to start with "disconnected" mode.

CRITICAL SKILL

14.2 Installing POP and IMAP on Red Hat

In order to install IMAP on Red Hat 8, look for the Mail Server option in the Servers section, either in the **redhat-config-packages** tool or during the initial install. If you're installing by hand, you'll want the **imap-2001a** rpm. Now, if you want to install a POP server, look for the Mail Servers option in the **redhat-config-packages** tool, or install the **imap-2001a** rpm. No, really. That's not a typo, the POP server also comes with the IMAP package. Both servers come as part of the University of Washington's IMAP server package (http://www.washington.edu/imap/). This is actually somewhat of an advantage if you're running both services on the same box, as we'll see later.

Configuring the POP and IMAP Servers

There is a file entitled **CONFIG** that comes with the UW IMAP distribution, and its contents begin with the following words: "The IMAP and POP3 servers are plug-and-play on standard UNIX systems. There is no special configuration needed. Please ignore all rumors to the effect that you need to create an IMAP configuration file." The remainder of the **CONFIG** file goes on to describe some minor source code tweaks that are possible at compile time, all of which are well beyond the scope of this book. (Perhaps, this will start to make up for having to deal with Sendmail's configuration in the last chapter.) So, now that you have your POP and IMAP servers configured, you probably want to make sure they start up when needed.

Starting the POP and IMAP Servers

Once again, starting the POP and IMAP servers when they're needed is the job of our old friend **xinetd**. As usual, you can adjust whether these services start in **xinetd** from the **redhat-config-services** tool (the Services option under the System Tools submenu). There are four entries in the GUI tool that are of interest to us: **imap**, **imaps**, **ipop3**, and **ipop2**. The **imap** entry, as you may have guessed, turns on the IMAP server. If you want to use **imap** wrapped in an encrypted SSL connection, then you'll want to enable the **imaps** option. POP version 3 is the newest and most used version of the POP protocol, and it can be enabled with the **ipop3** selection. The remaining selection, **ipop2**, refers to the much older version 2 of the POP protocol, and there is probably very little, if any, reason to turn it on.

If you're looking to enable these services by hand, you'll be looking for the corresponding service names in the **/etc/xinetd.d/** directory. For each of the four service entries you should find the corresponding **xinetd** file, and edit it. You'll want to change the **disable** directive to No for each service you want to have started. The resulting file should look similar to the following example:

```
# default: off
# description: The IMAPS service allows remote users to access their mail \
#              using an IMAP client with SSL support such as Netscape \
#              Communicator or fetchmail.
service imaps
{
        disable = no
        socket_type             = stream
        wait                    = no
        user                    = root
        server                  = /usr/sbin/imapd
        log_on_success  += HOST DURATION
        log_on_failure  += HOST
}
```

CRITICAL SKILL

14.3 # Reading Mail with Telnet

Each request to and response from the POP or IMAP server is in cleartext ASCII (not counting SSL enabled connections), which means it's very easy for us to test the functionality of a POP or IMAP server using Telnet. (This is especially useful when you have users who claim that the "mail server is broken," although the real problem is that they're unfamiliar with the system.) Like SMTP servers, POP or IMAP servers can be controlled with a very short list of commands.

To get a look at the most common commands, let's walk through the process of connecting to a server, logging in, listing available messages, reading one, and then dropping the connection.

 NOTE

We'll use the **telnet** command to read mail only as a means of seeing the actual commands being sent to the server and the server's responses. You'll rarely want to do this in the real world. Once the server has been set up, you can read your mail with a mail reader such as Evolution or Pine. Knowing the actual POP3 or IMAP commands is helpful, however, when you need to track down problems reported by your users. Often, it's easier to use Telnet to check quickly whether the POP or IMAP server is responding than to try to use a real mail client—especially if you suspect the mail client has a bug!

Reading POP Mail with Telnet

We begin by **telnet**ing to the POP3 server. The POP server listens for connections by default on port 110. From a command prompt, type (substituting your own values where applicable)

```
[root@redbox /root]# telnet pop3server.domain.com  110
```

The POP3 server responds as follows:

```
+OK POP3 pop3server.domain.com v2001.78rh server ready.
```

The server is now waiting for you to give it a command. (Don't worry that you don't see a prompt.) First, you want to log in, and then tell the server your login name via the **user** command:

```
user yourlogin
```

Here *yourlogin* is, of course, your login ID. The server responds with

```
+OK User name accepted, password please
```

Now tell the server your password, using the **pass** command:

CAUTION

The system will echo back your password, so don't do this if you have people looking over your shoulder!

```
pass yourpassword
```

where *yourpassword* is your password. The server responds with

```
+OK  Mailbox open, X messages
```

where *X* represents the number of messages in your mailbox. You're now logged in and can issue commands to read your mail.

Begin by listing the messages that are waiting, using the **list** command. Type

```
list
```

and the server will list all the messages in your mailbox. The first column represents the message number, and the second column represents the size of the message. The response for my mailbox currently looks like this:

```
+OK Mailbox scan listing follows
1 644
2 2303
3 2334
4 1599
5 2558
.
```

Now let's try to actually read a message, using the **retr** command. The only parameter that **retr** needs is the message number to read. We'll start simple: To read message 1, type

```
retr 1
```

The server responds with something like this:

```
+OK 644 octets
Return-Path: <michael@domain.com>
Delivered-To: michael@redbox.domain.com
Received: by redbox.domain.com (Postfix) with ESMTP id 2010D1ED3A
         for <michael@domain.com>; Mon, 28 Oct 2002 22:32:38 -0700
```

```
From: "michael" <michael@redbox.domain.com>
Message-Id: <20021028055811.E50CD1D017B @redbox.domain.com>
Subject: important message for you
Date: Mon, 28 Oct 2002 08:05:52 -0700 (PDT)
User-Agent: Gnus/5.090007 XEmacs/21.4 Linux/RedHat
MIME-Version: 1.0
Content-Type: text/plain; charset=us-ascii
Status: RO

Act now! Don't delay. Time could be running out. As seen on TV.
.
```

Normally, mail readers do us the service of parsing out the information and presenting it in a much more readable form than what you see here. But this example gives you an idea of whom the message is coming from, the subject line, and the date.

At this point, you can issue as many **retr** commands as you'd like to read your messages. Reading a message does not cause it to be deleted. To delete the message, you must explicitly issue a **dele** command, with a parameter specifying the message number. Now that we've read message 1, we can delete it by typing

```
dele 1
```

which gets this response from the server:

```
+OK Message deleted.
```

Like the **retr** command, you can issue the **dele** command as many times as necessary. The messages aren't actually deleted until you quit the session using the **quit** command.

```
quit
+OK Sayonara
```

And that's it. Now you know enough about POP3 commands to be able to test servers and, if really necessary, to read your mail without a proper mail reader!

Reading IMAP Mail with Telnet

Now we can do something very similar for testing your IMAP server. The IMAP server should be listening on port 143. Of course it goes without saying that we're dealing with the non-SSL wrapped version here. One difference in talking to IMAP servers is that every command you send is prefixed with a unique tag. Nearly any alphanumeric string can be used, but a simple ascending number is easiest for our purposes. After the server responds with any data associated with the request, it will include the same tag in its response so that you can always match up a particular response with the command it's responding to. The intervening data is considered "untagged" and is prefixed with an asterisk (*). The server's response to tagged commands should begin with OK if the command succeeded, NO if the command was attempted but failed, or BAD if the server didn't understand your request.

Let's start our example by **telnet**ing in.

```
[root@redbox /root]# telnet imap.domain.com 143
```

This should bring back a response from the server similar to the following:

```
* OK [CAPABILITY IMAP4REV1 LOGIN-REFERRALS STARTTLS AUTH=LOGIN] redbox.domain.com
IMAP4rev1 2001.315rh at Mon, 28 Oct 2002 01:07:15 -0700 (PDT)
```

You may notice the list in between the square brackets. This shows the capabilities that the server is willing to perform in its current state. This list will change over the course of the session. For example, there are more things the server is willing to do for you after you've logged in. The format for logging in is

login *username password*

Don't forget to prepend a unique tag, as we mentioned above (we're going to use numbers starting with 01 for the example).

```
01 login username password
```

When placing in your own *username* and *password*, remember the caution about the password being displayed as plain text. Your response should look similar to the following.

```
01 OK [CAPABILITY IMAP4REV1 IDLE NAMESPACE MAILBOX-REFERRALS SCAN SORT THREAD=REFERENCES
THREAD=ORDEREDSUBJECT MULTIAPPEND] User username authenticated
```

Since IMAP is capable of dealing with multiple mailboxes, we now have to specify which one we're interested in. The default mailbox for a user is called INBOX.

```
02 select INBOX
```

This should make INBOX the active target for commands that deal with messages within a mailbox. This will also return some information about the mailbox you've just selected.

```
* 5 EXISTS
* 1 RECENT
* OK [UIDVALIDITY 1031489397] UID validity status
* OK [UIDNEXT 6] Predicted next UID
* FLAGS (\Answered \Flagged \Deleted \Draft \Seen)
* OK [PERMANENTFLAGS (\* \Answered \Flagged \Deleted \Draft \Seen)] Permanent flags
```

```
* OK [UNSEEN 4] first unseen message in /var/spool/mail/michael
02 OK [READ-WRITE] SELECT completed
```

Among other things, this indicates that there are five messages in this mailbox (EXISTS), that one of them is new since the last time we checked mail (RECENT), and that first unread message has the ID of 4 (UNSEEN 4). Now let's retrieve a message:

```
03 fetch 4 rfc822
```

Remember that IMAP allows for retrieving portions of a message, such as just the header, or just one of many MIME parts. As a result, there are a good number of options for the **fetch** command. For our purposes here, we've specified to fetch message **4** in **rfc822** format, because this will give us nearly all of the message, and it's the closest thing to a human readable response from the available options.

```
* 4 FETCH (RFC822 {632}
Return-Path: <michael@domain.com>
Delivered-To: michael@redbox.domain.com
Received: by redbox.domain.com (Postfix) with ESMTP id 2010D1ED3A
        for <michael@domain.com>; Mon, 28 Oct 2002 22:32:38 -0700
To: michael@domain.com
From: "michael" <michael@redbox.domain.com>
Message-Id: <20021028055811.E50CD1D017B @redbox.domain.com>
Subject: important message for you
Date: Mon, 28 Oct 2002 08:05:52 -0700 (PDT)
User-Agent: Gnus/5.090007 XEmacs/21.4 Linux/RedHat
MIME-Version: 1.0
Content-Type: text/plain; charset=us-ascii
Status: RO

Act now! Don't delay. Time could be running out. As seen on TV.
FLAGS (\Seen))
03 OK FETCH completed
```

You'll notice at the end, the server also lets you know that it has marked this message as having been seen. Finally we can log out.

```
04 logout
* BYE redbox.domain.com IMAP4rev1 server terminating connection
04 OK LOGOUT completed
```

This barely scratches the surface of what IMAP is capable of, but is should be sufficient to test that your server is actually working as expected.

Testing IMAP Using Telnet

That was a lot of text and a lot of concepts to swallow. It's actually pretty easy to do, though. In this project we'll walk you through checking your IMAP server with Telnet quickly and easily. You'll need to have password authentication enabled on your IMAP server for this to work correctly. Remember to replace your actual information for the italicized items in the example steps.

Step by Step

1. First, **telnet** into your mail server on port 143.

   ```
   telnet my-mail-server.my-domain.com
   ```

2. Login to the IMAP server now using your real username and password. Remember to prefix each IMAP command with a unique prefix. We've used two-digit numbers in the example below, but any unique string will work.

   ```
   01 login my-username my-password
   ```

3. Make INBOX the active target for the following steps. You can use any mail folder that you know is on your system here, but INBOX is guaranteed to exist by default and is adequate for testing the server.

   ```
   02 select INBOX
   ```

4. If you've made it this far, you probably have a pretty good indication that IMAP is responding properly (or not, as the case may be). Just for thoroughness, we'll continue and actually pull a message up. Use the **fetch** command, followed by a message number, and the specifier **rfc822**. You don't really have to use the **rfc822** flag, but it'll make the output much easier to read.

   ```
   03 fetch 03
   ```

5. Log out when you're finished.

   ```
   04 logout
   ```

Project Summary

Hopefully, even if the explanatory text in the preceding section seemed complex, this project should illustrate how simple the actual steps involved are. Although you'll never want to actually read your mail like this, it's an invaluable tool for locating problems in your mail system.

Progress Check

1. List three distinct advantages of IMAP.

2. Why is knowing how to check your mail with Telnet important?

CRITICAL SKILL
14.4 Noticing IMAP Quirks

Since IMAP only specifies how messages get from the server to your e-mail client, it relies on other standards for some parts of its interaction with the outside world. Most notably, IMAP makes no attempt to define how mail is stored on the server. Instead, the server supports many of the common mail storage formats found on UNIX systems. Since none of these formats were designed with IMAP in mind, this sometimes makes for additional complications or places restrictions on what the server is capable of. For example, flat-file–based formats, such as the venerable mbox format, are incapable of supporting hierarchal subfolders. If you have concerns about these types of issues, you may want to pay special attention when creating additional mailbox folders to make sure the results are what you expected.

Don't Delete This Message

IMAP tracks a fair amount of additional information about e-mail messages and mailboxes that wasn't built in to the design of most mailbox storage formats. The server uses a number of tricks to make this possible, such as adding additional headers to messages to track status flags. One such trick is storing some mailbox information in the first message in the mailspool. Under certain circumstances this may require creating a special bogus "message" for such tracking. When this is done, the fake message will contain the Subject line "DON'T DELETE THIS MESSAGE—FOLDER INTERNAL DATA" and a message body that explains its purpose. You won't ever see this message in your IMAP client, but you may stumble across it if you examine your mailspool with other tools.

---

1. The distinct advantages of IMAP are that it allows
   - Multiple mail folders
   - Shared folders
   - Conservation of bandwidth
   - Consistent view of mail when accessed from multiple clients
   - Notification of new mail
   - Searching, which is built in to the protocol

2. Knowing how to check your mail with Telnet will help you find any bugs in your system that might have been reported to you, and that is especially useful in distinguishing server problems from client/user problems.

Most annoying is that some POP servers will unknowingly deliver this message along with the rest of your e-mail, thus removing it from the mailbox forcing IMAP to recreate it from scratch (resetting all values). Fortunately, the **ipop3** daemon that comes with the UW IMAP package is aware of this bogus file and will leave it intact. Although this is convenient when an IMAP user does hit her mailbox with a POP client one day, it's generally a good idea to keep users from switching back and forth between protocols. POP and IMAP approaches to dealing with your mailspool are different enough that they really don't play well together on the same mailbox.

TIP

Another feature of IMAP that can confuse some POP converts, if it's not totally hidden by their mail client, is the **delete** flag. We've talked before about the various flags that IMAP can attach to a message. When you delete a message with IMAP, it doesn't actually remove the message from the server; instead, it just marks it with a flag, in case you want to undelete it later. To actually remove deleted messages, you have to "**expunge**" your mailbox. Expunge is often presented as an "empty the trash" metaphor on many mail clients.

CRITICAL SKILL
14.5 Performing Special Authentication

One of the fundamental security flaws in both the basic IMAP and POP protocols is that they transmit passwords in cleartext over the network. This may seem acceptable on a small local area network (LAN), where you have tighter control of where the network can be tapped and by whom. However, the same can never be said about the Internet. Passwords in cleartext pose a real problem for remote users, who may need to access their e-mail from several remote locations.

To get around this security risk, a challenge/response mechanism is used to authenticate the user. For POP, the system used is called Authenticated POP, or APOP. For IMAP the Challenge-Response Authentication Mechanism is used with the MD5 digest algorithm, or CRAM-MD5 for short. Both systems use the same general idea. The server sends a generated string as a challenge, and the client combines this challenge with the password and generates an encrypted response using the MD5 algorithm. The server compares this response with its own calculated value, and if they match the client is authenticated.

Thankfully, the process of administering the APOP and CRAM-MD5 services is relatively straightforward. For the user, there is only the need to use a mail reader that supports the authentication method. No special work need otherwise be done.

The real disadvantage of using these mechanisms is that both the server and the client must keep plaintext copies of the password database—unlike the standard UNIX passwd/shadow scheme, which only stores encrypted passwords.

NOTE

Using one of these mechanisms will help protect your passwords from snoopers, but will do nothing to protect your data. E-mail itself will still transfer across the network as cleartext. If you wish to protect your e-mail data as well, it's recommended that you wrap your session with SSL. Enable the **imaps** server and turn on SSL support in your client. The POP server can also be set up to use SSL, but virtually no client support exists for this.

Setting Up APOP/CRAM-MD5 Users

Both APOP and CRAM-MD5 draw on the same password database for authentication. You'll need to create a simple text file named **/etc/cram-md5.pwd** and add a line for each user. The format is to have the username at the beginning of the line, followed by a single TAB and then the user's plaintext password. Comment lines begin with a pound symbol (#).

```
# database of user passwords for CRAM-MD5 authentication.
# remember to separate username and password with a single TAB
character
michael worUdgacWicA
amy     IbnisJark2
anie    FomwamEyt
```

The password need not be the same as their UNIX login password (if there is one); in fact, it's safer if it's not. If a user has an entry in the **cram-md5.pwd** file, that password will be used even for cleartext logins. All users must still have entries in **/etc/paswd** for **uid** and home directory lookups.

CAUTION

It's extremely important to protect this file. It contains unencrypted plain text passwords for all users' mail accounts. Performing a **chmod 0400 /etc/cram-md5.pwd** is strongly encouraged.

Module Summary

In this chapter, we examined and compared the POP and IMAP protocols for retrieving e-mail. The University of Washington's POP and IMAP servers are exceedingly simple to set up and use. Just like any other software, however, you'll want to keep up with security postings and patches.

Once you have the server running, the one important issue to address is authentication via cleartext passwords. The UW POP and IMAP servers support the use of APOP and CRAM-MD5, respectively, each of which should address this issue. In addition, you may want to consider running SSL-enabled IMAP. Most modern mail clients have support for these features.

For additional reading on the subject of IMAP, I would recommend *Managing IMAP* by Dianna Mullet and Kevin Mullet (O'Reilly & Associates, 2000).

In the case of POP, there isn't a heck of a lot more to know. RFC 1939, which documents the POP protocol, can be found at http://ietf.org/rfc/rfc1939.txt.

✓ Module 14 Mastery Check

1. What are POP and IMAP?

2. Which of the following send outgoing mail?

   A. POP

   B. IMAP

   C. SMTP

   D. All of the above

   E. A and B

3. Which of the following will work even if you don't have a permanent connection to the Internet?

   A. POP

   B. IMAP

   C. SMTP

   D. All of the above

   E. A and B

4. True or False? IMAP only transfers the actual messages you request.

5. True or False? Any client connected to the POP server can be sent a notification from the server of any new mail that arrives after the initial connection.

6. True or False? One way to install POP is to install the **imap-2001a** rpm.

7. Why should you be wary of using POP and IMAP together?

8. What is the name of the challenge/response mechanism that is available for POP to use?

9. What is the name of the challenge/response mechanism that is available for IMAP to use?

10. What is the disadvantage of using challenge/response mechanisms?

The answers to Module 14 Mastery Check can be found in the Appendix.

Module 15

The Secure Shell (SSH)

437

One unfortunate side effect of bringing your computer onto a public network (such as the Internet) is that, at one point or another, some folks out there will try to break into your system. Why? Because they stupidly think it's cool to do so. This is obviously not a good thing. If you think this won't happen to you, think again. If you have a server online, someone *will* try to get into it.

In Module 9, we discussed techniques for securing your Linux system, all of which are designed to limit remote access to your system to the bare essentials. But at some point, most systems administrators find the need to perform their duties from a remote site. Telnet is woefully insecure, because it transmits the entire session (logins, passwords, and all) in cleartext. How can you reap the benefits of a truly multiuser system if you can't securely log in to it?

To tackle the issue of remote login versus session security, a package called Secure Shell (SSH) was developed. It allows users to connect to a remote server just as they would using Telnet, except that the session is 100 percent encrypted. Someone using a packet sniffer merely sees garbage going by. Should they capture the garbage, decrypting it could take decades.

In this chapter, we'll take a very brief look at cryptography as it pertains to remote logins. Then we'll examine the versions of SSH and how to configure and use SSH.

Ask the Expert

Q: **What is cleartext and why is it important?**

A: Cleartext is data that is unencrypted. In any system, when passwords get sent over the line in cleartext, a packet sniffer may determine what a user's password is. This is especially problematic if that user is root!

Q: **Doesn't Windows handle this better? It has network logins that are encrypted by default, right?**

A: After authentication, the Primary Domain Controller (PDC) returns a token to the NT client for use in lieu of having to reauthenticate every time a user wants to access a network share that is used for the entire life of the login. Thus, if a packet sniffer captures the token, it can be reissued to a thief to gain access to servers. In short, a cracker doesn't even need the password to break in. In the immortal words of Homer J. Simpson, "D'OH!" Furthermore, it wasn't until Windows 2000 that the ability to log in to a host that is not in your local area network became available. Unfortunately, Windows 2000 only offers this feature through the insecure Telnet protocol.

NOTE

Most early versions of SSH were commercial products. The version we're going to use is OpenSSH, which has been completely implemented as free software by the folks from the OpenBSD group. The term "Open" refers to the fact that the source code is open to public inspection, and the resulting binaries can be used in both commercial and noncommercial use. For more information, see Critical Skill section 15.2, "Exploring SSH Versions and Distributions."

CRITICAL SKILL

15.1 Discussing Public Key Cryptography

Let me begin with a disclaimer: I am not a cryptography expert, and this chapter barely touches on cryptography and the depths it can cover. What you will find here is a general discussion along with some references to good books that approach the topic more thoroughly.

Secure Shell relies on a technology called *public key cryptography*. It works similarly to a safe deposit box at the bank: you need two keys in order to open the box. In the case of public key cryptography, you need two mathematical keys: a public one and a private one. Your public key can be published on a public web page, printed on a T-shirt, or posted on a billboard in the busiest part of town. Anyone who asks for it can have a copy of it. On the other hand, your private key must be protected to the best of your ability. It is this piece of information that makes the data you want to encrypt truly secure. Every public key/private key combination is unique.

The actual process of encrypting data with public key cryptography and sending it from one person to the next requires several steps. Let's watch Alice and Bob go through this process one step at a time in the following illustrations.

1. Alice fetches Bob's public key.

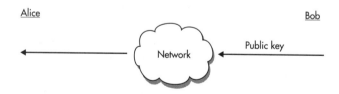

2. Alice uses Bob's public key along with her private key to encrypt the data.

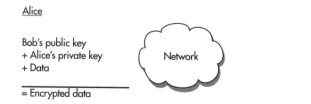

3. Alice sends the encrypted data to Bob.

4. Bob fetches Alice's public key.

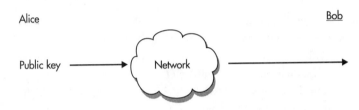

5. Bob uses Alice's public key along with his private key to decrypt the data.

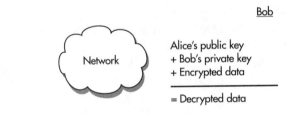

Looking at these steps, notice that at no point was the secret key sent over the network. Also note that once the data was encrypted with Bob's public key and Alice's private key, the only pair of keys that could decrypt it were Bob's private key and Alice's public key. Thus, if someone intercepted the data in the middle of the transmission, they wouldn't be able to decrypt the data without the private keys.

The ability to encrypt or decrypt with a given private key can also be taken as some measure of proof of identity. Public/private key pairs are used by SSH to identify both users and other machines.

To make things even more interesting, SSH regularly changes its private key so that the data stream gets encrypted differently every few minutes. Thus, even if someone happened to figure out the key for a transmission, that miracle would only be valid for a few minutes until the keys changed again.

Key Characteristics

So what exactly is a key? Essentially, a key is a very large number that has specific mathematical properties. Whether someone can break an encryption scheme depends on their ability to find out what the key is. Thus, the larger the key is, the harder it will be to discover it.

Low-grade encryption has 56 bits. This means there are 2^{56} possible keys (each being a unique number). To give you a sense of scale, 2^{32} (that is, the size of a 32-bit number) is equal to 4 billion, 2^{48} is equal to 256 trillion, and 2^{56} is equal to 65,536 trillion. While this seems like a significant number of possibilities, it has been demonstrated that a loose network of PCs dedicated to iterating through every possibility could conceivably break a low-grade encryption code in less than a month. In 1998, the Electronic Frontier Foundation (EFF) published designs for a (then) $250,000 computer capable of cracking 56-bit keys in a few seconds to demonstrate the need for higher-grade encryption. If $250,000 seems like a lot of money to you, think of the potential for credit card fraud if someone successfully used that computer for that purpose!

NOTE

The EFF published the aforementioned designs in an effort to convince the U.S. government that their laws that limited the export of cryptography software were sorely outdated and hurting the U.S., since so many companies were being forced to work in other countries. This finally paid off in 2000, when the laws were loosened up enough to allow the export of higher-grade cryptography. (Unfortunately, most of the companies doing cryptography work already were exporting their engineering to other countries.)

For a key to be sufficiently difficult to break, experts suggest no fewer than 128 bits. Because every extra bit effectively doubles the number of possibilities, 128 bits offers a genuine challenge. And if you want to really make the encryption solid, a key size of 512 bits or higher is recommended. SSH can use up to 1,024 bits to encrypt your data. The trade-off to using higher-bit encryption is that it requires more math processing power for the computer to churn through in order to validate a key. This takes time and therefore makes the authentication process a touch slower, but most feel this is a worthy bargain.

NOTE

It is a matter of public record that the National Security Agency (NSA), as well as the Chinese, the Russians, and the French, can break keys up to 1,024 bits (and probably higher). However, technology with enough processing power for such mathematics costs nearly $1 billion (USD). Plans exist that could break 1,024-bit encryption in seconds, although the price tags are still high. While 1,024-bit encryption will keep you safe from your average credit-card thieves, even 2,048 bits may not be enough to lock you down completely.

Cryptography References

SSH supports a variety of encryption algorithms. Public key encryption happens to be the most interesting and widely used method of performing encryption from site to site and is arguably the most secure. If you want to learn more about cryptography, here are some good books to look into:

- *PGP*, by Simon Garfinkel (O'Reilly and Associates, 1994)

- *Applied Cryptography: Protocols, Algorithms, and Source Code in C,* Second Edition, by Bruce Schneier (John Wiley & Sons, 1995)

- *SSH, The Secure Shell: The Definitive Guide,* by Daniel J. Barrett and Richard Silverman (O'Reilly and Associates, 2001)

- *Cryptography and Network Security: Principles and Practice,* Second Edition, by William Stallings (Prentice Hall, 1998)

The PGP book is specific to the PGP program, but it also contains a hefty amount of history and an excellent collection of general cryptography tutorials. The Applied Cryptography book might be a bit overwhelming to many, especially nonprogrammers, but it very successfully explains how actual cryptographic algorithms work. (This text is considered a bible among cypherheads.) Cryptography and network security are heavier on principles than on practice, but they're useful if you're interested in the theoretical aspects of cryptography rather than the code itself. The Secure Shell (SSH) is an in depth look at the SSH client and server for UNIX, Windows, and Macintosh—including installation, configuration, and troubleshooting, as well as the use of SSH for tunneling as a way to secure other applications.

CRITICAL SKILL
15.2 Exploring SSH Versions and Distributions

Until the middle of 2000, the U.S. government made it illegal to develop cryptographic software in the U.S. and export it to other countries. Since the laws have been relaxed, much more software has become available for export outside the U.S.

In addition to this change, there has been a lot of development of the OpenSSH package. This is a completely free implementation of the Secure Shell standard in terms of both the source code and its use. The first version of SSH was available under a fairly open license, but as time went by, it gradually became more and more restrictive. At that time, the SSH that was made available by DataFellows restricted free use of SSH to noncommercial activities. Commercial activities required that licenses be purchased. In early 1999, however, one of the old versions with its less-restrictive license resurfaced. Some of the folks from the OpenBSD project jumped on the chance to fork a totally free version of Secure Shell, and the OpenSSH project was born. More significant than the cost of the package is the fact that the source code to the package is completely open. This is important to cryptographic software, for it allows peers to examine the source code and make sure that there are not holes that may allow crackers to break the security. (In other words, serious cryptographers do not rely on security through obscurity.)

Because the SSH protocol has become an Internet Engineering Task Force (IETF) standard, there are also other developers actively working on SSH clients for other operating systems. There are many Windows, Macintosh, and Palm Pilot clients, in addition to the standard UNIX clients. You can find the version of OpenSSH that we will be discussing at http://www .openssh.org. You can find other implementations of SSH at http://www.ssh.com.

NOTE

As of this writing, we are up to SSH protocol version 2. Unfortunately, many non-UNIX clients support or enable only the SSH version 1 protocol. Thus it is important that your server side understand both versions. You should default to version 2 whenever possible because it is considered to be more secure than version 1. Use version 1 only in situations where version 2 is not available. If you plan to use OpenSSH, don't worry. It supports both.

OpenSSH and OpenBSD

The OpenSSH project is being spearheaded by the OpenBSD team. OpenBSD is a version of the BSD operating system (another UNIX variant) that strives for the best security of any operating system available. A quick trip to the OpenBSD web site (http://www.openbsd.org) shows that the organization has had only one remote hole in its default installation in nearly six years. Unfortunately, this comes at the expense of not having the most whiz-bang, feature-rich tools available, as the organization requires that anything added to its distribution get audited for security first. This has made OpenBSD a very popular foundation for applications such as firewalls.

The core of the OpenSSH package is considered part of the OpenBSD project and is, therefore, very simple and specific to the OpenBSD operating system. To make OpenSSH available to other operating systems, a separate group exists to make OpenSSH portable whenever new releases occur. Typically, this takes only a few days from the original release. (For instance, OpenSSH 3.4 and OpenSSH 3.4p1, the portable version—each containing support for both SSH1 and SSH2—were released the same day.)

NOTE

Since we are targeting Linux, we will use the versions suffixed with a *p* indicating that it has been ported.

Alternative Vendors for SSH Clients

Every day, many of you work with heterogeneous environments. It's impossible to ignore all of the Windows 95/98/NT, Solaris, and Mac OS systems out there. In order to allow these folks to work with a real operating system, they need some mechanism for logging in from remote sites. And because Telnet is not secure, SSH provides us with an answer.

Thankfully, DataFellows is not the only organization that makes an SSH client for non-UNIX operating systems. Here is a quick rundown of several SSH clients:

- **MacSSH for Mac OS (http://pro.wanadoo.fr/chombier/MacSSH/SSH_ info.html)** MacSSH is an award-winning Open Source SSH1 and SSH2 client for Macintosh published by the Free Software Foundation under the GNU General Public License (GPL). It is well documented and currently supported on Mac OS 7.5x and higher.

- **MindTerm (http://www.mindbright.se/mindterm)** MindTerm is a multiplatform, pure-Java implementation of an SSH client. It supports both SSH1 and SSH2 protocols and runs on Java-enabled browsers (specifically Netscape 4.7x and Internet Explorer 5.x). It is supported on Win 9x/NT/ME/2000, Mac OS 7+, Linux (kernel version not noted in documentation for UNIX environments), Solaris, and HP-UX. User licenses are charged on a per-user basis, and the application is distributed as binary only (sorry, no source code). Still, if a non-OS–dependent SSH client is needed, this may be useful.

- **TTSSH (http://www.zip.com.au/~roca/ttssh.html)** This package, a Windows client, is a Dynamic Link Library (DLL) extension to the TerraTerm Pro terminal emulator. Both the DLL and main package are free. It supports up to version 1.5 of the SSH protocol; however, the package maintainer does not intend to support SSH2 due to time constraints.

- **SecureCRT (http://www.vandyke.com/products/securecrt/index.html)** SecureCRT is a widely used commercial Windows SSH client that implements a Windows terminal emulator user interface to support both SSH1 and SSH2. SecureCRT is quite popular and is a robust and feature-rich client, despite its per-license charges and closed-source distribution.

- **PuTTY (http://www.chiark.greenend.org.uk/~sgtatham/putty/)** PuTTY is a widely used free (open source) Windows SSH client supporting SSH1 and SSH2. It also provides Telnet and Xterm capabilities. PuTTY is a simple but stable and effective client.

- **Top Gun SSH for Palm OS (http://www.ai/~iang/TGssh/)** If you've just gotta have connectivity from your personal digital assistant (PDA), Top Gun SSH provides SSH1 and SSH2 for any Palm OS PDA with a TCP/IP stack.

- **SSH Telnet Client v1.0 for the RIM 957 Blackberry (http://www.airstreamws.com/ourproducts/sshtelnet.html)** This client supports SSH1 and SSH2, as well as standard Telnet for the Blackberry PDA.

- **sshCE for PocketPC/WinCE (http://movsoftware.com/sshce.htm)** sshCE supports SSH1.5 for PDAs running Windows CE.

The Weakest Link

You've probably heard of the saying, "You're only as secure as your weakest link." This particular saying has an extremely significant meaning when it comes to OpenSSH and securing your network: OpenSSH is only as secure as the weakest connection between the user and the server. This means that if a user runs **telnet** from host A to host B and then uses **SSH** to connect to host C, the entire connection can be monitored from the link between host A and host B. The fact that the link between host B and C is encrypted becomes irrelevant. Be sure to explain this to your users when you enable logins via SSH.

For this reason, security-minded network administrators disable **telnet** altogether. Taking the time to tighten down your network will be a waste of time if users **telnet** to a host across the Internet so they can **ssh** into your server. And more often than not, they won't have the slightest idea why this is really bad. Furthermore, security-minded network administrators keep up-to-date with root-exploits and published "holes" in SSH, and apply patches as they are released.

CRITICAL SKILL
15.3 Performing Server Setup

The good news is that OpenSSH is a default part of the base Red Hat install. In all likelihood, it's already on your system. If for some strange reason it's not, you'll want to look for three packages. These are **openssh**, **openssh-server**, and **openssh-clients**. If you're working in X most of the time, you may also want either **openssh-askpass** or **openssh-askpass-gnome**. You should have both the client program **ssh** as well as the server daemon **sshd**, along with some helper tools that we'll discuss shortly.

Ask the Expert

Q: Won't using something like Telnet with Kerberos also protect my login session?

A: Kerberized Telnet will save your password from being passed to the server as cleartext, but it will not encrypt your session. Actions performed during your login session may also provide crackers with information useful for cracking your system. Although kerberized Telnet is arguably safer than plain Telnet, it's still nowhere near as secure as a fully encrypted session.

Server Startup and Shutdown

OpenSSH should already be enabled in the startup scripts, but you can double-check this by pulling up **redhat-config-services** (Services under the Server Settings submenu) and verifying that **sshd** is checked for the appropriate runlevel. Alternatively, you could look for the **S55sshd** symlink in the appropriate **rc** directory.

```
[root@brain root]# ls /etc/rc*.d/S55sshd
/etc/rc2.d/S55sshd  /etc/rc3.d/S55sshd  /etc/rc4.d/S55sshd  /etc/rc5.d/S55sshd
```

Configuration

The default configuration of SSH is pretty usable right out of the box. Digging into the configuration files will serve to reveal a number of cryptographic and security options, including changing what cryptography algorithms are used, whose subtleties are well beyond what we can convey here. But before you get scared away from the configuration options altogether, there are a few settings that may be worth examining.

If you look in the **/etc/ssh** directory among the many key files you'll find two configuration files, **ssh_config** and **sshd_config**. These contain the global options for using the **ssh** client from this machine and options for using the **ssh** server daemon, respectively. Comment lines begin with a pound symbol (#), and options are specified as key-value pairs separated by either white space or optional white space with a single equal sign (=).

SSH Client Configuration

The **ssh_config** file specifies global defaults for all users invoking **ssh** outbound from this machine. Users can of course override these defaults with settings in their own personal **config** file or with command-line options. Some of the more interesting options include:

```
ForwardAgent yes
```

This controls whether the connection to **ssh-agent** is forwarded to the remote machine for chaining to the next **ssh** connection. See the description of **ssh-agent** in the next section for more information. The default is "no."

```
ForwardX11 yes
```

With X11 forwarding turned on, you can start X-based applications on the machine you're shelled into and have them forwarded across the encrypted connection to display on your local workstation. This comes in handy if firewalls and/or security concerns would prevent you from using normal X forwarding. There is a corresponding server-side option that must also be enabled for this to work. The default is "no."

```
Protocol 2,1
```

Here you can limit which protocol version(s) are attempted and in which order. Multiple entries can be separated with a comma. For example, the default value of "2,1" means that protocol version 2 is tried first, and if that fails, version 1 is then tried.

```
StrictHostKeyChecking yes
```

Every machine running an **sshd** server has its own unique identity in the form of a public/private key pair. The public keys of machines you log in to are kept in a file, usually at **~/.ssh/known_hosts**. Every time you connect to a machine, its identity is compared to the key you have on file, and any discrepancy is flagged as a warning of something being possibly wrong. This configuration option comes into play when you try to connect to a host that doesn't have a key in your **known_hosts** file. If StrictHostKeyChecking is set to "yes," the server will refuse to connect. If it's set to "no," the server will blindly add the new key to your **known_hosts** file. The default setting is "ask," in which unknown keys will be added only if you approve the operation first.

```
Host shells*
```

This option will try to match its value with the host name you typed on the command line treating * and ? as wildcard characters. If the match is successful, all the options listed between here and the next Host directive will be applied. This is a powerful mechanism for setting nondefault options for specific hosts you log in to frequently and saving you a lot of typing at the command line.

```
HostName shells.example.com
```

Here you can specify the host name that you really want to log in to. When used in conjunction with the Host directive, this will allow you to set up abbreviations or aliases for commonly used machines. Just in case you want to connect to a nonstandard port on the remote machine.

```
Port 22
```

This is again probably most useful in conjunction with a Host directive. Default is the standard **SSH** port of 22.

```
User michael
```

Here's your chance to specify a username other than the one you're logged in to the current machine as. This is essentially the same as using the –l option on the command line.

The value of those last few options as entries in a **config** file might make more sense if you see them in context with a Host example.

```
# my personal ssh_config file
# first some global options
ForwardX11 yes
ForwardAgent yes

# ok, now some servers that I use a lot
# my setup for the host I call "brain"
Host brain
HostName shellserver.some.long.domain.com
User mt

# now for "pinky"
Host pinky*
HostName pinky.example.org
# what admin put this one on the wrong port?
Port 23
User Michael
```

Progress Check

1. What is the default port used by SSH?

2. How do you specify in the **ssh_config** file which protocol version to use?

3. What should you specify in **ssh_config** to allow X clients to forward back across the connection?

---

1. Port 22 is used by default.

2. Protocol *number* will specify the protocol version attempted on a connection. Multiple protocols can be separated by commas and will be tried in the order listed.

3. ForwardX11 yes.

SSHD Server Configuration

The **sshd** server has an even greater number of options than the **ssh** client, but again many of them are cryptographic or security subtleties with reasonable defaults. Nevertheless, some of the ones that you may wish to pay attention to are as follows:

```
Port 22
```

This specifies the port number that **sshd** listens on. The default is the standard **SSH** port, 22. Multiple options of this type are permitted if you want to listen for connections on more than one port.

```
ListenAddress 10.1.2.3:23
```

The default is for **sshd** to listen to all IP addresses assigned to the machine on port 22, or whichever ports you specified with the Port directive just mentioned. If you need to restrict which addresses are listened to, or use different ports on different addresses, then the **ListenAddress** option is for you. If you supply only an IP address value, then all the ports selected with the Port directive (or the default 22) will be used. Again, you can use this more than once.

```
Protocol 2,1
```

This is where you can specify which versions of the protocol the server will speak to. It specifies the protocol versions **sshd** should support. The default of "2,1" will support both versions of the protocol, and connections will be made based on which version the client tries to use first.

```
PasswordAuthentication yes
```

The **sshd** server is capable of authenticating users based on either their password, or based on a public/private key pair. This option specifies whether password-based authentication is allowed. The default is "yes." To specify whether or not public key authorization is allowed, you would use the following:

```
PubkeyAuthentication yes
```

Once again, the default is "yes." Note that this option only applies if protocol version 2 is being used.

```
PermitRootLogin yes
```

This specifies whether root can log in using **ssh**. The default is "yes," but some sites prefer to disallow this (by specifying "no") for an added measure of security. There is also the possibility of setting this to **without-password**, which restricts root to public authentication, even if other users are allowed password-based logins. Finally there is a **forced-commands-only** option that can be handy for administrative scripts, as it allows root to execute certain commands through **ssh**, but not log in interactively.

```
DenyUsers john sally *@windows.domain.com
```

The default is to allow all users with accounts on the machine to log in. You can restrict some of them from being able to log in with the **DenyUsers** option. The wildcard characters * and ? can be used, and you can also specify *user@host* for more fine-grained denials.

```
AllowUsers amy anie rachel@gorey
```

This is similar to the **DenyUsers** option, except that it reverses the sense. The default becomes to deny users except those specified here.

```
X11Forwarding yes
```

Enabling this allows users logged in to this machine to launch X-based applications and have them tunneled down the encrypted connection for display on their local workstations. Turning this off doesn't really add any security, as there are other ways to accomplish the same task. Nevertheless the default is "no."

```
StrictModes yes
```

Specifies whether **sshd** should check file modes and ownership of the user's files and home directory. If the permissions are too lax, **sshd** will deny them login. The default for this is "yes."

```
UsePrivilegeSeparation yes
```

Privilege separation is a new feature in OpenSSH. It tries to enhance security by having an unprivileged process listen for connections, and only after the user is authenticated does a process get created with the permissions of the authenticated user. The idea is to limit how much damage can be caused if a new vulnerability is discovered in the listening process. Although this is a really cool idea, it doesn't play well with some **pam** configurations. The default is "yes."

Progress Check

1. True or False? By default, root can log in through SSH just like any other user.

2. How would you set up **sshd_config** to allow users to only log in with public key authentication and not allow password-based logins?

3. If you want to limit which interfaces on the machine **sshd** will listen to, what would you add to **sshd_config**?

CRITICAL SKILL

15.4 Using Secure Shell (SSH)

With the **ssh** daemon started, you can simply use the **ssh** client to log in to a remote machine in the same manner that you would with Telnet. When you log in to a host for the first time, **ssh** may store the public key of the host in the **~.ssh/known_hosts** file, depending on the value you set for StrictHostKeyChecking, as mentioned earlier. If you're using the default of "ask," you will be prompted as follows:

```
[michael@brain michael]$ ssh pinky
The authenticity of host 'shells (10.1.1.2)' can't be established.
RSA key fingerprint is 60:ff:1b:c0:d8:b9:56:37:9b:30:44:7d:3f:93:d1:38.
Are you sure you want to continue connecting (yes/no)?
```

The main difference between **ssh** and Telnet is that **ssh** will not prompt you for your login, but instead will assume that you have the same login across both machines, which is typically the case. However, if you need to use a different login (for instance, if you are logged in as yourself on one host and want to **ssh** to another and log in to a different account), all you need to do is use either the **–l username** option or the *user@hostname* syntax. For example, if I want to log in to the machine shells.myhost.com from brain, I would do:

```
[michael@brain michael]$ ssh mt@shells.myhost.com
```

---

1. False. You must change the default in **sshd_config** if you want to allow root login.
2. PubkeyAuthentication, Yes; PasswordAuthentication, No
3. ListenAddress *ip-address*

and I would be prompted with a password prompt from shells for the user **mt**'s password. If you just want to log in to the remote host without having to change your login, you can simply run **ssh**, like so:

```
[michael@brain michael]$ ssh shells.myhost.com
```

If the host shells is within the same domain, or a domain specified in your **/etc/resolv.conf** file (see Module 10), the domain name does not need to be specified and you can log in as follows:

```
[michael@brain michael]# ssh shells
```

Public Key Logins

If you tried logging in to a machine just now by following the preceding examples, you were probably able to type in your password where prompted and gain access to the box. However, to get the most benefit and maximum security from SSH, you should really be taking advantage of its public key capabilities.

The first thing you'll need to do is create a key pair on the machine you'll be **ssh**ing from. The **ssh-keygen** program is used for this purpose. While **ssh-keygen** has a number of options, the only one that's required is the key type. Three types of keys can be generated from this program. The **rsa1** type is what you'll want if you expect to be accessing servers that use SSH protocol version 1. If you're going to access a server using SSH protocol version 2, you can select between the **rsa** and **dsa** key types. (Both are equally useful for our needs.) There's no reason you can't generate all three types, and even more if you want to represent different roles or identities. For now we'll just generate a **dsa** key pair.

```
[michael@pinky michael]$ ssh-keygen -t dsa
Generating public/private dsa key pair.
Enter file in which to save the key (/home/michael/.ssh/id_dsa):
Enter passphrase (empty for no passphrase):
Enter same passphrase again:
Your identification has been saved in /home/michael/.ssh/id_dsa.
Your public key has been saved in /home/michael/.ssh/id_dsa.pub.
The key fingerprint is:
f9:d3:0e:73:d8:5b:ad:01:72:46:fd:34:2b:8f:16:dd michael@pinky
```

The default file locations that it suggests are the correct choices.

A passphrase can be chosen to further protect your key. A passphrase is like a password, only typically much longer, like a sentence instead of a word. The same rules for picking good passwords apply here: plain English sentences are very bad choices. You can skip the passphrase, but then your key is only being protected by UNIX file permissions. That is not recommended unless you're absolutely certain that no one else will log in to your machine. Whatever you do, don't forget your passphrase. If you do, there's no way to recover your key, and you'll have to generate a new key from scratch.

Finally, you'll see that two files have been generated in your **.ssh** directory. The **id_dsa** file contains your private key and should be closely guarded. (You'll notice that it was created with permissions to be readable only by the owner.) The other file, **id_dsa.pub**, contains your public key, as you may have guessed. The contents of this file are the part that you can print on T-shirts and post on highway billboards, if it tickles your fancy, without jeopardizing your security. A better use for it, however, is to copy it to all the machines you plan to access via **ssh**, and append it to the **~/.ssh/authorized_keys** (creating it if it doesn't already exist). The key you copy into the **authorized_keys** file should be one long line—long enough that lines may wrap when displayed in your text editor. That's fine as long as no extraneous carriage returns are introduced. It must appear as one long line to the system.

Now if everything is set up correctly, keys are copied to where they belong, and all your file permissions are correct, you should be able to **ssh** into the target machine using public key cryptography. If you just rushed out and tried it, you're probably back here now thinking to yourself "Wow, that's cool that it worked, but I had to type in my passphrase to unlock my private key. Did I just trade in having to type my password for having to type an even longer passphrase?" Don't give up yet, though: we have an agent on our side.

The **ssh-agent** program keeps track of your SSH keys for you. The **ssh-agent** is designed to run at the beginning of your session, from **gdm**, or from your **.xsession** or your **.bash_profile**, or similar. If your entire session is a child process of **ssh-agent**, then any **ssh** connections you initiate will have the settings necessary to take advantage of the agent. If you want to just test out the agent quickly in a shell, you can run **ssh-agent** directly, and then execute the commands that it prints out. (These will set some environment variables to enable SSH to find the agent.) This will only be good for the shell you ran this in, but it'll be enough for a quick test without requiring you to log out and back in. Now for the final step, run the program **ssh-add** supplying the path to your private key. (Repeat the **ssh-add** step for any additional keys you wish to load into the agent.) Now you should be able to securely **ssh** anywhere that knows your public key without having to type your password or passphrase every time.

```
[michael@pinky michael]$ ssh-agent
SSH_AUTH_SOCK=/tmp/ssh-XXGC1yFo/agent.16056; export SSH_AUTH_SOCK;
SSH_AGENT_PID=16057; export SSH_AGENT_PID;
echo Agent pid 16057;
[michael@pinky michael]$ SSH_AUTH_SOCK=/tmp/ssh-XXGC1yFo/agent. 056;
[michael@pinky michael]$ export SSH_AUTH_SOCK;
[michael@pinky michael]$ SSH_AGENT_PID=16057; export SSH_AGENT_PID;
[michael@pinky michael]$ ssh-add .ssh/id_dsa
```

```
Enter passphrase for .ssh/id_dsa:
Identity added: .ssh/id_dsa (.ssh/id_dsa)
[michael@pinky michael]$ ssh brain
Last login: Sun Oct 27 21:43:19 2002 from localhost.localdomain
[michael@brain michael]$
```

Applications Related to SSH

The OpenSSH package actually comes with some additional programs that use the same encryption technology, such as Secure Copy Protocol (SCP) and Secure FTP.

The **scp** command is meant as a secure replacement for the **rcp** command, which allows you to do remote copies from one host to another. The most significant problem with the **rcp** command is that users tend to arrange their remote-access settings to allow far too much access into your system. To help mitigate this, instruct users to use the **scp** command instead. The format of **scp** is identical to **rcp**, so users shouldn't have problems with this transition. For example, if I'm logged in to shells as user **michael** and I want to copy the **amy.jpg** file from **brain**, I would type:

```
[michael@shells michael]$ scp michael@brain:amy.jpg /home/michael/images/
```

For SSH servers running protocol version 2, Secure FTP also allows you to copy files between hosts without transferring files or passwords in cleartext, only this time it mimics an FTP client, which may be more familiar for some users.

```
[michael@shells michael]$ sftp brain
Connecting to localhost...
sftp> cd pix
sftp> ls
drwxr-xr-x   54 michael   michael     3312 Sep  9 18:47 .
drwxr-xr-x   19 michael   users        712 Aug  5 23:34 ..
-rw-r--r--    1 michael   michael    14873 Jan  7  2002 safetux.jpg
-rw-r--r--    1 michael   michael    74378 Jan  4  2002 amy.jpg
-rw-r--r--    1 michael   michael    47558 May 21 17:05 wrongmuppet.jpg
sftp> get amy.jpg
Fetching /home/michael/pix/amy.jpg to amy.jpg
sftp> exit
```

Module Summary

The Secure Shell tool is a superior replacement to Telnet for remote logins. Adopting the OpenSSH package will put you in the company of many other sites that are disabling Telnet access altogether and allowing only OpenSSH access through their firewalls. Given the wide-open nature of the Internet, this change isn't an unreasonable thing to ask of your users.

Here are the key issues to keep in mind when you consider Secure Shell:

- SSH is very easy to set up and use.

- Replacing Telnet with SSH requires no significant learning curve.

- SSH exists on many platforms, not just UNIX.

- Without SSH, you are exposing your system to potential network attacks in which crackers can sniff passwords right off your Internet connections.

In closing, let me remind you that using OpenSSH doesn't make your system secure immediately. There is no replacement for a set of good security practices. Following the lessons from Module 9, you should disable all unnecessary services on any system that is exposed to networks that are not trusted (such as the Internet); allow only those services that are absolutely necessary. And that means that if you're running SSH, you should disable Telnet, **rlogin**, and **rsh**.

✓

Module 15 Mastery Check

1. If data is encrypted with a _____ key, it can only be decrypted with the corresponding _____ key.

2. What is SSH and what does it do?

3. If a cracker is using a sniffer (or similar tool) on a network connection, how will an SSH session appear to him?

4. True or False? Your public key can be given out to anyone at all, without compromising your security.

5. True or False? The fewer bits a key has, the harder it will be for a cracker to break it with a brute-force approach.

6. Why is open source software particularly important to security and security-related programs such as OpenSSH?

7. True or False? Installing SSH and disabling Telnet is sufficient to protect a server.

8. What does "strict mode" do when specified in **sshd_config**?

9. What program would you use to generate a key pair for yourself?

10. Name a utility program bundled with SSH that will allow you to securely copy files.

Part IV

Intranet Services

Module 16

Network File System (NFS)

The Network File System (NFS) concept is somewhat similar to that of Windows NT's disk sharing in that it allows you to attach to a disk and work with it as if it were a local drive—a very handy tool for sharing files or a large disk with coworkers. (Often, it's handy for both.)

Aside from their similar roles, there are some important differences between NFS and NT shares that require different approaches to their management. The tools that you use to control network drives are (of course) different, as well. In this module, we discuss those differences; however, the primary focus of the module is to show you how to deploy NFS in the Linux environment.

CRITICAL SKILL
16.1 # Examining the Mechanics of NFS

Module 7 covered the process of mounting and unmounting file systems. The same idea applies to NFS, except each mount request is qualified with the server from which the disk share is coming. Of course, the server must be configured to allow the requested partition to be shared with a client.

Let's look at an example. Making an NFS mount request for **/export/home** from the server gandalf, so that the share appears locally as the **/home** directory, is done as follows:

```
[root@frodo /root]# mount gandalf:/export/home /home
```

Assuming that the command was run from the host named frodo, all of the users on frodo would be able to view the contents of **/home** as if it were just another directory. Linux would take care of making all of the network requests to the server.

Remote procedure calls (RPCs) are responsible for handling the requests between the client and server. RPC technology provides a standard mechanism for any RPC client to contact the server and find out to which service the calls should be directed. Thus, whenever a service wants to make itself available on a server, it must register itself with the RPC service manager, portmapper. Portmapper tells the client where the actual service is located on the server.

Mounting and Accessing a Partition

Several steps are involved in a client's request to mount a server's partition:

1. The client contacts the server's portmapper to find out which network port is assigned as the NFS mount service.

2. The client contacts the mount service and requests to mount a partition. The mount service checks to see if the client has permission to mount the requested partition. (Permission for a client to mount a partition is based on the **/etc/exports** file.) If the client does have permission, the mount service returns an affirmative.

3. The client contacts the portmapper again, this time to find out on which port the NFS server is located. (Typically, this is port 2049.)

4. Whenever the client wants to make a request to the NFS server (for example, to read a directory), an RPC is sent to the NFS server.

5. When the client is done, it updates its own mount tables but doesn't inform the server.

NOTE

Notification to the server is unnecessary, because the server doesn't keep track of all clients that have mounted its file systems. Because the server doesn't maintain state information about clients and the clients don't maintain state information about the server, clients and servers can't tell the difference between a crashed system and a very slow system. Thus, if an NFS server is rebooted, all clients will automatically continue their operations with the server as soon as the server is back online.

Security Considerations for NFS

NFS was developed by Sun Microsystems, starting in the early 1980s, when network security was a much less visible issue than it has become today. Unfortunately, NFS is not a very secure method for sharing disks. The steps necessary to make NFS more secure are no different from those for securing any other system. The only catch is that you must be able to trust the users on the client system, especially the root user. If you're the root user on both the client and server, then there is a little less to worry about. The important thing in this case is to make sure non-root users don't become root—which is something you should be doing, anyway!

If you are in a situation where you cannot fully trust the person with whom you need to share a disk, it will be worth your time and effort to seek alternative methods of sharing resources (such as read-only sharing of the disk). Under no circumstances should you expose an NFS share to the Internet!

As always, stay up-to-date on the latest security bulletins coming from the Computer Emergency Response Team (CERT), at www.cert.org, and keep up with the all the patches from your distribution vendor.

Versions of NFS

NFS is not a static protocol. Standards committees have helped NFS evolve to take advantage of new technologies as well as changes in usage patterns. Today, the standards are up to version 3, with 4 in the works. Linux's NFS implementation has been known to lag behind the current standard, but this is showing signs of changing. Recent kernels fully support NFS versions 2 and 3 as a client, as well as support for running an NFS server (version 2 or 3) over the User Datagram Protocol (UDP). One of the new features introduced in version 3 was the ability to run over TCP, but Linux support for running a server over TCP is still considered experimental. Work is also being done at the University of Michigan to provide a reference implementation of NFS version 4 that runs on Linux (http://www.citi.umich.edu/projects/nfsv4/).

Enabling NFS

Red Hat comes with NFS installed by default. If for some reason you need to manually deal with it, the package name you're looking for is **nfs-utils**. Much of NFS is actually built in to your kernel, so what you're installing with that RPM is a collection of tools, daemons, and accessory programs that allow you to set up, manage, and use NFS mounts. That is why the package is called **nfs-utils** and not just **nfsd**.

If you want to run an NFS server, you'll want to look for the **nfs** option in the Service Configuration GUI tool (**redhat-config-services** if launched from the command line, or choose Services from the Server Settings submenu).

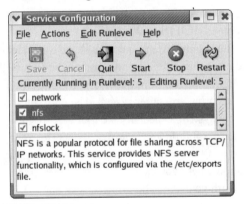

If you're adjusting the symlinks under **/etc/rc5.d/** by hand, then you'll probably want to use S60nfs or K20nfs.

If you aren't sure as to whether or not NFS is running, you can check by running **rpcinfo**, as follows:

```
[michael@gandalf michael]# rpcinfo -p
```

If NFS is running on your system, you'll see something like the following:

```
program vers proto   port
 100000    2   tcp    111  portmapper
 100000    2   udp    111  portmapper
 100024    1   udp  32768  status
 100024    1   tcp  32768  status
 391002    2   tcp  32769  sgi_fam
```

```
100011    1    udp    1021    rquotad
100011    2    udp    1021    rquotad
100011    1    tcp     600    rquotad
100011    2    tcp     600    rquotad
100003    2    udp    2049    nfs
100003    3    udp    2049    nfs
100021    1    udp   32771    nlockmgr
100021    3    udp   32771    nlockmgr
100021    4    udp   32771    nlockmgr
100005    1    udp   32772    mountd
100005    1    tcp   32793    mountd
100005    2    udp   32772    mountd
100005    2    tcp   32793    mountd
100005    3    udp   32772    mountd
100005    3    tcp   32793    mountd
```

If NFS isn't running on your system, the entries for **nfs** and **mountd** will be missing.

To start NFS without having to reboot, enter this command:

```
[root@gandalf /root]# /etc/init.d/nfs start
```

To stop NFS without having to shut down, enter this command:

```
[root@gandalf /root]# /etc/init.d/nfs stop
```

If you have NFS enabled for your runlevel, NFS will automatically start up every time you boot the system.

The Components of NFS

NFS under Linux is made up of five parts:

- **rpc.statd**   This daemon handles the file-locking issues between the client and the server.

- **rpc.quotad**   As its name suggests, **rpc.quotad** supplies the interface between NFS and the quota manager. Users will be held to the same restrictions regardless of whether they're working with their data through NFS.

- **rpc.mountd**   When a request to mount a partition is made, the **rpc.mountd** daemon takes care of verifying that the client has enough permission to make the request. This permission is stored in the **/etc/exports** file. (The upcoming "The /etc/exports Configuration File" section tells you more about the **/etc/exports** file.)

- **rpc.nfsd**   The main component to the NFS system, this process actually takes care of handling NFS requests.

- **rpc.lockd**   The **rpc.statd** daemon uses this daemon to handle lock recovery on crashed systems.

Ask the Expert

Q: So NFS is a user-space daemon, then? I thought I saw some kernel options for NFS?

A: The NFS server was originally a user-space process. That is, no special kernel support was necessary for it to work. With the introduction of the 2.2 kernel, an optional kernel mode NFS server was introduced, with critical parts of the process actually compiled into the kernel for performance reasons. Recently (particularly in 2.4 kernels) the user-space version of the NFS server has fallen by the wayside in favor of the kernel mode version. Because only critical parts of the server are compiled into the kernel, user-space daemons exist to handle the rest of the protocol.

Progress Check

1. What is the command to stop NFS without shutting the server down?

2. When a request to mount a partition is made, which file is consulted to determine access to the requested directory?

CRITICAL SKILL
16.3 Configuring NFS Servers

Setting up an NFS server is a two-step process. The first step is to create the **/etc/exports** file. This file defines which parts of your server's disk get shared with the rest of your network and the rules by which they get shared. (For example, is a client allowed only to read a partition or is it allowed to write to that partition?) The second step is to start the NFS server processes that read the **/etc/exports** file and follow the specifications. Pretty straightforward, isn't it?

TIP

For best security, you may also want to review your **/etc/hosts.allow** and **/etc/hosts.deny** files. See Module 9 for more information on **hosts.allow** and **hosts.deny**.

---

1. /etc/init.d/nfs stop.
2. The permission is stored in the **/etc/exports** file.

The /etc/exports Configuration File

NFS servers have only one configuration file: **/etc/exports**. This file lists the partitions that are sharable, the hosts they can be shared with, and with what permissions. Here is the format of each entry in the **/etc/exports** file:

```
/dir/to/export      client1(permissions) client2(permissions) \
                    client3(permissions) client4(permissions)
```

- **/dir/to/export** is the directory you want to share with other users; for example, **/export/home**.

- **client1**, **client2**, and so forth, are the host names of the NFS clients. The wildcard characters * and ? may be used. Netgroups may also be specified using the *@group* syntax. See Module 17 for more information on netgroups. Clients can also be specified by IP address or IP network block.

- **Permissions** are the corresponding permissions for each client.

  Table 16-1 describes the most useful permissions for each client.

Permission	Description
ro	Files are read-only. No files may be written to (or newly created) on this mount. This is the default.
rw	Allow both read and write requests to this volume. Useful for home directories, mail spools, etc.
async	This option attempts to improve performance by not waiting for the server to actually flush all data to the disk. If the server crashes at an inopportune time, this can result in data loss. Using this option without a specific reason is not recommended. In the past, this was the default, but recently the default has changed to **sync**.
sync	The opposite of the **async** option. Attempts to write data don't return until the data is actually flushed to disk. In order to match other NFS implementations, this is now the default. Because the default recently changed from **async** to **sync**, **exportfs** may issue a warning if neither option has been explicitly specified, so that admins are aware of the change.
anonuid	NFS supports the concept of an "anonymous" user, mostly in conjunction with the "squash" options listed next. By default this is mapped to the user **nobody**, but you can map this to a different user ID (UID) using the **anonuid** option. A corresponding **anongid** option also exists for remapping the anonymous group.

Table 16-1 Commonly Used Permissions for NFS Exports

Permission	Description
root_squash	Attempts to access files from the root user will be remapped as if they came from the anonymous user. Don't overestimate how much security this will buy you, however. Someone with root access on a client machine can always **su** to a user that does have access to a given file. What you may be able to get from this is a limited protection for files that are owned by root on the server, marked as only readable, writable, or executable by owner. This is the default.
no_root_squash	Disables the **root_squash** option just described. This is most useful on diskless workstations that mount their entire file tree over NFS, and preventing root access to some files (**/etc/shadow**, for example) causes its own problems.
all_squash	This works much like the **root_squash** option, except that all user access is remapped as if it came from the anonymous user.
insecure	By default, the NFS server will only accept connections from "secure" ports—that is, port numbers below 1024. If you need to allow non-root users to mount NFS exports, then you'll need to specify the **insecure** option.
no_wdelay	The NFS server tries to improve overall performance by not committing a write to disk if it suspects that a related write will arrive soon. This allows multiple write requests to be performed with a single disk operation. If you have a situation where lots of small unrelated writes are likely to occur, you may wish to turn this off by setting the **no_wdelay** option.
no_subtree_check	When the directory that you're exporting is only a portion of a disk volume, the NFS server checks to make sure that all requests refer to files that are in that subtree. If the directory that you're exporting involves an entire disk partition, you can speed things up by specifying **no_subtree_check**.
insecure_locks	Normally NFS will require authentication before honoring a lock request. Some older NFS implementations didn't have the concept of authenticating locks, so you may need to specify **insecure_locks** if you have to interoperate with one of these older implementations.

Table 16-1 Commonly Used Permissions for NFS Exports *(continued)*

A backslash at the end of the line indicates that the entry continues on to the next line. Comments can be added by using a pound symbol (#) at the beginning of the line.

CAUTION

Keep those UIDs in sync! Every NFS client request to an NFS server includes the UID of the user making the request. This UID is used by the server to verify that the user has permissions to access the requested file. However, in order for NFS permission-checking to work correctly, the UIDs of the users must be synchronized between the client and server. Having the same username on both systems is not enough. (You can compare this to keeping System IDs (SIDs) synchronized under Windows.) One way of keeping the UIDs in sync is to use the Network Information Service (NIS), as described in Module 17.

Following is an example of a complete NFS **/etc/exports** file:

```
#
# /etc/exports for gandalf.example.org
#
/export/home            frodo(rw) sam(rw) pippen(rw) \
                        @shire(rw) \
                        unixadmin(rw,no_root_squash)
/export/usr/local       legolas(rw) \
                        elrond(rw) galadriel(rw) \
                        192.168.3.0/24(ro,all_squash) \
                        *.rivendell.example.org (rw) \
                        unixadmin(rw,no_root_squash)
/export/anonftp         ftpserver(ro,all_squash,anuid=14,anongid=50)
```

Graphically configuring exports

Once again, Red Hat provides a graphical alternative for setting up your **/etc/exports** file. You can launch this GUI tool by selecting NFS Server from the Server Settings submenu or from the command line by typing **redhat-config-nfs**.

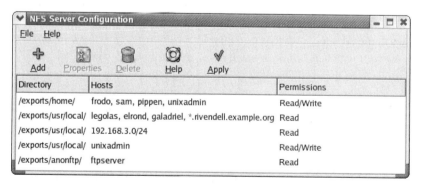

Adding exported directories from the main window is very straightforward. Either adding a new share or clicking on Properties for an existing share brings up a dialog box allowing you to adjust the options for that share.

The Basic tab holds settings for the hosts to which you want to export and settings for whether those hosts have write permissions. One of the oversights of the GUI tool is having to select either **ro** or **rw** for the entire list of hosts in the dialog box. If you want to mix **ro** and **rw** hosts, you have to make separate shares in the GUI tool.

Selecting the General Options tab brings up some additional selections that should seem familiar. The Allow Connections From Ports 1024 And Higher option corresponds to the insecure option mentioned earlier. You will probably recognize, without any difficulty, how to specify **insecure_locks**, **no_subtree_check**, and **sync** from the options presented on this tab. The last option, Force sync of write operations immediately, corresponds to the **no_wdelay** options.

Finally, the User Access tab lets you adjust the squash options. The Treat Remote Root User As Local Root option affects the **no_root_squash** setting, and Treat All Client Users As Anonymous Users is the **all_squash** setting. Notice that you can't change the **anonuid** or **anongid** options with only **root_squash** enabled; instead, **all_squash** has to be enabled.

As usual, the GUI tool provides no support for commenting your **/etc/exports** file and doesn't mix well with hand edits. In some cases, even a simple, valid, hand-edited **/etc/exports** file will prove to be unparsable by the GUI tool. As of this writing, the stability of this tool is not quite what it should be, and although we expect that to improve with future updates, you may want to make sure that you understand the format of the **exports** file in case you find yourself having to edit it by hand.

Telling the NFS Server Process About /etc/exports

Once you have an **/etc/exports** file written up, use the **exportfs** command to tell the NFS server processes to reread the configuration information. The parameters for **exportfs** are found in Table 16-2.

exportfs Command Option	Description
–a	Export all entries in the **/etc/exports** file.
–r	Re-export all entries in the **/etc/exports** file.
–u *client:/dir/to/mount*	Unexport the directory **/dir/to/mount** to the host **client**.
–o *options*	Options specified here are the same as described in Table 16-1 for client permissions. These **options** will apply only to the file system specified on the **exportfs** command line, not to those in **/etc/exports**.
–v	Be verbose.

Table 16-2 Command-Line Options for Use with the **exportfs** Command

Following are examples of **exportfs** command lines:

- To export all file systems:

  ```
  [root@gandalf /root]# exportfs -a
  ```

- To export the directory **/export/stuff** to the host **gollum** with the **read/write** and **no_root_squash** permissions:

  ```
  [root@gandalf /root]# exportfs -o rw,no_root_squash gollum:/export/stuff
  ```

 NOTE

In most instances, you will simply want to use **exportfs –ra**.

Common Problems

When exporting file systems, you may find that the server appears to be refusing the client access, even though the client is listed in the **/etc/exports** file. Typically, this happens because the server takes the IP address of the client connecting to it and resolves that address to the fully qualified domain name (FQDN), and the host name listed in the **/etc/exports** file isn't qualified. (For example, the server thinks the client host name is **balrog.example.com**, but the **/etc/exports** file lists just **balrog**.)

Another common problem is that the server's perception of the host name/IP pairing is not correct. This can occur because of an error in the **/etc/hosts** file or an error in the DNS tables. You'll need to verify that the pairing is correct.

Progress Check

1. What permission would you specify to prevent any files from being written to a mount?

2. Does NFS support the concept of an anonymous user?

CRITICAL SKILL
16.4 Configuring NFS Clients

NFS clients are remarkably easy to configure under Linux, because they don't require any new or additional software to be loaded. The only requirement is that the kernel be compiled to support NFS. (This feature is enabled by default.) Aside from the kernel, the only other change is to the options in the **mount** command.

The mount Command

The **mount** command was originally discussed in Module 7. Note two changes for NFS partition mounting: the specification of the NFS server name, and the options specified after the **–o** on the **mount** command line. Following is an example of a **mount** command line:

```
[root@gimli /root]# mount -o rw,bg,intr,soft gandalf:/export/home /home
```

TIP

Although you can explicitly specify the file type to the mount command with **–t nfs**, it's not actually necessary. The mount command will figure it out.

These **mount** options can also be used in the **/etc/fstab** file. This same entry in the **/etc/fstab** file would look like this:

```
gandalf:/export/home      /home      nfs      rw,bg,intr,soft   0   0
```

---

1. **ro**

2. Yes, and **anonuid** can be used to change which user an anonymous connection is treated as.

In the previous examples, **gandalf** is the NFS server name. The **–o** options are listed in Table 16-3.

NOTE

Remember that NFS servers can also be, at the same time, NFS clients.

Soft vs. Hard Mounts

By default, NFS operations are *hard,* which means they continue their attempts to contact the server indefinitely. This arrangement is not always beneficial, however. It causes a problem if an emergency shutdown of all systems is performed. If the servers happen to get shut down before the clients, the clients' shutdowns will stall while they wait for the servers to come back up. Enabling a *soft* mount allows the client to time out the connection after a number of retries. (The number of retries can be specified with the **retrans=***num* option.)

There is one exception to the preferred arrangement of having a soft mount with a **retrans=***num* value specified: Don't use this arrangement when you have data that must be

Option	Description
bg	Background mount. If the mount doesn't initially succeed, the **mount** command backgrounds itself to continue trying. This is especially useful for mounting at boot time, so that an unresponsive NFS server doesn't cause the entire boot to hang.
intr	Specifies an interruptible mount. If a process is pending I/O on a mounted partition, this option allows the process to be interrupted and the I/O call to be dropped. Note: See "The Importance of the intr Option" in this section.
soft	Enables a "soft" mount for this partition, allowing the client to time-out the connection after a number of retries (specified with the **retrans=***num* option). The default is to hard mount. Note: See "Soft vs. Hard Mounts" in this section.
retrans=*num*	Specify how many retries before timing out a soft mount to an unresponsive server. The default is 3.
nolock	As the name implies, this will disable locking. This may be necessary with some really old NFS servers that don't support file locking.
nfsvers=*num*	Specify a particular version of the NFS protocol, for servers that support more than one version. The default is version 2.
tcp	Use NFS over the TCP protocol, rather than UDP. This is a new feature available in NFS version 3. Not all NFS servers support NFS over TCP.
rsize=*num*	Sets the block size for read operations. See "Performance Tuning" in this section.
wsize=*num*	Sets the block size for write operations. See "Performance Tuning" in this section.

Table 16-3 Mount Options Specific to NFS

committed to disk no matter what and you don't want to return control to the application until the data has been committed. (NFS-mounted mail directories are typically mounted this way.)

Cross-Mounting Disks

Cross-mounting is the process of having server A NFS mounting server B's disks, and server B NFS mounting server A's disks. While this may appear innocuous at first, there is a subtle danger in doing this: If both servers crash, and if both servers require mounting the other's disk in order to boot correctly, you've got a chicken and egg problem. Server A won't boot until server B is done booting, but server B won't boot because server A isn't done booting.

To get around this problem, make sure you don't get yourself into a situation where this happens. All of your servers should be able to completely boot without needing to mount anyone else's disks for anything. However, this doesn't mean you can't cross-mount at all. There are legitimate reasons for needing to cross-mount, such as needing to make home directories available across all servers.

In these situations, make sure you set your **/etc/fstab** entries to use the **bg** mount option. By doing so, you will allow each server to background the **mount** process for any failed mounts, thus giving all of the servers a chance to complete the booting process and then properly make their NFS mountable partitions available.

The Importance of the intr Option

When a process makes a system call, the kernel takes over the action. During the time that the kernel is handling the system call, the process has no control over itself. In the event of a kernel access error, the process must continue to wait until the kernel request returns; the process can't give up and quit. In normal cases, the kernel's control isn't a problem, because typically, kernel requests get resolved very quickly. When there's an error, however, it can be quite a nuisance. Because of this, NFS has an option to mount partitions with the interruptible flag (the **intr** option), which allows a process that is waiting on an NFS request to give up and move on. In general, unless you have reason not to use the **intr** option, it is usually a good idea to do so.

Performance Tuning

NFS was designed to be resilient in a time of unstable networks. The default block size that gets transmitted with NFS has traditionally been 1K (some recent kernels now default to 4K). This is handy because if any packets get dropped, NFS has to retransmit very few packets. The downside to this block size is that it doesn't take advantage of the fact that most networking stacks are fast enough to keep up with segmenting larger blocks of data for transport, and that most modern networks are reliable enough that it is extremely rare to lose a block of data. Given these factors, it is often better to optimize for a fast networking stack and a reliable network, since that's what you're going to have 99 percent of the time.

The easiest way to do this with NFS is to use the **wsize** (write size) and **rsize** (read size) options. Unfortunately, there is no value that is good for all (or even most) cases. Old hardware and/or poorly written network drivers can have a drastic effect on the usefulness of raising these values. An often suggested size to use is 8K, which coincidentally is the maximum value under version 2 of the NFS protocol. Under version 3, the maximum size depends on what is compiled into the kernel on the NFS server. For most recent kernels (including the one supplied with Red Hat 8), this is set to 8K (although the experimental TCP server patches mentioned earlier change this value to 32K).

Although it's worth the time to play with these values in search of higher performance, the sad truth is that to really find the best values for your hardware and network, you'll need to spend a good deal of time with a good disk-benchmarking program, such as bonnie (http://www.textuality.com/bonnie/), bonnie++ (http://www.coker.com.au/bonnie++/), or IOzone (http://www.iozone.org/).

An example entry with **wsize** and **rsize** is as follows:

```
gandalf:/export/home   /home  nfs
rw,bg,intr,soft,wsize=8192,rsize=8192 0 0
```

CRITICAL SKILL

16.5 Learning Common Uses for NFS Partitions

The following examples give some reasons for using NFS partitions. Of course, they are just ideas. You are likely to have your own reasons for sharing disks via NFS.

- **To hold popular programs**   If you are accustomed to Windows, you've probably worked with applications that refuse to be installed on network shares. For one reason or another, these programs want every system to have its own copy of the software—a nuisance, especially if you have a lot of machines that need the software. Linux (and UNIX in general) rarely has such conditions prohibiting the installation of software on network disks. (The most common exceptions are high-performance databases.) Thus, many sites install heavily used software on a special partition that is exported to all hosts in a network. Often this partition is mounted on each client's **/usr/local** directory, since the partition contains software that is local to the site.

- **To hold home directories**   Another common use for NFS partitions is to hold home directories. By placing home directories on NFS-mountable partitions, it's possible to configure the automounter and NIS so that users can log in to any machine in the network and have their home directory available to them. Heterogeneous sites typically use this configuration so that users can seamlessly move from one variant of UNIX to another without worrying about having to carry their data around with them.

- **For shared mail spools** A disk residing on the mail server can be used to store all of the user mailboxes, and then NFS exports to all hosts on a network. Traditional UNIX mail readers then read a user's e-mail straight from the spool file. In the case of large mail servers, where multiple servers might be used for providing POP mailboxes, all the mailboxes can reside on an NFS partition that is shared with all of the servers.

CRITICAL SKILL
16.6 # Troubleshooting NFS

Like any major service, NFS has mechanisms to help it cope with error conditions. In this section, I'll discuss some common error cases and how NFS handles them.

Stale File Handles

If a file or directory is in use by the client and the server reboots, the client's identifier for the file it was using will no longer be valid. The error returned in this case is "Stale NFS Filehandle." The only fix for this is to unmount and remount the offending directory. You may have to cause the client program to stop using files in the mounted directory.

Permission Denied

You're likely to see the "Permission denied" message if you're logged in as root and are trying to access a file that is NFS mounted. Typically, this means that the server on which the file system is mounted is not acknowledging root's permissions. (Usually, this occurs for security reasons. See the discussion of the **root_squash** option earlier.)

The quick way around this problem is to become the user who owns the file you're trying to control. For example, if you're root and you're trying to access a file owned by the user **kim**, use the **su** command to become **kim**:

```
[root@gimli /root]# su - kim
```

When you're done working with the file, you can exit out of **kim**'s shell and return to root.

Note that this workaround assumes that **kim** exists as a user on the system and has the same UID on both the client and the server.

Another possibility is that you're not root and you don't really have access to the file in question. In that case, you need to discuss the problem with the administrator of the NFS server.

Hard vs. Soft Mounts

Although we covered hard and soft mounts in the section on configuring NFS clients, it's worth some additional comments here. When a server goes down, understanding the difference between hard and soft mounts over NFS is important to your troubleshooting efforts.

On an NFS file system that is *hard-mounted,* the client must commit all changes to the server before allowing other operations. The client will continue trying to contact the server, until the server sends back an acknowledgment. From the user's perspective, it may look like the client system has crashed when it hasn't.

The purpose of configuring a file system as hard-mounted is to make sure that data being accessed via NFS does not get lost. For crucial file systems (such as the mail spool), this is a very important attribute.

Soft mounts, on the other hand, aren't quite as persistent about getting data written to the NFS server's disk. The client will try to access the server and commit unwritten data, but after a specified timeout period (number of retries), the client will give up and return control to the user. Although this has the potential of causing data loss, it allows clients to handle failed NFS servers more gracefully.

Module Summary

In this module, we discussed the process of setting up an NFS server and client. This requires very little change, so sharing your disks this way should be relatively painless. Some key points to remember:

- NFS is a stateless protocol (although work is being done to change this in future versions). Clients can't tell the difference between a crashed server and a slow server; thus recovery is automatic when the server comes back up. (In the reverse situation, when the client crashes and the server stays up, recovery is also automatic.)

- The key server processes in NFS are **rpc.statd**, **rpc.quotad**, **rpc.mountd**, and **rpc.nfsd**.

- Use **rpcinfo –p** to view all the RPC services on your system.

- Use **exportfs –a** to export all the file systems specified in the **/etc/exports** file. (Use **exportfs –ra** after making changes.)

NFS is a powerful tool for sharing disks. Be sure to spend some time experimenting with it to meet your system's resource-sharing needs.

✓ *Module 16 Mastery Check*

1. What is NFS?

2. What does portmapper do?

3. Is notification to the server necessary after mounting?

4. In the **/etc/exports** configuration file, which of the following is a permission:

   A. **root_squash**

   B. **all_squash**

   C. **insecure**

   D. All of the above

5. List three command options that you can use when telling the NFS server process about **/ect/exports**, and explain what each does.

6. Name one problem that can occur when trying to export files with the NFS **/etc/exports** file.

7. When mounting NFS, which of the following does the **nolock** command do?

   A. Specifies an interruptible mount

   B. Sets the block size for write operation

   C. Disables the locking, which can be necessary with old NFS servers

   D. None of the above

8. When mounting NFS, what does the background **mount** command do?

   A. Specifies an interruptible mount

   B. Sets the block size for the write operation

   C. Disables the locking, which can be necessary with old NFS servers

   D. None of the above

9. True or False? If a file or directory is in use by the client and the server reboots, the client's identifier for the file it was using will no longer be valid. The error returned in this case is "Permission Denied."

10. True of False? The "Permission Denied" message will show if you are logged in as root and trying to access a file that is NFS-mounted with the **root_squash** option

11. During which type of mount must the client commit all changes to the server before allowing other operations?

    A. Hard

    B. Soft

    C. Wall

    D. A and B

Module 17

Network Information Service (NIS)

The Network Information Service (NIS) makes possible the sharing of data of critical files across the local area network. Typically, files such as **/etc/passwd** and **/etc/group**, which ideally would remain uniform across all hosts, are shared via NIS. In this way, every network machine that has a corresponding NIS client can read the data contained in these shared files and use the network versions of these files as extensions to the local versions. However, NIS is not limited to sharing just those two files. Any tabular file where at least one column has a unique value throughout the file can be shared via NIS. You'll find that many such files exist in your system, including the e-mail **/etc/aliases** file, the automounter files, and even the **/etc/services** file.

The main benefit achieved from using NIS is that you can maintain a central copy of the data, and whenever that data is updated, it automatically propagates to all of the network users. To your users, features of NIS give the appearance of a more uniform network—no matter what host they may be working on, all of their tools and files are always there.

If you're coming from a Windows NT background, you might think of NIS as a substantially more versatile Primary Domain Controller (PDC). In fact, NIS is actually much more in line with Windows 2000 directory services than PDCs.

This module explores NIS, how it works, and how it can benefit you. It then explains how to set up the client and server portions of the NIS configuration. Finally, it discusses some of the tools related to NIS.

NOTE

Sun Microsystems, the creators of NIS, have also developed NIS+ to address the needs for better security, more complex types of information, and better scalability. Unfortunately, NIS+ is rather beastly to manage on the server side, and has never achieved wide acceptance outside of Sun. It's been suggested that the replacement for NIS will be the Lightweight Directory Access Protocol (LDAP) rather than NIS+. Nevertheless, if you're on a network that already uses NIS+, Linux can act as an NIS+ client. The details of NIS+ are beyond the scope of this book.

CRITICAL SKILL
17.1 Looking Inside NIS

The Network Information Service (NIS) is really just a simple database that clients can query. It contains a series of independent tables. Each table originated as a straight text file, such as **/etc/passwd**, which is tabular in nature and has at least one column that is unique for every row (a database of key/pair values). NIS keeps track of these tables by name and allows querying to happen in one of two ways:

- Listing the entire table
- Pulling a specific entry based on a search for a given key

Once the databases are established on the server, clients can query the server for database entries. Typically this happens when a client is configured to look to the NIS *map* when an entry cannot be found in the client's local database. A host may have a simple file containing only those entries needed for the system to work in single-user mode (when there is no network connectivity)—for example, the **/etc/passwd** file. When a program makes a request to look up user password information, the client checks its local **passwd** file and sees that the user doesn't exist there; the client then makes a request to the NIS server to look for a corresponding entry in the **passwd** table. If NIS does have an entry, it is returned to the client and then to the program that requested the information in the first place. The program itself is unaware that NIS was used. The same is true if the NIS map returns an answer indicating that the user password entry does not exist. The program would be passed the information without knowing how much activity had happened in between.

This of course applies to all the files that we tell NIS to share. Other popular shared files include **/etc/group** and **/etc/hosts**.

NOTE

Although it is technically correct to refer to NIS's tables as a database, they are more typically called maps. (In this context, we are mapping keys to values.) Using the **/etc/passwd** file as an example, we map a user's login name (which we know is always unique) to the rest of the password entry.

The NIS Servers

NIS can have only one authoritative server where the original data files are kept (this is somewhat similar to DNS). This authoritative server is called the *master* NIS server. If your organization is large enough, you may need to distribute the load across more than one machine. This can be done by setting up one or more *secondary* (*slave*) NIS servers. In addition to helping distribute the load, secondary servers also provide a mechanism to better handle server failures. The secondary NIS server can continue answering queries even while the master or other secondary servers are down.

NOTE

A server can be both a server and a client at the same time.

Secondary NIS servers receive updates whenever the primary NIS server is updated, so that the masters and slaves remain in sync. The process of keeping the secondary servers in sync with the primary is called a *server push*. As part of its update scripts, the NIS master also pushes a copy of the map files to the secondary server. Upon receiving these files, the secondary servers update their databases, as well. The NIS master does not consider itself completely up-to-date until the secondary servers are up-to-date, as well.

NOTE

A server pull mechanism also exists for NIS. However, this solution is typically reserved for more complex configurations, such as when you have hundreds of slave servers. In a smaller network, this should not be an issue.

Domains

Primary NIS servers establish *domains* that are similar to the domains of a PDC. A significant difference is that the NIS domain does not require the NIS server administrator to explicitly allow a client to join. (Bear in mind that the NIS model assumes that all clients are members of the same administrative domain and are thus managed by the same systems administrators.) Furthermore, the NIS server only sends out data; it does not perform authentication. The process of authenticating users is left to each individual host; NIS merely provides a centralized list of users.

TIP

There is often much confusion as a result of the unfortunate overloading of the term "domain." There are security reasons why your NIS domain name should be different from your Internet domain name, but as an added bonus, you'll eliminate some confusion as well. You'll have a much easier time discussing your network domains with fellow administrators when everyone knows which is which.

CRITICAL SKILL
17.2 Installing and Configuring the NIS Servers

The client portion of NIS should already be a part of the default install, so you really only have to worry about adding the server. When you install your system or use the **redhat-config-packages** tool, look for the Network Servers option, and click Details. From the resulting list, make sure that the **ypserv** package is selected. If you're installing by hand, the RPMs you're looking for are **ypbind**, **yp-tools**, and **ypserv**.

Ask the Expert

Q: Why does everything related to NIS seem to start with the letters *yp* and not *nis*?

A: The NIS system was originally called "Yellow Pages," but it was soon pointed out that British Telecom held a trademark on the term "Yellow Pages," so the name was changed to the Network Information Service. Part of the legacy of this name change is that most NIS commands and tools still begin with the letters *yp*.

When you enable the NIS service in the **redhat-config-services** graphical user interface (GUI) tool, you're going to look for two entries, **ypserv** and **yppasswdd**. The **ypbind** entry is the client portion. We'll cover that later in this module in the section "Configuring an NIS Client." There is also an entry named **ypxfrd** that you don't need to worry about unless you decide to set up pull-based replication. The **ypserv** entry is the NIS server itself, and should be enabled on all NIS server machines. The other two entries will only be enabled on the master server. Enabling the **yppasswdd** service will allow users to change their passwords remotely (from a client machine, that is). If you're planning on manipulating the symlinks in the **rc** directories by hand, you'll probably want to use the same start and kill values that the GUI tool would use. That is S26ypserv and K74ypserv for the main server, and the password daemon would use S66yppasswdd and K34yppasswdd.

Once NIS is enabled, you'll need to configure it. There are four steps to doing this:

1. Establish the domain name.

2. Start the **ypserv** daemon to start NIS.

3. Edit the makefile.

4. Run **ypinit** to create the databases.

Establishing the Domain Name

Setting the NIS domain name is done with the **domainname** command. Let's say we're setting up a domain called **mydepartment.mycompany**; we can tell the system the name of the NIS domain like this:

```
[root@arrakis /root]# domainname mydepartment.mycompany
```

Of course, in order to have this established every time we reboot, we need to place the **domainname** command in an **rc** script. You can edit the **/etc/sysconfig/network** and add this line:

```
NIS_DOMAIN=mydepartment.mycompany
```

replacing **mydepartment.mycompany** with your own NIS domain name. Setting the domain name should occur before the NIS servers start.

Starting NIS

The **ypserv** daemon is responsible for handling NIS requests. If you are installing NIS onto a live server, most likely you will not want to reboot the server to complete the installation. Instead, you can simply run the **init** script yourself, like so:

```
[root@arrakis /root]# /etc/init.d/ypserv start
```

If you need to stop the NIS server at any time, you can do so with this command:

```
[root@arrakis /root]# /etc/init.d/ypserv stop
```

Editing the Makefile

You may be familiar with using the **make** command to compile programs. The **make** tool doesn't do the compilation, however—it simply keeps track of what files need to be compiled and then invokes the necessary program to perform the compilation. The file that actually contains the instructions for **make** is called a *makefile*.

The **make** tool is efficient because the programs it invokes are arbitrary. You can substitute your preferred compiler in place of the one that comes with your Linux distribution, for example. When **make** sees that a file's date and time have been modified, it takes that to mean that the file's contents have been modified. If the file has been modified, that tells **make** that the file needs to be recompiled.

Putting this concept to work on NIS is very straightforward. In this case, there's a series of straight text files that need to be converted into database format. We want a tool that will reconvert any files that have been changed—you can see how **make** fits the bill!

Changing over to the **/var/yp** directory, we see a file called **Makefile** (yes, all one word). This file lists the files that get shared via NIS, as well as some additional parameters for how they get shared and how much of each one gets shared. Open up **Makefile** with your favorite editor, and you can see all the configurable options. Let's step through the makefile options that apply to us.

Designating Slave Servers: NOPUSH

If you plan to have NIS slave servers, you'll need to tell the master NIS server to push the resulting maps to the slave servers. Change the NOPUSH variable to false if you want slave servers.

NOTE If you don't need slave servers now but think you will need them later, you can change this option when you do add the servers.

```
# If we have only one server, we don't have to push the maps to the
# slave servers (NOPUSH=true). If you have slave servers, change this
# to "NOPUSH=false" and put all hostnames of your slave servers in
# the file /var/yp/ypservers.
NOPUSH=true
```

Remember to list the host names of your slave servers in the **/var/yp/ypservers** file; and for each host name you list there, be sure to list a corresponding entry in the **/etc/hosts** file.

Minimum UIDs and GIDs: MINUID and MINGID

User accounts that are used by the system (rather than belonging to a real human) usually exist with lower numbers than the accounts created for actual users. When accounts are added, the minimum UID and GID created in **/etc/passwd** and **/etc/group** files will be different depending on your setup, but Red Hat defaults to starting at 500. You probably don't need or want to share system accounts across NIS, so be sure to set the minimum UID and GID values that you are willing to share. Obviously, you don't want to share the root entry via NIS, so the minimum should never be zero.

```
# We do not put password entries with lower UIDs (the root and system
# entries) in the NIS password database, for security. MINUID is the
# lowest uid that will be included in the password maps.
# MINGID is the lowest gid that will be included in the group maps.
MINUID=500
MINGID=500
```

Merging Shadow Passwords with Real Passwords: MERGE_PASSWD

So that NIS can be used for other systems to authenticate users, you will need to allow the encrypted password entries to be shared through NIS. If you are using shadow passwords, NIS will automatically handle this for you by taking the encrypted field from the **/etc/shadow** file and merging it into the NIS shared copy of **/etc/passwd**. There is a tradeoff here. Merging shadow entries back into the **passwd** list defeats most of the advantages of using shadow entries, but not doing so loses the ability to authenticate against the NIS database. Some systems support using the shadow entries directly as their own map, but this isn't supported by all systems and doesn't provide any real security advantage over merging since the data is sent unencrypted over the network.

```
# Should we merge the passwd file with the shadow file ?
# MERGE_PASSWD-truc|false
MERGE_PASSWD=true
```

Merging Group Shadow Passwords with Real Groups: MERGE_GROUP

The **/etc/group** file allows passwords to be applied to group settings. Since the **/etc/group** file needs to be publicly readable, some systems, including Red Hat, have taken to supporting shadow group files—these are similar in nature to shadow password files.

```
# Should we merge the group file with the gshadow file ?
# MERGE_GROUP=true|false
MERGE_GROUP=true
```

Designating Filenames

The following makefile segment shows the files that are preconfigured to be shared via NIS. Just because they are listed here, however, does not mean they are automatically shared. This listing simply establishes filenames for later use in the makefile.

Most of the entries start with

```
$(YPPWDDIR)
```

or

```
$(YPSRCDIR)
```

which are variables set up right before this section in the makefile. The default value for these variables is /etc, which means any occurrence of **$(YPSRCDIR)** will be replaced with /etc when the makefile is run. This allows you to point to where the files you want to share are located. **YPPWDDIR** is a separate variable, just in case the password-related entries you want to share are separate from your real system files on the server. (Do you really want all the users on your system to have a login on the NIS server?) By default, your real files in /etc are pointed to, thus GROUP will become equal to **/etc/group**, PASSWD will become **/etc/passwd**, and so forth.

```
# These are the files from which the NIS databases are built. You
# may edit these to taste in the event that you wish to keep your NIS
# source files separate from your NIS server's actual configuration
# files.
#
GROUP       = $(YPPWDDIR)/group
PASSWD      = $(YPPWDDIR)/passwd
SHADOW      = $(YPPWDDIR)/shadow
GSHADOW     = $(YPPWDDIR)/gshadow
ADJUNCT     = $(YPPWDDIR)/passwd.adjunct
#ALIASES    = $(YPSRCDIR)/aliases     # could be in /etc or/etc/mail
ALIASES     = /etc/aliases
ETHERS      = $(YPSRCDIR)/ethers      # ethernet addresses (for rarpd)
BOOTPARAMS  = $(YPSRCDIR)/bootparams # for booting Sun boxes (bootparamd)
HOSTS       = $(YPSRCDIR)/hosts
NETWORKS    = $(YPSRCDIR)/networks
PRINTCAP    = $(YPSRCDIR)/printcap
PROTOCOLS   = $(YPSRCDIR)/protocols
PUBLICKEYS  = $(YPSRCDIR)/publickey
RPC         = $(YPSRCDIR)/rpc
SERVICES    = $(YPSRCDIR)/services
NETGROUP    = $(YPSRCDIR)/netgroup
NETID       = $(YPSRCDIR)/netid
AMD_HOME    = $(YPSRCDIR)/amd.home
AUTO_MASTER = $(YPSRCDIR)/auto.master
AUTO_HOME   = $(YPSRCDIR)/auto.home
AUTO_LOCAL  = $(YPSRCDIR)/auto.local
TIMEZONE    = $(YPSRCDIR)/timezone
LOCALE      = $(YPSRCDIR)/locale
NETMASKS    = $(YPSRCDIR)/netmasks
```

What Gets Shared: The all Entry

In the following makefile entry, all of the maps listed after **all:** are the maps that get shared.

```
# If you don't want some of these maps built, feel free to comment
# them out from this list.

all:   passwd group hosts rpc services netid protocols mail \
       # netgrp shadow publickey networks ethers bootparams printcap \
       # amd.home auto.master auto.home passwd.adjunct \
       # timezone locale netmasks
```

Notice that the line continuation character, the backslash (\\), is used to ensure that the **make** program knows to treat the entire entry as one line, even though it is really three lines. In addition, note that the second line begins with a pound symbol (#), which means the rest of the line is commented out.

Based on this format, you can see that the maps configured to be shared are **passwd**, **group**, **hosts**, **rpc**, **services**, **netid**, **protocols**, and **mail**. These entries correspond to the filenames listed in the preceding section of the makefile. Of course, not all sites want these entries shared, or they want some additional maps shared (such as the **automounter** files, **auto.master** and **auto.home**). To change any of the maps you want shared, alter the line so that the maps you *don't* want shared are listed after a pound symbol (#).

For example, let's say you want only the **passwd**, **group**, **auto.master**, **auto.home**, and **netgrp** maps shared over NIS. You'd change the **all:** line to read as follows:

```
all: passwd group auto.master auto.home netgrp \
        # hosts rpc services netid protocols mail \
        # amd.home auto.local passwd.adjunct \
        # timezone locale netmasks
```

Note that the order in the **all:** line doesn't matter. The placement of the foregoing entries simply makes them easily read.

Using ypinit

Once you have the makefile ready, you need to initialize the NIS server using the **ypinit** command.

NOTE

Remember that you must already have the domain name set before you run the **ypinit** command. This is done with the **domainname** utility, as shown earlier in this module in the section "Establishing the Domain Name."

```
[root@arrakis yp]# /usr/lib/yp/ypinit -m
```

Here, the **–m** option tells **ypinit** to set the system up as a master NIS server. Assuming we are running this on a system named **arrakis.example.com**, we would see the system respond as follows:

```
At this point, we have to construct a list of the hosts that will run NIS servers.
arrakis.example.com is in the list of NIS server hosts. Please continue to add
the names for the other hosts, one per line. When you are done with the list,
type a <control-D>.
        next host to add:  arrakis.example.com
        next host to add:
```

Continue entering the name of all the secondary NIS servers. Press CTRL-D when you have added all necessary servers. These entries will be placed in the **/var/yp/ypservers** file for you; if needed, you can change them by editing the file later.

Once you are done, **ypinit** will run the **make** program automatically for you, to build the maps and push them to any secondary servers you have indicated.

Makefile Errors

If you made a mistake in the makefile, you may get an error when **ypinit** runs the **make** program. If you see this error:

```
gmake[1]: *** No rule to make target '/etc/shadow', needed by 'passwd.byname'.
Stop.
```

don't worry about it. This means you have specified a file to share that doesn't exist (in this error message, the file is **/etc/shadow**). You can either create the file or go back and edit the makefile so that the file is not shared. (See the previous section "What Gets Shared: The all Entry.")

Another common error message is

```
failed to send 'clear' to local ypserv: RPC: Program not registered
Updating passwd.byuid...
failed to send 'clear' to local ypserv: RPC: Program not registered
gmake[1]: *** No rule to make target '/etc/gshadow', needed by 'group.byname'.
Stop.
gmake[1]: Leaving directory '/var/yp/arrakis.example.com'
```

There are actually two error messages here. You can ignore the first one, which indicates that the NIS server hasn't been started yet. The second error message is the same one described in the preceding paragraph. Once you've fixed it, type in the following command to rebuild the maps, as described in the next section:

```
[root@arrakis yp]# cd /var/yp; make
```

Updating NIS Maps

If you have updated the files configured to be shared by NIS with the rest of your network, you need to rebuild the map files. (For example, you may have added a user to the **/etc/passwd** file.) To rebuild the maps, use the following **make** command:

```
[root@arrakis /root]# cd /var/yp; make
```

Progress Check

1. When installing the NIS server, what script can be run to initialize NIS?

2. Name an advantage of merging the **/etc/shadow** file and **/etc/passwd**?

CRITICAL SKILL
17.3 Configuring an NIS Client

Thankfully, NIS clients are much easier to configure than NIS servers! To set up an NIS client, you need to do the following:

1. Edit the **/etc/yp.conf** file.

2. Set up the startup script.

3. Edit the **/etc/nsswitch.conf** file.

Editing the /etc/yp.conf File

The **/etc/yp.conf** file contains the information necessary for the client-side daemon, **ypbind**, to start up and find the NIS server. You need to make a decision regarding how the client is going to find the server, by either using a broadcast or by specifying the host name of the server.

The broadcast technique is appropriate when you need to move a client around to various subnets and you don't want to have to reconfigure the client so long as an NIS server exists in the same subnet. One downside to this technique, of course, is that you must make sure that there is an NIS server in every subnet. (There are security issues with broadcasts as well, but as noted elsewhere, NIS is not the most secure system to begin with and should really only be used on trusted networks.)

---

1. To initialize NIS, you can run the following command:

```
/etc/init.d/ypserv start
```

2. An advantage of merging the **/etc/shadow** file and the **/etc/passwd** file is that it allows NIS to be able to authenticate the user.

NOTE

When you use the broadcast method, you must have an NIS server in every subnet because broadcasts do not span multiple subnets. If you are uncertain whether a particular NIS server is in the same subnet, you can find out by pinging the broadcast address. If the NIS server is one of the hosts that responds, then you know for sure that the broadcast method will work.

The other technique for client-to-server contact is specifying the host name of the server. This method works well when you need to subnet your network, but you don't need an NIS server in every subnet. This allows a client to move anywhere inside your network and still be able to find the NIS server—however, if you need to change a client so that it points to another NIS server (to balance the network load), you'll need to change that yourself.

- **Broadcast Method** If you choose the broadcast technique, edit the **/etc/yp.conf** file so that it reads as follows:

  ```
  domain my.nis.domainname broadcast
  ```

  where *my.nis.domainname* is the name of your NIS domain. Remember that if you need failover support, you will need to have two NIS servers in every subnet in order for **broadcast** to find the second server.

- **Server Hostname Method** If you want to specify the name of the NIS server directly, edit the **/etc/yp.conf** file so that it reads as follows:

  ```
  domain my.nis.domainname server servername
  ```

  where *my.nis.domainname* is the name of your NIS domain and *servername* is the name of the NIS server to which you want this client to refer. You can specify this option more than once if you want to point to redundant servers. If you specify both one or more servers by name and a broadcast option, **ypbind** will attempt to use the named servers first and fall back on the **broadcast** option only as a last resort.

NOTE

Remember that you also have to have an entry for *servername* in the **/etc/hosts** file. At the time NIS is started, you may not yet have access to DNS, and you most certainly don't have access to the NIS hosts table yet! For this reason, the client must be able to do the host name–to–IP resolution without the aid of any other services.

Setting Up the Startup Script

The NIS client runs a daemon called **ypbind** in order to communicate with the server. Typically, this is started in the **/etc/init.d/ypbind** startup script. This can be set to automatically start on boot using the **redhat-config-services** tool and selecting the **ypbind** entry. The equivelent symlinks for the **rc** directories would be S27ypbind and K73ypbind.

- To start the daemon without having to reboot, use this command:

  ```
  [root@caladan /root]# /etc/init.d/ypbind start
  ```

- If you need to stop the daemon, type

  ```
  [root@caladan /root]# /etc/init.d/ypbind stop
  ```

Editing the /etc/nsswitch.conf File

The **/etc/nsswitch.conf** file is responsible for telling the system the order in which to search for information. The format of the file is as follows:

```
filename:    servicename
```

where *filename* is the name of the file that needs to be referenced and *servicename* is the name of the service to use to find the file. Multiple services can be listed, separated by spaces. Here are the most important service entries:

files	Use the actual file on the host itself.
nis	Use NIS to perform the lookup.
yp	Use NIS to perform the lookup (**nis** is an alias for **yp**).
compat	This is a compatibility mode to enable features from earlier NIS implementations. (This applies only to **passwd**, **shadow**, and **group** entries.) See "Using NIS in Configuration Files," later in this module.
dns	Use DNS for the lookup (applies only to hosts).
[NOTFOUND=return]	Stop searching if the preceding entry resulted in a "not found" response. See the following text for more information.
nisplus	Use NIS+ (if you're on a network that requires it).

Here is an example entry in the **/etc/nsswitch.conf** file:

```
passwd:    files nis
```

This setting means search requests for password entries will first be done in the **/etc/passwd** file. If the requested entry isn't found there, NIS will then be checked.

The **/etc/passwd** file should already exist and contain most of the information needed. You may need to adjust the order in which certain *servicenames* are listed in the file.

The **[NOTFOUND=return]** entry occasionally causes some confusion, so here's one more example:

```
passwd:          nis [NOTFOUND=return] files
```

This time, NIS will be checked first. If NIS performs its search and says that the requested entry is not found, no further searching is performed. On the other hand, if the NIS lookup fails for some reason (perhaps the server is down), then the search continues by looking at the local **/etc/passwd** file.

Testing Your NIS Client Configuration

After the **/etc/yp.conf** and **/etc/nsswitch.conf** files are established and the **ypbind** client daemon is all set up, you should be able to use the **ypcat** command to dump a map from the NIS server to your screen. To do this, type the following command:

```
[michael@caladan michael]# ypcat passwd
```

which dumps the **passwd** map to your screen—that is, of course, *if* you are sharing your **passwd** map via NIS. If you aren't, pick a map that you *are* sharing and use the **ypcat** command with that filename.

If you don't see the map dumped out, you need to double-check your client and server configurations and try again.

Project 17-1 Setting Up a NIS Server

Now that we have looked at how NIS can help a network, let's walk through a simple server setup. We need to set up the master server first, but it will help if you already know if you're going to use slave servers and what their names will be. Make sure you know what domain name you plan to use and what maps you will want to share.

Step by Step

1. Establish your domain name. Set your NIS domain name right away using the **domainname** command.

2. With your favorite text editor, open the file **/etc/sysconfig/network** and change the line NIS_DOMAIN to reflect your chosen domain name.

(continued)

3. Run **/etc/init.d/ypserv start** to launch the server process.

4. Bring out your favorite text editor again, and edit **/var/yp/Makefile**.

5. Check the value of NOPUSH to make sure it matches your decision on slave servers.

6. Make sure that the value of MERGE_PASSWD and MERGE_GROUP are what you intend.

7. Change the value of the **all:** line to match the maps that you want shared out. Don't share out maps you don't need to share out. Remember that you can always change this later.

8. Save the makefile and exit your editor.

9. Run **/usr/lib/yp/ypinit –m** to initialize your master server.

10. When prompted, enter the names of your secondary servers. Press CTRL-D when finished.

11. Now check your server by using **ypcat** to display one of your shared maps.

Project Summary

This simple example is enough to get you up and running with a basic NIS server. From here you'll be able to add clients and slave servers to expand your network. As you work through the rest of this module, you can refer back to this server and build on what you've created here.

CRITICAL SKILL
17.4 Configuring a Secondary NIS Server

As your site grows, you'll undoubtedly find that there is a need to distribute the NIS service load to multiple hosts. NIS supports this through the use of secondary NIS servers. These servers require no additional maintenance once they are configured, because the master NIS server sends them updates whenever you rebuild the maps (with the **make** command, as described in "Editing the Makefile," earlier in this module).

There are three steps to setting up a secondary NIS server:

1. Set the domain name.

2. Set up the NIS master to push to the slave.

3. Run **ypinit** to initialize the slave server.

Setting the Domain Name

Like configuring a master NIS server, you establish the NIS domain name before starting up the actual initialization process for a secondary server:

```
[root@kaitain /root]# domainname mydepartment.mycompany
```

Of course, the secondary server's domain name must be set up so that it automatically becomes established at boot time, so edit your **/etc/sysconfig/network** file as you did for the master server and client machines.

NOTE

Be sure to set the domain name, by hand if necessary, before you continue with the **ypinit** step of the installation.

Setting Up the NIS Master to Push to Slaves

If you haven't already configured the master NIS server that will push to the slave NIS servers, you should do so now. This requires two tasks: First, edit the **/var/yp/ypservers** file so that it lists all the secondary NIS servers to which the master server will push maps. For example, if you want the master server to push maps to the hosts **geidiprime** and **kaitain**, you'll edit **/var/yp/ypservers** so that it looks like this:

```
geidiprime
kaitain
```

Second, you'll need to make sure the makefile contains the line **NOPUSH=false**. See the section, "Installing and Configuring the NIS Servers" for details.

Running ypinit

With these set-up steps accomplished, you're ready to run the **ypinit** command to initialize the secondary server. Type the following command:

```
[root@kaitain /root]# /usr/lib/yp/ypinit -s arrakis
```

where the **–s** option tells **ypinit** to configure the system as a slave server, and **arrakis** is the name of the NIS master server in our example.

The output of this command will complain about **ypxfrd** not running—you can ignore this. What the secondary server is trying to do is pull the maps from the master server down, using the **ypxfrd** daemon. This won't work, because you didn't configure the master NIS server to accept requests to pull maps down via **ypxfrd**. Rather, you configured the master server to push maps to the secondaries whenever the master has an update. The server process at this point must be started by hand. It's the same process as for the primary server: **ypserv**. To get it started, run this command:

```
[root@kaitain /root]# /etc/init.d/ypserv start
```

NOTE

Be sure to have the **ypserv** process start as part of the boot process. You can set this up the same way that you did for the master server.

To test the secondary server, go back to the master server and try to do a server-side push. Do this by running the **make** program again, as follows:

```
[root@arrakis /root]# cd /var/yp; make all
```

This should force all of the maps to be rebuilt and pushed to the secondary servers. The output will look something like this:

```
Updating passwd.byname....
Pushed passwd.byname map.
Updating passwd.byuid...
Pushed passwd.byuid map.
Updating hosts.byname...
Pushed hosts.byname...
[etc...]
```

The **[etc...]** on the last line means the listing will go on for all the maps that you are sharing.

CRITICAL SKILL
17.5 Discovering the NIS Tools

To help you work with NIS, a handful of tools have been written to let you extract information from the database via the command line:

- **ypcat**
- **ypwhich**
- **ypmatch**
- **yppasswd**

The first tool, **ypcat**, dumps the contents of an NIS map. This is useful for scripts that need to pull information out of NIS: **ypcat** can pull the entire map down, and then **grep** can be used to find a specific entry. The **ypcat** command is also useful for simple testing of services, as demonstrated earlier in this module.

The **ypwhich** command returns the name of the NIS server that is answering your requests. This is also a good diagnosis tool if NIS doesn't appear to be working as expected. For example, let's say you've made a change in the master NIS tables but your change can't be seen by a specific client. You can use **ypwhich** to see to which server the client is bound. If it's bound to a secondary server, it might be that the secondary server is not listed in the primary server's **/var/yp/ypservers** file. An example of **ypwhich** usage is as follows:

```
[michael@caladan michael]# ypwhich
arrakis.example.com
```

The **ypmatch** command is a close relative of **ypcat**. Rather than pulling an entire map down, however, you supply a key value to **ypmatch**, and only the entry corresponding to that key is pulled down. Using the **passwd** map as an example, you can pull down the entry to **paul** with this simple command:

```
[michael@caladan /root]# ypmatch paul passwd
paul:$1$sYnyCHmQ$zcKZp1FSaa66ɪY/GVyaIIΓ/:501:501::/home/paul:/bin/bash
```

The **yppasswd** command is the NIS version of the standard Linux **passwd** command. The difference between the two is that the **yppasswd** command allows users to set their passwords on the NIS server. The behavior is otherwise identical to **passwd**. In fact, many sites rename the standard **passwd** command to something like **passwd.local** and then create a symlink from **passwd** to **yppasswd**. Be sure that you've started **yppasswdd** on the master server.

Using Netgroups

NIS adds one more administrative tool to your arsenal. Netgroups are a way to collect similar hosts or users together for simplified administration. The file **/etc/netgroup** is typically where the groups are defined, and shared through the NIS specifier **netgrp**. The format for the netgroup file is the name of the group, followed by a space-separated list of its members. Members are specified either as another group or as a listing in the form (*host,user,domain*), where *host* is the name of a machine, *user* is the name of a user entry, and *domain* is the NIS domain in which the entry is valid. Any of the fields can also be blank, to match any value. For example:

```
admins (caladan,leto,) (,jessica,) (,duncan,)
users admins (,stilgar,) (,chani,)
badguys (,vladimir,) (,shaddam,)
servers (arrakis,,mydepartment.mydomain) (kaitain,,)
```

All of the entries in this example are valid in any NIS domain, except for **arrakis**, which is only in the servers group in the context of the **mydepartment.mycompany** domain. The group **users** also contains all the members of the group **admins**. Many applications only pay attention to either the host portion or the user portion. Using a netgroup in a **passwd** map, for example, only uses the user portion, because the host entry is not relevant in that context. In an NFS exports file, only the host portion would be relevant. For any application that uses both, they must match what is entered in the netgroup file. For example, when the **admins** group is used, **leto** only qualifies as an admin when logged into the host **caladan**.

Netgroups are only valid in NIS-aware contexts and are typically indicated by preceding the group name with an **@** sign to designate it as a netgroup instead of a regular entry. See the next section for an example of usage.

Using NIS in Configuration Files

One of the most popular uses of NIS is the sharing of the **/etc/passwd** file so that everyone can log in to all hosts on the network by making a single modification to the master **/etc/passwd**. In the past it was necessary to add an entry to the end of your local **/etc/passwd** file to indicate that you wanted to use NIS as well. The **nsswitch.conf** file was introduced as a cleaner way of establishing the relationship between NIS and local files, but it loses out on some of the configurability that the old syntax allowed. For this reason, the **compat** mode was introduced for use with **passwd**, **group**, and **shadow**. To use the syntax described in the following listing, change the **nis** entry in the client's **nsswitch.conf** file to **compat**.

```
passwd:        compat files
```

Here is the basic setting you would add to your client's **/etc/passwd** file to allow host login for all users listed in the NIS **passwd** list:

```
+::::::
```

Now here is where it starts to get interesting. Say that you want to override some fields in the password entry for NIS users. Here is the setting if you want NIS users to exist on this host (for permission lookups, for example), but you want to deny everyone from logging in to this host except for those listed explicitly in the **/etc/passwd** file:

```
+:::::::/bin/false
```

This overrides all the user's shell settings so that when login to the client is attempted, the login program tries to run **/bin/false** as the user's login program. Since **/bin/false** doesn't work as a shell, the user is immediately booted out of the system.

To allow a few, explicitly listed users into the system while still denying everyone else, use commands like these:

```
+paul
+duncan
+leto
+:::::::/bin/false
```

This allows only **paul**, **duncan**, and **leto**, specifically, to log in to the system. You can use netgroups here as well as individual usernames.

You can also specifically ignore some NIS entries by using a – sign instead of a + sign.

```
+paul
-feyd
+@admins
-@badguys
+::::::/bin/false
```

This example allows **paul** and everyone in the **admins** netgroup to log in normally; **feyd** and members of the **badguys** group don't exist on this system, and everyone else in NIS will exist but not be able to log in.

Progress Check

1. What tool dumps the contents of an NIS map?
2. What tool can you use to see to which server is client bound?

CRITICAL SKILL
17.6 Implementing NIS in a Real Network

In this section, we'll discuss deployment of NIS in real networked environments. This isn't so much a cookbook as it is a collection of samples. After all, we've already described the details of configuring and setting up NIS servers and clients. No need to repeat that!

Obviously, there will be exceptions to each scenario described here. Some small networks might generate an unusually high amount of NIS traffic, for some reason. Some large networks might have such light NIS traffic that only a single master is needed. In any case, apply a liberal dose of common sense to the following, and you should be fine.

A Small Network

We define a small network to be one with fewer than 30 to 40 UNIX systems, all of which exist on the same subnet. In this case, a single NIS master server is more than enough. Unless any of the systems in your network are generating an unreasonable amount of NIS requests, all of the other systems can be configured as clients to query the master server via either broadcast or direct connection. If you don't expect to segment your network, you'll probably want to stick with using the broadcast method, because it simplifies the process of adding hosts to the network.

---

1. Use **ypcat**.
2. Use **ypwhich**.

The NIS server itself shouldn't have to be too beefy. If you do have a powerful machine handling the task, don't be afraid to have it share the load with another lightweight service or two. Dynamic Host Configuration Protocol (DHCP) is often a good candidate for load sharing.

A Segmented Network

Segmented networks introduce complexity to the process of handling broadcast-style services such as Address Resolution Protocol (ARP) or DHCP. For a growing network, however, segmenting is likely to be a necessity. By segmenting your traffic into two or more discrete networks, you can better keep traffic on each segment down to a controllable level. Furthermore, this arrangement helps you impose tighter security for inside systems. For instance, you can put Accounting and Human Resources onto another subnet to make it harder for engineering to put sniffers on the network and get to confidential information.

For NIS, segmenting means two possible solutions. The first solution assumes that even though you have a large network, your network doesn't require a lot of NIS traffic. This is typically the case in heterogeneous networks where Microsoft Windows has made its way to many desktop workstations. In this case, keeping a single NIS master server is probably enough. In any event, this network's clients should be configured to contact the server directly instead of using broadcasts. This is because only those clients on the same subnet as the NIS server will be able to contact it via broadcasts, and it's much easier to keep all your client workstations configured consistently.

On the other hand, if you do think there is enough NIS traffic, splitting the load across multiple servers—one for each subnet—is a good idea. In this case, the master NIS server is configured to send updates to the secondaries whenever the maps are updated, and clients can be consistently configured to use broadcasts to find the correct NIS server. By using broadcasts, clients can be moved from one subnet to another without your having to reassign their NIS server.

Networks Bigger than Buildings

It isn't uncommon for networks to grow bigger than the buildings they're located in. Remote offices connected through a variety of methods mean a variety of administrative decisions— and not just concerning NIS!

For NIS, however, it is crucial that a server be located at each side of every wide area network (WAN) link. For example, if you have three campuses connected to each other in a mesh by T1 links, you should have at least three NIS servers, one for each campus. This arrangement is needed because NIS relies on low-latency links in order to perform well, especially given that it is a remote procedure call (RPC)–based protocol. (Issuing a simple **ls –l** command can result in hundreds of lookups, literally.) Furthermore, in the event one of the WAN links fails, it is important that each site be able to operate on its own until the link is reestablished.

Depending on the organization of your company and its administration, you may or may not want to split NIS so that multiple NIS domains exist. Once you get past this administrative decision, you can treat each campus as a single site and decide how many NIS servers need to be deployed. If you intend to keep a uniform NIS space, there should be only one NIS master server; the rest of the NIS servers at other campuses should be slaves.

Module Summary

In this module, we discussed the process of installing master NIS servers, slave NIS servers, and NIS clients, as well as how to use some of the tools available on these servers. Here are the key points to remember about NIS:

- NIS is a data-sharing and lookup service. NIS servers do not perform authentication.

- Because anyone in your network can join an NIS domain, it is assumed that your network is already secure. Most sites find that the benefits of this arrangement outweigh the risks.

- Once the makefile is set up and **ypinit** has been run, master NIS servers do not need additional setups. Changes to the files that you need to share via NIS (such as **/etc/passwd**) are updated and propagated by running **cd /var/yp;make**.

- NIS slave servers are listed on the master server's file, **/var/yp/ypservers**.

- NIS slave servers receive their information from the server via a server push.

- Setup of an NIS slave server is little more than running the **ypinit -s** command.

- NIS clients need their **/etc/yp.conf** and **/etc/nsswitch.conf** files to be adjusted, and then only the **ypbind** program is set running.

✓ Module 17 Mastery Check

1. Can NIS allow sharing on any tabular file?

2. What is the main benefit of using NIS?

3. What is one of the two ways that NIS can be queried for the data it keeps track of?

4. A NIS database can also be referred to as a

   A. Flag

   B. Map

   C. Cookie

   D. None of the above

5. True or False? The file that actually contains the instructions for changes to be compiled is called a makefile.

6. When configuring an NIS server for the list of maps, if you do not want maps to be shared, you can comment the line out with

A. A semicolon (;)

B. Two forward slashes (//)

C. A pound symbol (#)

D. A backquote (`)

E. All of the above

7. What does the **ypbind** daemon do?

8. True or False? The **yppassword** command returns the name of the NIS server that is answering your requests.

9. When using a netgroup, members are specified in what list form?

10. What advice does this module give for running NIS over a WAN link?

Module 18

Talking to Windows with Samba

Samba is a powerful tool for allowing UNIX-based systems (such as Linux) to interoperate with Windows-based systems. Samba does this by understanding the Microsoft networking protocol, Session Message Block (SMB). The SMB protocol is used by Windows machines for both file sharing and network printing. From a systems administrator's point of view, this means being able to deploy a UNIX-based server on a predominantly Windows network without having to install Network File System (NFS), the Line Printer Daemon (LPD), and some kind of UNIX-compatible authentication support on all the Windows clients. Instead, the clients can use their native tongue to talk to the server—which means fewer hassles for you and seamless integration for your users. No wonder Samba is so popular!

This chapter covers the procedure for installing and configuring Samba. Thankfully, Samba's default configuration requires little modification, so we'll concentrate on how to perform customary tasks with Samba and how to avoid some common pitfalls. In terms of administration, you'll get a short course on using the Samba Web Administration Tool (SWAT), the Red Hat graphical user interface (GUI) Samba configuration tool, and on the **smbclient** command-line utility. We'll end by documenting the process of using encrypted passwords.

No matter what task you've chosen for Samba to handle, be sure to take the time to read the program's documentation. For some reason, Red Hat has buried much of the best documentation in the SWAT package, so it's worth installing that even if you don't plan to use the web administration ability. The base Samba documentation is located in **/usr/share/doc/samba-2.2.5/**. The additional documentation is available through the SWAT interface (described later in this module in the section "Administering Samba with SWAT"), or you can find it directly under **/usr/share/swat/help/**. As a bonus, there is an entire book called *Using Samba,* by Robert Eckstein, David Collier-Brown, and Peter Kelly (O'Reilly & Associates, 1999) in electronic form accessible through the SWAT interface or under **/usr/share/swat/using_samba/**. All the documentation is well written, complete, and thorough. For the short afternoon it takes to get through most of it, you'll gain a substantial amount of knowledge.

NOTE

Samba has actually been ported to a significant number of platforms—almost any variant of UNIX you can imagine, and even several non-UNIX environments. In this discussion, we are of course most interested in Samba/Linux, but keep in mind that Samba can be deployed on your other UNIX systems, as well.

CRITICAL SKILL
18.1 Understanding the Mechanics of SMB

To fully understand the Linux/Samba/Windows relationship, you need to understand the relationships of both operating systems to their files, printers, users, and networks. To better see how these relationships compare, let's examine some of the fundamental issues of working with both Linux and Windows in the same environment.

Usernames and Passwords

The UNIX login/password mechanism is radically different from the Windows Primary Domain Controller (PDC) model and the Windows 2000 Active Directory model. Thus it's important for the systems administrator to maintain consistency in the logins and passwords across both systems. Users need to access both systems without having to worry about reauthentication or cached passwords that don't match a particular server.

You have several management options for handling username and password issues:

● **The Linux Password Authentication Module (PAM)**   Allows you to authenticate users against a PDC. This means you still have two user lists—one local and one on the PDC—but your users need only keep track of their passwords on the Windows system.

● **Samba as a PDC**   Allows you to keep all your logins and passwords on the Linux system, while all your Windows boxes authenticate with Samba.

● **Rolling your own solution using Perl**   Allows you to use your own custom script. For sites with a well-established system for maintaining logins and passwords, it isn't unreasonable to come up with a custom script. This would be done using WinPerl and the Perl modules that allow changes to the Security Access Manager (SAM), to update the PDC's password list. A Perl script on the Linux side can communicate with the WinPerl script to keep accounts synchronized.

In the worst-case situation, you can always maintain the two systems by hand (which some early systems administrators did indeed have to do!), but this method is error prone and not much fun to manage.

Encrypted Passwords

Starting with Windows NT 4/Service Pack 3, Windows 98, and Windows 95 OSR2, Windows uses encrypted passwords when communicating with the PDC and any server requiring authentication (including Linux and Samba). The encryption algorithm used by Windows is different from UNIX's, however, and therefore is not compatible. Here are your choices for handling this conflict:

● Edit the Registry on Windows clients to disable use of encrypted passwords. The Registry entries that need to be changed are listed in the **docs** directory in the Samba package.

● Configure Samba to use Windows-style encrypted passwords.

The first solution has the benefit of not pushing you over to a more-complex password scheme. On the other hand, you have to apply the Registry fix on all your clients. The second option, of course, has the opposite effect: For a little more complexity on the server side, you don't have to modify any of your clients.

The process of setting up Windows-style encrypted passwords is discussed in "Supporting Encrypted Passwords" later in this module.

Ask the Expert

Q: Active Directory uses the Domain Name System (DNS) for naming, so I shouldn't need nmdb anymore, right?

A: With the release of Windows 2000, Microsoft moved to a pure DNS naming convention as part of its support for Active Directory in an attempt to make name services more consistent between the Network Neighborhood and the host names that are published in DNS. In theory, you shouldn't need **nmbd** anymore, but the reality is that you will—especially if you intend to allow non–Windows 2000 hosts on your network to access your Samba shares. Unfortunately, it will be many years before we see the complete demise of the horror known as NetBIOS.

The Differences Between smbd and nmbd

The code of the Samba server is actually composed of two daemons: **smbd** and **nmbd**. The **smbd** daemon handles the actual sharing of file systems and printer services for clients. It starts by binding to port 139 and then listens for requests. Every time a client authenticates itself, **smbd** makes a copy of itself; the original goes back to listening to port 139 for new requests, and the copy handles the connection for the client. This new copy also changes its effective user ID from **root** to the authenticated user. (For example, if the user **michael** authenticated against **smbd**, the new copy would run with the permissions of **michael**, not the permissions of **root**.) The copy stays in memory as long as there is a connection from the client.

The **nmbd** daemon is responsible for handling NetBIOS name server requests. It begins by binding itself to port 137; unlike **smbd**, however, **nmbd** does not create a new instance of itself to handle every query. In addition to name server requests, **nmbd** also handles requests from master browsers, domain browsers, and Windows Internet Naming Service (WINS) servers.

Both daemons must be started for Samba to work properly.

CRITICAL SKILL
18.2 Installing Samba

First you will want to determine whether you need the ability to share local directories using Samba as a server, or only to mount other machines using Samba as a client. If you're taking the GUI approach, you'll want to either launch **redhat-config-packages** from the command line, or select Packages from the System Settings submenu. The Windows File Server option will allow you to install both the Samba package for the server and the Samba client package. The SWAT package is conspicuously missing from the list, probably in an attempt to encourage use of Red Hat's own GUI tool, so you'll have to install the RPM manually. As we mentioned earlier, it's probably worth installing the SWAT package for its documentation alone, even if you don't plan to use it for configuration purposes. The RPMs you'll want to look for are

samba-common, **samba**, **samba-client**, **samba-swat**, and **redhat-config-samba**. If you're only looking for a server installation, you'll need at least **samba** and **samba-common**. If you're only interested in acting as a client, then you'll want **samba-common** and **samba-client**. And if you don't want to set up the config files by hand, you'll want either **samba-swat** or **redhat-config-samba** if not both.

CRITICAL SKILL
18.3 Performing Samba Administration

This section describes some of the issues of administering Samba. We'll see how to start and stop Samba, how to do common administrative tasks with SWAT or **redhat-config-samba**, and how to use **smbclient**. Finally, we'll examine the process of using encrypted passwords.

Starting and Stopping Samba

If you want to manually control Samba, you can use the **/etc/init.d/smb** script to start and stop the services. This will handle both the **smbd** and **nmbd** services. For example, to explicitly start the service using this script, you would run:

```
[root@picard /root]# /etc/init.d/smb start
```

And to stop the service using this script, you would run:

```
[root@picard /root]# /etc/init.d/smb stop
```

To ensure that it starts at boot time, you can bring up the services GUI tool by selecting the Services tool from the Server Settings submenu, or type **redhat-config-services** on the command line. As you may have surmised from the previous example, the **smb** option will take care of both **smbd** and **nmbd**. The **swat** option can be turned on if you want to use the web-based configuration, or it can be left off it you only installed SWAT for the extra documentation.

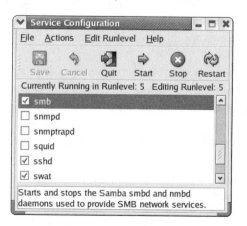

If you're looking to set this all up from the command line, you'll want to make sure you have the appropriate symlinks in the **/etc/rc3.d** and **/etc/rc5.d** directories pointing to the **/etc/init.d/smb** script. See Module 7 for details on checking for this and setting up the symlinks if you don't have them already. SWAT is typically started from **xinetd**, so you'll want to edit **/etc/xinetd.d/ swat** if you want to enable it. SWAT runs on port 901 by default, so you'll want to look at **/etc/services** if you really need to change that for some reason.

NOTE

If you make a change to the configuration of Samba, you'll need to stop and then restart Samba in order for those changes to take effect. It's the client's responsibility to reestablish the connection. This is part of the SMB protocol and not a limitation of Samba.

Progress Check

1. What is PAM?

2. What is one difference between **smbd** and **nmbd**?

CRITICAL SKILL
18.4 Administering Samba with SWAT

Prior to version 2 of Samba, the official way to configure it was by editing the **smb.conf** file. Though verbose in nature and easy to understand, this file was rather large and cumbersome. It also meant that setting up shares under Windows was still easier than setting up shares with Samba. Many individuals developed graphical front ends to the editing process. Many of these tools are still being maintained and enhanced—you can read more about them by visiting Samba's web site at http://www.samba.org. As of version 2, however, Samba ships with the Samba Web Administration Tool (SWAT).

Using SWAT is remarkably easy. All configuration is done via a web browser. SWAT then takes the information from the browser and builds an **smb.conf** file. For those who are used to editing configuration files, this may be a bit annoying because SWAT doesn't preserve comments in the configuration file itself. Therefore, server configuration documentation must remain external to Samba rather than embedded in the configuration file in the form of comments.

---

1. Password Authentication Module (PAM) allows you to authenticate users against a PDC.

2. **nmbd** handles name server requests from master browsers, domain, and WINS servers, whereas **smbd** handles the actual file sharing systems and printers.

NOTE

If you prefer maintaining comments in your configuration file or if you need to write some of your own tools to automate certain administration chores, you should not use SWAT. Herein lies the beauty of text-based configuration files. You have a choice: you don't have to use the GUI if you don't want to, and since the file format is public, anyone can write their own administration tool if they want to.

Setting Up SWAT

You can use SWAT to manage Samba through a browser interface. It's an excellent alternative to editing the Samba configuration files by hand, but don't let it make you believe that the configuration files are complex!

What makes SWAT a little different from other browser-based administration tools is that it does not rely on a web server (like Apache). Instead, SWAT performs all the needed web server functions without implementing a full web server. This is mostly accomplished by running through the **xinetd** daemon.

Simply point your web browser to your Samba server at port 901 to get a login prompt for entering SWAT. Note that the default configuration only allows you to connect to SWAT from the same machine on which you are running Samba. This was done for the purpose of security, since you don't want to allow random people to be able to probe at your machine remotely. If you have a web browser installed on the server, simply point it at http://localhost:901/. If you don't have a web browser installed on the local system, then you have to choose between using a different administration tool or enabling SWAT to be used across the network. If you want to use a local web browser but don't have X Window System installed on the Samba server, you can still use any of a number of text-based web browsers as well.

CAUTION

Logging in as **root** through SWAT causes the root password to be sent from the web browser to the Samba server. Therefore, avoid doing administration tasks across an untrusted network. Preferably, run a web browser on the server itself, or set up an SSH tunnel between the client host and the Samba server host.

Using SWAT from Other Hosts

If you used **xinetd**, then you already have TCP Wrappers functionality built into the configuration file. Changing the **only_from** option in **/etc/xinetd.d/swat** will allow you to add additional hosts with the ability to connect. Take a look at Module 8 for more information on how to limit which hosts can connect to your server.

The SWAT Menus

When you connect to SWAT and log in as **root**, you'll see the main menu shown in Figure 18-1. From here, you can find almost all the documentation you'll need for Samba's configuration files, daemons, and related programs. None of the links point to external web sites, so you can read them at your leisure without connecting to the Net. You'll also be able to access the Samba HowTo collection and the book *Using Samba*.

At the top of the window are buttons for the following menu choices:

Button Name	Description
Home	The main menu page
Globals	Configuration options that affect all operational aspects of Samba
Shares	For setting up disk shares and their respective options
Printers	For setting up printers to be accessible to NT clients
Status	The status of the **smbd** and **nmbd** processes, including a list of all clients connected to these processes and what they are doing (the same information that's listed in the **smbstatus** command-line program)
View	The resulting **smb.conf** file
Password	Password settings

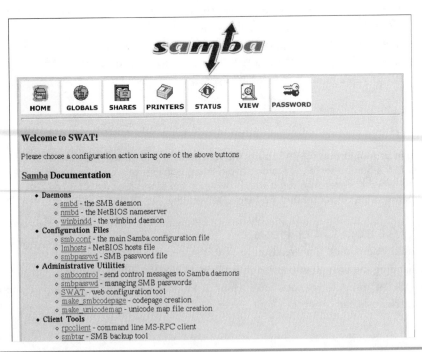

Figure 18-1 The main SWAT menu

Globals

The Globals page lists all settings that affect all aspects of Samba's operation. These settings are divided into seven groups: Base, Security, Logging, Tuning, Printing, Browse, and WINS. To the left of each option is a link to the relevant documentation of the setting and its values. If you're planning to share UNIX printers through Samba, you'll want to make sure you have your printing option set to use LPRng or Common Unix Printing System (CUPS), as appropriate.

Shares

Under Windows, setting up a *share* means creating a new folder, right-clicking it, and allowing it to be shared. Additional controls can be established by right-clicking the folder and selecting Properties.

Using SWAT, these same actions are accomplished by creating a new share. You can then select the share and click Choose Share. This brings up all the configurable parameters for the share.

Printers

Samba automatically makes all printers listed in your local printing setup—that is the **/etc/printcap** file, in the case of LPRng, or **/etc/cups/printers.conf**, in the case of CUPS (see Module 19), available for use via SMB to Windows clients. Through this series of menus, you can modify Samba's treatment of these printers or even add additional printers. The one thing you cannot do here is add printers to the main system. See Module 19 for more information on that process.

Status

The Status page shows the current status of the **smbd** and **nmbd** daemons, including information about what clients are connected and their actions. The page automatically updates every 30 seconds by default, but you can change this rate if you like (it's an option on the page itself). Along with status information, you can turn Samba on and off or ask it to reload its configuration file. This is necessary if you make any changes to the configuration.

View

As you change your Samba configuration, SWAT keeps track of the changes and figures out what information it needs to put into the **smb.conf** file. Open the View page, and you can see the file SWAT is putting together for you.

Password

Use the Password page if you intend to support encrypted passwords. You'll want to give your users a way to modify their own passwords without having to log in to the Linux server. This page allows users to do just that.

NOTE

It's almost always a good idea to disallow access to your servers for everyone except support personnel. This reduces the chances of mistakes being made that could affect the performance or stability of your server.

Project 18-1 Creating a Share with SWAT

The preceding section should have given you the basics needed to set up Samba effectively. This project will build on that knowledge and walk you step by step through the process of creating a share.

Step by Step

1. Click the Shares button on the main SWAT window. This displays a page like the one shown here.

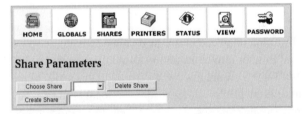

2. In the text box next to the Create Share button, enter the name of the share you want to create and click Create Share. For instance, to create a share called MYSHARE, the screen will look like this.

Share Parameters

Choose Share	myshare ▾	Delete Share
Create Share		
Commit Changes	Reset Values	Advanced View

Base Options

| Help | comment | | Set Default |
| Help | path | /exports/myshare | Set Default |

Security Options

Help	guest account	nobody	Set Default
Help	read only	Yes ▾	Set Default
Help	guest ok	No ▾	Set Default
Help	hosts allow		Set Default
Help	hosts deny		Set Default

Browse Options

| Help | browseable | Yes ▾ | Set Default |

Miscellaneous Options

| Help | available | Yes ▾ | Set Default |

(continued)

3. Change the settings for your share. You may want to customize the share's comment (which will show up in Windows Explorer), the directory where all the contents of the share should reside, and various security and browse options.

4. Once you've entered all the information, click the Commit Changes button near the top of the screen.

5. To make the changes appear to any systems that browse your server, restart the **smbd** daemon by going into the Status menu and clicking the Restart smbd button.

Project Summary

And that's it. You should now be able to see this share from Windows clients browsing the network. It may seem like a lot of work to set up at first, but once you've done a couple, they'll seem really easy. Don't forget that you can also use SWAT to go back and change your settings later.

CRITICAL SKILL
18.5 Sharing with redhat-config-samba

An alternative to using SWAT for setting up Samba shares is to use Red Hat's own GUI tool, **redhat-config-samba**. Although this tool will make it easy to share directories through Samba, it doesn't give you the fine-grained control over the various aspects of the Samba server that SWAT provides. Once again, the GUI tool is likely to destroy any attempt at commenting your config files.

Project 18-2   Creating a Share with redhat-config-samba

Since you understand the basics of Samba shares by now, you shouldn't have any trouble with this project.

Step by Step

1. Launch the tool either by typing **redhat-config-samba** on the command line or by selecting Samba Server from the Server Settings submenu.

Directory	Permissions	Description
/usr	Read Only	usr
/tmp	Read / Write	temp
/exports/	Read Only	shared stuff

Samba Server Configuration

Action   Preferences   Help

New   Properties   Delete   Help   Apply

(continued)

2. Click New to create a new Samba share.

3. Choose a directory either by typing the path into the appropriate text widget, or use the Browse button to select it.

4. Type a description of the share into the indicated text widget.

5. Choose whether or not to allow write access to this share by selecting the corresponding radio button.

6. Click OK when you're finished.

Project Summary

You can change any of the options you just set by selecting the share and clicking the Properties button. In addition, in the Preferences menu you'll find the options to change broader properties of your Samba server, such as your workgroup name. Although this tool doesn't have quite the variety of options that SWAT provides, it is effective in quickly and easily setting up a share.

CRITICAL SKILL
18.6 # Using smbclient

The **smbclient** program is a command-line tool that allows your Linux system to act as a Windows client. You can use this utility to connect to other Samba servers or even to real Windows NT/2000 servers. The **smbclient** program is very flexible and can be used to browse other servers, send and retrieve files from them, or even print to them. As you can imagine, this is also a great debugging tool since you can quickly and easily check whether a new Samba installation works correctly without having to find a Windows client to test it.

In this section, we'll show you how to do basic browsing, remote file access, and remote printer access with **smbclient**. However, remember that **smbclient** is a very flexible program, limited only by your imagination.

Browsing a Server

With so many graphical interfaces around, we've come to equate browsing to mean "point and click." But when your intention is to simply find out what a server has to offer, it's not enough of a reason in itself to support an entire GUI.

Using **smbclient** with the **–L** option allows you to view the offerings of an NT or Samba server without having to use a GUI. Here's the format of the command:

```
[root@picard root]# smbclient -L hostname
```

where *hostname* is the name of the server. For example, if you want to see what the host **locutus** has to offer, you would type:

```
[root@picard root]# smbclient -L locutus
```

This will return information that looks something like the following:

```
Added interface ip=192.168.1.1 bcast=192.168.1.255 nmask=255.255.255.0
Password:
Domain=[MYGROUP] OS=[UNIX] Server=[Samba 2.2.5]

        Sharename        Type       Comment
        ---------        ----       -------
        MYSHARE          Disk
        IPC$             IPC        IPC Service (Samba Server)
        lp               Printer

        Server                      Comment
        ---------                   -------
        LOCUTUS                        Samba Server

        Workgroup                   Master
        ---------                   -------
        MYGROUP
```

NOTE

Depending on server configuration, you might get prompted for a password. If the server allows guest browsing, you can simply press ENTER at the **password:** prompt and see the browse list. Otherwise, you'll need to enter your password.

Remote File Access

The **smbclient** utility allows you to access files on a Windows or Samba server with a command-line hybrid DOS/FTP client interface. For its most straightforward usage, you'll simply run the following:

```
[michael@picard ~]$ /usr/bin/smbclient //server/share
```

where *server* is the server name and *share* is the share name to which you want to connect. By default, Samba automatically sets up all users' home directories as shares. (For instance, the user **michael** can access his home directory on the server **picard** by going to //**picard/michael**.)

Once it's connected, you'll be able to browse directories using the **cd**, **dir**, and **ls** commands. You can also use **get**, **put**, **mget**, and **mput** to transfer files back and forth. The online help explains all of the commands in detail. Simply type **help** at the prompt to see what is available.

Following are some command-line parameters you may need to use with **smbclient** to connect to a server.

Parameter for smbclient	Description
–I *destIP*	The destination IP address to which you want to connect
–U *username*	The user you want to connect as, instead of the user you are logged in as
–W *name*	Sets the workgroup name to *name*
–D *directory*	Starts from *directory*

NOTE

The **smbclient** program has a **tar** mode as well. You'll find it is easier to access this mode from the **smbtar** command, since **smbtar** provides an interface much more consistent with regular **tar**. Obviously, this is most useful for interfacing with your backup system. The man page for **smbtar** will tell you more about it.

Remote Printer Access

So the head of Marketing got a brand-new color laser printer, but your request for a wrist brace to help with your carpal tunnel syndrome was turned down. It's only fair that you get to use the printer, right?

If that printer is sitting on an NT server that doesn't have **lpd** configured, but it does share the printer via SMB so other Windows workstations can print to it, you're in luck. You can use **smbclient** to submit print jobs to other NT or Samba servers just as a Windows client would.

To connect to a printer on a server using **smbclient**, use the **–P** parameter and specify the service name for the printer, as shown here:

```
[michael@picard michael]# smbclient //marketing/lp -P
```

This connects you to the service as a printer. You can then issue the **print** command along with the name of a local filename. For example, if you have a file called **blecker** in the directory from which you run **smbclient**, you can issue this command:

```
smb:> print deviousplan
```

to print the contents of the file **deviousplan**.

Possible uses for this remote printer access feature include setting up special filters in **/etc/printcap** files so that all files printed to a particular printer are automatically redirected to a Windows printer on the network. (For more information, see Module 19.)

CRITICAL SKILL

18.7 Mounting with smbmount

If your kernel is configured to support the SMB file system (as are most kernels that come with Linux distributions), you can actually mount a Windows or Samba share onto your system in much the same way you would mount an NFS partition. This is very handy for accessing a large disk on a remote server without having to shuffle individual files across the network.

To use **smbmount**, simply run this command:

```
[root@picard /mnt]# smbmount //locutus/michael /mnt/michael
```

where **//locutus/michael** is the share being mounted, and **/mnt/michael** is the directory to which it is being mounted. To unmount this directory, run **umount**:

```
[root@picard /mnt]# umount /mnt/michael
```

CRITICAL SKILL

18.8 Supporting Encrypted Passwords

Because Windows uses a password-hashing algorithm different from Linux's, Samba needs to maintain its own password file in order to support encrypted password support. The quick way to get a list of existing users in the **/etc/passwd** file for whom to implement encrypted password support is to use the **mksmbpasswd.sh** script that comes with Samba. You can find it in the **/usr/bin** directory (**/usr/bin/mksmbpasswd.sh**).

The **mksmbpasswd.sh** script's usage is as follows:

```
[root@picard /root]# cd /etc/samba/
[root@picard samba]# mksmbpasswd < /etc/passwd > smbpasswd
[root@picard samba]# chmod 600 smbpasswd
```

NOTE

If you are using NIS, you will want to use **ypcat passwd** to get the password list from the NIS server and store that to a file. Then, instead of using **/etc/passwd**, use the file containing the results from **ypcat passwd**.

The foregoing command will create the **smbpasswd** list with the appropriate file permissions. Unfortunately, because UNIX passwords cannot be reversed to generate a cleartext password that can then be rehashed to work under Samba, the **smbpasswd** file's list of users does not contain valid passwords. That needs to be set by the user using the **smbpasswd** command or via SWAT's interface.

Allowing NULL Passwords

If you have a need to allow users to have no passwords (which is a bad idea), you can do so by using the **smbpasswd** program with the **–n** option, like so:

```
[root@picard /root]# smbpasswd -n username
```

where *username* is the name of the user whose password you want to set to empty.

In addition to using **smbpasswd**, you can do this via the SWAT program.

Changing Passwords with smbpasswd

Users who prefer the command line over the web interface can use the **smbpasswd** command to change their Samba password. (Note that this is different from the **smbpasswd** file, which is in the **/etc/samba/** directory.) This program works just like the regular **passwd** program, except this program does not update the **/etc/passwd** or NIS **passwd** files. Because **smbpasswd** uses the standard protocol for communicating with the server regarding password changes, you can also use this to change your password on a remote Windows machine.

CRITICAL SKILL
18.9 Troubleshooting Samba

There are four typical solutions to connectivity problems with Samba.

- *Restart Samba.* This may be necessary because either Samba has entered an undefined state or, more likely, you've made changes to the configuration but forgot to restart Samba so that the changes take effect.

- *Make sure the configuration options are correct.* Errors in the **smb.conf** file are typically in directory names, usernames, network numbers, and host names. A common mistake is when a new client is added to a group that has special access to the server, but Samba isn't told the name of the new client being added.

- *Monitor encrypted passwords.* Passwords may be mismatched; the server is configured to use them, and the clients aren't—or, more likely, the clients are using encrypted passwords, and Samba hasn't been configured to use them.

If you're under the gun to get a client working, you may just want to disable client-side encryption using the **regedit** scripts that come with Samba's source code (see the **docs** subdirectory).

● *Monitor cached passwords.* Windows often caches passwords in files that end in **pwl**. Not only is this a security risk (the **pwl** files are poorly encrypted), but if your password has changed on the server, Windows may continue feeding the cached password instead of prompting you for a new one. Simply remove the **pwl** files to force Windows to prompt you for a password.

Module Summary

In this chapter, we discussed the process of compiling, installing, and configuring Samba so that your Linux server can integrate into a Windows-based network. Samba is a powerful tool with the potential to replace Windows servers dedicated to disk and printer sharing.

Reading through tons of documentation probably isn't your favorite way to pass the day, but you'll find the Samba documentation to be complete, helpful, and easy to read. At least skim through the files to see what's there, so you know where you can go to get additional information when you need it. Plus, with the entire *Using Samba* book (referred to in the introduction to this module) as part of the distribution, you should have everything you need for configuring even the most complex setup. If you would rather read more about Samba in print, you can purchase the same book that is shipped with the distribution.

✓ Module 18 Mastery Check

1. When dealing with encrypted passwords, what are two ways of handling the incompatibility between UNIX and Windows?

2. Do **smbd** and **nmbd** both have to be started in order for Samba to work?

3. What is Samba?

4. What is the main advantage of using Samba?

5. What does SMB stand for?

6. Give an example of command lines that start and stop Samba.

7. What is SWAT?

8. What are the "Globals" in the SWAT menu?

9. What is the Shares link on the SWAT menu used for?

10. What is the parameter for connecting the **smbclient** to a printer?

11. Which of the following are ways to troubleshoot Samba?

    A. Restart it.

    B. Verify configuration options.

    C. Monitor encrypted passwords.

    D. All of the above.

Module 19

Printing

The line printer daemon (**lpd**) is the traditional UNIX way of handling print requests. The name harkens back to **lpd**'s origins in the 1970s as a way of sending text to line printers. Over the years, support for other types of printers have been added (nearly any serial, parallel, or network printer can be supported) but the name remained. The **lpd** system can handle requests destined for printers attached to the immediate system or printers accessible via the network. These requests may originate locally or from other clients on the network.

The command that is used to request a print job be sent to the line printer daemon is **lpr**; and as a result, the **lpd** package is sometimes also referred to as **lpr**. One of the two printing systems that comes with Red Hat 8 is LPRng, the "next generation" print server for Linux. LPRng is a completely new implementation of the aging **lpd/lpr** system. What makes LPRng different from other implementations is that it is much more configurable, has a better filtering mechanism, scales to large numbers of printers, and is written with security in mind.

While **lpd** has been the standard for UNIX systems, other systems have come up with their own print systems. (We talked a bit about Windows printing in the previous module on Samba.) In the mid 1990s, a number of companies that had interest in a common printing system approached the Printer Working Group (**pwg**), which represented a number of printer manufacturers and venders. A printing project under development at IBM was combined with a joint effort underway between Novell and Xerox, and the result became the start of the Internet Printing Protocol (IPP). The goal of IPP is to provide a common protocol that can be used across systems, reduce the number of different standards that printers have to support, and cover most common printing situations. IPP enjoys widespread industry support and with time may become the standard network printing solution for all operating systems.

The Common UNIX Printing System (CUPS) is an implementation of IPP for UNIX that strives to be a complete modern printing system while maintaining compatibility with existing applications. Red Hat 8 ships with CUPS as an alternative to the LPRng printing system.

NOTE

On the other end of the process, printers come in a wide variety of models, with a wide variety of features, and very little compatibility with other manufacturers' printers. One notable attempt at device-independent printing is Adobe's PostScript. PostScript is actually a programming language that is focused on describing text and graphics on a page. The idea is that a PostScript interpreter can be built in to a printer (or other device). In theory, a PostScript file will then appear the same when printed on any PostScript-enabled device. We're not going to talk a lot about PostScript here, but you'll see the term pop up often enough when dealing with printers or printing systems that it helps to at least be aware of it.

CRITICAL SKILL

19.1 Knowing the Basics of lpd

The model used by **lpd** is actually similar to the e-mail process: The daemon quietly listens for print requests to come to it over the network. This means the daemon considers print requests coming from other hosts to be just the same as those originating from the same host as the daemon's, thus making the configuration files easier to manage.

For each print job that arrives, the file is first placed in a spool directory. Typically, this directory is **/var/spool/lpd/***printername*, where ***printername*** is the name of the printer to which the job is going. Once spooled, **lpd** gets the requested print job to the printer independently of the sender. This allows the sender to resume operation instead of the user having to stare at an hourglass icon.

Here are the steps of the **lpd** process for getting the print job to the printer:

1. Look up the printer configuration information in **/etc/printcap**.

2. If the printer requires that the job go through a print filter, send the file through the filter.

3. If the printer is physically attached to the server, send the filtered print request directly to the print device.

4. If the printer is remote (accessed via the network), contact the corresponding **lpd** server and send the filtered job to that server.

CRITICAL SKILL

19.2 Installing LPRng

When you launch **redhat-config-packages** you'll find an entry near the bottom of the list labeled Printing Support. Clicking on Details on the right will bring up a dialog box listing the printing-related packages you can install. At this point we're interested in the LPRng system and the **hpijs** printer drivers. The underlying RPMs installed are also named LPRng and **hpijs**.

The following table summarizes some of the programs and configuration files installed with the LPRng system, which we'll discuss in further detail in the following sections.

Program	Purpose
/usr/sbin/lpd	The print server daemon
/usr/bin/lpr	Used for submitting print jobs
/usr/bin/lpq	Checks the status of the print queues

Program	Purpose
/usr/bin/lprm	Removes print jobs sitting on the queue
/usr/sbin/lpc	Controls the print server daemon
/usr/bin/lpstat	Shows the status of the printers
/etc/printcap	Lists printers in the system
/etc/lpd.conf	Contains the LPRng configuration options used by both clients and servers
/etc/lpd.perms	Contains the permission information used by the **lpd** server to control user actions
/usr/sbin/checkpc	Checks the configuration of the print system

Starting LPRng on Boot

If you're changing the start or stop runlevels for LPRng from the GUI **redhat-config-services** tool, the entry you want to look for is **lpd**. If, on the other hand, you're looking to manipulate the symlinks by hand, you might consider using **S60lpd** and **K60lpd**, just to keep in sync with the GUI tool.

```
[root@scribe rc3.d]# rm K60lpd
[root@scribe rc3.d]# ln -s ../init.d/lpd S60lpd
```

CRITICAL SKILL
19.3 Configuring /etc/printcap

The **/etc/printcap** file tells the LPRng server daemon (**lpd**) the names and characteristics of all of its printers. Every printer has an entry that looks something like this:

```
printername1|printername2|printername3:
    :command=value:
    :command:
    :command=value:
```

where *printername1* is the name of the printer, and *printername2* and *printername3* are aliases to *printername1*. Each *command* may be followed by a value.

Before we see what the final **printcap** file will look like, take a look at Table 19-1, which gets into the details of what each parameter in the printer configuration means. Note that this is a simplified list. You can read about the complete configuration options in the LPRng-HOWTO guide at **/usr/share/doc/LPRng-3.8.9/LPRng-HOWTO.html**.

Command	Purpose/Value
sd	Spool directory pathname. This is where the **lpd** server will place files that are being sent to the printer. Since it is possible for it to receive a new file while one is still being printed, **lpd** will queue those new files in this specified directory. Typically, this directory is **/var/spool/lpd/*printername***, where *printername* is the name of the printer (e.g., **sd=/var/spool/lpd/plato**). As the files get printed, **lpd** will automatically remove them. If you expect a printer to get a lot of volume, you will want to be sure that this directory has enough space to hold all of the queued documents.
sh	Suppress header/banner pages. Banner pages show who printed the document and the name of the document. The idea behind this is to allow jobs arriving at high-volume printers to be easily sorted by whoever gets to the printer first. Most sites find that banner pages are not worth the wasted paper and prefer to keep this feature turned off.
rm	Specify the remote machine. Since **lpd** can redirect print jobs to other print servers, it must be possible to specify the name of the remote print server. This command lets you do so. This is typically used in conjunction with the **rp** command.
rp	Specify the remote printer queue. When redirecting print jobs to a remote print server, you need to specify the name of the remote print queue to which you want to submit the job, as well. Typically, this is because dedicated print servers control multiple printers. This command will let you specify the name of the print queue. (Note: If you are printing to a network-enabled printer, such as an HP LaserJet with JetDirect, you do not need to specify the remote print queue.)
mx	Specify the maximum job size in 1K blocks. 0 means no size limit.
lp	Specify the local output device (e.g., **/dev/lp0**). If your printer is connected locally, you need to specify the device name by which it can be accessed. Most printers that have a parallel port can be accessed through the **/dev/lp0** device. You will probably want to specify a filter with this parameter.
filter	Specify the filter to pass through before sending data to the local output device. You can consider a filter to be the logical equivalent of a printer driver under Windows. UNIX systems (Linux included) have a long history of working directly with PostScript, and because most of the original typesetters were driven by UNIX systems, PostScript became the de facto standard. (The "official" reason why UNIX was first developed at Bell Labs was so that the Patent Department could drive a typesetter. For more details, see Chapter 5 of the book *A Quarter Century of UNIX*, by Peter H. Salus (Addison-Wesley, 1994).) If your printer already understands PostScript, then you can probably leave this alone. On the other hand, if your printer does not understand PostScript, you will need a filter that converts PostScript into your printer's format.

Table 19-1   Printer Configuration Parameters

For example, in the following **/etc/printcap** file, the printer's name is **plato**, and its alias is **lp**:

```
plato|lp:
      :sd=/var/spool/lpd/plato:
      :sh:
      :rm=bookworm:
      :rp=plato:
```

You can have multiple printers listed in this file, like so:

```
orwell|lp:
      :sd=/var/spool/lpd/orwell:
      :sh:
      :rm=bookworm:
      :rp=laserprint:
poe|lp2:
      :sd=/var/spool/lpd/poe:
      :sh:
      :rm=bookworm:
      :rp=colorprint:
```

In this case, there are two printers: one is called **orwell**, and the other is called **poe**.

Sample /etc/printcap Files

Here are some example configuration files that have been tested and shown to work. As you can see, the configuration files on a per-printer basis are actually quite straightforward.

- An HP LaserJet that supports PostScript connected directly to your network:

```
orwell|lp:
      :sd=/var/spool/lpd/orwell:
      :mx#0:
      :rm=hplj:
```

- An HP DeskJet 550C connected directly to your parallel port:

```
carroll|lp:
      :sd=/var/spool/lpd/carroll:
      :mx#0:
      :lp=/dev/lp0:
      :ifhp=model=ghostscript,gs_device=cdj550
      :filter=/usr/libexec/filters/ifhp:
```

- A PostScript printer named **huxley** connected to a print server called **printserve**:

```
huxley|pslp:
      :sd=/var/spool/lpd/huxley:
      :mx#0:
```

```
:rm=printserve:
:rp=pslp:
```

Implementing Your Changes

There's one last catch you should be aware of before you run off to modify **/etc/printcap**. Unlike many versions of UNIX, the **/etc/printcap** file on Red Hat is actually a conglomeration of many sources. Certain events, such as using the GUI tool described in the next section, will cause the **/etc/printcap** file to be regenerated; and changes you've made by hand run the risk of being lost. If you want to make changes safely, you'll need to actually put them in **/etc/printcap.local**. This file will be merged verbatim into **/etc/printcap** when the latter is regenerated. Once you update the **/etc/printcap.local** file, you need to restart **lpd** in order for your changes to take effect.

```
[root@scribe /root]# /etc/init.d/lpd restart
```

Project 19-1 Graphical Printer Configuration

If you don't want to try to set this all up by hand, there is also a graphical tool that helps you get everything set up. Setting up a printer in the GUI tool will both create the queue and modify **/etc/printcap**, as well as give you the option to restart **lpd** and send a test page to the printer when you're finished.

Printers that you already have set up in **/etc/printcap.local** will not show up in the graphical tool, but can work alongside the printers you configure here. No attempt is made, however, to reconcile your graphically configured printers with those you've set up by hand, so it's easy for your graphical configuration to stomp on hand-edited changes. For this reason, you're strongly encouraged to use either hand configuration or graphical setup, but not both. This is particularly true in an environment with multiple admins.

Step by Step

1. You can bring up the printer GUI tool by selecting Printing from the System Settings menu, or by typing **redhat-config-printer** at the command line.

(continued)

2. Select New on the button bar to create a new print queue.

3. Click Forward to continue to the queue type selection dialog box.

4. Enter a name for your print queue.

5. Select the queue type depending on whether the printer is locally connected or whether it's being sent to a remote print server. If it is being sent to a remote print server, select the style of print server the remote machine is running.

6. If this is a local printer, select the device used by the local printer. For parallel printers, this is probably **/dev/lp0**. Alternatively, if this queue points to a remote server, you'll enter the server information at this point.

7. If your printer doesn't support PostScript directly, on the Driver page select the appropriate filter for your specific hardware, and then click the Forward button.

8. Examine the resulting setup and click Apply if it looks correct.

9. If you need to change values for an existing queue, select the queue and click Edit to change properties of an existing print queue. In addition to the values you entered, there is a tab for Driver Options where you can fine-tune some adjustments for your setup:

10. Select which print queue you want to be the default, and then click the Default button on the toolbar. The first column in the printer listings will show a green check mark next to the printer that is the default for commands that don't specify a print queue by name.

Project Summary

You can repeat this procedure for each printer you want to set up. Because any changes to **/etc/printcap** won't take effect until **lpd** is restarted, either clicking the Apply button on the toolbar or quitting the program will cause **lpd** to restart.

Progress Check

1. What is the purpose of the **/etc/printcap** file?

2. If you want to make changes to the **/etc/printcap** file, where should you make those changes?

CRITICAL SKILL

19.4 Understanding the /etc/lpd.perms File

The **/etc/lpd.perms** file allows you to control who can print to your print server. The file itself consists of a series of rules that are evaluated one at a time, in order. The first rule to match decides whether the request can or cannot be processed. The last rule should always indicate a default behavior. Any line in the **/etc/lpd.perms** file that begins with a pound symbol (#) is a comment.

The simplest configuration is to accept all requests. To accomplish this, the only uncommented line in the **/etc/lpd.perms** file should be

```
DEFAULT ACCEPT
```

The remainder of this section discusses more complex rules you can establish and ends with a sample set of rules you can use.

The Format of /etc/lpd.perms

The format of each rule line in the **/etc/lpd.perms** file can take one of the four following forms:

```
ACTION [not] KEY                assigned value
ACTION [not] KEY=pattern        substring match
ACTION [not] KEY=IP/mask        IP address (with optional netmask)
```

where *ACTION* is either ACCEPT or REJECT; the **not** keyword is optional and if present, it negates the *KEY*; and the *KEY* specifies the rule we are checking against with possible parameters (*pattern* or *IP/mask*).

Let's step through a quick example to see what's going on. Say you want to refuse connections from your gateway IP address. You would write a rule that looks like this:

```
REJECT SERVICE=X IFIP=192.168.1.1
```

---

1. The **/etc/printcap** file describes the names and characteristics of printers on a system.
2. You should make changes to the **/etc/printcap.local** file.

The action is to REJECT. There are two checks that need to match in order for the action to occur: first, the service must be a connection request (**SERVICE=X**); and second, the IP address must be 192.168.1.1 (your gateway). If these two are true, then the connection is rejected.

Taking the same example and making it more complex, let's say that you want to reject all connection requests not from your local area network (192.168.1.0/24), nor from the server itself. The rule would look like this:

```
REJECT SERVICE=X NOT IFIP=192.168.1.0/24,127.0.0.1/32
```

The action is REJECT. If the service is a connection request (**SERVICE=X**), the IP is not in the 192.168.1.0/24 network, and the IP is not 127.0.0.1, then the rule matches, and the connection is refused.

Defaults

The default behavior should always be defined. This one command breaks the standard rule format by starting with the command rather than the action. The format of **default** is as follows:

```
DEFAULT action
```

where *action* is either ACCEPT or REJECT.

Permission Keywords

With the exception out of the way, let's go through the most common keywords and their meanings. You can find the entire list and more examples in the LPRng **HOWTO** page.

- **SERVICE**   Tells us what services to match against. The types of services that can be matched are

Keyword	Request
C	**lpc** control request
M	**lprm** removal request
P	Printing
Q	**lpq** status request
R	**lpr** job transfer
X	Connection request

If you have an LPC request, you can add an **LPC=** clause to refine the permissions checking to allow or disallow **lpc** commands such as **lpc** status, **printcap**, and **active**. For example:

```
# Accept all lpq status requests
ACCEPT SERVICE=Q
# Reject requests to run lpc status
REJECT SERVICE=C LPC=status
# Accept everything
ACCEPT SERVICE=*
```

● **USER**   Specifies which user may perform (or be rejected) for certain services. For example, to reject print requests from all users except **root**, you would issue this command:

```
ACCEPT SERVICE=P USER=root
REJECT SERVICE=P
```

Remember that rules are evaluated in order. Thus if **root** submits a print job, the first rule will match, and the print request will be accepted. If the user is not **root**, the second line will be evaluated, and thus all print requests from other users will be rejected.

● **HOST**   Specifies hosts for a particular action. For example, if you only want connection requests from hosts in the **example.net domain**, you could say:

```
ACCEPT SERVICE=P HOST=*.example.net
REJECT SERVICE=P
```

Example of /etc/lpd.perms

A common configuration is to allow your local network users to submit jobs, remove jobs, and check the status of their jobs. However, you don't want any remote users controlling the printers, and you certainly don't want any nonlocal network users to be submitting print jobs. This is the resulting configuration file:

```
ACCEPT SERVICE=M HOST=192.168.1.0/24
ACCEPT SERVICE=P HOST=192.168.1.0/24
ACCEPT SERVICE=Q HOST=192.168.1.0/24
ACCEPT SERVICE=R HOST=192.168.1.0/24
ACCEPT SERVICE=X HOST=192.168.1.0/24
ACCEPT SERVICE=C HOST=127.0.0.1/32 USER=root
DEFAULT REJECT
```

CRITICAL SKILL
19.5 Examining the Client Programs of lpd

There are several peripheral tools that work along with **lpd** as clients. Many of them are discussed in the following sections.

lpr

Under Linux, **lpr** is the command-line tool for performing printing operations. Most applications that offer printing services actually just mask **lpr** behind a dialog box under the X Window System.

Using **lpr** is pretty straightforward; simply type

```
[michael@scribe michael]# lpr filename
```

where *filename* is the name of the file you want to print. This command sends the file to the default printer (the first printer listed in the **/etc/printcap** file). If you want to send the job to another printer, use the **–P** option, like so:

```
[michael@scribe michael]# lpr -P printername filename
```

where *printername* is the name of the printer and *filename* is the name of the file you want to print. The following table shows the most common options available for use with **lpr**.

Option	Description
–h	No banner or header for this job.
–J *jobname*	Specify the job name to print on the banner page. This defaults to the name of files in the job.
–K*copies*, **-#***copies*	Specify the number of copies of each file to be printed.
–P *printer*	Specify a printer to use other than the default printer.
–U *username*	The **–U** option is used to specify a username for the job. This is available only to root or users listed in the **allow_user_setting** configuration option. This is obviously a security loophole, but it is present to allow systems such as SAMBA to submit jobs on behalf of users.
–Y	Make a direct connection to the printer device and do not spool.
–Z *options*	Pass the specified options to the print spooler. Used when additional or specialized information must be provided to the spooler.

Most of the time, the only parameter you'll use with **lpr** is **–P**, which is helpful when you need to print to a printer other than your default.

lpq

The **lpq** program lists all jobs queued for the printer in the order in which they will be printed. Typically, the first job listed is actively printing. The exception is, of course, when there is a problem with the printer itself.

The only command-line parameter needed with **lpq** is the **–P** option, which is used to specify which printer's queue you want to see. The default for **lpq** is the first printer listed in the **/etc/printcap** file. Here's an example that shows what's listed in the queue for the printer **plato**:

```
[michael@scribe michael]# lpq -P plato
```

lprm

The **lprm** tool allows you to remove print jobs that have entered the print queue but have not yet been printed. Here are the command-line parameters for **lprm**.

lprm Parameter	Description
–P *printername*	Specifies the printer (*printername*) from which the print job should be removed. Otherwise, the default printer (the first one listed in the **/etc/printcap** file) is assumed.
–	Removes all jobs that the user owns from the specified printer.
number	Removes the job *number* from the queue. If you aren't sure what your job number is, use the **lpq** command to see what the print queue says.

Here's an example of an **lprm** command to remove job number **17** from the printer named **plato**:

```
[michael@scribe michael]# lprm -P plato 17
```

Progress Check

1. What command-line parameter can you use to specify which printer you'd like **lpq** to report on?

2. What command-line parameter can you use with the **lpr** command to suppress the creation of a banner page?

CRITICAL SKILL

19.6 Exploring CUPS

We've mentioned before that CUPS was based on the Internet Printing Protocol (IPP), which it is hoped will become a cross-platform standard for network printing. CUPS also provides some additional advantages besides just those presented by IPP.

---

1. The **–P** option is used to specify which printer's queue you want to see.
2. The **–h** option will suppress printing of banner pages.

The designers of CUPS have gone to great lengths to make it easy to use and easy to transition to. Administration is simplified through the use of a web-based front end to server configuration (although third-party GUI configuration tools exist as well) and clients often need no configuration at all. Printers are discovered automatically when possible. From the client's view of printing, CUPS will emulate many of the tools you've become used to under **lpd**-style systems (or System V, if you've worked with that elsewhere).

CUPS introduces the concept of *classes,* which allow you to send a print job to a group of printers, and have it printed on the first available machine in that group. This approach to load balancing and failover is carried further with *implicit classes,* which allow multiple servers to address the same physical printer. When two servers point to a printer of the same name, an implicit class is automatically created with no effort required from an administrator.

Printer *instances* allow multiple queues to point to the same printer with slightly different settings. This makes it really easy to choose between common features that your printer makes available.

By using pluggable *back ends* for the actual output from a queue, not only is it easy to support many types of printer hardware, but third parties can easily add support for output that isn't bundled in the core package. For example, Windows printing is handled by a back end provided by the Samba team. In addition, CUPS uses a text file called a PostScript Printer Description (PPD) to describe the features provided by a particular piece of printer hardware in a standardized way.

CRITICAL SKILL
19.7 Installing CUPS

Installing CUPS from the **redhat-config-packages** tool is very straightforward. Clicking the Details link next to Printing Support will bring up a dialog box with packages to select. In addition to the CUPS selection, you may find it useful to install **redhat-switch-printer**. For those that prefer the manual route, the RPMs you'll want are **cups**, **cups-libs**, **cups-drivers**, **cups-drivers-hpijs**, and **cups-drivers-pnm2ppa**.

Ask the Expert

Q: I keep seeing references to foomatic. What is that?

A: Although technically not a part of CUPS, *foomatic* is the name of a large collection of printer drivers available for use with free printing systems, including CUPS. Most of the printer drivers supplied with your CUPS installation come from the foomatic project. For more information about foomatic, see http://www.linuxprinting.org.

Switching Print Systems

To make it easy to switch your print system from LPRng to CUPS (or back again), Red Hat provides a tool to manage all the hard work. From the Extras menu, select the System Settings submenu and then select Print System Switcher. Alternatively you can launch **redhat-switch-printer** from the command line or **redhat-switch-printer-nox** if you're in a nongraphical environment.

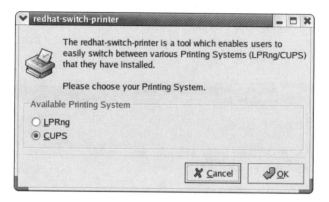

After you've selected your print system of choice, you'll still need to actually stop the old print system and start the new one by hand.

```
[root@scribe /root]# /etc/init.d/lpd stop
[root@scribe /root]# /etc/init.d/cups start
```

Don't forget to check your settings in **redhat-config-services** or the **rc** directories, as your settings from **lpd** don't carry over automatically.

```
[root@scribe rc3.d]# rm K10cups
[root@scribe rc3.d]# ln -s ../init.d/cups S90cups
```

CUPS Server Setup

The preferred method for setting up a CUPS server is to use the web-based administration interface. Unlike GUI tools that were attached as an afterthought by a third party, the CUPS web interface is thoroughly integrated into the CUPS system and is as capable as any other configuration method (although CUPS has its share of third-party GUI tools as well). Command-line tools also exist for CUPS configuration if you're working in a nongraphical environment. Directly editing the configuration files is rarely ever necessary.

Web-Based Administration

Launch your web browser and point it at http://localhost:631/ to bring up the administration interface. You'll need to log in as **root** with the password for the root account on that machine. The toolbar across the top will bring you to the various items you'll need to configure. The Administration link is slightly redundant, bringing you a menu of the same options that the toolbar provides. The links on either end of the toolbar will take you to the web sites of Easy Software Products, the developers of the CUPS system, and the cups.org main web site. The Help link will bring up the extensive documentation available for CUPS. It'll be worth your time to peruse the available documentation, even if you don't read it in depth quite yet. The remaining links will take you to the tools for managing printers, classes, and print jobs.

From the Printers page you can add new printers or manage existing printers. When you click the Add Printer button, you'll be presented with a simple form requesting the name, location, and description of the new printer. The name of the printer is what you'll use to identify it when performing any administration. The location is any text string you want to use to describe the printer's physical placement, such as "East side of the building near the coffee maker." The description is any additional text you want to use to further identify the printer. After clicking the Continue button, you'll be given a chance to select the back end for your printer from the Device drop-down box. Selecting a local back end, such as a parallel port, will lead you to choosing a Make and Model for your printer so the correct filter can be applied. Alternatively selecting a remote print server will first prompt you to enter the location in the form of a uniform resource identifier (URI). A URI is a more general form of a URL, much like what you would use in your web browser. For example, if the remote print server is running **lpd**, you would specify the server name and queue name in the format **lpd://*servername/queue***.

Once you've finished, your printer will show up in the list on the Printer page. Selecting the Configure Printer button will let you fine-tune the specifics for that particular print device. You'll also have the option here to stop the printer or tell it to reject jobs. If you select Reject Jobs, the printer will stop accepting new print requests but will still finish the jobs already in its queue. Using this as a prelude to completely stopping the printer is a bit gentler on your users.

Configuring classes of printers is easy as entering the name, location, and description, and then selecting which printers should be a part of the class. Classes can be stopped and started as well as set to reject or accept jobs much the same way that individual printers can. Individual jobs can be put on hold or cancelled from the Jobs page.

Implicit classes will be created automatically when two servers point to a printer with the same name. These provide load balancing and failover without any special configuration needing to be performed on either the server or the client.

Command-Line Configuration

CUPS provides a number of command-line utilities to configure your server in the absence of a graphical environment. The most important tool in the suite is **lpadmin**. With this command you can create, remove, and manage printers and classes. The following table summarizes some of the most used options to **lpadmin**.

Option	Description
-h *servername*	Specifies the server if the machine on which you're running this command isn't the print server itself. This allows for remote administration of printers and print servers.
-p *printername*	Specifies the name of the printer you want to create or modify. This is needed with all other options except **-d** or **-x**.
-L *location text*	Specifies the location of the printer.
-D *description*	Provides additional text information about the printer.
-c *class*	Adds the printer to this class. If the class doesn't already exist, it will be created.
-r *class*	Removes the printer from the specified class. If the class is left empty, it, too, is removed.

Option	Description
–v *URI*	Specifies the device back end in URI form.
–u *allow*|*deny:user, user*	Changes user permissions for the printer. (See Critical Skill section 19.8 on setting user permissions.)
–vd *printername*	Changes the default printer to the one specified.
–x *printername*	Deletes the named printer.
–E	Starts the printer and sets it to accept print jobs.

An example is in order to show how this works, but before we get to that, let's introduce a couple of other useful commands. The **lpinfo** command is closely related to adding and modifying printers with **lpadmin**. When using the web interface you will be presented a list of options for printer model and back-end device. Using the command line, you may not be sure which models and devices are supported on a particular setup. The **lpinfo** command can list for you the models and devices that a particular server supports. Specifying the **–m** option to **lpinfo** will list the models (in the form of a path to the **.ppd** file) that you can pass to **lpadmin**'s **–m** option. Likewise, specifying **–v** to **lpinfo** will list the back-end devices available to pass to **lpadmin**'s **–v** option.

The **lpstat** command can be used to gather information on configured printers, classes, and pending print jobs. There are a number of options for selecting what output is returned from **lpstat**, and the man page will tell you all about them, but for our purposes we're just going to use the **–s** option. Using **lpstat** with the **–s** option will list the classes and printers that have been set up, along with the devices associated with each printer and will tell you which printer is the default. It's worth mentioning that the **–t** option will show you all information that **lpstat** is capable of displaying.

To illustrate how **lpadmin** is used, look at the following example. We're going to create a printer named **asimov**, which is an HP LaserJet 4 connected to the local parallel port, and make it part of the class named **lasers**. Then just for the purpose of illustration, we'll delete the printer.

NOTE

Due to the size of the printed page of this edition, line lengths shown in the following code listing may not match your printout. Where overlong lines break onto another line, they have been indented three spaces.

```
[root@scribe root]# lpinfo -m |grep -i 'LaserJet 6P'
foomatic/HP/HP-LaserJet_6P-gimp-print-cups.ppd.gz HP LaserJet 6P,
   Foomatic + gimp-print
foomatic/HP/HP-LaserJet_6P-gimp-print-ijs-cups.ppd.gz HP LaserJet 6P,
   Foomatic + gimp-print-ijs
```

```
foomatic/HP/HP-LaserJet_6P-ljet4-cups.ppd.gz HP LaserJet 6P,
   Foomatic + ljet4
[root@scribe root]# lpinfo -v |grep -i parallel
direct parallel:/dev/lp0
[root@scribe root]# lpadmin -p asimov -m
   foomatic/HP/HP-LaserJet_6P-ljet4-cups.ppd.gz -v parallel:/dev/lp0
[root@scribe root]# lpadmin -p asimov -c lasers
[root@scribe root]# lpstat -s
system default destination: asimov
members of class lasers:
        asimov
device for asimov: parallel:/dev/lp0
[root@scribe root]# lpadmin -x asimov
[root@scribe root]# lpstat -s
no system default destination
```

Controlling access to printers under CUPS comes in two basic forms. For the truly paranoid, you can set up encryption of all print jobs and only allow access to clients presenting cryptographically secure signed certificates. If you really need this level of security, we recommend that you carefully read the documentation. Setting this up is beyond the scope of this book.

TIP

Before you completely write off print job encryption as paranoia, ask yourself if your payroll department uses a networked printer? How about your CEO?

Simple control of which users can access your machine is much simpler. The **lpadmin** utility allows you to specify a list of users, using the **–u** option, that can or can't access a particular printer. The following examples will show how this is used.

```
[root@scribe root]# lpadmin -p orwell -u allow:alice,bob
```

This will make the printer **orwell** accessible only to **alice** and **bob**, and deny everyone else.

```
[root@scribe root]# lpadmin -p orwell -u deny:eve,mallory
```

This will replace our previous list of allowed users on **orwell**. Now the printer will be accessible to everyone except **eve** and **mallory**. Notice that the specified list isn't cumulative, but replaces the previously held list. Also note that the default becomes the opposite of the list you specified. Now let's return **orwell** to a state where it will accept print jobs from anybody.

```
[root@scribe root]# lpadmin -p orwell -u allow:all
```

You also could have specified **deny:none** for the same effect.

Progress Check

1. Controlling access to printers under CUPS comes in what two basic forms?

2. What command will show you what classes and printers have been set up?

CRITICAL SKILL
19.8 Configuring Clients for CUPS

The CUPS RPMs are not divided along client/server boundaries, so installing CUPS on a client machine matches what we did for the server; you just won't configure any local printers. If your print server is on the same subnet on your client, then when a new printer is added to the server, on the client machine you will... do nothing. Your new printer should show up as available to your client within about 30 seconds or so. Wasn't that easier than messing with **/etc/printcap**?

TIP

As you may have surmised, printer discovery involves sending data to the broadcast address. Although the data involved is very small, about 80 bytes per printer, if you have a large number of printers or print servers on the same subnet you may want to use the **BrowseInterval** and **BrowseTimeout** directives to tune your network usage. The details of tuning at that level are not covered here, but are fully described in the CUPS documentation.

Unfortunately, if you want your client to talk to a printer that isn't on the same subnet, you have to actually edit a configuration file. Although we've been trying to spare you from it up until now, CUPS really does have configuration files. We're not going to cover them thoroughly here, because you really should be using the supplied tools whenever possible. We will show you how to point your client at a server across the network, though.

The configuration file we're most interested in here is **/etc/cups/cupsd.conf**. There are two directives in this file that we'll cover. The first is **BrowsePoll**. The argument supplied to **BrowsePoll** is an additional print server that you want your client to use.

```
BrowsePoll scribe.example.com
BrowsePoll plagiarist.example.com
```

1. Two basic forms of controlling printer access in CUPS are encryption and user access control.
2. You can find out what classes and printers have been set up by using **lpstat –s**.

This example adds two print servers for the client to use in addition to what is on its local subnet. Printers added or deleted from those print servers will be noticed by the client just like those on the local subnet; that is, you don't need to do anything extra on the client.

Now, one more step to make our lives as administrators easier. You probably don't want to have to perform the configuration to every other client on this subnet just so they can also see the two print servers, so let's relay the information to the rest of our subnet.

```
BrowseRelay 127.0.0.1 192.168.42.255
```

This entry will tell CUPS to relay any printer browsing information that it has on the local interface (including the information from **scribe** and **plagiarist**) to the rest of the subnet. The first argument to **BrowseRelay** is the IP address we're relaying from, in this case the local interface. The second argument is the broadcast address of the subnet for which we're going to relay. Now none of your other clients on this subnet need to change their configuration from the default at all. If you have a client that has network interfaces on more than one subnet, you can replace the local address in the first argument with the address on another subnet and relay printers from the subnet that you're not even listening for locally (that is, printers on servers not listed in a **BrowsePoll** option).

TIP

Remember that your print server is itself probably a client. If you set up a print server on the local subnet to do the relaying from other subnets as just mentioned, then you don't have to single out a workstation as the client to have the special configuration.

As a last resort, if you really need to set up access to a printer by hand, you can use the **lpadmin** command. Specify the **–E** option to enable a printer, the printer name, and specify an IPP-style URI to point to the print queue. The format of an IPP URI is **ipp://*server*/printers/*printer*** where *server* and *printer* are replaced with the actual names of your print server and your print queue. For example:

```
[root@client root]# lpadmin -p orwell -E -v
ipp://scribe.example.com/printers/orwell
```

would set up a client to print to the printer called **orwell** on the server **scribe**.

Client Tools

As part of CUPS' attempt to make transition from **lpd**-like systems as painless as possible, printing from the command line will work much like it does under LPRng. In particular, **lpr**, **lpq**, and **lprm** will work just as we described them in the previous sections.

```
[michael@client michael]# lpr file.ps
[michael@client michael]# lprm
[michael@client michael]# lpq -P plato
plato is ready
no entries
```

Module Summary

This module explained how to set up printer server software under Red Hat Linux, and described the corresponding client tools for use along with the software. We covered both LPRng, a replacement for the traditional UNIX **lpd** system, and CUPS, a newer system built around the Internet Printing Protocol. We also discussed the required configuration for securing your printer, **/etc/lpd.perms** (in the case of LPRng), and **lpadmin** (in the case of CUPS). A discussion of both **/etc/printcap** and CUPS' web-based configuration was included. However, we were only able to scratch the surface of the feature list for either of these tools. I highly recommend you read the documentation provided with whichever system you choose to use. It's long, but well worth the read, as it includes more details on security options and integration with Windows environments via Samba.

Once you have printing set up on your Linux server, you'll find that it does its job very nicely and lets you focus on new and interesting challenges. Problems that arise with printing services afterward typically point to problems with the printer itself, such as paper jams and user abuse.

✔ Module 19 Mastery Check

1. What does IPP stand for?

2. What is the goal of the IPP?

3. Why is PostScript notable?

4. Describe the purpose of banner pages and why you would want to suppress them.

5. Describe the difference between **rm** and **rp** in **/etc/printcap** when dealing with remote printers?

6. True or False? The **/etc/lpd.perms** file shows the stats of the printer.

7. True or False? The permission keyword **C** represents LPC control when used in the **/etc/lpd.perms** file.

8. What is the preferred method for setting up the CUPS server?

9. _____ will be created automatically when two servers point to a printer with the same name.

10. A new printer is added to a CUPS print server on your subnet. What do you have to do to make the client see the new printer?

11. Which printing system uses the **/etc/printcap** file?

    A. LPRng

    B. CUPS

    C. Both

12. Which printing system supports automatic printer discovery?

    A. LPRng

    B. CUPS

    C. Both

Module 20

Host Configuration with DHCP

543

Configuring IP addresses for a handful of servers is a fairly simple task. However, manually configuring IP addresses for an entire department, building, or enterprise of heterogeneous systems can be daunting.

The DHCP (Dynamic Host Configuration Protocol) client and server can assist with these tasks. The client machine is configured to obtain its IP address from the network. When the DHCP client software is started, it broadcasts a request onto the network for an IP address. If all goes well, a DHCP server on the network will respond, issuing an address and other necessary information to complete the client's network configuration.

Such dynamic addressing is also useful for configuring mobile or temporary machines. Folks who travel from office to office can plug their machines into the local network and obtain an appropriate address for their location.

This module will cover the process of configuring a DHCP server and client. At the end of the module, we'll step through a complete sample configuration.

CRITICAL SKILL
20.1 Discovering BOOTP and the Roots of DHCP

Once upon a time, when hard disks were expensive, it was fashionable to create diskless machines that would mount their file system across the network from a server that is usually shared. While having diskless stations provided some—mostly financial—advantages, they also presented their own challenges. One of the chicken-and-egg sort of problems with this scheme was how to get enough networking set up to mount remote file systems before you can consult the configuration files that contain your IP address, and so on. One piece of the puzzle was addressed with the Bootstrap Protocol (BOOTP). Each Ethernet network interface

Ask the Expert

Q: How well will DHCP work with non-Linux systems?

A: DHCP is a standard; thus, any operating system that can communicate with other DHCP servers and clients can work with the Linux DHCP tools. One common solution that includes using the Linux DHCP server component is in office environments where there are a large number of Windows-based clients. The Windows systems can be configured to use DHCP and contact the Linux server to get their IP address. This reduces the need for yet another Windows server and the associated licensing costs surrounding it.

contains a unique identifier built into its hardware known as its MAC address. When a diskless machine that supported BOOTP started up, even though it didn't know its network identity, it could at least broadcast to the network as a whole (or at least its segment of the network). A broadcast packet that contained the machine's MAC address would go out, and a BOOTP server could match that MAC address to a specific network configuration, including the IP address and any other parameters needed for network setup, and send an answer back. Performing this transaction with a single packet exchange was important for keeping broadcast traffic from getting out of hand on a busy network.

In the early 1990s, DHCP was proposed as a direct extension to BOOTP. Because DHCP is built on top of BOOTP, servers can easily accommodate older BOOTP clients as well as direct DHCP clients. DHCP offers a number of additional features over BOOTP, but the most important is its ability to hand out addresses from a given range to machines for which MAC addresses were previously unknown to the server. This makes it very useful even in cases where the client isn't a diskless machine. Addresses can be handed out either as a permanent assignment, as in a workstation that discovers its IP address during an automated install, or they can be "leased" for a period of time, such as to support a laptop that is only occasionally on the network. This is a huge boon to administrators of large or very dynamic networks. In addition to its popularity among laptop users, DHCP is gaining widespread use as more "network-aware" devices, such as network printers, show up on the scene.

CRITICAL SKILL
20.2 Viewing the Mechanics of DHCP

When a client is configured to obtain its address from the network, it asks for an address in the form of a DHCP request. A DHCP server listens for client requests. Once a request is received, it checks its local database and issues an appropriate response. The response always includes the address and can include other information such as name servers, a network mask, and a default gateway. The client accepts the response from the server and configures its local settings accordingly.

The DHCP server maintains a list of addresses it can issue. Each address is issued with an associated *lease*, which dictates how long a client is allowed to use the address before it must contact the server to renew the address. If the lease expires, the client is not allowed to continue to use the address.

The implementation of the Linux DHCP server includes several key features common to many DHCP server implementations. The server can be configured to issue any free address from a pool of addresses or to issue a specific address to a specific machine. In addition to serving DHCP requests, the DHCP server also serves BOOTP requests.

20.3 Investigating the DHCP Server

DHCPD, the DHCP server, is responsible for serving IP addresses and other relevant information upon client request. Since the DHCP protocol is broadcast based, a server will have to be present on each subnet for which DHCP service is to be provided.

Installing the DHCP Server

The Internet Software Consortium's (ISC) DHCP server is the de facto implementation for UNIX machines. It's not one of the defaults on the Red Hat 8 install, but if you open up the Details section of the Network Servers option from the packages tool, you'll find **dhcp** pretty easily. If you're installing by hand, the rpm you're looking for is predictably named **dhcp**.

Configuring the DHCP Server

The default primary configuration file of the ISC DHCP server is **/etc/dhcpd.conf**. The configuration file encapsulates two components:

- A set of declarations to describe the networks, hosts, or groups attached to the system and possibly the range of addresses available to be issued to each respective entity. Multiple declarations can be used to describe multiple groups of clients. Declarations can also be nested in one another when multiple concepts are needed to describe a set of clients or hosts.

- A set of parameters that describe the behavior of the server and configure appropriate responses. Parameters can be global, or local to a set of declarations.

NOTE

Since every site has a unique network with unique addresses, it is necessary that every site be set up with its own configuration file. If this is the first time you are dealing with DHCP, you might want to start with the sample configuration file presented toward the end of this module and modify it to match your network's characteristics.

Like most configuration files in UNIX, the file is ASCII text and can be modified using your favorite text editor. The general structure of the configuration file is as follows:

```
Global parameters;
Declaration1
    [parameters related to declaration1]
```

```
    [nested sub declaration]

Declaration2
    [parameters related to declaration2]
    [nested sub declaration]
```

As this outline indicates, a declaration block groups a set of clients. Different parameters can be applied to each block of the declaration.

Declarations

We may want to group different clients for several reasons, such as organizational requirements, network layout, and administrative domains. To assist with grouping these clients, we introduce the following declarations.

Group Individually listing parameters and declarations for each host again and again can make the configuration file difficult to manage. The **group** declaration allows you to apply a set of parameters and declarations to a list of clients, shared networks, or subnets. The syntax for the **group** declaration is as follows:

```
group label
    [parameters]
    [subdeclarations]
```

where *label* is a user-defined name for identifying the group. The *parameters* block contains a list of parameters that are applied to the group. The *subdeclarations* are used in the event that a further level of granularity is needed to describe any additional clients that may be a member of the current declaration.

Ignore the parameter field for now. We will go into further detail about it in the upcoming "Parameters" section.

Host A **host** declaration is used to apply a set of parameters and declarations to a particular host in addition to the parameters specified for the group. This is commonly used for fixed address booting or for the BOOTP clients. The syntax for a **host** declaration is as follows:

```
host label
    [parameters]
    [subdeclarations]
```

The *label* is the user-defined name for the host group. The *parameters* and *subdeclarations* are as described in the **group** declaration.

Shared-Network A **shared-network** declaration groups a set of addresses of members of the same physical network. This allows parameters and declarations to be grouped for administrative purposes. The syntax is as follows:

```
shared-network label
    [parameters]
    [subdeclarations]
```

The *label* is the user-defined name for the shared network. The *parameters* and *subdeclarations* are as described in the previous declaration.

Subnet The **subnet** declaration is used to apply a set of parameters and/or declarations to a set of addresses that match the description of this declaration. The syntax is as follows:

```
subnet subnet-number netmask netmask
    [parameters]
    [subdeclarations]
```

The **subnet-number** is the network that you want to declare as being the source of IP addresses for giving to individual hosts. The **netmask** is the netmask for the subnet. The *parameters* and *subdeclarations* are as described in the previous declaration.

Range For dynamic booting, the **range** declaration specifies the range of addresses that are valid to issue to clients. The syntax is as follows:

```
range [dynamic-bootp] starting-address [ending-address] ;
```

The **dynamic-bootp** keyword is used to alert the server that the following range of addresses is for the BOOTP protocol. The *starting-address* and optional *ending-address* fields are the actual addresses of the starting and ending blocks of IP addresses. The blocks are assumed to be consecutive and in the same subnet of addresses.

Parameters

We introduced this concept briefly earlier in the module. Turning on these parameters will alter the behavior of the server for the relevant group of clients. We'll discuss these parameters in the following section.

always-reply-rfc1048 This parameter's syntax is as follows:

```
always-reply-rfc1048;
```

This is used primarily for BOOTP clients. There are BOOTP clients that require the response from the server to be fully BOOTP Request For Comment (RFC)–compliant. Turning on this parameter ensures that this requirement is met.

authoritative
This parameter's syntax is as follows:

```
authoritative;
not authoritative;
```

The **authoritative** parameter is used to tag a particular network as "authoritative." By default, the server will assume that it's authoritative. When a network segment is "not authoritative," the server will send a DHCPNAK message back to a client to indicate this. The client will presumably retry its request at that time.

default-lease-time
This parameter's syntax is as follows:

```
default-lease-time seconds;
```

The value of *seconds* is the lease time allocated to the issued IP address if the client did not request any duration. The lease time is a tradeoff between server traffic and releasing addresses for reuse.

dynamic-bootp-lease-cutoff
This parameter's syntax is as follows:

```
dynamic-bootp-lease-cutoff date;
```

BOOTP clients are not aware of the *lease* concept. By default, the DHCP server assigns an IP address that never expires. There are certain situations where it may be useful to have the server stop issuing addresses for a set of BOOTP clients. In those cases, this parameter is used.

The *date* is specified in the form *W YYYY/MM/DD HH:MM:SS*, where *W* is the day of the week in cron format (0=Sunday, 6=Saturday), *YYYY* is the year, *MM* is the month (01=January, 12=December), *DD* is the date in two-digit format, *HH* is a two-digit hour in 24-hour format (0=Midnight, 23=11pm), *MM* is a two-digit representation of minutes; and *SS* is a two-digit representation of the seconds.

dynamic-bootp-lease-length
This parameter's syntax is as follows:

```
dynamic-bootp-lease-length seconds;
```

Although the BOOTP clients don't have a mechanism for expiring the addresses they receive, it's sometimes safe to have the server assume that they aren't using the address anymore, thus freeing it for further use. This is useful if the BOOTP application is known to be short in duration. If so, the server can set the number of *seconds* accordingly and expire it after that time has past.

CAUTION

Use caution with this option, as it may introduce problems if it issues an address before another host has stopped using it.

filename   This parameter's syntax is as follows:

```
filcname filename;
```

In some applications, the DHCP client may need to know the name of a file to use to boot. This is often combined with **next-server** to retrieve a remote file for installation configuration or diskless booting.

fixed-address   This parameter's syntax is as follows:

```
fixed-address  address [, address …];
```

This parameter appears only under the **host** declaration. It specifies the set of addresses assignable to the client.

get-lease-hostname   This parameter's syntax is as follows:

```
get-lease-hostname [true | false];
```

If set to true, the server will resolve all addresses in the declaration scope and use that for the **hostname** option.

hardware   This parameter's syntax is as follows:

```
hardware [ethernet|token-ring] hardware-address;
```

In order for the server to identify a specific host, the **hardware** parameter must be used. The *hardware-address* (sometimes referred to as the MAC address) is the physical address of the interface, typically a set of hexadecimal octets delimited by colons. This parameter is used for fixed-address DHCP clients and is required for BOOTP clients.

max-lease-time

max-lease-time   This parameter's syntax is as follows:

```
max-lease-time seconds;
```

A client has the option to request the duration of the lease. The request is granted as long as the lease time doesn't exceed the number of seconds specified by this option. Otherwise, it's granted a lease to the maximum of the number of seconds specified here.

next-server   This parameter's syntax is as follows:

```
next-server server-name;
```

When booting from the network, a client can be given a filename (specified by the **filename** parameter) and a server from which to obtain booting information. This server is specified with the **next-server** parameter.

server-identifier   This parameter's syntax is as follows:

```
server-identifier hostname;
```

Part of the DHCP response is the address for the server. On multihomed systems, the DHCP server issues the address of the first interface. Unfortunately, this interface may not be reachable by all clients of a server or declaration scope. In those rare instances, this parameter can be used to send the IP of the proper interface that the client should communicate to the server.

server-name   This parameter's syntax is as follows:

```
server-name name;
```

where *name* is the host name of the server that is being booted by a remote booting client. This parameter is used for remote clients or network install applications.

use-host-decl-names   This parameter's syntax is as follows:

```
use-host-decl-names [true|false];
```

This parameter is used in the same scope of other host declarations. It will add the **host-name** option to the **host** declaration, using the host name in the declaration for the option host.

use-lease-addr-for-default-route   This parameter's syntax is as follows:

```
use-lease-addr-for-default-route [true|false];
```

Some network configurations use a technique known as ProxyARP so that a host can keep track of other hosts that are outside its subnet. If your network is configured to support ProxyARP, you'll want to configure your client to use itself as a default route. This will force it to use ARP (the Address Resolution Protocol) to find all remote (off the subnet) addresses.

CAUTION

The **use-lease-addr-for-default-route** command should be used with caution. Not every client can be configured to use its own interface as a default route.

Options

Currently, the DHCP server supports more than 60 options. The general syntax of an option is as follows:

```
option option-name [modifiers]
```

Table 20-1 summarizes the most commonly used DHCP options. Some examples of these in use will be seen Project 20-1.

Option Name	Description
broadcast-address	An address on the client's subnet specified as the broadcast address
domain-name	The domain name the client should use as the local domain name when performing host lookups
domain-name servers	The list of DNS servers for the client to use to resolve host names
host-name	The string used to identify the name of the client
nis-domains	The Network Information Service (NIS) domain name (see Module 17)
nis-servers	A list of the available NIS servers to bind to
routers	A list of routers the client is to use in order of preference
subnet-mask	The netmask the client is to use

Table 20-1 Common Options Used in DHCP Server Configuration

Progress Check

1. When configuring a DHCP server, what does the **shared-network** declaration stand for?

2. What is the MAC address?

Project 20-1   Setting Up a DHCP Server

Now that you have the basics needed to create a running DHCP configuration, let's work through an example. In this project you'll create a simple **dhcp.conf** file that your can modify to fit you own needs. By completing this project you should gain a clearer understanding of how the options and parameters presented in the preceding section fit together.

Step by Step

1. Using your favorite text editor, open **/etc/dhcpd.conf**.

2. Set your network.

```
subnt 192.168.1.0 netmask 255.255.255.0
        # Options
        option routers 192.168.1.1;
        option subnet-mask 255.255.255.0;
```

3. Enter your domain name and DNS servers.

```
        option domain-name "example.com";
        option domain-name-servers delirium.example.com;
```

4. Choose your lease times.

```
        # Parameters
        default-lease-time 21600;
        max-lease-time 43200;
```

5. Create a range of addresses to hand out.

```
        # Declarations
        range dynamic-bootp 192.168.1.25 192.168.1.49;
```

---

1. A **shared-network** declaration groups a set of addresses of members of the same physical network. This allows parameters and declarations to be grouped for administrative purposes.

2. The MAC address is an Ethernet card's permanent hardware address.

6. Enter any fixed addresses you may need.

```
# Nested declarations
host vertigo
        hardware ethernet 00:80:c6:f6:72:00;
        fixed-address 192.168.1.50;
```

7. Save the file.

8. Start the DHCP service.

```
/etc/init.d/dhcpd start
```

Project Summary

In this example, a single subnet is defined. The DHCP clients are instructed to use 192.168.1.1 as their default route, and 255.255.255.0 as their subnet mask. DNS information is passed to the clients; they will use **example.com** as their domain name and **delirium.example.com** as their DNS server. A lease time of 21,600 seconds is set, but if the clients request a longer lease, they may be granted a lease that can last as long as 43,200 seconds. The range of IP addresses issued starts at 192.168.1.25 and can go as high as 192.168.1.49. The machine with a MAC address of 00:80:c6:f6:72:00 will always get assigned the IP address 192.168.1.50.

TIP

If the lease time expires, the client can no longer use its acquired address. In order to avoid last-minute desperate requests, the client actually starts trying to renew its lease at a time well before the actual expiration time arrives (by default, when half of its lease time has expired). This is useful to keep in mind when trying to balance lease times with network traffic on busy subnets.

General Runtime Behavior

Once started, the daemon patiently waits for a client request to arrive prior to performing any processing. When a request is processed and an address is issued, it keeps track of the address in a file called **dhcpd.leases**. In the event of a server failure, the contents of this file are used to keep track of the addresses that have been issued to specific clients.

CRITICAL SKILL
20.4 Knowing the DHClient

DHClient is the program used to obtain configuration info from the server described in the previous sections. If invoked, it will attempt to obtain an address from an available DHCP server and then set up its networking configuration accordingly. This client is part of the standard Red Hat install, and so you probably already have it installed on your machine. You may have even used it during your Red Hat install to get an IP address for the machine if you already have a DHCP server on your network. On the off chance that you have a reason to manipulate the rpms manually, **dhclient** is the package you're looking for.

Client Configuration

Setting up your machine to obtain an address automatically is very easy. If you prefer the graphical user interface (GUI) option, select the System Tools menu and then the Network Device Control option. On the resulting dialog box, select the interface you're interested in if you have more than one, and click Configure. The window that comes up is the same one you'd see if you launched the **redhat-config-network** tool from the command line. From here you can select your interface and click Edit. On the General tab, shown in the following illustration, you'll see a radio button to select Automatically Obtain IP Address Setting With:, followed by a drop-down box where you can select **dhcp**. In addition, you can optionally specify a host name to provide to the DHCP server, and select whether you want to use the DHCP server–provided DNS server.

If you're going the route of directly editing the config files on your machine, then you'll want to look in the **/etc/sysconfig/network-scripts/** directory. You'll find a script named

ifcfg-*dev* where *dev* is the system's name for your network interface. For example, the first Ethernet device would be represented by a script called **ifcfg-eth0**. Inside this script there may exist a line that reads **BOOTPROTO=*method*** where *method* is one of **dhcp**, **bootp**, or **none**. You'll want to change that to read **BOOTPROTO=dhcp** if it doesn't already.

Advanced Client Configuration

The preceding section should be everything you need to start using that DHCP server on your network. If, however, you do have a client with special needs, you can provide a configuration file for **dhclient**. In the file **/etc/dhclient.conf** you can specify what information to request from the server, defaults to use if the server is unable to provide certain information, overrides for some information the server sends, and even fall-back addresses to use on networks without a DHCP server. The format is essentially the same as the server configuration file, except with its own settings. The most common settings are summarized in Table 20-2.

Setting	Description
timeout *time*	How long should the client keep trying before giving up? The default is 60 seconds.
reboot *time*	This specifies how long after a reboot the client should try to get the same address it had before, After this time passes, if the client hasn't been able to renew its old address, it gives up and tries to acquire a new address normally. The default is 10 seconds.
request *option, option, …*	The **request** statement causes the client to seek specific information from the server. The *options* listed here correspond to the options available to be specified in the server. The defaults are **subnet-mask**, **broadcast-address**, **time-offset**, **routers**, **domain-name**, **domain-name-servers**, **host-name**, **nis-domain**, **nis-servers**, and **ntp-servers**.
require *option, option, …*	Options listed here must be included in the servers offer, or the offer is ignored.
send {*option declaration, …*}	Here the client can supply options to which it already knows the answers, in which case it helps the server differentiate it from other clients.
default *option declaration*	Specify a value for *option* in case the server doesn't supply one.

Table 20-2 Common Settings Used in DHCP Client Configuration

Setting	Description
supersede *option declaration*	Override the servers answer for *option* with the local value.
lease { *lease-declaration ...* }	The DHCP client maintains a leases file, just as the server does. If the client reboots and it has some leases that haven't expired, it will try to renew those first. This keyword block is primarily for use in the **dhclient.leases** file, but you can predefine a lease in the **conf** file if you have a need to. See the man pages for **dhclient.leases** and **dhclient.conf** for more information.
reject *ip-address*	This allows you to reject a specified IP address handed out by a server. Before you use this option you may want to consider if the right thing to do is to fix the server instead.

Table 20-2 Common Settings Used in DHCP Client Configuration *(continued)*

Module Summary

DHCP is a useful tool for dynamically configuring the addresses for large groups of machines or a mobile workstation. Since DHCP is an open protocol, the architecture and platform of the server and the client are irrelevant.

A computer running Linux can serve DHCP requests. The software to do this is highly configurable and has mechanisms to persist after machine failures.

Software also exists to configure the networking of a Linux machine from a DHCP server on the network.

✓

Module 20 Mastery Check

1. What does DHCP do?

2. True or False? The DHCP server can still answer BOOTP style requests.

3. True or False? The ISC DHCP server is the de facto implementation for UNIX machines.

4. What did BOOTP do?

5. What is a major advantage of DHCP over BOOTP?

6. What happens when a lease expires?

7. When configuring the DHCP server, what does the **group** declaration do?

8. What is the general syntax of the DHCP server options?

9. What does the DHCP server option **host-name** do?

10. Which of the client options for configuring advanced DHCP options specifies how long after restarting the client should try to get the same address it had before?

11. Which of the client options for configuring advanced DHCP options allows you to reject a specified IP handed out by a server?

Module 21

Backups

A server that is not backed up is a disaster waiting to happen. Performing backups is a critical part of any server's maintenance, no matter what operating system you use. This module discusses the backup options that come with Red Hat Linux. Many commercial packages exist as well, and you can purchase them for anywhere from a few hundred to many thousands of dollars. The best package for you depends on your site and its needs.

CRITICAL SKILL
21.1 Evaluating Your Backup Needs

Developing a backup solution is no trivial task. It requires that you consider the interactions among all the parts of your network, the servers, and the resources distributed among them. Even trickier is deciding the order in which backups are performed. For example, if you want to back up multiple partitions in parallel, you could end up losing the benefits of that parallelism if there is contention on the SCSI (Small Computer System Interface) bus! And, of course, you must arrange for backups to occur regularly and to be verified regularly.

Unfortunately, no cookbook solution exists for setting up network backup. Every organization has different needs based on its site(s), its network, and its growth pattern. To make an educated decision, you need to consider the following questions.

How Much Data?

Determining an accurate count of the data to be backed up is the most important issue for estimating your network backup needs. What makes this question tough to answer is that you must include anticipated growth in your determination. Given that most shops have tight purse strings, when planning for backup, it's always wise to try to plan as far ahead as financially possible.

It is also important to consider how often your data changes and with what frequency. Data that changes often (such as databases) need to be backed up frequently and quickly, whereas data that rarely if ever changes (such as the **/etc** directory) doesn't need to be backed up often (if ever).

What Kind of Hardware?

Selecting the backup media can be tricky. Many of the high-density options are appealing for the obvious reason that you can cram more data onto a single tape. Of course, high-capacity tapes typically cost more. Work toward finding an optimum solution that backs up the most system data at the best price, balanced with your requirements for media capacity.

NOTE

Many advertisements for tape drives boast impressive capacities, but keep in mind that these numbers are for the compressed data on the tape, not the actual data. The amount of uncompressed data on the tape is usually about half the compressed capacity. This is important to note, because compression algorithms achieve various levels of compression depending on the type of data being compressed. For example, textual data compresses very well. Certain graphics or sound formats get little to no compression at all. When you estimate the amount of data you can store on a single unit, be sure to consider the mix of data on your servers.

Another aspect of hardware to consider is your tape drive and its relationship to the backup server. Will the tape drive be in contention with other peripherals on the system? For instance, will the tape drive be on the same SCSI chain as a disk that's being backed up? This is extremely important because it can significantly affect the time it takes to back up a site.

And finally, are you able to feed data to the tape drive fast enough so that it can stream? If the tape drive cannot stream, it will stop writing until it gets more data. This pause may be as long as several seconds on a slow mechanism while the drive realigns itself with the tape and finds the next available position to write data. Even if the pause is brief, when it occurs thousands of times during a single backup, it can increase your backup runtimes by many hours.

How Much Network Throughput?

Unfortunately, network throughput is easily forgotten in the planning of backup operations. But what good do you get from a really fast backup server and tape drive if you feed in the data through a thin straw?

Take the necessary time to understand your network infrastructure. Look at where the data is coming from and where it's going. Use Simple Network Management Protocol (SNMP) tools, such as Multi Router Traffic Grapher (MRTG) (http://www.mrtg.org), to collect statistics about your switches and routers. If you need to back up machines that are connected via hubs, consider a backup sequence that won't back up two machines on the same collision domain at the same time.

Gathering all this information will help you estimate the bandwidth necessary to perform backups. With your analysis done, you'll be able to figure out which upgrades will net you the best return for your money.

What Speed of Recovery?

When requests to restore data from tape arrive, you're likely to be under the gun to get the data back to the user as quickly as possible. How long your users have to wait will depend on the tool used for backup. This means you need to incorporate the cost of response time into your backup evaluation. How much are you willing to spend to get the response time you need for a restore? Obviously, faster restores typically mean higher prices.

NOTE

Although this module mentions only tape backups, the issues covered here apply to backup on any other media, such as CD-Recordable (CD-R) discs or even Zip disks. Each medium has its advantages and disadvantages. CD-Rs offer quick access to data, but they lack the high capacity of tape drives. Pick the medium that works best for your system's needs.

How Often Do I Need to Recover?

Unfortunately, this is a question that too often gets lost in the shuffle. If you have data that needs recovery only once in a blue moon and the speed at which you recover the file is not critical, then you can get away with investing in a less-capable system. On the other hand, if you suspect that you'll be doing recoveries often (typically the case in office environments), then investing in a tape drive that gives you the necessary performance on reads is just as important as how quickly you can move the data to the tape in the first place. Having a manager loom over your shoulder while you wait for the tape drive to find a file is never fun.

CAUTION

Always test your backups to make certain that you can restore valid files from them. Not testing your disaster recovery plan ahead of time is a guarantee that it won't work as expected when you most need it to.

What Kind of Tape Management?

As the size of your backups grows, so will the need to manage the data you back up. This is where commercial tools often come into play. When evaluating your choices, be sure to consider their indexing and tape management. It does you no good to have 50 tapes worth of data if you can't find the right file. And unfortunately, this problem only gets worse as you start needing more tapes for each night's backups.

Project 21-1 Creating a Backup Plan

Now that we have gone through what needs to be considered before your backup has begun, let's sit down with pencil and paper and decide what needs to be done for your system backup. Once you complete this project, you will know what steps need to be taken by you or your company in order to ensure that your system will have a backup when you need it.

Step by Step

On a piece of paper with a pencil—or for those geeks among us, on a text editor screen—begin to answer the following questions:

1. How much data do you need to back up?

2. What kind of hardware will you use for the backup process?

3. How much network bandwidth will you need to support your backup process?

4. How quickly must the data be recovered?

5. How often is data expected to be recovered?

6. What kind of media management do you need?

7. What is your plan for testing recovery?

Project Summary

With this information in hand, you should be in a position to evaluate your resource requirements, including your backup software. Don't just try to jump in and figure it out as you go along, or you'll find yourself missing pieces and retracing steps. Make sure you have a comprehensive plan before you start.

CRITICAL SKILL
21.2 Managing the Backup Device and Files

The tape device interacts with Linux just as most other devices do: as a file. The filename will depend on the type of tape drive, your chosen mode of operation (autorewind or nonrewind), and how many drives are attached to the system.

SCSI tape drives, for example, use the following naming scheme:

Device Name	Purpose
/dev/st*X*	Autorewinding SCSI tape device; *X* is the number of the tape drive. Numbering of tape drives is in the order of the drives on the SCSI chain.
/dev/nst*X*	Nonrewinding SCSI tape device; *X* is the number of the tape drive. Numbering of tape drives is in the order of the drives on the SCSI chain.

Let's say you have a single SCSI tape drive. You can access it using either of these filenames: **/dev/st0** or **/dev/nst0**. If you use **/dev/st0**, the drive will automatically rewind the tape after each file is written to it. If you use **/dev/nst0**, on the other hand, you can write a

Project
21-1

Create a Backup Plan

single file to the tape, mark the end of file, and then stay at the tape's current position. This lets you write multiple files onto a single tape.

NOTE

Non-SCSI devices will obviously use a different naming scheme. Unfortunately, there is no standard for naming backup devices if they are not SCSI devices. The QIC-02 tape controller, for example, uses the **/dev/tpqic*** series of filenames. If you use a non-SCSI tape device (a rare thing these days), you will need to find its corresponding driver documentation to see what device name it will use.

You may find it handy to create a symbolic link from **/dev/tape** to the appropriate device name for the rewinding mode and a link from **/dev/nrtape** for the nonrewinding mode (for example, **/dev/tape** → **/dev/st0** and **/dev/nrtape** → **/dev/nst0**). This will make it easier to remember the name of the tape device when issuing commands. See Module 6 for information on using the **ln** command to create symbolic links.

What makes these backup device files different from disk files is that there is no file-system structure. Files are continuously written to the tape until it's full or until an end-of-file marker is written. If a tape device is in nonrewind mode, the write head is left in the position immediately after the last end-of-file marker, ready for the next file to be written.

Think of tape devices as similar to a book with chapters. The book's binding and the paper, like the tape itself, provide a place to put the words (the files). It is the markings of the publisher (the backup application) that separate the entire book into smaller subsections (files). If you (the reader) were an autorewinding tape drive, you would close the tape every time you were done with a single file and then have to search through the tape to find the next position (chapter) when you were ready to read it. If, however, you were a nonrewinding tape drive, you would leave the tape open to the last page you read.

Manipulating the Tape Device with mt

The **mt** program provides simple controls for the tape drive, such as rewinding the tape, ejecting the tape, or seeking a particular file on the tape. In the context of backups, **mt** is most useful as a mechanism for rewinding and seeking.

All of the **mt** actions are specified on the command line. Table 21-1 shows some of the most used parameters for the command. Note that not all parameters are valid for all tape drives. Be sure to check your documentation carefully.

mt Command Parameter	Description
–f *tape_device*	Specifies the tape device. The first nonrewinding SCSI tape device is **/dev/nst0**.
fsf *count*	Forward-spaces a number (*count*) of files. The tape is positioned on the first block of the next file; for example, **fsf 1** would leave the head ready to read the second file of the tape.
asf *count*	Positions the tape at the beginning of the file indicated by *count*. Positioning is done by first rewinding the tape and then forward-spacing over *count* file marks.
rewind	Rewinds the tape.
erase	Erases the tape.
status	Gives the status of the tape.
offline or **eject**	Brings the tape offline and, if applicable, unloads the tape.
load	Loads the tape (applies to tape changers).
lock	Locks the drive door (only applies to certain tape drives).
unlock	Unlocks the drive door (only applies to certain tape drives).

Table 21-1 Commonly Used Options for the mt Command

NOTE

If you do not use a nonrewinding tape device, the tape drive will automatically rewind after you perform your operation with **mt**. This can be rather frustrating if you are seeking to a specific file!

- To rewind the tape in **/dev/nst0**, use this command:

  ```
  [root@scribe /root]# mt -f /dev/nst0 rewind
  ```

- To move the head so that it is ready to read the third file on the tape, use this command:

  ```
  [root@scribe /root]# mt -f /dev/nst0 asf 2
  ```

CRITICAL SKILL
21.3 # Exploring Command-Line Tools

Linux comes with several tools that help you perform backups. Though they lack administrative front ends, they are simple to use—and they do the job. Many formal backup packages actually use these utilities as their underlying backup mechanism.

dump and restore

The **dump** tool works by making a copy of an entire file system. The **restore** tool can then take this copy and pull any and all files from it.

To support incremental backups, **dump** uses the concept of *dump levels*. A dump level of 0 means a full backup. Any dump level above 0 is an incremental relative to the last time a dump with a lower dump level occurred. For example, a dump level of 1 covers all the changes to the file system since the last level 0 dump, a dump level of 2 covers all of the changes to the file system since the last level 1 dump, and so on—all the way through dump level 9.

Consider a case in which you have three dumps: the first is a level 0, the second is a level 1, and the third is also a level 1. The first dump is, of course, a full backup. The second dump (level 1) contains all the changes made since the first dump. The third dump (also a level 1) *also* has all the changes.

The **dump** utility stores all the information about its dumps in the **/etc/dumpdates** file. This file lists each backed-up file system, when it was backed up, and at what dump level. Given this information, you can determine which tape to use for a restore. For example, if you perform level 0 dumps on Monday, level 1 incrementals on Tuesday and Wednesday, and then level 2 incrementals on Thursday and Friday, a file that was last modified on Tuesday but got accidentally erased on Friday can be restored from Tuesday night's incremental backup. A file that was last modified during the preceding week will be on Monday's level 0 tape.

NOTE

The **dump** tool is file-system dependent, and the version that comes with Red Hat is only for use with ext2/ext3. If you are using a different file system, be sure to find out what backup tools are appropriate.

Using dump

The **dump** tool is a command-line utility. It takes many parameters, but the most relevant are as shown in Table 21-2.

For example, here is the command to perform a level 0 dump to **/dev/st0** of the **/dev/hda1** file system:

```
[root@scribe /root]# dump -0  -f /dev/st0 /dev/hda1
```

dump Parameter	Description
–n	Specifies the dump level, where *n* is a number between 0 and 9. For example, **–0** would perform a full backup.
–b *blocksize*	Sets the dump block size to *blocksize*, which is measured in kilobytes. If you are backing up many large files, using a larger block size will increase performance. You may need to carefully adjust this to match the capabilities of your tape system.
–B *count*	Specifies a number (*count*) of records per tape to be dumped. If there is more data to dump than there is tape space, **dump** will prompt you to insert a new tape.
–f *filename*	Specifies a location (*filename*) for the resulting dump file. You can make the dump file a normal file that resides on another file system, or you can write the dump file to the tape device. The SCSI tape device is **/dev/st0**.
–u	Updates the **/etc/dumpdates** file after a successful dump.
–d *density*	Specifies the *density* of the tape in bits per inch.
–s *size*	Specifies the *size* of the tape in feet.
–a	Bypasses all tape-length calculations and writes until an end-of-media signal is returned. This works best for most modern tape drives and is particularly useful for appending data to existing tapes. This is the default mode.
–z or –j	Compresses each data block. The **–z** parameter uses zlib compression, while **–j** uses bzlib. Either option can be immediately followed with a number, if you want to specify the compression level, or white space, if you want to accept the default compression level of 2. Your tape drive must be able to support variable-length blocks to be able to use this feature. If your tape system has hardware compression built in, don't use both the hardware compression and this option together, or your files will likely increase in size.

Table 21-2 Common Options Used with the dump Command

Using dump to Back Up an Entire System

The **dump** utility works by making an archive of one file system. If your entire system comprises multiple file systems, you need to run **dump** for every file system. Since **dump** creates its output as a single, large file, you can store multiple dumps to a single tape by using a nonrewinding tape device.

Assuming we're backing up to a SCSI tape device, **/dev/nst0**, we must first decide which file systems we're backing up. This information is in the **/etc/fstab** file. Obviously, we don't want to back up files such as **/dev/cdrom**, so we skip those. Depending on our data, we may or may not want to back up certain partitions (such as **swap** and /tmp).

Let's assume this leaves us with **/dev/hda1**, **/dev/hda3**, **/dev/hda5**, and **/dev/hda6**. To back up these to **/dev/nst0**, compressing them along the way, we would issue the following series of commands:

```
[root@scribe /root]# mt -f /dev/nst0 rewind
[root@scribe /root]# dump -0uz -f /dev/nst0 /dev/hda1
[root@scribe /root]# dump -0uz -f /dev/nst0 /dev/hda3
[root@scribe /root]# dump -0uz -f /dev/nst0 /dev/hda5
[root@scribe /root]# dump -0uz -f /dev/nst0 /dev/hda6
[root@scribe /root]# mt -f /dev/nst0 rewind
[root@scribe /root]# mt -f /dev/nst0 eject
```

The first **mt** command is to make sure the tape is completely rewound and ready to accept data. Then come all the **dump** commands, which are run on the partitions using zlib compression. We finally rewind the tape and eject it.

CAUTION

It's considered dangerous to dump file systems that are being actively used. The only way to be 100 percent sure that a file system is not in use is by unmounting it first. Unfortunately, very few people can afford the luxury of unmounting a system for the time necessary to do a backup. The next best thing is to go through the unappealing task of verifying backups on a regular basis. Verification is best done by testing to see if the **restore** program (discussed in the next section, "Using restore") can completely read the tape and extract files from it. It's tedious, and it isn't fun. But many a systems administrator has lost a job over bad backups—don't be one of them!

Using restore

The **restore** program reads the dump files created by **dump** and extracts individual files and directories from them. Although **restore** is a command-line tool, it does offer a more intuitive interactive mode that lets you go through your directory structure from the tape.

Table 21-3 shows many of the command-line options for the **restore** utility.

restore Option	Description
–I	Enables interactive mode for **restore**. The utility will read the directory contents of the tape and then give you a shell-like interface in which you can move directories around and tag files you want to recover. When you've tagged all the files you want, **restore** will go through the dump and restore those files. This mode is handy for recovering individual files, especially if you aren't sure which directory they're in.

Table 21-3 Common Options for the restore Command

restore Option	Description
−r	Rebuilds a file system. In the event you lose everything in a file system (a disk failure, for instance), you can simply re-create an empty file system and restore all the files and directories of the dump.
−b *blocksize*	Sets the dump's block size to *blocksize* kilobytes. If you don't supply this information, **restore** will figure it out for you.
−f *filename*	Reads the dump from the file *filename*.
−T *directory*	Specifies the temporary workspace (*directory*) for the restore. The default is **/tmp.**
−v	Verbosely shows you each step **restore** is taking.
−y	In the event of an error, automatically retries instead of asking users if they want to retry.

Table 21-3 Common Options for the restore Command *(continued)*

A Typical Restore   A typical invocation of **restore** is as follows:

```
[root@scribe /root]# restore -ivf /dev/st0
```

This will pull the dump file from the device **/dev/st0** (the first SCSI tape device), print out each step **restore** takes, and then provide an interactive session for you to decide which files from the dump get restored.

A Complete Restore   Should a complete file system be lost, you can re-create the file system using the **mke2fs** command and then **restore** to populate the file system. For example, let's say our external SCSI drive (**/dev/sda**), which has a single partition on it (**/dev/sda1**), fails. After replacing it with a new drive, we would re-create the file system, like so:

```
[root@scribe /root]# mke2fs /dev/sda1
```

Next, we have to mount the partition in the appropriate location. We'll assume this is the **/home** partition, so we type the following:

```
[root@scribe /root]# mount /dev/sda1 /home
```

Finally, with the dump tape in the SCSI tape drive (**/dev/st0**), we perform the restoration using the following command:

```
[root@scribe /root]# cd /home; restore -rf /dev/st0
```

tar

In Module 6, we discussed the use of **tar** for creating archives of files. What we didn't discuss is the fact that **tar** was originally meant to create archives of files onto tape (**tar** = *t*ape *ar*chive). Because of Linux's flexible approach of treating devices the same as files, we've been using **tar** as a means to archive and unarchive a group of files into a single disk file. Those same **tar** commands could be rewritten to send the files to tape instead.

The **tar** command can archive a subset of files much more easily than **dump** can. The **dump** utility works only with complete file systems, but **tar** can work on mere directories. Does this mean **tar** is better than **dump** for backups? Well, sometimes…

Overall, **dump** turns out to be much more efficient than **tar** at backing up entire file systems. Furthermore, **dump** stores more information about the file, which means that it requires a little more tape space but makes recovery that much easier. On the other hand, **tar** is truly cross-platform—a **tar** file created under Linux can be read by the **tar** command under any other UNIX system. And **gzip**ped **tar** files can even be read by the WinZip program!

Whether you are better off with **tar** or **dump** depends on your environment and needs.

NOTE

For more information on using **tar**, see Module 6.

Progress Check

1. What program provides simple controls for the tape drive?

A. mt

B. tapetls

C. tar

D. All of the above

2. Do you need to take a partition offline in order for **dump** to copy and back up your data?

---

1. **A.** The **mt** program provides simple controls for the tape drive.

2. While not absolutely required, unmounting a partition before dumping it will ensure that you get a clean dump. If you don't, you run the risk of not correctly capturing files that are in use.

CRITICAL SKILL
21.4 Using Amanda

Although **dump** can be used to send backups to a remote tape server, it needs to be run as **root** to do so, and it's still not really the program's strong point. When it comes to systems that were designed for client/server-style backups, Amanda is the best known among the open source choices. It's also the one that's included with Red Hat 8.

The Advanced Maryland Automatic Network Disk Archiver (Amanda) was developed at the University of Maryland. While it lacks some of the features that the expensive commercial alternatives boast, such as hot backups of databases, it does work well for many types of networks. Amanda is very configurable and is actually built on top of existing UNIX components such as **dump** and **tar**.

If you've worked with other backup systems before, it may take awhile to get used to the idea that Amanda will manage your tapes for you. In most other backup solutions, you decide that you're going to do a full backup on Mondays, for example, and incremental backups the rest of the week. Then, if you need to do a restore on Thursday, you grab the full backup tape from Monday and the incremental tapes from Tuesday and Wednesday. In contrast, with Amanda, you specify how often you would like a full backup. You also tell Amanda the size of the tape you're using and how much time you have to run backups. Using the same example as above, let's assume that Amanda did a full backup on Monday of a given file system. Then on Wednesday, Amanda finds that one of the file systems it has been asked to back up has a lot of changes. It may "promote" the full backup of that one file system, performing it earlier than normal, assuming there is enough time and tape to do so. This means that the administrator may not know which day's tapes contain a full backup of a given file system and which contain only incrementals. That's OK though. When Thursday comes around and you have to do that unexpected restore, Amanda will tell you exactly which tapes you need to grab. And since you may be getting full backups more often than the minimum you specified, you may need to grab fewer tapes to do that restore.

The Amanda backup cycle is triggered by a **cron** entry. There are usually (at least) two entries in **cron** for an Amanda server. The first checks that everything is ready for the day's backups, including the correct tapes being available and clients being reachable on the network. If something is not right, an e-mail will be sent to the administrator alerting her about the situation. At some point later, the actual backup process starts and the server connects to the clients to pull data for backing up.

Although it's not required, the best efficiency is achieved if the Amanda server has a portion of its hard drive set aside for temporary holding space. This allows Amanda to back up multiple clients in parallel as fast as the network bandwidth you've allocated to it will allow. Then Amanda can flush the backups to tape as fast as your tape drive will allow. If you don't use a holding space, you run the risk of an input/output (I/O) bottleneck slowing down the entire procedure. In addition, if there is a problem writing to tape, you still have the backups on disk and can flush them to tape when the problem is corrected.

Installing Amanda

The Amanda system will require you to install programs on both your server and your client machines. When you bring up the packages tool, either from the System Settings menu or by typing **redhat-config-packages** on the command line, you'll want to look at two different sections. The Network Servers section contains the option for **amanda-server**, while the System Tools section has the option for **amanda-client**. Keep in mind that your server will most likely be a client as well. If you're managing your packages by hand, there are three rpms you'll want to look for: **amanda**, **amanda-client**, and **amanda-server**. The package called simply **amanda** has core components needed by both the server and the client, and will need to be installed in conjunction with one or both of the other packages.

The Amanda Server

Amanda allows you to have multiple different configurations set up simultaneously, with each configuration having its own subdirectory beneath the **/etc/amanda** directory. The example configuration that comes with the Amanda package is called DailySet1 and can be copied as a template for your own Amanda configuration.

```
[root@scribe /root]# cp -r /etc/amanda/DailySet1/ /etc/amanda/MyBackups
```

Inside each configuration directory are two files of interest to the administrator. The first is **amanda.conf**.

TIP

The nature of Amanda's tape rotation means that you'll have to rethink many of the archival, off-site, or long-term storage plans you may have used with other systems. This is where having multiple configurations can come in really handy. A separate configuration can be set up to handle archives, for example.

The **amanda.conf** file is quite readable and very well commented. Most configuration statements are a single line, with a few special ones containing multiline blocks surrounded by curly braces. Most of the values have reasonable defaults, but you will want to pay special attention to things like the list of administrators to e-mail with reports (the **mailto** variable), and the name of your tape device (the **tapedev** variable). Be sure that you specify the nonrewinding version of your tape device. You will also need to set your **tapetype** variable, which is discussed in a bit more detail later in this section.

A few of the parameters that pertain to Amanda's scheduling cycle should probably be examined as well. The **dumpcycle** variable specifies how many days are in a backup cycle. This affects how often full backups are performed. Setting this to **1 week**, for example, will mean that every file system will receive a full backup at least once per week (though perhaps more, as explained earlier). The parameter **runspercycle** specifies how many times you'll actually perform backups during a backup cycle. This defaults to being the same as **dumpcycle**, but you can change that if you don't do a backup everyday. Perhaps you skip weekends, and so you have a **dumpcycle** of **1 week** and **runspercycle** of **5**. You'll set **tapecycle** to the number of tapes you use before overwriting old ones. This must be at least one larger than the number of tapes you'll use in each **dumpcycle**, but you may want to pad a few extras in to allow for schedule changes or unforeseen circumstances. Amanda ensures that all tapes used are marked ahead of time with a special label as an identifier. You can specify with the **labelstr** what identifier Amanda should check against to be sure it's not overwriting the wrong tape. This is especially useful if you're running multiple configurations on the same server, as each will have its own label string.

If you want to fine-tune Amanda's performance, you'll want to look at some of the network parameters available. Setting **netusage** can limit the maximum amount of bandwidth that Amanda will be allowed to use at once. In addition, you can limit the number of backups performed at once by setting the **inparallel** option to a number other than its default of 10. The **maxdumps** setting can limit the number of simultaneous file systems being backed up from the same client at once.

Further down in the file you'll find a number of block options, where multiple statements are grouped together with curly braces to define a single setting. One of these will describe your holding space.

```
holdingdisk hd1 {
    comment "main holding disk"
     directory "/var/tmp/amanda"  # where the holding disk is
     use 1024 Mb   # how much space can we use on it
}
```

You can change the size or location of your holding disk, or you can specify more than one if you want to spread the load (presumably to different physical disks). Any backup that won't fit into a holding disk will be written directly to tape.

Another set of block sections will define parameters for a number of common types of tapes. These all begin with the words "**define tapetype**," followed by a name and a block of parameters. You probably won't want to mess with these but instead just make a note of which one fits your hardware. Then take the name of that definition (the name is the string after the keyword **tapetype** and before the curly brace), and set the variable **tapetype** with this value.

```
tapetype DLT # what kind of tape it is (see tapetypes below)

define tapetype DLT {
    comment "DLT tape drives"
    length 20000 mbytes           # 20 Gig tapes
    filemark 2000 kbytes
    speed 1536 kbytes             # 1.5 Mb/s
}
```

The final block parameters are near the bottom, and they define **dumptype**s. You may want to come back and adjust these when you're a bit more comfortable with Amanda, but for now, just find one that best matches your needs, and make a note of its name; you'll need it for the next file. This brings us to the **disklist** file.

Each entry in the **disklist** file specifies a device on a client machine to back up, along with the **dumptype** to use. The **dumptype** is simply the name of a type defined in the **amanda.conf** file. Adding a new client to the backup schedule can be as simple as adding a line for each of its file systems into the **disklist** file.

TIP

You may have noticed that many of the **dumptype**s support compression. Amanda is capable of performing software compression on either the client or the server. If you're trying to decide between hardware compression on your tape device, or software compression in Amanda, there are a few points to keep in mind. Software compression will give Amanda a better insight into how well the data compresses, which helps in scheduling tapes. Client-side compression will also reduce the amount of network traffic required for a backup. The tradeoff is, of course, CPU usage on whichever machine performs the compression. Whatever you decide, remember not to use both software and hardware compression on the same data.

The Amanda Client

Setting up the client side of Amanda is exceptionally easy. The Amanda process will have a specified user to run as. Red Hat uses a user named **amanda** for this purpose. In this user's home directory, which is **/var/lib/amanda** by default, there is a file called **.amandahosts**. You must add a line to this file that specifies the name of the server that is allowed to connect, and what username on that server is allowed.

```
scribe.example.com amanda
```

Make sure that the **amanda** user has permissions to read the file systems you plan to back up. The default on Red Hat is to have the **amanda** user as part of the group **disk** for exactly that reason.

Starting the Amanda Service

Now it's time to bring up our old friend **redhat-config-services**, either from the command line or by selecting Services from the System Settings submenu. The Amanda services are all run from **xinetd**, so you'll want to make sure that's activated if it isn't already. On your server you'll want to turn on **amandaidx** and **amidxtape**, and on all of your client machines you'll want to turn on the **amanda** service. Don't forget that your server is probably a client as well.

If you prefer to make these adjustments by hand, head over to the **/etc/xinetd.d** directory and edit the appropriate service files, named exactly as they are in the graphical user interface (GUI) tool, setting **disable = no** in each. Don't forget to restart **xinetd**.

```
[root@scribe /root]# /etc/init.d/xinetd restart
```

Finally, you'll want to put an entry into **cron** to run the backups automatically at regular intervals. There are two commands you will want to place in **crontab**. The first is **amcheck**. This is the program that determines if everything is set up for the next backup run. Even if you run your backups unattended at night, you'll want to run this check while someone is still around to fix any problems it discovers. Passing the **-m** option will send e-mail to the systems administrators if any errors are detected. You'll also specify which configuration to use. The second entry in **cron** is the **amdump** program. This starts the actual backup and will be passed the name of a configuration.

```
0 16 * * 1-5    /usr/sbin/amcheck -m MyBackups
45 0 * * 2-6    /usr/sbin/amdump MyBackups
```

Amanda Utilities

The Amanda system is actually made up of a number of small programs that work together. Many of these you'll never have to invoke directly, but a few of them are worth attention. You met two of them in the last section, **amcheck** and **amdump**. The next most important command would be **amrecover**.

Running **amrecover** on a client machine will connect to the server and present you with a command-line environment from which you can browse a virtual file system and decide what files to restore. It's easiest to navigate to the place on the client where you want the files restored to before you invoke **amrecover**. Browsing through the virtual file system is much like using FTP in that you can use commands like **cd**, **pwd**, **ls**, **lpwd**, and **lcd** to navigate and find what you need. When you find what you're looking for, you can use the **add** command to put a file or directory on the list of things to be restored. Items can be removed from the restore list with the **delete** command. If you want to review what's slated to be restored, you can issue the **list** command. Once you're satisfied with your list, you issue the **extract** command, and Amanda will walk you through the restoration, including telling you which tapes are needed.

Other utilities that you may find useful are listed in Table 21-4.

Amanda is a fairly powerful tool, and you're strongly encouraged to read the accompanying documentation, particularly if you want to create advanced configurations such as using tape changers or encrypted backups.

Utility	Description
amflush	Flushes backups from the holding disk to tape. This is normally handled automatically by **amdump**. If, however, something prevents **amdump** from writing to tape, you may have to flush the disk manually after correcting the problem.
amcleanup	Cleans up after an interrupted **amdump**. This is only needed in rare circumstances, such as after a server crash.
amrestore	Restores a backup from tape. This is less interactive than **amrecover** and expects you to have a bit more knowledge of what you're looking for and where to find it. This may be easier to use when restoring an entire system.
amlabel	Labels tapes. All tapes must be labeled before Amanda will write to them. Run this on any new tapes you add to the system.
amadmin	Performs a variety of administrative tasks, such as forcing hosts to do a full backup or looking at scheduling information.
amverify	Checks backup tapes for problems. This essentially reads the tape back in but doesn't write the result to disk.
amstatus	Reports the status of a running or finished **amdump**.
amplot	Generates utilization plots to aid in performance tuning.

Table 21-4 Utilities That Make Up the Amanda System.

Module Summary

Backups are one of the most important aspects of system maintenance. Your systems may be superbly designed and maintained, but without solid backups, the whole package could be gone in a flash. Think of backups as your site's insurance policy.

This module covered the fundamentals of tape drives under Linux, along with some of the command-line tools for controlling tape drives and for backing up data to tape drives. With this information, you should be able to perform a complete backup of your system. Thankfully, **dump**, **restore**, and **tar** are not your only options for backup under Linux. Many commercial and noncommercial backup packages exist as well. We touched briefly on **amanda** as one option that ships with Red Hat 8. High-end packages such as Legato and Veritas have also provided Linux backup support for quite some time now and offer some impressive solutions. However you decide to go about the task of backing up your data (and testing those backups), just make sure that you do it.

✔

Module 21 Mastery Check

1. What are some things to consider when deciding how much data you need to back up?

2. Why should the data stream be fast enough to ensure that pauses do not occur when writing to tape?

3. What are some of the simple controls for the tape drive that the **mt** program provides?

4. What is **tar**?

5. Explain the relationship between the **dump** and **restore** tools.

6. True or False? The **tar** program was originally meant to create archives onto tape.

7. True or False? Amanda's way of scheduling backups is unusual.

8. What does Amanda stand for?

9. Does the Amanda program utilize other programs in order to run more efficiently?

10. Can the same **dump** program be used for all file system types?

Appendix

Answers to Mastery Checks

Module 1: Technical Summary of Linux Distributions and Windows

1. Linux is an operating system kernel.

2. The included utilities, applications, and tools distinguish distributions from one another. Bonus points if you know that the philosophy and support options also distinguish distributions.

3. **A** and **B.** The GPL requires access to the program source code, and it requires the distributor to allow redistribution of the software (still under the GPL). Technical support and the software itself do not need to be provided without a cost.

4. Single-user systems are designed to be run by one user from one console. Multiuser systems are designed to be run by multiple users from multiple access points. Network-user systems provide services to users on a network without logging them in.

5. The Windows family of products was developed as a single-user system.

6. Linux (like UNIX) was developed as a multiuser system.

7. Both Windows and Linux can run services that support network users.

8. While integration into the kernel provides some performance benefit to the GUI, the integration also prevents a system from running without the GUI code. Separating the GUI from the kernel allows servers that don't need GUIs to run more efficiently and stably.

9. **C** and **D.** The Network File System (NFS) is used by Linux systems to provide network access to directories and files. The Distributed File System (Dfs) provides the same functionality on a Windows server.

10. Linux configuration files are usually found in the **/etc** directory or its subdirectories.

11. The Network Information Service (NIS) is a commonly used domain security system in UNIX and Linux networks.

12. A Domain Controller authenticates users; NIS leaves authentication to individual applications.

13. The Lightweight Directory Access Protocol (LDAP) is available on Linux and is compatible with Active Directory.

14. One good place to look for Linux information is http://www.linux.org.

Module 2: Installing Linux in a Server Configuration

1. The Hardware Compatibility List is a database of hardware certified for use with Red Hat Linux 8.0. Using hardware that is not on the HCL can sometimes cause problems when installing and running Linux.

2. Stability means the server continues operating as it is supposed to. Availability means its resources can be used as intended. Performance is its speed in performing its assigned tasks.

3. **B** and **C.** While recompiling the server's kernel may provide some benefits, doing so is not ordinarily necessary. Liquid nitrogen, while fun to play with, isn't often a practical means for cooling servers. And while loading as many kernel modules as possible will make those functions available, it will also bloat the kernel with unneeded features. The name of the game is foregoing any functionality that isn't needed.

4. The **uptime** command gives the time elapsed since the system last started up.

5. The Linux Documentation Project at http://www.linuxdoc.org.

6. The **rawrite** utility can be used on a Windows system to create a boot disk for Red Hat Linux 8.0.

7. The three utilities are **redhat-config-xfree86**, **redhat-config-keyboard**, and **redhat-config-mouse**. The X Window System configuration tool is a bit of a trick question, as was mentioned in passing in Module 1.

8. The root directory on a Linux system is /.

9. The four directories are **/usr**, **/var**, **/home**, and **/tmp**.

10. **B.**

11. After initial installation, an SMP system will have two options: the default SMP-enabled kernel, and a uniprocessor kernel as a fallback.

12. The Red Hat Linux **–up** option does not include multiprocessor functionality, so it can be selected in the unhappy event that the normal SMP kernel causes problems on a multiprocessing system.

13. The **su** command can be used to become the root user. It can also be used to become any other user.

14. A shadow password is an encrypted password stored in the **/etc/shadow** file rather than the **/etc/passwd** file. Because access to the **/etc/shadow** file is more restricted, shadow passwords are more secure.

15. **A, B, C,** and **E.** Access authentication via a RADIUS server is not configurable during Red Hat Linux installation.

16. It can be damaged and broken, although this is less likely than it used to be. All the same, it's good to know your monitor's specifications: horizontal and vertical sync values.

Module 3: GNOME and KDE

1. Zero percent of the GUI is built into the kernel. Separation of the user interface from the kernel is a distinctive design characteristic of Linux.

2. A program that draws borders, sets colors, and performs other implementation details for windowing systems. A window manager is separate from X itself.

3. Yes, as long as any KDE-related libraries the applications rely upon are installed on the system. But you don't have to be *running* KDE to use KDE applications. Likewise, GNOME applications will run under KDE, as long as any necessary libraries are installed.

4. The command used to start the GUI in Red Hat Linux 8.0 is **startx**.

5. On a user-by-user basis, you can change ~/.**xinitrc** to include either **gnome-session** or **startkde**. On a system-wide basis, change **/usr/sysconfig/desktop** to refer to the desired GUI.

6. Neither **D**, the System Monitor, nor **G**, the Terminal Emulator, are included by default on a Red Hat Linux desktop.

7. Right-click on a blank space on the panel, and select the Add to Panel option. Many options will be available!

8. The GNOME project's primary web site is http://www.gnome.org.

9. Among the available resources for GNOME themes are http://art.gnome.org, http://themes.freshmeat.net, and http://www.themedepot.org.

10. The primary KDE web site is http://www.kde.org.

11. KDE themes are available at www.kde-look.org, http://themes.freshmeat.net, and http://www.themedepot.org.

12. Right-click on a blank space on the panel and select the Add option.

13. New in Red Hat Linux 8.0 is the Bluecurve theme and its various elements: icons, backgrounds, etc.

14. On a user-by-user basis, ~/.**fonts** can be used as a repository for new fonts. To make fonts available system-wide, use the **/usr/share/fonts** directory instead.

15. Run the **fc-cache** script, specifying the font directory, to add new fonts to the system.

Module 4: Installing Software

1. To install a package, use **rpm –i** *rpmfile*. To upgrade a package, use **rpm –U** *rpmfile*. To delete a package, use **rpm –e** *rpmfile*.

2. To determine which package owns **/bin/gzip**, use **rpm –qf /bin/gzip**.

3. You could look at the packagename returned by **rpm –qf /bin/gzip** (namely **gzip**) and run **rpm –e gzip**. The **gzip** utility is very useful, though, so don't try this on a system you care about.

4. If you're sure you want to install a recalcitrant package despite the reasons the RPM tool gives you, use the **rpm –i --force** command.

5. Use the **rpm –i --test** command to test a package installation without actually pulling the trigger.

6. The correct answer is **C**. The **rpm –qlp bc** command is invalid because the **–p** option is used to look at a package file, not an installed package, and **bc** is not a valid RPM filename. The **rpm –ql**

bc-1.06-10.i386.rpm command specifies a package file, so it needs a **–p** option, and it wouldn't check installed packages. The **rpm –qa | grep "mysql"** command will list all installed packages with "mysql" in their package names, but it won't list the files contained in any of those packages.

7. The **redhat-config-packages** tool is a package manager that works in both desktop environments.

8. From the Red Hat menu, select System Settings, then Packages to run the tool without resorting to the command line.

9. Not to be too obvious, but http://www.redhat.com is one place to start. You can also look at http://www.rpmfind.net, http://freshrpms.net, http://www.linuxapps.com, http://freshmeat.net, and others.

10. A tarball is a single-file, compressed archive of one or (usually) more files and directories. The **tar** command is used to create the archive, which can be compressed using several different compression utilities.

11. Tarballs usually use one of the following extensions: **.tar.gz** or **.tgz** for a gzipped tar archive, or **.tar.bz2** for a bzip2-compressed tar archive.

12. The **configure** script often recognizes the --**help** argument as a cry for help with the available options, so use ./**configure** --**help**. You could also look at the contents of the ./**configure** file using a text editor or even **more ./configure**.

13. Only the root user can manipulate files in **/usr/local/src** unless you change its permissions, which means you have to copy, configure, and build software as **root**, which shouldn't be necessary and isn't always wise.

14. The correct answer is **D**. First run the configure script, then make the software, install it, and clean up afterward.

15. Use the **echo $PATH** command to see what directories are in the current path.

16. Use the **rm –rf** command to delete a directory and all its subdirectories and all their contents. It's like a nuclear weapon for directories, so be careful!

Module 5: Managing Users

1. A GID is a group ID, which is a unique identifier assigned to each user group.

2. A UID is a user ID, a unique numeric identifier assigned to each user account.

3. The MD5 encryption scheme can (and should) be installed on Red Hat Linux 8.0 systems.

4. The **/etc/shadow** file contains the MD5-encrypted passwords for the system.

5. On a properly configured system, only the root user can view the contents of the **/etc/shadow** file.

6. I suggest adding the asterisk (*) character to the password field to disable login. Furthermore, I suggest adding a brief text description of the reason the password was disabled.

7. The default location for the default user configuration files is **/etc/skel**. The contents of this directory may be altered, or you can set the **adduser** command to use another directory for the default configuration files.

8. Use the **groupadd –r** command to request the next available system group ID.

9. Use the **userdel –r** command to delete an account and remove all files owned by the user from the user's home directory.

10. Only **B** is correct; use the **redhat-config-users** command from X to graphically manage user and group accounts. I made up the other program names.

11. Certain executable files have a permission setting that indicates that when they are run, they run with the authority of the user who owns them. If that owner is the root user, the file is said to be SetUID root.

12. The **sudo** command has more configuration and limitation options, including finer-grained control over who can use it, and is less easily exploited than SetUID root.

13. The **visudo** command should be used to edit the **/etc/sudoers** file. While **/etc/sudoers** is a text file, the **visudo** editor provides safety features that should be used.

14. If a directory listing shows a number for a file's owner user or group, it means that the user or group that owned the file has been deleted. The number is the UID or GID of the dearly departed user or group.

15. The **/etc/pam.d** directory holds configuration files for each program that uses PAM.

16. An **auth** module requires a password from the user and conveys user and group privileges. An **account** module does not authenticate the user; it restricts or permits access depending on other factors. A **session** module indicates the actions required before or after login. A **password** module allows users to change their passwords.

17. A **requisite** module must successfully authenticate the user or the process is terminated immediately and fails. A **required** module must successfully authenticate the user or the process fails. A **sufficient** module that successfully authenticates a user causes the process to succeed if no other required or sufficient flags must be dealt with. An **optional** module can fail to authenticate the user without causing the whole process to fail.

Module 6: The Command Line

1. Use the **jobs** command to see the names and job numbers of jobs that have been started in the session.

2. Run the **fg** command with the number of the job to bring to the foreground.

3. The matches are

    A. command < file

    B. `command`

    C. command > file

D. command 1 | command 2

E. command 1 ; command 2

F. command &

4. Because program documentation is in man section 1, the default, you can use either **man passwd** or **man 1 passwd**.

5. Because configuration file documentation is in section 5, use the **man 5 passwd** command.

6. These form the contents of the directory listing:

A. The normal file is **usage.out**.

B. The directory is **routerconfig**.

C. The symbolic link is **a.txt**.

D. The block device is **xdb9**.

E. The character device is **zqft2**.

F. The named pipe is **flicker**.

G. The user **rwhite** owns the **routerconfig** directory.

H. The group **rwhite** owns the **usage.out** file.

I. The **usage.out** file is readable only to user **root**.

J. The **routerconfig** directory can be read or written to by the admin group.

7. Use the commands **chown rwhite README** and **chgrp rwhite README**. If you read the man page for **chown**, you'll find that you can also perform both operations in one step using the **chown** command: **chown rwhite.rwhite README**.

8. Use the **chmod** command with the following values: **chmod 664 README**.

9. The **find** command can be used: **find /usr -name README**.

10. Use the **tar** command as root: **tar /root/etc.tar.gz/etc/**.

11. To identify the executable file that runs when you enter **top**, use **which top**.

12. Find the free space on local disks this way: **df –l**.

13. Use the **kill –9** command with the process number of the process you wish to terminate. It absolutely will not stop, ever, until the process is dead. Usually.

14. Run the **who** command to see who is logged in, or the **w** command to see who is logged in and more about what they're up to.

15. Use the CTRL-H combination to get help in **emacs**.

16. Use the **:help** command to get help with **vi**.

Module 7: File Systems

1. I-nodes provide a layer of indirection to the file system, storing information about files rather than the contents of the files. The i-nodes point to other i-nodes (thus the indirection) or directly to the locations the data is stored.

2. The superblock contains data about the disk's physical attributes, its contents, and the location of the first i-node.

3. The ext3 file system is essentially the same as the ext2 file system, but it has journaling support. It is designed to be very compatible with ext2; you can freely convert a single partition between the two file systems.

4. Information on how to mount a system's partition is contained in **/etc/fstab**.

5. The six entries in the **/etc/fstab** file are the partition to be mounted, the directory in which to mount that partition's file system, the file system type, any optional mount parameters to be used, how frequently the **dump** command needs to back up this partition's contents, and the relative priority of the partition's **fsck** check.

6. The **mount** command is used to for mounting, and the **umount** command is used to unmount.

7. You could either **umount /dev/hda5** and then **mount –o ro /dev/hda5 /opt**, or simply **mount –o ro,remount /dev/hda5**.

8. The **e2fsck –f** command will force a check. Be sure the file system is unmounted or mounted read-only first.

9. Bits of files that cannot be restored to wholeness are placed in that partition's **lost+found** directory. In this case, "files" don't have to be normal files; directories and other special files can end up in **lost+found**, too.

10. The fifth SCSI disk would be **/dev/sde**, and its first partition would be **/dev/sde1**.

11. The **fdisk** utility is an interactive tool for deleting and creating partitions.

12. Within **fdisk**, one must specify a system type of **82** to designate a partition as a Linux swap.

13. The **mkswap** command is used to create the swap file system on a Linux swap partition.

14. To create an ext3 file system on **/dev/hda1**, run the command **mke2fs –j /dev/hda1**.

15. Using NFS, **mount gregory:/export/foo /mnt/foo** would mount the server gregory's **/export/foo** directory in the local system's **/mnt/foo** directory.

16. The **autofs** daemon's primary configuration file is **/etc/auto.master**. This file points to other configuration files called **mapfiles**, each of which tells **autofs** what to mount in a particular directory.

17. The correct answer is **D**. First, edit the **/etc/fstab** file to add the **usrquota** and/or **grpquota** options, then run **quotacheck** to initialize the quota system, and then run **edquota** to set quota parameters. Extra point if you remember that you'll want to run **quotacheck** periodically thereafter.

18. Use the **repquota** command to generate a report on quota usage.

Module 8: Core System Services

1. The four core Linux services are **init**, **xinetd**, **syslog**, and **cron**.

2. The number of **title** commands in the configuration file will determine the number of menu entries.

3. In GRUB-speak, the fourth partition on the first hard disk is **hd0,3**.

4. Press the ESC key to bring up the hidden GRUB boot menu.

5. Sorry, this is a trick question. GRUB doesn't require any notification of configuration changes; it just reads the altered configuration file when booting. LILO, on the other hand requires you to run **lilo** after editing the **lilo.conf** file.

6. Runlevel 5 boots into a graphical login screen.

7. To change the runlevel to single-user mode, **telinit 1**.

8. The four fields in the **/etc/inittab** entry give the service **id**, the **runlevels** that run the service, the **action** taken, and the **process** that runs when starting this runlevel.

9. The **initdefault** action determines the default runlevel.

10. The **ctrlaltdel** action determines how the system responds to CTRL-ALT-DEL.

11. Edit the **/etc/xinetd.conf** file and in the **defaults** section, set **instances=20**.

12. Edit the **/etc/xinetd.conf** file and in the **defaults** section, set **cps=5 60**.

13. Set **syslogd** to run with the **–m 60** to set the frequency of default log entries to one hour.

14. The **debug** priority is likely to be the most verbose but generate the least vital messages.

15. To run **foo** twice a week, you can put it in **/etc/cron.weekly**, or set up a **cron** job of its own.

16. At startup, K files run first, and progress in numerical order, and then S files follow suit. Thus, these **rc** files would run in this order: **B**, then **D**, then **C**, then **A**.

Module 9: Securing an Individual Server

1. The **up2date** command is used to collect updates from the Red Hat Network.

2. The **rhnsd** process must be running for a system to be able to receive updates ordered via the RHN web site.

3. The RHN website is **http://rhn.redhat.com**.

4. Use the **up2date-config** command to configure proxy settings, download options, and set package skipping rules.

5. The **rpm –K ./foobar-server.2.3–4.rpm** command, run from the directory in which the RPM package was downloaded, works admirably.

6. The ports from **0** to **1023** are reserved for system use.

7. The **–a** option lists all listening or connected ports, while **–t** specifies TCP ports only and **–p** reports on the listening or active process names, so **netstat –atp** would produce this result.

8. When determining which services to enable on a server, ask: Do I need the service? Is it secure by default? Does the service need updates? Bonus points if you think to ask: Do I feel lucky?

9. Use the **service xinetd stop** command to shut down the service altogether.

10. The syslog port is port **514**, which is used to transmit and receive syslog reports from remote systems (if **syslogd** was started with the **–r** option).

11. The Tripwire program creates a checksum for each protected file and sends a notification whenever any of those files are changed.

12. The Nessus server process is **nessusd**.

13. Security through obscurity is a type of wishful thinking by which people convince themselves that if nobody is told how something works, they'll have a more difficult time breaking or breaking into that something. I don't know how well it works, but it's a weak idea conceptually, since there are many ways to attack even the least illuminated of black boxes.

14. Social engineering is a type of salesmanship by which a cracker attempts to gather useful information about an intended target system or user. It's the computer version of the person who stole your wallet calling you up, claiming he's from the bank, and asking for your ATM PIN. Many people have been suckered into giving up PINs or passwords by confident, unethical predators.

15. Your answers may vary, but I'll provide a few. Lock the door and restrict access to the key. Leave floppy disk drives, USB ports, and other means of getting access to the system unconnected, or disabled via a password-protected BIOS. Use locking racks. Don't store expensive equipment or data in your cubicle.

Module 10: The Domain Name Service (DNS)

1. A primary name server for a domain is simply a DNS server that knows about all hosts and subdomains existing under its domain.

2. The root servers.

3. Subdomains are used to further divide domains into smaller sections for ease of administration.

4. The three types are

   Primary servers are authoritative for a particular domain; all domain configuration files reside here.

   Secondary servers work as backups and as load distributors.

   Caching servers contain no configuration files for any particular domain but keep a local copy of the result from a query.

5. The server statement tells BIND specific information about other name servers it might be dealing with.

6. Possible answers may include:

SOA: Start of Authority   The SOA record starts the description of a site's DNS entries.

NS: Name Server   The NS record is used for specifying which name servers maintain records for this zone.

A: Address Record   The A record is used for providing a mapping from host name to IP address.

PTR: Pointer Record   The PTR record is for performing reverse name resolution.

MX: Mail Exchanger   The MX record is in charge of telling other sites about your zone's mail server.

CNAME: Canonical Name   The CNAME records allow you to create aliases for host names.

RP and TXT   The Documentation Entries—the TXT record is a free-form text entry into which you can place whatever information you deem fit. The RP record was created as an explicit container for a host's contact information.

7. CNAME allows you to alias expected names to a server whose real name is something else.

8. BIND is the Berkeley Internet Name Domain server, the defacto DNS server on the Internet.

9. True.

10. You would precede it with an exclamation mark (!).

Module 11: Transferring Files with FTP

1. In a passive transfer, the client is responsible for opening the control connection and the data connection. In an active transfer, the server opens the data connection back to the client.

2. You should double-check your configuration and test it before going live because crackers can break into insecure FTP servers.

3. Users can be allowed to log in as themselves, and you can restrict your server to only anonymous password-less logins.

4. The user's e-mail address.

5. False.

6. True.

7. File Transfer Protocol is a method for transferring files from one computer to another.

8. The Very Secure FTP daemon is used by Red Hat because it has a lightweight design, and has proven itself to be stable and scalable under heavy usage. In addition, it is believed to be more secure than the alternatives.

9. /usr/share/doc/vsftpd-1.1.0/

10. The **ftpd_banner** option allows you to change the message displayed when you first connect to the server.

11. The anon_world_readable_only default is set to "yes" as a precaution to keep anonymous users from downloading anything that is not explicitly world readable. This is useful if a number of files are owned by the user that **vsftpd** is running.

12. Setting the configuration option for userlist_enable allows the server to limit who can log in based on a list in a file. It can either allow only those names listed, or can deny those listed.

13. Placing an entry in the **/etc/hosts.allow** or **/etc/hosts.deny** files will allow you to explictly control access to a number of services, including **vsftpd**.

14. Using passive mode will allow access for clients behind a firewall that doesn't specially handle FTP connections.

15. Yes. However, each virtual server must have a unique IP address.

16. No. **vsftpd** must be run from **xinetd** (or **inetd**).

Module 12: Setting Up Your Web Server Using Apache

1. The server name directive allows you to match the machine name returned by a web server to a CNAME instead of the actual machine name. This can be useful if your machine name does not happen to be **www**.

2. Apache will start a number of processes and have them wait around for incoming connections. The number of running processes will be increased or decreased according to load.

3. You can include one MPM module on a server.

4. Apache provides modules that allow you to extend Apache's features.

5. D is the correct answer.

6. HTTP is the Hypertext Transfer Protocol, and it is used to move web pages from the server to your browser.

7. It is stable. Several major web sites, including www.amazon.com and www.generalelectric.com, are using it.
   The entire program and related components are open source.
   It works on a large number of platforms (all popular variants of UNIX, some of the not-so-popular variants of UNIX, and even Windows).
   It is extremely flexible.
   It has shown itself to be more secure than most of the alternatives.

8. False.

9. True.

10. True.

Module 13: Sending Mail with SMTP

1. The SMTP protocol defines the method by which mail is sent from one host to another.

2. **B.**

3. SMTP is a transport protocol for sending messages only. A user cannot connect to an SMTP server to read his or her mail. POP and IMAP are just the opposite. A client can use POP or IMAP to read mail off of a server, but the client host cannot send e-mail with POP or IMAP.

4. Sendmail now ships the package in a very tight security mode and leaves it to consumers to loosen up only what they wish.

5. IMAP.

6. Mail transfer agent (MTA), mail delivery agent (MDA), and mail user agent (MUA).

7. **C.**

8. **myorigin**.

9. Sendmail maintains only one queue, and it is stored in **/var/spool/mqueue**; spools are stored in **/var/spool/mail**. Postfix delivers to **/var/spool/mail** by default; it uses subdirectories under **/var/spool/postfix** for each of its spools.

10. True.

11. False.

Module 14: Using POP and IMAP for E-Mail Retrieval

1. The Post Office Protocol (POP) and the Internet Message Access Protocol (IMAP) are protocols for receiving mail from a server for reading.

2. **C.**

3. **E.**

4. True.

5. False.

6. True.

7. Basically, IMAP keeps your messages in a mailbox on the server. POP thinks that whatever is on the server is just temporary storage for mail you haven't picked up yet. So when you send your mail through POP, those messages are removed from the server when they're sent to your client. Then IMAP comes in later and sees no messages on the server. (POP already removed them.)

8. The name of the challenge/response mechanism that is available for POP is called Authenticated POP (APOP).

9. The name of the challenge/response mechanism that is available for IMAP is called Challenge-Response Authentication Mechanism (CRAM or CRAM-MD5).

10. Challenge/response mechanisms keep plain text copies of the password database on the server, causing your data to be unprotected there.

Module 15: The Secure Shell (SSH)

1. If data is encrypted with a public key, it can only be decrypted with the corresponding or private key (or vice versa).

2. SSH is the Secure Shell, and it allows users to connect to a remote server with a session that is 100 percent encrypted.

3. The session will appear much like random garbage going by.

4. True.

5. False.

6. It allows peers to examine the source code and make sure that there aren't any holes that may allow crackers to break the security. The protocols used are in no way weakened by someone viewing how they work.

7. False. Users must also be educated not to compromise security in other ways.

8. It specifies whether **sshd** should check file modes and ownership of the user's files and home directory. If the permissions are too lax, **sshd** will deny them login.

9. **ssh-keygen**.

10. **scp** or **sftp**.

Module 16: Network File System (NFS)

1. Network File System (NFS) is the UNIX way of sharing files and applications across the network.

2. Portmapper is the RPC service manager, and it takes care of telling the client where the actual service is located on the server.

3. Notification to the server is unnecessary because the server does not keep track of all clients that have mounted its file systems.

4. **D.** All of the above.

5. The possible commands are

    –a exports all entries in the **/etc/exports** file.

    –r re-exports all entries in the **/etc/exports** file.

 −u *client*: **/dir/to/mount** unexports the directory */dir/to/mount* to the host client.

 −v verbosely prints messages about what it is doing.

6. Possible problems that can occur are

 The server can confuse a file with a fully qualified domain name.

 The server's perception of the host name/IP pairing is not correct.

7. **C.** Disables the locking.

8. **D.** None of the above.

9. False.

10. True.

11. **A.** Hard.

Module 17: Network Information Service (NIS)

1. As long as the tabular file has at least one column with a unique value throughout, NIS can use it to share information.

2. The main benefit achieved from using NIS is that you can maintain a central copy of the data; and whenever that data is updated, it automatically propagates to all of the network users.

3. You can query NIS either by listing the entire table or by pulling a specific entry based on a search for a given key.

4. **B.**

5. True.

6. **C.**

7. The **ypbind** daemon is used to find and connect to an NIS server.

8. False. The **ypwhich** command returns the name of the NIS server that is answering your requests. The **yppasswd** command allows you to change your password entry on the NIS system.

9. When using a netgroup, members are specified in the form *host,user,domain.*

10. Place at least one NIS server on each end of the WAN connection.

Module 18: Talking to Windows with Samba

1. Two ways of handling the incompatibility between UNIX and Windows are

 Edit the Registry on Windows clients to disable the use of encrypted passwords. The Registry entries that need to be changed are listed in the **docs** directory in the Samba package.

 Configure Samba to use Windows-style encrypted passwords.

2. Yes.

3. Samba is a tool for allowing UNIX to share files and printers with Windows-based systems.

4. Samba allows UNIX clients to talk to Windows servers using their native tongue, which means fewer hassles and seamless integration for your users.

5. SMB stands for Session Message Block.

6. Possible answers are **/etc/init.d/smb start** and **/etc/init.d/smb stop**.

7. SWAT is the Samba Web Administration tool; it is a web-based interface for administering Samba.

8. The Globals page lists all settings that affect Samba's operation. These settings are divided into seven groups: Base, Security, Logging, Tuning, Printing, Browse, and WINS.

9. Shares on the SWAT menu are for setting up disk shares and their respective options.

10. The parameter for connecting the **smbclient** to the printer is **–P**.

11. **D.**

Module 19: Printing

1. The Internet Printing Protocol.

2. The goal of IPP is to provide a common protocol that can be used across systems, reduce the number of different standards that printers have to support, and cover most printing situations.

3. PostScript is a programming language that is focused on describing text and graphics on a page. This is notable because a PostScript file will appear the same when printed on any printer that supports PostScript.

4. Banner pages show who printed the document and the name of the document. Most sites find that the banner pages are not worth the wasted paper and prefer to keep this feature turned off.

5. The **rm** command specifies the remote print server, and **rp** specifies the printer queue on that server.

6. False. The **/etc/lpd.stats** file shows the stats of the printer.

7. True.

8. The preferred method for setting up the CUPS server is to use a web-based administration interface.

9. An implicit class.

10. Nothing.

11. **A.** LPRng

12. **B.** CUPS

Module 20: Host Configuration with DHCP

1. DHCP is a protocol for obtaining IP addresses and related information for a machine on your network.

2. True.

3. True.

4. BOOTP, or Bootstrap Protocol, allowed a server to inform each machine of a corresponding IP address by matching the MAC address in a presupplied table.

5. An advantage of DHCP over BOOTP is that DHCP can hand out addresses from a given range to machines whose MAC addresses were previously unknown to the server.

6. When a lease expires, the client is no longer allowed to use that address, and the server may reallocate it to another client.

7. The **group** declaration allows you to apply a set of parameters and declarations to a list of clients, shared networks, or subnets.

8. **option** *option-name* [*modifiers*]

9. The option **host-name** is the string used to identify the name of the client.

10. **reboot**.

11. **reject**.

Module 21: Backups

1. Growth, financial or legal issues, and frequency of data changes.

2. If your data stream is not fast enough, pauses can occur. Even a small pause in the data stream can cause the tape mechanism to realign itself, causing a large delay in the backup runtime.

3. Rewinding the tape, ejecting the tape, and seeking a particular file on the tape.

4. It is a command that stands for *tape ar*chive; the **tar** command can archive a selection of files into a single file.

5. The **dump** tool works by making a copy of an entire file system. The **restore** tool retrieves the copy and pulls selected files from it.

6. True.

7. True.

8. Amanda stands for Advanced Maryland Automatic Network Disk Archiver.

9. Yes. The Amanda program uses both **tar** and **dump** in order to more efficiently keep track, back up, and restore data. It can be configured to use other utilities as well.

10. No. The version of **dump** supplied with Red Hat 8 is specific to ext2/ext3 file systems. If you have another type of file system, you must find a version of **dump** written by the provider of that file system.

Index

E

Q

INTERNATIONAL CONTACT INFORMATION

AUSTRALIA
McGraw-Hill Book Company Australia Pty. Ltd.
TEL +61-2-9900-1800
FAX +61-2-9878-8881
http://www.mcgraw-hill.com.au
books-it_sydney@mcgraw-hill.com

CANADA
McGraw-Hill Ryerson Ltd.
TEL +905-430-5000
FAX +905-430-5020
http://www.mcgraw-hill.ca

GREECE, MIDDLE EAST, & AFRICA
(Excluding South Africa)
McGraw-Hill Hellas
TEL +30-210-6560-990
TEL +30-210-6560-993
TEL +30-210-6560-994
FAX +30-210-6545-525

MEXICO (Also serving Latin America)
McGraw-Hill Interamericana Editores S.A. de C.V.
TEL +525-117-1583
FAX +525-117-1589
http://www.mcgraw-hill.com.mx
fernando_castellanos@mcgraw-hill.com

SINGAPORE (Serving Asia)
McGraw-Hill Book Company
TEL +65-863-1580
FAX +65-862-3354
http://www.mcgraw-hill.com.sg
mghasia@mcgraw-hill.com

SOUTH AFRICA
McGraw-Hill South Africa
TEL +27-11-622-7512
FAX +27-11-622-9045
robyn_swanepoel@mcgraw-hill.com

SPAIN
McGraw-Hill/Interamericana de España, S.A.U.
TEL +34-91-180-3000
FAX +34-91-372-8513
http://www.mcgraw-hill.es
professional@mcgraw-hill.es

UNITED KINGDOM, NORTHERN,
EASTERN, & CENTRAL EUROPE
McGraw-Hill Education Europe
TEL +44-1-628-502500
FAX +44-1-628-770224
http://www.mcgraw-hill.co.uk
computing_neurope@mcgraw-hill.com

ALL OTHER INQUIRIES Contact:
Osborne/McGraw-Hill
TEL +1-510-549-6600
FAX +1-510-883-7600
http://www.osborne.com
omg_international@mcgraw-hill.com